Clausewitz

RAYMOND ARON

Translated by
Christine Booker and Norman Stone

Prentice-Hall, Inc., Englewood Cliffs, New Jersey 07632

© 1985 by Editions Gallimard

First published in 1976 as *Penser la guerre, Clausewitz* by
Editions Gallimard. 1983 translation published by Routledge &
Kegan Paul plc, London, England. This edition published 1985
by Prentice-Hall, Inc., Englewood Cliffs, New Jersey 07632.

Printed in the United States of America

10 9 8 7 6 5 4 3 2 1

This book is available at a special discount when
ordered in bulk quantities. Contact Prentice-Hall, Inc.,
General Publishing Division, Special Sales,
Englewood Cliffs, N.J. 07632.

Library of Congress Cataloging in Publication Data
Aron, Raymond   (date).
    Clausewitz, philosopher of war.
    Translation of: Penser la guerre, Clausewitz.
    Includes index.
    1. Clausewitz, Carl von, 1780–1831.   2. War.
3. Military art and science.   I. Title.
U21.2.C54A7613   1985   355'.02   84-26569
ISBN 0-13-136342-5

Prentice-Hall International, Inc., *London*
Prentice-Hall of Australia Pty. Limited, *Sydney*
Prentice-Hall Canada Inc., *Toronto*
Prentice-Hall Hispanoamericana, S.A., *Mexico*
Prentice Hall of India Private Limited, *New Delhi*
Prentice Hall of Japan, Inc., *Tokyo*
Prentice-Hall of Southeast Asia Pte. Ltd., *Singapore*
Whitehall Books Limited, *Wellington, New Zealand*
Editora Prentice-Hall do Brasil Ltda., *Rio de Janeiro*

ISBN 0-13-136342-5

Contents

Preface

I first came across Clausewitz forty years ago. In the two years before Hitler's rise to power I was acquainted with a historian in Berlin who had a special interest in military affairs, strategy and army organization – Herbert Rosinski. As far as I can remember, he did not at the time intend to specialize in the study of war. We were discussing a famous article by Carl Schmitt, 'The Concept of Politics', which he harshly criticized; he alluded to his favourite author, Carl von Clausewitz, on whom he planned to write a book, the definitive book. He got no further than an article which appears in all the bibliographies, even today. The article appeared in the *Historische Zeitschrift* in 1935 and attempted, perhaps for the first time, to reconstruct the stages of Clausewitzian thought in the period between Koblenz (1816) and 1830 in the light of four notes written by the general himself, which the editor of the posthumous work, Marie von Clausewitz, had included at the beginning of the first volume. For the most part, the hypotheses of my companion have been confirmed by later research. But to my knowledge he never expanded the mysterious suggestions which he makes at the end of his article. According to him, the thought of Clausewitz had progressed between 1827 and 1830 and, at the time the manuscript was sealed, new horizons were opening for the theorist. What progress? What horizons? Rosinski did not answer these questions. The difficulties he experienced during emigration, accompanied perhaps by personal difficulties, prevented him from writing the book he had already dreamt of in 1932.

I doubt whether he communicated his enthusiasm for Clausewitz to me because I do not remember reading *Vom Kriege* before the war. But by a strange coincidence the offprint of his 1935 article survived events and moving house; I found it intact thirty years later when I decided to give a course of lectures at the Collège de France on the most celebrated and yet perhaps the least well-known (especially in France) of military writers.

Meanwhile I had met another passionate student of *Vom Kriege*, this time in London – a Pole from the Teschen region, Stalislas Szymonczyk. He was writing studies in German on military affairs for *La France Libre*, founded by André Labarthe, which I was translating into French. He readily made use of Clausewitzian phrases to enhance the tone and style of strict analysis. I do not remember having read the Treatise (i.e. *Vom Kriege*) at this time, but I do remember having read H. Delbrück's *Die Geschichte der Kriegskunst in Rahmen der politischen Geschichte*.

I read Clausewitz's masterpiece for the first time in about 1955 when the French translation by Mme Naville appeared. At the time I was reflecting on the politico-strategic consequences of nuclear weapons. In the atomic age the subordination of the military leaders to the leaders of the state or government becomes a manifest and essential feature. The formula 'war is the continuation of policy by other means', so often misconstrued, takes on its original significance. I included in one of the essays of *Espoir et peur du siècle* the sentence from Book VIII: 'The whole of the art of war becomes mere prudence whose principal object will be to prevent the unstable balance from suddenly turning to our disadvantage and to prevent half-war from being transformed into a complete one.'

A great work, particularly of political philosophy, always lends itself to many interpretations. In order immediately to enlighten those who intend to follow me to the end, let me say that I regard as a matter of fundamental importance the idea that Clausewitz probably only grasped at the end of his research: the possibility of a movement in the opposite direction from a rise to extremes, a movement extrinsic to war in the narrow sense of a trial of strength, but intrinsic to war according to its full definition, no longer something autonomous but part of the political whole.

This third, yet first direct, encounter with the man and the work developed into lasting familiarity. In London the Treatise was for me, as for so many others, a treasury of quotations. From 1955 onwards I sought to find in it the theoretical formulation of an area of study. I used it (in a way which I now consider to be unsatisfactory) in *Paix de Guerre entre les nations*. The initial definition of war given in the first page of the Treatise implies that states resort to violence when they seek to impose their will on others. Such a definition has no originality. It repeats the hypothesis common to the classical philosophers of relations between states, from Hobbes to Montesquieu and from Rousseau to Hegel. I prefer to turn to Clausewitz's because he allows for the introduction into the same conceptual system of the changing modalities of armed conflicts, or even conflicts reduced to armed observation, tests of will in the shadow of violence.

The contrast between the 'cabinet' wars of the eighteenth century and the wars of the Revolution and Empire supplied a point of departure for his thought; the hyperbolic magnitude of the wars unleashed in 1914 and 1939, followed by the threat of nuclear arms, forces the citizen, the observer and the sociologist to ask when and why wars develop into extremes, if and how men can limit them. Did Clausewitz concern himself with this limitation? At this point I was again faced with the article of Herbert Rosinski and the long polemic, unknown in France but well known in Germany, on the Foreword of 1827 and on the two types of war.

With a view to resolving the matter and forming my own opinion I decided to devote one of my courses of lectures at the Collège de France to Clausewitz. What attracted me initially was the philosophical problem, the effort required to grasp the nature of war, to formulate a theory which would not be confused with a doctrine, in other words which would teach the strategist to understand his task without entertaining any absurd claim to communicate the secret of victory.

Once launched into the study of the texts with a view to determining dates and distinguishing the successive stages of his thought, I felt the pleasure that would result from reading a detective story, shorn of its last chapter: each reader solves the mystery in his own way. Whether one will or no, the teaching of Clausewitz remains and will always remain ambiguous. The interpretation that I shall give to it accords with my own views about the generations that lived through the wars of the twentieth century. I also believe that this interpretation is in accord with the final thoughts of Clausewitz, or at least with one of the trends of his final thoughts. But for reasons that will be revealed in this book, doubts subsist and will subsist. Besides, there will always be pacifists to remind us that a theoretician is never innocent. Under the pretext of grasping the essence of the phenomenon of war, he paints a fixed picture of the world: generals and statesmen will then act in conformity with this representation of reality. After all, men of action create in part the reality to which they give the impression of submitting. For those who are able to read the whole of Clausewitz, he advocates neither boldness in the quest for an annihilating victory, nor prudence with a view to reducing wars to armed observation; or rather, he advocates both boldness and prudence, the destruction of enemy armed forces as first among military objectives, but also the subordination of the conduct of military operations to policy. Who in Germany could quote him as their authority after 1918, or after 1945? Who in the USA could do so after the disaster in Vietnam? The quarrels between the experts on Clausewitz led straight into universal historical debate.

As nobody who spends years in a kind of intimate dialogue with another mind can help seeing things in the light of that silent and insistent interlocutor, it is only right that I should confess my sympathy with him. I have never denied that my 'intellectual portraits' lacked objectivity if by this one means an 'affected neutrality'.

Some passages, not many, should have irritated me. For example, 'Bonaparte is as grasping as a Jew and just as cynical'. The passages which express hatred or scorn of the French are innumerable. But none of these moves me because they reveal a Clausewitz stripped of his genius and similar to so many of his contemporaries. They allow him to speak in the spirit of his age, *Zeitgeist*. I have more difficulty in tolerating the song of joy of 4 April 1813:

> I am in good health and the days are full of happiness; this is essentially the news that I have for you. To be part of a delightful little army with my friends at its head, to cross magnificent countryside in the summer months, and for such a goal, is just about the ideal longed for in earthly existence (if you consider it transitory and as a path to other existences). My friend G. [Gneisenau] looks like a god in his general's uniform. The troops are full of life and sing 'Auf, Auf Kameraden' and other similar songs, others yodel to perfection.

Did Clausewitz believe in other existences, or did he use the phrase in response to the religious ideas of his wife? I can understand and tolerate the passion for combat and glory which animated the young Prussian officer as a state of being or of feeling. It is found across the centuries and it does not disappear, but rather assumes different forms. Is the mob that attacked the Bastille, in which Sartre saw humanity tearing off its shackles, of any greater worth than French or German soldiers singing when marching to death and to victory? The answer varies according to the times and the prevailing mood.

A Frenchman has only to remember his own experiences between 1940 and 1945 to sympathize with the attitude of Clausewitz between 1806 and 1815. Not that I should want by this to compare Napoleon with Hitler: but the German patriot did not resist French domination over Europe any the less. In resisting, Clausewitz refused to accept the peace of surrender with an eloquence that moves men of my generation: 'I shall never accept this peace which brings submission. If I cannot live in a free and respected state and enjoy the golden fruits of peace in your arms, then let peace depart for ever from my heart.'

After the disaster, while a prisoner in France, he wrote to his fiancée on 28 June 1807:

> There is nothing which I fear more than peace; the stronger the desire to bring it about the more dangerous it will be. It is the weariness of a man who is in danger of losing his life in a paralysing cold such that, if he gives in to the pressing needs of the moment, he will never revive.

Resisting when others hesitated or despaired, he did not give way to impure thoughts of revenge on his return to Paris as victor.

> In the eyes of history the English will appear in the most favourable light in this catastrophe because they do not give the impression of having come here fired by a thirst for vengeance and reprisals, as we do. They appear as a master who punishes with a proud calmness and an impeccable integrity – in short, they have more distinction than us.
>
> The long marches which we have made have prevented us from maintaining a strict discipline everywhere, but even amongst our officers there has often been displayed a spirit of covetousness for which we have so often decried the French; I cannot say how much that saddens me. But this is entirely due to the role we are playing and which I had imagined more honourable.

And further, 'My most pressing wish is that this epilogue will quickly come to an end because I find it repugnant to my feelings to hold another by the throat while the interminable conflict of interests and parties is repugnant to my reason.'

I am moved by Clausewitz's letters to Marie, his fiancée and, from 1806 until 1831, his wife, even more than by the nobility of soul shown by the above. The correspondence is singular and perhaps unique, bearing witness to a passionate and constant love. The follower of Machiavelli here betrays the two souls within him, a will for action and a quivering sensibility. Perhaps the juxtaposition of several quotations will enable the reader to see the sympathy which I can feel towards this enemy of Napoleon and of France. 'No man in the world feels more than I the need for the honour and dignity of the nation.' Nevertheless he is, no more than Machiavelli, a believer in the immutability of political matters.

> The highest institutions of civil organization, however many centuries they may have lasted, contain within themselves the seeds of their own destruction. . . . If religious feeling in its elementary purity will haunt man eternally, no actual religion will last forever. . . . While the artist has within him the elating and strongly

satisfying feeling that the object of his aspirations lies far outside all convention, not only in time and place, but also in the eternal and infinite, . . . urban man must take refuge in strict conventions to lay the corner-stone of his own building; he will scrupulously demarcate his territory in time and space to gauge the modest role of his work, voluntarily limited in its duration and perfection. Everywhere he must distinguish, separate, class, choose, exclude and, with what boldness, lay a hand on this sacred unity which is the supreme good of reason and perhaps the only good recognized in this world, without knowing whether it does good or ill.

Clausewitz was a man of action with all his soul, but he also wanted to think out with all his soul his own activity, and action in general. In the peace that reigned in Europe between 1816 and 1830, this Prussian officer, who in fact belonged to a family of theologians and professors, devoted his energy and spare time to a work which he did not envisage would be published in his lifetime but which he proudly and modestly bequeathed to future generations:

Despite its incomplete form, I think that a reader who is not prejudiced and who seeks truth and certainty will not fail to recognize in the first six books the fruits of many years of reflection and of an ardent study of war; he may perhaps find ideas in them which guide him towards a revolution of theory.

To search for truth and to die at the moment of attaining it, to defend passing values, which unfaithful followers corrupted a century later – such was the fate of Carl von Clausewitz.

There is no need to be a German, a Prussian or an officer to share the adventure of this gifted soul.

Introduction to Parts I, II and III

On the Interpretation of History

Interpretation in the widest sense and for whatever its object, dreams or *Capital*, has been one of the favourite themes of French philosophers in the last few years. Claude Lefort devoted over one hundred pages in his monumental book on Machiavelli to formulating a theory of interpretation before putting it into practice. In the following few pages, in which I set out my method, I do not aim so high. The same theory of interpretation does not hold good for all authors, and each interpreter retains his freedom. Alain liked to say that the true Descartes is the Descartes who is true − a formula which is both arrogant (who, if not Alain, made the distinction between truth and falsity in Cartesian writings) and anti-historic; thinkers belong to their age even when they go beyond it.

The method which seems to me best suited to the subject chosen will no doubt be judged simplistic, indeed − the highest insult − positivist. Clausewitz published nothing in his lifetime except the article against H. von Bülow in the *Neue Bellona*, the letters on the Prussian defeat of 1806 in *Minerva*, and a commentary on the campaign of 1813 until the armistice − three anonymous writings.

His masterpiece remained unfinished and he did not want it published in his lifetime. Why? He had, perhaps, not lost all hope of playing a historic role should unforeseen circumstances occur. As a general he could have published any of his works without loss of prestige: Scharnhorst had done so. But the Treatise was not like an artillery manual, it was fundamentally different from the works on strategy which he knew well and rejected. In military circles he was already considered a penman, a scribbler, an intellectual; the publication of the Treatise would have confirmed a reputation which was harming him and which was not deserved: while he certainly possessed a superior mind he also knew how to wield the sword.

Apart from these motives, Clausewitz never dreamt of publication because he was aware of the grandeur of his work and because he suffered in advance from the criticisms that he foresaw. Too sensitive to face the lack of understanding without bitterness, too proud to defend his writings, he wrote for posterity. The difficulties that meet the interpreter of Machiavelli − whom did the old collaborator of Soderini want to deceive? − are not found in this case: Clausewitz wrote for himself, for those who would be prepared to study him; he felt no need to tread warily. The man who devoted so much passion to his struggle against Napoleon and the French takes care not to characterize peoples and generals according to their nationality. If he does not spare his criticisms of the man he calls Bonaparte, he also calls him the 'god of war', and he does not refrain from

1

criticizing Frederick II either. The author of the Treatise aims to be a scientist or a philosopher – he does not always distinguish between science and philosophy. To interpret him is above all to understand what he said, starting from the sensible hypothesis that he said what he wanted to say.

Where do the uncertainties arise? Why does his 'discourse', to use the fashionable word, lend itself to divergent, indeed contradictory, interpretations? The Treatise was never finished. In the final note, written probably on the eve of sealing the chest which contained the whole of the manuscript, he declared himself entirely satisfied only with the first chapter of Book I. On the other hand, it is known that he worked on the Treatise from 1816 onwards and the last interpreter who had the whole of the archive at his disposal, W. M. Schering, specifies the dates at which the different parts of the Treatise were written, unfortunately without distinguishing between hypotheses, suggested by content and style, and assertions supported by philological arguments. In any case, the fact that the Treatise was never completed, and the intention to revise the manuscript which Clausewitz expressed until his death, compel us to take a first step which was once classical: to begin with a study of the formation of his thought. The chapter entitled 'The Life of Clausewitz' was not indispensable; I could have only written about the stages of his career and the battles in which he had taken part or at which he had been present. Without explaining the work through the writer and the theoretician through the soldier, it seemed to me that the texts on action or the letters to his fiancée or wife, between 1806 and 1815, would help the reader, particularly one who does not read German and who does not know the literature of the 'war of liberation', to sympathize with a typical representative of an elite, an elite which was both rationalist and romantic, more German than Prussian, and which refused to despair at the time of collapse and prepared the way for recovery.

Of more consequence than this brief account of his experiences are the following two chapters where I try to follow the formation of Clausewitz's thought between 1804 – the first notes on strategy written by the 24-year-old officer were published in 1937 – and 1830. These texts force us to accept two assertions which provide the basis for interpretation: Clausewitz conceived several of his themes, several of the guiding principles which historians attribute to him, very early on; it was late in his life that he completed the systematic organization of his thought and, in all probability, it was only in the last three years of his life, between 1828 and 1830, that he fully grasped the distinction between concept and reality, or, to express it in his own terms, the unreal character of absolute war. This allowed him to progress from his first definition of war, which is always quoted, to the threefold (trinitarian) definition, the final state of his thought.

In other words, the interpretation of the Clausewitzian system requires an ordering of texts according to their date. A second rule emerges from this first one: the current practice, even among serious-minded historians, of juxtaposing quotations taken from different chapters of the Treatise seems to me to be, if not condemned, at least dangerous. Owing to his method, Clausewitz does not take into account in each of his analyses all the elements of a problem. He emphasizes one element, or else he follows the logic of one line of reasoning. In order to make a valid comparison of the different passages in which he deals with the same problem, it is necessary to approach the whole and not to take phrases out of their context; for example, the proof of the need for the greater force in defence appears in Chapter 2 (Book I), Book VI and the *Principles of Instruction* given to the Crown Prince.

Clausewitz, as we shall see, continually uses the relation between the means and the end, and he constantly refers to the purpose or to the objective of actors. The interpretation of Clausewitz, like that of every actor — in this case an actor in relation to his work — likewise makes it necessary for us to discover his object or purpose. What did he want to say to posterity? What was the intention behind his discourse? The answer is to be found in the texts themselves, but studying these texts involves the risk of inducing error should they not be placed in a historical context, or should the meaning given to words by his contemporaries not be brought to light. In short, the old and trusted methods of the history of ideas still remain indispensable today, at least as a preliminary step, if we wish to understand the 'true Clausewitz'; in other words, to reconstruct as faithfully as possible what he thought.

There are some people who retort that the historian loses himself in a vicious circle between the age and the work. He construes the age through which he then explains the work, without taking heed of the fact that he only knows the age through the works, and these reveal to him what he claims to explain. This real but not insurmountable difficulty marks the limits of the historical method of explanation, it does not entitle us to exclude it. Clausewitz's experiences of the years from 1792 to 1815 do not explain what places the Treatise above all other books by military writers, nor do they explain why we passionately take sides for or against *The Prince* or *Capital*. But every interpretation which respects and honours its subject cannot and should not avoid diversion through the age, the environment or any other expression that might be chosen to define the historical field. Of course, there is a coming and going between the work and its age, between the works and the events of the age which might perhaps be called the hermeneutic circle — a circle which is not vicious.

Machiavelli, Marx and Clausewitz pondered certain problems and tried to answer some of the questions posed by their contemporaries, the society to which they belonged. They gave to the words they used a meaning which the historian discovers by studying not only their works but those of their adversaries and supporters as well. This perfectly historical means of interpretation does not exhaust the content of any great work, b⋅ nevertheless averts what continues to appear to me to be an inte⋅ error and an ethical fault: the translation of the thought of an a⋅ language or conceptual system which was either foreign to h⋅ a different tone (or a different meaning) in his age th⋅ To take a single example: Clausewitz was not un⋅ revolutionary repercussions of arming the people⋅ to overthrow a weak and corrupted state, as ⋅ in the extension of Clausewitzian thought. Lik⋅ the capitalist system incites wars, and that these defensive character according to the nature of the⋅

the formula, but the author of the Treatise would have rejected it, because he would have considered it incompatible with historical experience.

It follows that a twofold distinction is imposed here: between the framework of the thought of Clausewitz the man and the framework of his system, between the interpretation of his system in relation to the historical environment and the interpretation in relation to our present age. Clausewitz considered wars between states to be a normal phenomenon; in the Treatise he accepts the fact of a duel, two fighters each seeking to impose their will on the other by violence. The fight assumes its own form, of a greater or lesser intensity, in each historical setting. In other words the historical (or political, if one prefers) setting contains in itself the features of the war: this idea appears self-evident to him and, for that matter, banal. Could any witness of the wars of the Revolution or Empire have not been aware of this? On the other hand, he would have greeted with scepticism Lenin's idea that wars would disappear at the same time as capitalism (or the monarchy or despotism). By starting from the premise of the test of will and of force between states, he implicity discounts an irenic vision of the future. Yet nothing prevents us from inserting into the framework of a historical sociology, originating from Chapter 3(B) of Book VIII, some of Lenin's hypotheses, which are moreover false, on the relationship between the economic system and conflicts between states. Furthermore, it is only proper, out of respect for the author, not to confuse what he actually thought with the extended meanings that later events give to his analyses.

The distinction between the thought of the man and the logic of the work remains simple in the abstract, at least in the examples I have just chosen. It is very different when we examine the logic of the work itself. This raises a fundamental ambiguity, as in any philosophy of politics and therefore of action: is it a logic of what is desired or a logic of what is real? How does the transition from the real to the desirable take place? When does the analysis of what has happened suggest what should have happened according to efficacy and morality? This kind of uncertainty in one form or another feeds inexhaustible debate on the ultimate aims of Machiavelli. Once the two extremes are put to one side – the instruction on despotism for the princes, the instruction on liberty and distrust for the people – what is the role that should be ascribed in each of the analyses to the melancholy statement that 'such is the course of human affairs', to the hidden indignation against villainy, to the counsels of prudence, courage or trickery? More profoundly, was Machiavelli in all conscience opposed to what Leo Strauss calls classical philosophy, or was he simply extracting from his experiences in the Italian cities, in the light of a semi-mythological past, a political sociology without illusion and a praxology for all alike, peoples and princes, good and bad: a catechism of success?

We know only too well that the same ambiguity affects the system of Marxist thought. The synthesis, characteristic of the doctrinaires of the Second International, between the laws of historical development and the action of the working class, has not stood up to the test of time. It required a certain conformity between the future development of the capitalist system (a deepening of working-class discontent or of economic contradictions) and the actual evolution of European and American societies.

Macrohistoric determinism is not incompatible with the role of men, classes and their will. But determinism is in danger of sinking into voluntarism if the action of the masses or their leaders breaks free of any determination by the historical setting, which is itself the crystallization of men and their relation with things. The latest interpretation of Marx which is at present fashionable in Parisian circles resolves the antinomy in an original way in that it radically dissociates two themes which previous interpreters usually linked; systematic determinism and inexorable development. According to the theory of Althusser, determinism only applies to the functioning of the system, to the synchronic relationship between the parts. At a stroke, auto-reproduction ceases to run into a barrier whose resistance would cause the explosion of the system itself. This explosion, or, in other words, revolution ceases to flow from the structural laws of the system; it is determined by the combination of many, possibly accidental, causes.

The same ambiguity of the relationship between the real and the desirable, between determinism and will, has weighed time and again on the interpretation of Clausewitz. However, Clausewitz in this respect imposes stricter limits on the fantasy or imagination of interpreters. The ultimate purpose of Machiavelli the man or of Machiavellian discourse will always remain unclear. The ultimate purpose of Marx the man or of Marxist discourse escapes clear definition because prophetism and science, faith and the quest for truth, in turn or simultaneously, inspire a work which is all the more fascinating as it discourages rigorous formulation.

The purpose of Clausewitz can be easily seen if you are prepared to read him carefully. (I should add that there have not been many careful readers.) Over a period of some fifteen years he sought to formulate a conceptual system, a theory (in the sense that we speak of economic theory today) which enables the concept of war (or real wars) to be thought out with lucidity. At the age of 25, influenced by Scharnhorst and events, he already knew which types of theory to reject as being contrary to the nature of things and as offering bad advice: namely those which failed to recognize the role of emotion, of military virtues and of passions; in short, of the human side of war and its conduct, those which put forward strict rules and claim to have discovered one rule amongst them all which is responsible for victory or defeat, those which failed to take heed of the singularity of each combination of events, and exclude the part played by accident and good or bad luck. But of what worth is a theory that bears no resemblance to unilateral, pseudo-rational, illusory, deadly doctrines? Clausewitz pondered for fifteen years before he gave a definitive answer which none the less remains ambiguous in certain respects. He, too, could have quoted after Montesquieu the Latin adage: *proles sine matre creata*. Like the author of *De l'esprit des lois*, who perhaps influenced him more than the Germans thought, he sought the theory of a praxis amenable to changes in history, to the hazards of fate and to human passions.

While the purpose is not in doubt, the same cannot be said for the unfinished work. On certain important points – the two types of war, the connection between the two definitions of war at the beginning and end of Chapter 1 of Book 1, the revision that he intended of Book VI – the debate continues and to my mind will continue indefinitely for two reasons.

5

Clausewitz himself never succeeded in entirely clarifying his own ideas; his conceptual system suggests many precepts but at quite different levels and in terms of quite different arguments; sometimes precepts necessarily flow from concepts or principles and present an abstract truth, sometimes they are based upon historical experience and have no validity beyond that limited experience, and at other times they follow from the logic of a type of war in the same way that in Montesquieu certain laws follow from the nature or from the principle of a type of government. Finally, the interpreter wonders on many occasions whether Clausewitz the man always expresses himself in a language which accords with the logic of his system.

The large number of possible interpretations of Clausewitz in his time is vastly multiplied when we examine what remains of Clausewitz in our own age. The strategist certainly is limited to a smaller field of action than Machiavelli or Marx. He does not lend himself to as many transfigurations as the Florentine secretary of state or the mythical ancestor of the Soviet regimes. However, he has not escaped the misunderstandings that he foresaw and against which he warned his readers.

The fact that there is a mass of contradictory or at least incompatible interpretations between Machiavelli and Marx and ourselves does not mean, contrary to what Claude Lefort suggests, that we should not go straight to Machiavelli, Marx or Clausewitz. It is the contemporaries and predecessors and not the heirs, legitimate or illegitimate, who provide the necessary approach. To understand what Machiavelli or Marx meant to say one must turn to their characters, their purpose and their age. The understanding of their discourses will help us to understand later interpretations – an understanding which itself calls for reference to their age and intentions. Historical study does not make it possible to decide categorically in favour of any particular interpretation of Machiavelli or Marx because the purpose of each remains ambiguous or because the work puts together diverse elements amongst which each selects, emphasizing some elements and ignoring others.

The interpretation of Clausewitz in the light of Lenin or of Mao Tse-tung, or in relation to the realities of the nuclear age, seems to me legitimate, but at least for those who respect the prerequisites of historical knowledge – on condition that two quite different tasks are not confused: on the one hand there is the interpretation of what Clausewitz meant to say to those who belonged to his world, to those who shared the same historical experience and who gave the same meanings to words, and on the other, there is the interpretation of the meaning or meanings which his work and system retain or take on for us, in terms of our own world and our own experiences. Whoever confuses the two tasks violates the rules of historical dialogue. If the interpreter, firmly placed in time as he is, does not manage to become detached from himself in order to go and meet the other, what is the good of questioning an interlocutor who will only send us back our own words, like an echo?

In short, I would answer those who ask me from which position I examine Clausewitz as follows: from my willingness to read and to listen while detaching myself from my own position – perhaps an unattainable ideal but not an inconsistent desire. The hermeneutic circle between the parts and the whole, between the man and his age, between experiences and a work, effectively presupposes that the interpreter is free and accessible. If he studies a philosophical work he can pursue his formulation and his intelligible reconstruction of the work to an end without worrying himself about his own situation. If, on the other hand, he seeks the living nucleus, the ultimate inspiration, the guiding principles, the continuing message of Machiavelli or Marx, he cannot fail to find what he is seeking; he will insist on what he thinks odious if he is fighting Machiavellians or Marxists and will insist on what he will always consider admirable if he sees himself as fighting for the same goal.

Furthermore, a distinction must be made between the subjective reinterpretations which are characterized by the predilections of the interpreter of historic events. By referring to current economic science, the interpreter legitimately brings out consequences or implications which Marx himself had not clearly perceived. The theory of today gives a richer meaning to the theory of yesterday. The practice of today enables one to grasp the full significance of an analysis which a century ago met a lack of curiosity bordering on indifference. I shall have occasion to outline such reinterpretations in Parts IV and V.

Yet this has nothing in common with the interpretations which contradict some of the most categorical assertions of Clausewitz. Whoever asserts the autonomy of military calculation, whoever rejects the intervention of politics in the conduct of operations, whoever puts absolute war into the same category as total war, whoever postulates absolute war as an ideal to be attained, does not interpret; he falsifies. Between the reinterpretations which are strictly faithful to the letter of the texts, or to the logic of the system, and deliberate or unintentional falsification, there are many intermediates, to use an expression dear to Clausewitz himself.

Part I
From Writer to Writings

The Treatise comprises three of the ten volumes of the *Hinterlassene Werke*. If the seven other volumes of correspondence, political articles and the course on guerilla warfare are added to it, the major work only forms a fragment of the writings of Clausewitz. Yet, for reasons which will immediately become apparent, I intend particularly to clarify and elucidate the Treatise.

I have chosen a seemingly circuitous route. Some will say that the third part, 'The Theoretical Scheme', would have been better placed at the beginning. In fact, it is the very logic of my undertaking that has led me to the structure which I have ultimately adopted.

Clausewitz only published unsigned articles in his lifetime, he never perfected the Treatise and he wrote, before sealing the manuscript, that the latter in its existing form lent itself to all sorts of misunderstandings. Consequently, I believe it suitable in the first instance to follow the stages of his thought, not only before 1815, but also during the years 1816 to 1830. The method adopted is not a simple one for the reader who suddenly, without preparation, is asked to penetrate Clausewitz's universe. In particular, the first paragraphs of Chapter 3 require, in their expounding of the final thesis, close attention. The significance of these paragraphs will become clearer to the reader who is willing to return to them having read to the end of Part III of this work.

The order which I have followed in the account, or commentary, does have one limitation. Since, as I believe, Clausewitz only fully mastered his own system at the time when he wrote the first chapter of Book I, it is advisable to read and interpret the whole in the light of what I sometimes call the final synthesis or intellectual testament. In the final note, drawn up before resigning his appointment as director of the military academy, he himself expressly indicated that he only felt satisfied with the first chapter of Book I. I therefore had to retrace fully the broad lines of the evolution of Clausewitz's thought before analysing the 'dialectic' of 'The Theoretical Scheme'.

On the whole, I kept strictly to the texts themselves and to the military writers known by Clausewitz, and I willingly disregarded the commentators except to set their interpretations against mine. I made only one exception which seemed to me indispensable, even though I appreciate the drawbacks, notably the 'strategic debate' which was started by Hans Delbrück. He inextricably threw into confusion a discussion on the thought of Clausewitz with a debate on the two kinds of war or strategy. Without referring to it I could not discuss the Foreword of 1827. Nor could I report the analysis of the strategic debate without coming back to

Clausewitz himself. Any other solution would only have led to more complications than the one I finally chose.

In Parts II and III, I did not intend to reproduce in detail Clausewitz's strategic or tactical ideas. In particular, I have hardly used the 'Outline of a Theory of Combat or Tactics'. This text, entirely neglected by French readers before 1914, would have prevented them from making errors. As my main purpose is to draw out the way of thinking and, so to speak, the mental structure of Clausewitz, this text supplies almost nothing which cannot be found in the Treatise itself. The method is at once conceptual and empirical.

The following account – analysis and commentary – does not aim to replace the actual reading of the Treatise but to make it easier. Its aim is to guide the reader in his exploration of a text notoriously irksome for all but military readers. I trust it will not provoke in its turn as many misunderstandings! Anyway, that danger is now more remote than in the past as Clausewitz has found his natural home: the universities.

Chapter 1

The Life of Clausewitz

Carl von Clausewitz, the fourth son of Friedrich Gabriel Clausewitz, entered the Prussian army at the age of 12, in 1792, as a *Fahnenjunker* (ensign). He died in 1831, after reaching the rank of general at the end of a brilliant career. He knew of no existence other than that of the soldier, he received no teaching other than that of the military academy, where, admitted in the autumn of 1801, he met Scharnhorst, his spiritual father. He owed his education to extensive reading and reflection.

Between 1792 and 1831, Carl von Clausewitz passed, with his generation, through two epochs of history. First, the Europe of the wars of the Revolution and Empire – from 1793–4 as a 13-year-old soldier, until the campaign of 1815 when as colonel he served as chief of staff to General von Thielmann who was commandant of the Prussian corps positioned opposite Grouchy after the battle of Ligny. Then, the Europe of the peace of the Holy Alliance which, while offering officers in search of exploits few opportunities, encouraged reflection on the lessons for the future, to be drawn from recent events.

Inseparable from mainstream history, Clausewitz's life also divides into two periods: one devoted above all to action and the other to writing. Indeed, the young officer measured himself against theoreticians while he attended the military academy and while he had served as aide-de-camp to Prince August. The 'Strategy' of 1804 bears witness to an astonishing maturity of mind, and many of the themes or methods characteristic of the Treatise appear in it. In 1810–11, he taught for two years in Berlin, at the establishment where he had met his master during a course on guerilla warfare. He was made responsible for the military education of the crown prince (1810–12). This led him to write a memoir, dated 1811, before leaving the service of the king to fight Napoleon in Russia. This memoir helps us to follow the development of his thought between the first notes of 1804 and the Treatise. However, after 1815, Clausewitz probably did not consider that circumstances excluded him from action for good. In the wake of the French Revolution of 1830 and the Polish Revolt, having resigned the directorate of the military academy, Clausewitz was not only appointed inspector general of artillery, he was also appointed chief of staff to Field Marshal von Gneisenau, then in command of the Prussian army on the eastern front. He had lost none of the passions against the French which had animated him since his childhood, nor had he lost his taste for the plans of campaign which were buried in the drawers in his bureau.

I accept the reservations which the biographers of Clausewitz express about the distinction between the two periods: *Geist und Tat* (to adopt the

11

title of a small volume of miscellany published by W.M. Schering). The soldier never separated thought and action and, similarly, he did not separate war from politics nor understanding from sensibility. If, despite this, I maintain the distinction in a limited sense, it is because circumstances have so dictated, creating a situation comparable to that in which Thucydides or Machiavelli wrote their works or, at any rate, their principal works. It seems that we owe the great books on action to men of action whom fate deprived of their crowning achievement, men who arrived at a subtle blend of engagement and detachment which left them capable of recognizing the constraints and shackles of the soldier or the politician and also capable of looking from outside, not indifferently but calmly, at the irony of fate and the unforeseeable play of forces that no will can control. Philosophy presents an image of pessimism. For what, may one ask, makes victories precarious and the state unstable? Whoever devotes himself to the state chooses to build sandcastles. There remains for him only the hope of Thucydides or that of Clausewitz: 'My ambition was to write a book which could not be forgotten after two or three years but which could be taken up several times when required by those who take an interest in this subject.'

Can one compare Vom Kriege with the Peloponnesian War? Indeed one can, but only to contrast them. Thucydides related the great war and inserted, even in the narrative, the lessons which he drew from it. The interpretation of men and events constitutes the articulation of the narrative itself. Clausewitz related several of Napoleon's campaigns: the Treatise uses the narratives to raise a conceptual edifice, a theory of strategy. To the extent that this theory is based on historic experience and tends to pass beyond it in order to formulate eternally true or valid propositions, it persuades the interpreter to bring to mind the personal experience of the theoretician and the material data which the latter did not recall on each occasion because he assumed they were known.

It seems to me both impossible and fruitless to write a political and military account of the wars of the Revolution and Empire. It seems equally futile to narrate once more the Prussian collapse after Jena, the work of the Reformers, the alliance with Napoleon in 1812, the War of Liberation after the disaster of the Grande Armée and the participation of the revived Prussian troops in the battles of 1814 and 1815. Nor do I intend to offer in a single chapter a summary biography of Clausewitz. By letting him speak, by using and abusing fragments of his correspondence and occasional writings, I hope to help the reader to understand the man, his twofold passion, the stages of his career, his tribulations, his farsightedness. Followers of pure theory will judge this biographical sketch unproductive. Perhaps they are right; let them – if they find the concept of abstract or absolute war fascinating, or if Marie von Brühl bores them – jump to the following chapter.

1 Origins and personality. Clausewitz and Marie von Brühl

The father of Clausewitz, Friedrich Gabriel Clausewitz – no 'von' – was born on 13 February 1740 in Halle, the only son of the Professor Benedictus Gottlieb Clausewitz's second marriage. At the age of 9, following the death of his father, he was brought up by the second husband of his mother, Major von der Hundt. The latter made him recognize a nobility which his parents and grandparents, professors of theology and philosophy or pastors, had renounced. This claim to nobility was based on connections with a Freiherr von Clausewitz of Silesia whose origins could be traced back to the end of the seventeenth century. Recent research, particularly that of E. Kessel, shows that the family had no right to nobility at all. Friedrich Gabriel Clausewitz served in the army of Frederick II when the latter, during the Seven Years' War, must have relaxed the rule by which only 'blue blood' authorized entry to the officer corps. Once peace had returned, according to the version given by Carl, an injury to his hand forced him to leave the service. Deprived of his uniform, he occupied a mediocre position in fiscal administration, tied body and soul to the institution which had dismissed him. If Carl is to be believed, his father's comrades continued to frequent the house of the old officer who reacted to personal frustration with an exaggerated patriotism and spirit of militarism. He brought up his four sons in veneration of Frederick II of Prussia and of the army. Three of them chose a career in arms, surviving the wars to end up as generals. Carl himself, despite the moroseness which darkened his last years, had a fast-moving career; major at 30, colonel at 34, general at 38.

German authors have led erudite researches into the origins of the family; some have also raised the question which arises from the psychology of inscrutabilities: was the personality of Carl marked by an uncertain ancestry? Let us read the letter written to his fiancée on 13 December 1806, after the disastrous defeat at Jena in October:

> After careful thought, dear Marie, it seems to me that it would be better to bring to an end now, in this letter, the subject of conversation that we have recently broached. This subject is only painful in that circumstances prevent me from saying everything, which cannot be done in a letter. I was going to wait until later before speaking to you about it. There was no reason for it, it was a feeling I had: there are so many things that have to be left to uncertain intuitive perception. Now, the way you spoke to me about it and the trustful intimacy of our souls, growing stronger day by day, makes me happy to tell you everything now.

Clausewitz then wrote that his father descended from a noble family from Upper Silesia whose last representative lived at Jägerndorf at the end of the seventeenth century. The latter's children 'seem to have adopted the status of commoner, since my grandfather was a professor at the university of Halle'. The family no longer dreamt of nobility,

> only my father, the youngest of the family, was of a different opinion. Anxious not to lose the definitive right to our privileges, he wrote to Frederick the Great and, declaring his noble status, he applied for a military post which suited his many qualities. The king, giving effect to his request, drafted him to the Nassau regiment.

Now we come to the official version: the father takes part in the Seven Years' War; injured in the right hand, he is forced to leave the army. The elder son is studying theology and experiences such aversion for his situation that, too old to become a soldier, he enters the civil service. The

13

fate of the three other sons is decided by the father himself. Writing to the king he ensures that, in Carl's words,

it is thus that the three younger sons, as we were, owe our enlistment to our status as gentlemen; my third brother and myself found ourselves in a regiment (bearing the name Prince Ferdinand) where only members of the nobility were admitted. Now since we had a parentage which did not seem to be of noble origin, we quite naturally came to fear that, if discovered, we should be taken for usurpers. I cannot say how repugnant this idea was to us, for we well knew that there was not a single drop of mendacious blood in us. In fact, we did not have the least apprehension: to whoever was ill-advised enough to challenge our title to nobility, we would have replied with the sword which sheltered us from complete humiliation; but in relations which needed more tact, every allusion to a usurpation was unbearable for us while a detailed exposition of circumstances could not brush it aside (as at this moment) and show us as free from all suspicion as we felt from the bottom of our heart.

Carl finally explains that his father had wanted to ask the king for confirmation of his nobility, that his friends, Rüchel in particular, had dissuaded him, arguing that nobody doubted it. The events of the war diverted them further from this step. Carl finally ends with this confession:

From the moment that our relations made me envisage the possibility that you would one day be mine, this matter began to weigh on my heart; but, knowing that the strength of the bond that unites us would not fail to give me an opportunity to explain myself in detail, I was not too worried with regard to you even though it was always painful to raise the subject only to gloss over it.

I swear that the idea of passing as a usurper or an adventurer and the idea that I could be suspected of being ashamed of my parentage, all people of extreme probity, hurt me to the depths of my heart, like pointed arrows, rousing in me the most unspeakable of feelings. You could hardly have had the first of these ideas; but it is possible that you might have been unable to defend yourself against the other at some stage. I hope, Marie, that you are also now freed from this idea and that you again belong to me with all your soul and with a relieved soul. I am too moved now to add anything else, let me leave it there. Tomorrow, I hope that I shall see you again, that I shall see your exquisite face, your heavenly face.

The letter bears witness to an ill-restrained emotion, to insoluble contradictions, to a wounded pride. To be sure, Carl does not want to doubt that his father is connected with the family from Upper Silesia whose nobility has, so to speak, fallen into desuetude by the conversions of two generations of professors to the bourgeois state. The letter, vibrant with love and suffering, betrays doubt in the denial of doubt. Doubt and denial were equally distressing for Clausewitz who, according to his own scale of values, should have brushed aside this obsession with 'blue blood' that did not run in the veins of Scharnhorst. Yet, in the Prussian army of the nineteenth century, which remained largely unchanged until the beginning of the next century, Clausewitz could not show indifference to his ancestry without passing as a cavalier of fortune, or without escaping from the morality of the Prussian universe, in whose light his father had raised his three younger sons. To doubt his nobility would mean accusing his father, doubting his word. Marie von Brühl herself belonged to a great Saxon family of imperial nobility. How could Marie's mother easily consent to marriage with this poor officer if he did not even possess a legitimate nobility and at the same time was guilty of usurping an officer's rank.

I have lingered for a few moments on this letter, a witness to a worried soul, deprived of inner peace to his last day. This uncertain nobility – bastardy in the words of Sartre – left its mark on the personality where the taste for concepts and abstract constructions, proper for theologians, is found in the theoretician. After all, in addition to a philosopher of war, Clausewitz could be called a theologian of war. He questions the existence of war no more than the theologian questions the existence of God. He puts in a rigorous form the ideas which involve the nature of the reality or of the idea to a greater or lesser extent confused.

In spite of his obscure origins, a peculiar destiny compelled Carl to spend the greater part of his life, from 1803, in the company of the illustrious. Following his return from the French campaign (1793–4), he was garrisoned for eight years in the small town of Neu-Ruppin – eight years in which the young lieutenant schooled himself to pass the entrance examination of the military academy. The two years in Berlin, at the academy, mark a turning point. Emerging as top of his year, he became, on the recommendation of Scharnhorst, aide-de-camp to Prince August whom he accompanied during the campaign of 1806 and his subsequent captivity in France. He only left the prince, in 1808, to rejoin Scharnhorst when he was instituting the reorganization of the Prussian army. Many of the circulars or instructions, published by Professor Hahlweg, are from the hand of Clausewitz who, among the Reformers, so to speak, held the pen. It was he who drafted the famous *Professions of Faith*.

The contrast between his origins and his surroundings – the environment of the court and the trappings of great nobility – must have accentuated his inclination to retire into himself, to withdraw into silence and seriousness. It seems that Carl was very soon aware of his intellectual superiority, not in relation to some – Scharnhorst and Gneisenau he both respected and admired – but in relation to most of those with whom he associated in the company of the prince.

In a letter of 29 September 1806, the eve of the disaster at Jena, he wrote to his fiancée:

> When I draw a conclusion from all the observations that I have occasion to make, I always arrive at the probability that it is we who are going to win the next great battle; little though the weight of reasons which balance the scales on the side of hope might be, it is enough to give me and you, equally, cause for severity.
> Probability would become certainty, hope would be transformed into conviction if I had complete freedom to organize the conduct of all this war and to organize each of the armies as I understand them.

The man who writes these lines is only 26. Perhaps he feels the confidence that he expresses. Which officer, which patriot resigns himself to despair before even fighting? Yet certainly, by this thought, he puts himself in the position of *Feldherr* or of a warlord, so promising his beloved a victory which 'will save Germany and Europe', clearly rendering him worthy of his adorable Marie.

The poor officer, inclined to intellectual speculation, aware of his worth, does not take part in the gaiety and diversions of those who surround him, particularly the courageous but frivolous Prince August.

It is a strange thing, this tense gravity that nature has put in me and from which I am completely incapable of freeing myself. I could not be induced at any price to take part in a masquerade, to play an entertaining role in society. I know that this is commonly known as pedantry, but it would be wrong, for as far as I am concerned, it happens completely against my will, or at least irrespective of it.

Many of those who met him in society or in the service responded to his seriousness, to his lack of vivacity, with hostility, indeed with that irony which is often directed towards the intellectual officer. As if this officer lacked martial virtues! His conduct at Prenzlau and in the battles of 1814 is enough to banish such suspicions.

In fact, Clausewitz passed judgment free from indulgence on his contemporaries and those whom he saw in higher positions. The portraits of the leaders of the Prussian state, on the eve of the disaster, remind me of some of the portraits that Alexis de Tocqueville left us in his Memoirs. A comparison in some respects is paradoxical: Clausewitz raised himself, thanks to his intelligence, above his status, de Tocqueville belonged to the old nobility. Moreover, both played secondary roles when they felt, despite themselves, superior: one in 1806 and the other in 1848, one dreaming of himself as a war leader, the other as statesman, one conceiving campaign plans, the other drawing up the model of a democratic and moderate regime; the one following Prince August, the other Odilon Barrot (who still remembers the leader of the dynastic opposition?). They were both considered distant, proud and, even though it concealed timidity, to possess a personality ill-reconciled with itself (the Norman aristocrat rallied to democracy with the head rather than the heart). When they let their pen run freely on paper, the ferocity of their judgment justified, in a certain way, the antipathy which they aroused. All things considered, those who accuse them of arrogance are not mistaken: these two men of thought, who wanted to be and were men of action, cast their eyes on the majority of others with the pitiless glance, just or unjust, of a misunderstood genius (or of the genius who believes himself to be misunderstood).

Yet, it cannot be said that Clausewitz was misunderstood by the few superiors to whom he was devoted. Scharnhorst immediately discerned his talents; he was loved by Marie, so distant from him by birth. The letter of 9 April 1807, written from Soissons, which might raise a smile, accurately discloses the two passions of the young man:

> But there are two facts in my life which have left an impression of joy that nothing has caused to disturb or weaken and that, at least on some occasions, has made me forget everything else. The first is the distinction which falls upon me when placed at the head of forty

16

young people, all jealous to surpass each other in qualities of mind and military science. Without making me think that I was superior to all the others by the qualities of my mind, this privilege did at least convince me that my thoughts came closest to those of the head of this institution, a man whom I judge well able to assume the responsibilities extended over the theatre of great events; I should add that I cannot say how flattering this reward appeared to me. The second fact is to have won your love. You will never believe, dear Marie, what progress I find that I have made, thanks to this, in the direction of the goal for which I aim. It was a need for me to love, and what sensitive man would not understand this fine aspiration? Yet, a love which would have enclosed me in the humdrum circle of life would only have roused bitterness and dissatisfaction in me; it is love directed towards a quite exceptional being that accelerates our passage along a noble career. Without going as far as that, the feeling that I have acquired an asset so rare and of such distinction is enough to make me celebrate our bond with undiluted joy; for the riches of your soul are a guarantee of the duration of my own love; my reason tells me this as plainly as my heart.

His reason and his heart were not mistaken: the love between Marie and Carl lasted until death. The last letters, sent in 1831 from Posen, although the tone has changed, bear witness to the same unbroken intimacy between two souls, to the same pride, to the same confidence.

What influence did Marie have over Carl? As a prisoner in France, he visits the Louvre and conveys his impressions to her. She gave to this 'son of the camp' (*Sohn des Lagers*) the taste for art, for paintings, for music that perhaps he had in him but which he developed and enriched in communion with her. The man who wrote on 3 October 1807:

What feelings asleep within me does this music not awaken! It is like a new world which is reborn in you. To try to convey this by words would be to claim to separate air and mist with the help of a strainer. I can only bring together the impression of the whole in the indescribable expression of love and nostalgia that makes me want to press you to my heart, my very dear wife.

Perhaps the comparisons with art which are such a feature of the Treatise owe something to the artistic initiation which Marie encouraged.

Did Carl share the religion of his loved one? Certain biographers assert this, in particular, P. Roques. On various occasions he speaks of another existence, but such expression is commonplace and does not prove genuine faith. The text most often quoted in favour of the opposite thesis is no more convincing:

I realize that we, discerning nothing, or at least little of the totality of its plan, have no right to incriminate it. Yet, it is clearly because our heart will never turn aside from the generations we see carrying faithfully the burden of life over the centuries, to find peace in faith, that our reason itself cannot completely detach itself from this earth and turn towards heaven. Moreover, it falls neither to our heart nor our reason to do it. Our view of the world must not be distracted by religion; it is a heavenly power which allies with all that is noble here below, and I, for my part, have never been spurred to some good deed and without feeling the desire, even the hope, of carrying out a great one. This, in my view, justifies my inability to take my eyes off the earth and secular history, and reconciles the feelings of my heart with the conclusions of my feeble mind.

Idealism, the philosophy of the Enlightenment, does not exclude this religious ethos – the belief in providence, albeit an inscrutable providence. What singles out Clausewitz and gives him a place on his own is that religious sentiment fired his will to act. One cannot say that politics or war have a sacred character, but the idea that man takes part in the work of providence, through his joys and sufferings, victories and defeats, is in danger of slipping, in another context and in another age, into oblivion, or at least a falsification of that idealism still alive at the time of the Reformers.

Carl and Marie did not have children. Only once in his correspondence did Carl express sadness:

> It makes me very sad to see our house empty and I must confess to you that this sadness grows from day to day, not so much because I am deprived of this good fortune but because I cannot console myself with the thought that you, the most lovable and noble wife that there is, may be left without descendants.

In a home without children Carl and Marie lived for each other, through each other; she stimulated by public affairs, he capable of following her into a world of beauty; she spontaneously serene, well balanced, he always worried and as if torn apart, plagued by anxiety. In 1807, she spoke to him of this 'passionate and unhappy nature which feeds on itself and which clings to yourself rather than to others'. Carl replied that this disposition was

> baleful and buried in myself but indisputably true; it feeds on itself, seeing that it is not nourished from an outside source and that the ravaging flame attacks myself. All this has become much clearer in the situation which has befallen me since the time of our misfortune; I spend all my time trying to find distraction and at no time have I experienced the pleasure which I occasionally felt in the past as a reward for my work. All things considered, I only know real joy in your conversation, for the rights of the heart proudly assert themselves indefeasible.

Two years later, in a letter of 9 January 1809, Marie wrote, 'As long as you are alive and love me I cannot be completely unhappy.' A little further on she cites Madame de Staël:

> No doubt the woman who has met a man whose energy has not erased sensibility; a man who cannot bear the thought of another's misery and also brings honour into kindness; a man faithful to the vows that public opinion does not guarantee, and who needs constancy to enjoy the true happiness of love; the woman who is the sole friend of such a man would be a triumph, in the bosom of bliss, over all the systems of reason.

She finally concludes:

> This rare union of very different and so often incompatible qualities that I admire in you is also what attracts me towards it so

inexorably . . . likewise you also, my Carl, attract the esteem of
your friends by your knowledge, by your activity and the
seriousness of your will, while the depth of feeling in your good
soul satisfies the least expectations of a loving, heart-rending choice
which was not to be avoided.

They had to wait more than five years for permission from Marie's
mother. Fifteen months after the marriage Carl left, abandoning the
service of his king to fight Napoleon in Russia. Previously, Marie had
given him not so much permission as an order:

your love is my only possession, my supreme possession. Yet,
should I be impossible to console on account of my person, opinion
or desires so that you were to consent to some sacrifice which you
would later regret? You must think of yourself and your own future
and to encourage you in that let me cite the Diotima of Hyperion:
it is for you to act, I am ready to suffer everything'.

2 Defeat and resistance

Clausewitz, aide-de-camp to Prince August, followed him to France,
finally capturing the laurels that had been his dream.

Before the battle, on 11 September 1806, at the age of 26, he wrote to
Marie:

If I fail to accomplish [noble deeds of heroism], I shall always have
the feeling of having robbed heaven by possessing this love without
sharing it and by being the subject of your deepest feelings. If I find
it impossible to eliminate from the circle of my thoughts this idea of
having usurped an unmerited possession, it is not because I lack
noble pride, it is not the result of any pusillanimity, for, since
childhood, my heart has been preoccupied with the desire to carry
my efforts to the top. Yet, I would never have been able to reconcile
myself with destiny if I had seen you fall to a man who would not
have raised himself above others in so far as his fate raised him
above the common fortune of this world.

He should earn his good fortune by the noble deeds which ensure his
conquest.

Several days later, he experiences an 'aesthetic impression' at the sight of
the troops and, curiously, he notes that individuals, each with their own
characteristics, stand out in spite of everything in this crowd.

This mass of individuals which the smallest military unit presents to
the eye, united in a common long and painful journey, which
should lead it to the theatre where a thousand threats of death
await it, the exalted and sacred goal that they are pursuing, all this
makes my soul find in this sight a significance which moves it
deeply.

A little further, in the same letter, we read, 'War is necessary for my
country. Moreover, when all is said and done, it is war alone that can make
me attain happiness.'

Neither love nor patriotism emerge unscathed from the catastrophe:
they even express themselves in a tone, in a style, with which the reader of
today will more easily sympathize. He is aware — and the account of the
last engagement at Prenzlau proves this — of having conducted himself as a

soldier, in the midst of danger.

I have had some distressing experiences, and my soul has endured many bloody wounds, but the rock on which I have based my hopes, on which I have relied with certainty, this rock is still standing, solid and intact . . . for, as regards my inner state, if I am not bringing back a booty rich in great exploits, I am at least free from the burden of blame; so I can say to myself that I have not been unworthy of the modest hopes that you, my generous friend, have placed in me. I can thus return to you holding my head high . . .

Before leaving for France as a prisoner, he wrote two letters, published in the review *Minerva*, in which he endeavours to explain the disaster. On the way to France he also wrote a letter, and it ends with the following lines:

Thus are the high hopes and all this fine friendship that bound us to Germany crushed. Deprived of civil happiness, every career closed to us and our troops forced to inaction, we are feeling the weight of the unjust reprobation of all Europe. I do not feel the least desire to cry out to all Germans: 'Keep up your dignity, that is to say: do not despair of your destiny.'

He rejects the fate of the Athenians under Roman domination. The memory of greatness does not console him in his abasement. On the contrary, the memory of the still very recent past makes his present impotence unbearable, inspiring him to become courageous and confident: how could his people have degenerated to the point of resigning themselves to life under the yoke? At times he, too, like all 'rebels', judges his own nation harshly:

The mentality of the Germans seems to become more and more deplorable, one sees manifested everywhere such a lack of character, such a weakening of the spirit that it nearly brings tears to the eyes. I write this with infinite sadness; for there is no man in the world who values more than me the honour and dignity of his nation; but one cannot delude oneself about a phenomenon that no one could deny.

In truth, his national passion is more often than not directed against the French. In his letters, he multiplies the comparisons between the French and the Germans, even with regard to the institute for deaf-mutes. He treats this at length in two articles, one drafted at Coppet, when Prince August, returning from captivity, stopped at Madame de Staël's and met Madame Récamier, the other drafted probably in 1807, some months later. To begin with, I would like to cite several passages so that the French and Germans of today do not forget the wrath that drove superior minds towards the twin vices of hatred and scorn.

I shall take the passage from the extract 'The French and the Germans' where Clausewitz refutes the admirers of the Revolution, those who attribute the élan and victories of the republican army to the enthusiasm of liberty.

Those who have studied Machiavelli with great care will have foreseen the outcome of this revolution. A people of corrupted morals is not capable of liberty. Such was the nature of the enthusiasm in a political field. Such is the nature of what they have already demonstrated in war. What if the French took up arms? If they trembled before a government of terror, their driving force can be proved to have little to do with either élan or liberty. That a man, whose home is haunted by the ghost of brothers, fathers, mothers and sons all guillotined, happy to leave this bloody abode, runs to war where at least murder is appeased by murder – what proof of driving incentive is this?

What of the victories of the revolutionary armies? The republic has thrown a million men to its frontiers, 'men hungry for spoils and pillage who have fought, with mixed fortunes, armies four times smaller in number. Fear was thus the sole driving force and the empire of this demon can only be of short duration'. The Revolution has not ennobled the French nation, only despotism has resulted:

This cold spirit of despotism, of a mortal in uniform, leans with all his weight on the whole nation which he takes good care not to stir up by thoughtless or tyrannical measures, so stifling all by sheer logic and cold ability. Where is the slightest sign here that France has raised herself morally above her previous condition? It is a fall that she has experienced, of that there is no doubt.

From this follows a twofold conclusion. France owes her success in arms (force of numbers aside) to the talent of her generals and above all Bonaparte. Furthermore, it is a popular error to think that a nation can fundamentally change its nature in one generation – a popular error because the only knowledge the people have is of today and yesterday. They cannot look beyond the immediate, they cannot escape the illusions of the moment to perceive the import of sense impressions.

Whatever the virulence of this fighting text, comparable in its excesses to the propaganda we knew during the first and second wars of the twentieth century, it would be wrong not to discern a simple and valid idea: the French owe their success not to superiority as a people but to superiority of numbers, to the new means of playing the deadly games of combat and to the talents of their generals united under the genius of Napoleon. With the calm of a theoretician, Clausewitz says just this in the Treatise.

The tract entitled 'The French and the Germans' need not detain us any longer. It has interest for the historian of ideas and the specialist in national prejudices and stereotypes. French characteristics, including sociability or mundanity, superficial politeness, the importance of language, vanity, excitability and shallowness, are all enumerated by Clausewitz. Classic at the time, the work is without particular originality but full of a malevolence that his experiences as a prisoner render understandable.

Let us just remind ourselves of a few ideas, banal at the time, yet startling a century later. The national sense (*Nationalsinn*), writes Clausewitz, is not to be confused with either national character or nationality. What is lacking in the Germans is the national sense.

And this tendency in our spirit which destroys the national sense, making us all cosmopolitans, this is precisely a constituent element of our nationality. We have too few beneficial prejudices; this truly critical spirit that is in us, wherever it is applied, is heedful of the good just as much as of the bad; by which I mean it recognizes the merits of other nations and exposes the faults of ours. This destroys the national spirit, which draws its strength from prejudice. I should add that reasoning in our country, far from being content to suppress salutary prejudices, has also undermined character to the extent that it has been well and truly abused.

The contemporary of the two twentieth-century wars does not attribute to the German a lack of 'prejudices' – prejudices which cement nations together. It was the French who, in 1940, accused the intellect of having eroded character. At least they did not picture themselves as the Greeks against Romans. Such historical myths not only lack originality, they also enjoy rare repetition.

The spirit of the Germans does not suit the citizens (Bürger) of a great monarchy. It would adapt to the republican form of government:

> If there is a form of government which is the least contrary to it, it is the republican regime, where its critical spirit would find its place and where a legal participation in government would fasten its attention more to its country and would put limits on its natural cosmopolitanism.

In a federative constitution, it would find itself in its true element, and it could give vent to its natural inclinations. Sadly, on the continent, large republics are impossible, particularly for Germany, by reason alone of her geographical situation, surrounded by other states.

> That is why it needs an extreme uniformity of political tasks and institutions. A splintering into parts, which can gave beneficial consequences in other countries, will necessarily lead in Germany, this country over which the foreigner never ceases to quarrel, to great divisions which will cause this empire to collapse.

The inclination of the Germans towards cosmopolitanism, towards criticism, and towards reasoning – from this, Clausewitz denies the inevitability of a strong power's existence. On the contrary, the federal constitution which has lasted so long seems to him the proper outlet for these inclinations of the German Geist – an outlet encouraging free expression. It is politics and geography that force the desire for a quite contrary constitution. The psychology of national character comes to apply in this way to the canons of geopolitical analysis:

> What, then, is the final result of these observations? They must establish that the French, by nature of limited vision and of little ambition, and, moreover, vain, are nevertheless much easier to integrate into a uniform whole, conforming as they do to the goals of their government, so producing a much better instrument of politics than the Germans, whose spirit remains intolerant of all restrictions. The diversity and originality of their individual characters give them a taste for reasoning and unflagging aspiration which make them seek the lofty goal which they have set themselves.

Curiously, for us, the comparison between the French and the Germans ends with parallel drawn between the Greeks and the Romans. The superiority over the Germans that Clausewitz recognizes in the French 'in the practice of political life', he also attributes to the Romans over the

Greeks, even though one cannot deny that the latter possessed 'a richer and finer individuality' than can be ascribed to the Germans. Clausewitz finally notes that the greatness of the Greeks lasted only 150 years, that of the Romans 800 to 900 years.

Let us now leave these transient writings, these variations on themes in vogue, which were created by the passions of the patriot and fired by the bitterness of the prisoner. Some months after his return from captivity, Clausewitz left Prince August with evident satisfaction. The levity of the prince in France, or at least what his aide-de-camp judged as such (the frequenting of salons and theatres, mundane conversations, not to mention the episode at Coppet and the love for Madame Récamier), irritated the earnest and serious patriot. Furthermore, his post near the prince, while bringing him into contact with the illustrious and the court, detached him from proper military service. Coming back to Scharnhorst, a new world was opened to him. 'It is the first time in my life', he wrote to his fiancée on 10 August 1808, 'that the forces of my soul have been lifted above the limits which mark the activities of a cramped private life.' Scharnhorst spoke to him in complete confidence on matters of the highest importance. When, on 1 March 1809, Prince August, as the recently appointed brigadier-general and chief of artillery, assumed his new offices, Clausewitz, now promoted to the rank of captain and placed at the major-general's disposal, worked in daily and intimate co-operation with the Reformers, and in particular their leader Scharnhorst. The role of Clausewitz, from this time until his departure for Russia, is difficult to separate from that of the group of military chiefs, Scharnhorst, Gneisenau, and Grolman Boyen, who were training the army of 1813–15.

However, we would leave the body of this biographical sketch if we were to try to analyse or even to summarize the conceptions and accomplishments of the Reformers in order to discover the proper role of Clausewitz. Let us limit ourselves to two famous texts, the one which suggests the measures to be taken at the Ministry of War, the other indicative of our patriot's state of mind. In the article entitled 'Über das Leben und den Charakter von Scharnhorst', Clausewitz himself summarized the fundamental ideas of the work accomplished by his master and friend:

> 1. Setting up an organization, armament and equipment to conform with the new form of war. 2. Improvement of the quality of the component units and raising the spirit of the troops. Hence the abolition of the system of enlisting foreigners, and the setting up of an organization which involves compulsory military service for all, the abolition of corporal punishment, the founding of good institutes for military education. 3. A careful appointment of officers to be placed at the head of large units. 4. New decorations, adapted to the needs of modern war.

More famous still are the texts called *Bekenntnisse* (*Professions of Faith*) in which Clausewitz, in February 1812, holding the pen for all the Reformers, in the most eloquent and most rigorous manner gave expression to the sentiments and arguments of those who rejected alliance with imperial France against Russia.

The first profession of faith begins with a merciless denunciation of public opinion which, with almost no exceptions, does not believe that resistance to France is possible. The different classes live in this spirit of capitulation each in its own way, in its own style. 'The distinguished classes are those which are corrupted, the officials of the state and of the court more so than all the others.' 'Thus did French patriots charge the leading classes, the bourgeoisie, during the last war.' Clausewitz denounces these cowards who, not content with sacrificing duty for tranquillity, pursue with unforgivable hate those who do not despair.

The first profession of faith ends with a piece of eloquence from which I shall cite a few lines:

I solemnly disavow the ill-considered hope of deliverance from the hand of chance . . . The uncertain expectation of a future which the apathetic mind refuses to envisage. . . . The puerile hope of warding off the anger of the tyrant by voluntary disarmament; the hope of gaining his confidence by vile submission and base flattery. . . . I believe and profess . . . that the mark of infamy from a cowardly submission is for ever iradicable. . . . That this drop of poison mixed into the blood of a people passes to its descendants to paralyse and undermine the energies of the generations to come. . . . That the honour of the king and of the government is incorporated into the honour of the people and that it is the sole guarantee of salvation.

The second profession of faith analyses the conduct of Napoleon with regard to Prussia, and the advantages and drawbacks of an alliance with France. Yet the patriot refuses to recognize any advantages. Security of existence would not be assured, nor would the threat of war be removed or even delayed. By an alliance with France, Prussia would humiliate herself and the nation in fighting alongside a country which is

our worst enemy. It would rob us of our greatness and would cause us extreme ill-treatment. Even more, it would surrender us, bound hand and foot, to the will of the French emperor. The people whose king has lost honour and liberty, has also lost them . . . it will be self-hating, sinking lower with the passing of each day. Such will be the fate of a prince and people who surrender, with hands voluntarily bound, to their natural and unyielding foe, a hereditary enemy who could have been overcome had there been a final and courageous resistance.

Clausewitz conceded that 'the probability of success lay against us'. In the margin, Gneisenau wrote: 'This is contrary to my conviction.'

The third profession of faith enumerates the means of fighting still possessed by Prussian soldiers, and officers: arms, guns, munitions, horses, clothes, food and money. Clausewitz then quotes the famous text of Guibert: 'Suppose that there grew up in Europe a people strong in genius, means and government. . . . We would have this people conquer its neighbours and see it overturn our weak constitutions as easily as the north wind bends fragile reeds.' He then outlines a plan of campaign which is only of secondary interest. On the other hand, he sets out the essential ideas of popular war – ideas which the Prussian general staff were to forget during the following century, but which seem to us, in the twentieth century, ahead of their time. *Landsturm* can be called up – i.e. arming a whole people for the immediate defence of a country. All men capable of bearing arms, between the ages of 18 and 60, who do not serve in the standing army or in the reserves, are armed and belong to the people in arms. He alludes to the Tyrol and Vendée.

> Two or three communities join together and form a troop or company, the name does not matter; the companies from the same district form a column or territorial brigade and these brigades from an entire province constitute a small army. At the head of these formations, there will be chiefs responsible for the communities and districts respectively, most often elected, but sometimes appointed by the king. The commander-in-chief *(Landeshauptmann)* of all the militia levied in the territory of a province is chosen from the inhabitants of that province. Nevertheless, the chiefs of the territorial brigades are invested with the ranks of army officers as soon as they take up office.

Such a scheme tends to create a popular army but not a revolutionary one because the officer corps constitutes the sanction of the monarch.

Clausewitz continues by describing war between irregulars and an enemy's standing army, even picturing the detail of operations in a region. With a pitiless prescience and cold objectivity, he foresees the cruelty of repression by an enemy and he answers the objection:

> as if we could not be as cruel as the enemy. The enemy will not hesitate to take extreme measures in repression, and at whose disadvantage? Those who have the least men at their disposal, who are fighting with regular armies alone. Let us accept the risk of repaying cruelty with cruelty, of answering violence with more violence. It will be easy for us to overtake the enemy and to draw him back within the limits of moderation and humanity.

After a comparison between the French and the Germans, in order to repeat once again that the latter are inferior to no one militarily or with regard to valour, Clausewitz rejects the classic objections that 'the Germans are not the Spanish . . . popular war will be bloody . . . it will entail dangers for the established order'. Moreover, Clausewitz replies, 'The government which itself sets up this movement will keep control of it.'

These professions of faith, which I have roughly summarized in order to give the reader the desire to read them fully, generate an ambiguous response in me. The decision of the king, which historians have usually treated without leniency, was justified by the course of events. The general insurrection dreamt of by the patriots in 1812, that the king himself ordered in 1813, at Königsberg after the disaster of the Grande Armée, did not take place. The territorial militia and the reserve army took part in battles with the standing army and performed well. The people did not rise up, they did not take up arms; the Germans left the fighting to the soldiers.

The arguments against alliance with France were refuted by the facts. The war was fought outside Prussian territory. Moreover, by allying herself with France, Prussia gave Napoleon the supplementary means of launching the assault against Russia, so precipitating his downfall. Now Clausewitz had always foreseen that Napoleon would not succeed in conquering Russia. We can share the feelings of the Reformers readily if we put ourselves in their place and look with their eyes at the empire of Napoleon and the 'arrogance' of the French. We still understand their rhetoric, even admiring it in parts. We also perceive the voice of the passions, noble and fatal, which tore apart the tissues of European civilization, which smashed the fragile barriers of custom and opened the floodgates to the ferocity of war. Whose fault, exclaims Clausewitz? The conquerors', to be sure. The analyst does not create the history that he interprets. The last lines added to the end of the *Professions of Faith* formulate with perfect clarity one of the conclusions of the Treatise and of history.

In as much as this great remedy is the natural manifestation of national forces subjected to excessive pressure and not the result of certain schemes, so will it cease to be necessary when the men of Europe, thanks to it, will have pulled themselves out of the chaos in order to set up organic states, according to the law of nature.

In addition, when the time returns when no people will be forced to resort to the ultimate and desperate remedy of national revolt, these times will not consider war any less a great national cause. It will be conducted in this spirit, and the degree of effort produced will be determined by the strength of national character and that of the government.

3. From the Russian campaign to Waterloo

During the years 1808–19, between the appointment to the Ministry of War and the departure for Russia, rather than come close to the illustrious without participating in their activities or influencing it, Clausewitz worked at the reconstruction of the army which now embodied the spirit of the nation. Moreover, he was put in charge of the course on guerilla warfare. Two years later, at the military academy, the strategy of guerilla war could be understood by partisans as well as by regular contingents of the army. He was granted the honour of teaching the principles of war to the crown prince – which gave Clausewitz the opportunity of drawing up, just before he left the king's service, the text entitled, 'Übersicht des Sr. Königlichen Hoheit dem Kronprinzen in den Jahren 1810–1812 vom Erfasser erteilten militärischen Unterrichts'.

On every occasion that he saw, or thought he saw, a chance for Prussia to take up the fight, he drew up a plan of operations. He prepared one in the months which passed between his return from capitivity and the start of his appointment at the Ministry of War (between November 1807 and March 1808). The following phrase is taken from it, raising echoes, too, for the Frenchman who remembers 1940: 'my idea is to sacrifice entirely the state which we can no longer defend, in order to save the army'. A little further on:

> Thus, if the Prussian army cannot attach itself to the state without falling with it, if the loss of the state is inevitable, then it seems to me that we can detach the army from the state and prove that it is wiser to entrust the powers of the monarch to the former than to bind them to the latter.

In 1809, he keeps an eye on events, always hoping for a German revolt that might be triggered off by a setback for Napoleon; in letters to his fiancée, he mentions time and again the Spanish war which undermines the strength of the emperor – were not half of the French forces, some 300,000 troops, retained in the peninsula? He admires Major von Schill who, on his own initiative, took up arms against the French but whose venture rapidly came to an end. The elders condemned it; to him it inspired respect because it bore witness to an exceptional strength of mind. 'The end crowns virtue and even makes virtuous that which, to begin with, we held to be a violation of the law and sense of duty.' The Reformer – nothing less than a revolutionary but exasperated by those who feared revolution more than the enemy – continues: 'It seems that the men of the old guard fear the terrors of the revolution and so pull long pale faces.'

From day to day, Clausewitz alternates between hope and despair; at one time he sees the glorious moment draw near when all Germans, following the Prussians and Austrians, will rise up together against the despot; at another time he dreams of dying with honour, in a supreme and vain fight; and at another, he expresses himself in the vocabulary of the philosopher. In peaceful times, there would be some nobility in giving up the display of eternal honour which rewards the vanity of those who occupy high positions. That does not apply today. If only the struggle between virtue and misfortune were openly declared, it would give us strength and would save us from the abyss into which we are gradually sinking. 'I do not mind disappearing into it. But we must fight. By fight I mean nothing short of a vast exertion of strength.'

Let me cite further the letter which is the most beautiful, the most profound and the most revealing of the contrasting passions of Clause-witz, that of 21 May 1809, when the outcome of the war between Austria and France was not yet decided but when the hopes of a German insurrection had already vanished.

> Europe will not escape a great revolution of general scope, whoever the final conqueror might be. It will be less bloody and of shorter duration if Austria and Germany gain victory. If the reverse occurs, our generation may well disappear before the real crisis emerges. In this great and universal revolution (which, it must be said in passing, need not be a French Revolution) even an insurrection of the German people would only be an early symptom of impending catastrophe; only kings able to grasp the true spirit of this great reform could retain power.

Clausewitz then attacks the small-minded men who want to stem the tide, who blame men and conspiracies for the inevitable consequences of the last fifteen years' events. 'They plot little intrigues against the men of our time and against those who are marked out by destiny, fancying that they can trick destiny itself. Ah! its vengeance will only be the more frightful.'

Yet, if unrest among the people were one day to endanger the king, Clausewitz would happily throw himself into the midst of the mob and sacrifice his life for his monarch.

> I would do it, without hope or fear, for revolution demands very different remedies from the heroic sacrifice of a few individuals; it is also why I would ask myself: What am I doing there? I am acting from pride, to prove that I am capable of a noble sacrifice for the person of His Majesty. Yet if Your Majesty relies on such means, the cause is lost.

27

No other text of Clausewitz's expresses with such clear passion the contradiction felt by the conservative in a revolutionary epoch. From his youth, from his father and perhaps from his uncertain origins, Carl maintains an unconditional loyalty towards the sovereign – a loyalty to the state embodied in the king or a quasi-feudal loyalty to the very person of the monarch. On the other hand, he has too much historical foresight not to recognize the significance of the revolutionary crisis. Thus, he shared the destiny of the Reformers: he, too, contributed to the creation of the army which finally, in 1815, pursued Napoleon to Paris. After 1815, reaction set in, and the Prussian, later the German, army, which dominated nineteenth-century Europe, stopped the revolution that Clausewitz described one day in 1809, gripped by the exasperation that was roused in him by the passivity of his compatriots. Such was the irresistible wave that swept individuals aside, like chaff.

The loyalism of Clausewitz did not go as far as fighting alongside the enemy. From 1808 to 1811, he forecasts that circumstances may perhaps one day lead Prussia to sign a treaty of alliance with France: he will never fight against his country, and he will never be content to take the role of an observer. He dreams of entering the service of Austria. Yet, in 1812, Austria was also on Napoleon's side. He asks for and obtains permission to leave the Prussian army. With a letter of recommendation from Gneisenau, he leaves for Russia and enters the service of the Tsar.

Did Clausewitz have a major influence over the course of events? Does he deserve the credit for the retreat of the Russian army which, in the final analysis, precipitated disaster for the Grande Armée? Whoever refers to Clausewitz's own account of the Russian campaign will without hesitation answer negatively. Certainly, he recommended, in the discussions around Alexander, that battles should be avoided. He then asserted that Napoleon was heading for defeat if he attempted the adventure. He harshly criticized Colonel Pfuhl, who prayed for battle. He visited the camp on the Dvina where Pfuhl advised the Tsar to establish the Russian army. He came away convinced that the advice of his chief, wrapped in his theories, could only lead to disaster. He made an ambiguous report to the Tsar, endeavouring to betray neither his superior nor the truth. This suggests that, no less than in 1941, the strategy finally adopted in 1812 resulted less from a carefully considered decision than from indecision and circumstance. Far from highlighting the will of men and the role of genius, he never ceases to wonder at the irony of destiny. 'It is thus that the frivolity and charlatanism of this humbug became more useful than the integrity of Barclay.'

The judgment given on the role of Kutuzov in the battle of Borodino raises a smile when one remembers Tolstoy's novel.

In our opinion, Kutuzov was anything but brilliant in this role and showed himself to be very much less good than we could have hoped for, judging from his previous actions. The author has not come close enough to the person of Kutuzov to speak with complete certainty about his personal activity. He only saw him for a moment during the battle of Borodino and thus can only know what the contemporary opinion in the army was immediately after the battle. According to this, his role during the various phases of the action was nil. He seemed to possess neither internal power nor a clear vision of the events which occurred; he gave neither sign of vigorous intervention nor personal action. He let those who had the matter in hand act and did not seem, as far as the details of the battle were concerned, to be much more than an abstraction of authority.

He himself considered that he had been unable to distinguish himself in Russia on account of his lacking a necessary understanding of the language. Yet he does not underestimate the importance of the convention of Tauroggen. He does not credit himself with it, notwithstanding his participation in the discussions between the Russian command and General von Yorck who had been chosen by Frederick William to command 20,000 troops, placed earlier by Napoleon under the command of Marshal Macdonald to guard his left flank. The Prussian general had not received the order from his sovereign to cease fighting, or orders to disobey the French marshal or to change sides. Once informed of the emperor's rout, what should they have done? Historians and philosophers have pondered at length over this matter of conscience; did General von Yorck have the right to set himself up as a judge of the political circumstances governing the national interest, instead of following the instructions of his king? Although Napoleon had numerous followers in Prussia, as long as his power seemed to be irresistible, he, the general, was close to the patriots; Napoleon and the French obviously remained, in his eyes, enemies even when force of circumstance drove Prussia temporarily into the despot's camp.

But, two of Clausewitz's brothers served in the Prussian army. The commanding officer, C.L.H. von Tiedemann, another contemporary of Clausewitz's at the military academy, fell in the Tsar's service, ironically hit by a Prussian bullet. In his account, Clausewitz evokes the painful pleasure that he felt upon hearing the Uhlans speaking German even though they were in the other camp. The vast majority of Prussian officers blamed the 'dissidents', and only a few put their hatred of the French or of Napoleon above their duty to obey. Who, therefore, was the traitor? The question was not yet posed in the same terms as those employed during the Second World War, but it was asked nevertheless. Unlike the members of the Resistance movement in the twentieth century, Clausewitz wanted to leave to the Russians themselves the business of treaty-making with the commander of the Prussian forces. He knew, he wrote in his memoirs, that the majority of his companions in arms blamed him. He therefore considered himself ill-qualified to take the initiative in the negotiations and act as an intermediary. Between compatriots who see their duty in different terms, the tension only makes dialogue more difficult if they represent the two states, former and future allies, Russian and Prussian in 1812, British and French in 1942.

One must bear in mind the difference between the two ages and their differing violence of passion. The Prussians in the service of the Tsar did not claim to embody their country; they were following their consciences. Finally, at the request of the Russian General Diebitsch, Clausewitz went to General von Yorck who let himself be convinced. The latter had manoeuvred in such a way that the military situation, having gradually grown worse, justified his decision and allowed him to accuse his French superior, Marshal Macdonald, of having abandoned him. He declared himself neutral. Several months later, the King of Prussia launched his famous appeal to his people, proclaiming national insurrection, conceived and prepared by the Reformers. The great hope of the patriots was finally being realized.

In his account, written some ten years after the events, Clausewitz illustrates, on several occasions through examples, some of the concepts, some of the fundamental ideas of the Treatise. Let us consider one passage of the work where he writes as if he were another rebel, speaking of himself in the third person.

> The vastness of Russia makes it impossible for the assailant to cover and occupy strategically the area that he leaves behind him by the sole circumstance of his movement forward. In studying this thought, the author has come to the conclusion that a large country of European civilization cannot be conquered without the help of internal discord.

In the campaigns of 1813, 1814 and 1815, Clausewitz served first of all in the headquarters of Blücher, where he rejoined his friends; he took part in the battle of Lützen, where Scharnhorst received a wound from which he died a few weeks later. Clausewitz himself was wounded behind the ear and only just avoided being taken prisoner. After the armistice, which was deplored by the Reformers, Clausewitz, at the request of his friends, wrote an article to justify the suspension of hostilities. In 1814 the king still refused to reinstate him in the Prussian army and he filled the post of chief of staff to Count Wallmoden, commander of the Prussian legion integrated into the Russian army. In 1815, restored to the rank of colonel in the Prussian army, he filled the same post of chief of staff to General von Thielmann who commanded the corps opposite Grouchy after the battle of Ligny. The retreat which he advised his superior to make, even though he was aware of Napoleon's defeat at Waterloo, has caused controversy ever since.

Without claiming to settle the controversy, let me say that Clausewitz himself never regretted the decision or considered that any other was possible. The following is his account of events, taken from a letter written on 29 June 1815 from Le Plessis-Piquet:

> At ten o'clock we were sent a letter from General von Pirch informing us of his brilliant victory and that he was going to cut off from the rear the forces that were opposite us. Yet, the points at which he envisaged carrying out this operation were so distant that it could not be of any help to us. Cut off from the main part of the army by the turning movement of the enemy, we were left to ourselves. Moreover, we had some 45,000 men under the able command of Vandamme and Grouchy against us. We could have held on for one hour and still no General von Pirch. Furthermore, an error which I have never been able to explain had caused General Borcke to rejoin the main part of the army with our largest brigade, without which we could never have survived. At eleven, we began our withdrawal to Louvain, without loss – if this means few casualties.

In the account in Chapter XLVI, written some twelve years later, he has

30

explained the decision of General von Thielmann in the same way. He adds a further detail: the Prussian general had hoped that the enemy, knowing of the defeat of the main army, would itself have retreated for fear of being cut off. 'General von Thielmann consequently made his troops shout out victoriously and seem joyful, but this ruse did not work. The enemy still pressed them. General von Thielmann consequently had to accept further withdrawal and finally order a general retreat.' The polemic relates at the same time to the expediency of the stratagem and to the psychology of Clausewitz. Was not the latter overcome by a pessimism which made him see above all the unfavourable elements of the situation, and which prompted him to incline towards an excess of prudence foreign to the theorist who always extolled boldness?

The discussions of Clausewitz with his friends after the occupation of Paris and the final defeat of Napoleon interest us further because they characterize both the man and politics. Whereas Blücher and even Gneisenau wanted Napoleon to be executed, he seems spontaneously hostile to vengeance or revenge. He opposes the plan of Blücher to blow up the bridge at Jena, he is disturbed for political reasons that the Prussians decide not to support Louis XVIII openly since, in the final analysis, he ought to govern France. He does not want the peasants of the west to be called upon to disarm 'for it would drive to the limits of exasperation the people who took up arms for the same cause as us, only with more enthusiasm and boldness'. Perhaps, apart from noble sentiments, and apart from political considerations, he even ended up feeling a sort of respect for the French, whom he continued to detest for their 'arrogance' until the end of his life but whom he feared for their obstinacy and perhaps admired, deep down, for their refusal to lower themselves or to admit defeat.

4 The period of meditation

With the return of European peace, the period of action came to an end. Clausewitz spent three years at Coblenz, at first under the orders of his friend Gneisenau, to whom he swore almost the same friendship as his master Scharnhorst, then under the orders of a pedantic, authoritarian general, Hake, whom the colonel, accustomed to meeting superiors who recognized that his qualities were out of the ordinary, considered unbearable. On 9 May 1818 he was appointed commandant of the military academy and on the 19th of the same month he was promoted to the rank of general. He was to run the school until 1830 when, on 19 August, he became inspector of artillery at Breslau. On 6 March 1831 Gneisenau received the command of the four army units stationed in the east by reason of the Polish revolt. He chose Clausewitz as chief of staff and came close to action for the last time. Of course, Clausewitz once more drew up campaign plans against the French while regularly sending to his wife letters full – as ever – of politics and love. On 24 August, Gneisenau died of cholera. On the following 7 November, Clausewitz returned to Breslau. On the 16th, attacked in turn by cholera, he died in a few hours. According to the statement of the doctor, his death was due more to the state of his nerves, shaken by a deep pain in his soul, than to the illness.

Concerning these sixteen years, between the end of Napoleon and the end of the man who had so hated the 'god of war', the years of the writing of the Treatise, three questions call for close examination. How did Clausewitz view the evolution of Prussia, Germany and Europe? What sort of man did he become once the fury of the patriot had been appeased? What was the state of his mind at the time of his death? Can we distil the essence of what historians of a generation or two ago called moral collapse or inner torture, and those of today, neurosis?

An unfinished text written at Coblenz entitled 'Umtriebe' offers, in my opinion, suitable guidance. I quoted above a passage in a letter in which the Prussian officer admired the greatness of the revolutionary epoch. How did he interpret the French Revolution, once the storm subsided?

Clausewitz's interpretation essentially uses class concepts in the sense of estate (*Stand*). The origin of the historic crisis, in his view, is to be found in the constitution of the monarchistic states in the seventeenth and eighteenth centuries, which had radically transformed the position of the nobility. The nobility had guarded its rights with regard to its subjects, but not with regard to the prince. It no longer took part in sovereignty, and in relation to the king it no longer differed from the rest of the population. On the other hand, it preserved its rights in relation to the peasants, rights which were derived from the continuation of its privileges.

At the same time, another estate, the middle class (*Mittelstand*) had acquired wealth, business sense and self-awareness. Society was divided into three estates: the nobility, the middle class and the subjects of the nobility. The great mass of subjects did not count. This organization which 'had been the constitution of all peoples in a certain state of nature, notably that of the celebrated ancient republics, is being transformed to the extent that the position, the power and the wealth of the estates are changing'.

The nobility was progressively ruining itself. It owed its fortune to the sword and knew of no other means of enriching itself. Now this means was gradually eroded without the nobility's ever having to renounce its luxurious life-style and seek other sources of money. Even the posts in the administration and at court were of no use as long as the nobles did not understand the principles of the economic order. 'As for subsisting through industry or trade, the nobility banished the thought. There was thus no means for them to compensate for the losses suffered.'

It is worth citing the following passage which shows that Clausewitz was very aware of the stark contrast between the seignorial life of the past and the industrial exploitation of the present.

> We remember our youth and the crowd of servants, the luxury of liverymen, clothes and utensils which a noble household did not believe it could do without; it is only in the most recent times that we see gentlemen exploit their land by industrial methods and even lower themselves, if necessary, to the point of being manufacturers and traders in agricultural products.

Because of its way of life, spending much and not working, the nobility condemned itself to decline. By their way of life, working and saving, the middle class and also the peasantry grew in strength, in number and in wealth. Though nearer to each other in reality, and united within the state, the classes entered into conflict due to the very existence of the inequality of rights and duties resulting from history. Learned men and philosophers who had formerly belonged to the nobility spoke for the middle class. They became the spokesmen for the latter and for the peasantry. They appealed to humanity and to their rights: the peasants by their number, the middle class by its industry and culture, represented humanity better than the nobility. Thus the rights of the nobility appeared 'as exorbitant privileges and its position in the state as a veritable usurpation'.

Clausewitz adds that this privileged position of the nobility only constituted the survival of a social organization on the path to extinction. The nobility had lost its unique privilege of defending the country alone. Even though it provided most of the officer corps, it appeared inevitably favoured; after all, is it not an advantage to serve as an officer rather than a soldier? The nobility in the army was only another example of privilege. Finally, instead of land, the nobility received from the sovereign the grant of administrative posts, pensions and revenues. Clausewitz adds a phrase in which his twofold philosophy, rationalism and historic sense, comes to light:

> It was clear, to the tribunal of reason, that there was an abuse; but these abuses which arise from familiar notions find solid support therein and it should not surprise us much that the princes and nobility did not immediately give the philosophers credit for this point, and that they did not consider it so unreasonable that the state could be at their service without their serving the state.

The tension between the classes, resulting in the decline of the nobility and the rise of the bourgeoisie, would resolve itself either suddenly by violence or progressively by agreed changes. The tension was heightened for a second reason, the abuses of the administration. Clausewitz analyses with much acuteness the evolution towards a monetary economy: 'Money is to be considered like a lubricant which, by reducing all natural frictions, allows a much greater diversity and mobility of all forces.'

Money replaced personal services. The powers of the state or of the princes were gradually extended. Absolutism of the monarchy and growing complexity of administration progressed simultaneously. Sovereigns found themselves faced with tasks that they could not succeed in mastering.

> The rights and theoretical claims of the lower classes, which gradually emerged from initially confused aspirations, did not yet have, in the eyes of the princes, that urgent character which the claims of the nobility and of towns possessed when they required compensation for agreed sacrifices in the form of favours and privileges.

Hence the conclusion:

> Our opinion is, consequently, that the French Revolution originates from two essential causes. The first is the tension between estates or social classes, the very privileged position of the nobility, the great subjection and, in truth, the particularly strong oppression of the peasant class. The second is the disorder and favouritism and wastage which haunts the administration of this government.

This analysis, exclaimed Delbrück in an excess of enthusiasm, while perhaps not untainted by nationalism, contains in a few pages or in a few

33

lines the principal ideas of 'L'Ancien Régime et la Révolution'.

Clausewitz only puts forward his explanation of the French Revolution in order to judge and condemn the vain agitation of the post-revolutionary period. Conditions in Germany, although comparable in many ways to those in France, had not deteriorated to the same extent. There were some prodigal princes, a territorial nobility and a multiplicity of small states which limited the abuses of the administration, but there was no absolute monarchy. Germany had no need of a revolution. Only men of culture and philosophers allowed themselves to be carried away by abstract ideas. Hostility towards intellectuals finds expression under the pen of Clausewitz with a force as passionate as under that of de Tocqueville and, a half century later, that of Taine:

> The scholars who, in Germany, go wandering among several Greek and Roman authors, their heads stuffed with ancient liberty and ancient constitutions of which they understand nothing (as nobody does, for that matter), understand no more than people living about two or three thousand years ago. Philosophers, who are right about everything by dint of universal concepts and who have minds which are too distinguished to have some respect for local and historic particularities, let themselves be strongly influenced by Parisian philosophy and politics, the majority of them taking quite different roles in the whirl of revolutionary ideas.

Of course, Clausewitz discusses the intellectuals to show how they were guilty of having sympathized with the ideas of the Revolution and, at an early stage, with the French themselves. But he also expounds a philosophy which, derived from the rationalism of the Enlightenment (he refers many times to the *gesunder Menschenverstand*, to common sense), stresses the singularity of time and place. The whole of the Treatise, like *De l'esprit des lois*, aims to overcome the dichotomy between the universal and the historic.

Certainly, he does not deny that contradictions, responsible for the revolutionary explosion in France, also tormented the social organization of Germany, but the Reformer of 1809 considered the reforms essentially completed:

> Let us recapitulate the reforms carried out in Prussia and in the South German states from 1805. The great mass of the nobility lost the privileges which exempted them from taxes and personal services; the monopolies and restrictions regulating the practice of the professions were abolished. The commoner could henceforward apply for any position. Taxation, falling heavily only on the shoulders of certain classes, was abolished in favour of dues whose burden could be spread over all. All these measures had been the objectives of the French Revolution; these very same objectives were now obtained in Germany without violent upheaval.

As for the two objectives that fired the imagination of German youth once peace had returned, Clausewitz treats them both in his merciless style. German unification?

> There is, for Germany, only one way that will lead it to political unity, and that is the sword, if one of its states is to bring all the others into submission. Yet, the time is not ripe for such subjection

34

and, should it ever arise, it is not at present possible to foresee which of these German states will hold sway over the others.

Clausewitz gives greater weight to the discussion of the second objective of the youth movement, what was called an 'estates-constitution' (*Ständische Verfassung*), but not because he sympathizes with the views of those sovereigns who had allowed Napoleon to trample over the whole of Europe. It was rather because Germany or the Germans could not assert their authority more worthily abroad that the youth had called for a constitution.

Clausewitz asserts first of all that action abroad does not immediately, essentially, depend on its constitution within. Under Elizabeth and Cromwell, the English at least enjoyed liberty; they played their most effective role abroad. The Swiss have for a long time accepted political insignificance; the North Americans have not always shown themselves worthy of the great continent that they represent. According to each case, the deliberations of Parliament strengthen or paralyse the workings of the government. The geographical position of the state is of great importance. England, North America, the Netherlands benefit from a certain independence. On the other hand, a country surrounded by dangers can only triumph by secrecy, resolution and cunning – qualities which do not easily accompany the deliberations of assemblies. The institutions recommended are called 'ministry' and 'council of state': a grouping of ministers in a ministry and a council composed of distinguished personalities. Such are the – to say the least, cautious – propositions with which Clausewitz concludes.

Nothing is more striking in this text, or so characteristic of the nationalist-liberal Germans, than the sarcastic denunciation of parliamentary life, combined with an awareness of the necessary participation of all citizens in the state and its great interests.

Here is an example of his polemic:

> In such bodies there is constant life and movement, intrigue and debate, strife and success, fear and hope, terror and joy, a solidarity amongst friends and a relentlessness in hunting down the enemy; there is an enthusiasm that excites an individual and sweeps along others, finally causing some kind of activity as cunning as it is violent – a rich and flourishing political life which calls to mind the forum of ancient Rome and the market-places of Athens. In the light of such a scene of civil life the fact of quietly attending to private affairs necessarily takes on the appearance of stagnation.

Though hostile to parliamentarianism, Clausewitz desires even less a mutual confidence between subjects and the government. The subject can only belong to the state in a real sense on the condition that he is acquainted with its important and lasting interests, 'and it is at the level of this lasting orientation that the participation of the citizen will be found. The government will recognize its guiding stars and will allow it to set its course with all the more ease and celerity'. Governments need popular support, but 'this thoughtless agitation, this disordered participation, prejudiced against the government, which holds the most active prisoners of a circle in constant motion, is a true anomaly copied from the image of certain very turbulent small republics'.

Liberal but, unlike de Tocqeville, not converted to the democratic idea, he angrily denounces the student movement (festival at Wartburg in 1817, assassination of Kotzebue in 1819) in which an impassioned hatred is directed against those who deviate: e.g. the Levellers of Cromwell's time whom he would call philistines.

The short article entitled 'Über die politischen Vortheile und Nachtheile der Preussischen Landewehr', according to Schwartz, must have been written towards the end of the 1820s. Today, authors date it at the end of the previous decade so placing it a few months after the article 'Über unsere Kriegs-Verfassung' 'On our Military System'). Indeed, it was in December 1819 that King Frederick William III carried out a reorganization of the *Landwehr* or militia, the dissolution of thirty-four battalions and the incorporation, in time of peace, of sixteen brigades as divisions of the line in the standing army. The decision of the king marked the victory of the reactionaries over the Reformers (whom the former called revolutionaries). The war minister, H. von Boyen, and the chief of staff, Grolman, who both belonged to the group of Reformers, resigned in protest. In the first article Clausewitz defended the work of his friends. In the second, rising above the event, he proclaims his philosophy. Should the arming of the people be feared or not? Applying historical experience and reason, as was his custom, he answers: no.

The militia increases the threat of revolution but, by dissolving this threat, the danger is increased. What is to be feared most, revolution or invasion? We have never known a real rebellion in Germany. Can it be said that we know nothing about invasion?

The French people did not have arms in 1789. The standing army did not save Louis XVI. The Tyrolese, though armed, remained loyal subjects of the Austrian crown. Peace within – the stability of the state – does not depend on the armament or disarmament of the people. If in the final analysis, faced with an oppressed people, the government has to maintain itself by the sword, this will be identified with the martial personality of the king or his family, in liaison with a virtuous entourage. Neither the standing army nor an arming of the people constitutes the heart of the peril. Without a wise and honest government well-disposed towards the army, the militia and the people, there cannot be faithful attachment or security in the state.

Why does the government experience so much anxiety? Because it feels isolated and because it senses popular dissatisfaction. It fears the day when that dissatisfaction will explode into a refusal to obey, when the force of the army will be reduced to nothing by a militia double its size. Where should the state find its support?

In the government collecting around it the representatives of the people, chosen from those who share the true interests of the government without being strangers to the people. Ironically, this council was its mainstay, both a friend and aid in the same way that for centuries Parliament was for the King of England.

Never did Clausewitz, in defending the work of his friends, use language so close to that of the democrats.

In the final analysis, the general returns to Prussia and her military system. By devoting a greater proportion of her resources to the army than

36

most other states were prepared to, Prussia matched the most powerful. Yet were she to slacken her efforts, all those who envy her would seize the first opportunity to bring her down. To the end, Clausewitz remains faithful to the idea of the nation in arms, the result of the Prussian tradition mixing with the French example, cultivated by reactionaries who, though not accepting the work of the Reformers and the liberals, dreamt of German unity and parliamentary institutions.

After 1945, the national liberals went back to the glorious period of the War of Liberation to find the origins of a destiny that was ultimately tragic. Did the reforms of the Steins and the Scharnhorsts create the framework within which bourgeois and industrial society could develop harmoniously? The noble class, which monopolized the officer ranks as, according to Clausewitz, the French nobility had done, embodied the nation in arms. The Reformers had prepared for the rise of the last properly warlike class of bourgeois Europe which was to lead German soldiers to so many vain victories and eventually to a twilight of the gods.

By all accounts, Clausewitz's mood darkened during the years when he ran the military academy. He did not have the authority which would have allowed him to reform the school or its teaching. He, who had taught in 1810 at the age of 30, no longer gave lectures. In charge of the administration, hardly known among the pupils – among whom was the future victor at Sedan – he led a withdrawn life with his Marie, writing. There was no shortage of reasons for sadness. He suspected the king of never having pardoned his 'desertion' of 1812; he blamed himself for not having given Scharnhorst the tribute that the personality and accomplishments of that master deserved. Accepting the post of ambassador to London, he resigned when opposition arose, and was both too proud to indulge in manoeuvres and yet too sensitive not to feel some bitterness.

More than ever, in society he appeared distant and silent, disciplined but intransigent and dissatisfied with an obscure existence. Although continuing to love with the same passion the woman with whom he had enjoyed a happy intimacy, he was always aware of his intellectual superiority, and he felt condemned by his view of the world to nurture a nostalgia for the glory of arms rather than seek the fame of letters. Finally, in 1827, the king made indisputable a nobility the origins of which had weighed heavily on his early years.

Despite this, are we to conclude that he was a victim, until the end, of that tension between ideas and ambitions which divided his mind and personality? Should we accept the evidence of his doctor and his wife, according to which he died less from cholera than from the exhaustion of his will to live? I do not know. I should only like to add a few questions as a footnote to this touching and enlightening account.

Certainly, Clausewitz experienced personal disappointment with the return in force of the reactionaries whom the revolutionary wave had swept away but whom the counter-revolution gradually restored to the fore. Withdrawn into himself, he hardly spoke to the world, writing to Gneisenau, not with affected modesty but with conviction: 'Every man should keep to his rank to maintain the equilibrium of the whole.' Conservative in opinion, he also proved himself not only a difficult personality but also a trouble-maker or a spoil-sport, so forcefully did he insist on his opinion when convinced of its validity.

He suffered for years from nerves; in 1808 on his return from France he speaks of an infectious fever; he used to take the waters for rheumatism. Occasionally, a short spell of depression or melancholy would take hold of him only to be lifted by the presence of his beloved. Any number of interpretations can be constructed with the help of devices which explain the depths of profound depression. Personally, I am content to refer to a letter of 18 May 1821 which recalls, with a trembling and shy sensibility, the child of 12 whom his father is going to take to cadet school, the child who perhaps never entirely overcomes the trauma of this rupture:

> Potsdam awakens in me all sorts of heavy and saddening responses, but I am used to it. It has always been thus, and it is also rather natural since I always feel foreign and alone there. I recognized the house where I lived with my father when he took me to the regiment, twenty-nine years ago. It is not without very great emotion and enormous gratitude towards fate that I think of all the good fortune that has befallen me since then and how that journey laid the first stone. Yet I also retain a very clear picture of the melancholy feelings which especially at that time beset my heart, and which have never completely left me. Certainly, fortune has smiled so much in life that I have come to consider it as a pledge. All the same, I shall no doubt never wholly free myself from this feeling.

It may be that with age, this deep sadness, this melancholy, perhaps the price he paid to fate, was, despite Marie's presence, to darken more often than not Clausewitz's everyday life.

Yet one should believe Marie. She stood by his bedside until the very end. She wrote,

> At least his last moments were peaceful without suffering, though yet there was something anguished in the expression and the sound of his last gasps. It was as if he had decided to reject the burden of life which had become too heavy for him. Soon his features were peaceful and composed. Yet, an hour later, when I saw him for the last time, his countenance was again tormented, marked by a terrible suffering.

The thesis of the old man, weary of life, is found in two sources: the letters and his activity during the period at Posen where he was reappointed chief of staff to Gneisenau. The officer shows then, by all accounts, the same zeal, precision and efficacy as fifteen years before. The revolution of 1830 in Paris awakened his fierce hatred of France, or at least a fear lest France should again abuse her power to the disadvantage of the other European nations. In this respect, he lacked foresight. To distaste for the despised French was added a burning scorn of Poland. Two articles of 1831, subsequent to the July days of 1830, bear this out: 'Die Verhältnisse Europas seit der Teilung Polens' and 'Zurückführung der vielen politischen Fragen, welche Deutschland beschäftigen auf die unserer Gesamtexistenz'. Neither thought, tone nor style reveal the slightest hint of weakness.

These two articles spring from a sort of principle, namely that it is France and France alone which since Louis XIV – albeit with an interlude of twenty-four years during which she had feeble and peaceful governments – has placed the equilibrium of Europe at risk. From the Revolution onwards, and particularly under Napoleon, France wanted to proceed from supremacy (*Vorherrschaft*) to all-powerful empire (*Alleinherrschaft*). When France abused her power and victories to destroy historic boundaries, so arbitrarily carving out artificial states, her victorious enemies only recovered her conquests but refused to reduce her in size. 'Beneath the formula that France must be strong was concealed a conviction that a violent and aggravated reaction amongst the French must be avoided.' But what is the result of this moderation? It is that France though defeated and disarmed, will never cease to have at her disposal the means which guarantee her autonomy and independence. France possesses the qualities of a nation which is homogeneous and undivided as well as well situated, warlike and full of spirit. ... Consequently, Clausewitz examines all the questions of Belgium, Poland and Italy posed in 1831 from the narrow viewpoint of German national interest, confused, thanks to history, with all the interests of the European balance of power because France alone threatened the latter.

Was Poland to be restored to satisfy the philosophers and the fashion of the day? The loss of the territories claimed by Poland would weaken Austria as well as Prussia. The new state would become a natural and permanent ally of France. At least a hundred years would be needed for it to shed off its barbarism and attain the nobility of a European state. Belgian independence? This formed an outer defence for Germany. France could attempt to invade Belgium, and control of Belgium, of the left bank of the Rhine, would again give France the capacity to threaten the peace of Europe. What the French call natural frontiers concerns not the security of their state, but the security of their supremacy. Similarly, the revolt of the Italians is considered from a strategic perspective. Italy becomes another outer wall for Germany. Will Italy one day achieve her unity? Nobody knows, and in any case the reply belongs to the distant future. For the moment what is important is that the Italians, lightweight and disunited, do not give the French added means to attack that centre of gravity which is at the heart of European resistance, namely Germany.

Political analysis yields to the calculation of armed forces. With regard to liberal or national ideas, the uprisings of the Belgians, Poles and Italians are treated by Clausewitz with the contempt of the realist, faced with the profligacy of the philosopher or public opinion. At the same time, there transpires a philosophy of relations between European states to which Clausewitz adhered right up to the end of his life – the philosophy of opposition and equilibrium.

What is the natural opposition in Europe to England? Clearly, France. Do the philosophers consider that there is no need for such opposition? That would hardly be a philosophic opinion, for physical and moral nature is wholly maintained in equilibrium only by opposition. As for the opposition between political principles, the so-called liberalism of the west opposed to the so-called despotism of the east, that is only a matter of opinion (*Glaubenssache*) which must be separated by consideration of the relations which condition the outside security of states.

Even if principles and opinions of a political and religious order were regularly allied to material interests and outside security, they could never replace them. Suppose that what has come to be known as despotism completely disappears; all peoples are as free and happy as Paris now is and as Dresden still was until a few months ago. In this way will relations between peoples be idyllically peaceful, and will that confrontation of interests and passions which never ceases to threaten external peace be reduced to silence? Of course not! It is therefore not in maxims that we must seek opposition between peoples, but in the totality of their spiritual and material relations. Thus, on this point, it is important to consult history.

Nothing in his writings betrays the anguish or the pain of living. The passions continue to burn. The call to 'faithfulness to our princes, to our country, and to ourselves' maintains the same emphasis as at the time of disaster and shame. Just as the patriot refuses to lay down his arms, the writer does not put down his pen.

Let us not forget, either, that his masterpiece – the first chapter of Book I – dates from 1829 or 1830. In other words, the man whom historians, following Marie, show us to be morally crushed had never possessed such mastery of thought and language. According to several interpreters, in 1829 he discovered new horizons of theory. Should one therefore imagine the officer at this point as being indifferent to his work? That he wanted to be a man of action first is clear. That he did not feel the desire to pursue his patient meditation, of which the strategy of 1804 marks the first step, to its ultimate conclusion, I find difficult to believe. Inclined to melancholy, with a lively sensibility and a rigorous intelligence, borne along by the romanticism of glory and a career in arms, wounded by the contrasts, even minor, of social life, poor amidst the rich, of a doubtful nobility amidst the most lofty trappings of aristocracy, the career of this luckless lieutenant from Neu-Ruppin was deceptive. The intimacy of Scharnhorst and Gneisenau combined with the inherited qualities of his father and his own intelligence to destine Clausewitz to a role on the field of battle. He suffered from torments, yet despite these he did not succumb to the contradictions between cosmopolitanism and nationalism, between the ideals and cruelties of politics, between reformers and reactionaries, his organism, the physical embodiment of his will, finally fell victim to the ravages of cholera.

Chapter 2

The Formation of Thought (1804–30)

The biographical sketch in the preceding chapter will perhaps help the reader to sympathize with the author of the Treatise – sympathize in the etymological sense of the word which excludes neither distance nor hostility; to sympathize without having a fixed interpretation of the theory. It describes the personal experiences of a staff officer, one of the first representatives of that illustrious phalanx, typical of the Prussian and German army of the nineteenth and twentieth centuries. Hardly known in his lifetime though admired by some great soldiers, this officer raised an intellectual edifice which continues to inspire respect after a century and a half.

The personal experiences of Clausewitz contained a lesson which we find repeated in the Treatise. How could anyone fail to see the ties within the organization of armies, a mode of fighting on the one hand, and the politico-social structures on the other, at a time when the makeshift troops of the revolution introduced or generalized methods, tactics and logistics which were partly new, notably *tirailleurs*, deep columns and requisitions, while other methods – the thin infantry line, rigid formations – fell into disuse? Clausewitz could not fail to discover and observe the diversity of wars according to the times, and their risks. The Prussian collapse after Jena, the performance of Prussian troops in combat in 1813, 1814 and during the year of Waterloo: all these contrasts would have taught him the importance of morale had he needed to be so instructed.

We should not conclude from this that Clausewitz confined himself to formulating the lessons of a tumultuous quarter of a century between the cannonade of Valmy and the defeat of Napoleon at Waterloo.

We must reject such a superficial interpretation and take into consideration the strategic writings of Clausewitz prior to the Treatise. We may not possess them all, but the 'Strategy' of 1804, completed in 1808, the article in the *Neue Bellona* (1805), the fragments drawn from the archives by K. Schwartz, H. Rothfels and W.M. Schering, and the summary of the *Principles of Instruction* given to the crown prince (1812) allow us to follow the formation of his thought.

1 The criticism of H. von Bülow and the theory of definitions

What strikes the reader of the texts of 1804–5 is not so much the expression of certain ideas, certain themes, later elaborated in the Treatise, as the rigour of the thought and style. The 25-year-old lieutenant criticizes a known, almost famous, theorist with sovereign scorn and a self-conscious superiority. The intellectual arrogance suspected by those who spoke to him, and which was concealed by his silence, is manifested here without restraint. Consequently, T. von Bernhardi attributed the article in the *Neue Bellona* to Clausewitz before finding the manuscript in the family archives.

The book which Clausewitz takes as his target is called *Lehrsätze des neueren Krieges oder reine und angewandte Strategie aus dem Geist des neueren Kriegssystems, hergeleitet von dem Verfasser des neueren Kriegssystems und des Feldzuges von 1800* published in 1805. The author, Heinrich Dietrich von Bülow, brother of the general who took part in the campaign of 1815, led the life of an adventurer and suffered a tragic end. He had published *The Spirit of the System of Modern Warfare* in 1798, and a few years later (1801) a critical history of the campaign of 1800. The book of 1805 picks up the main principles of the first of these books and takes examples from the second. Yet the 1805 book, torn to shreds by Clausewitz, differs in many respects from the two earlier short treatises from which it is drawn.

The Spirit of the System of Modern Warfare appeared in a French translation, in modified form, in 1801. Although, in the Preface to the 1805 book, Bülow complains that the translation rendered incomprehensible some of his conclusions, the French version alters neither the principles nor the arguments of the author. Consequently, the hypotheses remain the same, at least with regard to strategy, from 1798 to 1805.

The first book was divided into two parts whose titles or summaries suffice to disclose their desired objects. After an account of armament and firearms comes the hypothesis of the base as fundamental to the conduct of operations. In the second part Bülow describes the most ambitious, if not the most extravagant, consequences of modern armament. Here, are the main steps of the proof taken from the French version: (a) The mass, that is to say the greatest number of fighters and the largest quantity of appropriate elements to wage war, will sooner or later decide success in modern wars; not, as in wars of the past, superiority of discipline or courage. (b) A consequence of this is that small states in the future will no longer conquer the large. On the contrary, they will become their prey. (c) Europe will one day be divided into several large states. (d) Since military forces belonging to states are not unlimited, it follows from the principle of the base that, as they move further from their region, they will diminish. They can only act in a predominant manner within certain natural limits. (e) It follows that the system of modern warfare puts force of numbers above the intrinsic worth and excellence of the fighters and that the advantage today always lies on the side of justice and liberty; that is to say that this order of things favours defensive war and the insurrection of citizens (in the case of oppression) rather than a regular and disciplined army. (f) As sooner or later the various states of Europe will stretch to their natural limits, because it is useless and dangerous for a government to operate outside nature's prescribed frontiers, there necessarily results from this order of things a perpetual peace.

All of this second part of *The Spirit of the System of Modern Warfare* disappeared from the work of 1805 and Clausewitz alludes to this when he writes that he considers the author too intelligent to believe seriously the intellectual games of his youth. The first part, namely the development of the strategic theory of the base, thus constitutes the sole object of Clausewitz's criticism. But if one intends to give transhistoric significance to the Bülow–Clausewitz dialogue, the second part of *The Spirit of the System of Modern Warfare* should be borne in mind. Bülow is a theorist who not only deduces rules of the conduct of operations from the new requirements of supply, created by armaments (the discovery of gunpowder, leading to guns, cannons, the need not only for bread but bullets, etc.). He is also a man who bases on the technical progress of weapons a theory of the factors of power, a diplomatic prospective and, in the final analysis, an anticipation of perpetual peace according to the dream of the philosophers – a dream in which he himself ceased to believe having transfigured it into an alleged science. Contrary to all those – and there remain a few today – who count on technical progress to lead humanity to peace, Clausewitz embodies the pitiless wisdom or renunciation of hope of the thinker without illusion: wars, as conflicts of great interests, which are decided by blood, take on various forms through time without changing essentially in nature. Conflict's instruments, from the spade to nuclear arms, modify the phenomena of battle without eliminating war itself.

Bülow reproduced the definitions and theories in 1805 as they stood in the first part of *The Spirit of the System of Modern Warfare*. The definitions, three in number, concern (a) the operation of war (movement of an army which has the enemy as its immediate object), (b) the line of operations (the space across which the armies move between the subject and object of operations) and, finally, (c) 'strategy' and 'tactics'.

The criticism of the definition of 'strategy' and 'tactics' holds a dual interest for us; it reveals Clausewitz's conception of science while dissecting the objectives of war.

It must be said forcefully, as interpreters have a tendency to see only the difference between the two men, that Clausewitz shares with Bülow a taste for abstraction and rigour as regards definitions, in short what they both call science. Against the scepticism of the man who inspired them by provoking them, Georg Heinrich von Bernhorst, they both want to affirm the laws of science, to reconstruct an intellectual edifice, only they conceive it quite differently. Moreover, Clausewitz confesses that for some time he was among Bülow's disciples: after all, who is not tempted to adhere to a doctrine which, in a few hours, converts one to strategy and which captivates the reader with its clarity and simplicity of argument?

In what does the science, or the scientific character, of the study of war consist? First and foremost, in the elaboration of concepts or, to use the language of Clausewitz in 1805, of general notions (*allgemeine Vorstellungen*). 'We shall apply ourselves to general notions above all, because in the constitution of a science it is to them that we shall above all return.' The prime importance of concepts is expressed and confirmed in the insistence on definitions.

Bülow defines strategy as 'the science of the movements of war outside the field of vision of the enemy, tactics being within their vision'. In the French version, the translator uses the following formula:

I call strategy the movements of war of the two armies outside the reciprocal visual circle or, if you like, outside the effect of cannon. The science of movements within the presence of the enemy so that they can be seen, and reached by artillery: that science is tactics. The formulation in the book of 1805, in German, remains the same. Field of vision and range of cannon mark the boundary between strategic and tactical movements, thus differentiating the science of the one from that of the other.

Clausewitz heaps criticism upon these definitions. They illegitimately reduce all warlike activity to movements, they base the distinction on a tangible characteristic – the field of vision or the range of artillery – and not on an abstract characteristic; they do not therefore lead to a distinction which is rationally satisfactory. How can such a distinction be reached? Usage cannot settle it since the current meaning of words, which vary with time, is not determined by philosophical principles. From this follows the positive assertion: 'Die Sache muss entscheiden' (the matter must decide).

In order for the matter to decide, it must itself comprise a structure and internal differentiation which the scholar, far from creating it artificially, actually discovers carefully by studying the subject-matter upon which usage has imposed certain limits; if he is led some of the way by this principle of the vaguely conceived division, he should finally reach the point where the nature of the subject-matter experiences a modification that is generally perceived only at its most striking, i.e. at extremes. In other words, and as it were, most perfect form, the boundary thus arising at the point where the principle of the distinction manifests itself.

All his life, Clausewitz practised the method put forward in 1805, or rather half of this method; namely he chose, as the point of departure, extremes or complete antitheses. There is hardly a trace of the search for boundaries in the Treatise.

It should be noted once more that, in order to give clarity, precision and force to notions, only complete antitheses [vollkommene Gegensätze] have been taken to represent the objects of our consideration. On the other hand, the concrete example of war is more often found in the environment and is guided by extremes only to the extent that they become more closely involved with it.

In contrasting the precision and force of the concept with approximate reality, Clausewitz suggests parallels with the ideal types of Max Weber – parallels which nevertheless require reservations: the distinction between concepts, which take the extreme case, and reality, which approximately approaches it, is the same as that between a more or less confused reality and the rationalized mental picture. The Clausewitzian distinction, at least at this point, implies a rough scale, whereas the Weberian thought contrasts a diffused or equivocal reality with a concept illuminated by understanding. Moreover, Clausewitz by no means accepted the freedom of the analyst and his legitimately arbitrary intellectual constructions: the matter itself decides. The definition grasps the nature of the subject: this nature seizes the mind which seeks the definition.

How does Clausewitz refute Bülow's definition? He begins by substituting the notion of art (Kunst) for that of science. 'The object of art is to use available means in the achievement of an end that one has in mind.' The theory of war is thus the theory of an art or of a practice (in modern terminology, a praxis). As regards the definitions of tactics and strategy, they emerge without difficulty from the definition of art – in other words, from the conceptual duel of means and end.

Strategy is nothing without combat; for combat is the matter which it utilizes, the means which it applies. Just as tactics are the use of armed forces in combat, strategy is the use of combat – that is to say the linking of single engagements into a whole – with a view to the ultimate objectives of the war.

Resorting to the duel of means and end, itself demanded by the comparison with art, alone allows the rational dissection of theory. Tactics and strategy each have a particular means (armed forces and combat respectively). If one accepts the method of extremes or of complete anti theses, the dispatch of a patrol results from tactics, the plan of campaign arises from strategy; in the one case men make use of the means or of the matter, in the other of victories, the destruction of enemy forces and the occupation of their territory. Instead of tangible criteria – the range of vision or of cannon – there come conceptual criteria.

In fact, Clausewitz does not immediately draw on the notion of art (as he could have done), or on the two definitions of strategy and tactics; he shows rather that Bülow becomes entangled in insoluble contradictions by taking the field of vision as the distinguishing criterion; he therefore attributes to tactics such movements as a column advance which in no way distinguish themselves from other strategic manoeuvres. What interests us, and also interests Clausewitz, is that the tangible criteria, in spite of appearances, lead to an arbitrary division (*Zerschneiden*) instead of an organic dissection (*Zergliedern*).

Of course, the pages between the introduction of the notion of art and the definitions of strategy and tactics also fulfil one of Clausewitz's major intentions. The eleven theorems that Bülow formulated in 'Der Geist des neueren Kriegssystems', reproduced in the work of 1805, appear to Clausewitz not only false but derisory, almost grotesque, in any case incompatible with the theory conceived by Clausewitz in 1805 and repeated twenty-five years later when he wrote the last lines of the Treatise.

I will not go into the eleven theorems in detail, but I should point out that the first lays down that the dependence of a modern army on the depots or arsenals from which that army draws its provisions exercises a decisive influence on the course of operations. From this comes the third theory: 'Operations conducted along a single line which, having a base on a single plan of operations, enters enemy territory, have an insufficient base and cannot succeed unless the enemy have neglected all counter-movements.' The most famous of the theorems is the fifth: 'Operations which are contained in a triangle or in an arc of a circle of 60 degrees or less must [*müssen*] fail according to the rule that they cannot lead to their objectives if the enemy makes use of his advantages, because they have no base.' The eighth theorem completes the fifth: 'Operations enclosed in an obtuse triangle or an arc of a circle of 90 degrees or more are the best as they have a sufficient base.'

Which of Clausewitz's major objections have retained such significance

45

today that the theorems of Bülow stand only as a historic curiosity? First and foremost, it is absurd to deduce from one element – the consequences of provisioning – strategic theorems for which two truths, scientific and practical, are hazarded. The study of the influence which provision requirements have over the movement of armies is legitimate; the dogmatism on which the geometric forms are based, the angle made by the lines of operations drawn from the edges of the base up to the objective, lends itself to a refutation too easy to be worth developing. Clausewitz hates Bülow's fascination for the strategic geometric forms just as he hates any form of dogmatism. Not only does Bülow embody geometric dogmatism, he also embodies strategic dogmatism, or, more precisely, he commits a cardinal error in the relationship between strategy and tactics. He claims repeatedly that the combats of the day no longer decide anything; he even writes that battle is no longer joined. All his theorems thus rest on the hypothesis that combats (and therefore tactics) no longer retain their ancient significance. The modern system based upon provisioning contrasts radically with that of antiquity, based on combat. Clausewitz answers this with an idea which expresses itself in the two definitions of strategy and tactics just as it governs all his work: it is that tactics ultimately produce the decisions. Strategy should prepare for or invite battle in well-chosen localities at the propitious moment, in favourable conditions; it can neither be a substitute for combat nor render it useless nor guarantee success. Clausewitz appears hostile to manoeuvre; in fact, he opposes theories in which manoeuvre is anything other than choosing the locality, moment and conditions for combat, and simultaneously exploiting them and organizing them with a view, first to the military goal, and then to the political objective of the campaign or war. He never wrote or thought that the movement of armies across land, according to the demands of time that is to say, strategic manoeuvre in the widest sense – were without influence over the outcome of war.

In Bülow's work, Clausewitz discovered in a pure and almost perfect state those concepts and that philosophy which the French armies of the Revolution, by their victories, had proved to be inherently false. The method of requisitioning reduces the dependence of armies on their arsenals; action along lines of communication only takes effect slowly whereas success in combat immediately takes effect, with all its weight. Bülow asserted that the modern army obtains fewer results from war than the ancient army at the very time when the French Republic was refuting this thesis. He bases his politico-historical forecasts – the disappearance of small states, the organization of Europe into a reduced number of large states, perpetual peace – on the inevitable victory of big battalions, in short, on the distribution of material forces. He concludes: 'The excuse of being too weak in relation to the enemy can well justify the general but not the government, since it is foolish to wage war against an enemy obviously superior in numbers [dem man nicht gewachsen ist].'

The process of enumerating Bülow's errors reveals some of the fundamental themes of Clausewitzian thought. On the distribution of forces he agrees, but thinks that non-physical elements must be considered. Strategy does not just teach the weaker party to sign the peace treaty. On the contrary, it encourages him to compensate for his material inferiority with moral virtues. Can we object that strategy or strategic science becomes impossible as soon as non-material factors are taken into consideration? The young Clausewitz replies, as he would have done a quarter of a century later, that he would rather confess to artistic atheism than confuse art with an object that does not merit its name.

On one point alone Clausewitz's thought, as expressed in the 1805 article in the *Neue Bellona*, is considered, in the eyes of some interpreters, as fettered by illusions, nurtured by the environment and the spirit of the times. It concerns the following lines: 'It seems to us that the object of the development of the art of war consists solely in submitting events (generally speaking: the action of forces) more and more to the deliberate control of a reasonable will, so that they are for ever free from the risks of chance.' This definition of progress gave rise to contradictory comments: some saw in it a survival of rationalism, others put the emphasis on will rather than on rationalism, so exposing the consistency of Clausewitzian thought.

It seems to me that one need only follow Clausewitz's thought process to support the second school. Bülow proves, or claims to prove, the superiority of the ancients by a single argument: unlike modern battles the battles between Greeks or Romans produced results which were militarily or politically decisive. In our age, days, months or years after a defeat, an army resumes hostilities unless the state introduces another army into the line. So, what is the use of these sterile encounters? A pacifist's argument pervades the military judgment. Clausewitz replies that the perfection of the art lies not in the relationship between cause and effect, between the means employed and the results obtained. He opposes the tendency of enlightened rationalism and the economic way of thinking: the art of war cannot be reduced to a calculation of cost and return. To this first proviso he adds a second: inasmuch as defence belongs to the art, it is not surprising that it does not produce more important results. By definition, defence tends to maintain balance; he offers to speak later of this negative end, concluding with a definition of the progress of the art of war by the mastery of rational will.

This definition is in my view truly Clausewitzian, because it falls between the scepticism of Bernhorst and the false science of Bülow. The former tirelessly recalled that fate, or chance, trifles with men and their plans. Frederick II confessed that he had to be thankful to fate ('wie viel ich dem Schicksaal zu verdanken habe'). The Prussians reaped victory in Leuthen in spite of the art (*der Kunst zum Hohn*). Only the military writers Bernhorst and Folard find favour in the eyes of Bülow. He wants to raise strategy to the level of a science by eliminating battles and by basing the art of operations on theorems. Clausewitz, though refuting the false science of Bülow, does not return to Bernhorst's scepticism. The art of the strategist really aims for this mastery of the rational will over the forces which have broken loose and, in this sense, for a reduction of the role left to fate. What he does not state in the passage – although he does not deny it either – is that mastery of will cannot obliterate chance. No war leader escapes the whims of fortune although the scientific or philosophical study of war, as conceived by Clausewitz, effectively assists will, enlightened by understanding (or understanding stimulated by will), to control the blind action of forces or circumstances.

I have commented at length on this short article without exhausting its content, because it seems in many respects to follow the historic form of a dialogue found in all ages. Clausewitz, at the age of 25, would have opposed the eternal temptation, to which Bülow succumbed, with the quiet certainty of 'eternal truths'. What is this temptation? It is the temptation of practical dogmatism, that is to say the transfiguration of a factor or particular experience into a unique factor or definitive rule. As regards action in war or politics, to deduce a comprehensive set of pseudo-scientific rules and mechanical precepts from provisioning, from the angle of the lines of operation or from some other different principle, is to commit a sin against mind. Choosing another principle resulting in another strategic system, would be no better. 'Those who do this or that permanently, without consideration of the circumstances, without criticism, without judgment, are equally at fault. They both display a poverty of spirit of which neither the one nor the other has reason to be proud.'

Has the antidogmatism of Clausewitz degenerated into a new dogmatism? Has the refusal to recognize provisioning and strategic movements as the unique factors in the art resulted in a dogmatism for combat and antimanoeuvre, as a number of interpreters, both favourable and hostile, have asserted? Is the eternal truth of Clausewitz simply antidogmatism or the principle of combat, the destruction of enemy armed forces, as the supreme objective of operations?

2 The themes of the 'Strategy' of 1804

The 'Strategy' of 1804 may, at first sight, surprise the reader because the short chapters appear disordered, and the first, curiously to our eyes, concerns mountain operations. Clausewitz's interest in mountain warfare was shared by many of his predecessors and contemporaries and can be explained on several grounds.

Since that time, historians have shown that the book *Principes de la guerre de montagnes* by Bourcet, who was chief of staff to Marshal de Maillebois and commanded operations in the Alps in 1745–6, contributed in no small way to the military training of Napoleon. The 1799 campaign, to which Clausewitz devoted a long study towards the end of his life, was the subject of much debate in both academies and military journals. Moreover, space figured in his thought as one of the factors of the strategic equation: the nature of the terrain, in particular the accidents of the terrain – mountains, rivers, marshes, and forests – influenced not only tactics, the way of fighting, but also strategy, the disposition of the troops, concentrated or dispersed in front or behind these natural obstacles.

Clausewitz advises against mountain warfare, except in the case of popular insurrection, because the troops escape from the will and control of their leader. In the mountains, the leader gains victory thanks to his army, while on the plains the army gains victory thanks to its leader. In the account of the 1799 campaign, probably written after 1827, he explains the French successes in terms of the spirit of the revolutionary troops. 'The French, led by the spirit of the Revolution to break all barriers and only to expect results from bold actions, obeyed this impulse when they did not find any other solutions.' In that type of war the units enjoy an autonomy, and this gave the French, inspired by revolutionary dynamism, a formidable advantage. As early as 1804, mountain warfare, the permanent characteristics of which had been illustrated by the 1799 campaign, gave Clausewitz the opportunity to apply some of his concepts and to perceive a few general propositions: the judgment on the lines of minor posts stationed on the defensive flank and their vulnerability, and consequently the mistake of defending on the ridges instead of waiting for the attacker where the valley opens, the opportunity for the attacker to concentrate his forces, etc.

More generally, we readily find in the paragraphs of the 'Strategy' of 1804 some of the themes of the Treatise – those which may properly be extracted from the article in the *Neue Bellona* and which I shall now recall briefly. First of all, Clausewitz, in opposition to the system builders, marks the limits within which theory can claim to formulate precepts:

Therefore, the side of strategy dealing with combinations of combats will perforce be restricted to a free and not a systematic reasoning and to particular considerations which indicate points of view and can give the proper direction. Any further development of theory is not only useless, but also results in lowering a noble object, in ridiculing it unintentionally as an insult to common sense.

Amidst the scattered notes of 1804, most of the notions appear which will help to construct the conceptual edifice of the Treatise: strategy and tactics, attack and defence, material forces and moral forces, the means and the end, the rules, the genius, boldness and caution, the virtue of success and the virtue of risks, the qualities of mind and the qualities of character needed by the war leader. At this point the question which is asked, or rather one which one would like to ask, is a fundamental one: does the young Clausewitz differ in his philosophy from the man who, in 1830, leaving the unfinished Treatise, put the reader on his guard against misunderstandings which could so easily haunt this long-thought-out work? In fact, the notes of 1804, showing Clausewitz in possession of his method and his major ideas, make it impossible to give a categorical answer.

Take, for example, note 12: 'I should not venture to have this printed, but I must admit to myself that a general cannot be too bold in his plans, provided he is in full possession of his faculties [*bei Sinnen ist*] and only sets himself aims which he himself is convinced he is able to reach.' No limit to boldness on the one hand, but nevertheless one reservation: it is the leader himself who must take the measure of his forces and consequently choose his objectives. If that is so, the principle of always choosing the most decisive operation within the range of one's forces flows from the spirit possessed by the art of war. Yet that does not exclude a defensive conduct of the war; although defence should always be active. Furthermore, a defensive conduct of war, if it is not to be open to error (*Fehlerhaft*), may (*darf*) only be adopted when forces are insufficient for offensive conduct, that is to say when the most decisive operations within the capability of our forces 'are not conducive to the offensive, in other words to an attack in the theatre of war'. In this instance, the desire to gain time does not contradict the principle formulated above (i.e. to attack with the desire for a decisive operation).

At this point, the offensive strategy is defined by the invasion of the enemy's territory of operations. The adoption of the defensive apparently only finds justification on the grounds of inferiority in numbers. Now, in paragraph 4, where he writes about the propitious moment for battle and where, quoting Machiavelli, he stresses the moral superiority which an army draws from a first victory, he makes an important reservation: 'If Bonaparte one day advances as far as Poland he will be easier to beat than in Italy and in Russia; I should consider his defeat assured.' Many times afterwards he comes back to the difficulty of conquests in Europe, conquests which were thought impossible before Bonaparte. In the Treatise, he gives expression to this constant idea and completes it by an analysis of the European balance of power. But this makes the reader wonder about the connection between the calls to boldness and offensives on the one hand, and the difficulties which space and men pose for conquest on the other.

In 1804 he notes that, to avoid battle, one must give up territory; an inevitable but not necessarily too high price to pay, for example in the case of Russian frontier territory. In the war plan against France of 1807, he comes to the extreme formula: to abandon the country in order to save the army, to separate the army from the state and put the invading army at the disadvantage of having to fight defensively on enemy soil, to operate in complete freedom with one invaluable advantage, surprise. Now, 'in war, surprise is the soul of fortune'.

These quotations from 1804 and 1807 only serve to confirm a thesis essential for the interpretation of Clausewitz's thought: two tendencies which interpreters often consider divergent, if not incompatible, emerge at all times. On the other hand, at least in the analysis of strategy and tactics, the influence of politics rarely appears. Not that the connection between war and politics escaped the young Clausewitz. In his war plan against France of 1807, the first paragraph analyses at length the possible attitudes of the various powers in the event of a new war between Prussia and France. Neither the conceptual system nor military considerations completely integrate the political element.

Paragraph 13 of the 'Strategy' of 1804 makes a distinction between the objectives of war (equivalent to political ends) and the objective in war (*im Kriege*). These two types of ends become, respectively, the political object (*der politische Zweck*) and the military objective (*das Ziel*). The political object is presented in 1804 in the form of an alternative: either completely destroy the enemy, bringing to an end his existence as a state, or, at the conclusion of peace, dictate terms to him. He writes that the intention (*Absicht*) must be to paralyse the enemy forces so that they can in no way carry on with the war or so that they can do so only by endangering their very existence. The alternative of 1804 becomes one of the terms of another alternative in the 'Warning' of 1827. In other words, destroy the enemy or dictate peace terms to him: these two forms of victory both belong to one type of war. So on this point the thought of Clausewitz has changed. Now, this point is decisive: the political object (or the modality of the return to peace) controls the whole conduct of the war. In spite of his mistakes Delbrück had the merit of underlining the importance of the second type of war that Clausewitz had not clearly envisaged in the texts prior to his last years.

On another, equally important point, the text of the 'Strategy' of 1804 was to be revised subsequently without Clausewitz ever arriving at an entirely satisfactory version. The abstract notion – the destruction of enemy forces – suggests three concrete objectives: occupation of territory, destruction of war reserves (*Kriegsvorräte*) or direct destruction of the army itself. In the *Principles of Instruction* (1812) the enumeration of objectives does not remain the same: he adds public opinion to armed forces and the sources of the army; in Book VIII of the Treatise the centres of gravity vary according to the country and the war. The objectives indicated in Book I, Chapter 2, of the Treatise – military forces, territory and the will of the army – come close to the above trinity but take on a new significance in the final system.

What conclusions are to be drawn from these first texts, for the most part written before the direct experience of battles? Though not unaware of the paradox, I shall suggest two: on the one hand, Clausewitz already seems to have mastered his method and to have grasped the major ideas; on the other, the idea which more than any other contributed to his glory, namely that war is the continuation of politics by other means, either does not appear or appears only as a pattern without affecting purely military considerations. These conclusions naturally lead to two propositions. To begin with, the meditation of Clausewitz between 1804 and 1830 had as its object and result, in most cases, a probing into themes, an elaboration of concepts. The research tended less towards invention than towards perfecting expression, rigour of analysis, and the enumeration of reservations demanded by a general proposition (exceptions which a general rule calls for); finally and above all, towards the grasping of a whole or interrelation within a whole or, in short, what he calls *Zusammenhang*, the inner order, the structure of the subject. The notes of 1804 contain, scattered about the paper, a good number of the ideas and formulae that are found in the Treatise. But science, as Clausewitz understands it, requires a high degree of abstraction: the definition of concepts which suit the appropriate matter and, on the other hand, the organization of concepts, or, in vulgar language, a system. It is the systematic character of the Treatise which has sometimes made superficial readers confuse it with dogmatism. In reality, the systematization alone permits the definitive refutation of dogmatism since all the elements of strategy find their place in the whole, and consequently none of them can claim an exclusive or disproportionate importance.

For a quarter of a century, in the midst of action or retreat, Clausewitz thought out the ideas that Scharnhorst had suggested to him, in his lectures, actions and genius. Should one add that this long meditation also led him to the leading principle, namely the exact understanding of the relationship between politics and war? If one is to believe one of the most penetrating interpreters of Clausewitz, W.M. Schering, this understanding dates from 1827, when the first six books had already been written and the last two were in outline or skeleton form.

Certainly, W. Hahlweg is not mistaken in finding in the appendices to the *Bekenntnisse*, sent by Clausewitz to Gneisenau, the leading principles of ideas developed in Book VIII. Taking all the evidence, no contemporary of the wars of the Revolution or Empire could ignore the influence of circumstances or political conditions on military events, the differences between cabinet war and popular war. All there was left to do was to fit these personal experiences into a theory. There is nothing to prove that Clausewitz achieved this before the end of his life, the years of peace having allowed him to look back at Napoleon and at the Prussian catastrophe. Twenty years after Jena, ten years after Waterloo, wars to the death had become the exception rather than the rule.

One can still argue that he always knew this, as is shown by the last lines of the appendices just mentioned. From now on, mass popular insurrection is the only means people will have of fighting each other.

May heaven keep us from this. . . . This supreme way to salvation will cease to be necessary when, with its help, the men of Europe, having emerged from the chaos, will have moulded themselves into organic states according to the laws of nature.

Any war will none the less be considered as a national matter (*National-sache*). This last forecast has effectively been confirmed by history. It does not solve the question which can be formulated in the following terms: is it possible to elaborate a theory or a strategic doctrine, disregarding political circumstances and the political intention or end or, according to Clausewitz's vocabulary, disregarding politics as the brain of the personified state? Now, if the objectives of war, by which I mean the object which is to be reached by war, figure both in the 'Strategy' of 1804 and in the article in the *Neue Bellona*, if the texts on combat from 1807 to 1812 take into account the obvious link between the historical context and the modality of the war, nowhere do strategic considerations seem to be affected by politics – except in the limited sense that the violence of the struggle and the degree of effort depend on circumstances, and that the arming of the people corresponds to the monstrosity of the Napoleonic ambitions and conquests.

The summary of the *Principles of Instruction* to the crown prince (1812) could apparently serve as an intermediate link between the 'Strategy' of 1804 and the Treatise. It certainly offers an authentic interest, but from a different point of view from the one I have adopted. Because of its didacticism, it comes closer to the military writings of classical form; it helps one to understand the precepts that the theory justifies inasmuch as they are founded on the generality of cases. But it does not make it possible to solve the major problems which fascinate interpreters, that is to say the two kinds of war, and the link between war and politics. Clausewitz expressed himself as a teacher, specifically for the crown prince. Being responsible for purely military instruction, he could hardly speculate on the various forms taken by wars according to historical circumstances. Of necessity, he called Napoleon the Emperor of the French and not, as in the Treatise, Bonaparte. In these conditions, it is better to go straight to the controversy about the chronology of the various parts of the Treatise, if need be comparing the text of 1812 with the precepts which are implicit in the unfinished work.

3 The elaboration of the Treatise according to the notes. The final question

It has been conclusively established that Clausewitz started writing the Treatise during his period at Coblenz, between 1816 and 1818. Some of the texts published by Hahlweg and drawn from the Gneisenau archives prove that he never gave up the work of elaboration which finally led to the manuscript which we possess. For instance, the dialectic analysis of defence and attack, at the tactical and strategic level, in a style closer to that of the Treatise than to that of the *Principles of Instruction*, figures in one of the appendices to the *Bekenntnisse*.

If the date at which Clausewitz started writing the Treatise is of little interest, the same docs not apply to the dates at which he wrote the various parts. Depending on which hypothesis we adopt, the evolution, indeed the final meaning, of his thought is revealed in a different light. We need, therefore, to enter into the philological controversies which started in the 1930s and, because of the loss of the Clausewitz archives during the Second World War, will never be solved with certainty.

The controversy developed, it seems to me, from the article published in 1935 by the friend of my youth, Herbert Rosinski, shortly before he left Germany. Not that the previous interpreters had disregarded the fact that the Treatise had been written at various times between 1816 and 1830: Delbrück and his opponents, in the course of the long polemic 'Über die doppelte Art des Krieges' ('On the Two Kinds of War'), had used and commented upon the third note which I call the 'Warning' of 1827 (dated, in fact, 10 July 1827). However, it seems to me that nobody had rigorously studied the connection with the three other notes: the one in which he alludes to Montesquieu, which I shall call the first note; the one in which he declares that only the first chapter of Book I gives him satisfaction, which I shall call the final note; finally, the author's Preface which figures at the start of the book. These texts figured unaltered in the first volume of the posthumous works published by Marie von Clausewitz in 1832.

Rosinski referred the first note and the Preface to the Coblenz period, and thought that the final note was written after Clausewitz, appointed as inspector of artillery, had sealed the box containing his manuscript, fearing that he would never come back to it. So Rosinski expressed the judgment that the author held for his work when he abandoned it. The Preface would be roughly contemporary with the first note, probably dating from the end of the Coblenz period, thus 1818. So, two texts, the first note and the Preface, relate to a first manuscript which we do not have but of which some chapters have perhaps been integrated into the texts we do possess. The 'Warning' of 1827 and the final note inform us about the ultimate stage of Clausewitz's thought and are of a key interest.

The hypotheses of Rosinski which, he claims, agreed with those of K. Linnebach, were confirmed by the last commentators to have studied the family archives, W.M. Schering before and E. Kessel after the last war, and allow us to say that Clausewitz may first have written a small work to which the remarks of the first note would apply, and a second work made up from the first six books, finished in 1826 or 1827. At a time of illness in 1827, he would have written the 'Warning'. At that time, the manuscript already included the eight books of the published manuscript. Books III,

IV and V would not have been revised; Book VII, a mere sketch, would have remained unaltered; some chapters of Books I, II and perhaps VI were revised or added to between 1827 and 1830. As for Book VIII, some authors assert that it had also been revised; others take issue with them.

Let us try at the same time to distinguish accepted points from doubtful ones and to bring out the significance of these scholarly debates. It seems to me to be accepted that the Treatise went through three stages or assumed three forms. One volume was composed of short chapters in the style of Montesquieu: Marie von Clausewitz bears witness to this first undertaking: 'he put his ideas [*Ansichten*] on paper in the form of short articles which were only connected in a loose manner'. Whoever remembers the 'Strategy' of 1804 accepts without difficulty this first form of the Treatise. Some chapters of the final text are in keeping with one of the sentences of the first note: 'The manner in which Montesquieu had treated his subject floated vaguely in my mind.' The parallel with Montesquieu, which will at first surprise the French reader accustomed to comments about the 'metaphysical haze' of Clausewitz, presents no problem, at least for those who read German: chapters 4 and 5 of Book I and Chapter 5 of Book III effectively belong, by their style, to the tradition of *De l'esprit des lois* as far as the different geniuses of the two languages allows. I would add that the conceptualization of Clausewitz resembles that of Montesquieu far more closely than anybody has ever suggested, and far more than any similarity it may bear to the works of Hegel or Kant.

Having accepted the existence of this manuscript as perhaps complete and ready for printing (*druckreif*) in the eyes of Clausewitz himself, the specialists continue to argue about a point which for me is of secondary importance. Have some of the chapters of 1816–18 been incorporated unchanged in the final manuscript? Or is there nothing left in the Treatise which was written at Coblenz? Schering attributes Chapters 4, 5, 6 and 7 of Book I and all the chapters of Book III, with the exception of the first two, to the first version: a plausible hypothesis in accord with the description given by Clausewitz himself of this version. On the other hand, Kessel asserts that none of the Coblenz chapters is found unaltered in the book at our disposal. I see no sure way of deciding the issue. None of the problems of interpretation is affected by the acceptance of either hypothesis.

A second point remains controversial. Does the Preface also date from the Coblenz period? Analysis of the style, of the 'manner', makes such an assumption plausible. Schering asserts this without, unfortunately, defining the data on which he relies. He adds that Clausewitz himself had placed this Preface of 1818 at the head of the manuscript of 1827 or 1830. Should that be surprising? I think not.

The Preface defines 'scientificity' as the attempt to penetrate (*erforschen*) the essence of the war phenomenon, to show its link with the matter which makes it up. This effort towards abstraction, towards the essential definition, in accordance with the reality of the matter, was already demanded in the 'Strategy' of 1804 as a criterion of science (or philosophy). Moreover, as was pointed out by Rosinski, the Preface deals with the connection between philosophy (or abstract theory) and experience in terms akin to those used by Clausewitz in the portrait of his master

54

Scharnhorst, written in 1818. 'The author never evaded the demands of philosophical rigour, but when the thread of the latter became too thin, the author preferred to break it and to turn to the corresponding phenomena of experience.' A little further on: 'Abstract analysis and observation, philosophy and experience, must not scorn or exclude each other: they safeguard each other.' Whether or not this text dates from 1818, it expresses Clausewitz's conception.

As for the ironic criticism in respect of the 'system builders', it is aimed at the Bülows or the Jominis; the quotation of Lichtenberg has no other object than to ridicule them or to suggest the triviality of 'strategic systems on paper'. For 'if a house is on fire, we must above all seek to protect the right-hand wall of the house on the left and the left-hand wall of the house on the right. . . .'.

Clausewitz, in this Preface, has absolutely no doubt about the systematic character of the Treatise (as he understands it), that is to say the conceptual elaboration of the war objective, the combination of necessary ideas and experience which peculiarizes his work and gives it its value or truth. Either he makes an ironic concession to those who cannot read or he affects modesty when he evokes the greater mind which 'will know how to present, instead of these scattered particles, a whole in a single cast, free from alloy'.

The first note makes perfectly clear the nature of the work achieved during the creative years. From one scheme – short chapters, pithy formulae sculptured in marble – the author lets himself be drawn by the irresistible tendency of his mind to develop a system: not a system comparable to that of Bülow – that is to say precepts about the angles of lines of operation from the base – but a system of notions and propositions which are linked and which translates into ideas the structure of the object. Let us say, in modern terms, that Clausewitz aims at reaching the plane of the systematic theorist, he takes into account both the mental experience, comparable to that of pure economics, and the historical experience of which the historical school avails itself: as a doctrinaire, he aims at being radically antidogmatic. It is the theory which indicates that the responsibility for decision is thrown back on the man of action.

Let us come now to the major argument which caused much ink to flow: the 'Warning' of 1827 and the final note. Here it is not so much a question of dates as the thought itself. Let us first put to one side the secondary points, the minor questions. In 1827 Clausewitz, in the 'Warning', described in these words the state of the book which deals with the war plan: 'As for Book VIII, the war plan, that is to say the overall preparation of a war, there are already several sketched out chapters, but these cannot even be considered as real material, they only amount to mere rough work.'

Is this description of Book VIII compatible with the state of the book in its present form? Certainly; therefore some historians have considered that the elaboration of the book did not progress after 1827. Others, greater in number, hold the opposite opinion, with which I concur, but without conviction. In any case, Clausewitz did not follow the plan of work which he had set himself (according to the 'Warning'): that is to say he did not first write Book VII, devoted to attack (or offensives), then perfect Book

VIII in the light of the two major ideas indicated at the beginning of the 'Warning' (i.e. two types of wars, and war defined as the pursuance of politics by other means), and finally revise all the first six books by introducing the same spirit in them. As Schering asserts, and as the study of the texts makes probable, he first worked on Book VIII and not on Book VII. Then, even before finishing Book VIII, he undertook the revision of the first six books. Chapter 1 of Book I was written after Book VIII and the possible revision of the latter: the proof, if there is need of one, can be found in Chapter 1 of Book I and mentions considerations which do not figure in the present version. In Book VIII, Clausewitz has finished a paragraph on the famous formula: 'War possesses, it is true, its own grammar but not its own logic.' He amplifies the idea and goes on:

> War can never be separated from political relations [politische Verkehr], and if this separation occurs anywhere in the study, all the threads of the relations are broken in one way or another and there only remains a thing without meaning or purpose. This way of thinking would be indispensable even if war was nothing but war, nothing but the element of unleashed hostility; for all the components on which it is based and which determine its principal trends – one's own power, the enemy's power, the respective allies, the conflicting character of the people and the governments, etc., which we have enumerated in the first chapter of Book I [underlined by R.A.] – are they not of a political nature?

There is no trace left of this enumeration in the first chapter which would have dealt with the political context which conditions war before analysing the end and the means in war (Chapter 2). The approach would be close to that of Jomini in his Précis on the art of war.

The final note, which specifies that only Chapter 1 of Book I should be considered complete, confirms, therefore, as Linnebach and Rosinski thought and as Schering asserted, that it was written after the 'Warning' of 1827 and the actual reduction of Book VIII (whatever work may have been done by Clausewitz on Book VIII between 1827 and 1830).

Why argue about the dates when Clausewitz, as I, following several others, have repeated already, seems to have had mastery over his method and several of his governing ideas at the age of 25? The reader may have anticipated the answer. We do not find here expressed, or explained, the two ideas which according to the 'Warning' were to direct the revision of the first six books: neither the two types of war nor war as the continuation of political relations with the adjunction of other means.

The philological controversy leads to the essential question: What does the distinction between the two types of war mean? Does the primacy of politics involve modifying the strategic ideas expressed above which can be found, hardly changed, in the manuscript that we possess? The whole of this book endeavours to give an answer to these two questions. For the moment I would like to analyse more closely the two ideas of the 'Warning'.

Forgetting the hundreds of pages covered by the contenders in the great quarrel – two wars or two strategies? – let me quote the definition of the two types of war.

These two types of war are, on the one hand, that in which the

56

object is to overthrow the enemy [*niederwerfen*], either with a view to annihilating him politically or to disarming him [*wehrlos machen*] and thus compelling him to accept any conditions of peace; and, on the other hand, that in which one only wants to make conquests at the frontiers of one's own state with a view to keeping them or using them as a means of exchange at the time of peace. The intermediate stages between one type and the other should remain, but the entirely different nature of the two undertakings should penetrate everywhere and separate the irreconcilable.

Let us now recall the method of the definitions: first let us grasp the extremes where the distinction is crystal clear. Where is the principle of this distinction? On reading the text, the answer seems straightforward: in the object of the war. The distinction between tactics and strategy results both from the means and the end, the end of tactics becoming the means of strategy. Here, only the end differs: in the first case, war seeks to overthrow the enemy; in the second, to keep occupied territory or exploit limited conquests as a means of exchange. Comparing war with boxing, one could say the difference lies between a knockout victory and a points victory. Since the ultimate end of war cannot be separated from a certain type of peace, the modality of the return to peace becomes the criterion of the alternative: in the case of 'knockout', the winner imposes on the prostrate enemy any conditions, including even the disappearance of the state, indeed the physical elimination of the population; in the other case, he treats with an enemy who agrees to abandon one province (as Maria-Theresa was forced to abandon Silesia to Frederick), or he exchanges the province which he has occupied for another. Thus, imposed or dictated peace (*Diktat*) on the one hand, negotiated peace on the other.

This interpretation, which clearly emerges from the text, itself resolves some of the difficulties in which the commentators Delbrück and his opponents have been embroiled. It concerns an opposition not between two strategies but between two kinds of political end of war, considered in its totality. Or, to use the words of the 'Strategy' of 1804, the opposition relates to the end of war and not to the ends of war. There is no doubt that the former influences the latter, or, in the words of Book VIII, that the end of war influences the objective in war (i.e. military objectives). In fact, Clausewitz analyses the limitation of objectives and indecisive campaigns more than the breaking–curbing or the dictating–negotiating duality. But the governing idea apparently arises from politics and affects the modality of the return to peace or the character of relations between enemies at the time when hostilities cease.

Following from this, one understands immediately the multiplicity of the intermediate stages. States wage war when their wills conflict. At the end of hostilities one or the other will have won, but it can happen that neither of them has won to the extent of attaining all its ends. A draw, in the true sense of the word, seems logically to be excluded: one of the two opponents inevitably will have taken the initiative with a view to seizing an advantage. If he must sign a treaty without having obtained an advantage, the other, who has gained nothing either, has none the less frustrated the conquering will of the aggressor. One would have to imagine a war entered

57

into by accident or for fun, with no intention of gain, purely for the pleasure of combat, which ends on equal terms, to make a true draw possible. In all other cases, war of the second type always gives the advantage to one or other of belligerents, but for all that it is not capable of destroying the existence of the vanquished state, it does not compel it to subscribe to whatever conditions are imposed, it does not give the victor the opportunity to dictate (*vorschreiben*) any conditions whatever. There are degrees in the relation of inequality between the victor and the vanquished. The latter has still some means and the former has not overthrown his enemy, either because he could not or because he did not want to. The method – first of all to grasp extreme cases from which the principle of oppposition clearly emerges, without failing to recognize the intermediate cases – explains the first paragraph of the 'Warning'.

It seems to me that this same interpretation also answers a question discussed at length by commentators: Why does the distinction between the two types of war precede the assertion that war is nothing less than the continuation of the policy of a state by other means. Schering states, with his usual tendency to express correct ideas in an exaggerated form, that Clausewitz had not conceived this crucial idea – an idea which in fact established his fame – before 1826 or 1827. This thesis is justified provided that it clearly specifies what constitutes the originality of the idea.

Clausewitz never failed to recognize the links between politics and war, between the interests of states and the way in which each conducted operations, between the character of the peoples and their way of fighting. In the notes from his youth, he eulogizes Machiavelli, derides petty intellectuals or tender souls who accuse the Florentine of cynicism when the very statesmen who condemned him in fact followed his teaching.

No reading is more necessary than that of Machiavelli; those who affect to be shocked by his principles are nothing but petty intellectuals posing as humanists [*eine Art humanistische petit-maître*]. . . . Some of this writer's pages have become antiquated; others reflect eternal truths. Frederick II wrote his 'Anti Machiavelli' while remaining a faithful Machiavelli disciple: if he pretended to condemn him, it was only to cling to him with greater ease, and Voltaire very rightly said that he spat on him to disgust others.

In the same way, in 1811 and 1812, when he was writing the *Bekenntnisse*, when he was thinking about popular war, he explained the arming of the people by political circumstances, by the total character of the state. He was bold enough to foresee that all the wars of the century to come would remain national wars yet without mobilizing the entire population.

Having said this – and we come here to a comment based on common sense which may seem paradoxical – I should add that the essential was lacking: elaborating the concept or, if preferred, making clear the meaning and the consequences of the links between politics and war. Now, he took this decisive step late, and suddenly the whole of what he had thought and written for more than twenty years demanded revision. In a philosophy of action governed by the duality of the means and the end, how can the means not change when the end changes? Strategy has only one means, combat, but the use of combat includes marches, the choice of time and

58

place, the refusal or acceptance of battle, the choice of real combat or fictitious or simulated combat (*vorgespiegelt*), the crossing of rivers, the lines of invasion, outflanking or enveloping movements, etc. In short, in either type of war, the definition of strategy as the use of combat with a view to the end of the war remains valid; however, what calls for reflection is the possible modification of strategy (or conduct of operations) in relation to the end (to overthrow the enemy or not). Clearly, the change of end has an influence on the conduct of operations: what influence? This is the real problem which has puzzled the commentators and which, in my opinion, obsesses Clausewitz in the course of his last years, between 1827 and 1830. Has he ever fully solved it? I am not sure. However, it is certainly with a view to solving it that he elaborated the system in Chapter 1 of Book I.

Schering reproduced a note by Clausewitz in the volume of texts entitled *Geist und Tat* which does not figure in the Treatise and which would belong to an older version. It could also be, quite simply, a working note in which Clausewitz wrote down for himself the difficult questions.

Is one war of the same nature as another? Is the objective of the enterprise of war distinguishable from its political end? What is the size of force which must be mobilized in a war? What amount of energy must be deployed in the conduct of the war? What is the reason for the many pauses during hostilities: are they important parts of the latter or real anomalies? Do the wars of the seventeenth and eighteenth centuries with a restricted force, or the wanderings of half-civilized Tartars, or the destructive wars of the nineteenth century conform to the phenomenon itself? Or is the nature of the war conditioned by the nature of the relations, and what are these relations and these conditions? The substance of these questions does not appear in any of the books written about war, in particular in those which have been written recently on the conduct of the war in its overall perspective, that is to say strategy.

The interest of this text lies in the focusing of most of the questions which Clausewitz deals with in Book VIII and Chapter 1 of Book I; in short, all those which arise from the contraposition of the summary of Principles of Instruction and the Treatise. In all the texts written before 1827, political considerations are not absent but they never seem to influence the conduct of war directly. The principles do not refer to a particular war but to war *qua* war: only the relation of forces – inferiority or superiority – seems to some extent to determine strategy, offensive or defensive. However, the above quotation poses two major questions: the relation between the political end and the military objective, and the effect of circumstances determining the form assumed by war. Chapter 3 of Book VIII develops this last question, Chapter 6 of the same book the first. On the one hand, politics – the brain of the personified state – determines the military objective in terms of the end of the war; on the other, circumstances condition the historical diversity of wars. Politics only adequately determine the end provided that the nature of the war is exactly appreciated in terms of the circumstances which condition it.

During his last years – as the text that I have just quoted, but also Chapter 2 of Book I, and the whole of Book VIII, support – Clausewitz reflects on what I shall call the problem posed by Montesquieu: how to reconcile the concept – the definition – of war in terms of its own permanent nature with the diversity of wars. Is this a problem of praxis as well as of theory? The two types of war represent extreme ends: to impose peace or negotiate it. But how is one to pass from these two political ends to the military objectives that they govern?

The answer given by Clausewitz to these problems can essentially be found in Book I (of which he revised at least the first two chapters) and in Book VIII, but is the answer the same in Book VIII and in Book I (written last)? Do the limited objectives of Book VIII mean the same thing as the indecisive defence of Book VI, which Clausewitz intended to revise, according to the final note? We know what Clausewitz was pondering in these last years: do we know the final results of his reflections?

Chapter 3

The Final Synthesis and the Strategic Debate

I specified earlier, by a simple reading of the texts, the meaning which Clausewitz seems to give to the formula 'two types of war': a distinction directly related to the end sought, regardless of whether this involves the overthrow of the enemy or not. If the vanquished is prostrate, the victor dictates peace terms; if neither of the adversaries has reduced the other to impotence, both must negotiate. Such abstractly defined situations historically take on characters of such a diverse kind that, between disarmament of the vanquished and a draw, many intermediate stages emerge.

Such an interpretation, although closest to the text, nevertheless presents difficulties. Does the duality relate to the political end or the military objective? Even if one admits, as I do, that it relates to the political end, this governs, at least partially, the military objective. In fact, in Book VIII, Clausewitz, with regard to the war plan, deals with the limitation of the objective (*Ziel*) in Chapters 5, 7 and 8, but interpreters have not always resisted the temptation to substitute *Ziel* for *Zweck*, the military objective and political end, thus failing to recognize any other reason for limiting, apart from lack of means, the military objective. Furthermore, a second type of war, though not defined, is characterized by the conquest of a province at the frontier – which again suggests to the careless reader the military objective as much as any political end.

We can only resolve these difficulties by a comparative study of Books VI (where, in Chapter 30, the duality of the two types of war appears), VIII and I, using the final synthesis of the only finished chapter (Book I, Chapter 1) as a guide and mentor in the case of uncertainty. Having interpreted and clarified the final synthesis, I shall then compare the results obtained with the two contending parties in what is called the strategic conflict (*der Strategiestreit*).

1 The conceptual system

Chapter 1 of Book I stands out from the rest of the book because of its rigour of analysis and perfection of form. It lets us imagine what the result might have been had the writer pursued his work for a few more years. It gives expression to the last state of a thought which was until the end obsessed with a search for itself. By good fortune, it reveals the complete conceptual apparatus which structures the theory.

Essentially, this chapter goes from a definition of war in two term, 'War is an act of violence intended to compel the enemy to fulfil our will' (I, 1, 2), to a definition in three terms:

A strange trinity composed, firstly, of an inherently original violence which can be likened to a blind natural impulse; second, of the play of probability and chance which make it a free activity of the soul; and finally, of its subordinate nature to the instruments of politics through which it belongs to pure understanding (I, 1, 28).

At each stage of the path that leads from the original definition to the threefold definition, new key concepts enrich the analysis.

The initial definition is derived from a comparison between war and the duel, in the meaning of a two-man contest. The reader should imagine two wrestlers at grips with each other, each trying to throw the other onto the ground (the word *niederwerfen* here keeps its original physical meaning), thus rendering him incapable of resistance.

This definition involves three major concepts, which are: violence, objective and end. By introducing the concept of violence in the definition of war – for 'there is no moral violence outside the concept of the state or of the law' (I, 1, 2) – Clausewitz, unlike modern authors, postulates *a priori* a radical opposition between war and peace; he also postulates – what has escaped the notice of many interpreters – that the end of war is peace. What sort of peace? Let us postpone the reply, as Clausewitz himself did. The immediate end, the imminent objective of war itself as an act of violence, is to disarm the enemy – disarming being the equivalent, in the contest between states, to grounding one's opponent in wrestling. One of the adversaries, whether wrestler or state, finds himself incapable of continuing the contest. As the state has armed itself with the invention of the arts and sciences to carry on the contest, to overthrow the state is also to disarm it.

According to the scheme of the concept, the 'overthrow' constitutes the true objective of the struggle as a trial of strength. What we want to impose on the adversary once he is on the ground or disarmed, we shall provisionally regard as something outside the war, since it results from a collision between opposing forces. Now, if we disregard all that precedes or follows the contest itself, the circumstances from which it arises, the end that it seeks, clearly its goal is, in concept, the overthrow of an adversary.

Many interpreters have quoted, isolating them from their context, such formulae as 'these things [social conditions] do not belong to war itself and one cannot introduce a principle of moderation into war without committing an absurdity' (I, 1, 3) or 'the objective takes the place of the end and rejects it in some way as if it were something that did not belong to war itself' (I, 1, 2) as if they were the last word in Clausewitz's thought. In other words, they make him say the opposite of what he wanted to say; the propositions which are true at this initial stage of the analysis, at the conceptual level, are not definitive. They apply to war in the abstract, separated from its origins and ends, and not to real war: now, Clausewitz precisely wants to prove that one cannot and should not separate a real war from its origins and ends.

Why does war, according to this abstract consideration, necessarily lead to extremes? Why is this escalation derived from the logic, or the essence, of the duel or of the contest? The reason for the latter lies in the reciprocal action of forces and wills in the struggle, as each side seeks to impose its law on the other.

This reciprocal action (*Wechselwirkung*) assumes three forms, or is articulated according to three reasonings. Let us distinguish hostile intention (*Absicht*) from hostile feeling. Of intention and feeling, it is intention which is the more important. Intention, in effect, does not implicate feeling whereas the latter always accompanies intention. It is possible for passions to subside without hostile intentions disappearing. Moreover, the latter inevitably react upon the former. Men and races who at first fight without mutual hatred end up by hating each other by reason of the fighting. The degree of violence does not depend, in the final analysis, on the degree of civilization but on the 'importance and duration of the enemy interests' (I, 1, 3). To discover the first truth, it is enough to scatter the illusions of the doctrinaires of the *ancien régime* whom events have called to order: violence as such does not admit of intrinsic limits, and since each of the contenders seeks to impose its will on the other, since neither of them can do less than the other, they will both logically be pushed to act to the maximum.

The two other reciprocal actions divide the first, one taking into account the physical, the other the moral aspect of the fight. As long as I have not thrown the enemy onto the ground, I must fear that he will throw me to the ground. In effect, only the 'overthrow', the disarmament of the adversary, gives me security; but he reasons as I do. Security for one implies that the other loses the means to defend himself. If each reasons in the same way, each outdoes the other until they come to extremes. The resistance of the adversary depends on the strength of his means and his will. Whereas, if need be, one can approximately gauge the means at his disposal, moral force escapes calculation. Let us say that the motive for the fight allows me to evaluate approximately the force of resistance into which I shall run: I shall engage a slightly superior force in order to overcome the resistance. But my adversary will do the same, and once again, effort after effort, we shall both condemn ourselves to go to the limit, so raising ourselves to the extremes.

This first stage of the analysis suggests a series of paired concepts – military objectives with political ends, hostile intentions with feelings of hostility, understanding with sensibility (*Gemüt*), material means with moral strength – ascending to extremes. Finally, and above all, none of the formulae which figure in the first five paragraphs of Book I, Chapter 1, applies to real wars; they all apply to war in terms of the concept or the philosophy, to the act of violence detached from the social environment which conditions it and from the end that each player seeks to attain, in other words they are separated from the political in its two meanings (relating to politics and to policy).

The second stage of the path that leads from the monistic to the trinitarian definition begins with the opposition of concept (or of abstract definition) with reality according to a stated method of modification. For the trial of strength between two wrestlers let us substitute war between states: at once we bring back space, time and policy. Clausewitz by method had separated the latter (implied by the first definition of war, i.e. to compel the other to fulfil our will) in order to analyse the logic of the taking to extremes, resulting from the reciprocal action of two violently opposed wills. At the start of paragraph 11, Clausewitz recalls that he had separated them previously.

The contenders, when they take the form of states, have territory, resources and allies. War develops across space, it takes time, it does not appear as a flash of lightning, it projects into the activity of interstate relations. In victory or defeat, it rarely displays an absolute or definitive character. The belligerents know each other, they each know approximately what to fear or hope for from the other. Here we have returned from the absolute concept to the probabilities of the real world and, accordingly, are obliged to follow a policy giving the reasons for the conflict, defining precisely the role of its desired end.

The reintroduction of policy, while not necessitating the opposite of a rise to extremes, does make possible the descent to armed observation. The rise to extremes is an abstract development while the descent to 'mere armed observation' (*blosse bewaffnete Beobachtung*) (I, 1, 11) concerns reality. Let us first substitute real states for ideal wrestlers. 'Each of the two sides will deduce, according to the laws of probability, the conduct of the other from the character, institutions of state and situation of the adversary so determining his own in terms of these probable deductions.' Let us bring back the political end that we have put to one side. This, as the initial reason for the war, determines the military objective and the efforts which it demands, but with one important reservation: the reasons for war do not concern dead matter but human beings. It is thus possible that there is so much tension, such an aggregate of hostile elements between two peoples or two states, that a minor reason for war can provoke violence out of all proportion to it. The proportional relationship between the reason and the amount of effort (or the violence of the war) becomes all the more distorted as more become involved.

We find in paragraph 11 the definition of the second type of war. The military objective can become confused with the political end, e.g. the conquest of a province. Sometimes, this confusion is impossible; in this case the military objective should be equivalent to the political end and represent it at the time of peace. However, owing to popular passions and hostile feelings between the states, it is possible that a limited political advantage demands considerable effort. Paragraph 11 thus recalls the second type of war, but instead of opposing the two types, so following his usual method, Clausewitz prefers to emphasize different degrees of violence between the extremes of annihilation and armed observation.

This second state reinforces the unreal character of absolute war, of the rise to extremes:

> One must recognize that the human mind would hardly yield to such logical dreaming [*logische Träumerei*]. There would often be a useless outlay of forces which would be counteracted by other principles in the art of government; a tension of the will would be required that would be entirely out of proportion to the proposed end which could consequently never be realized – for human will never draws its strength from logical subtleties (I, 1, 6).

I cannot overemphasize this text, the only one where Clausewitz incontestably and explicitly warns against a false interpretation of his concepts and method: far from absolute war being an ideal which should be reached, the balance between the interests at stake and efforts expended is kept by the art of politics. The abstract necessity for the rise to extremes to no extent constitutes a practical imperative. As soon as real wars are considered, the possibility of descent determines or should (*soll*) determine conduct just as much as the abstract possibility necessitates a rise.

The second stage, according to the method of modification, moves from the abstract to reality, from which the following concepts or themes emerge, including absolute war and real war, the relationship between political end and military objectives, trends in the proportional relationship between the scale of the former and the importance of the latter, the influence of passions and tensions on this relationship, and the laws of probability with the evolution of the war in space and time.

At the third stage, Clausewitz introduces the inequality of defence and attack with a view to explaining a phenomenon which he at first considered logically incomprehensible: the suspension of hostilities. How is it possible that the two belligerents can simultaneously profit from suspending operations? It would seem in effect that if the advantage of one lies in waiting, it would be to the advantage of the other to act or to conclude peace. Now, continuous operations would give operations a continuity, a causal connection which would make them more dangerous. The use of the same word – *Äusserstes* – common in Clausewitz, even in his letters, should not surprise us: 'to go to the extreme' does not imply total mobilization but simply the release of energy, an extreme form of violence.

Clausewitz resolves the paradox of the suspension of hostilities in two ways: first, in an abstract manner, by an analysis of polarities, then by a method of modification or, in other words, by considering real belligerents rather than ideal duellists. The logical difficulty comes from the implicit hypothesis that the advantage of one is the disadvantage of the other; that if one would rather suspend hostilities, the other should prefer to fight. Even the equilibrium of forces does not explain the suspension of hostilities: the one who seeks a positive object, i.e. whose motivation is strongest, ought to take the initiative and attack.

The mistake in this reasoning lies in the illegitimate extension of the principle of polarity. Polarity in the exact meaning of the word – the advantage of the one equals the disadvantage of the other or the gain of the one equals the loss of the other – is not valid for all the steps taken by opponents. In Chapter 1, paragraph 15, polarity applies to the battle in which, by definition, the victory of the one equals the defeat of the other since each wants victory: it therefore also applies to the decision (I, 1, 16). Yet polarity, or the advantage of the one equalling the disadvantage of the other, does not apply to attack in relation to defence because the two forms of war have an unequal force.

Side A deems it advantageous to postpone attack for a few weeks; side B would prefer this attack to happen now. It does not mean that it would be to its advantage to attack. Indeed, it could be that Side A is superior, without this advantage sufficing to match the forces of the defensive side.

Let us imagine this first solution to the paradox to be valid even in the event of strictly rational actors. Nevertheless, war leaders can never play such roles because they are never in possession of all the relevant information. So, in the uncertainty, each tends to overestimate the forces of his adversary and his own weaknesses (because he knows them). Normally, the lack of information leads to a lessening of the violence and the duration of hostilities, and to the widening of the gap between absolute war and real war; it increases the role of probability calculation. War takes on the character of a game as chance plays an increasingly greater part. Consequently, it calls for fundamentally different qualities from those of understanding – above all courage, the supreme virtue in the middle of danger. Courage does not exclude shrewd calculation (*Kluge Berechnung*) but it draws its strength from different sources. The taste for risk, trust in fortune and boldness all emanate from courage. Any theory which on principle ignores moral forces, the human aspect of war, would be useless in reality.

This third stage thus introduces the concept of polarity, the asymmetry of attack and defence, the opposition of intellect and emotion, of understanding and moral qualities. The latter are not only opposed to material forces, they are also opposed to the abstractions of pure theory and calculations of the mind.

Taking up an idea I have already discussed, we come to the fourth and last stage, to the conclusion: policy. The meanings of policy and politics are clearly distinguished: war between civilized peoples arises from a political situation and is instigated by a motive of policy (I, 1, 23). It is therefore the political end which is the supreme consideration in the conduct of the war. It would only be otherwise if the war, once engaged, only obeyed its own laws, being thereafter independent of the policy which instigated it; in this case war would be comparable to an explosion which is determined solely by the preparations which precede its release. This traditional conception, Clausewitz writes, is radically wrong, although it has been accepted until now. Real war cannot be compared with the total and blind unleashing of violence because it unfolds slowly enough to remain in submission to the will of a directing intelligence (*Willen einer leitenden Intelligenz*).

The primacy of moral virtues (courage, boldness, trust in fortune) over the qualities of the mind, apparent in the third stage, is reversed at the following stage when war finally submits to policy. The instrument, the means, certainly exercises a counteracting influence over the political intention, which is the end; 'war is the means and never can the means be conceived without the end' (I, 1, 24).

Once again Clausewitz comes back to the duality of war, this time to underline that war remains just as political in its determination in the one type as in the other (I, 1, 26). 'Indeed, if one considers policy as the intelligence of the personified state, there may be, amidst all the constellations that it must include in its calculations, the nature of all circumstances which condition a war of the first type.' Paragraphs 20 to 27 of Chapter 1 contain the main substance of the development in Chapters 3 and 6 of Book VIII.

The conceptual analysis leads to the threefold definition stated opposite. Does this final definition radically differ from the initial definition of war as 'an act of violence intended to compel the enemy to fulfil our will'? Clash of wills, trial of strength: the initial definition subsists in the final definition. Yet, the will becomes no longer that of a wrestler but that of the state; now, the will of a state is determined in relation to circumstances, by an appraising of the major characteristic of a given conflict. The primacy of policy, inasmuch as it determines the end, is implicit in the initial definition. The means, that is to say the act of violence, includes material force and moral force, passion and intelligence. The image of the two wrestlers did not suggest the duality of popular passions and the free play of probabilities and chance, but it would have been enough to substitute for this contest between two people a battle between two teams in order to be able to perceive, in the fight itself, the duality of blind passion and boldly thought-out initiatives.

The threefold definition none the less brings a decisive innovation: it alone is valid for all real wars, and although wars may deviate more or less from absolute war, they are nevertheless war from the moment that one refers to the threefold definition which is the basis of theory, history and doctrine.

2 The threefold definition, the result of the conceptualization

Let us first discard a thesis formulated by an excellent historian, Otto Hinze: that in the 'Warning' of 1827, Clausewitz opposed the two types of war, whereas in Book I he distinguished all the degrees of violence between total overthrow of the enemy and armed observation. Clausewitz's method makes it impossible to hold such a thesis. From the article in the *Neue Bellona* to the 'Warning' of 1827, Clausewitz applied the same method: first, to grasp in their extreme form the antitheses when they appear clearly, and then to go gradually from the pure to the borderline cases which in reality separate the two concepts or types. Besides, in the 'Warning', having postulated the two extremes, he accepts the intermediate stages.

If Chapter 1 of Book I has a different tone from the 'Warning', it is not because of the gradation of violence between the will to annihilate and the caution of armed observation, but because of the subordination of the two major ideas of the 'Warning' to an idea which does not figure in any of the unrevised books, from III to VI, and which, even in VIII, does not emerge clearly: namely the abstract, unreal, philosophical, ideal character of war consonant with Clausewitz's concept (he uses all these adjectives according to the circumstances).

However surprising this statement may seem, Clausewitz only laid the foundation of his conceptual edifice, namely the unreality of absolute war, in the last years of his life, between 1827 and 1830. Neither in 1804 nor in 1812 does he hesitate to formulate precepts or maxims of action. Can it be said in any war that energy and boldness are the characteristics of a leader destined for victory? This can be accepted. Nevertheless, Books III, IV and V on strategy, combat and armed forces bear no trace of any of the important ideas of the final synthesis, of the two types of war, of the duality which results from the primacy of policy, a primacy which itself reduces the rise to extremes to a game of logic.

The evolution of Clausewitz's thought, in the course of these last years, could be summed up in the following way. The contrast between the manner of waging war in the seventeenth century and that in the eighteenth strikes him in the course of his historical studies. He therefore conceives the duality of types. He then expresses this duality by referring to the Napoleonic practice – to overthrow the enemy – a practice which until now he considered as normal, logical, necessary, the other practices

67

appearing to him all the more degenerate in that they bore the responsibility for the defeats suffered by the allies and the victories of revolutionary and imperial France.

Of course, he had not ignored the political conditions of cabinet wars – the indifference of the peoples – any more than he had ignored the participation of the entire populace during the subsequent period. What it lacks is any approximation of the war which tends towards the extreme form – the annihilation of armed forces and the overthrow of the enemy state – to the war furthest from it – the conquest of a province at the frontiers or armed observation. In his youth, he introduced moral forces into his theory; in his maturity, he introduced the conceptual distinction needed to reconcile the transhistoric theory with history, in other words the two extreme forms of war, each one conditioned or determined by circumstances or political intentions. In order to establish the equality of status in the two types of war, he had to recognize the unreality of absolute war which in many texts he represented as the only one consistent with the concept.

In this respect are there differences, whether obvious or not, between Book VIII and Chapter 1 of Book I? There is no clear answer because of the incomplete state of Book VIII which, though perhaps revised after 1827, is much closer to the outline mentioned by Clausewitz than to the formal perfection of Chapter 1 (Book I). Certainly Book VIII, Chapter 2, clearly contrasts real war with absolute war. Clausewitz takes the decisive step: the advice which he seemed to give to the war leaders, in his youth, is only conditionally valid, provided that real war is consistent with its abstract or ideal nature. In that sense, the Clausewitzian duality of the concept (or of the ideal nature) and of the reality figures in Book VIII as well as in Book I but with a substantial, indeed major, difference: there is no trace, in Book VIII, of the threefold definition of war. Clausewitz has no right to use the expression *Halbding* or *Halbheit* (half-way affair) to characterize wars of little energy, or wars of the second type, unless he ignores the threefold definition. To the extent that all wars contain the three elements – original violence, free activity of the spirit and political understanding – cabinet wars do not deserve the name of half-war, they are only wars in which the third element dominates and the first tends to fade out because of the social organization (i.e. participation of the army rather than the people). In other words, the language of Book VIII seems to me to be behind the conceptualization of Book I. The vocabulary of Book VIII wavers between two conceptions: only the wars aimed at overthrowing the enemy are real wars, all wars both minor and great are wars, limited wars as well as unlimited wars are consistent not with abstract nature (that of the initial definition) but with the concrete and complex nature in which all three elements act together, although with variable force.

Everything happens as if the choice between the two possible solutions had been set out by Clausewitz himself in Chapter 2 of Book VIII. Just as he refused to exclude moral forces and friction from theory – this exclusion would have created such a gap between reality and theory that the latter would have become useless and sterile – he likewise refuses to exclude half-wars (or rather, what he calls half-wars) from it for the same reason. What would a theory mean which did not take into account the

68

most numerous wars in history, which were closer to armed observation than to Napoleonic campaigns? What would a theory mean which, however strong in its logic, nevertheless proved false in the wars of tomorrow, as in those of the past, though not perhaps the recent past?

From the beginning of Book VIII onwards, Clausewitz's choice is clear; he justifies without formulating it the threefold definition. However, on many occasions in Book VIII, the representation of absolute or ideal war seems to give it a privileged status. In Chapter 2 the theory aims to bring to the fore the absolute form in order to use it as a point of general reference. In Chapter 3, of these two kinds of notion (one in which the final result decides everything, the other in which the outcome results from small successes or defeats) the first, as the fundamental notion, should be the base and the second should be used 'as a modification of the first, justified by circumstances'. Does the primacy of absolute war and the way of thinking that goes with it correspond with the logic of Book I, Chapter 1?

The answer seems to be the following: absolute war corresponds with the concept, with the nature, with the truth of war *qua* war, in other words with war separated from its origins and its end, thus separated from policy as a condition of finality. In this sense, even in Chapter 1 it keeps a primacy, the character of a fundamental notion, of a logical necessity which is deduced, first, abstractly from the reciprocal action of clashing wills, and then concretely from unleashed passions. In Book VIII, the first kind of representation owes its truth to the nature of the thing, whereas we find the truth of the second kind in history; on the other hand, in Book I, Chapter 1, the threefold definition, valid for all real wars, marks the definitive split with the old idea that only wars which completely overthrow the enemy arise from the concept whereas imperfect wars, almost like games, are solely found in history. This way of expressing himself suggests that Clausewitz hesitated in the light of his own thoughtful logic.

There is no absolute war in reality, it only exists in the world of concepts of ideals. Yet, wars approaching absolute war are not perfect wars as opposed to imperfect wars mixed with policy. This opposition between total wars and wars affected by policy, still latent in Book VIII, is explicitly rejected by Clausewitz in Chapters 1 and 2 of Book I. A war which approached perfection is neither more nor less political than any other: it is policy itself which determines its absolute character. In other words, perfect war, which in Book VIII is used as a fundamental concept, becomes in Book I, Chapter 1, the simple logic of a war cut off from its causes and objects, doubly unreal, one could say. Thus, in Book VIII, the unreality of absolute war arises from the inevitable gap between the concept and the phenomenon; in Book I it arises from an incomplete definition of war.

At the same time, the opposition between the necessity for a rise to extremes and the possibility of an implicit understanding to prevent this rise loses its significance in reality: the three elements are features of all wars. Never does the element of blind violence and hate alone become unleashed in wars between civilized people. The magnitude of conflicting interests, the intensity of tensions and the political understanding, responsible for the choice of objects, all combine to determine the character of the phenomenon created by hostilities.

The final synthesis, as set out before us in Chapter 1 of Book I, allows us

69

to understand simultaneously the diversity of wars, of a greater or lesser intensity, and the opposition of the two types, each characterized by its manner of restoring peace – dictated in one case after the overthrow of the enemy or after negotiated peace in the other.

Now, the interpreter may ask why the strategic debate or conflict aroused such passion and lasted for so many years. What position does Clausewitz himself take in relation to Delbrück and his adversaries? To answer these questions the reader must be asked to read, not Clausewitz himself, but Delbrück and his countless adversaries.

3 Delbrück and the strategy of Frederick the Great

The link between the interpretation of Clausewitzian thought and the strategic controversy results from the play of chance on one person: Hans Delbrück. In a review of the biography of Clausewitz written by K. Schwartz, Delbrück formulated for the first time, in 1878, the distinction between two strategies which he called respectively the strategy of annihilation (*Vernichtungsstrategie*) or overthrow (*Niederwerfesstrategie*) and the strategy of attrition (*Ermattungsstrategie*), attributing to Clausewitz himself the authorship of this alternative. In other words, he likened the two types of war in the 'Warning' to two strategies, as he understood them.

A few years later (1886), he used the distinction between the two strategies to contrast the approach of Frederick II with that of Napoleon. The great king, a national hero, became in the eyes of the historian an exponent of the strategy of attrition. To characterize the latter he used a second alternative: war leaders have two means available, battle and manoeuvre; a strategy which aims resolutely and almost unconditionally towards battle heads for a single pole, whereas the strategy which combines manoeuvre and battle deserves to be called bipolar.

From then on passions were kindled, not really for reasons linked with the enigma of the final synthesis and with the secret of Clausewitz's thought, but with the cult of Frederick and with the victories of 1866 and 1870. The German generals, the great general staff, proudly followed the doctrine that Napoleon had inaugurated, that Clausewitz had taught and that the victor of Sadowa and Sedan brilliantly put into practice. Delbrück violated a taboo; he cast a slur on a national glory by attributing to Frederick the theory and practice of another strategy, inevitably inferior since the annihilation of enemy armies in a few decisive battles had assured the glory of both Napoleon and Moltke.

Then, the strategic debate inextricably confused the three following considerations:

(a) How much did Frederick's strategy differ from that of Napoleon? Is this difference characterized exactly by the two concepts of overthrow and attrition, by unipolar–bipolar alternatives? These questions remain essentially historical ones, but they lead to a theoretical question since Delbrück resorts to transhistorical concepts to define the two strategies of Frederick and Napoleon.

(b) Hence to a question which belongs to the history of ideas: How exactly does Delbrück interpret Clausewitz when he attributes the distinction to him? Can these strategies be likened to the two types of war of the 'Warning' of 1827? Is it legitimate to confuse two strategies and two types of war?

(c) Whether one accepts this confusion or not, Clausewitz recognizes a type of war in which the natural objective of hostilities – the annihilation of enemy forces, the overthrow of the adversary – is neither sought nor achieved. Now, which circumstances justify the abandonment of this objective and yet are consonant with the nature or concept of war? This last question not only referred to the past, it also anticipated the uncertainties of the future. The comparison between Pericles and Frederick the Great led to a comparison between Athens on the eve of the Peloponnesian War and Germany at the end of the nineteenth century. Delbrück was already critical of the strategy of annihilation or decisive victory which the Hindenburg–Ludendorff command was to adopt until the summer of 1918 and the final catastrophe.

Let us consider, as briefly as possible, the problems of the first rubric which we qualified as historical. Let us take as a starting point the article of 1886 which considers Frederick and Napoleon without referring to Clausewitz. Delbrück attempts to demonstrate that the strategic system as thought out and applied by Frederick differed in its principles from that of Napoleon.

As a historian and not a philosopher or theoretician, he first recalls the facts. First and foremost, the element which changed between the campaigns of Frederick and those of Napoleon was the number of combatants. The largest army which Frederick ever fielded in a single sphere of operations, the one which crossed the frontiers of Austria in 1757, numbered less than 100,000 men. Napoleon crossed the frontiers of Russia in 1812 with 467,000 men, in the autumn of 1813 he was still in command of some 440,000 troops.

Numbers had increased and the cost diminished owing to the change in the mode of recruitment. Conscription supplied the generals of the Revolution with soldiers whose upkeep involved lesser financial burdens than the professionals who, in the eighteenth century, waged small wars while the populace remained indifferent.

This professional army, whose gaps were filled by Frederick with prisoners, required a fearsome discipline; according to a famous saying, soldiers feared their officers more than the enemy. The strength of the Prussian army came from the coherence of the tactical units. Recruitment and organization determined to a large extent the mode of combat: the long, rigid lines which moved as a single man and fired their salvoes on command. The soldiers of the Revolution, on the other hand, because of their number and lack of education, acted as *tirailleurs* or in deep columns. The army of Frederick did not ignore *das Tiraillieren* but only used it on rare occasions as a last resort.

According to Delbrück, the fear of desertion radically excluded requisitioning, which was the practice of the Revolutionary armies who lived off the land: it was discipline's greatest problem for, though more or less controlled, it inevitably degenerated into pillage. Frederick did not go far from his arsenals except for a few marches and on principle he refused requisitioning. With linear tactics, he did not have the means either to force an enemy army occupying a well-defended position or to turn this position by rapid march. To wage battle he had to choose even terrain. The battle, conducted according to traditional tactics, was even more bloody than that of Napoleon, losses running sometimes as high as a third of the effective forces.

As a historian, Delbrück deduces from the socio-political data and the resulting military organization the system which he associates with the old monarchy.

Resources available are not sufficient to overthrow entirely the enemy state by combat. Even after the greatest victory, one would not be in a position to destroy totally its armed forces, to occupy the capital and most of the provinces. It is therefore necessary to compel him to yield and to conclude peace, not by surrendering unconditionally, but by wearing him out. If we take a frontier province and a few strongholds, if we choose a position from which he has no hope of expelling us by force, he will in the end come to accept our peace terms after a certain time of tension and after his financial resources have been exhausted.

The system of the old monarchy, which in the above quotation is defined as attrition (of will rather than force), is characterized, strategically, by the duality of poles or means. But modern or Napoleonic strategy leans towards a single pole, battle. Delbrück quotes Napoleon's saying: 'I only know three things in war, which are to cover ten leagues a day, to fight and to rest.' Moreover he concludes, 'Never did Frederick call for battle in such an unconditional way. Napoleon demands it absolutely and unconditionally; Frederick only relatively, as a desperate resort, a means of salvation in difficult circumstances.'

As for manoeuvre, Delbrück understands it, as the case may be, in two ways. In the narrow meaning, it describes 'all the movements which are designed to ensure advantages without shedding too much blood, in contrast with movements which are designed to create as far as possible favourable conditions for the next battle'. Manoeuvre in the widest sense, in particular in the pamphlet on Pericles, includes other means than the movement of armies, namely blockage and the devastation of territories; in short, all the means which make it possible to ensure advantages without joining battle. Concerning not so much the wars of the eighteenth century as the personality and mind of Frederick II himself, Delbrück's thesis seems to provoke an insuperable objection: had not Frederick – inevitably, according to Clausewitz – been in matters of battle the most offensive of war leaders? Did not his brother, Prince Henry, who was closer to the doctrines of the age, reproach him for always wanting to *Bataillieren* and for directing all his wisdom to the art of war?

Delbrück clearly does not intend to deny the differences between Frederick and the general opposed to him, between Frederick and his advisers of the old school (or Prince Henry whom the great king described as a 'general without fault'). He also extols the battles of which he was, more than any other, the chronicler. 'A victory, a victory in a great battle lives for ever. One cannot conceive the temperament of a truly great war leader as other than driven, by some kind of passion, to challenge a great decision of destiny.' He thus recognizes in Frederick the warlike temperament and vitality of soul necessary to face trials and take decisions which are wise because of their boldness (to paraphrase Clausewitz).

His superiority over all his contemporaries is to be found in that specifically warlike quality of boldness which carries him way above them; owing to this quality, he tends consistently towards the pole of battle (to use the same image) whereas his contemporaries incline towards the opposite pole of manoeuvre.

In this form, Delbrück's thesis, as a historical interpretation of Frederick, does not justify the passions that it has aroused. Delbrück concedes to his adversaries (he calls them such: *Gegner*) that Frederick, more than his brother Henry or his advisers, inclined towards the pole of battle. On the other hand, it is difficult to see how the exponents of the opposite thesis can deny that Frederick often and extensively manoeuvred (in the eighteenth-century meaning of the term), and that he often had recourse to 'jealousies' and 'umbrage'. When reduced to the defensive, however, he operated quite differently from Napoleon who, in 1814, never ceased to join battle.

Can one end the debate by attributing to Frederick the genius of Napoleon, constrained by the trappings of Frederick's age? Delbrück would probably have subscribed to this formula because he concedes in his reply to his first critic, the future Marshal Colmar von der Goltz, that Frederick, with the means of Napoleon, would have thought differently from the way he did, whereas, according to Delbrück, he remained, in theory and in practice, within the system of the ancient monarchy. Strategic doctrine is not historically separated from available means.

The details of the controversy need not concern us. Delbrück's critics reproached him for 'idealizing' the revolutionary armies, for belittling those of Frederick, for simplifying to the point of caricature Napoleonic strategy, for exaggerating Frederick's 'aversion' for battle, for failing to recognize the combined use, in all wars, of all means. They did not deny the qualitative and quantitative differences between Napoleon and the Prussian king's armies, but whereas Delbrück tends to pass from the conditioning to the determination of strategy by the military instrument, his adversaries stress the margin of initiative kept by the war leader in relation to the ideas of the age and armaments.

On the system of thought of the ancient monarchy and that of Frederick himself, the exchange of texts and arguments still continues today. According to the period of writing, Frederick moved towards caution or towards boldness, towards manoeuvre or towards battle. In his 'Military Testament' after the Seven Years' War he counsels caution, but this emphasis is perhaps explained by political reasons. What is certainly clear is that Frederick never professed a doctrine comparable to that of Napoleon, especially if one interprets the latter in the light of Clausewitz himself or in the light of Moltke or certain other texts. On the whole, Frederick considered battle neither as an evil nor as a permanent imperative nor as an exclusive means. If, in the *General Principles of War* (1747), he lists the reasons for which a general can justify the decision to join battle, it is because he writes in an age when those who are considered wise advise against the exposure to risks which battle involves.

If Frederick remains, in theory, within the system of the ancient monarchy, did he in action break this system? This question leads to another, more limited question, which nevertheless perhaps constitutes a reply: how should one interpret the campaign of 1757 or, if you prefer it, that of 1756–7 (regarding the two campaigns, separated by winter quarters, as a single one). Indeed, after the defeat at Kolin and the failure of the 1757 campaign, even the victories of Rossbach and Leuthen, which saved Frederick, did not give him any chance of a crushing victory. On the other hand, all the critics recognize that he would have gained a unique victory in the annals of contemporary military history had he managed to defeat the Austrians at Kolin and capture the Habsburg army at Prague.

Theodor von Bernhardi attaches a decisive significance to the first years of the Seven Years' War – which seems predictable in view of the thesis that the author wishes to defend. It was, indeed, in 1756–7 that Frederick possessed, according to him, the necessary forces to act in conformity with his own conceptions, in other words to seek total victory 'as Napoleon did in each of his campaigns during the Imperial period'.

Delbrück attempts to refute Bernhardi's interpretation, even when limited to the campaign of 1756–7. Frederick, according to Delbrück could not expect such a victory unless he foresaw incredible mistakes on his opponents' part. Moreover, in 1756, he was checked by the camp at Pirna, occupied by Saxony; he did not take it by assault or outflank it in the manner of Napoleon; he laid siege to it and, after the surrender of the camp, he set up winter quarters. The plan of the concentric attack on Bohemia cannot have been conceived by the king himself, and in any case this campaign, the least consistent with the practice of the age, remains far from the Napoleonic model. Consequently, Delbrück on many occasions lays stress on the faults committed by the king since he supposes that the latter conformed to the principles within a strategy of annihilation.

Whatever the judgment of historians on Frederick's plan of 1757, I see little difficulty in reconciling the objective of a great victory, in order to end the war as quickly as possible, with the general doctrine of a two-pole strategy. In 1756–7, Frederick had numerical superiority with an army of better quality. He was not unaware of the limitations of Prussian resources and he hoped for 'short and sharp' wars. That he envisaged in advance, or only after the first success, the near destruction of the Austrian army does not seem to me to put in question the two judgments found in the Treatise: Frederick, precursor of Napoleon, owes his greatness as much to virtues which enabled him, in spite of inferior forces, to attain his ends, as to the few battles which assured his salvation in times of extreme peril.

4 Delbrück and Clausewitz. Vocabulary and ideas

We now come to the second category of problems. To what extent does the distinction between Delbrück's two strategies reproduce the distinction between the two types of war? The critics have all asserted that Delbrück's concepts and ideas differed profoundly from those of Clausewitz. I think that the critics, in the final analysis, are entitled to stress the difference between the thought of the theoretician and that of the historian. Yet, I would first like to show that the historian as such is not as wrong as his opponents would maintain.

Let us first consider the definition of manoeuvre in its narrow meaning: the movements of armies which tend not to create conditions propitious for combat. How does Clausewitz define *das Manövrieren*? 'Manoeuvre is not only in contrast with the violent execution of attack but also with all forms of the attack's execution which flow directly from the means of attack, even an action against the enemy's lines of communication, or against his retreat or as a feint, etc.' It is a curious definition since it seems to exclude from manoeuvre action against the enemy's lines of communication or retreat.

The obscurity disappears when we come to distinguish *das Manövrieren* and *das Manöver*, in other words, the strategy which consists in manoeuvring and a manoeuvre which prepares for combat. Clausewitz does not mean that the action on enemy lines of communication does not belong to manoeuvre since, a little later, he includes lines of communication and retreat among the objects or supports of such an action. He excludes from manoeuvre all that is an integral part of attack, including even, as in Napoleon's campaigns, the threat against the enemy's lines of communication or retreat.

He would not have accepted that the famous campaign which led to the surrender of Ulm was an example of such a mode of operations: this campaign, unique in the French emperor's career, was a sort of aftermath, a second harvest from his earlier victories. It was the memory of his famous campaigns and the mistakes of his adversaries which assured him a victory through deception, without shedding blood. (He had, after all, shed it beforehand.)

Manoeuvring, separated from attack itself, inasmuch as the latter tends towards combats or battle, shows at least some analogy with Delbrück's narrow meaning of manoeuvre. In both cases the war leaders seek minor objects or advantages. In Chapter 13 of Book VII, Clausewitz enumerates five objectives or applications of manoeuvre involving action: cutting off or limiting the provisioning of the enemy, preventing the junction of enemy corps, threatening the enemy's communications with the interior of the country or other armies, threatening the lines of retreat, attacking at certain points with superior forces. Clearly, he is thinking of the methods of the generals of the *ancien régime*. This kind of manoeuvring far from preparing for attack or achieving the decision, is found, so to speak, within a situation of equilibrium.

> If we restrict ourselves to practice, there is in the concept of manoeuvre an efficacy which, from nothing, or from a situation of equilibrium, only comes about through the faults that the enemy can be made to commit. They are the first moves in a game of chess, which is also a game of equal forces. . . .

This chapter, inserted in the book on attack, explicitly refers to the end of Chapter 30 of Book VI where the notion of 'the balanced game of forces' is analysed more rigorously (*gleichgewichtiges Spiel der Kräfte*). Clausewitz elaborates the idea: from the time that there is no movement of the whole, that no one has important goals in view, one can consider the two sides, even if of unequal strength, to be in equilibrium. 'Out of this equilibrium of the whole there arise the peculiar motifs of small actions and minor goals.' Clausewitz finds that excessive importance has been placed on this manoeuvring, but he recognizes no less (a proof that his book belongs to a late phase) that most wars between civilized states have mutual observation as their object rather than overthrow, and consequently that most campaigns necessarily evolve according to the strategy of manoeuvre.

Here, the conceptualization of Delbrück does not fundamentally differ from that of Clausewitz. Both, observing the same historical reality, arrive at the same notions: at one extreme, movements which relate to battle, at the other, movements which, in a situation of equilibrium, characterized by the denial of the decision (denial common to both sides), only aim for moderate objects and for indirect efficacy.

That wars in which manoeuvre predominates belong to the second type cannot be doubted. Mutual observation or armed observation characterize hostilities and limit the objective. It is clearly a historical form that accords with the definition of the second type of war since neither of the belligerents seeks to overthrow his enemy, and consequently peace will be negotiated between the adversaries and not dictated sovereignly by one of the two.

In Chapter 3(A) of Book VIII, Clausewitz once again considers the opposition between the two types of war, and he does so in terms which recall Frederick and Delbrück (or, if you prefer it, Frederick as interpreted by Delbrück). We could say that what defines a war is the internal structure, the relation between the two sides. All war constitutes a totality, but there are two types of totality: either the totality is represented by the ultimate event; or it is constituted progressively by the consecutive addition of partial results. In one case, nothing is won, nothing is lost before the final result.

The outcome [das Ende] crowns the work. In this representation, war is an indivisible whole whose constituent parts (separate results) have no value except in relation to the whole.

To this representation of the structure of results in war, which may be regarded as extreme, stands opposed another extreme representation according to which war is composed of separate results, each independent, each previous result exercising no influence on the following ones, as in a game of cards. Everything here amounts to the sum total of results and one can place each alongside the others, like counters.

Clausewitz immediately adds (as I indicated above) that the first representation derives its truth from the nature of the thing, whereas it is history which reveals the second to us; in other words, he does not put, at least in Book VIII, 'the nature of the thing' and 'historical modalities' on the same plane. Delbrück also found the idea of final victory by an accumulation of small results in history in the writings of Frederick II. Delbrück quotes a passage from the Introduction to the History of the Seven Years' War:

It is very probable that the Austrian generals will not deviate from the method of General Daun, which is unquestionably the right one, and that in the first war we will find them as careful to take up good positions as they have been in this one. This makes me observe that a general will do badly if he rushes into attacking the enemy in mountain positions or in broken-up terrain. Force of circumstance has sometimes compelled me to go to this extremity, but when war is waged between equal powers more certain advantages can be gained by ruse and cunning. Without being exposed to the same degree of risk, and acccumulating many small advantages, their sum total makes them great. (Introduction to the *History of the Seven Years' War*, Historical Works, Vol. IV, p. xviii)

I do not claim that Clausewitz interprets Frederick's strategy in exactly the same way as Delbrück. However, it does seem closer to Delbrück than to Bernhardi. The idea of victory by an accumulation of small advantages, characteristic of one type of war according to Chapter 3 of Book VIII, is found in the writings of Frederick and in the interpretation of Frederick by Delbrück.

Even the classical criticism which Schering takes up after so many others – that Delbrück confused the two types of war with the two types of strategy – does not really carry weight. Indeed, if Clausewitz distinguishes two types of war, this distinction derives from the political finality and, in turn, from the alternative: to overthrow the enemy in order to dictate peace or to ensure a certain number of pawns in order to negotiate an advantageous peace. From the political finality is derived the military objective. From the military objective is derived strategy since Clausewitz includes in strategy the whole conduct of the war. By what miracle could the same strategy be correct in a war in which the final result alone counts and in a war in which the final result simply represents the accumulation of partial results? Of Delbrück who does not distinguish the dual type of war and the dual type of strategy on the one hand, and Bernhardi and Schering who deny the dependence of strategy in relation to the type of war on the other, it is Delbrück who is nearer to the truth than his adversaries.

On the other hand, the term *Ermattung* and the notion of *Ermattungsstrategie* belong neither to the vocabulary nor to the conceptual system of Clausewitz. Certainly Clausewitz uses two closely related words, *Ermüdung* (action of tiring the opponent or of tiring oneself) and *Erschöpfung* (exhaustion). But the first of these terms does not directly correlate with the war of the second type even though it holds an important place in two analyses of the Treatise.

In Chapter 8 of Book VIII, Clausewitz denies that the objective of the defensive as such can be to tire the adversary. Indeed, generally, we have the right to say that the forces of the attacker wear out the adversary more than those of the defender. The attack will slacken if the defence can prolong things to a point where, even after a great victory, the ratios are reversed.

But if such a reversal does not happen it is the defender who loses the most whether, by reason of inferior forces, the same losses become relatively greater, or whether the attacker takes a part of his territory or resources away from him. Clausewitz does not conclude that the side that remains on the defensive and exposes itself to the blows of the adversary without itself striking, as in 1812, will in all probability finish by being exhausted and succumbing. He expresses himself in different terms: the side which does nothing but defend has no counter-weight to balance the danger that one of the adversary's blows might succeed. Then the immediate result, he adds, that exhaustion or rather the wearing out of the stronger side has on several occasions ensured peace, 'the cause being the incomplete [*Halbheit*] character most often assumed by war'. Wearing out the enemy is not and cannot be thought of as the general and final objective of any defence; it is the waiting that constitutes the characteristic. When there is nothing to hope for from military circumstances there remains the possibility of political changes. Clausewitz is thinking of Frederick II in the Seven Years' War, having no other objective than to hold out, to gain time, even giving up waging battles because they, even though victories, cost him dear. To this defence which is, so to speak, reduced to the economical use of force, Clausewitz, according to his method of extremes, contrasts the example of the Tsar in 1812 who could count on the reversal in the relation of forces after the zenith of victory.

In this analysis the attempt to wear out the superior enemy only represents one of the extreme possibilities open to the defence, victorious in the final analysis, of the weaker side, but it is a possibility immanent in a war of the second type in which neither of the belligerents is animated by a strong resolve to overthrow the enemy.

The second analysis in which the same notion appears seems to me to be still more interesting. Clausewitz, in Book I, Chapter 2, examines the motives that could induce the enemy to conclude peace even though it still has the means to pursue the war. He distinguishes two: the improbability of success and the excessive price of success. How can you raise the price of victory for the enemy? By forcing him to deploy greater strength, either by inflicting losses on his armed forces or by conquering a part of his territory. After these means (*Mittel*), which are self-evident, Clausewitz indicates three other ways (*Wege*). The first is the invasion of enemy provinces, not to keep them, but to inflict damage on them, to raise contributions or even simply to devastate them. The second way, which in reality is only a variant of the first, consists of directing attacks against objectives to increase the damage. Here Clausewitz specifies – and this specification is enough to demonstrate the heterogeneity of operations according to the type of war – that the appropriate directions given to armed forces will differ according to whether or not the aim is to overthrow the enemy.

We finally come to the third way, that of wearing out, by far the most important because of the number of cases that arise from it.

> The concept of wearing out [*ermüden*] in battle incorporates the exhaustion of the physical forces and of the will, gradually produced by the duration of the action. . . . If we want to hold out longer than the enemy, we have to be content with minor goals because they are less expensive and because the risk of failure is less. It is a question of inflicting enough losses on the enemy to make him give up his offensive designs. The negative intention, which constitutes the principle of 'pure resistance', is the natural means to succeed against the adversary in the duration of the struggle.

In other words, this third way, that which tends to tire out the adversary, that which exploits to the full the advantages of defence, of the negative intention, covers the majority of cases in which the weaker resists the stronger. If, in this case, Clausewitz evokes the whole range of means, it is within the compass of a pure resistance – a strategy which is found in the opposite extreme to the one which he considers doctrinaire, namely the direct offensive with a view to annihilation in battle.

Here again Clausewitz takes, as an example of attrition, the strategy of Frederick II.

He was never in a position to overthrow the Austrian monarchy; and even had he tried, in the manner of Charles XII, he would have inevitably precipitated his downfall. But when the skill with which he knew how to put into practice a wise economy of forces became evident during seven years, the powers which were allied against him, realizing that their expenditure of forces far exceeded their forecasts, decided to make peace.

The attempt to wear out the enemy, even in this text which in all probability was written later than Chapter 8 of Book VIII, is not the sole way to execute the second type of war; it nevertheless becomes the way *par excellence* which the weaker side in any case should follow, and perhaps even any belligerent whenever the outcome depends on his capacity to hold out longer than the adversary. Now in the twentieth century, with the memory of the First World War, we are inclined to connect the notion of the 'last quarter of an hour' with ruthless conflicts in which states engage all their resources. Clausewitz, on the contrary, connected this notion with hostilities without military decision, in which the belligerents only mobilized limited resources for the very reason of the limitation of the stakes. It is thus to the second type of war that the principle of the economy of forces applies.

Here again, Delbrück has at least partly revealed Clausewitz's thoughts. In his book on the strategy of Pericles, he suggests that, instead of opposing battle and manoeuvre, we could oppose 'law of boldness' with 'law of the economy of forces'. 'Where it is not possible to overthrow the enemy, the thing is to know which one will first be exhausted [*ermattet*], not so much to smash the enemy forces as to save our own, so as to keep the last thaler in our pocket.'

My defence and explanation of Delbrück, who was condemned by all German critics who prided themselves on their philosophy, is intended quite simply to show that Delbrück discovered, by historical study, ideas which Clausewitz reached at the end of his life, probably also by reflecting on history. Furthermore, they analysed the same historical cases, the one to elaborate the concept of the strategy of attrition and the other to elaborate the notion of the second type of war. Even if Frederick II, as a war leader, assumes the role of precursor of Napoleon in Clausewitz's eyes, the latter brings out the details of the wars of the second type by taking as an example the conflicts of the eighteenth century. It is not surprising, then, that the two men, as historians, lead in different languages to neighbouring conclusions.

Yet on what points do Delbrück's critics have the last word? The historian has not articulated the conceptual system of the theoretician. The latter begins, firstly, by opposing absolute war and real war; the opposition between the two kinds of war is located at a different level, that of historical diversity, even though Clausewitz is sometimes inclined to confuse absolute war and war of the first type. In the second place, the wars of the second type should not be identified, in Delbrück's way, with a historical form (the wars of the *ancien régime*) or with a defined strategy (bipolar). The wars of the eighteenth century illustrate the transhistoric character of a war of the second type which is brought to a close by negotiated peace. Possibly, similar examples can be found in other centuries and socio-political contexts. Delbrück himself was close to drawing out the essential when he compared Frederick and Pericles, both of whom adopted a strategy aimed at not losing and not defeating decisively. Clausewitz for his part does not always rigorously differentiate historical particularities from the transhistoric character.

Would Clausewitz have accepted that the system of the ancient monarchy and that of Napoleon were opposed respectively as 'unipolar' and 'bipolar'? It does not seem so. Certainly, manoeuvre had a more important place in the strategy of the old monarchy than in that of Napoleon. Yet, I doubt whether he would have accepted the simplification: of either, exclusively, battle or else the choice, according to circumstances, between battle and manoeuvre (in the narrow or broad sense), or on the one side battle and on the other everything else. To include blockade, occupation or devastation in the notion of manoeuvre would have appeared a strange conception to him.

Delbrück's description of 'unipolar' strategy caricatures, or falsifies, the Clausewitzian description of Napoleonic strategy. Even on the material level, battle does not constitute the sole principle of annihilation: space, climate, lack of provision, guerillas sometimes 'destroy as much as or even more than battle'. In Chapter 2 of Book I the references to combat or battle represent a conceptual truth which can be deduced from the definitions: in reality, there are many ways which lead to the goal, and imagined or simulated battles can take the place of battles actually waged. Clausewitz would not have called a strategy of attrition a strategy which, more often than not, leads to peace when the belligerents retain the material means to pursue hostilities. Or, at least, he would have underlined the moral (or psychological) character of attrition – the wearing out of the will rather than the exhaustion of physical resources.

He would no more have forgone, it seems to me, a transhistoric typology of the matter to which the action of war relates. He did not always enumerate the various types of matter in the same terms, but in the *Principles of Instruction* (1812) he recognizes three, and in the Treatise he rigorously elaborates this not strange, but logical trinity. They are: armed forces, material and human resources necessary for the upkeep of these forces, morale. In the abstract analysis, he puts armed forces above the others: the immediate subject-matter, by definition, of the action of war. According to the logic of the final synthesis, if not according to the letter of the Treatise, the relative importance of these three types varies with the ages, depending on the methods of combat and of the instrument, and also depending on political circumstances.

If Delbrück convinced nobody, it is partly because of his lack of conceptual rigour, and above all on account of an internal ambiguity in Clausewitz's thought that the final, outline, synthesis could not clear up. How can the two types of war, the two strategies, be made equivalent when the Treatise sets the overthrow of the state or the destruction of armed forces as the natural and ideal objective of war as such?

So we come to the third group of problems: which circumstances determine or explain the transition from one type of war to another?

5 Why wars of the second type?

Why do we discuss wars of the second type, namely real wars which do not conform with the nature of war, which betray it more than they reveal it? In the strategy of Pericles, Delbrück writes that a certain weakness (*Schwäche*) of will or of force (*Kraft*) induces the transition from one type to another. He considers without clearly separating them, the inadequacy of the military instrument (a professional army weighed down and paralysed by the transportation of provisions) and numerical disadvantage. During the second part of the Seven Years' War, Frederick found himself in such a position of inferiority that he could contemplate neither a decisive victory nor the overthrow of the Austrian empire.

Clausewitz also does not rigorously distinguish between the various determinates – instrument, relation of forces, object (or political finality). In Chapter 3 of Book VIII the phenomenal characteristics of real wars seem to be determined above all by political circumstances, in which he includes the constitution of states, the relation between government and people, and the quality and quantity of troops. Chapter 3(B) (Book VIII) considers the theme of Delbrück's major book, the history of the art of war within the framework of political history. It is here, rather than in the 'Warning' of 1827, that he could have found his governing ideas. The features of war are inscribed in politics like the characteristics of a living being in the embryo. On this historical, objective or permanent truth are based the precepts which hold first place in Clausewitzian praxology: the judgment which arises from policy (in the subjective sense), and the personified intelligence of the state which discerns the nature of this war following an analysis of the historical environment (or objective politics).

In Chapter 6 of the same Book, Clausewitz takes up the analysis of policy, no longer in the objective sense (the historical environment out of which war rises), but in the subjective sense: the determination of the war plan according, first, to judgment as to the major characteristic of the conflict, and then to many heterogeneous considerations, a determination at this point so complex that it would defy the genius of a Euclid or a Newton. It is thus, in Chapter 6, that Clausewitz passes on from the conditioning of war by policy to the decisive idea of political action through arms, a superior point of view which is a basis for the unity of the concept of war in spite of the diversity of wars and the duality of types. It is not the initial conception of absolute war which allows the historical diversity of wars to be subsumed under a single concept, but the intrinsically political nature of war. Whether Marshal Saxe often avoids battle or whether Napoleon always seeks it, war remains war because, in both cases, the states act politically by violence, whatever the methods might be.

The title of the second part of Chapter 3 concerning the magnitude of the object of war and of the efforts to be made, and that of the second part of Chapter 6, concerning an instrument of policy, confirm without leaving any doubt that historical circumstances and the ends of the belligerents determine the magnitude of effort or, as we might say today, the coefficient of mobilization and the relentlessness of the struggle. Still, the condition-

81

ing of hostilities by the military instrument does not exclude a margin of freedom, evidenced by a Gustavus Adolphus or a Frederick.

On another side, in Chapter 5, the limited objective, which is opposed to the natural objective of overthrow, is explained or justified by two circumstances: an objective one, the lack of necessary forces to achieve overthrow; and a subjective one, the lack of boldness, the rejection of great enterprises. These expressions bring to mind those of Delbrück cited above, a certain weakness of will or of strength. However, a general proposition can be based on this chapter alone since it ends with the formula: 'We have hitherto deduced that the modification of the objectives of war is sometimes due to military motives, and sometimes to political reasons.' Chapter 6 of Book VIII confirms this interpretation.

However, Chapters 7 and 8, which deal with the offensive or defensive plan with a limited objective, return to military analyses. Chapter 7 analyses attacks such as were carried out in the eighteenth century and examines the weakening, felt to a greater or lesser extent, that affected the attacker from the fact of his conquests. Clausewitz alludes to the high point of victory, but this concerns above all, if not exclusively, the other type of war. In the wars of the old monarchy the consequences of limited conquests varied according to the geographical situation of occupied territory. The conqueror could not be disinterested, as in decisive campaigns, in the other parts of the country. Once again the example of Frederick in the Seven Years' War illustrates the case of defensive war with a limited objective. This kind of defensive war contrasts with that waged by the Russians in 1812 leading to Napoleon's decision to withdraw. Clausewitz attempts, as he writes elsewhere, to illuminate, to 'intellectualize' (vergeistigen), military analysis by referring to the opposition between the two types of war.

What can one conclude? The adversaries in the strategic debate have sought the answers to two questions, which the texts neither give nor enable to be given. Does the decision to limit the objective of war, to thus abandon overthrow, depend on objective circumstances, on the instrument or on the intentions of the belligerents? According to the logic of the system, if one takes the whole of the texts into consideration, Clausewitz did not choose between these different explanations. He can isolate none of them: the instrument limits the possibilities of Frederick but he, with his small army, succeeds in surprising the Austrians and attaining his ends. The relation of forces, by itself alone, does not decide anything. If it were decisive by itself, the struggle of the weak against the strong would become inconceivable, absurd. Now it is strategic theory which must come to the help of the weaker.

Rosinski unearths another difficulty in his article: the character of war and the war plan depend on two kinds of consideration – the intensity of political tension on the one hand, and the relation of forces on the other. Now, the first kind of consideration suggests a scale of violence, with many intermediate points; the second imposes the alternative of yes or no: either one has or one does not have sufficient forces to overthrow the enemy. I do not subscribe to this line of argument. Rarely does the head of state have the knowledge of the relation of forces which would allow him to settle, by yes or no, the question: Are the forces sufficient to overthrow the enemy? Even if one supposes perfect information, the war leader must still ask which victory he needs in order to attain his political ends. In the abstract, the alternative of victory by 'knockout' or victory on points asserts itself; in reality, it only indicates two extreme points between which are inserted many intermediates.

Rosinski is right to assert that one can pass from a war which aims at the overthrow of an enemy state to war with a limited objective for strictly military reasons, because of the relation of forces. The comparison between the war plan against the French, in Chapter 9 of Book VIII, and the war plan conceived in 1831 with the hypothesis of the non-participation of Austria, bears witness to the possible determination of the military objective by the relation of forces. It does not prove that one must aim for the extreme objective that available forces sanction.

Delbrück, as well as his adversaries, wonders why all wars do not belong to the first type. Thus, implicitly, they are all adopting the conceptualization of Book VIII rather than that of Chapter 1 of Book I. Or, again, to express the same idea in another way, they start from the initial or monist definition of war and not from the threefold definition. Since all real wars comprise, but in different proportions, the three elements – passion of the people, free activity of the soul of the war leader, political understanding and direction of the war by the state – why not look for the causes of the war which rises to extremes as well as those of wars which descend to armed observation?

This seems to me to be implicitly the problem raised by the Treatise: Clausewitz attributes the victories and the conquests of France not to the virtues of the French but to the Revolution and its sequel, in other words to political tensions, induced by internal upheaval, freeing all the energies of a people. Chapter 6 of Book VI, on the European tendency towards equilibrium, suggests the abnormality of the crisis which drove Napoleon to Moscow and then to St Helena. It is thus not the limitation of hostilities but the rise to extremes that calls for explanation.

Delbrück and his adversaries can nevertheless put forward one excuse; the following question is often asked, both in the Treatise and by them: Why does real war not conform to its own nature? Why are the belligerents satisfied with minor successes and why do they abandon attempts at overwhelming victory? As has been said, the Treatise remains unfinished and does not resolve its own enigma. Let us read the last lines of Chapter 3 (Book VIII).

> This is why we must state that the objective which is fixed by whoever undertakes war, and the means which he mobilizes, are determined according to the strictly individual characteristics of the situation; but that they must also bear the character of the age and of the general circumstances; and lastly, that they must remain subject to the general consequences which must be deduced from the nature of war.

The last phrase, underlined by Clausewitz himself, contains the enigma and not the solution. Which consequences must be deduced from the nature (that is to say from the essence, from the concept) of war? Is the principle of annihilation of armed forces as the prime objective predominant? No doubt it is, but what remains of the general consequences, which are deduced from the concept and from the point when the latter only applies to a fictitious war, separate from what precedes and from what follows it, i.e. from the point when policy fixes the military objective, controls operations and decides in the last instance? What is the value of precepts deduced from a definition of war that is fictitiously autonomous?

We have finally come to the decisive question: is there not a fundamental divergence and perhaps incompatibility between the principle of annihilation and the supremacy of policy? Clausewitz, obsessed by the memory of 1806, ceaselessly recalls the danger of underestimating the resolution of the adversary, of opposing with the dagger the heavy sword of the knight, or in short of committing an error by default. But the supremacy of policy also teaches us not to indulge in logical reveries, not to confuse the abstract necessity of a rise to extremes with an imperative for action. Moderation demands implicit accord between the two adversaries: does not the survival of the system of European states prove the possibility of this accord? The war which ends without either of the belligerents being overthrown, the most frequent in history, finally appears normal – only on condition that the adversaries know each other and know approximately what they have to fear and hope for from each other. Did Clausewitz, at the end of his life, also fear errors due to excess? The logic of his thought was leading him in this direction, even if he himself did stop, disconcerted, before the unknown perspectives which were opening out in front of him.

I would like to mark the end of Part I by comparing my conclusions with those of W.M. Schering.

The distinction between the three stages in the composition of the Treatise or of the three versions no longer raises controversy: the octavo of Coblenz, a rhapsody of short chapters in the style of Montesquieu; the bulky volume written between 1823 and 1826, with the first six books, the sketch of the seventh, the outline of the eighth; the revision of 1828–30 which involved the whole of the first and probably a part of the second book and perhaps the eighth. That some chapters from the octavo of Coblenz might have passed unaltered into the manuscript published after his death is only of minor importance.

In 1827, Clausewitz announced his scheme to revise the manuscript by introducing throughout the distinction between the two types of war, and also the idea that war serves as an instrument of policy. For unknown reasons, he fails to complete his scheme; he does not write Book VII as he had expressly intended, he perhaps revises Book VIII and certainly the first book and probably a part of the second. Marie von Clausewitz writes in her Preface that her brother discovered the revised text amongst Carl's papers and inserted it in the first book at convenient points.

From these given facts, can we accept Schering's theses which I shall summarize in the following terms. Was it only in 1827 that Clausewitz discovered, or at least thought out clearly, the two ideas of the 'Warning' (two types of war, subordination of war to policy)? Now, these two ideas involved not only a deepening but also a reorientation of a thought which had been apparently fully-fledged for twenty years. The revision which these two ideas make necessary is not taken to its limit because he goes beyond the 'dualist' definition of war just as he had passed beyond the 'monist' definition in 1827.

According to Schering, the first version, that of Coblenz, was written in a light, ironic tone, and had as its object 'the vivid presentation of the vital element or atmosphere of war in which moral greatness freely moves'. The endeavour to portray the sight and feel of the reality of war remains in the final version. In the *Principles of Instruction*, he recommends that one should read the accounts of the combatants themselves rather than history books.

The far more developed version, written between 1823 and 1826, is thought to retain an essential idea from the initial version: the annihilation of enemy armed forces is not separate from the end, of overthrow by the state against which war is waged. Logically Clausewitz should have distinguished, from this time onwards, between the abstract notion of overthrow and the divers concrete manifestations of this notion. The political end – overthrow – and the military objective which is the means – destruction of the enemy armed forces – are intertwined. It is in this sense that Schering calls monist the theory or definition of war present in the book of 1823–6 as in the 'Strategy' of 1804 or in the *Principles of Instruction*.

This theory, he thinks, became dualist with the 'Warning' of 1827, itself the result of historical studies pursued by Clausewitz during the 1820s. History exposes to view wars too different in their intensity and in their evolution to enable us to hold to a law of extremes, to the principle of annihilation. Theory should not only include wars consistent with what appears to be the essence of wars, but all wars. The same respect for experience which compels him to take moral greatness into account in the theory now compels him not to neglect, in the theory, wars conducted passively, with limited military objectives, without the political object of destroying or overthrowing the enemy state. Furthermore, he establishes that wars distant from the essence are far more numerous than 'perfect wars'.

In the 'Warning' of 1827, he announces the scheme to revise his book taking into account the diversity of wars, in particular the two types of war, at the same time as the primacy of the political object, the origin of this duality.

From 1827 onwards, he reflected on this decisive set of problems. The letters to Major Roeder bear witness to his research. Should he say that wars very distant from those of Napoleon are not *der Sache angemessen*, in other words that they do not conform to the nature of war? If he replies that they do not belong to the nature of war, the theory loses contact with historic reality since these kinds of war are the most common. But, if he gives the opposite reply, he must at least substitute the dualist conception, the two types of the 'Warning', for the monist conception.

From the dualist conception follows, in the final stage, in Chapter 1 of Book I, the definition of the strange trinity: original violence (people), free activity of the spirit (war leader), supremacy of understanding (government). This threefold definition marks the outcome of Clausewitzian thought but does not preclude the dualist theory. The three elements of the strange trinity, present in each war, determine by their respective force and their relations, that war's particular character. The threefold definition is

85

opposed not to the duality of types which is found at the level of historical experience but to the monist definition which always supposes political overthrow and military destruction.

The meaning of the discovery of 1827 – transition from the monist conception to the dualist conception – seems to me simple and clear. Clausewitz did not discover belatedly the political conditioning of wars, he did not retain the innocence of the soldier, indifferent or hostile to political considerations, until 1827. Quite the reverse: as reader of Machiavelli and Montesquieu, as spectator or actor in the revolutionary wars, as analyst of coalitions, he never separated the phenomena of war from the historical totality. The problem was to harmonize a definition of war which applied to the enterprises of the conquerors and great commanders with innumerable wars apparently incompatible with the actual nature of war. The duality of types and the supremacy of policy resolve – and resolve definitively – this problem.

What is the meaning of the transition from the dualist conception to the threefold definition? Personally, I would reply that this definition represents progress in the conceptual elaboration; it incorporates the distinction, necessary in the abstract and common in reality, between the military leader and the head of state, the first being subject to the second; the first having access to greatness owing to the free activity of the soul (the virtues of the senses in the midst of physical dangers), the second charged from the beginning with the supreme responsibility, of first giving judgment on the nature of the war that he is going to wage or have waged by his army chief, and then with maintaining the control of intelligence over unleashed passions or the decisions, which are inevitably adventurous, of the military command. At the same time it integrates the duality of the people and the state, the one symbolizing the passion and hate of which war is born or to which war gives birth, the other which channels passions, sometimes excites them, always controls them.

Up to here, I do not see any major difficulty. On the other hand, the conclusions which Schering draws from the threefold conception seem to me to warp the very meaning (both the signification and the orientation) of the intellectual evolution of Clausewitz. According to Schering, even out of the threefold definition which figures at the end of the first Chapter of Book I, Clausewitz had arrived at a philosophy of action, or at a philosophy of *Hier und Jetzt*. Certainly, at all the stages of his career, Clausewitz, intensely aware of the gap between the speculations of the strategists and the decisions of the war leader in the middle of the action, understood and extolled the greatness of the man who, alone, had to take, in the teeth of danger, a decision – here and now – for the salvation of all. But the threefold definition does not stress the voluntaristic or irrational aspect of Clausewitzian thought. On the contrary, it refines it by subordinating the *Freie Seelentätigheit* to *Verstand*, gambling to calculation, adventure to wisdom, the military to the civil, the army chief to the head of state. By putting the head of state on the side of understanding, Clausewitz does not approach the false rationalism of a Bülow but the true rationalism of action: the authentic rationalism which gives prime importance to political intelligence because war, in its essence, is policy with a mixture of other means.

So what, at this point, remains ambiguous? To sum it up in one question: up to what point is the monist definition, the supreme principle of a decision by arms, of the destruction of enemy armed forces, reconcilable with the two types of war, with the threefold definition of war, with the primacy of policy?

Clausewitz wanted to, and believed he could, reconcile the book of 1826, his previous ideas, with his ultimate thoughts by distinguishing the idea from the reality, wars according to the monist (or abstract or absolute) definition from real wars. Inevitably the reader constantly wonders whether the implicit propositions or precepts are valid for war according to the idea, for wars which approach 'perfection' or for all wars. If the destruction of enemy armed forces remains valid as a prime, if not exclusive, objective, what becomes of the subordination of the war plan to the intelligence of the head of state? If the priority of destruction becomes logical in the sense that it is derived from the definition of war as such, separated from its origins and ends, it loses the praxological implications that have usually been given to it. Towards which side of this alternative does Clausewitz himself incline? The interpreters of the Treatise are themselves divided, too, into two schools, one of which is predominant at the time of victories while the other emerges only after defeats – not to mention, of course, those who have not even understood the question, inevitably the greatest number.

Part II
The Dialectic

The Plan of the Treatise

The Treatise, in the form that it has reached us, is organized according to a plan which, it seems to me, becomes apparent as one reads. The first book defines war, its nature and its end; it elaborates the principal concepts of the system and, by contrasting the abstraction of the analyses with the description of the field of battle, it emphasizes the contrast between armchair strategy and strategy on the ground. At the same time, the reference to policy and the refusal to consider war as an autonomous reality provide the conceptual basis of the distinction between ideal or absolute war and real wars. The contrast between pseudo-scientific speculation and live combat goes back to Clausewitz's youth and certainly appears in the Coblenz manuscript. On the other hand, the subordination of the war to policy, or, to be more exact, the essentially political nature of war as such, only acquires its full significance, as we have seen, in the texts of the last years, in particular of Chapter 1 of Book I.

The second book constitutes the equivalent of an epistemology, of a 'theory of theory', not without enriching, here and there, the definition of war itself. What is the nature of knowledge and power? What comprises the theory of an art (*Kunst*)? In what sense can the action of war, in particular that of the leader, be likened to an art? As for Book VIII, it deals with the plan of war, in other words with a decision that is inseparably political and military; it thus takes up the central problem of Book I, making use of the military studies contained in the intermediate books, or at least it would have done had Clausewitz been able to perfect it after having given a definitive form to the first two books. In its existing form, Book VIII leads us into the workshop of Clausewitz, according to a formula of W.M. Schering, but it does not yield a completed theory.

The intermediate books divide into two categories. Books VI and VII, 'Defence' and 'Attack', bear the stamp of the thinker's originality. Other military writers, although not unaware of the classical opposition of defence–attack, have not considered these forms themselves, or the intrinsic force of each in the light of a series of conceptual pairs: keeping–taking, gaining time–losing space, repelling–advancing, political defence –military attack, strategic defence–tactical attack.

Of the other books, Book III, entitled 'On Strategy in General', contains many chapters, almost half, which deal only with moral forces, so that the whole book is finally organized around the moral–physical pair of strength of will and strength of numbers. Books IV and V, the most classical, having combat and armed forces as their subjects, deal with the means of strategy and the means of tactics, in their phenomenal or historical manifestation. War implies combat, but the concrete modalities of combat vary according to the age. War is a chameleon in two senses: it is diverse in itself because of the strange trinity; it is diverse in its expression. What is true of battle in 1815 will not necessarily be true of battle in 1945.

Proceeding from this summary, how should we order our own account without following the example of the French commentators, La Barre Duparcq or Palat, who followed the text of the Treatise? It is self-evident that the reply depends on the end that one sets for oneself. My purpose is threefold: I first want to make clear Clausewitz's way of thinking, his method of analysis, of reasoning; then to bring out his guiding political and military ideas; then, having become acquainted with the method and the theses, I shall finally examine the heritage of Clausewitz. This last question necessitates research into the final stage of his thought, the logical consequences of the principles set down in the first chapter of Book I.

The means to attain these ends – to borrow my author's language – seems to me to be as follows. Most commentators have recognized that Clausewitz thought dialectically, in the precise sense that he brought pairs of opposed concepts into play, and it is by choosing the essential oppositions or antitheses that one has the best chance of elucidating at one and the same time the manner and matter of this book, written by a strange chief of staff who resolved never to surrender his work to the public in his lifetime and who was convinced, deep down, that he was writing for posterity.

After much hesitation I have retained three antitheses and I am surprised, after the event, at this hesitation: moral–physical, means–end, defence–attack are the three conceptual pairs around which the system develops.

The first goes back to the reflections of the young officer, and to the rejection of the pseudo-science of H. von Bülow and of all the geometries of strategy. The introduction of moral influences into theory seems, at first, to render the theory itself impossible. But, in the final analysis, we may as well give up all theory rather than elaborate one so far removed from reality that it ceases to be of any use for the actors. War effectively develops across space and time; strategy thus implies a combination of these two important factors. But this concerns combinations so simple in themselves that these calculations do not constitute the essential. In other words, the moral–physical opposition leads us to the thing itself, the action of men in conflict with each other across space and time, the leader assuming the responsibility of moving the mass despite the friction, of imposing on events the guidance of an intelligent will.

The first antithesis leads immediately and logically to the second, that of the means and the end. This was implied, as early as the article in the *Neue Bellona*, by the definition of tactics and strategy, each using different material with a view to a specific end: the first, armed forces with a view to victory; the second, combats or, to be more precise, the results of combats with a view to the end sought by the campaign and by the war itself. These definitions, by their abstract character, characterize one dimension – the

90

intelligent dimension of war. This, to use the vocabulary of Max Weber, is *par excellence zweckrational*, governed by final rationality. At all levels, the leader asks and must ask the question: In view of what? What is the end that I want to attain by the shooting, by the charge, by the shock, by the combat, by the battle, by the campaign, by the war? Reference to final rationality ends logically in the subordination of war to policy as of the means to the end; at the other extreme, it forces the actor to take into consideration the nature of the means — troops or arms — in determining the end. The latter remains the supreme but not despotic legislator, bound, in part, by the constraint of the means.

The third antithesis, that of defence–attack, is to be found at a lower level in relation to the two others, since the first two relate to the very nature of war and since strategic theory takes rational consideration (*vernünftige Betrachtung*) as its subject. The two concepts of defence and attack penetrate the whole field but they only come into play, in the first chapter, after the initial definition, test of will by violence, which to all intents and purposes contains the two preceding antitheses. At the highest level of abstraction, one could say that the two concepts of defence and attack are themselves also implied by the test of will, one of the fighters wanting something positive, the other having the negative end of not ceding what the former strives to seize from him. In that case, the third antithesis would have been presented in and by the original model of the fighters.

Clausewitz reasons differently. If we disregard the origin and the end of the struggle, there remains only the clash of wills, each wanting to impose by violence its law on the other. Consequently, the distinction between defence and attack results from the spatio-temporal conditions in which the struggle unfolds. As a result the positivity or negativity of the political intention, without being completely eliminated, appears only occasionally, marginally, the connection with space and time becoming the substitute of intention.

Is the above enumeration exhaustive? Does it allow the exposition of the whole of the Treatise, the development of all the major ideas? I shall reply, Yes, on condition that we agree to separate the intellectual system from the historical phenomena which Clausewitz considers. The first two chapters of Book I and the whole of Book VIII relate to the very nature of war, to the relations between the military objective and the political end, to the duality of the objective and the end, or perhaps to the duality of the relation between the objective and the end according to the type of war.

Book III, 'Of Strategy in General', like Chapters 3–7 of Book I, has as a central theme the antithesis of the moral and the physical, the latter often embodied in numbers. The whole of Book III suggests a confrontation of moral force and material force; other factors, such as the geometry of movements or the lines of operation, are reduced to a subordinate role. As regards Books VI and VII, they have defence and attack as their title and their subject — which confirms that all the problems that beset strategists are to be found in the body of this antithesis.

What remains outside this survey of the Treatise? Two books, one, Book IV, on combat (*Gefecht*), the other, Book V, on armed forces. Now both of these, though indispensable to the whole, differ manifestly from the other books in their relation to history. Combat is the means *par excellence*, according to some texts the sole means, of strategy. But, in Book IV, the second chapter brings out the characteristics of contemporary battle as if to warn the reader against putting a transhistoric interpretation on the analyses or descriptions. As for the book devoted to armed forces, to the disposition of troops, in relation to various weapons, it perhaps does retain some significance in its method. But how would Clausewitz have suddenly failed to recognize the incessant transformation of arms and of organization, the contest of shell and armour, of defence and attack? Even supposing that he believed, as did many others, in the lasting, if not permanent, character of the armies of his age, he would correct himself by deducing the consequences of the principles that he had expounded. Books IV and V are to be found, to a large extent, within the bounds of strategy and tactics; they illustrate the principles, and the methods. Combat represents the material of strategical artists or the means of the war leader. Book IV will find a place without difficulty in the rubric means—end, just as Book V, which deals with armed forces, supplies indispensable knowledge to whoever is in command of a battle that has itself been given a role in the campaign by a leader of higher rank.

As regards the two ideas of the 'Warning' of 1827 in the light of which he intended to revise his manuscript, they are found in the extension of the thought on the relation of the means to the end. What does the dual type of war mean, if not the realization, by Clausewitz himself, that one cannot deal with war, even from a strictly military point of view, without referring to the end of the war, at least at the meeting point of the military objective and the political end that constitute the ways of the return to peace? This duality of types precedes the subordination of war to policy because Clausewitz, in a book on strategy, cannot study in detail the diverse ends sought by the belligerents; but he does meet major opposition in the form of decisive victory and relative advantage.

By reason of the above, the three chapters on the three major antitheses will allow us both to bring out the characteristics of Clausewitzian dialectic and to seek the reasons for his dissatisfaction at the end of his life. Why did Book VI on defence then appear imperfect to him? What would the revision of the book have entailed in the light of what I call the final synthesis, the intellectual testament or the conceptual edifice, namely the first chapter of Book I?

The only book which has not yet been mentioned in this reconstruction is the second, entitled 'On the Theory of War'. In fact, I think that it is essentially distinguishable from the others since it contains not a fragment of theory but a sketch of the 'theory of theory'. Furthermore, the author who makes clear the theory of his own theory, or elaborates the epistemology of his research, always risks making a mistake, I mean doing something other than he believes he is doing. Even Max Weber, anxious to make his practice understood, is found by readers of today to have not always made the practice of his theory conform to the theory of his practice. It thus seems to me legitimate or even necessary to reserve consideration of Book II, provisionally. Part III of this work will be devoted to it.

To my knowledge only one author has attempted a reconstruction comparable with the one I have just outlined. Schering, in his book on Clausewitz's philosophy, attempts this. I agree with him on some points, but I must differ on others. I reach a radically different interpretation from his without hiding from myself the fact that he also believed himself 'generous' in attributing to Clausewitz ideas which were closest to those he held as true, those most in harmony with the *Zeitgeist*, the spirit of the age.

Schering propounds a more complex structure in using both the three elements of the strange trinity (passion, free activity of the spirit, understanding) and the three themes he considers to be most important, namely laws and rules, moral greatness, means and ends. To each of these themes he devotes a chapter, itself divided into three parts, each of which is devoted to one of the elements of the strange trinity: thus we have the laws and rules of elementary violence, of the free activity of the spirit, of understanding (or of policy). By this expedient, Schering manages to refer each of the chapters of the Treatise to one of the nine rubrics created by the multiplication of one trinity by the other, the first prescribed by the author, the second constructed by the interpreter.

Without denying that with a little ingenuity one could arrive at such an arrangement, it raises many difficulties. The theory of laws and rules is found scattered among the various chapters of the Treatise, without the nature of the various laws, mentioned here and there, appearing clearly. In theory, in Book II, Clausewitz, following commonplace logic, distinguishes natural laws and prescriptive laws (positive or negative imperative, order or prohibition to act). Yet, many laws escape this alternative and seem, as in *De l'esprit des lois*, to draw their substance from the nature of things.

The strange trinity is only explicitly analysed in Chapter 1 of Book I; it does appear implicitly in some passages of Book VIII, Chapter 6 in particular, when Clausewitz introduces the distinction between the war leader and the cabinet, the concrete translation of the abstract distinction between the free activity of the spirit and understanding. In the rest of the book, this distinction remains implicit and the war leader (*Feldherr*) appears as the commander of the armies or else as responsible for both policy and operations. I doubt whether one could discern laws and rules which specifically apply to one or other of the elements of the strange trinity.

The major objection is directed at the heterogeneity of the trinity – law and rules, moral greatness, means–end – constructed by Schering. The whole antithesis of means–end intellectually structures the whole politico-military field: human action comprises using materials with an end in view, political or military action also uses materials but in the face of an adversary who is doing the same and aims at opposed ends. Moral virtues should not be considered in isolation but in opposition to quantities or matter, above all numbers, in order that the interaction of will and material, on one side as on the other, defines in the final analysis the relation of the forces.

The concepts of the means and the end, by their formal character, are found at the highest level of abstraction: complementary and not opposed, they are as indispensable for the actor in making a decision as they are for the observer in understanding. They govern, at each stage, the relation of the part to the whole and, at the same time, of war to peace, since in the final analysis the end of war is peace or a certain type of peace.

Moral virtues and material resources are less complementary than opposed but it is only a conceptual opposition. According to the circumstances, the state of mind compensates for material inferiority or increases it; the destruction of the armed forces is more in accord with the moral sense than with the material. Violence, in the final analysis, aims at the enemy's state of mind, even though it only attains this by shedding blood.

Defence and attack, in the field of military operations, are key concepts for two reasons. They substitute for the apparent symmetry of fighters, each wishing to overthrow the other, a dissymmetry that is political (one wants to alter the *status quo*) and military (one takes the initiative in invading the other's territory). Furthermore, these two concepts react on the two preceding pairs by recalling the reciprocal action of the duellists, in that it involves choosing an end or imposing moral force. It is in relation to the other that the actor decides. Now, the relation between the adversaries is fashioned by the dissymmetry of defence and attack.

The theory of laws and rules clearly does not belong to the same category as these three conceptual pairs. Moreover, it seems to me difficult to differentiate the laws and rules as they apply to one or other of the elements of the strange trinity. Or, at the very least, the only radical distinction is that between inevitable laws and the laws of probability. Now, the former are valid neither for events nor for the future; for *das Geschehen*, as Schering suggests, they are only valid for intellectual subjects, for ideal or intellectual reality.

The reconstruction that I propose seems to me more coherent. It is more in conformity with the thought of Clausewitz than with that of Schering. The strange trinity reminds us of the triple nature of the belligerents (a people, a military leader, a leader of state), the virtues peculiar to each of the constituent parts, but also, and above all, the indissoluble link between these parts. I consider the distinction of rules and laws, peculiar to each of these three elements, to be artificial and the dissection of the theory of the means and the end in terms of the strange trinity somewhat arbitrary. The true implications of the strange trinity will appear by themselves in the three following chapters.

I shall thus try to bring out the articulation of the system and the major ideas by organizing my account around the three conceptual pairs of means–end, moral–physical, defence–attack. In the same way, I hope to discern the play of thought that is justly called dialectic. Consequently, it attempts to grasp the duel of the belligerents and to think out conceptual or real oppositions, inscribed in the field of action.

Chapter 4

The Means and the Ends

Gesunder Menschenverstand: good sense or common sense: Clausewitz never ceases to assert it. The man whom the first French readers sometimes judged the most German of Germans, enshrouded in metaphysical haze, is nurtured on French culture. He likes nothing as much as clarity and he attempts less to contrive than to spotlight the structure of his object of study. This object, composed of human actions, owes its unity to two circumstances: the hierarchic organization of the command of the army of each of the belligerent states; the duel between these states, delimited in space and above all in time, which entails by its nature the result of the victor imposing his will on the vanquished.

This structure thus itself forms an analysis, in terms of the categories of means and end, from the top to the bottom of the ladder: the same question, 'In view of what?', is asked by the patrol commander when he fights the action, by the head of state when he declares war and by the leading general when he establishes his plan of operations. Such is the idea of good sense that the Weberian notion of final rationality (*Zweckrationalität*) popularized, and which analytical philosophers have taken up to characterize human conduct as such.

From the 'Strategy' of 1804 onwards, Clausewitz uses his mode of analysis to distinguish tactics and strategy. He still uses it twenty years later to specify the relations between war and policy. The two pairs of tactics–strategy and war–policy will serve as examples and illustrations of the most formal pair: means–end.

1 The Dissection of the object. Tactics and strategy
Clausewitz, as I have shown above, defined tactics and strategy for the first time in the article in the *Neue Bellona* and in the 'Strategy' of 1804, in other words at the age of 24. He never altered these definitions.

At the start of his course on small-scale warfare, in a text little used by commentators until now, Clausewitz takes up the distinction of tactics–strategy in order to place this partial theory in the total theory.

Small-scale warfare is distinguished from large-scale by the number of troops involved. Small-scale – guerilla – warfare is understood to mean the use of units composed of a small number of men. 'Combats involving 20, 50, 100 or 300 or 400 men, if they form a part of more important combats, belong to small-scale warfare.' Although Clausewitz recognizes that this definition could be taken as mechanical rather than philosophical, he asserts that it is the true one if usage is taken into consideration. He adds that it would take too long to show that it is the only possible one.

This definition does not allow a precise line of demarcation to be drawn

95

between small- and large-scale warfare. He concedes this inevitable defect in a theory which, unlike mathematics or philosophy, does not create its own insights and consequently adheres to what is again that which most frequently occurs, equivalent to the general.

Why is it legitimate to devote a special study to small-scale warfare? Because it reveals specific characteristics, which Clausewitz enumerates at length: a small number of troops can go anywhere, find provisions without difficulty, hide themselves, move about rapidly, retreat even in the absence of roads, etc. Furthermore, they often have neither an offensive nor a defensive end, but wage a war of observation. These particular characteristics of small-scale or guerilla warfare determine the moral qualities required by the troops, and the spirit in which they must be led. 'Small-scale warfare has the peculiar characteristic that it exposes, alongside boldness and temerity of the highest order, a greater fear of danger than in large-scale warfare.'

At one and the same time Clausewitz describes, as it were, the concrete or material characteristics of small-scale warfare and the moral forces which are therein expressed (which refers us to the following chapter). Nevertheless he does not forget that the art of war divides into two parts, and into two parts alone, tactics and strategy. Which of the two applies to small-scale warfare? Strategy makes use of combats, determines the place, the time and the strength of troops committed to the extent that these three influence the end. Now, clearly, place, time and strength are also important in small-scale warfare: must one therefore speak of a strategy of small-scale warfare? Clausewitz replies in the negative: the ends of small-scale refer to the large-scale war, thus to the strategy or the tactics of the latter. Now it is the tactics rather than the strategy of the large-scale war that governs the choice of time, place and strength to be engaged in a combat of small-scale warfare.

> It could thus be said that the strategy of small-scale warfare is governed by tactics and, as the tactics of small-scale warfare should certainly be part of tactics as such, it follows that the whole of small-scale warfare falls into the realm of tactics, in other words that it forms a category of its own.

Logically, one could also distinguish the tactics and strategy of large-scale and small-scale warfare respectively, but since most determinations of place, time and strength of combats in small-scale warfare arise from tactics, it would be better to devote special attention to small-scale warfare, alongside strategy and tactics, even though it is, in the final analysis, essentially a part of the latter.

Why this refusal to add a third heading to strategy and tactics? The reason is always the same: the two concepts of means and end, and they alone, allow action and, in particular, the action of war to be thought out. The knowledge or theory of action consists of as many categories as the latter consists of distinct means or ends. Now, Clausewitz only knows two essentially different means: armed forces and combats. It is thus by reference to the means rather than the ends that strategy and tactics are differentiated. The latter makes use of armed forces, the former concerns combats or the results of combats. From the fact that armed forces are used, it follows logically that combat is always considered possible. It is in this sense that combat becomes the equivalent of payment in kind in commercial or financial transactions. But these formulae do not imply that combat should be the end of all warlike activity. Clausewitz, in 1810–11, at a time when according to most interpreters he had not yet fully worked out his guiding ideas, explicitly specifies that strategy, in view of its particular ends, makes use of combat as a means.

Thus what is problematic in Clausewitz's theory is the determination of the ends, in tactics as in strategy. Now, he writes in the Introduction to *Small-Scale Warfare*:

If we determine (define) strategy according to its means and not according to its ends, the reason is that the means (namely combat), used by strategy in a very general way, are unique and can never be eliminated by the mind without destroying the very concept of war, while the possible ends (of strategy) are varied and do not allow themselves to be exhausted.

The means reveal a character that is not normative but conceptual. From the concept of war armed forces are inferred, and from these the continual possibility of combat. Finally, combat itself becomes the means *par excellence* of a strategy which postulates various ends. Clausewitz reserves the notion of victory (*Sieg*) for tactics. If strategy has one end, it could be summarized in a single word: peace. The end of strategy or of the conduct of the war is peace, not military victory, even though each of the belligerents clearly wants a different peace or conceives of peace in different terms.

Can it be said that tactics, or the use of armed forces, unlike strategy, can be determined or defined by its end (victory) at the same time as by its means? In a sense, yes: by definition, as the end in a combat is to prevail, to conquer. The means of tactics are armed forces; the end is victory. But the fact that the enemy leaves the battlefield is still only an indication of victory. The latter takes on a different character or content according to the end that strategy has given the combat.

By the medium of victory, strategy attains the end which it has devised for the combat and which gives it its proper significance. This significance exercises some influence on the nature of the victory. A victory which aims to weaken the armed forces of the enemy is something other than a victory which only enables us to occupy a position.

Following this line of thought, it appears that the superior end – that which strategy aims at by a particular combat – governs the dispositions taken by tactics. Moreover, since war forms an organic whole, the ultimate ends of strategy, in other words the objectives which lead immediately to peace, govern the use of combats or of successes. The means–end relation, combined with the duality of tactics and strategy, each with its specific definition, results in the picture of war as a structured entity structured by the hierarchy of means and ends and by the search at each level for the final rationality. This is always subordinate to the finality of the higher level of small-scale warfare to that of large-scale warfare, that of tactics to that of strategy, that of the means in war to that of the ends of war.

In the Treatise, the same distinction is formulated in almost the same way at the start of Book III. If the text of Book III, Chapter 1, is compared with paragraph 23 of the 'Strategy' of 1804, we establish that, of the five subdivisions enumerated in the notes from his youth, only the first two apparently subsist in the Treatise. In fact, the evolution is more apparent than real. Indeed, the three heads of strategy which have apparently disappeared from the Treatise concern respectively the organization of the army, the provisioning of troops and the fortification of towns (the fortification of the countryside belongs to tactics). Now, Book V of the Treatise deals with the organization of armies and their provisioning. The question of fortified towns appears here and there, particularly in Book VI, without it becoming the theme of a separate chapter on strategy. 'Strategy' in the Treatise as well as in 1804, thus essentially takes into account on the one hand tactical successes (the effect of small combats and great battles, of combats in the plain and in the mountains, of a defensive victory or an offensive victory, etc.), and on the other the co-ordination of particular combats with a view to the objective of the war. This combination implies the determination of time, place for combat or for battle, strength of troops engaged and the exploitation of the success obtained.

Clausewitz, with yet more vigour in the Treatise (Book II, Chapter 1) than in paragraph 33 of the 'Strategy' of 1804 endeavours to show that the tactics–strategy duality, as he explains it, covers the whole of the field of study and exhausts the art of war or the conduct of war. Why does he attach so much importance to a distinction and to definitions which fanatics of Clausewitz admire and justify, yet which many military writers accept or reject with some indifference?

The first reason for the insistence with which Clausewitz clings to the definitions elaborated in his youth results from the theoretical scheme itself. Occasionally, the distribution of the matter into chapters comes down to a question of expediency or convenience. In such a way the fortified towns, which in 1804 figured under the same title as the organization of the army in one of the five principal chapters on strategy, have so to speak disappeared from the Treatise. On the other hand, some of the dissections reflect the natural articulation of the subject-matter and guide the mind, preventing it from falling into confusion: thus the strategy–tactics duality. At the same time the kinship between the art of war and other arts and skilled activities is asserted. Finally, the tangible or spatial principle of discriminating between tactics, large-scale tactics and strategy is replaced by an intellectual principle. The material and the means are not the same. The same applies to the higher level; the material and the means are not the same for policy as for war.

Clausewitz is not unaware of this; he explicitly recognizes that the clear opposition of two poles risks becoming confused in the intermediate zones. For example, where do the spatial and temporal boundaries of a particular combat lie? A particular combat extends in space as far as the personal command, in time until the moment, characteristic of all combats, when the crisis has passed. Clausewitz adds that there are, of course, doubtful cases where the separation of different combats lends itself to discussion, where the total unity of the combat can be conceived in one manner or another, and consequently the same action could be counted as strategic or tactical without it being possible to settle the matter decisively either way.

Likewise, the march arises from tactics or strategy depending on the case in point; the act of marching in the combat, even though it does not yet involve the use of arms, is an integral part of the latter. On the other hand, the march outside combat will take place. The march outside combat also obeys the laws of tactics in that the troops must constantly be prepared to fight. In reality, the distinctions, conceptually clear-cut, give way to doubtful cases or even to mixed cases. Clausewitz does not see real objections in these remarks: the distinction, conceptually valid, does not preclude uncertain boundaries in reality.

The art of war includes strategy and tactics, both of which make use of armed force, the one at a distance, the other immediately. Clausewitz agrees to extend the art of war to include the levying, arming, equipping and training the troops. He prefers the narrow meaning according to which this art consists of using arms, combats and their results with a view to the end of the campaign or of the war. He does not want to admit any intermediate area between tactics and strategy because in his eyes one makes use of either armed forces or combats: at this level of abstraction, proceeding from the definition of war, there cannot be a third term.

At the same time, the two arts, strategy and tactics, rebound from each other in a reciprocal action that it is tempting to call dialectic. In the 'Strategy' of 1804, Clausewitz reserved the prerogative of the decision to tactics when the latter did not accord with strategy because in the final analysis it can only attain its objectives by successful combats. But this remark was to be found in the paragraph relating to the organization of the army. With regard to this, organizational strategy, he wrote, assumes the task of creating a structure in such a way that independent parts are formed, so that the whole splits up into autonomous elements; a structure which gives flexibility to the whole and allows fragmentary combats and whole campaigns to be combined in the most satisfactory manner.

In another sense, the prerogative of the decision belongs to strategy since it is strategy which determines the place, time and strength of the combat. However, it behoves strategy not to make bad use of this prerogative, in other words not to prescribe combat in conditions which offer no chance of success. The reciprocity of the action between strategy and tactics resembles that of policy and war: it is the first, strategy or policy, which settles the aims and organizes the whole in terms of these.

In paragraph 33 of the 'Strategy' of 1804 as well as in Books II, I, and III, Clausewitz educes the consequences of the definitions laid down in the *Neue Bellona* article and bases the totality of war on the relation of means to end, on the combination of combats with a view to the end fixed by the strategist, without then differentiating what the Germans called operational strategy or the conduct of operations. Was he unaware of what these expressions meant or did he not want to give them an independent status? I have no doubt about the reply: it is the second alternative which corresponds to his thought.

Marches or manoeuvres, as he writes in Chapter 1 of Book II, simply form the concrete expression of the concept of the 'combination or ordering of combats with a view to the end of the campaign or the war'. If he persists in using the abstract concept of the use of combats and their results, it is so as not to create the illusion that the movements are self-sufficient and contain their own principle of efficiency. But it would be wrong to draw the conclusion that he is unaware of or scorns marches or manoeuvres which allow battles to be fought in conditions favourable to success and the exploitation of success. What he does believe is that manoeuvres, with their geometric form and in their abstract expression, are so simple that theory should be more concerned with the difficulties of execution and the moral qualities necessary for this.

The division of the art of war under two, and only two, heads entails another consequence: the tendency to confuse policy, conduct of the war and strategy. In other words, if all the decisions above those taken by the army chief in the field arise from strategy, the latter includes the conduct of the war, together with the whole of the means, violent and non-violent, material and moral, from the war plan to the decision to wage battle in a particular place or at a particular moment, to withdraw to the interior of the country or push forward to the capital. Clausewitz, as the case may be, uses the expressions 'conduct of the war', 'policy' and 'strategy' but he does not clearly and distinctly distinguish between these terms. Inadvertently or through lack of elaboration? Neither, I think.

From a practical point of view, it may be convenient to distinguish tactics, large-scale tactics, operational strategy, the war plan, the total conduct of the war. I think that Clausewitz would have had no difficulty in accepting the graded levels of strategy as secondary headings. He could not give them the same theoretical status as the duality of tactics and strategy because this duality is derived, at conceptual level, from its nature rather than from specific means and natural end. The specific means of tactics, the material of the artist tactician, are armed forces. The end is victory and beyond that the destruction, physical or moral, of the opposing force. The specific means of strategy are combats, real or simulated, and their results; the natural end is not victory but the objects which lead immediately to peace.

The totality of war, inseparable from the hierarchy of ends, does not allow the conceptual dissociation of operations of the military, and, above that, political, finality of the whole war. Even before taking into consideration the political intention, central in all actions of war, the definitions of tactics and strategy, combined with the scheme of the ultimate rationality and with the heterogeneity of the material and work, contain the seeds of the notorious Formula: War is the continuance of policy by other means or moreover, with a mixture of other means. This formula is better since policy – dealings between states by non-violent means – continues whereas hostilities lapse.

2 'The Formula': war and policy

The range, both theoretical and practical, of the structuration of the field of war through the relation of the means to the end is clearly revealed if we go to the last link of the chain of means and ends. The Formula, though overlaid with innumerable quotations and contradictory interpretations, reveals a sort of clarity in Clausewitz's thought even though he had so much difficulty in fully grasping its scope and its very meaning. War using acts of violence with a view to imposing one side's will on the other, thus incorporating a means, violence, and an end, a settlement by policy. But since the end subjects violence to intelligence, that is to say policy, the latter never ceases to induce the unleashing of violence. Let us substitute states for fighters facing each other in the middle of an enclosed field: the will emanates from objectivized policy from the whole of politico-social relations in the heart of which are traced the clandestine features of the armed conflict. Between 1804 and 1807, Clausewitz became fully aware that the ends of war should control the ends in war. If many readers are amazed today that Clausewitz stressed this banal, indeed trivial, idea so heavily, it is because he justifiably held that other theoreticians neglected this consideration which was in his eyes decisive, and that they therefore had nothing to say about the essential, historical diversity of wars and the inherent heterogeneity they possess.

The best way to refute the accusation of banality or triviality, is, it seems to me, to follow an indirect route and review some of the false interpretations. I myself thought for a long time, owing to the use made of the Formula by propaganda on many occasions, that it expresses or presupposes a militarist philosophy of international relations. From time to time it is still said that Clausewitz rarely speaks of peace, that he did not understand that 'the true object of war is peace, not victory, and that peace is consequently the guiding area of policy and that victory is only a means for attaining it'. What else did Clausewitz mean if not this? That war is the means of policy implies that it is the means for the restoration of peace. Does he not show that the acceptance of peace by Alexander, after the taking of Moscow, was Napoleon's sole chance of success? The substitution of victory for peace as the ultimate objective of war would result in the autonomy (*Selbständigkeit*) of war. As soon as war ceases to be an 'independent thing' it has no ultimate objective other than peace.

A sceptic will interpose a certain type of peace. Certainly, since war exists – a conflict of great interests ruled by blood – belligerents want to attain incompatible ends (the very definition of the conflict of great interests). Clausewitz ascertains that such conflicts exist by the study of history. He does not wish to be a philosopher of war in the sense that Kant, author of the treatise on perpetual peace, is considered a philosopher of war. He neither condemns nor approves of war, he takes it as a given primary fact. To be sure, he implicitly admits the normal character of settlement by blood, but this perception is no more immoral than that of the theoretician of economic equilibrium. I shall return later to this aspect of the debate. What we are left with, from this starting point, is that by reducing the act of violence, war, to a means of policy, Clausewitz gives as its end not victory but the return to peace.

The sceptic, accepting the theory on the logical plane, will retort that the peace aimed at by policy will consequently simply be the means of another war, the accretion of resources with a view to the next trial of strength. Now, A. Rapoport asserts,

> if Clausewitz's conception of the relation between war and politics is examined with reference to the ends and means of each, it appears that the two are interchangeable. The function of the military is to implement the will of the state; the will of the state is tacitly assumed to be directed towards continually increasing its power *vis-à-vis* other states, hence to seek and seize opportunities to gain strategic advantages for future struggles. In short, the

101

interests of the state and of the army coincide in Clausewitz's conception of war.

I believe this interpretation, which is in fairly wide circulation in England and the USA, to be incompatible with the texts, with the logic of Clausewitz's thought, with all that we know of his political philosophy. The subordination of the military leader to the cabinet or to the sovereign is in effect justifiable, first of all, by pragmatic considerations. The military leader is a specialist, whereas the statesman takes in the whole of political as well as military circumstances of which some will normally escape the attention of someone who has no other experience of, or other task than, the conduct of armies on the battlefield.

As a witness of a war of coalition, Clausewitz saw and understood the divergence of interest between states officially united against the same enemy. He examined the best method of distributing the allied troops, he recommended that each army be entrusted with its own theatre of operations that interest it directly, since the absolute unity of the troops of different states is shown to be impossible to achieve. He speculated on two possible methods; either a single command, or the autonomy of each national army in the light of a war plan worked out by the cabinets together, which responds to the always different and often divergent intentions of the allies. Can one conclude from this, as Rapoport does, that the head of state becomes a sort of supreme general who enforces his authority over the commander-in-chief in the same way that the latter enforces his will over his subordinates? In a sense, this hierarchy of command, inseparable from the chain of the means and the end, corresponds to Clausewitzian logic: but Rapoport is wrong to assert that the military and politics are interchangeable and that politics is permanently placed at the service of the military force, in the same way that, in time of war, the latter is placed at the service of politics.

To my mind, nothing justifies such a hypothesis. Let me quote the famous formula from Chapter 6 of Book VIII:

> That policy unites in itself and balances all the interests of internal administration, those also of humanity and everything of philosophical understanding, can still be asserted, granting our hypothesis, for policy is nothing other than the plain administrator of all interests vis-à-vis other states.

Such a text certainly does not suggest that the political direction of the war is restricted to the military implications of diplomatic relations or to the calculations of strength with a view to the next war. Furthermore, at no time in the chain of means and ends does a reversal intervene, the inferior end governing the superior end in the way that the latter normally governs the former. By postulating that the military and the political are interchangeable, Rapoport insists at the same time that Clausewitz is breaking the logic of his thought at a decisive level, namely the highest level. If Clausewitz had written that policy has no other end than military strength, that is to say the instrument of violence, he would have failed to recognize the conclusions of his own reasoning. Not only did he not say it, he explicitly stated the reverse.

As a reader of Montesquieu and of Voltaire, Clausewitz remained to the end a theoretician of some sort of European equilibrium. The European system is defined, in his eyes, by the tendency of states to react when one of their number inclines towards domination and threatens to accede to universal monarchy. In Chapter 6 of Book VI, he sees in this spontaneous coalition against the disturber or the conqueror a promise of support for the one amongst them who loses the first battles or whom ill-fortune overwhelms.

Consequently, the republic of the states of Europe forms a whole, an entirety or a system, a tangle of great and small interests of great and small states. A state on the defensive, short of living in a state of tension with the whole, will find more interests leagued in its favour than against it. This equilibrium is not static, it neither excludes nor prevents changes, but each of these must only offend some states, not the majority of them; for the states in the majority consider their own preservation to be represented and guaranteed by the interests common to all, by the interests of the whole. In a language less elegant and sometimes more technical than his predecessors, Clausewitz outlines an interpretation of the society of European states which, it seems to me, links up with that of Montesquieu, Voltaire or Gentz. It is to Voltaire or Montesquieu that he probably alludes in recalling the precept of a great French writer: we must raise ourselves above the anecdotal level to make history intelligible, this millennial history during which European states, and nearly the same ones, have coexisted without having been incorporated into an empire. Far from being able to deduce from his admiration of Napoleon the thesis that the military and political ends are interchangeable, he explains the final defeat by the extent of the emperor's ambitions and his exclusive confidence in the force of arms. The tendency towards equilibrium is not enough to prevent the temporary superiority of one state over all the others; that state ends up by perishing by fault of its very success, since it ranges against itself the majority of the other members of the European republic.

One event alone seems to contradict the rules deducible from history for whoever, above the anecdote, aims at general relations which are alone capable of making a millennium of European history intelligible: the disappearance of Poland. With regard to this, Clausewitz, in his letters, his private diary and his political studies, reveals hostility and even scorn. In the Treatise, where he expresses himself as a thinker, he explains but never justifies the partition of Poland. The Tartar state, situated not on the shores of the Black Sea, at the frontier of the European zone, but on the Vistula, had not played any role for a century; she had lost the substance of independence. Had partition not taken place, she would have become a Russian province; incapable of defending herself, she would have complicated the task of the three states who had united in order to divide her and facilitated that of the three states – France, Turkey, Sweden – interested in her preservation. 'If the preservation [*Erhaltung*] of a state must be assured wholly from outside, it is certainly too much to ask for.' As a theoretician of European equilibrium and a doctrinaire of national defence, Clausewitz never expressed himself as if the accumulation of military means constituted the ultimate end of politics.

Could it be said that these considerations of equilibrium arise from pragmatic calculation, with reference to the relation of forces? They do indeed, but Clausewitz does not write a treatise on politics or morals, he

103

thinks out the fact of war and, unlike most military writers, he refuses to acknowledge its autonomy. As a consequence, he lays down two principles which are directly contrary to the militarist philosophy that Rapoport attributes to him: the plurality of ends at the strategic level, and the subordination of the commander-in-chief of the armies to the civil power during the actual course of hostilities.

There is a strange omission by the commentators: I do not think that any have stressed a curiosity in the vocabulary that I indicated a little earlier. The word for victory (*Sieg*) belongs to the vocabulary of tactics, not of strategy. Victory, a strictly military concept, only appears as a means with a view to the true end, namely peace. The plurality of political ends and the non-determination of these ends correspond very exactly to Fuller's requirement: to think of war not in itself but in relation to peace.

If Clausewitz also returns often to this idea, but exclusively in the parts of the book written or revised after 1827, it is because, on the day that he fully grasped the idea that war is a policy which wages battles instead of sending notes, he finally resolved simultaneously the two problems posed by his historical experience and his philosophical concern: how to subsume under the same concept phenomena as varied as the wars of the ancient cities, those of the *condottieri*, those of the cabinets, those of the Revolution and Empire. Obsessed since his youth with the desire to discover the nature of things (in Montesquieu's sense of the phrase), Clausewitz finds unity no longer in the unleashing of extreme violence but in a superior point of view: war rises out of policy, it is this policy which determines its intensity, which gives rise to its motive, which delineates its main features, which settles its ends and, at the same time, its military objectives. The solution to the theoretical problem governs that of the praxological problem or problems.

Current opinion is that the military leaders who most want to throw off the yoke of civil leaders finally acknowledge, after discussion, that the beginning and the end, the declaration of war and the conclusion of peace, are the responsibility of the head of state or the government. They do not deny that they receive their means, above all their armed forces, from the civil authority, and that the latter remains competent at the time when the greatest advantage must be drawn from successes on the battlefield or when it is necessary to make the best of defeats suffered. What lends itself to dispute is the part played respectively by the supreme commander of armies and the head of state in the conduct of the war, thus both in the working out of the war plan and in the direction of operations after the commencement of hostilities. Now, the man who lived in uniform all his life, devoted with all his soul to Scharnhorst, then to Gneisenau, loyal to his king but not to the point of serving a slave-prince forced to ally with Napoleon, settles these two problems in favour of what we call the civil power.

Let us quote the crucial text:

> In consequence of this view, the distinction, according to which a great military event, or the plan of such an event, should be left to a purely military judgment, such as cabinets make, is absurd; but still more absurd is the demand of theoreticians that the available means of war should be entrusted to the war leader [*Feldherr*] so

that he may lay down a purely military plan for the war or the campaign in accordance with those means of war. In fact, the leading lines of war have always been determined by cabinets, a practice which is fully in accord with the 'nature of things' since none of the principal plans for the war can be separated from political considerations.

What must have shocked the officers at main headquarters even more than this intervention of politics, and thus of the head of state, at the start of the war and in the plan of the whole, was the persistence of this intervention during the course of operations. Consequently, it is not surprising that Clausewitz's text was falsified after the second edition. In this same chapter (VIII, 6), Clausewitz contemplates the possibility of the sovereign and the commander-in-chief not being united in one and the same person. It is then appropriate, he writes, that the war leader (*Feldherr*) should become a member of the cabinet in order that the latter could participate at decisive times in the action of the former. It was enough in German to replace 'es' (*das Kabinett*) with 'er' (*der Feldherr*) to give the passage a meaning completely contrary to the author's intention. Clausewitz thus recommends that the cabinet or the sovereign remain close to the battlefield so that the necessary political decisions do not incur a waste of time.

It goes without saying that general formulae do not allow the precise determination of when and how the cabinet decides in the course of operations. What does not lend itself to doubt is that Clausewitz, at least at the end of his life, never subscribed to the doctrine that all the German war leaders would have preferred: freedom of action between the first firing of the cannon and peace negotiations. Clausewitz explicitly rejects this doctrine. Now, although he accepts that politics does not permeate as far as the detail of combats (a patrol is not sent for political reasons), *a priori* he fixes no limit to the influence of politics – not only because it settles the end but also because it alone creates the unity which can grasp the whole. As for the competence required from the minister superior to the war leader, it is not even specifically military. 'France was never worse advised in its political and military affairs than by the Belle-Isle brothers and the Duke of Choiseul, even though all three were good soldiers.'

3 The supreme law and the supremacy of policy

It seems impossible, if we follow this line of thought, to place the absolute form of war on the highest plane; but what about the destruction of the enemy's armed forces, the principle of annihilation, the guiding idea of the military thought of Clausewitz? Countless interpreters, without denying that war was the instrument of policy, have failed to draw the same conclusions from the means–end relation at the highest level.

From which texts is it possible to develop an interpretation contrary to the one that I have just outlined? Let us put to one side the formula in which Clausewitz concedes – that real, effective policy does not always satisfactorily fulfil the task which falls to it. He not only refrains from denying that defeat may be due to policy, but he explicitly affirms it with regard to the defeats suffered by the old monarchies in the revolutionary wars. Policy caused the defeats because it was mistaken; it had cast a judgment on the real war that was contrary to the nature that it assumed. Another text goes a little further: 'The political end is no despotic legislator; it must adapt to the nature of the means and often, as a result of this, it is completely transformed' (II, 1, 23). All the texts from Book VIII, quoted above, offer the commentator the simple proposition: the action is defined by the end, but it can only attain this end by using expedient, efficacious means. In case of war, the means is confused with violence; now, does this not imply a decision by arms (*Waffenentscheidung*)? War does not have its own logic but it has its own grammar: how does the grammar influence the logic?

The chapter which lends itself best to both interpretations at the same time seems to me to be Chapter 2 of Book I, probably revised in 1828–9 although the revision did not achieve the perfection of Chapter 1. It is, indeed, in this chapter that the means apparently carry the most imperative implications for the conduct of the war.

First of all, let us reason along the lines of the Clausewitzian concepts. What is war if not a struggle (*Kampf*)? States oppose each other in the manner of fighters. Now, states which make war by definition possess armed forces. The clash of armed forces that we call combat constitutes the means *par excellence*, the sole means, if you like, of war. Why the sole means? Because armed forces are made for combat and all the rest – recruitment, clothing, organization, provisioning, fortifications – only has a meaning or, better still, an end in relation to combat. 'The decision by arms is for all operations in war, great and small, what cash payment is for credit transactions.'

The idea goes back to Clausewitz's first reflections because the same formula figures in the 'Strategy' of 1804. It marks Clausewitz's original and continuing opposition to the antiquity of the eighteenth century, to the idea of a war without combat when only the leader without talent waged war. Theoretically or, if one prefers it in the abstract, the idea is implied by the nature of the struggle and of the fighters. In a struggle between armed forces, combat represents the first priority and, in a sense, the exclusive means.

I have just used the two words 'priority' and 'exclusive' because certain of Clausewitz's texts sanction this. 'Priority' means that

> every important decision by arms, that is the destruction of the
> enemy armed forces, reflects on all the preceding [decisions]
> because they tend, like a liquid, to bring themselves to a level. Thus
> the destruction of the enemy forces always appears as the superior,
> more effectual, means to which all the others must give way.

'Exclusive' means that 'we have seen that in war . . . combat is the sole means and that, as a result, everything is subject to a supreme law, that of the decision by arms. . . .' But in the very sentence in which he asserts that there is only a single means in war, he recalls that several ways lead to the objective (*Ziel*). In other words, they allow us indirectly to attain our political end. Plurality of ways and singleness of means: a strange way to philosophize, as Engels would say.

Why is there only one means? Or rather, in what sense is there only one means? At what level of the analysis does this proposition assert itself? Clearly at the ideal or abstract level. Since all activity is defined, in its rational structure, by its means and its end, tactics has only one material or means at its disposal, armed force. Likewise, strategy which uses the ends of the inferior activity to attain its own ends has only one means, combats or battles. Decision by arms becomes the supreme law: not that it alone should govern all the decisions of the war leader, not that it should always materialize; the supreme law enters the first of the two categories distinguished by Clausewitz. 'As an object of cognition, law is the relation of things and their effects upon each other; as a subject of the will it is a determination of action – and thus equivalent to command and prohibition.' One cannot help thinking of Montesquieu: law is a necessary relation which derives from the nature of things.

It remains to be seen whether this concerns things as they appear or evolve concretely in the world, or things whose pure, abstract, ideal nature has been grasped by the mind. Now, there is no doubt on this point: the supreme law of decision by arms is derived from the abstract nature of war. In reality there are always several ways.

The apparently subtle opposition of the one means and several ways falls into line quite easily with the final stage of Clausewitz's thought. Combat constitutes the sole means of strategy on condition that there is included in the notion of use of combat everything that concerns the choice of time and place, and also the distribution of troops between theatres of operations. From the plan of war to the decision to wage a decisive battle or avoid it, strategy embraces the conduct of the war, in the art of which combat represents primary material. Finally, the comparison with art is corrected by the analogy with commerce – a clear advance since commerce implies two exchangers whereas the artist models or manipulates inanimate material. At the same time war, without losing its violent character, is found to be inserted in the course of relations between states, a course which does not interrupt the eruption of violence. Combat should thus, according to the logic of war-commerce, lose its character of being the exclusive means. It possesses this character only in relation to the specific characteristic of war, namely the recourse to violence. Yet, since the relations between states continue during hostilities, the means of peace continue to be available in times of war. Battle is waged rather than notes sent, but notes or their equivalents continue to be sent during battle. Furthermore, we could say that Clausewitz in the Treatise only managed to save the definitions elaborated in his youth by limiting their validity to an abstract war which for the leaders of the war or of the state does not constitute an exclusive reference.

This reasoning, which conforms to the logic of Clausewitz himself, thus limits the scope of the formula of combat being the exclusive means. In yet another way, the scope of the formula is singularly reduced. Clausewitz, as we know, was always troubled by the most difficult question, that of the relation between the ends of war and the ends in war, to use the words of 1804, or between the military objectives and the political end to use the words of the Treatise. He always recognized that the enemy army constitutes the primary objective, not the exclusive objective, which can be and should be aimed at. It clearly results from this that, to the extent that military objectives, in the hierarchical system of means and ends, constitute the means with a view to the political ends, the war leader retains the option between many military objectives. In other words, the plurality of ways is equivalent to the plurality of military objectives and these, as the means of the political end, reduce the exclusivity of combat, or the supreme law of the decision by arms, to an abstract truth.

Indeed, it is enough to say that, in most wars, the victor does not go as far as the total disarmament of the enemy in order for the diversity of possible strategies (or possible ways in which the war can be conducted) to be substituted for the supreme law (if at all events this confuses decision by arms and the destruction of the enemy). Indeed war, a relation between two states, resembles commerce in its inevitable outcome and also in the calculations of the adversaries / traders. Adversaries can treat before either of them have exhausted their resources; one may consider success too improbable, or one or the other may consider the price of continuation of the war too high. Clausewitz thus analyses, according to his usual method, the various means of increasing the improbability of success and the price of war. He comes to the conclusion that there are many ways which lead to this objective and that all do not aim at the overthrow of the enemy – the conquest of enemy provinces, simple occupation of these, enterprises which aim directly at political relations, finally a passive awaiting of the blows of the enemy – and he concludes that this is a question of means in which the various ways are orientated to represent the means of attaining the political ends.

Nothing seems more contrary to the logic of Clausewitz's reasoning, therefore, in Chapter 2 of Book I, than to confer on the supreme law a different validity than that of an abstract truth and an always necessary warning. Decisions, in the real world, represent a choice between various military objectives capable of leading to political ends; it falls to the war leader to choose between the various ways and also to the head of state (or to the cabinet) to modify these ends according to the outcome of operations. Thus, to the extent that strategy and the conduct of the war are not distinct, strategy necessarily changes according to the political end. The choice of strategy lies at the intersection of political consideration and military considerations. To decree, therefore, as Bernhardi and Schering do, that there are not two strategies but only a good one and a bad one, does not refute Delbrück but wavers between a commonplace and a mistake: a commonplace, if one means that strategy always consists of choosing the means adapted to the ends that one aims at; a mistake if one means that, whatever the nature of the war, the same choice must be made, the same risk taken, the same battle waged. The means–end relation, as used by Clausewitz, gives a rational structure to fragmented action and to the whole simultaneously, it subordinates the rationality of the former to the nature of the latter. Now, it is policy which collectively specifies the whole and which consequently determines strategy in the broad meaning of the word, the plan as much as the conduct of the war.

Just as Clausewitz draws from the notion of disarmament of the enemy its absolute validity by using the distinction between the concept and the reality, so, in Chapter 4 of Book VIII, he seeks the real equivalents of overthrow in order to determine the centres of gravity (*Schwerpunkte*) against which blows should be directed. The notion of a centre of gravity has been retained by German soldiers both in strategy and in tactics.

Clausewitz also uses it in a political sense to translate, in real terms, the notion of overthrow. From this comes the well-known list: the centre of gravity of Alexander, Gustavus Adolphus, Charles XIII and Frederick the Great is the army; that of states torn apart by party struggles is the capital; that of small states which rely on the support of the great is the army of their allies; that of alliances is the unity of interests; that of a people in arms is the main leader and public opinion. Here again, he follows his usual method and recognizes the historical diversity of the concrete objectives needed to be attained to overthrow the enemy and ensure the return to peace – a diversity of objectives which does not, as is usually the case exclude the remainder of the ancient and, in a sense, continuing concept that 'victory over the armed force of the enemy represents the surest commencement and, in all cases, a very important part of war'.

A more systematic formulation would have been possible. In the final analysis, the logical selection of the objects that can be taken as targets may be found at the start of Chapter 2 of Book I: either to destroy the enemy army or to conquer the country, or to break the will of the enemy. The army fights, the country provides resources, men and material for the army; the will to continue to fight would prevent the conclusion of the matter, that is to say the return to peace. Of the objectives against which the different ways (separate from the disarmament of the enemy) are directed, some relate to the army (improbability of success) but with the replacement of real combats by imagined or simulated combats (which must be considered as the equivalent of real combats), others relate to resources (occupation or devastation of a country); all have as their object, indirect or direct, the will of the enemy since this should give way to what we aspire to gain before having exhausted its physical capacity to resist.

With regard to the centres of gravity that I have listed, they could be deduced from a theory of states or of their bases. In fact, all the examples come down to either the army (of the state itself or of the allies of a small state) or to the capital, particularly when the government of the enemy state is not certain of its legitimacy. This latter case arises from the political or moral order, in the same way as an alliance which does not offer resistance to the divergence of interests of the associated powers. The allusion to the armament of the people, to guerilla warfare, also arises from the moral order or will of the people.

Nowhere does disarmament or overthrow – the finality of war closest to its perfect form – imply annihilation, in the physical sense, of soldiers or the destruction of the country. The image remains that of throwing to the ground. A people, like a wrestler, can rise up again: no decision is definitive.

Why, in spite of everything, does a doubt remain in our mind? First of all, Clausewitz sometimes expresses himself, almost involuntarily, as if his sensibility leant towards the side of the war leader who seeks a bloody decision. Although he certainly changed morally, the young man who could not imagine success outside the battlefield, who dreamt of armed glory to fulfil himself, survived in the mature man, disappointed by an existence in the shadow of distinguished commanders. In speaking of generals who avoid the grandiose and bloody outcome, he uses words which, without being pejorative, place them beneath heroes. He recognizes the greatness of Frederick II even though he had most often to save his forces and not annihilate those of the enemy. The man who wrote in 1804, 'the war leader can never be too bold', the man who, in 1830–1, drew up war plans against France by gathering together on paper hundreds of thousands of men, remains at the very least divided between the taste for vast enterprises and worry about useless losses. Next, the supreme law of decision by arms derives from the nature of things, in other words from the essence of war, from the reciprocal action of wills at grips since these confront each other with arms. Hostile intention, because it is more general than hostile passion, is of the highest order, but war itself creates the passions which feed it. The logical dialectic of the rise to extremes is realized in reality by the unleashing of passions. This explains why the participation of peoples in wars between states tends to draw real wars to what they would be if they conformed to the concept of absolute war. At the same time, this explains the ambiguity of the judgments of Clausewitz himself, aware that future European wars will be national wars, desirous also that they do not put the European equilibrium in doubt and do not force kings to arm their peoples or the peoples to arm themselves in order to safeguard the nation's independence.

Everything takes place as if Clausewitz had for a long time been tempted by another theoretical solution: only wars close to perfect or absolute war would truly have been wars. He rejected this solution with a growing firmness. But, in the whole manuscript as it has reached us, sentiments which are at the least ambivalent run through, though involuntarily, the abstractions of the Treatise. The use of the concept of war, sometimes according to the initial narrow definition, sometimes according to the complete (or threefold) definition, sustains the ambiguity.

Finally – and this reason seems to me the most important – there is nothing to prove that Clausewitz ever drew all the logical consequences from the final synthesis. The method of conceptualization that he adopted, the modification of abstract truths by reality and policy, inevitably leaves uncertainty. From the nature of war follows the supreme law of the decision by arms. From this law certain praxological consequences also follow. The limitation of the violence of war requires the consent of both of the duellists.

> We should not avoid pointing out at once that the violent discharge of the crisis, the effort to annihilate the armed force, is the first-born son of war. When the political ends are modest, when the motives are weak, the tensions between forces reduced, a circumspect war leader may skilfully seek out all the ways to peace on the field and in the cabinets, without a great crisis and bloody solution, owing to the particular weaknesses of his adversary; we have no right to find fault with him, when his hypotheses are sufficiently well-founded and justify his confidence in success; however, we must still require him to remain aware of the fact that he is treading on slippery slopes on which the god of war may trap him, to keep his eye continually fixed on the enemy lest, at the time the enemy brandishes the heavy sword, he has nothing to oppose him with other than the dress rapier.

As a fragmented expression separated from the whole, this passage, that one of Clausewitz's editors, Linnebach, cited in 1940 to explain or illustrate the victory of the Third Reich over France in May–June 1940, adds nothing to the idea which I expounded in Chapter 1, I : i.e. to avoid the rise to extremes, to keep war at a moderated level, there needs to be an agreement between the adversaries which is only ever implied; the decision taken in this sense, on one side as on the other, is based on probabilities. A mistake might be fatal, as happened to Prussia in 1806. In short, each imposes its law on the other not only in the abstraction of war but also in real wars.

Apart from this consequence, evidence in itself, Clausewitz's texts as they have reached us allow two interpretations. The first bases itself essentially on Book III and Book IV, in other words on the books written before 1826 and unrevised. For example· 'Combat is the real activity of war, everything else is only its auxiliary.' And again: 'Combat means fighting, and in this fight, the end is to destroy or conquer the enemy; now, in any particular combat, the enemy is the armed force which stands opposed to us.' To destroy the enemy thus becomes the imminent end of warlike activity or combat. Or again,

> As long as we disregard all the particular ends of combat, we can consider the complete or partial destruction of the enemy as the sole end of all combats. Now, we maintain that in the majority of cases, and especially in great combats, the particular end by which the combat is individualized and bound up with the great whole [*grosses Ganzes*] is only a weak modification of that general end. . . .

On the other hand, let us refer to Chapter 30 of Book VI. 'There can be such a difference between one battle and another that it can no longer be regarded as the same instrument.' This chapter brings to an end the manuscript completed in 1826, unless it was added later (which seems to me improbable). He introduces, illustrates and analyses the distinction between the two types of war. It thus expresses better the final state of Clausewitz's thought. It confirms our own interpretation, whereas the comparison with the texts of Book IV explains the two possible orientations of the commentators.

4 Two interpretations: E. Weill and W.M. Schering

Eric Weill, in a brilliant and profound article, defended an original and partly true thesis, which I shall briefly discuss to clarify the significance of both the means–end and the war–policy pairs. Weill asserts that the two fundamental concepts which structure the field of analysis are those of totality and polarity. As regards the means–end pair:

> here are two other essential concepts in the thought of Clausewitz. They are on a different level from the foremost pair, formed by the concepts of totality and polarity; they are not philosophically fundamental; nevertheless, it is only with their assistance that the reality can be thought out on the level of the decision, in the coherent details of its structure.

This thesis causes surprise to the commentator for a primary reason: the means–end pair figures in all the texts after those of 1804. The totality–polarity pair never appear as such. From the *Neue Bellona* article

111

onwards, the means–end pair is used to dissect the war object, to define tactics and strategy. Clausewitz borrows it from art and from craftsmen. Now, he endeavours to elaborate the theory of a practice, not a philosophy of history. What he sought all his life was to think out reality on the level of the decision. The hierarchical inversion, totality at the higher level, the means–end relation at the lower level, belongs to the philosophy of Eric Weill, and perhaps to the logic of Clausewitz but not to his explicit thought. At the very most it would lead to the implications of the final synthesis: to the extent that war only constitutes an episode in the relations between states, it constitutes a partial totality, introduced into a wider totality, policy. But, in fact, these two methods of consideration linked to the two meanings, objective and subjective, of politics and policy are intertwined. Even in his intellectual testament, Clausewitz goes from the subjective meaning to the objective, from the violent contest between two wills to the social relations from which this contest emanates.

The second part of the thesis, namely the polarity between war and policy, seems to me wholly incompatible with the Treatise. The word polarity is rarely used. Clausewitz does, however, state his intention, in Book I, Chapter 1, to devote a whole chapter to it (which does not exist). It is thus advisable to specify the meaning he gives the concept. Now the reply seems to me simple and undeniable, corresponding exactly to what we today call the structure of a goal-less draw: the advantage of one equals the disadvantage of the other; what one side wants, the other does not want; the gain to the one is equivalent to the loss of the other to the same extent. Clausewitz adds that there is no direct polarity between defence and attack; polarity thus ranges over what both relate to, namely the decision.

In the account of the Russian campaign he uses the word *Polarität* and he also specifies that it relates to the end, not to the means. The idea is the same as in the first chapter of the Treatise and one can see why Clausewitz intended to devote an entire chapter to it. In the two texts that I have just quoted, the reference to polarity serves to limit, to circumscribe its field of application. The contenders can simultaneously have an interest in suspending hostilities, in neither of them wanting to attack, in turning towards the same direction. In short, the analysis will have brought to light everything that, in the action of the belligerents, does not fall under the principle of polarity or does so only indirectly.

If Clausewitzian polarity is defined in this way – and no text to my knowledge justifies any other – the relation between war and policy is not an example of polarity. Policy, in the subjective sense, as the intelligent will, resorts to violence in times of war without, for all that, renouncing other means; policy, the exchange of notes, negotiations, speeches, continues during the hostilities, whereas by definition, hostilities cease on the signing of peace. It is in this sense that violence, characteristic of war, is added to the means that policy is constantly using. Since violence possesses its own law, policy cannot rule it despotically, it cannot give it unlimited tasks or ignore the rules which belong to it. This relation, dialectic if you like, lies at the opposite extreme to polarity: a relation of complementarity and of differentiation, never a direct radical opposition.

Clausewitz, as I have said, toys with concepts and conceptual pairs. But the relation between these concepts changes from one pair to another.

It is legitimate to raise the dialectic of defence and attack, of the physical and the moral, of the means and the end, but not to confuse this dialectic with the principle of polarity. Furthermore, these three dialectics have a common characteristic, which is incompatible with polarity: there is no attack without defence, no physical force without moral components, no military end which does not become a political means, thus no violence which is not necessarily subjected to the intelligent will. Perhaps the intended chapter on polarity would have included the analysis of the different modalities of the opposition between the combatants, in the course of hostilities, between the logic of the rise to extremes and that of the descent to armed observation. Whether one departs from the totality or from the relation of means–end, the latter sanctions the role of intelligence in the fight at the same time as it justifies the comparison of strategy with an art.

Amongst the interpreters of Clausewitz, Schering, to whom I have often referred, places a quite different significance on the means–end relation. If he is to be believed, the two words *Mittel* and *Zweck* would not strike the ear of a twentieth-century man in the same way that they would have a man living a century and a half ago. A reader of Clausewitz would have given these notions, later corrupted by usage, a richness of meaning which they have now lost. Schering believes it would be better to replace *Mittel* with *Leistung* (production, performance) and *Zweck* with *Wille* (Will). Writing in the climate of the 1930s, and sympathetic to the cause of national socialism, this interpreter pursues the remnants of rationalism that he believes to exist in Clausewitzian thought: the structuring of the action of war by the hierarchy of the means and the ends, the political end as the ultimate end of the totality of war, both appeared to him to be rightly full of rational, if not rationalist, implications. To repeat the most paradoxical formula, the goal of strategy is not victory on the battlefield but the preparation for this victory (or for these victories) with a view to the ends of the war (and not in the war). For what is meant is precisely this union of the rational, that is to say understanding, with the irrational, that is to say will.

I do not think that the words 'means' and 'end' meant anything different in 1830 than a century later. Without doubt the means–end relation, classical in the theory of art in the eighteenth century, essential in the *Critique of Judgment*, is inspired by a certain rationalism, that of Kant rather than that of Bülow. This rationalism serves as a basis for the understanding of the historical world, as a light to the man of action which, without depriving him of his liberty, allows him to challenge the hostile and uncertain environment he must face. Of course, the analysis of available means and of the end sought does not produce the decision alone; it never reduces it to a strict calculation of probability. The specific characteristics of the decision remain, which cannot be reduced to those of an act of pure thought. The genius of war requires other qualities than those of the scholar and the scientist, qualities of will and of character which, moreover, only blossom when coaxed by the light of understanding.

If Schering had limited himself to taking up the opposition of the artist at grips with the material and of the strategist at grips with another will, to recalling that every decision (*Entschluss*) is born from resolution (*Entschlossenheit*) which bring together the virtues of the intelligence and those of courage, he would not have renewed the theme or made any mistake. The choice of an end by the head of state, the commander of armies or the officer in charge of a patrol results from a decision, but this must not be confused with the end conceived by understanding and probably after a comparison with other possible ends. What forbids the confusion between the end and the decision (or the translation of end by decision), is that the means–end relation governs each fragment of the totality of war as well as this totality itself. The oscillation between politics and policy suggests the twofold usage of the means–end relation: it is indispensable to the historian to think out *das Geschehen*, the outcome of events, and indispensable to the war leader once he has raised himself, with civilization, above the elementary blind unleashing of hate and violence. The same relation clarifies the intelligibility of the real and the decision of the actors, because the real is confused with objectivized, crystallized actions, and because the actions derive from the means that society makes available to the combatants and from the ends which the latter fix in view of prevailing interests and accepted ideas.

Furthermore, the role of understanding broadens out and asserts itself in the final texts. Interpreters have rarely given the last paragraphs of Chapter 1, Book I the attention that they deserve. The three elements internal to every chameleon-like war – passion and hatred; free activity of the spirit; and understanding – are answered by the three constituent parts of the real fighter – the state (namely the people), the military chief, the cabinet or the sovereign. Thus an essential distinction appears between the free activity of the soul and understanding, between the activity pertaining to the command of the army and that which falls to the responsibility of the state. Now, in no other text does this distinction appear so clearly. In Book VIII, Clausewitz considers the possibility of the commander of the armies not being the same person as the head of state, and he forcefully asserts that in this event the task of taking decisions belongs to the cabinet which, in doing this, should closely follow the movements of the armies. Most often the man whom he calls commander-in-chief (*Feldherr*) fulfils both functions. Even in Chapter (6 B) of Book VIII, where Clausewitz most heavily stresses the supremacy of the cabinet, he puts forward the opposition between the partial importance of the military and the global importance of policy without any allusion to the contrast between free activity of the soul and understanding. The military chief must not leave his domain, which is limited in two ways: war is waged with other means besides armed forces; the war as conceived by the soldier stops at the objective; now, the latter remains the means with a view to peace which, as the ultimate end, governs the use of the means with a view to the intermediate ends.

In Book I, war as an instrument of politics falls to the share of pure understanding.

> The passions which are inflamed during the war must already be latent in the peoples: the range which the exercise of courage and talent will assume in the realm of the probabilities of chance

depends on the particular characteristics of the commander-in-chief and of the army; the political ends belong to the government alone. (I, 1, 128)

A convergence of the state and understanding, the exclusive choice of the ends of the war by the government: how can one avoid concluding that the determination of the ultimate ends, the exclusive prerogative of the state, necessitates above all clarity of understanding? To the extent that operations will evolve in the real world of armies, with the inevitable friction caused by human machines, incomplete information, and good and bad luck, the head of state does not escape uncertainties. In the midst of these, ranges the free activity of the soul. In taking on war, the head of state takes on risks: he also gambles, like the commander in chief. It is symbolic of his understanding to place only reasonable bets. He must not demand from the instrument more than it can give, and must not use it in a way which contradicts specific laws. By placing politics above war, by reserving the responsibility for political decisions to understanding, Clausewitz extolled prudence as much, if not more, than boldness. The man of 50 who writes his testament in the first chapter has overcome the ardour of the young officer in the eyes of whom no general could be too audacious.

If the substitution of decision for end seems to me unjustified, that of performance (*Leistung*) for means seems to me even more devoid of significance. It stands to reason that, in the conduct of operations, the means employed by whatever commander, inferior or superior, cannot be identified with inanimate objects, with arms. To ensure the safety of his unit, the lieutenant or captain will carefully determine the number and location of guard posts, of sentries on watch night and day. The performance of these actors, at the lower level of the hierarchy, will alone allow the ends determined by the commander of the unit, in terms of the ends that a superior commander has ordered the unit to attain. In this sense, the transition from means to performance is reasonable since the means are embodied in human actions. But, in another sense, Schering radically falsifies Clausewitz's approach. The concept of means is applied indiscriminately to things and to beings, to courage and to cannons. It does not characterize the material substance of the instrument, or the material, but the rationalizable, if not rational, relation intrinsic in all craft, in all art, in all practice. The rifle is the means of the infantryman, victorious combat the means of the strategist and war the means of policy. This method of analysis is universally valid, disregarding the distinction between matter and men, armed forces and combats, battles and notes.

The dialectic of the means and the end thus does not involve contradictory or incompatible concepts: the end of an inferior activity becomes the means of a superior activity. It could thus be called both the dialectic of intelligent action and the dialectic of the totality. The hierarchy of the means and the ends restores, thanks to understanding, the unity of the totality of war, a unity spontaneously realized by the blind clash of untamed peoples and seemingly broken up by the multiplication of dispersed combats. But the dialectic of the means and the end re-establishes this total unity in two radically different ways: either, by concentrating the campaign into one decisive battle, the commander-in-chief rediscovers, thanks to the resources of the art, a form apparently close to the contest

115

between man and man or between people and people; or, on the contrary, he accepts the game in which the number of points, at the time of settlement, designates the victor; in this latter case, it is the absence of organic unity which will give the campaign or the war its dispersed or incoherent structure, a structure which, despite all theory, remains nevertheless intelligible.

In the collection of articles entitled *Thoughts of a Soldier*, General von Seeckt twice quotes the Formula, which had become a cliché (*Schlagwort*). He corrects this quotation by taking one of the formulae from Book VIII of the Treatise, 'continuation of political relations with a mixture of other means'. He gives two meanings to this, of which one holds an eternal truth and the other must be revised according to experience.

It remains true that at all times and in every place political activity and diplomacy continue during the course of hostilities. On the other hand, the idea that the conduct of the war will be all the more forceful when the policy of the state is itself more forceful, more aware of its ends – an idea that the Napoleonic victories would have suggested to Clausewitz – is not unreservedly valid.

In fact, this second idea, in the form expressed by General von Seeckt, was not originated by Clausewitz. He explained the French victories by the consequences of the French Revolution, by the liberation of all the national energies; he did not deduce any law out of this, at most an empirical norm; there usually is a proportionality between the size of the stakes and the intensity of the struggle and between the tensions within the states and the outbreak of war.

After this distinction between the eternal truth and the historical truth, General von Seeckt, pretending to adhere to the authentic thought of Clausewitz, writes: 'The quotation is misunderstood, since, having become a cliché, it obscures the teaching of Clausewitz himself on the subject of the true essence of war with the annihilation of the enemy as its objective.' With extraordinary naivety, he immediately adds that war is not a thing by itself, that it is inserted according to its own proper laws into the organic life of peoples – without recognizing the contradiction between the supremacy of policy and the unconditional imperative of the annihilation of the armed forces and the overthrow of the enemy state.

Elsewhere, he himself contrasts the Formula with another cliché, dear to American authors: war is the failure of politics. At the same time, he illustrates the two themes in the debate which are aroused and maintained by the application of the means–end pair (or of the final rationality) to the relation of policy and war: how does the true finality of war (or principle of annihilation) fit in with the supremacy of the political end? Does policy incline towards the same ends in times of peace as in times of war even though it does not use the same means? Clausewitz did not give a clear theoretical or general reply to these two questions: his readers have given many and contradictory interpretations to prolong the posthumous fate of this posthumous work.

Chapter 5

The Moral and the Physical

Clausewitz is often considered, rightly, as a military writer who introduced into military theory the notion of morale or moral forces
(*moralische Potenzen*). Even the least favourably disposed interpreters,
including Liddell Hart, cannot fail to concede him this merit.

This theme has also given rise to misunderstandings. Machine-gunners
mow down the waves of assault in open ground, whatever the morale of
the soldiers. Firing kills the bravest men. The madness of the commanders
of 1914, even though they quoted some of the formulae of the Treatise, is
not derived from the Prussian strategist. On this subject, as all the others
the system must be rediscovered if we are to understand it, the partial
analyses must be placed within the whole; the first chapter of Book I will
be our guide and our mentor.

1 The origins of the moral element

At which points does the opposition of the moral and the physical appear
in the course of the conceptual development of this key chapter? It seems to
me to appear on three occasions: first, in the initial definition of war; a
second time from paragraph 18 to paragraph 21, when Clausewitz
attempts to mark the divergence between war as a concept and real war;
and finally, in the conclusion, the threefold definition of war. At each of
these points, another aspect, another significance of the moral–physical
antithesis, comes to light.

The simplified model which Clausewitz puts forward at the beginning,
that of the wrestling match, contains in itself this duality. The contest
brings wills into conflict and not only bodies: analytically but not concretely discernible in the case of the wrestlers, these two terms separate as
soon as one substitutes arms for bodies and community for individuals. An
English author, J.C. Fuller, has made the observation that one need only
substitute fencing for wrestling to give a completely different picture of
war. True enough, but the objection does not hold weight for two reasons.
Alexander and Genghis Khan do not resemble fencers: by taking, as a
model, adversaries who use the same means and compete in subtlety,
Clausewitz would have prevented himself from reaching the concept of
war capable of integrating all the forms that it assumes. To understand
war from the most simple model, one must recognize its nature – war is a
relation between human wills – and its specific character, the resort to
physical violence. Where the theoreticians of today would rather find fault
with Clausewitz, is to have specified the dialectic of wills by the resort to
violence when they themselves use the notion of the duel without specify-
ing the means employed by the duellists.

117

The duality of the means – violence – and the end – to bring the adversary to do what we want him to do – immediately implies taking moral virtues into consideration. What force will our adversary deploy? To what point will his capacity to resist extend? The dialectic of the rise to extremes partly results from the indetermination of moral force. All the banal formulae of today ('Only he who recognizes defeat is beaten'; victory falls to 'the one who holds out for the last quarter of an hour') are based on the principle laid down in the first pages of the Treatise: we gauge the weight of a wrestler, but not, in advance, his resistance, his tenacity, in a word his moral strength. If Clausewitz forced strategists to neglect moral virtues no longer, it is not because of a chance intuition that he conceived the notion or discovered an unknown element, it is because he went back to the true nature of the phenomenon of war, to its human significance. Men fight each other, and states make war against each other, with weapons that civilization puts into their hands: neither men nor states resemble armchair strategists, those who calculate the angles made by the lines of operations with the base. It can happen that in certain historical situations wars between states resemble a court fencing contest. If we can understand the court fencing contest from the struggle to the bitter end, we still cannot understand the latter from the former: firstly, incompatible wills using possibly unlimited violence, then, according to circumstances, the limitation, stylization and legalization of violence.

The second point at which moral force appears seems antithetical to the first: the indetermination of the will as a moral force in theory contributes to the rise to extremes. How is it possible not to push to the limit since one can never know to what extremity the other resolves to go? Indetermination again figures at the second point but with an apparently opposite function. The halting of military operations, or the suspension of hostilities in the very course of the war, contradicts logic. If the advantage of the one lies in doing nothing, that of the other ought to lie in action. At this point, Clausewitz discovers, simultaneously, polarity (the equality between the advantage of the one and the loss of the other), the limitation of polarity to the ends or to the decision and not to the means and, finally, the dissymmetry of defence and attack. This is a necessary and adequate solution to the rational schematism of war consonant with its nature, but too distant from the real to satisfy the double Clausewitzian requirement of abstraction and realism.

Just as economists very often assume, in their theory, a perfect knowledge on their subjects' part, strategists, in order to confer on their theory an apparent scientificity, have neglected one of the characteristics of real war, the uncertainty over the relation of forces, over the intentions of the adversary. Once this is considered, the rational calculation of simplified theory is transformed into the calculation of probability; the struggle becomes a game in the sense that one speaks of a game of cards. The players still oppose each other and intelligence plays a role: but chance intervenes. Furthermore, in war the uncertainty of the game assumes the form of danger. Once the actor is forced to use the calculation of probabilities, he is condemned to gamble. The gamble in the face of danger, the resolve to try one's luck, requires courage.

Real war shows us the virtues needed by the commander-in-chief, not only the naked force of the will which would logically lead to the extreme, but also the precise qualities of mind and character which are demanded by this singular activity of men at grips with their fellow men, all armed with instruments that human science places at their disposal.

In other words, the moral element first comes into play in the most simplified theory, comparable to pure economy: the will to conquer, to make the other yield, plays the same role as the will of maximization in economics. This moral element intervenes a second time when the theoretician has passed from rigorous calculation to the calculation of probabilities and has reintegrated into his subject the duality of objective and subjective. Uncertainty comes into play with both, the one linked to material circumstances, the other to human circumstances, an uncertainty which challenges courage and which multiplies the very response to courage.

The threefold definition takes up and completes these two analytical points. At the beginning of the chapter, the rise to extremes seems above all to arise from a rational dialectic. At the end, the element of war, which involves the hyperbolic violence of real wars, hatred and hostility, inclines rather towards the people, whereas moral forces, mentioned at the second point, the game of courage in the field of probabilities and chance, pertain above all to the commander-in-chief. It is to him, the head of state, that free activity of the soul and the determination of the ends reverts, i.e. the struggle for supremacy, since war must obey policy as the tool obeys the worker or the means obeys the end.

In every real war, these three elements are to be found, but with an unequal force according to the particular circumstances: sometimes policy uneasily channels popular passions in order to make them conform to what is at stake. Sometimes it experiences difficulty in inflaming popular passions which the safety of the nation justifies and requires. Sometimes the hostility reaches a point where policy seems to disappear and hostilities resemble a blind clash of unleashed forces; at other times, on the contrary, political considerations – the limitation of the stake, or rivalry between allies – permeates the course of operations. The least that can be said is that, by its passion or indifference, the people always play a part; the military leader always makes decisions in the midst of danger and, by gambling, the head of state always bears the higher responsibility, that of appraising the true character of the particular war.

With the threefold definition, Clausewitz lays down the foundations of the conceptual system into which the partial analyses must be inserted. Take, for example, the duality *Gemüt–Verstand*, that is to say (approximately) emotionalism (or affectivity)/understanding. The head of state, in determining the ends, should evince intelligence, have a thorough knowledge of the conjuncture, and compare his resources with those of his adversaries or his allies as well as understand his time. But, if intelligence governs at the highest level, it still does not rule alone. It is not intelligence alone which gives the courage to decide. If a small state finds itself in conflict with a stronger one, must it not take the initiative if the future offers nothing but a deterioration in the relation of forces? The man who has the supreme responsibility in this case needs no less courage, resolve, indeed boldness than the general on the battlefield. There is a difference as he does not expose himself to physical danger, but the courage needed to fulfil his responsibilities does not appear to Clausewitz as an inferior form of courage.

If the duality of emotionalism (affectivity) and understanding governs the theory of the military leader as much as that of the head of state, the two sometimes united in the commander-in-chief (*Feldherr*), is there not the same duality when we come to the people and the army? Certainly at each level of the military hierarchy the same complementarity, but in different proportions, of emotionality and understanding remains necessary. On the other hand, the spirit of the peoples which constitutes one of the moral powers (*moralische Hauptpotenzen*) only partially results from analysis in terms of intelligence and emotionality.

The people, as the motivator of opinion, constitutes one of the targets of enemy action at the same time as being a condition of resistance or victory. Since war brings states and armies into conflict, the moral elements that theory should include dominate the leaders and their instruments which owe their effectiveness to the collective action of men, the relation between those who execute them becomes dialectic: policy has the last word which it expresses in terms of the weapon, in other words in terms of the army that it controls. The military leader gives the orders: the loyalty and the confidence of the troops condition the decision that he takes and the results that he obtains.

In short, Clausewitz's emphasis on moral forces results from his interpretation of war as a social activity in which men are involved as a whole people – army, military leaders, head of state – all interdependent, the moral union of the people and the sovereign constituting the ultimate foundation of the state.

These three appearances of the moral element in the first chapter lead us to three themes.

(a) The initial definition of war implies that the outcome of a combat, battle or war depends on the respective strength of wills in conflict. When Clausewitz speaks of inferiority or superiority, he always includes the moral element which, consequently, is opposed to the material element *par excellence*, numbers. Since the moral and the material elements are inseparable both can become targets; destruction or annihilation aims as much at the will as at the instrument. When the will of the soldiers or leaders gives way, the instrument, made up of men, no longer exists as such. In this line of thought lies the study of the moral element as subject and as object, as a condition of superiority and as a vulnerable objective, one of the factors of victory and defeat.

(b) The second appearance of the moral element, to relate the suspension of operations in war, leads us to the concept of friction which is dealt with above all in Book I but is traced through the whole work: the incessant movement to and fro between concept and experience, the rejection of theory in the old meaning of the word.

(c) The threefold definition of war is itself found, in some degree, throughout the whole of the Treatise. Now, the three constituent elements in every war – the passion of the people, the free activity of the spirit of the military leader, the understanding of the state – are particularized by a moral notion, one would be tempted to say by a faculty or combination of faculties. In this way we can explain why Book III, devoted to strategy as such, contains so many chapters which consider psychology or morale. Let us examine these three themes in turn, in the reverse order.

2 The warlike virtue of the army

If we wish to summarize in one formula the originality of Clausewitz in relation to the theoreticians to whom he is opposed, Bülow or Jomini, the following would seem to me to be valid: in a book on strategy as such, the other theoreticians would have analysed above all the movements of armies, the bases, the lines of communication or of retreat; Clausewitz deals above all with moral forces and opposes to these, numbers. The rest, including the geometry of campaigns or of battles, does not disappear but passes to the secondary level and becomes a subordinate method of consideration.

Let us read Book III in the light of this formula and, in particular, the short Chapter 2 entitled 'Elements of Strategy'. Taking up current distinctions, he lists the moral, physical, mathematical, geographical, statistical elements which he could, it seems to me, have analysed separately. He admits that these elements are thought out separately in order to give some clarity to the notions and to appraise, in passing, the greater or lesser worth of each case. But he immediately notes that the worth of a base depends less on the angle which it forms with the operation lines than on the roads and the country through which they pass. In that case the analysis of the geometric form, taken in isolation, would produce radically false ideas. The man who, among strategists, is rightly considered the most abstract, the most inclined to concepts thus evokes the phenomenon in its totality.

We want to remain within the world of phenomena considered in their totality and not pursue our analyses further than is from time to time necessary for the comprehension of an idea which we wish to convey and which we have conceived, not by speculative research but through the impression made by the phenomena of war in their entirety.

Why does the analyst of the first chapter of Book I suddenly seem to jump to the opposite pole, comprehension, the grasp of the total phenomenon? The following chapter gives the answer: because of moral virtues. Physical and moral forces merge in such a way that no chemistry will dissolve the alloy. No proposition relating to physical force can be asserted which deliberately disregards what, to simplify matters, we shall call morale. The requirement of totality does not exclude analytical distinctions, but forbids rules or precepts which are based on one element alone and ignore the essential, namely the activity of the spirit. Clausewitz uses the word *Geist* in its widest meaning, incorporating various faculties or qualities: affection, understanding, courage. What he never ceases to say is that everything emanates from man and everything comes back to man.

As if in passing, he outlines a classification of the three dimensions of moral forces: (a) The spirit and the other moral qualities of the army, military leader and governments. (b) The state of mind in the provinces in which war is being waged. (c) The moral effect of a victory or defeat. Book

III, 'Of Strategy in General', deals especially with the first and third dimensions which moreover he does not separate in the following chapters.

Each combatant in a war comprises a people, an army and a leader: from this results the three principal power factors of a moral order, the talents of the commander-in-chief, the military virtue of the army, and its military spirit. The pages which Clausewitz devotes to these three factors (or powers) take up ideas which go back to the start of his career. For example, he analyses the part played respectively by the commander and the army according to the nature of the territory. Now, from 1809, he wrote that in mountain warfare the commander-in-chief is less in control of his troops than on level terrain.

> In the mountains it is rather the armies who confront each other, on the plain the commanders-in-chief. But what gives the army its worth, in mountain warfare, is not its training on the parade ground, for this only makes it a more perfect mechanical instrument in the hands of an intelligence which remains outside it. This intelligence is the commander-in-chief. This is why such armies are more suitable for the plain where they serve the glory of the commander-in-chief, as we have just said. In mountain warfare, the warlike spirit and experience of the armies measure their strength and face each other.

Clausewitz at once concludes from this that mountainous terrain favours popular insurrection. On the plain, the lack of tactical formation of the insurgents ensures the superiority of the regular armies; in the mountains, the spirit of the insurgent troops, normally superior to that of regular armies, reaches the point where one would willingly entrust it with the welfare of the country.

In his account of the 1799 campaigns, written late, Clausewitz illustrates the same ideas from history. The French had an advantage because, in that kind of war, the enthusiasm, and the martial spirit of each fighter, from privates to commander-in-chief, played a greater role. Each unit retained a certain independence.

> The French, borne by the spirit of the Revolution to break all shackles and to reach results only by bold acts, followed this impulse when they saw no other way out. The Austrians, reared on the subordination of the will, accustomed to rules, paralysed by the worry of their responsibilities, remained inactive when faced with difficulties.

In this way, convincingly, the superiority of the French is explained, as well as that of the Austrians – when they obeyed their leaders.

The Treatise takes up, elaborates and amplifies these views, remaining at the same time 'incomplete and rhapsodic' in order to avoid commonplaces and platitudes. Clausewitz defines or characterizes the popular spirit of the army by enthusiasm, 'fanatical zeal, faith and opinion'; he writes under the influence of the wars of the Revolution but also of liberation. He no longer opposes the plan of campaign on the plain, the privileged territory of professionals, to the mountains, the natural place for popular insurrection; he interposes undulation, broken country between the mountains and the plain, and this gives the commander-in-chief the greatest scope for action. In the mountains, he has insufficient mastery over the different parts, and the control of the different parts is beyond his powers: in the plain it is too easy and does not fully stretch these powers.

Let us stop for a moment at these analyses, in particular at Chapter 5, 'The Military Virtue of an Army', which completes the above on the principal power-factors of a moral order. Clausewitz will not ignore the psychological factors of the fight, but he also will not calculate, with a false rigour, the weight of each. Only history authorizes propositions to be formulated when they are not universally valid. The Treatise at this point refers to the state of the science or military art as it emerged from the wars of the Revolution and Empire. Armies reached the same level of facility of execution (*Fertigkeit*) and training; the conduct of the war developed in method to the point corresponding to its nature, to use an expression of the philosophers, so that one could no longer expect, on the part of the commander-in-chief, the application of certain artifices, in the limited sense (such as Frederick II's oblique order). 'It cannot be denied that, as matters now stand, an even greater field of action [*Spielraum*] is afforded to the spirit of the people and habituation to war.'

This text seems to me essential if we are to avoid misunderstandings. The respective influence of the various factors in victory depends on many circumstances which constantly change across history ('war is a true chameleon'). The theoretician conceptualizes these factors, he enumerates them, he compares them, he does not attribute to them, once and for all, a given weight. This historical variability is too often forgotten by interpreters, particularly with regard to numbers.

The thoughts on the 'military virtue of an army' have a lasting significance because they emanate from a historical experience which has recurred several times (the clash between irregulars and professional armies), and because they touch on the very essence of the army or of the war, the relation between the part and the whole, partial units and the total unity, individuals and the entirety. Lenin read the chapter carefully precisely because, without neglecting the worth of the people in arms, it brings to light the specificity of the military career and of military virtue as such. The citizen will never be confused with the soldier: in the recognition of this duality and the true appraisement of the professional and the partisan is expressed the spirit of the enlightened Reformers who forged the Prussian army of 1814 and 1815. Should we also add the German army which, from victory to victory, forged the empire with fire and iron, to be finally lost in an apocalyptic catastrophe?

Here, firstly, is a description, a dark passage, which combines literary talent with a sense of abstract rigour:

> An army which keeps to its ordinary formations under the most devastating fire; which does not give way to imaginary fears, and which resists, foot by foot, in the face of well-grounded fears; which, proud in its victories, retains in the adversity of defeat its sense of obedience, its respect for its leaders and its confidence in them; an army whose physical powers are drained by privations and effort, like the muscles of an athlete; an army which sees its efforts as a means of victory and not as a curse attached to its standards, and in which the short catechism of one idea, that of the

123

honour of arms, is enough to remind it of its duties and virtues; such an army is imbued with the military spirit.

This description, which contains analysis and instruction, in itself illustrates Clausewitz's constant endeavour to conceptualize personal experience. From his first writings he reflected on the qualities needed by a commander (because he dreamt of being one), and above all on what escapes so-called rational calculation. Thus, he borrows a remark from Machiavelli, in the 'Strategy' of 1804, on the moral effect of victory.

Machiavelli, who has a very sound judgment in military affairs, asserts that it is more difficult to defeat with fresh troops an army which has just been victorious than to defeat it beforehand. He bases this assertion on several examples and very rightly asserts that the moral advantage obtained fully compensates for losses incurred.

The moral effect of victory and defeat, during and after battle in the course of the campaign, remains one of Clausewitz's essential themes in Book III as in Book IV. But, in Book III, in the chapter we are studying, the duality of regular armies and of the people in arms, of professionals and of partisans, is combined with the duality of the army and its leader, comparable to that of the instrument and the will, of the mass and the spirit.

The commander uses the instrument but he controls, and can only control, the whole. 'Military virtue is at all times for the parts what the commander is for the whole. The commander can only control the whole, not each part, and where he cannot control the part, military virtue must serve as the guide.' The comparison between the army and an instrument under the orders of the intelligence (the commander) is not valid without reservations: the instrument is made up of men, organized at each level according to a hierarchy. As one approaches its base the capacity of the leaders becomes more uncertain and the capacities of the people compensate for the shortcomings of the commanders.

Clausewitz does not fail to recognize either the bravery of the Vendéens or the exploits of the Swiss and the Americans; a standing army, such as that of Marlborough, did not possess military virtue. The standing army as such was never characterized by this virtue. When opposed by another standing army, it can even do without this virtue. It represents the supreme achievement of the military career, of the specific activity of the combatant. It is only engendered by special training, possible in peacetime, and by habituation to danger and effort which only war itself brings.

How is the true soldier born, made, represented? It seems to me that the Treatise answers this question in two words: drill and experience. Neither bravery nor enthusiasm make a soldier; at most they constitute primary material, a natural aptitude which will favour the cultivation of specific qualities. The military virtue of an army appears as a definite moral factor, which can be extracted by thought, whose influence can thus be estimated, hence it is an instrument whose power can be calculated.

The first stage in the education of the soldier comes to an end: each has a second nature, each succeeds in submitting himself naturally to the law of the whole; cohesion is based on the spontaneous adherence felt by each to all and by all to the common enterprises. The second stage, which is decisive, is war itself, victories, ordeals, sufferings accepted and overcome.

Clausewitz pinpoints the Macedonians under Alexander, the Romans under Caesar, the Spanish under Alexander Farnese, the Swedes under Gustavus Adolphus and Charles XII, the Prussians under Frederick the Great, and the French under Bonaparte. He compares this last army, the unrivalled instrument of the commander, to the molten metal which emerges from the refinery, one could almost say the processing of a mineral to create a precious stone. It is primary material, but primary human material which only becomes comparable to a mechanism with the permanent influence of the intelligence, with the submission of spontaneous impulses to the constraints of organization. In Clausewitz's eyes, the conscript is not dehumanized by this apprenticeship but converted or transformed into a professional, into a soldier.

Some lessons are implied in these analyses: depending on the nature of the instrument, depending on the qualities of the soldier and the army, the steps to be taken change. Instead of calculating the angles from the base to the operation lines, one will estimate the part played by the enthusiasm of a people who arm themselves in defence; and one chooses suitable country, and appropriate tactics, so that the qualities of the combatants may be fully expressed.

On the level of objective study in the dialectical thought of Clausewitz, to what are moral factors opposed? Without doubt, to numbers. In this way we come to a debate to which a great part of Clausewitzian literature is devoted. The same Liddell Hart who greeted the introduction of moral forces into theory, denounces the prophet of mass armies, the strategist obsessed by quantity. It seems that he did not take care to unravel the thread, to follow the method of abstractions and antitheses to unveil the link between what he praises and what he censures.

3 Numbers and the other factors of victory

Book III, which according to the title deals with strategy as such, seems to me to be constructed around the antithesis of the moral and of numbers, a putting into concrete form, in a particular historical conjuncture, of the antithesis of spirit and of matter.

In order to interpret correctly the weight which Clausewitz attaches to numbers, we must follow the approach by which he comes to consider it as the apparently decisive factor in success. The Treatise more often than not presupposes armies equipped in approximately the same way, born of people in a comparable state of civilization. He thus puts to one side, by hypothesis or by convention, the differences in armament, technical means, organization and training. What, therefore, remains? First, moral forces: let us eliminate these by a mental process. There then remains strategy. It is certainly this 'which determines at which point, at which moment and with what forces the battle will be waged; by this triple determination it exercises a very important influence on the outcome of the combat'. If we make a further mental elimination, we end up with a single residue: numbers.

If we strip the combat of all modifications which it may undergo according to its determination and the circumstances from which it proceeds, if we finally disregard the valour of the troops because that is a given quantity, there only remains the bare concept of

125

combat, that is a fight without form in which we distinguish nothing but the number of combatants.

Once again, it is permissible to criticize this method or to argue with the style of the account. But the benevolent or simply honest interpreter will not conclude from it that Clausewitz recognizes numbers alone or remains, after the wars of the Revolution and Empire, obsessed with numbers.

Let us first recall that in the account of Frederick's campaigns, with regard to Leuthen, where 30,000 Prussians, owing to the oblique order, triumphed over 80,000 Austrians, he mentions in passing that numbers at the time weighed less heavily than in modern warfare. The importance of numbers thus lies in the way in which modern wars and battles are fought.

Without doubt, Clausewitz considers irrational and absurd the conception of an optimum size of the army, arguing that an army which is too large would escape the authority of the commander, and would lose the capacity to manoeuvre, while a small army would always victoriously oppose the masses. Clausewitz, like Napoleon, ascribes to the god of combat a propensity for large battalions: in this respect, he is neither first nor alone. Although by giving, in hypothesis, the same armaments to both sides, he prevented himself from bringing another factor of success to light, his historical diagnosis of the European wars was sadly confirmed as much as it was contradicted in the following century, until 1945.

In the penultimate chapter of Book III, he calls to mind Napoleon, destroying major states at almost one blow: the Spaniards pursuing their resistance to the end: Russia showing that a vast country cannot be conquered and that a state can become stronger within its own territory in spite of losing battles and provinces, and even the capital itself; and lastly, Prussia multiplying the effectives of its army by six owing to the militia and using this enlarged army abroad.

> . . . now that all these cases have shown to what extent the heart and sentiment [*Gesinnung*] of a nation can be a prodigious factor in its performance, that it affects the forces of the state, the war or the army; now that today all governments have learnt to use these aids, we cannot expect them to refrain from using them in future wars when danger threatens their own existence or when burning ambition drives them on.

Wars waged with the whole weight of national forces obey different principles from those in which standing armies alone take part; the latter resemble fleets and the art of terrestrial warfare borrows something from naval tactics.

War between peoples makes the old notion of an optimum size of armies anachronistic. There is no lack of examples of victories won by small battalions. At Rossbach Frederick defeated 50,000 allied troops with 25,000 soldiers. But at Kolin his 30,000 men were defeated by Daun's 50,000, and at Leipzig, Napoleon was overcome with 160,000 against 280,000.

Experience thus teaches that the greatest commander has hardly any chance of success with one against two. Not that Clausewitz draws the lesson from this that the weaker must submit to the law of the stronger. On the contrary, strategy has the task of helping the weaker (the strong can, if need be, dispense with it), of teaching him not to despair, indeed of reminding him of Frederick's example at Leuthen: in some circumstances supreme boldness accords with supreme prudence.

Clausewitz certainly stresses numbers as a factor of victory, even if we accept that, in the notion of inferiority or superiority, he introduces a moral element: the same force, with a Frederick or a Napoleon, imbued with the military spirit, becomes as it were more numerous. The commander and military spirit can compensate for quantitative inferiority, but only within certain limits. Does not the criticism of Liddell Hart retain a certain validity?

It can again be emphasized that the military chapters of the Treatise above all reflect a particular historical experience, even those in which Clausewitz does not explicitly specify that the analyses are only valid for a particular epoque, characterized by a particular armament and organization. Let us also recall the method of mental experiment, the elimination through thought of other factors in success in order to isolate numbers. It is after all not by chance that he comes to isolate numbers after having listed moral factors as if to set up, in all its simplicity, in all its greatness, the antithesis of mind and of matter.

From this comes the reputation of Clausewitz amongst American and English authors: he is seen as representing anti-Lloyd, the strategy of the direct and brutal clash, of the attack of the strong against the strong rather than the strong against the weak; he is thought to be unaware of manoeuvre, stratagem, unexpected movements, the 'indirect approach', to take up the concept (somewhat equivocal) of Liddell Hart. This is the teaching that they attribute to Napoleon's adversary, suggesting an interpretation which is partial, if not erroneous.

Let us try to clarify Clausewitz's thought and his approach before judging it. Superiority or inferiority of numbers, unlike the military virtue of the army, and unlike armament, does not constitute a given fact for the commander. The total number of troops placed at the headquarters' disposal depends on the head of state or the cabinet. But the relation of numbers in a particular combat, in a particular battle, far from falling to the responsibility of the military, remains undecided until the last moment. Strategy consists precisely of ensuring numerical superiority in a certain point, at a certain time. In other words, numbers – or matter – becomes the instrument at the disposal of the mind – the commander; it is tactical success, as we know, which decides everything. In combat or in battle, it is the material force and morale – numbers corrected by moral powers – which, all things being equal, carry the decision. Defined as the use of combats with a view to the final objective of the campaign, strategy thus seeks to exploit the maximum advantage of numbers, therefore it looks everywhere or at least into the whole range of possibilities.

Was there failure to recognize manoeuvre? The meaning of words must be agreed upon. As we have seen, Clausewitz most often reserves the word 'manoeuvre' (and especially 'manoeuvrity') for the conduct of the campaigns of the eighteenth century. But in strategy, the 'use of combat with a view to the ultimate objective of the campaign', he includes the movements of armies, their transfer, the choice of country, the distribution of forces, all that prepares for combat or battle in favourable conditions, all that will

127

have the greatest influence on success. Since it concerns the concentration of force at the opportune place and time, all strategy could be presented as a combination of time and space. Clausewitz does not deny this fact, but he rejects this formulation because it involves an intellectual calculation, always easy as such, whereas the true difficulties, the true talents, belong to another category altogether.

The correct appreciation of their adversary [Daun or Schwarzenberg], the audacity to leave only a weak force for some time opposite him, the energy of the forced marches, boldness in rapid attacks, the augmented activity of great souls in the hour of danger, these are the reasons for victories – and what have these to do with the ability to calculate exactly two such simple things as space and time?

In other words, it is true that strategy governs combat in time and space, but a radically false idea is conveyed when it is presented as a calculation of distances and of durations because this calculation is simple and because the difficulty lies in the qualities required from the commander: correct intuition about the opponent, boldness, energy, in short the free activity of the spirit, one of the elements of the strange trinity.

Superiority in numbers becomes a goal which strategy by its own means endeavours to attain. What are these means? The two chapters which follow on from the above quotations – on surprise and stratagem – provide an answer which is at the least partial and a justification of the criticism of the Liddell Hart school. To begin with, he acknowledges that 'surprise is the basis of all these enterprises'; as a qualification he adds immediately but in very different degrees according to the nature of the enterprise and other circumstances. He continues to claim that it is extremely rare for a state to surprise another by war or by the direction of the whole of its troops. Equally rare are surprises which, during campaigns, yield great results. The effect of surprise requires favourable circumstances: the victory of Bonaparte over Blücher in 1814, when one isolated Prussian unit after another was defeated, depended on placements adopted by Blücher of which Bonaparte was unaware.

What conclusions can be drawn from these scattered remarks? Surprise rarely determines the results of a war of campaign. At the lower level it results above all from the psychological relation between the two parties and from accidental and unforeseen circumstances. The one who impresses the other with his prestige, with his reputation, has the best chance of causing surprise because the effect of surprise seems in turn to be the cause and effect of moral superiority.

Stratagem plays a still lesser role than surprise in Clausewitzian thought. In this respect, the Chinese and the Prussian – Sun-tzu and Clausewitz – are found at opposite poles. The latter recalls the definition of strategy (the regulating of combat with the measures which relate to them) in order to exclude conduct which consists only of words, or declarations. In other passages he does not disregard the importance of public opinion or the morale of the combatants. None the less, he excludes from so-called strategy feigned information, plans and orders, false reports, or at least considers them only of insignificant effect. It may be said that, on the whole, he believes in combat rather than shows of force, in soundness of

128

judgment and energy rather than stratagem (even though it spoils nothing as long as it adds to the other qualities of the leader and does not detract from them).

If he returns to the concentration of forces in space and time after having considered surprise and stratagem, it is because, as Liddell Hart thinks, superiority of forces, a combination of numbers and morale, constitutes the decisive factor and because strategy obeys a supreme imperative: to ensure this superiority. Clausewitz's strategic principles effectively follow from this notion of superiority: the concentration of forces in space and time, not without substantial modifications according to what he considers to be tactics or strategy.

Within the framework of strategy the idea of reserves seems to him absurd, to the extent that it postulates leaving inactive a part of one's forces when the decisive battle is taking place. He believes entirely in the principle of Napoleon – that you can never be strong enough at the decisive point – even if he perhaps pushed its application too far in the Russian campaign. The surplus forces need not entail any inconvenience strategically if they prove to be useless, since the excess forces are not engaged and consequently are not used up. On the other hand, tactically, reserves are indispensable for the progressive engagement of troops – not only to ward off enemy attempts to envelop, not only to redress the situation in case of any unforeseen enemy success at one point or another, but also because of the very nature of modern battle as conceived and described by Clausewitz.

The penultimate chapter of Book III is entitled 'On the Character of Modern Wars'; proceeding from the unfortunately correct idea that wars are becoming national, he concludes that armies are growing larger in proportion to the resources of belligerent states. In the second chapter of the following book, he deals with 'the character of the modern battle'. Now, what emerges from this description? To summarize what seems to me to be the central idea: victory comes to the one who holds out a moment longer than the other, who keeps reserves capable of engagement at the moment of decision: it is a battle (as it were) of attrition which ends, in favourable cases, with the annihilation of the enemy less during the combat itself than as a consequence of it.

If the reader will forgive a lengthy quotation:

> What actually happens in a great battle? A position is methodically occupied with great masses arranged alongside and behind one another. Only a relatively small part of the whole is deployed, and it is left to be worn out for several hours in the fire of the combat, only interrupted from time to time by some smaller activity from bayonet or cavalry charges, which result in some movement in one way or another. When this part of the army has in this way gradually exhausted its warlike ardour and there remains nothing but cinders, it is withdrawn and replaced by another. So the battle burns, with an element of moderation, slowly away like wet powder.
>
> When the veil of night prescribes rest, because nobody can see any longer and neither side wants to be left in the hands of blind chance, they take stock of the remaining masses which can be

129

thought to be effective, that is those which have not yet totally collapsed like extinct volcanoes; account is taken of what has been gained or lost and of the position of the rear's security; these results are joined with the particular impressions of courage and cowardice, of intelligence and stupidity, which are thought to have been observed on the one side or the other, and all these add up to a single, principal impression from which arises the decision: to abandon the battlefield or resume combat on the following?

Of course, Clausewitz immediately adds, the above are the characteristics of great battles rather than of ordinary fighting. In the following chapters, he develops this prescription, taking into account the efforts of both parties to turn their opponent, to protect their reserves from fire. He nevertheless concludes that modern battles have assumed and will keep this character because nations, at the same level of civilization, with the same institutions and art of warfare, have allowed the warlike element, unleashed by conflicts of great interests, to follow its natural paths – the nature of war as such, not subject to moderating factors. Surprising though the proposition may seem at first, this theoretician of the strategy of annihilation conceives attrition by battle as the means of weakening enemy forces before the *coup de grâce*, on the battlefield or during retreat.

French military writers, Camon in particular, have vigorously criticized this prosaic description of Napoleonic battle. Clausewitz, they wrote, understood nothing of Napoleon, who conceived a plan of battle and decided in advance the point at which the principal effort would be made in the attempt to break through. Austerlitz certainly does not accord with the Clausewitzian description. But Eylau or Borodino do not fit any better Camon's description of a Napoleonic battle. Which battles did Clausewitz witness? He witnessed Auerstädt where the Prussians, having a great numerical superiority over Davoût's army, would have gained victory, according to him, if the king, instead of ordering retreat, had engaged the 20,000 men kept in reserve. He was witness to the rout in 1806 in which an army, which was retreating in good order, was swept aside by a defeated force. The losses, more or less equal between the armies during the fight, became enormous, entailing the destruction of the army in retreat.

The second great battle in which Clausewitz took part was Borodino. The man who is supposed to overvalue the role of the commander or genius calmly writes that in the whole battle one found not 'a single trace of an art or superior intelligence'. He notes once more that the forces methodically measured their strength against each other (*ruhiges Abmessen der Kräfte*) and that the balance gradually leant on the side of the more resolute leader and of the more seasoned army. The almost perfect equality of numbers confirms the value of the theory. The Russian army withdrew from the battle undefeated.

Clausewitz also participated, alongside Scharnhorst who was fatally wounded, in the battle which the Germans call Gross Görschen (we speak of Lützen). Napoleon was successful but, for lack of cavalry, the victory bore no fruit as he was unable to destroy the Prussian army. Once again, Clausewitz found, in this, confirmation of the decisive role of numbers and of the thesis that the destruction of the army occurs during retreat rather than in battle. He noted no manoeuvre, no initiative on the part of the commanders.

Finally, as chief of staff to General von Thielmann, he took part in the battle of Ligny on the eve of Waterloo, and on the day following the French disaster he had a hand in the decision to pull back the Prussian corps standing opposite General Grouchy. During the 1815 campaign, what was decisive first and foremost was the decision of Blücher, on the advice of Gneisenau, to move towards Wellington and not towards Namur which seemed the natural line of retreat. That Napoleon was unable to defeat decisively Wellington's army before the arrival of the Prussians was above all due to tactical errors committed by Ney, to a delay of several hours in the start of the battle, to accidental circumstances, to frictions. On both sides, 'all was simple but the simple was difficult'. As for the perseverance of Napoleon in prolonging a lost battle and transforming it into a total disaster, in the vain hope of reversing the decision of fate, Clausewitz takes it as a proof of the very intensity needed in military virtues.

There is a point beyond which perseverance can only be termed folly, of which no critic could approve. In that most celebrated of all battles, that of Waterloo, Bonaparte engaged his last forces to retrieve a battle which could no longer be retrieved. He spent his last farthing and was then forced to abandon both battlefield and Empire, as a pauper.

After 1870, the French readers of Clausewitz saw in such a text proof of the hatred felt by the Prussian towards Napoleon. Admittedly the harshness of the text brings emotions to the surface which are usually withheld. On the critical plane, Clausewitz is right: the battle of Waterloo ended in disaster because Napoleon was unable to bring himself to retreat while there was still time. The only objection that Clausewitz could have made against his own verdict arises from policy. The 'usurper' neither could be satisfied with a half-victory nor could he survive a half-defeat. But such an objection would condemn the return from Elba as well as the perpetration of the battle of Waterloo.

To conclude this section: the propositions relating to the predominant importance of numbers clearly refer to a historical period, characterized by the similarity of armies, of arms and of organization. In such conditions, there alone remain, as factors in victory, moral powers and quantity. The quantitative relation between troops in conflict is not a given fact, it also depends on the commander. It was the line of retreat chosen by Blücher or Gneisenau that resulted in the superiority of the coalition over Napoleon at Waterloo. Energy, the concentration of forces in space or time, often resulted in Napoleon's numerical superiority on the field. The genius of the commander often creates a quantitative advantage, a principle of victory, in the same way that he manages to compensate for numerical inferiority on the field by the military virtue of an army. We should add, nevertheless, that Clausewitz further stresses the importance of large battalions for two reasons. He describes modern battle in such a way that the outcome appears largely to be determined by the wearing down of forces before the *coup de grâce*. He does not scorn the art of strategy and manoeuvre in the wide sense but he hardly believes either in strategic surprise or in the effectiveness of geometrical forms of operation lines. 'We do not hesitate to consider as an established truth that in strategy the number and plenitude of victorious combats are more important than the drawing of great lines by which they are connected with each other.'

4 Military genius, science and natural gifts

Clausewitz enumerates three moral power factors: to the military virtue which the army acquires in combat, and which becomes second nature, is opposed the talent of the commander, popular spirit lying between the two since it must animate the whole but scattered people, and since consequently it presupposes among the partisans some ardour and initiative in the individual. In the army of Frederick or Napoleon each soldier becomes comparable to a fragment of refined metal, to the wheels of a mechanism; in popular insurrection or in mountain warfare, the soldiers, and the commanders of small units, rediscover autonomy, initiative and responsibility.

Of the three moral factors, it is that of the commander which is analysed at greatest length in the Treatise. This is hardly surprising: the theory of large-scale warfare is by definition directed towards the commander, since he, in the current vocabulary of the Treatise, represents both the head of state and the commander of operational forces, hence he is the man who both formulates the plan of war and controls operations. Because he dreamt of becoming commander, because the antithesis of genius and rules was one of the themes of aesthetic theory in his time, Clausewitz, from the 'Strategy' of 1804 until his last years, reflected and wrote much on the part played respectively by nature and education, by sensibility and intelligence among the great leaders. The chapter on military genius deals at length with these two themes: Which men possess the temperament and constitution which affords greatness of action? What knowledge must a gifted man acquire in order to assume effectively supreme responsibility?

First, a few words on the vocabulary. Clausewitz uses the word spirit (Geist) or soul (Seele) to indicate the whole which includes understanding (Verstand) and sensibility (Gemüt) or sentiments (Gefühle). At one point in the analysis, he uses a classification of temperaments (or various types of sensibility) equivalent to that of Kant in anthropology. He distinguishes between individuals of lifeless sensibility, whom he calls phlegmatic or indolent, those in whom sensibility is alive but whose sentiments rarely go beyond a certain strength (he calls them sensitive but timid), those who react quickly and strongly but whose emotions are extinguished as readily as they are inflamed, and finally those who only react slowly but whose sentiments can be both powerful and lasting. It is among the latter, animated with energetic passions, hidden in the depths, that more often than not the great leaders will be found.

What place does the portrait of military genius, in Chapter 3 of Book I, occupy in the general organization of the Treatise? It seems to me that this chapter completes the two preceding ones and that all three contain the totality of guiding ideas and major antitheses. The chapter on the relation between means and ends analyses the intellectual structure of warlike activity; the following chapter, added in his later years (if Schering is to be believed), shows in which concrete conditions the activity of understanding operates. It could, perhaps, more logically have been placed after the four short chapters that now follow it. But one can understand that, having later written or revised the synthetical chapters of the first book, Clausewitz should have retained the short chapters written several years beforehand in the style of Montesquieu.

Be that as it may, the reflection on military genius, constant throughout Clausewitz's itinerary, makes up an integral part of the theory as conceived by both the young officer who examines the qualities of the commander and the inactive general who meditates upon his experience and upon history.

The theory applies to real war and not to geometrical designs or the cabinet's calculations. Now, in real war, the commander, Frederick or Napoleon, has a role which nobody can be unaware of without being blind. Not that Clausewitz sacrifices himself to the cult of the hero: he does not hesitate to criticize Frederick whom he somewhere calls *eigensinnig*, a word to which he gives a pejorative meaning. He does not attribute to military genius a role that is always decisive in victory; he underestimates neither the spirit of the people, nor the military virtue of the army, nor the importance of numbers. If he continues to accord military genius such a role in the theory, it is because the genius embodies the duality intrinsic to military action, it alone unites apparently opposed qualities, it alone resolves the problems whose complexity baffles the greatest minds and thus, in spite of everything, it presents one of the great and noble expressions of humanity.

Clausewitz fights, so to speak, on two fronts: on the one hand against the pseudo-rationalists who claim to reduce strategy, in theory and in practice, to a strictly rational exercise; on the other, against the sabre-rattling hussars who, scorning science, distrust any officer immersed in books. He willingly concedes that the man of study is a different type from the man of action. This banal formula leads to two kinds of consideration, one relatively straightforward: What knowledge is needed by the commander? The other is extremely complex: How are the qualities of mind and sensibility translated in the commander?

The main examples of the first kind of consideration are found in the 'Strategy' of 1804 as well as in Chapter 2 of Book II. The supreme commander has no need (and would find it impossible) to know everything that his subordinates ought to know at the different levels where they operate. He has no use for the knowledge of the engineer who makes bullets and cannon-balls for the simple reason that war is not waged with coal, sulphur, saltpetre, copper or lead but with powder, rifles and cannons. Likewise, in our age, the head of state can remain unaware of the physical laws which explain the working of nuclear arms: he only has to know the effects of these arms, the destruction which they cause. As one progressively rises in the hierarchy, the required knowledge is simplified without becoming easier. The military commander, in so far as he directs, animates, leads the whole, must understand the different arms, the efficacy of each of them, their combinations, the use of fortresses or fortified

133

camps, without besides having to address his mind to the details relating to the construction of the fortifications or to the use of artillery at the tactical level.

At the end of Chapter 2 of Book II, Clausewitz summarizes in a few lines the knowledge required by the commander.

The commander is required to be neither an erudite historian nor a publicist. But he must be familiar with the higher affairs of state; he must know and correctly judge trends, customs, interests affected, questions at issue, dynamic personalities; he need not be a shrewd observer of men, a rigorous analyser of human character but he must [*muss*] know the character, the way of thinking, the habits, the peculiar faults and qualities of those whom he has to [*soll*] command. He need not understand anything about the construction of a carriage or the harness of a battery horse, but he must [*muss*] be capable of judging exactly the duration of the march of a column according to different circumstances.

This last phrase is a striking reminder of the practical scope of these theoretical distinctions. As one rises level by level in the hierarchy, the knowledge required by the commander tends to become simplified, to become transformed. It remains to be determined which elements of knowledge, indispensable at the lower level, must be possessed by the commander.

Let us turn to the divergence between the reality of the combat experienced by the soldiers in 1914 and the picture which had been retained too long by the generals, who were prisoners of ideas formed and hardened into dogma during the years of peace. Let us turn in particular to the peremptory formulae of the first chapter. The political end governs the war, but it is not 'a despotic lawgiver, it must adapt itself to the nature of the means, and is often modified'. The specificity of the war depends on the specific nature of the means. The art of war and the commander are thus justified in requiring that the orientations and the intentions of policy are not in contradiction with these means; now, 'this demand is not a trifling one'.

It is not too difficult to deduce from the knowledge required for virtuosity the type of mind which can meet the demands of the art: whether we concentrate on the intelligible object or on experience, we would choose critical rather than creative minds, those which embrace the whole rather than those which look in one direction alone, cool rather than impassioned heads and, in a fine formula, Clausewitz concludes: 'it is to these to which in time of war we should entrust the welfare of our brothers and children, the honour and safety of the fatherland'.

These lines are found at the end of Chapter 3 Book IV; they conclude the analysis of the military genius, recalling one of the great Clausewitzian themes: warlike activity, at all levels but particularly at the highest, is of an intellectual order or, in other words, requires the participation of an informed understanding. This assertion, necessary to correct the blind pretensions of the swordsmen, is of less significance to him than the other, directed against the armchair strategists – strategists whom German commentators have christened rationalists, i.e. who exaggerate the role of abstract intelligence or who present the decisions of the commander as though strategy were a question of trigonometry. Two sentences, both equally well-known, disclose by their juxtaposition the core of the theory: 'In war everything is simple, but the simplest thing is difficult.' 'Bonaparte was right when he said that many of the decisions which commanders have to face would make problems of mathematical calculation worthy of the powers of a Newton or a Euclid.' This second formula returns in Book VIII. In both cases, it applies to the commander in the exercise of his double function as head of state and head of the armies. It invokes *per contra* the sentence from Book II: the complexity of the equation that the commander must resolve is no less than that of the equations faced by Newton or Euclid, 'but life, despite the riches of its teaching, will never produce another Newton or Euclid, though it may bring forth great calculators like Condé or Frederick the Great'.

In other words, comparison of the calculations of a commander and those of a physicist or mathematician reveals less the similarity than the distinction between them. The similarity arises as the plurality of variables escapes, strict calculation because many of them are of a moral nature and others are unknowns. If, in real war, the calculation of a Condé or Frederick can be called the calculation of probabilities, it is in the sense that we today speak of subjective probabilities; in the midst of a mass of facts and contradictory arguments, the mind grasps intuitively the correct path, that which offers the best chances. The notion of probability serves above all to highlight the uncertainty in which the art of war is exercised, the difficulty of that which appears simple and the simplicity of those decisions which finally resolve mathematically insoluble equations. It is not intelligence alone but the entire soul which undertakes the reply to fate.

In war intelligence must triumph over danger, physical effort, uncertainty and chance. One could just as well say that emotionality must triumph over its four enemies. In fact, understanding only triumphs if enlightened by emotion. The chapters which follow the chapter on military genius are respectively entitled 'Of Danger in War', 'Of Physical Effort in War', 'Information in War'. These correspond exactly to the elements which, in Chapter 3, make up the atmosphere of war (danger, physical effort, uncertainty). Friction covers a wider ground than chance, but the latter is no less an effect and symbol of the whole indicated by the word friction. Having established the two antithetical terms – the atmosphere of war, the role of understanding – Clausewitz seeks to characterize, step by step, the qualities which allow the commander to triumph not over the enemy but over its elements, in other words the qualities of emotional response and character, owing to which understanding remains supreme.

We need not follow in detail Clausewitz's analysis, but I shall refer to some parts of it which to my eyes seem particularly characteristic. Since danger is always near in war, courage (*Mut*) is of the first importance, the original virtue. But courage assumes two forms: courage in risking one's life and courage to take on one's responsibilities, the second scarcer and more precious than the first. As for courage itself, either it is a state of the soul born of the intelligence, of contempt for life, of habit, or it is an emotion, fired by positive motives, ambition, patriotism, enthusiasm of one kind or another. According to the dialectic method, the first kind of courage is more certain because it has become second nature; the second leads further: the former breeds constancy or steadfastness, the latter boldness. The union of the two – which does not constitute a synthesis – creates the most perfect type.

The later stage, in my eyes the most important, takes us from courage (*Mut*) to resolution (*Entschlossenheit*), courage not in the face of physical danger but in the face of responsibility (*Verantwortung*) and, so to speak, in the face of danger of the soul (*Seelengefahr*). Danger, physical effort makes the task of understanding more burdensome. The challenge which understanding must take up is really a moral one: it is the challenge of uncertainty. Courage in the face of danger of the soul has often been called spiritual courage 'because it springs from understanding' though it is not really an act of understanding but an emotional response, a matter of *Gemüt*. Understanding alone is still not courage, for we often see the most intelligent men devoid of resolution. Understanding must therefore first awaken the feelings of courage and be supported and guided by it because feelings sway man more than thoughts at the critical moment.

I have kept the genealogy of resolution (to use one of Clausewitz's expressions) in order to confirm the thesis of a certain rationalism or, if you prefer it, the decisive role of understanding. It is not enough that men easily take decisions for them to deserve to be called resolute: their decisions must undergo reflection and overcome doubt. Resolution is understanding which, being fully aware of the reasons giving rise to doubts, has recognized the necessity of decision and the fatal consequences of hesitation. Resolution is the achievement of solid rather than brilliant brains. *Coup d'œil* in the sense of good judgment and *presence d'esprit* (presence of mind): these French expressions used by Clausewitz are united in resolution and together define what I shall call the virtue of intelligence in the commander.

Proceeding from this, there remains to be determined, by the typical backward and forward movement of the dialectic between understanding and emotion, the qualities of the latter which make possible a *coup d'œil*, presence of mind, resolution, courage in the face of danger to the soul and decision when fully aware of uncertainty. In the 'genealogy', understanding itself inculcated resolution in that it revealed the fatal consequences of hesitation. At the following stage, it is the emotional quality which governs the moral or psychological equilibrium, and is itself conditioned by the supremacy of intelligence which is still ever-present. Energy, steadfastness, constancy, force of sensitivity or character, these are the virtues the commander must possess in order to overcome trials, i.e. the prolongation of combat, the harrowing sight of bloody sacrifices, the many contradictory impressions which beset him; in other words, the qualities of sensitivity remain indispensable for the mind to continue to obey understanding and be governed by it.

It is at this point that there arises the classification of the temperaments to which I have alluded, and which reveals a kinship with the anthropology of Kant. Some temperaments lend themselves better than others to the virtues which benefit the commander. Artists of genius are not created out of any temperament in the same way that military genius presupposes a favourable disposition.

136

A strong sensitivity is not one which is only capable of strong emotion, but one which maintains equilibrium under the influence of the most powerful emotions in such a way that, despite the storms raging within, perception and conviction continue to act with the same subtlety as the needle of a compass in a storm-tossed ship.

Another antithesis is formulated in the second part of the analysis: that between lasting convictions of established principles at any particular moment, and relative circumstances. Nobody can face a storm without a compass: danger, suffering, uncertainty, threaten to cloud judgment, to strengthen doubt, to paralyse resolution; intuition must give understanding the strength to remain faithful to itself and to give it the courage of its carefully acquired convictions which are consolidated by experience. In instances of doubt, to follow one's principles rather than one's impressions, and only to give way when compelled to do so by a clear conviction, is what defines character (in the sense of having character); but constancy degenerates into obstinacy when the commander refuses to recognize his mistake or the facts, not because of intellectual shortcomings but because of the will to be right and to impose his will on others.

The tone of the chapter on military genius differs, it seems to me, from that of Chapter 6 (Book III) on *Kühnheit*, which I would translate as boldness (or daring) rather than as intrepidity. In the one case the emphasis is placed on perspicacity, in the other on the acceptance of risk. Perhaps, as has often been said, the young Clausewitz was inclined towards the one meaning, and the older Clausewitz towards the other. Greatness and confidence of success are contrasted. Whoever aims for great success must run great risks. Clausewitz's particular method does not, however, permit us to discern an evolution of thought between the chapter on boldness and the later chapter on military genius. After all, he lays equal stress in Book III on the increasing role of intelligence; as the soldier rises in the hierarchy, he needs certain intellectual qualities. Nevertheless, boldness (*Kühnheit*) is not amongst the qualities of military genius in Book I, whereas it does seem to assume a central part in Book III. Perhaps the following passage reveals both the constancy of the thought and its nuances:

> When a young man leaps across a deep ravine to show his skill in horsemanship, he is being bold; if he does this to escape from a troop of head-chopping janissaries, he is resolute. The further the necessity is from the action, the greater the number of circumstances which understanding must consider in order to realize the necessity, and by so much the less does necessity reduce the part played by boldness. When Frederick the Great in 1756 saw that war was inevitable and that he could only escape disaster by taking the lead over his enemies, it was necessary but at the same time bold for him to commence war, for few men in his position would have resolved to do so.

In this context, resolution is derived from boldness, hence from a quality of sensitivity; furthermore, in Book I, resolution (*Entschlossenheit*) emanates from an understanding which has become convinced of the urgency of action. In spite of the differences in expression – and Chapter 3 of Book I bears witness to a deeper maturity than Chapter 6 of

137

Book III – the same idea appears here and there with different words. Resolution, courage in the face of responsibility, becomes more difficult and still less dispensable as one goes up the hierarchy. 'Tel brille au second qui s'éclipse au premier.' This saying of Voltaire, which Clausewitz quotes in Book III, expresses the idea in Book I. If he places boldness above all else at the highest level, he none the less requires (also in Book III) that it should not violate the laws of probability and that it should not launch itself in a challenge contrary to nature. 'Boldness directed by a superior [*vorherrschend*] mind is the stamp of the hero.'

The change of vocabulary – the substitution of *Entschlossenheit* for *Kühnheit* – further implies a difference of psychological interpretation, a greater part attributed finally to understanding than to sensitivity in the capacity to face up to fear of the soul. It is not easy to say categorically why. Basically, Clausewitz bears in mind at all times two models, two heroes: Frederick II and Napoleon (or Alexander). In the eyes of Clausewitz it is Frederick who always had the supreme merit of adapting his enterprises to his means, of rising to greatness by wisdom, even brilliantly demonstrating at Leuthen that in certain circumstances supreme boldness becomes supreme prudence. Lacking the means, because of the military organization and spirit of the times, he never launched like Alexander or Napoleon into grandiose enterprises. Leaving the battles of Rossbach and above all Leuthen on one side, he attained his ends in managing to survive, despite his inferiority. In addition, the portrait of the commander must accord with the two antithetical figures of the hero – an accord achieved better in Book I than in Book III.

Still, even in Book III, he does admit:

> Each time that boldness encounters irresolution [*Zaghaftigheit*], the probability of success is necessarily in its favour because irresolution already amounts to a loss of equilibrium. It is only when it launches itself against considered prudence, which one could say is no less bold, and in all events is just as strong and solid as boldness, that it finds itself at a disadvantage.

He adds that such cases are rare; the prudent are usually recruited from the timid. In the same way that, in the 'Strategy' of 1804, he ascribed the successful strategy of Fabius not to lucidity but to temperament, in Book III he always believes that prudence rarely emanates from a superior wisdom. Resolution, taking the place of boldness, also suggests evolution. The subordination of war to policy must have revealed to him the risk of error by excess as much as by default.

5 Military genius and political genius: Frederick and Napoleon

Does the portrait of military genius take into account the dual type of war? Had he completed the schedule which he had set for himself in the Foreword of 1827, would Clausewitz have had to finish or correct the chapters on which I have commented in the preceding pages? With some hesitation and reservation, I would say no to this question.

At the end of Chapter 3, he explicitly requires of the military genius both the wisdom of the statesman and the resolution of the commander – a distinction which confirms the hypothesis that it was written late.

We do not bestow upon Charles XII the title of a great genius: he could not make the power of his arms subservient to a higher vision and wisdom, he did not know how to achieve a brilliant objective. Thus the term, military genius, only applies to the man who possesses at one and the same time the qualities necessary for the free activity of the soul and the qualities necessary for the intelligence of the personified state. The commander becomes statesman but he must not [*darf nicht*] cease to be commander: on the one hand, his vision must embrace all the relations between states; on the other, he must remain fully aware of what he can accomplish with the means at his disposal.

This balance of moral and intellectual forces, of emotionality and understanding, of resolution and prudence, is characterized more than any other by Frederick II. If, in Book VIII, Clausewitz presents Gustavus Adolphus, Charles XII, and Frederick II as new Alexanders, sovereigns of small states wanting to establish great monarchies with their armies of limited size but of qualitative superiority, precursors of Napoleon as regards the risks that can be run in war, this comparison does not remain valid when we turn to consider the virtues of the statesman. The formula of Book VIII, three new Alexanders, ambitious of establishing great monarchies, hardly applies to Frederick; a conqueror he was indeed, but with a view to rounding off his territory: but he did not have in view grandiose objects incompatible with the European balance of power, but an awareness of the need to maintain a reasonable balance between the base of original power and the ultimate end. The historical reality as well as the thought of Clausewitz is better expressed in the text of Book VIII:

Being at the head of a small state, which was similar to any other in nearly every respect, with the exception of some branches of administration, he could not become an Alexander, and if he had acted in the same manner as Charles XII, he would have suffered the same fate and would himself have been dashed to pieces. Consequently, we find in his conduct of the war, a controlled power, always well balanced, that never slackens the pressure, which in the most critical moments rises to astonishing deeds, and the next moment continues to oscillate calmly in subordination to the play of the slightest political influence. Neither vanity, nor ambition, nor the thirst for vengeance could make him turn from this course, and it was this course alone which led him to the fortunate outcome of the contest.

Does not the assertion that Frederick II belongs to the select number of heroes, of military geniuses, suffice to refute Delbrück's interpretation of the dual type of war, and show that the same virtues which raised the commander to greatness in the age of the old monarchy also do so today? The argument deserves close attention. The comparison – both similarities and contrasts – between Frederick and Napoleon is drawn throughout the length of the Treatise: the same spirit in the offensive, the same virtuosity in marches and counter-marches, the same resolution, the same strength of soul, the same capacity to take risks; conversely, the instruments are different, likewise the system of provisioning. Hostilities in the age of Frederick assumed a different spirit, conforming to different customs. Finally and above all, Frederick more often than not found himself in the

139

same situation as that of Napoleon in 1814 as regards the balance of forces. He therefore displayed the virtues of the defender, who resists to the end, who more often than the conqueror prevents his adversaries from attaining their end.

There is no point in taking up again the quarrel between Delbrück and the supporters of the great commander: the differences between the strategy of Frederick and that of Napoleon must be attributed to the balance of forces, to the nature of the instrument or to the type of war. What I find interesting here is that Clausewitz refuses the title of military genius to Charles XII because he overreached himself, whereas he accords Napoleon that title even though he could have reproached him for exactly the same reason. He also finally lost his head in adventure, like Charles XII, though in a different style. I would say that Clausewitz, contrary to what most French commentators have thought, is more indulgent towards Napoleon than his own theory would imply. The determination of ends in terms of a correct estimate of means characterizes, without exhausting it, the political genius of the commander. Using this criterion, which appears the greater, Frederick or Napoleon?

I could go further. Among the campaigns of Napoleon, Clausewitz returned to none more often than the campaign of 1812, and no thesis is sustained with greater insistence than approval of the emperor's plan to conquer Russia. Napoleon had to march straight to Moscow; he was in no position to undertake a methodical campaign, a gradual conquest, or to spend winter quarters at the latitude of Smolensk. Whatever he was, whatever Europe imagined him to be, he had no choice; he would not have changed the disastrous outcome of the adventure by avoiding the secondary errors which he made. The vastness of Russian space was an insurmountable obstacle. Napoleon gambled on Alexander's treating after the fall of Moscow. He did not do so, and the gambler lost his stake because he misjudged his opponent. Now, Clausewitz goes further: the preceding campaigns did not differ in substance from this one. He succeeded before 1812 and failed in 1812 for a simple reason. In the earlier case he was not mistaken, but in the other he was mistaken as to those he was fighting. Thereby he finds kinship with Frederick who, in some circumstances, pushed misreading of reality and scorn of the enemy too far.

The question still remains: Napoleon's career ended in catastrophe; the Spanish resistance and the Russian disaster were foreseeable; why then accord him the political dimension of military genius? Because Napoleon experienced years of glory and fortune? Because he acted for a long time in truly political capacities? Because he continued the age-old aspirations of France for supremacy? Because Clausewitz himself dreams of a new Alexander? Of all these answers the last seems to be excluded because of his conception of the European equilibrium. In truth, Clausewitz (and many Germans after him) was to the end under the fascination of Napoleon, and he never grasped the contradiction between his own definition of the military genius and the genius of Napoleon. The latter lacked, as head of state, the major virtue which assured the ultimate success of Frederick.

This fascination came from the 'perfection' to which the art of war was raised when Napoleon subjected the instrument forged by the Revolution to his imperious will. As a theoretician of war in the narrow meaning of the initial definition, of the pure concept, Clausewitz cannot help admiring the decisive battle and its bloody sacrifices. He denounces in advance those who, in the future, would consider them as 'barbaric' and almost absurd. However, he also writes that most wars between civilized states have mutual observation rather than overthrow as their end. Does the commander need the same qualities in both cases?

Is the answer yes or no? Frederick revealed the same virtues as Napoleon because he boldly seized the initiative in invading Silesia, in starting the war in 1756, in attacking at Leuthen with 30,000 against 80,000 men, because he inculcated his small army with his own will, reserved the force of his soul for the most critical moments, succeeded in overcoming the friction of the machine, and because he could shut off his heart from the sufferings of his soldiers, his ears from their cries. In short, the virtues of the king differed in no respect from those which he analyses in the portrait of the military genius; they do not characterize one type of war or, at least, if they do, they characterize the type which approaches absolute war, according to his concept. But in a war of the second type, the virtues appropriate for absolute war sometimes become necessary.

On two occasions the Treatise mentions the qualities needed for wars of the *ancien régime*, and on two occasions, though in less brutal terms the second time round, he disparages them. In Chapter 16 of Book III, he describes with a condescension tainted with irony the methods followed by the generals during the cabinet wars which did not involve popular participation. This traditional conduct of the war did not rule out a kind of intelligence or astuteness (*Klugheit*). The game was more varied and more prolonged: 'The game of hazard played with gold coins changes into a game of commerce with pounds, shillings and pence.' He derides the theorists who see as the height of the art only feints, parries and quarter thrusts as if this tame war assured the triumph of mind over matter, whereas recent wars marked a relapse into barbarism. Such an opinion is as frivolous as the object to which it relates. Where great forces and great passions are wanting, it is easier for an agile intelligence to show its skills. But is not the command of great forces, the navigation of ships in the midst of tempest and raging seas, a higher exercise of the mind? Does the captain summon up the whirlwind just so as to have the opportunity of bringing his virtuosity into action?

The swordsman must, of course, fear that his opponent will arm himself with a sword. Therefore, 'woe to the cabinet which, with a half-hearted policy and a limited art of war, confronts an opponent who, in principle obeys only the laws intrinsic to himself.' Clausewitz never expressed the complementary idea: woe to the man who, in a system of equilibrium between states, unleashes the whirlwind.

In Chapter 30 of Book VI, in the course of dealing with the defence of an indecisive theatre of operations, in other words when analysing the military operations in the second type of war, he considers the qualities of the commander involved, not in a test where everything is at stake, but in a battle of skill (*Kampf der Geschicklichkeit*). He recognizes that intelligence plays a greater role when there are many combinations in time and space instead of a single act, a great battle. The strategy of manoeuvre, where there is a balance of forces, because activity is reduced to minor operations, proportionate to moderate ends, gives free reign and a dominant importance to astute calculation (*kluge Berechnung*). If the latter gains importance at the expense of chance on the one hand, it gains on the other at the expense of the virtues of the soul attributed to the military genius, courage, strength, resolution and composure. Now, these virtues also, in certain circumstances, limit the influence of chance. It is not astuteness and skill which master the violence of the elements at times of great decisions, but the virtues of the soul, the *élan* of the mind which immediately sees through a difficult situation, the great impulses which raise men above themselves, in short understanding animated by sentiments, or feelings enlightened by the perception.

Up to this point, the text of Book VI, although less scornful of the 'virtue of skilfulness', expresses ideas which are similar to those of Book III. That aspect of the strategy of manoeuvre has been given a false importance. But on the following page, Clausewitz presents contemporary war, the war introduced by the Revolution and perfected by Napoleon, as being just as historically conditioned as cabinet wars. Cabinets had made the mistake of thinking that the ways of their time were eternal; contemporaries may well be making a similar mistake if they think that the wars of the future will all have the same character – whether Napoleon's wars or the knife attacks of savages. To see in fencing, in the duel with buttoned foils, or in the game of balanced forces, the expression of a culture or a superior art is to sin against logic and philosophy. But the opposite idea, according to which the game of war definitely belongs to the past, reveals a lack of thought or, in non-Clausewitzian terms, a lack of historical sense.

Of the new phenomena in the art of war, very few should be attributed to new inventions or to new intellectual tendencies; most arise from new situations and social relations. The latter, having emerged during the crisis of a society in upheaval, must not be taken as a norm either; one cannot doubt therefore that many of the methods of war of the past will appear again.

Decisive and indecisive hostilities therefore form two historical types on the same level, although the first type is closer to the absolute concept and is the only one which allows military genius to display its entire virtuosity. Moreover, on the following page, Clausewitz goes as far as refusing to say whether Daun's or Frederick's method is better – whether extension and careful choice of position or concentration of the army, instant readiness for improvisation or constant harassing the enemy.

The two methods did not only derive from nature but also from circumstances; improvisation is easier for a king than for a commander who is responsible to a superior. Let me once more stress that criticism has no right to consider the different ways or methods of attaining levels of unequal perfection, to subordinate one to the other: they must be equated, and in each case their use must be left to judgment.

Taken literally, this text reveals that Clausewitz's thinking was in the direction of historical relativism, whereas most texts (in particular in Books III and IV) show him to be in a different light, glorifying wars of annihilation, the only real wars, and the only wars which conform to the

142

concept. Can Daun's method be put on the same level as that of Frederick when, according to the text of Chapter 3 (B), Book VIII, it was he more than anyone else who enabled Frederick to attain his will, such that Maria Theresa failed to attain her end? Of course, in this latter text, too, he states that according to the ideas of the time General Daun 'must have been considered a great commander' because criticism accepted 'greatness and perfection of all kinds'. But here he himself rejects this sort of criticism which neglects the beginning and end of the war, in other words what gives a meaning, a *raison d'être* to the hostilities themselves.

What is lacking in the Clausewitzian analysis? It is any explicit discrimination between historical and transhistorical criteria. The modes of conducting war are historically conditioned, the expression of the ideas and institutions of each specific time; the ways in which operations are conducted cannot be organized in a hierarchy at whose apogee are the fencing flourishes so dear to cabinet wars, the rationalists and humanitarians, and the brutal shock of the épée, the clashes of peoples. But, in each age, whatever the instrument, one wins (and therefore attains his end) and the other loses. Within a type of war, within a given way of fighting, one side is better than the other. To justify any refusal to put Frederick above Daun we should have to say either that Frederick was superior to his age or that, between a general responsible to the sovereign and a commander who is at the same time a head of state, comparison is unfair. Clausewitz puts forward these two ideas but he never manages to discriminate explicitly between historical and transhistorical criticism. Nor did Montesquieu, who condemned slavery and the arms race only in eloquent or ironically striking passages.

Chapter 6

Defence and Attack

Clausewitz introduces the concepts of defence and attack for the first time in paragraph 16 of Chapter 1 (Book I) in order to make us understand why, in (by and large) rational conduct of war, hostilities are sometimes suspended. Why do both adversaries have an interest, at the same time, in waiting? Polarity, to use Clausewitz's concept – what one gains, the other loses – seems to involve, logically, a continuity of operations. Of course, Clausewitz could have accounted for the lack of continuity by friction, by men's weakness, by the shortage of information, or by one or other of the concrete circumstances which differentiate abstract natural war and real wars. He believed he had found a cause, in that 'warlike activity is divided into two forms which, as we shall show in depth in the following, are very different and of unequal force. Polarity exists in relation to the object common to both, namely the decision. But not where attack and defence are themselves concerned'. These sentences give rise to two essential themes: on one hand, reciprocity of action between attack and defence (if one attacks, the other defends); and on the other hand, the asymmetry (or non-polarity) of these two forms due to the superior force of defence.

A little further on, at the start of the second chapter of the same book, the distinction between attack and defence is introduced at the end of the analysis upon which I have already commented, and which considers the means of increasing the improbability of success and the cost of the fight for the adversary.

The last means envisaged, the third way (*der dritte Weg*), seeks to wear out the adversary. It is not, Clausewitz indicates, a metaphorical question; to wear out the enemy is to bring about the gradual exhaustion of his physical forces and his will. To hold out longer than him, we have to make do with ends that are as limited as possible and, at the extreme, to stage simple resistance, 'combat with no positive intention'. Such negativity can only lead to pure passivity, contrary to the very concept of war, but resistance, in such a case, has no end other than to inflict heavier losses on the enemy than those which one's own side suffers.

Here Clausewitz uses the notion of negative intention, linked with the notion of defence, to point to an act of war, a combat which has no end other than to prevent the enemy from attaining his own end. Whoever intends to wear out the enemy – that is to say, to defeat him by holding out longer – must limit risks; if greatness and certainty of success are inversely proportional to each other, if only small successes can be certain, the side which seeks victory by attrition will compensate for the limits of each success by the overall number of successes; in other words, it will gamble

144

on a continuation of hostilities. It is at this point that Clausewitz for the second time draws the distinction between attack and defence which governs the entire range of war.

This second reference leads us to equally important themes and concepts; positive or negative intention; the contradiction between the size of victory and security; a method of defence; and pure resistance (*Widerstand*) by the side with inferior forces. The strategy of Frederick II in the final stage of the Seven Years' War provides the example cited several times of this method of defence, with the minimum of activity or of positive aims.

This theme is central to Clausewitzian thought, and is the subject of Books VI and VII, the latter remaining in draft form, as it was in 1827, at the time of the writing of the Foreword. The sixth book, by far the longest of the Treatise (almost a quarter of the whole), is today considered the least interesting because it deals at length with military and even technical questions: defence of mountains, rivers, forests and marshes. It also contains well-known chapters, e.g. the sixth, on arming the people and the guerilla fighter.

In his final note, Clausewitz speaks of Book VI with a severity that is at first surprising. Book VI, he writes, must be considered as simply an essay (*Versuch*). 'I would have entirely revised [*umarbeiten*] it and I would have sought the way out [*Ausweg*] in a different manner.' The translation of this sentence lends itself to discussion. In the French text, *Versuch* becomes *esquisse* (sketch). Can one call thirty chapters, which altogether take up more than 200 pages and which number amongst the most developed of the Treatise, a sketch? Clausewitz considers that this essay about a theory of defence is not yet in shape. There is another more serious difficulty: what should be understood by *Ausweg* ('way out')? Do we translate *Ausweg* as 'conclusion'? Does Clausewitz intend to follow another path to arrive at the object (as is suggested by the words *anders den Weg suchen*)? In other words, what is it that dissatisfies him, the premises of his ideas, the order followed or the arguments raised?

To my knowledge, none of the commentators, even the most erudite and inclined towards philosophical reflection, has devoted a rigorous and detailed study to these problems. Rosinski, in the article cited earlier, attached much importance to this passage of the final note since he reproached General von Cammerer with having adopted the argument of Book VI to justify the thesis of the superior force of the defence, an argument which Clausewitz would have explicitly rejected – and which seems to me, from the facts before us, an unfounded assertion. The final note mentions, amongst the clear propositions, the one according to which defence is the form of war with the most negative end. The dialectic and the asymmetry of attack and defence certainly remain valid for Clausewitz, even in the last stage of his thought. Therefore what would the revision of the whole have entailed? What would have been the way out or the route followed?

I would not claim to unravel the riddle but to set the problem: if we accept that the revision of the first two books dates from after 1827, what calls for revision in Book VI in terms of the final development of Clausewitz's thought? In order at least to hypothesize, I have adopted the following method: I shall begin by stating, as rigorously and as systematically as possible, the guiding ideas of Book VI as they appear to me; I shall next seek to find faults which become apparent from the text itself, in relation to Clausewitz's requirements of analysis and exposition; and finally, I shall examine whether the revision, as far as we can predict, would have involved the order, the putting into shape or the modification of some of the principal arguments.

1 The dialectic of defensive and offensive

Book VI is divided into three sections. The first, containing the first nine chapters, has the most abstract character. It defines the concepts, the reciprocal action of defence and attack, the different tactical and strategic levels — battle, theatre of operations and war — in which this dialectic comes into play, and finally the elements of the strength of defence and of the diversity of methods of resistance. In this first part, the thesis of the superiority of defence is established both in the abstract and by reference to historical experience. In the second section, Clausewitz studies in detail some of the means of defence (fortresses, defensive positions), the utilization of natural obstacles (mountains, rivers, forests, marshes) and likewise some strategic operations (flank position, action on the flank, retreat to the interior of the country, arming of the people). The whole of the last four chapters seems to seek to define defence according to which kind of decision the theatre of operations involves. In Chapter 1, Book I, both attack and defence are shown to lead to a decision; Chapter 30, Book VI, studies at length what happens when neither of the belligerents seeks a decision; the last two chapters (29 and 30) clearly thematically approach the Foreword of 1827 and Book VIII.

The first and last sections are of especial interest. Supposing that some of the technical analysis, strategic or tactical, had appeared imperfect to Clausewitz, only a specialist military historian would be in a position to see the points at which the self-criticism might have been directed. On the other hand, since we know that Clausewitz's thinking at the end of his life concerned the essential nature of war, the relation between concept and reality, the intervention of policy into the detail of military operations, the desire to effect a revision (assuming that this went beyond better presentation) was probably aimed at sections 1 and 3, where the main difficulty occurs. What should you say about war as such once you have realized that it is not modified by policy, but is itself an act of policy?

Without forcing ourselves to follow the order of the presentation of Books VI and VII, let us try to establish as clearly as possible, while respecting the vocabulary of the author, the principal propositions of the first section of Book VI.

How should defence be defined? By its aim? In this case it consists of waiting (*abwarten*). A passive waiting, doing nothing, which would not lead to an attack (for that would inflict a setback), would no longer be part of war: defence, according to the concept, repulses (*abwehren*) the attacker or resists him. Clausewitz does not use the two words *abwehren* and *Widerstand* indifferently. The first is the more general and apposite. It signifies the act which effectively opposes the attack, thus the act which faces it, which brings about a setback. To repulse an assault, to ward off a blow, allows the end of defence to be attained, namely to keep or to preserve.

Clausewitz apparently uses three notions to define defence, They are repulsing, waiting and preserving, the first being concept (*Begriff*), the second characteristic (*Merkmal*) and the third goal. In reality, according to him, the first notion – repulsing – is tantamount to preserving, and implies the second, waiting. He returns in Chapter 8 to the unbreakable link between repulsing and waiting; he emphasizes the extreme importance of the latter concept, never before elaborated by the theoreticians. He does not conceptually distinguish defence and defensive, but defence must mean action according to space, countryside, or theatre of operations, and defensive means position, according to time, war, the campaign or the battle. To defend oneself is to leave to the other the initiative of the attack (or of the offensive), to wait with a view to repulsing him.

From these initial definitions there follow two apparently divergent consequences which in reality are compatible and even complementary. The concept of attack is itself a complete concept.

Defence cannot be thought of without counterattack [*Rückstoss*]; the latter is a necessary part of defence. The same cannot be said of attack; the blow or the act of attacking is in itself a complete [*vollständig*] concept, but defence is not a necessary part as such, though space and time, to which attack is linked impose defence on it as a necessary evil.

Defence is thus doubly complex: waiting is part of defence since the attacker has the initiative and since the defence thus results, initially, from the introduction by Clausewitz of the concept of waiting. On the other hand, defence in the full meaning of the word implies that the blows which are received are returned in a later phase and that it is not enough to ward them off. Defence is only successful when the blows are returned with the counterattack.

There emerges from this analysis, it seems to me, a distinction between the two concepts of defence: the more general and stricter concept would be defined by the act of repulsing the attack or of warding off the blows, whereas waiting for an attack is an act intended to preserve. The attacker, having reached the zenith of victory, will no longer have sufficient forces at his disposal to continue his venture, and will thus be reduced to the defensive: he waits, and prepares to repulse the counterattack of the defender with whom he has changed roles. Defence, as a complete concept, waits for or wards off the blows with a view to returning them. Attack in fact always comprises elements of defence, but of a weak defence because it evolves in conditions which lack all its principles of efficacy.

The second inference drawn from the definitions of attack and defence is that the latter always has priority; in reality it is clear that attack determines defence and vice versa. The trial of strength and will, characteristic of war or even, more generally, all conflicts, requires the attacker to attain his ends. It remains to be decided which of the two concepts should be selected as the point of departure.

The answer given by Clausewitz, which delighted one of his most illustrious readers, Lenin, is one formulated on two occasions, with several pages in between: that defence should be taken as the point of departure, not attack.

147

War is imposed upon the defender rather than the conqueror for it is invasion by the latter which brings about defence and, at the same time, war. The conqueror always likes peace (as Bonaparte constantly claimed); he would willingly peacefully invade our state; to prevent him from doing this, we must be ready and also prepare for war; in other words: it is precisely the weak, restricted to the defensive, who must [sollen] always be ready and not allow themselves to be taken by surprise. This is what is required by the art of war.

Clausewitz does not jest, even though Lenin considered this remark as having been made in jest, and though his followers have offered much proof of a love of peace, superior yet similar in style to Napoleon's. The choice of the point of departure follows from the very concepts, or rather from the objectives of the two actions. If attack leads to conquering, it does not contain within itself the idea of war or contest; it has, as its end, the taking of possession.

If we think philosophically about the origins of war, the proper concept of the latter is not born in attack because this has as its absolute end not so much the struggle as the taking of possession. It is born in defence, for this has struggle as the immediate end, because repulsion and struggle are manifestly the same.

Is this a conceptual game? Does the order of the two notions entail theoretical or praxological consequences? Conquering and preserving are opposed, word for word, only to the extent that conquest is tantamount to the taking of possession of any object. As military operations progress spatially, Clausewitz implicitly confuses in his initial definitions the intention or positive goal with invasion of the other's space. According to him, the side which is more advanced in preparation appears first in the theatre of operations. It is the respective state of preparation of the belligerents rather than offensive or defensive intention which determines entry into the theatre of operations. It is nevertheless true that, strategically, attack is carried out by movement towards the territory of the enemy state. Taking of possession of space becomes the goal of attack.

A defender, as described in Chapter 5 of Book VI, with fortresses, an army and a commander, thus lays down the first laws of the war; he forces the attacker to establish his plan in terms of the interior preparations of his enemy. The defender at the same time retains the advantage of playing second. According to this analysis the temporal priority of defence over attack has praxological implications. In the reciprocal action, by nature undefined, the defender benefits from the double advantage of starting the war and of being the last to lay his cards on the table.

This summary and these initial analyses enable us to perceive several kinds of complementarity and asymmetry between the concepts and the acts which they indicate. Defence calls for attack in order to become a complete concept in terms of the very nature of war: it would be contrary to the nature of war to receive blows without returning them. Attack calls for defence, not in the abstract but in the real world, because it takes place in time and space and progressively loses the superiority upon which it is based. Attack seeks to conquer, not to fight; only defence has struggle as its immediate and absolute end. There is necessarily a reciprocal action

148

between attack and defence once the action has commenced: each wants to realize his intention, positive if conquering, negative if preserving. The negative intention is defined by the negation, the annihilation of the positive intention of the attacker. That the latter does not conquer what he wanted to conquer, and the defender has at the same time realized his intention, is a formulation which, as such, in these first chapters, Clausewitz does not consider sufficient to conform with the concept of war.

A final dialectic and the most important one is the relation of contrary concepts with incessant transitions from one to another, and it follows from the dimensions in space and time of what the defender wants to preserve, territory, theatre of operations, field of battle. Once we postulate that defence is derived from the position of waiting adopted by one of the sides, that the defender awaits the attacker in front of his position, in his theatre of operations, or in his territory, it becomes clear, looking from a different point of view, that every defence involves elements of attack. Across his territory, in the theatre of operations, or on the battlefield, the defender in turn uses the method of attack or that of defence. The whole totality of defensive war involves offensive combats. The combat or battle involves defence and attack. It is the waiting for the attacker on one's own soil – territory, theatre of operations or battlefield – which is the essential element of defence. When the other element – action – survives, defence tends to dissolve into attack or the distinction becomes blurred.

In a defensive campaign one can therefore carry out offensive actions, in a defensive battle one can use some of one's divisions offensively, and when simply in place to face an enemy assault, one can launch artillery attacks. The defensive form of the conduct of war is thus not a shield created by skilful blows.

These relations, partly conceptual and partly real, introduce the formula, or rather the two formulae, which summarize the relative force of defence and attack. According to the final note, defence is the stronger form with the negative aim, and attack is the weaker with its positive end. According to the text of Chapter 8 (Book VI), defence is the stronger form of war because it can more certainly bring victory over the adversary (*die stärkere Form des Krieges, um den Gegner um so sicherer zu besiegen*). These two formulae apparently contradict each other, the latter being more in accord with defence than the former. If defence, the stronger form, leads more surely to victory it enjoys the combined advantages of security and greatness of success. Assuming that it faithfully expresses Clausewitz's thought it only applies to the total concept of defence which integrates not only action or counterattack but the decision as well. It cannot apply to defence in the narrow meaning of the word, which is satisfied by waiting or repelling.

Why is defence the stronger form of war? Clausewitz gives two arguments of a general character which, in his eyes, are clear features. The first is that it is easier to preserve than to take. That applies in time of war as in lawsuits: *beati sunt possidentes*. The second reason results both from experience and from reasoning. Does not history reveal that the weaker side almost invariably chooses the defensive? Is this not proof that this form tends to compensate for inferiority and that it is thus inherently stronger than the other? Furthermore, if attack, which seeks a positive end were at the same time the stronger form, why would one of the sides ever remain on the defensive? If the one is resigned to a negative end, to prevent the other from attaining his ends, it is because, in waiting for the enemy and in repulsing him, he is counting on gradually reaching the point when the relation of forces will be reversed.

Beyond these two arguments, which make good sense, Clausewitz moves on to analyses which, though not self-contradictory, lack a rigorous organization and were, perhaps, written at different times. We can distinguish Chapters 2, 3 and 4, a comparison of the respective advantages of attack and defence, by means of a description of the factors which affect each form differently. Chapters 6 and 8, on the range of means of defence and methods of resistance, make use of a slightly different vocabulary (means on the one hand, types or methods of resistance (*Widerstandsarten*) on the other). Not only does Clausewitz draw a distinction between the different types of resistance, but he also discovers two types of reaction, two sorts of decision, according to whether the cause of the attacker's defeat lies in the sword of the defender or in his own efforts. The way matters are presented suggests that Clausewitz (whose German disciples really extracted a doctrine of out-and-out offensive for a victory of annihilation) was little interested in the offensive in the Treatise, since as the only principle, it offered little material for analysis.

The analytical proof of the superior strength of the defensive first requires a description of the causes or factors which affect the outcome of a battle, campaign or war and whose influences vary according to the chosen form, offensive or defensive. Clausewitz finds three of these factors at the level of tactics, six at the level of strategy. The three factors which affect the results of tactics – the factors unaffected by the choice of attack and defence being excluded – are (a) surprise, (b) advantage of the lie of the land or terrain (*Gegend*) and (c) attack launched simultaneously from different sides. From the strategical point of view three more factors are added: (d) support from the theatre of operations due to fortresses and everything that goes with this, (e) support by the people, (f) the use of the great moral forces.

In the Treatise, devoted to war on a large scale, Clausewitz only peripherally touches upon tactical problems, where the strategic analysis cannot be completed without reference to a combat which finally decides everything. Tactically, the attacker would benefit a little from the first and third principles of victory, but not at all from the second. The side taking the offensive benefits from the advantage of the surprise attack of the whole on the whole (of strength against strength). However, the defender can in the course of combat constantly surprise by the form and force of his attacks. Finally, it goes without saying that the defender has the advantage of terrain because it is he who has chosen the site.

In Book 6 Chapter 2 what seems to me more intrinsically interesting than these passing remarks, is the study of the successive changes of defence and attack, according to the popular model of the contest of armour and sword. In the Thirty Years' War and the war of the Spanish Succession, deployment and disposition of the troops were of the essence. As a general rule, the defender had the advantage as he was the first to carry out these operations. The advantage disappeared when the attacker acquired the ability to manoeuvre. The defender regained superiority by sheltering behind mountains, rivers and deep valleys. This superiority of the defender disappeared yet again when the attacker acquired a mobility and a skill which enabled him to expose himself on broken (or uneven) terrain, and to attack in separate columns. As a result, the attacker could turn the defender. So the latter was compelled to stretch his lines more and more thinly. The attacker regained superiority as he succeeded in breaking these lines by concentrating his forces on a small number of points. During the last war (that is to say, the wars of the Revolution and Empire) the defence again adapted itself to this new style of attack; it, too, concentrated undeployed, covered masses who were ready to parry any action taken by the attacker as it occurred. For all that, partially passive defence of the terrain is not excluded; it offers too many advantages not to occur many a time in the course of a campaign, but it is no longer generally the main feature.

Clausewitz therefore opposes the idea that a battle once accepted, and therefore of a defensive nature, is already half lost, but as a tactician he is far from the doctrinaires of the offensive at all costs. Moreover, such a text reveals the best side of Clausewitz's mind, the permanent value of the lessons he gives us: antidogmatism, a sense of history and the constant reviewing of methods. The doctrinal theses which put forward the tactical superiority of defence or attack arise from an unjustified generalization of a moment which is transitory in the art of war.

But, it will be said, if there is no permanent superiority of attack or defence in the field of battle tactics, why should there be in the field of strategy?

The answer, which Clausewitz did not explicitly formulate seems to me to be as follows. Most of the advantages which benefit defence – the choice of terrain, the support of the people, the wearing down of the attack – are not or are only marginally affected by historical changes. On the other hand, attack and tactical defence, in a constant dialectic, are each ensured of superiority in turn. The invariability of strategic principles does not contradict the radical originality of each constellation – an originality which excludes any dogmatic teaching; in the same way the mutability of tactical methods does not at any given time, prevent teaching based upon constants.

Of the three principles of victory, the second, the terrain, lies in strategy on the side of the defender supported by two others: fortresses and the theatre of operations generally, and the support of the people. If the defender has allowed the attacker to advance, the latter will be fighting in hostile country, and when the attack has exhausted the forces available the attacker will have to take the offensive in the most unfavourable conditions. Two other principles remain to be considered: surprise and concentric attack.

It is hardly necessary to say that, in the period which separates the writing of the Treatise and the writing of this book, these two principles have played a historically decisive role. 'A surprise attack [*Überfall*] in strategy has often ended an entire war at one go. Yet it must again be stressed that the use of this means can assume, on the part of the enemy,

151

serious, decisive and rare mistakes.' It is more important, therefore, in certain circumstances, in strategy rather than in tactics. In strategy, no less than in tactics, concentration of forces belongs to the attacker alone. By choosing his position carefully, the defender has every chance of seeing the attacker appear in front of him in order to wage battle. Even the attacker will have to split his forces because of supply problems, and the defender will then be in a position to attack, with massed forces, a fraction of the forces of the attacker. The third principle, which can be analysed in greatest depth in strategy, is the principle of attack from several sides, in other words the role attributed to the movements of troops in order to turn, to envelop and to encircle the enemy. At this point Clausewitz rediscovers the classical controversies about outer and inner lines, about the eccentricity of defence and the convergence of attack. He returns several times to this series of problems.

Principles (d) and (e) – support from the theatre of operations and support by the people – clearly favour the defender. Fortresses, rivers and mountains slow down movement, and thus check the attacker who wholly relies on speed and momentum leading to victory. The people, unless they receive the attacker with sympathy, being hostile to their state or to their princes, inevitably assist defence, at the very least by the creation of a propitious environment and by the information which they offer, and in extreme cases by arming themselves and taking part in small-scale war-fare.

As regards the last principle, the use of moral forces, Clausewitz recognizes that it favours the attacker at first; elsewhere he even asserts that it favours the attacker for the most part. But, in Chapter 3, he concludes the review of the six principles with the following lines:

> Moreover, there remains to be stated a secondary [klein] principle which we have not yet considered. This is courage, the feeling of superiority which the army, aware of belonging to the attacking side, experiences. In itself the idea is genuine but this feeling soon disappears in the more general and stronger feeling which inspires an army in its victories and defeats, the skill or incapability of its commander.

It seems to me to be proper to divide these principles into three categories: the first, which we shall properly call 'strategic', encompasses surprise and envelopment, in other words the movements of troops by which each side attempts to surprise the enemy by concentrating its forces at a certain point; or movements by which each side attempts to join battle in conditions most favourable for the scope for and security of success and for the exploitation of the victory. In this chapter, Clausewitz hits upon classic controversies, both of his own and later ages, about operation lines.

The second category involves the material means used by the defender to raise obstacles for the attacker, whether the means are provided by nature (mountains, rivers, marshes) or prepared by man (fortresses).

The third category includes moral forces, whether of the people when roused to greater or lesser activity by the attacker, or of the army, initially borne by lust for conquest but soon worn down by the trials of the venture as it runs into difficulties.

It is relatively easy to explain Clausewitz's principal ideas by organizing, as I have just done, the list of principles for victory in a different way from in Chapters 3 and 6 of Book VI. But these two chapters have a strictly analytical or abstract character: Clausewitz draws out the consequences from the nature of the thing or from the thing itself (*Natur der Sache, Sache selbst*). The propositions which are reached at the end of these analyses are not only generally true, 'all things being otherwise equal', but even in isolation. The defender normally has the advantage of terrain since he has chosen it, but the decision and the timing from then on belong to the attacker. It can happen that the attacker besieges fortresses and thereby forces the sending of a relief army and this passes over to positive action. In other words, we must always beware of considering analyses as valid bases for precepts when they are based both on concepts and historical examples but only partially. The theoretical analysis of attack and defence is by itself no more praxological than the economic analysis of supply and demand.

2 Types of resistance; flank positions; the two types of war

In the first section of Book VI, Chapter 8 stands out by itself. It deals with a subject taken up in the last section of the book, beginning at Chapter 27. It analyses not defensive means in the abstract or separately, but the types of resistance.

By defence (or defensive), Clausewitz means, at the highest level of abstraction, the attitude of the party which intends to hold on to what it possesses, its armed forces, its territory, its state. If the object of attack appears to aim specifically at the conquest of space, defence generally comes down to the preservation of territory. Arising from the fact that military operations take place and evolve in space, defence often entails the sacrifice of a part of territory in order to postpone the moment of battle.

Resistance (*Widerstand*) lies at a less elevated level of abstraction; it encompasses the whole of actions, possibly including partial or local attacks, aimed at the proper end of the defensive conduct of the war. Consequently, Clausewitz contrasts the means of defence (analysis of the separate means in order to consider them one after another) with the types of resistance, distinct methods of strategy.

According to W.M. Schering, Chapter 8 ('Types of Resistance') must have been taken from a very old version of the Treatise (the Coblenz version). Leaving aside arguments based on manuscripts of which we do not know and probably never shall, the style here and there resembles that of the short chapters of Book I which Schering likewise attributes to the same period. For example, the style of the formulae, both concrete and abstract, gives certain passages a strange and almost savage beauty:

> It is not the great number of unassailable positions which one
> comes across everywhere, nor the terrifying sight of the dark
> mountainous mass which hangs over the theatre of war, nor the
> wide river which passes through it, nor the ease with which some
> combinations of actions actually paralyse the muscle destined to
> knock out our strength – these things are not the cause of the
> success often achieved by the defender without shedding blood: the
> cause is found in the weakness of the will with which the attacker
> hesitatingly takes a step.

The idea as well as the style suggests that it is a relatively old text. Not

153

that the idea expressed – it is the weakness of the will of the attacker which allows the defender to succeed without fighting, by straightforward strategic combinations – does not survive in the final state of thought, but in this form it dates from before the realization of the plurality, of the historic heterogeneity of wars, wars resulting from minor tensions being no less wars than those which approach absolute war. Clausewitz already recognized the political conditioning of wars, but not the penetration of the whole of the act of war by policy. He still expresses himself as if war was becoming incomplete (*Halbding*) owing to the multiplicity of political considerations that it involved. The tone of scorn in respect of this *Halbding*, of these strategic combinations without blood being shed, is more in line with Clausewitz's mood following the Napoleonic epic than with his state of mind in the last period.

Moreover, some phrases of this chapter seem to be almost incompatible with the contents of the preceding chapters. Thus, in the middle of the chapter, he suddenly writes:

> We hope in this way to have covered and weighed up the whole field of defence. It is true that there remain enough sufficiently important subjects in defence to create separate sections, in other words to become the focal point in systems of ideas which we must also study – the nature and influence of fortresses, of entrenched camps, of the defence of mountains and rivers, of flank action, etc. We shall deal with these in the following chapters, but all these subjects do not appear to us as outside the series of notions which we have just considered; they are merely a more detailed application to places and to circumstances. This series of notions has been extracted for us from the concept of defence and its relation with attack; we have linked simple notions with reality and have thus shown by which route one can return from reality to these simple notions and thus establish a solid foundation which protects our reasoning from the constraint of seeking refuge in supposed fixed points which themselves float in the air.

While he did not mention fortresses or mountains in Chapter 8, he did consider them in preceding chapters, namely 2 and 6, among the principles favourable for defence. Had he rewritten Chapter 8 after the preceding chapters, he would not presumably have written that he had omitted these natural or artificial obstacles but would have noted that he had already mentioned them.

At the start of Chapter 27, Clausewitz writes:

> We might perhaps have been content to speak of the most important means of defence and only touched upon the manner [*die Art*] in which these means are linked to the whole of the war plan in the last book, where we consider the war plan; for not only does every secondary plan of attack and defence follow the war plan and is broadly determined by it, but also in many cases the war plan itself is nothing other than the offensive or the defensive in the principal theatre of war.

On the point of devoting three chapters to the defence of a decisive theatre of operations followed by a long chapter on the defence of an indecisive theatre of operations, he expresses himself as if Chapter 8 did

154

not exist, as if all the previous chapters dealt exclusively with the means of defence, each analysed separately. Chapter 8, which has in mind synthetically the types of resistance, which distinguishes the two principal types, which demonstrates the penetration of the principle of waiting across the whole system of thought, anticipates Chapters 27 and 30 which do not take it into account.

Can the opposite hypothesis be formulated, namely that Chapter 8 was added later? This hypothesis seems to me at the least improbable. The style and the content characterize an earlier period, 1823–6, if not 1816–18. Moreover, the vocabulary and the themes of Chapters 27–30 approximate to those of Book VIII, written later, to such a point that doubt becomes impossible. The last chapters of Book VI mark the transition from the analysis of the means of defence to the synthetic study of types of resistance (or of the defensive), a study which in itself marks a transition towards the war plan.

The precise theme of Chapter 8 as presented by Clausewitz confirms this interpretation.

> In order to determine notions in terms of a simple subject, we put to one side, until the chapter concerning war plans, the case of the defence of a country in which a greater diversity and a greater influence of political conditions come into play; from another point of view, the act of defence of a position or in a battle is a subject of tactics, a subject which only forms the basis of strategic activity when taken as a whole; this is why the defence of a theatre of operations is the subject which allows us to show the conditions of the defensive in the best manner.

In other words, the defence of a position or a battlefield springs from tactics; the war plan includes many political considerations. Amongst these, the defence of a theatre of operations considered as a whole, which means can no longer be the means of defence separately analysed, must be treated as a whole – types of resistance, the methods of defensive strategy, the various ways of combining the means with a view to the next object and the preservation of the theatre of operations. In this text, Clausewitz, in the light of mental experience or of a case study, seeks a total military action as little influenced by politics as possible, in other words in which the commander has full freedom. The start of Chapter 27 takes up the same idea in terms that are hardly different.

The defence of a theatre of operations constitutes a veritable whole in the combat, battles and war plan, involving waiting and action *(Handeln)* and embracing the reaction *(Rückstoss)* as well: the flash of the sword of retribution and the supreme moment of defence. In order to restore harmony between the formulae, let us say that defence, considered as a whole, necessarily includes, in terms of the intrinsic logic of the idea, reaction, counterattack and the transition to the offensive.

Likewise, if defence conceived in this way is the strongest form of war, there is no reason to add 'with the negative aim' since defence, including counterattack, becomes the strongest form of war for being all the more certain of conquering the enemy. It again seems that Clausewitz's thought has not found its definitive form, or that he simultaneously uses two definitions of defence, one according to which defence aims at preservation and is pursued by repulsion, the other according to which defence begins by waiting and is completed by counterattack. In this chapter, Clausewitz retains the second definition, not without doubt. The idea of reprisals (*Widervergeltung*) lies at the very foundation of the notion of defence; without this idea the dynamic relation between attack and defence would be unbalanced since the attacker would intend to inflict greater harm on the defender than the defender would intend to inflict on the attacker. But at the same time he writes that he leaves it to circumstances to decide whether or not the victory goes further than the object to which the defence related. 'Furthermore, to the extent that defence consists of waiting, it only indirectly aims at victory; it confines itself to preservation and it only benefits from the advantages of being the strongest form to the extent that it is satisfied with this more modest end.' In other words the defensive includes, not ambiguously, strategic counterattack but, in this second phase, it loses some of the intrinsic advantages of defence; the assistance of the people, of the region, of the allies continues for the defender who, after a retreat towards the interior of the country, passes over to the attack and brandishes the sword of retribution.

The analysis of Chapter 8 is based on the same space–time relation as the 'Strategy' of 1804: sacrifice space to gain time. It also distinguishes four kinds of resistance – in fact essentially two, according to the extent of the sacrifice of space. The first type includes: (a) the offensive battle as soon as the enemy crosses the frontier; (b) the offensive battle as soon as the enemy appears before the position chosen by the defender; (c) waiting for the enemy attack against the chosen position. (d) Retreat towards the interior of the country by itself constitutes another type of resistance.

These four types of resistance represent as many successive stages of the defensive, each involving a greater sacrifice for the defender but at the further expense of the attacker, with this circumstance favourable to the defender which he borrows and which the enemy pays for in cash. Loss of territory will weaken the defender in the future; the advance weakens the attacker at once. Clausewitz clearly conceives the notion of the turning point of victory (although he does not use the expression), the point at which the relation of the forces is overturned and at which the attacker loses the superiority which had allowed him to take the initiative and invade the defender's theatre of operations.

The Russian campaign serves as an illustration of both the fourth type of defence and the duality of the principles of decision. Although, in the abstract, it is always the sword of the defender which brings about the losses of the attacker by the combats that are offered, if not fought in practice, an army may succumb by its own efforts as, for example, the army of Napoleon did in Russia. The principle of strength on the side of defence, the principle of weakness on the side of the attacker becomes, in this limited case, clear; every attack wears itself out by its own advance. It is not only natural obstacles – mountains, rivers, forests, marshes – which slow down the momentum and come to the help of the defender, it is the distance itself. The time inexorably arrives when the relation of forces, which had caused the defender to abandon terrain, is reversed in favour of the latter. The attacker must turn to the defensive, but in worse conditions. The hour of retribution strikes.

This chapter, showing the two types of resistance, does not contradict the previous chapters or arguments as to respective advantages of defence and attack, but Clausewitz makes no further use of, or even reference to them. He contrasts the defence of a theatre of operations not far from the frontiers (the Prussian strategy in 1806) with retreat into the interior. As for the choice of the method of resistance, it depends on the many circumstances, material and moral, which theory may consider in the abstract. Only judgment on the spot can and should appreciate the relative importance of these in given circumstances in order to choose the most appropriate method.

The two principles of decision – the sword of the defender and the efforts of the attacker – lead Clausewitz to devote several passages to attacks which fail owing to lack of vigour and resolution. He refers to the wars of the eighteenth century and denounces pretences, delusions and illusory justifications in them. Commanders and historians gave pseudo-rational or theoretical reasons for decisions which came from policy itself and from the weakness of the military element because of extraneous complications.

These passages in Chapter 8 correspond to Chapter 30, namely the defence of a theatre of operations without a decision, but they do not involve the distortion of two types of war. Thus Clausewitz recalls the fundamental principles of the theory: strategic combinations themselves produce nothing; everything comes down to tactical success; with one stroke Bonaparte would have torn apart the spider's web which Prussian arms offered against Daun during the Seven Years' War. Combat, whether bloody or not, whether offered or fought, remains the supreme and only arbiter. You have to be certain of your own superiority or of the moral weakness of the enemy to hope for anything to emerge from strategic trickery alone.

These remarks (written in any case before 1827) show us the meaning of the Foreword and the intended revision. Daun's method of fighting, the contrast between this method and that of Napoleon, the dependence of the method on political conditions were all ideas that Clausewitz acquired before his last years, but he failed to conceptualize them clearly. He did equate the wars of Bonaparte and those of Daun as historical types. He gave weight, as proper illustrations of the concept, to Bonaparte's alone. The ideas, the examples and the appraisals do not change, or at least they change little: on the other hand, the conceptual presentation becomes more rigorous.

In Chapter 27, Clausewitz begins by repeating, as he had done in Chapter 8, that he will return to the strategic totality of the defensive, influenced by political circumstances, in the chapter on the war plan. He could, he writes, keep to the analysis of the means of defence, the method of resistance being only one method of the war plan. In fact, he deals with the same problem only in Chapter 8 though in different form.

The concept of *abwehren*, repulsing or parrying, does not appear in Chapter 27. The initial formulae are as follows:

> According to our way of thinking, the defensive is nothing other
> than the strongest form of the context. The conservation of our
> own forces, the destruction of enemy forces, in a word victory, is

the object of the contest; but it is not the ultimate end. The preservation of our own state and the overthrow of the other is the ultimate end. Peace will be obtained because the conflict is resolved and completed in a way affecting both.

Many of Clausewitz's critics should have read these lines: military victory is not the ultimate end, it is only the means to the true end, peace, in which opposed wills unite. Here we have reached the final state of Clausewitz's thought, if we are to believe his testament in Chapter 1, Book I.

The duel, originally the conflict between two wills, is between two states which, in the abstract, mutually desire to overthrow each other. Each state is divided into armed forces and territory, the latter indispensable for maintaining, supplying and regenerating the former. Army and territory do not exhaust the totality of the state but they remain the dominant (*vorherrschend*) elements, which as a general rule are superior to all the others.

Clausewitz has no difficulty in rediscovering the dialectic of territory and armed forces, a dialectic comprising both the reciprocal action of the two elements and the asymmetry of the effects of each on the other; the destruction of armed forces assures the possession of territory but not vice versa.

As long as attack was defined as taking possession or conquest – which would suggest a spatial relationship – the conceptual presentation would suffer from a visible defect. Attack seemed to aim at territories whereas in fact it aimed above all at the army. By moving away from wills at grips with each other, the difficulty is easily resolved. The contest takes place between two states; each wants to impose its will on the other. In a war, according to this concept, the wills aim at the overthrow of the enemy state. Since each state consists of territory and an army, both are objects of attack and defence. Each wants to preserve itself and destroy what the other possesses. As territory is controlled by the army but not the reverse, at least in the short term, the primary target of whichever side wants to conquer the other is the armed forces of the enemy.

From this, Clausewitz introduces the concept which is indispensable for a satisfactory definition of the theatre of operations, that of the centre of gravity. This concept retains the idea contained in the simplified representation of the contest: that of unity. But a war or campaign is seemingly split up into an indefinite number of separate combats. The effects of a victory are only felt in a limited range; a victory does not normally come from a decision at a stroke, but the more it affects the troops the wider its range. In war, as in mechanics, there are centres of gravity 'whose movement and direction govern other points'. He immediately adds, in order to conform to the method of for and against: 'Just as in the world of inert bodies action against the centre of gravity is measured and limited by the composition of the parts, so can it be in war: here and there, one blow can easily have more force than it needed to overcome resistance. The result is a waste of force.'

Clausewitz, according to the formula of the final note, believes that great successes determine small successes at the time. It is thus appropriate to concentrate strategic actions on a small number of centres of gravity, but he does not forget that this unification of war also involves limits. Even with concentration of forces, there must be limits. In this case, the opposition becomes that between defence of territory, which implies the division of forces, and attack against the centre of gravity of the enemy force, which implies concentration of forces. In this way the notion of the theatre of operations is defined according to Clausewitzian rules within the system of fundamental principles. The theatre of operations extends as far as the direct effects of a victory or of a decision over the principal force of the enemy. Such a victory represents the best defence of a theatre of operations since it ensures possession. By substituting for the preserving–conquering pair, the preserving–destroying variation (the priority of armed forces instead of the priority of space or territory), everything becomes clear and ordered.

This step in effect leads to the next stage which begins with the question: How can we suppose that the combatants seek a decision? Chapter 28 thus differs from Chapter 8 in the initial determination of the conditions in which the methods of resistance evolve. In Chapter 8, Clausewitz hypothetically eliminates the political circumstances which always influence real wars in order to restrict himself to a strictly military consideration, as far as possible. In Chapter 28, conforming to the Foreword of 1827, he abandons the distinction between wars where one or other or both of the belligerents seek a decision, and wars where neither seeks it.

The distinction between the two types of war is not formulated in the exact terms of the Foreword of 1827. The vocabulary approaches much more that of Chapter 1 of Book I. At one extreme is the rise to extremes and the fight to the death, at the other is armed observation. Now the majority of wars in the past, he writes, were closer to armed observation than to the fight to the death and perhaps the wars of the future will have the same character. A theory which only recognized wars of the first type would be too far removed from real life to be of any use.

The study of the defence of a theatre of operations falls into different categories according to whether at least one of the belligerents seeks the decision or whether neither of the two seeks it.

Once defence refers to the possibility of the decision, it is no longer divided into waiting and action but into waiting and decision. The defender by definition postpones the moment of the decision, and generally he postpones it more or less according to the time which he needs to restore the balance of forces in his favour. He adopts one of the methods of resistance: he takes up a position near to or further from the frontier, he more or less exploits the advantages of the terrain, and he relies on a defensive or offensive battle, or on the support of fortresses, in the light of many considerations which the theoretician can only enumerate and which may be quickly grasped. The theoretician elaborates truths which the military genius has always known, though without formulating them.

The analyses of Chapter 8 tally with those of Chapter 28, writes Clausewitz: the former distinguishes between the various stages of defence, the latter adds the consideration of the centre of gravity, and hence the principle of the concentration of forces; at the same time, there appears a major difficulty for the side on the defensive: how can one be sure of striking at the centre of gravity of the attacker? Following from this, Chapter 28, while adhering strictly to Chapter 8 and sometimes commenting upon the same historical examples, first of all poses a problem not touched upon before: How can one choose a position that will force the attacker to join battle at the place chosen by the defender? What resources should the latter deploy if the attacker, despite everything, has pushed ahead and, without fighting, has passed by the army on the defensive? Before giving the answers to these two questions, let me return to the basics of the theory. Without entering upon details of the strictly military analyses, we can briefly resume the causes of the superiority that Clausewitz attributes to defence before studying in depth the particular case of flank positions.

The object of strategy is to give to tactics the opportunity of waging battle in material and moral conditions which are propitious for victory and for the exploitation of the latter. The terrain, natural obstacles, entrenchment, fortresses are among the material conditions, together with numbers. Strategy is thus placed at the service of tactics so that the latter may bring about the decision – which does not exclude the fact that in another sense tactics obey strategy which arranges and organizes the combats in the light of its own ends.

Among the principles of the superiority of the defensive, some act at once and do not require the retreat into the interior. Clausewitz, in spite of his reputation as a doctrinaire proponent of the offensive, attaches extreme importance to the site, to defensive tactics. Certain fortified positions, he writes, are impregnable. Whoever correctly chooses his battlefield benefits from the advantage of terrain even before distance, people, the wearing down of the offensive act in his favour.

The other major reason, apart from terrain, which causes him to prefer defensive strategy is the scepticism which he feels for the concentric attack, launched on several sides at the same time with a view to turning, cutting off, encircling the enemy. As we have seen, a surprise decisive victory over the strategic plan assumes exceptional faults on the part of the defender. At the start of the campaign, the occasion rarely presents itself to cut off the defender's lines of communication. The attacker does not always possess the freedom of choosing between the concentric form and another form: 'When the defence is stretched in a straight line from one sea to another or from one neutral territory to another, the strong points or bases of operations of the two extremities are absolutely secure.' Moreover, eccentric action or manoeuvre along interior lines more than compensates for the advantages of the concentric offensive: 'movement along interior lines can become such a multiplier of forces that the attacker cannot expose himself to this disadvantage unless he is vastly superior'.

Consideration of defensive positions and flank positions is inserted into this whole. In Chapters 8, 12, 14 and 28 Clausewitz examines the necessary characteristics for the defensive position. He lists four in Chapter 12: (a) that the enemy cannot pass by without attacking; (b) that in the struggle for the lines of communication, the position secures the advantage for the defender; (c) that the relationship between the lines of communication of the two armies exerts favourable influences on the configuration of the combat; (d) that the terrain exerts a favourable influence on the whole.

One of the defensive positions particularly interests him, that which he calls according to custom the flank position (*Flankenstellung*). He gives this name to a defensive position because it can be held even if the enemy passes in front of it without attacking it. All fortified camps and fortresses are by definition, so to speak, flank positions. But what of defensive positions which are not impregnable but which the enemy can skirt or bypass, even frontally? The campaign of 1806 provides an example of this and Clausewitz refers to it on two occasions (Chapters 14 and 28). The deployment of Prussian troops on the right bank of the river Saale was, in relation to Bonaparte, arriving on the road from Hof, a flank position provided that the Prussian troops faced the Saale and awaited events.

In Chapter 14, as in Chapter 28, he emphasizes the strategic advantages from which the Prussian army benefited. 'Nothing would have prevented the Duke of Brunswick from taking up positions on the 13th so that on the 14th, at dawn, 80,000 men would have found themselves opposite the 60,000 that Bonaparte had ordered across the Saale at Jena and Dornburg.' The analysis, which is more complex in character in Chapter 28, lists the options which were open to the Prussian command, to attack the enemy if they crossed the Saale, to engage the Prussian army there, to stay where they were and take action against the enemy lines of communication, or finally, if found possible and opportune, to hurry by a flank march to intercept the enemy at Leipzig. If the Prussian command had kept the first two options open the position would have truly become a flank position. The duke finally decided on the third, but too late, and he was forced to wage the two battles of Jena and Auerstädt. The strength of the position was not relieved by the duke being able to annihilate the right wing of his adversary at Auerstädt; there was no bold resolution to win the obvious victory, and at Jena there was a belief in a victory which was in reality impossible. Despite everything, Clausewitz concedes that the choice of a position susceptible to being attacked, as a flank, is a strategy which is as dangerous as it is effective if successful. In Chapter 14, he concludes that it is especially valuable against a cautious adversary and in wars of observation. In Chapter 28, having distinguished between defence with and without decision, he concludes differently since the chosen position must lead to the decision. Consequently, he lists the five options open to the defender where the enemy has passed in front of the position chosen without attacking. Of the five options, the last (do to the enemy exactly what he has done to us – in other words, counterattack in his theatre of operations) fits uneasily with the hypothesis of the defensive, namely the superiority of the enemy. The fourth, to take action against the enemy lines of communication, does not lead to the decision. The first, to divide forces from the start so as to be certain of attacking with at least part of one's troops while hastening to bring up the rest, involves the danger of dispersion, or of a war of small bodies. The second, to answer the enemy advance by a march on the flank, to get round at speed, to intercept and force a battle, does not correspond to the needs of a defensive battle. Thus, there finally remains the third, to attack the enemy on the flank, joining battle with fronts reversed – an advantageous strategy. It is in the light of these problems (what should be done if the enemy advances beyond a defensive position which is not impregnable?) that Clausewitz once more returns to the campaign of 1806.

Comparison of chapters 14 and 28 brings to light the implications of the duality of wars and, at the same time, the import of one of the intended revisions. In chapter 14, the conclusion contrasts the danger of the flank position faced by an enemy in search of the decision (such as Bonaparte) with the possible effectiveness of the same position opposed by a cautious enemy and in wars of observation. In Chapter 28, the distinction of defence with or without decision is established from the start: the analysis of the various options constantly relates to the end implied, namely the decision.

This last observation will serve as a transition towards the essential idea that I wish to extract from the comparison of Chapters 28 and 30: the profound, often radical, difference between the two types of war. History proves that wars to the death are not only not the only wars, but that they represent the exception, and can appear to be anomalies. The majority of real wars lie between the two extremes of indiscriminate violence and armed observation, but the distinction between the two types is made necessary because the same decision, right for one of the two types, would be fatal in the other. Of the innumerable examples of this contrast, let us take one, the most abstract and the most decisive: when one side or the other seeks the decision, the defender abandons some space in order to create favourable conditions for the decision. When the attacker does not seek the decision, the defender has no reason to abandon anything further especially as when peace is concluded the counters in the pockets of each will be added up. Or again: when one takes action with a view to the decision, one joins battle behind fortresses since this deprives the enemy of some troops. If there is no question of decision, one normally places troops in front of them – which is enough to dissuade the enemy against the siege that was intended and which would now only become possible after a battle which would probably be difficult.

In the course of this chapter, Clausewitz is led to an analysis of strategy in the eighteenth century, in a style which corresponds at least in part to Delbrück's interpretation. If the decision is not sought – he means here the destruction of the enemy armed forces – the object of attack varies: provinces, depots or fortresses become the targets that the defender must protect; natural obstacles and terrain assume an increased importance. The general staff use their topographical knowledge and draw up a system of rules in the light of choice and the preparation of positions and approach routes.

In this type of war, the difference between attack and defence tends finally to disappear. At the start, one of the two appears in the theatre of operations of the other; but it can happen that soon he will be defending his own territory on the territory of the other. When some sort of equilibrium is reached, with each side lacking great ambition and only aiming at small advantages cheaply won, there only remains what Clausewitz calls *Manövrieren*, manoeuvring with a view to minor successes. All the campaigns in which neither of the contenders seeks the decision tend towards manoeuvre in this sense. This balanced game of forces, this sort of war which is not war, is precisely what the young Clausewitz, awoken from the slumbering dogmatism of a false rationalism by the thunderclap of the Revolution, denounced from his youth and which he accepts in the Treatise as one of the metamorphoses of the war-chameleon.

For all that, he did not diverge on two points which, more than any other, were close to his heart. In this type of war, there are not principles, rules or methods (*Grundsätze, Regeln, Methoden*) whose regular application can be revealed by history.

War for great decision is not only much more straightforward but it also conforms more to nature, stripped of infernal contradictions. It is more objective and linked together by an internal law of necessity. This is why reason [*Vernunft*] can impose forms or laws on it; in this type of war, all this seems much more difficult.

As for the two fundamental principles of the theories of the time, the width of the base according to Bülow and manoeuvre along interior lines according to Jomini, he declines to find confirmation of these in experience.

The second point which is dear to him is the danger of trying the esquire's dagger while the enemy brandishes the heavy sword of the knight. In other words, never fail to know the enemy. Now, even in campaigns without decision, the commander never refuses to accept successes which are offered to him. Should the occasion arise, he will exploit a favourable position or a victory whose extent may surprise even him. A commander must especially examine the every intention; if he thinks the latter wants a great victory through the use of great resources he must not use small means and subtle methods which tend to favour equilibrium and inaction. 'The first requirement is that the commander take the correct measure of his enemy and organize his work accordingly.'

3 What revision did Clausewitz contemplate?

Let us return to the questions I asked at the beginning: Why did Clausewitz contemplate a total revision of Book VI? What does he mean by seeking different ways out or seeking the way out by another route?

(a) Our first hypothesis may be struck out. Nothing in the final thoughts of Clausewitz as expressed in Book VIII and the revised chapters of Book I suggests a different military conception of defence or a different justification of the intrinsically greater force of defence. True, Clausewitz writes on two occasions in Book VIII that time does not always operate in favour of the weaker, but he specifies 'time as such'. Furthermore, the idea was already present in the old texts in a different form (Book III, Chapter 12). The duration of the combat wears down the engaged forces; time does not wear them down in the same way in strategy. The idea that in certain circumstances the weaker side takes the initiative, even though the attack further accentuates his inferiority, tallies with the ideas in Book VI and the analysis of the relation between times of attack and defence.

(b) A second hypothesis, in itself credible but insufficient, is a basis of the Foreword of 1827. Clausewitz would have wanted to take into account, in the book devoted to defence, the two types of war and the Formula. That this revision would have appeared to him as more necessary in this book than in the previous ones is easily explained. The first two books were at least partially revised, the third, devoted to the dialectic of the physical and the moral, seems little affected by the two ideas of the Foreword. As for Books IV and V, they oscillate between historical studies and the implications of the concept of the duel contest or of the war. Descriptive or analytical, they do not call for revision to the same extent as Book VI. For the latter deals with two forms which, so to speak, reflect two methods in which war may be conducted. The ideas of the Foreword manifestly and directly affect the forms of war more especially as at the higher level, that of the defence of a theatre of operations, the type chosen (*Widerstandsart*) becomes closer to the plan of campaign, itself dependent on the war plan. In other words, we already find an undeniable reason for the desire to revise: you cannot deal with defence and attack without taking into consideration both the alternatives of final goals (to conquer or not) and the continuance of policy in war.

The existing text of Book VII leaves no doubt on this point. Chapter 8, the types of resistance, is of a synthetic character; it distinguishes the two extremes of plans of defence according to whether battle is joined close to the frontier or whether the army withdraws to the interior of the country; according to whether the defender counts above all on destroying the enemy with his forces or whether he relies on the self-destruction of the enemy. Likewise, the last chapters of the book, starting at Chapter 27, take into consideration the whole of the theatre of operations and, proceeding from this, highlight the alternative, with or without decision, which is not confused with that of the two types of war, though depending on it. If war is waged with a view to overthrowing the enemy state, a decisive victory must be won over the opposed forces, and they must be destroyed. As the first twenty-six chapters more or less explicitly presupposed the intention, common to both sides, of gaining a decision, Clausewitz would probably have introduced from the beginning the distinction, with or without decision, hence that of the two types of war.

It is perhaps appropriate to add that Book VI, the most important with Books I and VIII, seems to me also the furthest away from the perfection of Chapter 1 of Book I. The truly military studies (fortifications, fortresses, the crossing of rivers and mountains) are related to a particular state of arms, even if a reader of today, such as Camille Rougeron, can still draw lessons from them. They approximate to tactics to the extent that it is troops which prohibit the crossing of a river or the penetration of a forest. Alongside these chapters on military art, the analytical chapters of the first section, or Chapter 26 on the arming of the people, retain the same freshness for us as for contemporaries; perhaps the scope of Chapter 26 is only wholly disclosed to the reader of today.

(c) We thus come to a third hypothesis. We know that Clausewitz directed his efforts to the conceptualization of ideas and themes which he had conceived when very young. The theme of the superior force of the defence, it is true, does not appear in the 'Strategy' of 1804, but Clausewitz had already grasped it in 1812 when he wrote the *Bekenntnisse* and took part in the Russian campaign. Perhaps he would have rewritten the chapters in the first section, particularly those which review the various factors in success and analyse the relation of each with defence and attack. All that I can indicate, by way of hypothesis, is the imperfection of the conceptual structure which he would perhaps have corrected.

In the *Principles of Instruction*, Clausewitz distinguishes politically a defensive war, which is waged for independence, from a strategically defensive war in which one simply fights the enemy in the theatre of operations indicated for this purpose. The notion of politically defensive

164

war is not taken up in Book VI, nor for that matter in Book VIII (at least not explicitly). This omission is perhaps justified by an idea which he expressed elsewhere:

> Political defence, which consists of what a nation does to fight for its importance and its maintenance, i.e. not with a view to conquest (the form of which is of little importance), is of no concern to war in its true meaning, even though it may have a significant influence on the spirit of the army, and to this extent may become important.

Yet in Chapter 5, Clausewitz does not define strategic attack, apart from the political intention of the parties. If the conqueror makes up his mind earlier than the defender it is because he wants to modify politically the *status quo*. The formula which delighted Lenin – that the defender really starts the war because the conqueror would prefer to seize without fighting – clearly relates to the higher level of policy. In the light of the Foreword, Clausewitz could have more clearly differentiated attack, in the sense of the political intention of seizing something, from the offensive form of strategy, which manifests itself in the initiative of operations or the appearance in the enemy's theatre of operations. A politically defensive war can be waged in a strategically offensive manner – a dialectic implicit, but not elaborated, in Book VI.

The truly conceptual analysis presents other difficulties. It develops from two different premises· either from the notion of repulsing or parrying (*abwehren*), or from the more abstract notion of preserving (*erhalten*).

If we begin with the first notion, we discover from it the idea of waiting. By just parrying blows or repulsing attacks, one leaves the other the initiative of striking first. Waiting, combined with space, leads successively to tactical defence (of a position), defensive battle, and defence of a theatre of operations. Each of these defences entails offensive actions. The reference to space allows us, in Chapter 8, to classify the types of resistance. Clausewitz then uses the definition of war to stress that the main object of defence – repulsing or parrying – is not enough by itself, but that the object of the defence or the defensive war is no different from the goal of every war, namely the destruction of enemy forces.

He attempts to prove this proposition in many ways: 'It would be in contradiction of the same concept if we meant that defence would be passive not only as the whole but in each of its parts.' But if we mean defence as a whole to include counter-offensive and victory, we can no longer speak of negative ends; the correct formula is the one which Clausewitz himself sometimes uses: defence is the strongest form because it is more likely to defeat the enemy. Clausewitz asks, without answering the question: To what extent does defence remain the advantages of waiting in position, or parrying, when it passes over to counterattack? The reply given in Chapter 8 is negative – which seems to me to betray the thought of Clausewitz: counterattack on one's own soil retains certain advantages of the defensive, whilst the defensive of the attacker on enemy soil suffers only disadvantages. The other premise, preserving and not repulsing or parrying, lies at a higher level of abstraction since the term does not imply any reference to space and since one preserves one's troops just as much as one's territory. At the beginning of Chapter 5, Clausewitz does repeat that the intention to preserve, to maintain the *status quo*, does not imply any reference to space, since one preserves one's troops just as much as one's territories, which militarily, would only use repelling attacks. The opposition of preserving and seizing (or destroying) is no less valid both in relation to political intentions and in relation to military means – which was not the case with the more concrete concept of parrying or repulsing, simply the means of preserving.

As regards armed forces or territory, the terms which are opposed to preserving are destroying (annihilating) or conquering (seizing). As regards armed forces, the two intentions of preserving one's own and destroying the other are inseparable but, according to whether the one or the other predominates, the positive end (destroying) or the negative end (preserving), we choose attack or defence. Taken to the extreme, the attempt to preserve our forces results in pure resistance. In the same way that a parry is limited to repulsing attacks, a defence which is limited to the preservation of our forces is confined to dashing the adversary's intentions.

The text of Book VI, Chapter 27, echoes Book I, Chapter 2: preserve our forces, destroy those of the adversary – these are the objects of the fight. It always goes beyond defence in the narrow sense. But even this victory is not the ultimate end because the true conflict opposes states: maintain our own state, defeat the enemy state. As Clausewitz adds, 'from the peace that one seeks', a new uncertainty arises because all wars do not have as their object the defeat of the enemy state, nor therefore as the immediate or necessary end the destruction of opposed armed forces.

These two pairs, parrying–striking and preserving–seizing (conquering – this being a logical premise), could have been integrated by Clausewitz into a single and more intellectually satisfactory system. Likewise, of the circumstances which favour defence, it would have been preferable to distinguish those which pertain to matters of politics and even particular matters such as the trend towards equilibrium in Europe. Finally, it would have been appropriate to distinguish rigorously between defence with a negative end and the defensive which aims for the destruction of enemy armed forces, and which thus has an ultimate or conditional end that is not negative, and is quite as positive as attack. This last misunderstanding seems to me the most serious: why, politically, is it not sufficient to break the enemy's will to seize (or to destroy)? Supposing that the very concept of war must not be confined to this negative will, it is a question of pure concept, not subject to political laws. Whoever repulses the enemy and keeps what he wanted to take, has imposed his will on the enemy. That the defender must also want to destroy the armed forces which have led the attack belongs to the logic of absolute war and not to the logic of a real war.

As regards tactics, Clausewitz twice returns to the opposition of attack and defence. The first time, in paragraphs 73–5, he develops the dialectic that we know:

> Attack is the positive intention, defence the negative. The former seeks to chase the adversary, the latter only to preserve. But as preserving [erhalten] consists not only of holding out [aushalten] but of suffering passively [leiden], preservation depends on a reaction. This reaction is the annihilation of the attacking armed

force. It is thus only the end which must be considered as negative, not the means.

Here, Clausewitz asserts – incontestably – that attack and defence have the same end, namely victory. This proposition is implied in the very notion of fighting. One must not thus ascribe to the victory of the defender a negative character, or at least must not include this negative character in the concept of defence. But he seems to contradict himself a few pages later. The defender accepts combat because he wants to prevent the attacker from attaining his end, because he wants to maintain the *status quo*. He adds: 'that is the immediate and necessary intention of the defender; whatever is connected but goes beyond it is not necessary. The necessary part of it is negative.' Waiting represents the specific means of this specific intention. The defender hopes that nothing will happen and thus leaves the initiative to the attacker. Once the combat has begun, the positive intention of victory arises out of the combat itself for the defender, but policy does not necessarily go beyond the maintenance of the *status quo*. In other words, if we refer to the specific intention of defence, it is confined to preserving. But as defence is drawn into the fight, it aims at victory, and the retreat of the enemy is the sign of victory, the destruction of enemy forces being its essential content. But just as the conduct of a campaign or of a battle cannot be deduced from the concept of war, the defensive which in theory, as a form of war, leads to the destruction of enemy forces can in real circumstances continue parrying to a greater or lesser extent beyond the preservation of its territory, state and forces.

(d) From these remarks, can we picture what Clausewitz meant by 'seeking the way out in a different manner'? The word *Ausweg* in the Treatise indicates way out, sometimes in the concrete meaning, sometimes in the abstract. It is the abstract use which interests us since it alone can bring to light the meaning of the final note.

In Chapter 6 of Book II, Clausewitz compares the in-depth analysis of facts with the illustration of an idea by many examples.

> When a detailed analysis of fact is not possible, we have already
> conceded that the demonstrative power which is lacking can be
> made good by the number of cases quoted; equally, such a way of
> escaping [*Ausweg*] from the difficulty is dangerous and lends itself
> to frequent abuse.

I have made the comment earlier that *Ausweg* can be translated as 'getting out of the difficulty'. It could be translated as 'expedient'. It is a case here of replacing the desirable – the circumstantial analysis of a historical example – by the listing of numerous not fully understood examples.

Another use, in Chapter 6(A) of Book VIII, confirms the meaning of this word in Clausewitzian dialectic – the way of getting out of a difficulty or of an opposition. Clausewitz has just analysed the descent into simple armed observation and negotiation.

> The theory of war, if it is to be and remain a philosophical study,
> finds itself in difficulty here since all that is inherent in the concept
> of war seems to fly from it. But the natural outlet soon shows itself.
> The more a modifying principle influences the act of war, the
> weaker the motives of action become and the more the action will
> tend to be transformed into passivity; the less eventful it will

become, the less in need of principles. The art of war becomes mere prudence with the principal object of preventing the unstable equilibrium from suddenly turning to one's disadvantage and the half-war from changing into a whole one.

The solution does not restore to real war the necessary elements contained in the abstract concept of war, it gives the theory of war its philosophical character: the weakness of the action reflects the weakness of the motives, of the hostile intention and of the will to act. The rationality of the total concept of war, with its three elements, is substituted for the rationality of the abstract concept of war. The first hypothesis would refer to the Foreword of 1827 and would adopt what I have formulated somewhat earlier. The last four chapters represent the conclusion of Book VI. In Chapter 27, he introduces the notion of the centre of gravity; in Chapter 28, he contrasts, within the notion of defence, the decision with waiting, whereas he ordinarily contrasts action with waiting. In Chapter 29, he considers the successive engagement of forces in connection with the retreat towards the interior of the country. For the most part these chapters take up problems already dealt with in previous chapters, notably Chapter 8, and lead back to the latter which stands out from the rest of the book because the hypothesis of a campaign without a decision had never been considered before. At the same time, the distinction between defence and attack tends to blur. One sometimes wonders who is attacking and who is defending; the situation becomes that of a balanced play of forces. Had Clausewitz been aware of the opposition 'with or without decision' in all his arguments, Chapter 30 would not have provided the way out. This hypothesis gives *Ausweg* an almost concrete, material meaning, and suggests to me another more probable hypothesis. What constitutes the Clausewitzian hypothesis *par excellence* – not Kantian antinomy but the balancing of opposed terms – is that the strongest form aims for a negative end and the weakest form aims for a positive end. Unlike Schering, who curiously thinks that the negative end does not signify a weakening but a strengthening of the superiority of defence, I think that Clausewitz opposes the negative character of the end with the intrinsically superior force of defence. Not that this negative character weakens or, indeed, strengthens defence. But a positive end prevails over a negative end; to take is more difficult than to keep. But if it is easier to keep than to take, it is more meritorious to take than to keep. In this sense, this is an antithesis comparable to that of the grandeur of success and the risk incurred.

Book VI should logically have ended with the solution to this antithesis: an intrinsically stronger form with lesser results as against greater results with an intrinsically weaker form. The way out being the substitution of the synthesis by a dialectic which does not bring about a reconciliation of opposed terms, by a theory which remains in doubt between the contrary issues, the revision should have led to a conclusion comparable to the strange trinity of Chapter 1 of Book I or the new theory of Chapter 3 of Book II.

Book VI does not offer this conclusion or systematic organization because certain essential points remain in the background: do not the advantages of defence remain, during the second stage, when the defender, not satisfied with merely stopping the attack or parrying the blows, in turn decides to strike or destroy? Nothing prevents one from using the same concepts of defence and attack in strategy and in tactics, in a context of combat, battle or campaign. But there remains to be determined the relation between the specific end of defence or attack and the end of the war as such on the one hand, and, on the other, the particular end of the whole to which the combat, battle or campaign belongs. Every campaign, as an episode in the contest, has the aim, in all contests, of destroying the enemy armed forces, at least such is the priority. But as part of a war, it effectively has no goal other than that set for it by the war plan. Two notions of defence emerge, albeit imperfectly, from the texts of Books I, VI and VIII: one which has the same end by virtue of having the same objective as attack, namely the destruction of the enemy armed forces, by the means of waiting and by postponing the attack; and the other, which seeks to annihilate, not the armed forces of the enemy, but his positive intention, i.e. what, by combat, continues to maintain the *status quo*. This second kind of defence, more appropriate for the dialectic of political wills than that of armed forces, was confusedly sought by Delbrück in the two types of war where it was not to be found. It was implicit when the term annihilation was applied to the will, not to the armed forces of the enemy.

Between the 24-year-old officer who wrote the notes on the 'Strategy' of 1804 and the melancholy general who took leave of his work, between the young man who dreamt of glory and the disillusioned hero who warned posterity against misunderstanding, the constancy, indeed the continuity, remains. Paragraphs 12 and 13 of the 'Strategy' of 1804 do have a different tone from the first chapters of Book VI. Between boldness and caution, the lieutenant, incapable of finding happiness outside the battlefield, without hesitation chooses boldness; the man of 50 attempts to give each its due. At least partially, he justifies a way of fighting that he earlier wrote off as weakness of character, by historical circumstances and political intention.

What he sought to introduce into the whole book was the guiding idea that military action remains, as such, political. Once military operations lose their autonomy, or policy is not satisfied by setting the ends to be attained by the war, all the strictly military analyses assume a conditional character. Principles or precepts are valid if the results that they promise answer the intentions of the head of state. The alternative of dictated peace or negotiated peace is sufficient to exclude the universal validity of imperatives drawn from the concept of absolute war. The more that defensive and offensive, as strategy, approximate to the war plan or to the overall conduct of hostilities, the more Clausewitz would have considered unsatisfactory a version written before the realization of the identity of the nature between war and policy, before the formulation of the threefold definition of war.

To summarize this lengthy study: at the most abstract level, defence and attack are defined by their end, their unchanging goal, to preserve on the one hand, to conquer or take on the other. Politically, the one who wants to keep what he has is on the defensive; the one who wants to take what the other possesses stages the offensive. The political aim of the war does not determine its conduct, offensive or defensive. This results from many factors, above all from the relation of the forces, but also from the respective state of advancement of the belligerents' preparations. As hostilities are directed towards two principal material objectives, armed forces and territory, defence may seek to preserve either forces or territory. The negative intention of preserving – forces or territory – leads to the notion of waiting. It is thus the other who takes the initiative, conquers space or through battle seeks the destruction of the enemy armed forces. Defence, in the narrow sense, aims at neither of these two ends; to the extent that war as such implies these ends, the defensive conduct of war seeks them too, but indirectly, beyond the stage of waiting.

According to the extent of the retreat – of the sacrifice of space – we can distinguish types of resistance. But a different distinction between the types of resistance results from their aims. Frederick wanted to discourage Maria-Theresa's will to win, while Tsar Alexander destroyed the Grande Armée. The balance of forces compelled Frederick to hold back his ambitions; could not policy, in other circumstances, impose the same moderation? Why should a state, aiming to keep what it possesses and having destroyed the enemy's will to conquer which is responsible for the war, give itself another goal?

In any case, one can suitably distinguish between the advantages of politically defensive war – even if this takes place on enemy territory – and the military advantages of fighting on one's own soil. In the European state system, the agitator, the one who threatens the balance, normally creates a hostile coalition against him. On the other hand, when one considers the assistance given to defence by the land, people and national insurrection, it is the theatre of operations which is of sole importance.

As for the concept of repulsing, in its strategic meaning, it is equivalent to the annihilation of the positive (or conquering) intention of the enemy. At all levels, the action of repulsing implies waiting: it is the enemy who strikes, we parry the blows and strike him in turn.

On the level of military strategy, the Clausewitzian revision should probably have inserted not at the end but at the beginning of the book the distinction of the two types of war, the different conduct of operations according to whether one or other or both of the belligerents seek a decision. At the same time, the political intention as well as the concrete circumstances (nature of the armies, method of supply, governing ideas) must be taken into consideration. The types of resistance do not differ from war plans or, at least, cannot be separated from them, and war plans, as we know, express both policy and politics. It is in Book VI that military analysis becomes difficult once policy and politics are disregarded. Is this not, in the final analysis, the reason why the book requires in Clausewitz's eyes, a complete revision? Not because he rejected any of the analytically separated arguments by which he justifies the superior force of defence. What is lacking is the equivalent of the threefold definition of Book I, Chapter 1.

Interpreters have rarely concerned themselves with these theoretical subtleties. Some have held the idea of the defensive–offensive strategy as based on the web of Hegelian dialectic. Others more numerous, in Germany, have wanted to refute the thesis of the intrinsically greater strength of the defensive. Others still have accepted it, particularly as regards tactics, without for all that adopting a defensive strategy. We had to wait for Mao Tse-tung for Chapter 26 of Book VI, on the arming of the people, to acquire a central place in strategic thinking, and likewise with the dialectic of defence and attack, when defensive strategy and offensive tactics create a progressive reversal of the relation of forces up to the annihilation of the enemy by a defender who passes over to attack. Mao Tse-tung grasped all the Clausewitzian themes, including the annihilation of enemy forces as the goal of defence: a logical interpretation of the prolonged conflict, at the end of which one side or other in a civil war must seize power. Transposed to the rivalry between nuclear states, this same interpretation would lead to a fight to the death in which the two belligerents would perish altogether. At this point, the other interpretation returns: it is enough for defence to succeed in destroying, not the armed forces of the enemy, but his intention of destroying.

Part III
The Theoretical Scheme

Jomini and Clausewitz: the significance of the theoretical revolution
In the *Summary of the Art of War*, dating from after the posthumous publication of the Treatise, Baron Jomini wrote the following lines:

No one could deny General von Clausewitz's great learning and fluent pen, but this pen, sometimes a little vagrant, is too pretentious, especially for a didactic discussion in which simplicity and clarity should be the foremost merits. Apart from that, the author reveals himself to be far too sceptical about military science; his first volume is only a tirade against all the theory of war, whereas the two following volumes, full of theoretical maxims, prove that the author believes in the efficacy of his own doctrine even if he does not believe in that of others.

For myself, I must confess that I could find only a small number of illuminating ideas and remarkable articles in this learned labyrinth; and far from my sharing the scepticism of the author, no work has contributed more than his to make me feel the necessity and usefulness of good theories if I ever have doubted this. It can only do good to understand the limits that one should place on them to prevent oneself from falling into a pedantry worse than ignorance.

General Jomini, Swiss in origin, who served for a long time in the French army and was chief of staff to Marshal Ney before going over to the other side after the Russian campaign, enjoyed a high reputation in his lifetime. He prided himself on being the first and only person to have seen through Napoleon's strategy, to the point of predicting his actions with certainty. His writings, according to W. Rustow were, with those of Willisen, studied and commented upon more than any other in the staff schools of the nineteenth century. Today, they are no longer of interest except to specialists in military history, whereas the Treatise continues to be evoked by the followers of Napoleon, Lenin and Mao, admired by some, but anathema to others. As Clausewitz himself hoped, the book still appeals today, and will appeal to generations to come as much as to contemporaries.

Nevertheless we should not underestimate the *Summary*. The first part contains pertinent distinctions between the various kinds of war; Jomini recognized, under the title 'wars of opinion', wars which we call ideological; he dealt with national and guerilla wars with moderation and good sense. Nor did he fail to appreciate the dependence of war on the political context, on the motives of the belligerents, on their ends. He begins his third chapter, relating to strategy, by asserting the need for generals to

173

agree with the government on the nature of the war. He none the less develops from this the casuistry of lines and strategic points with as many abstract minutiae as H. von Bülow himself.

It is true that he, too, recognizes that 'war is a drama on a grand scale in which a thousand moral physical forces play a lesser or greater part and which one cannot reduce to mathematical calculations', but he does not draw the consequences that can be logically deduced from the action of moral forces. He states from the outset: 'by applying, through strategy, to the whole chessboard of war, the same principle that Frederick had applied to battles, one should have the key to the whole science of war'. Here lies the centre of debate between Clausewitz and the military writers of his time: does 'a key to the science of war' exist? Does it exist in the sense that a theory would try to reveal the secrets of victory to generals? What would happen if the leaders on both sides held this key?

Is Clausewitz 'sceptical about military science'? He is indeed, if one persists in considering science as maxims of action or schemes of manoeuvres which are universally valid across time and space. A theory of action is not the same as a science of matter. The theory of art is not enough to create artists: it is artists of genius who, sometimes unconsciously, create according to the rules of art.

No more than he grasped the positive significance of the Clausewitzian scepticism did Jomini interpret in depth the interdependence between policy and strategy. He writes, for example:

> Yet, the geographical position of our capital, the political relations of the belligerent powers with neighbouring powers, the respective resources, whether actual or allied, form so many strange combinations at the basis of the science of combat: but they are all intimately linked, nevertheless, with operations, plans and whether an army should shrink from making for the enemy's capital.

Such a formula should suggest that the responsibility and the supreme authority belong to whoever politically conducts the war. At the same time, the expression 'strange combinations at the basis of the science of combat' suggests the autonomy of the science of combat. Clausewitz hesitated between these two assertions: the supreme authority of the head of state and the autonomy of the science (or the art) of combat. But at the end of his life, he finally overcame his hesitation and resolved the antinomy: war is as such a political thing – which excludes the autonomy of the military conduct of operations.

Finally, Jomini did not even suspect Clausewitz's central problem, i.e. the relation of concepts to history. He indiscriminately declared that the principles of strategy remain the same, under Scipio and Caesar as well as Peter the Great, Frederick the Great, and Napoleon. For, he adds, they are independent of the nature of arms and the organization of troops. Clausewitz, on the other hand, writes that each age develops, in a sense, its own strategic doctrine.

This brief comparison between Jomini and Clausewitz reminds us first of all that the first readers of the Treatise found in its text no dogmatism at all but, on the contrary, a rejection of science, a kind of scepticism. Pseudo-Clausewitzian dogmatism dates from the end of the century, after the victories of Moltke.

The main question thus bears on the very notion of theoretical revolution. What comprises Clausewitz's scheme? What gives it effect? Which ambiguities remain?

Chapter 7

The Art of War

Book II, as I have said, differs from the other books of the Treatise because it contains a kind of methodological or epistemological commentary on the whole work.

The first chapter is devoted to establishing the divisions of the art of war. The following two chapters, one long and later revised, the other very short, deal simultaneously with war and the science or art of war which is the nature of the theory. Chapters 5 and 6 concern methodology since they specify the rules of criticism and the use of examples. The intermediate chapter, entitled 'Method', combines two themes: on the one hand definition of notions (laws, principles, rules, etc.), and on the other the function of method in a theory that condemns methodology as a method. This cannot be regarded as intellectually fully satisfactory; in particular, we wonder why the division of the art of war precedes the question: art or science. We also wonder why the definition of war itself, which occurs in Chapter 3, comes after the dialectic (thesis–antithesis) resolution of Chapter 2, relating to the theory of war.

1 The three conceptions of theory

The first chapter serves as an introduction; moreover Clausewitz takes up ideas already formulated in 1809, namely the division of the art of war into two parts, tactics and strategy, each defined by its means or its material, armed forces for combat in one case, combat or the results of combat in the other. The conduct of war in the narrow sense does not have, and cannot comprise, another chapter since the use of armed forces is immediate (in tactics) or indirect (in strategy). The commander orders a combat or a battle; he orders combat or battle with a view to the end of the campaign.

In the text of 1809, the art of war, in the wide sense, also includes three other chapters, on the organization of armies, the supplying of troops, the fortification and assault of towns (fortified positions being to strategy what field entrenchments are to tactics). In the Treatise, these three chapters no longer belong to the art of war which is here considered in the narrow sense (or to the conduct of war, or to the theory of the use of armed forces, all equivalent expressions). Chapters 3, 4 and 5 of the note of 1809 have not, for all that, disappeared; they become auxiliary though indispensable supplements, recognitions of the art of war in the narrow sense. The artist who makes use of armed forces must clearly know how they have been recruited, armed and trained. Yet, if the theory took as its point of departure a particular organization of armed forces, it would only apply in those circumstances where such an organization existed. Thus theory, in order to remain valid in the majority of cases (and never unusable), must be based on the most general characteristics of forces and on their most important results. We shall find in the following chapter this same problem, that of the historicity of strategy. It indirectly makes use of an instrument which changes with time. To what extent does theory remain constant despite historical changes?

At this point of the theory Clausewitz is preoccupied with isolating the true subject of his reflection, namely the conduct of war – which implies the conduct of war at the highest level, military or (and) political. He thus reviews the activities external to combat, in semblance or in reality. Some, such as provisioning, care for the injured, replacement of arms or equipment, whatever their importance, are not connected with combat itself and therefore remain outside theory. Others, such as marches, camps or quarters, are connected with combat, indirectly or directly, and thus emanate from the art of war.

This is an abstract distinction, sometimes difficult to place in the real world. In some cases, the distance of hospitals or arms and munitions depots exerts a considerable influence on strategic decisions. However, Clausewitz considers these cases to be too rare for the theory of war to have to include the ways and means, elaborated by theory, of these auxiliary activities. He does concede one exception of great significance. The methods of provisioning, providing magazines, or requisitioning, are an integral part of the theory of war in the narrow sense.

This introduction to the theory of the theory calls for several remarks. The text was probably not revised after 1827, and was perhaps even an old one (although Schering asserts the contrary). Indeed, the second page has a reference to Chapter 1 of Book I. Now the version of the chapter that we possess does not contain the analysis stated, namely the analysis of the unit of combats as totalities. The division of the campaign into a multiplicity of combats and battles, or the principles, of time and space, of the unit of combat or of battle, do not appear in Chapter 1 of Book I. Moreover, two pages later, Clausewitz refers to Chapter 3 of Book I, whereas he should have referred to Chapter 2. (This latter could perhaps have been caused by a misreading of the manuscript.)

The tone and the content of this chapter tallies more with those of Books III–VI, in other words with the 1823–6 version, before Clausewitz became aware of the two types of war and the intrinsically political character of war itself. This explains why the distinction between strategy and tactics remains very similar to that of the 'Strategy' of 1804. Strategy is the indirect use of armed forces, as if the latter were the only means or the sole target. In other words strategy is still defined in a strictly military way; it resembles what we call today the conduct of operations.

In spite of this, Clausewitz was able to leave this chapter as it was, as an introduction to his theory of theory, because it contained the two essential ideas for the sequel. The theory that he wants to create bears on the conduct of war, separated from all subsidiary branches of knowledge, from all the techniques of organization, of supply, of fortification. The conduct of war comes under two heads and can come under two alone: since war is a contest and the contest between states relates to combat, the conduct of war consists of the art of ordinary combat and the art of co-ordinating combats with a view to the end of the campaign. That tactical acts are sometimes difficult to distinguish in reality from strategic acts, takes nothing away from the distinction between the concepts. Clausewitz teaches us to think of the confusion of the concrete because of the rigour of the notions.

Chapter 2 offers one of the most striking examples of Clausewitzian dialectic, with three stages, one thesis, one antithesis and then a resolution (*Ausweg*). The thesis is introduced at the end of a quick summary of the different forms assumed by the art or science of war. Clausewitz recalls the different areas of knowledge which result from the study of war, a knowledge which covers all material elements – armed forces, arms, siege – to the limit of tactical methods. What is lacking at this initial stage is the essential, namely the conduct of war. To fill in this gap, some have tried to establish a positive doctrine (or positive instruction) which in their eyes took the form of science. Between those who confuse the science of war with the knowledge needed by armament engineers or builders of fortifications and a Heinrich von Bülow and a Jomini, Clausewitz sees deep down a kinship: all fail to recognize the free activity of the mind which characterizes all art and inspires every artist.

The theoreticians, whom Clausewitz indefatigably criticized from his youth until his death, nourished the illusory and fatal ambition of reducing strategy to several material facts, to several geometric forms, and of preaching rules which, if respected, would guarantee victory. Material facts, the superiority of numbers and the supply of troops: thus, geometric forms, the connection of the base with operation lines (Bülow) or manoeuvre along interior lines (Jomini). Admittedly, Clausewitz does not deny that progress has been made in analytical thought owing to the elaboration of notions which he himself uses. He reproaches the followers of such a positive instruction with four mistakes: (a) the exclusive, unilateral consideration of one variable among the facts of a complex problem; (b) the refusal to take moral forces into account; (c) the illusion of scientificity by measuring amounts that are incapable of quantification; (d) finally, the omission of the reciprocity of action. The last mistake, which is fundamentally the most serious because it is based on the confusion of the art of war with one of the fine arts, is made clear in Chapter 3 by developing the definition of war laid down in Chapter 2.

The antithesis results from the criticism of the thesis. Theory must respect the proper nature and complexity of its subject; once it neglects the human dimension, the clash of wills, it loses contact with reality and becomes altogether useless or, worse still, harmful. Under the pretext of science, it encourages a misunderstanding of the essential. But, in the opposite sense, does a theory not become impossible if it must take into consideration the forces and actions of a moral order, the reactions of human beings and the uncertainties of all the given facts? There are no two strictly similar situations; theory only embodies classes of phenomena; now, nothing is more individual than the effect on an enemy of a measure that we take. Likewise, the individuality of the leaders is expressed in the multiplicity of ways which they choose to attain their ends. Conclusion: positive instruction is incompatible with the nature of the subject. Supposing that one could construct such a doctrinal edifice (*Lehrgebäude*), the actor, on every occasion where he has to rely on his skill, would ignore the instruction. Skill and genius would act outside the laws yet the theory would stand against reality.

Two resolutions of this emerge: first of all, the difficulties of theory are not equally great at all points. The part played respectively by courage, intelligence, judgment varies according to the levels of the hierarchy, and the number and uncertainty of the given facts similarly vary. The role of the physical increases and that of the moral decreases as one descends towards tactics. Regularities appear. The second way out completes the first: a theory does not need, to merit such a title, to have the ability to give instructions to the actors. Every activity which uses the same means with a view to the same ends gives rise to a rational study. An analytical study of the subject, in its natural organization, leads to a refined knowledge, to fine distinctions; applied to experience, in this case to history, it creates a true familiarity with one's subject.

A specialist who devotes half his life to cleaning up an obscure subject thoroughly will know more about it than a person who seeks to familiarize himself with it in a short time. Theory should develop the mind of the future leader in war, or rather it should guide him in his education and not accompany him on the battlefield; just as a wise tutor will direct and facilitate the mental development of his pupil without keeping a tight rein on him all his life.

The 'theory of the theory', defined in this way, seems perfectly clear. The conduct of war cannot support the formulation of a positive instruction for three major reasons: the reciprocal action of forces, the influence and indefiniteness of moral virtues, the uniqueness and complexity of each situation in which the actor takes his decisions.

This activity lends itself no less to an analytical study because structurally it presents certain characteristics: the number of means and ends, in tactics as well as strategy, appears limited; so are the number of circumstances (country and place, time of day, meteorological conditions) which influence the specific means and ends of strategy; so again are the number of combinations to be found in history, equivalent to experience. Moreover, strategy only considers the result of combats in relation to the military objective and, beyond that, to the peace which will bring the war to an end. The commander has no need to know all that his subordinates should know; the necessary knowledge is simplified as one ascends the hierarchy of command – a simplification which explains why a Condé or a Frederick, but not a Newton or a Euclid, can owe their education to life.

In this form, the theory of the conduct of war (or of the art of war) compares with the theory of fine arts but differs from it. The fragments published by H. Rothfels and by W.M. Schering on the theory of art reveal one of the origins of Clausewitz's thought. The latter, in the fragment entitled 'Über Kunst and Kunsthistorie', reflects on the art of war in the light of other arts. Careful, as usual, about precise definitions, he examines a twofold distinction, that of art and the theory of art, even though the same word sometimes refers to both, and that of art and of science. Finally, in the fragment as well as in Chapter 3 of Book II, he brings to light the link between knowing and being able (practical knowledge) and at the same time he maintains the distinction between the goals.

180

According to his usual method, he attempts to review the current use of words and to distinguish concepts clearly. Usage does not always distinguish between art and the theory of art. For example, architecture designates the act of construction as well as the theory of construction (or the knowledge needed by persons who want to construct). He explains this tendency by the confusion caused by the inevitable presence of art (or application) in science and of a science (or knowledge) in art. All thought is composed of judgment and, in this sense, it is art. The art of calculation depends on mathematical knowledge, but the latter also involves an element of art (or of *savoir-faire*). The only way of defining a rigorous opposition between knowledge and capacity in this case, is by reference to the goal. Science aims, in the final analysis, at knowledge; art, in the final analysis, at creation or production. At the same time, the kinship between the art of war and other arts appears, and the expression 'art or conduct of war' seems preferable to that of 'science of war'. There remains no less a theory of war, as there exists a theory of architecture, in order to indicate the whole of the knowledge required for the conduct of war. Clausewitz is in favour of scientific effort to elaborate the major concepts of this activity, in other words to think out this activity clearly and distinctly.

In relation to the fine arts – architecture, painting and music – to which Clausewitz compares the art of war, the latter shows an originality which radically separates it from all the others: the artist does not manipulate inert forces, he tackles another will. The will in war is exercised neither against dead matter nor against submissive or passive minds. The painter or the architect directs his work towards minds or sensibilities which will abandon themselves and in some cases submit to his work; the soldier aims to break or bend a will which, by nature, is opposed to his.

When Clausewitz suddenly writes, in Chapter 3 of Book II, that war belongs to neither the field of sciences nor that of arts, but to that of social life, one wonders why he did not begin from there. Indeed, although his thoughts are unequivocal, the same cannot be said for his ways of expressing them. Having stated that war can be compared with commerce, which is also a conflict of interests and of human activities, that it is still much closer to politics which can be considered a sort of commerce on a grand scale, the distinction of knowledge and capacity, of science and art continues to apply to this social activity. Whereas science differs from art in its own finality (knowledge), war differs from politics in its specific means, violence. The specificity of the means – violence – and the indefinability of the ends – which policy alone determines – explains the difficulty of a theory of the conduct of war. Indeed, this theory stops at the end which results from the specificity of the means and which remains logically subordinate to the ultimate end, of a political nature, imposed on strategy and in many respects indeterminate.

What remains of the comparison between the fine arts and the art of war in the final thought of Clausewitz? The unity of an art or of an application lies either in the end or in the means: the unity of architecture is its end, that of painting is its means; war is opposed to politics by the means, not necessarily by the end. All art presupposes an innate skill, even if study or practice alone allow the natural talent to be developed. The need for the work, the beauty of the finished product do not happen by chance, but nor do they result from the application of laws or rules. Assuming that the beauty conforms to laws or rules, it is genius, it is the artist himself who applies them spontaneously, without having learnt them. The similarity of the art of war with the fine arts serves, as it were, as a base for the conception of the military genius.

By this expedient, Clausewitz returns to the fundamental antithesis of Chapter 2 in whose final paragraphs the solution is to be found. What prevents a science of war, as understood by certain of his contemporaries, or as we would say today, a doctrinal system, is on the one hand the totality of the concrete data which differentiates real combat from simulated or imagined combat: the uncertainty of information, moral forces, friction of the military school or machine, thus of the human machine. On the other hand, it is the reciprocal action of conflicting wills, the action of one will, not on dead matter, but on another will, which often reacts in an unpredictable manner. From these two causes can be deduced the singular, unique character of every situation in which the commander commits himself and his forces.

Now, the theory of a practice must, as we know, be of use to this practice. It cannot provide a recipe, it must educate the mind. It must offer a satisfactory solution for the overall commander of the war but not for the hundreds or thousands of chiefs who lie between the supreme command and the corporal. Clausewitz thus goes on to make conceptual distinctions from which the praxological implications of theory considered as a rational study are deduced.

In Chapter 4 of Book II, Clausewitz first distinguishes the two classical meanings of the word 'law'. As a subject of knowledge, law is the relation of things and their effects on one another; as a subject of the will, it is a determination of conduct, it is equivalent to a command or prohibition to do something. Principle (*Grundsatz*) represents an attenuated form of law for action. It keeps the spirit and meaning of law without assuming a definitive form, without imposing itself unconditionally. It allows more freedom of application for judgment which must decide, in the midst of the complexity of the real, whether it is appropriate or not to apply the principle. Directions and instructions (*Vorschriften und Anweisungen*) determine action as regards a multiplicity of circumstances that are too numerous and of too little importance to lend themselves to laws. Finally, the method or mode of acting is a constant process selected from several possible ones; methodology does not consist of an attachment to principles or to particular instructions, but of the constant applications of a method.

Chapter 4 ends with two conclusions which, when brought together, are of a paradoxical nature. We could dispense with the concept of law in the theory of war. Phenomena are too complex and not regular enough or, if regular, not complex enough for one to be able to speak of laws of knowledge. We cannot use the notion of law, either, as meaning a command 'because the variableness and the diversity of phenomena prevent one from finding sufficiently general determinations to deserve the name of law'. The other conclusion concerns method, in other words the constant application of a certain method of acting. Clausewitz considers this inevitable and justified in the lower levels of the hierarchy in tactics. One cannot grant to all leaders, from the top to the bottom of the ladder, the free activity of the soul which belongs as of right to the artist, to the military genius. Furthermore, while condemning blind adherence to a particular method in the highest echelon, he foresees the excesses that will result if there is no valid theory or no rational consideration of the conduct of war.

To what extent does the theoretical revolution, effected by Clausewitz himself, allow the scope of methodism to be limited? An answer will only be possible at the end of this account. On the other hand, the other conclusion – that we can dispense with the notion of law in the theory of war – calls for an immediate examination. Indeed, Clausewitz repeatedly uses, in different senses, the concept of law. Must it be said that the practice of the theory does not always conform with the theory of the practice?

2 Necessary laws and laws of probability

A first antithesis, typical of Clausewitzian dialectic, occurs on several occasions, that of necessary laws and laws of probability.

Returning to the analysis of the rise to extremes, however: 'In the abstract field of simple concept, reflective understanding cannot find rest as long as it has not reached the extremes, because it is concerned with an extreme, with a conflict of forces left to themselves which follow no other laws than their extreme personal laws.' Which laws are these? Prescribed laws? Certainly not. Laws of physical nature? No again: forces, beyond the control of understanding, are unleashed according to their own internal law, in conformity with their nature. The curious conciliation of logical necessity and of the unleashing of passions operates through a notion of law which seems to me to underlie the thought of Clausewitz but which he has not elucidated. Internal laws are derived from the nature of things, they express this nature, they characterize the manner of existence or the acting of an entity either abstract or real.

The highest law of the decision by arms – the formula used in Chapter 2 of Book I and so often quoted by commentators – falls hardly more easily into the alternative: natural (necessary) law or prescribed law. The diversity of ways prevents this. Is it natural law? Must we compare the supreme law of decision by arms with the law of gravity, a law of the real world which governs more particular laws? Perhaps Clausewitz vaguely thought of such a comparison but I hardly believe this for the simple reason that, according to him, most wars do not bring about a decision, at least great decisions by arms. What, then, is the solution? In my opinion, it is abstract truth expressing the necessary relations which result from the nature of things.

From the characteristic of war, perhaps the essential component, violence, it follows that combat is its sole means. The definition of tactics implies this proposition which is suggested at least by that of strategy. One must include in 'combats' both those which have taken place and those which are offered, simulated, conceived and proffered. Since war opposes armed wills, combat or the clash of arms becomes the specific means and, if you like, alone in forcing decisions. It is the sole means not because the belligerents necessarily and in all circumstances have recourse to it, but

183

because it serves as a reference to settlements concluded between enemies who have recoiled before the supreme test. The famous sentence, so often quoted in the wrong sense, illustrates the logical significance of the sole means. 'The decision by arms is for all operations in war, great and small, what cash payment is in credit transactions; however remote the relations may be, however seldom realization may take place, they are never totally absent.' The relation to the decision by arms never disappears, no more than bill or credit transactions remain valid, disregarding the contingent settlement in cash. In similar terms, one would also draw the conclusion that the great battle plays the same role as, not so long ago, gold did in the vaults of the Bank of France. Besides, the English fleet in the past century only maintained its supremacy by credit: no enemy defied it and forced it to honour its bill by a cash payment.

The supreme law thus seems to me not at all a law of *Geschehen*, of the real natural or human world, whatever Schering may say; it is a law which I would call, for want of a better term, abstract or ideal; it emerges from the conceptual analysis, in the same way as the law of the rise to extremes (even though the latter at least partly translates, in the ideal universe, from internal laws into unleashed forces). In paragraph 10 (Chapter 1, Book I) Clausewitz speaks of 'the rigorous law of forces exerted to the extreme': an abstract or logical structure. It does not follow that one or other of these laws – the rise to extremes or the decision by arms – does not exercise an influence over events or over the conduct which the commanders adopt or should adopt. I only assert that the means which are used in operation may not consciously be chosen in terms of the ideal scheme, i.e. in the 'real' case, as distinct from the conceptual, absolute one, which supplies the ideal type from which there may be deviation.

Logical laws, sometimes compared to mathematical laws, are contrasted with the laws of probability: a contrast which, by itself, enlightens us on the probability Clausewitz has in mind – not mathematical probability, which results from the determination of frequency, but the capacity of the mind to grasp, according to probability, the character of the war, the intention of the enemy, the means at his disposal or what he will mobilize. Two passages clearly illustrate the central idea: the antithesis of necessity and probability, which is merged into the antithesis of pure concept and of reality. In Chapter 2, Book I, 'war must [*muss*] break free from the rigorous law of internal necessity and surrender itself to calculations of probability'. More important still is the passage from Chapter 1 of Book I (paragraph 10): 'If the extreme is no longer to be apprehended nor sought, it is left to judgment to determine the limits for the agreed efforts to be made in place of it, which can only be accomplished on the data furnished by the phenomena of the real world according to the laws of probability.' The antithesis necessity–probability re-emerges in full light: necessary laws do not belong to the real world but to the ideal world, that of concepts. All the praxological conclusions deduced from the conceptual world are suddenly found condemned by the logic of the final thought of Clausewitz, since they are not based on the data and probabilities of the real world. The essence and the ambiguity of the thought lies in the distance between concepts and reality.

The paragraph which follows the one from which the above extract is taken explains, with still greater precision, the thesis towards which our commentary is leading: 'From the character, the institutions, the situation, the conditions of the adversary, each side will draw conclusions, according to the laws of probability, as to the conduct of the other and will consequently determine his own.' By this indirect means we discover the fundamental antithesis even though the majority of commentators neglect it; the rise necessarily develops because it belongs to the conceptual world; the descent cannot be necessary because it develops in the real world and because the latter does not involve necessity. The descent suggests and requires a probable judgment by each side about the intentions and capacities found in the other. From this follows the famous formula of Book VIII: the initial step which governs everything is the appreciation of the nature of war as sets of circumstances make probable. Although Clausewitz did not say so explicitly, the mutual understanding of the adversaries, hence a certain kind of communication, alone allows each of them to escape the catastrophe which struck Prussia in 1806, and also allows both to limit the devastation of the war. Clausewitz, following his personal experience, possessed to the end the obsession with misfortune which strikes the duellist who is unaware of circumstances and who does not wage the same kind of war as his enemy.

He often stresses the complexity of circumstances, the multiplicity of variables which the commander as head of state must take into consideration. Yet, although he speaks of laws of probability, although he invokes Newton and Euclid, the analysis of politico-military judgment, at the higher level, leads the mind in a quite different direction. The commander must grasp at a stroke, by a kind of intuition, the truth in the midst of an extraordinary confusion of possibly contradictory facts. If a Newton himself would have flinched before such a calculation, it is because the indeterminateness of the quantities and the singularity of each situation forbid calculation, in the strict meaning of the word. A historical situation does not result from the addition of data; it owes its significance, its singularity to one major fact.

Genius (or good sense) is exercised less in the calculation of that which does not lend itself to calculation than in the discernment of the essential. The judgment over the nature of war did not resemble a conclusion discerned from premises, but an appreciation by a man of experience of circumstances which have no exact equivalent in the past, which nevertheless sufficiently resemble a past experience to allow foresight of what he must fear or hope for.

From the contrast between the wars of the *ancien régime* and the wars of today, Clausewitz finally draws out a half-explicit conception which I shall express in a style that is not unintentional but intentional and paradoxical. The exceptional character of war conforms to its concept, of absolute war which breaks all fetters. Civilized states, in particular European states within a system which tends towards equilibrium, rarely launch themselves into a struggle to the death, into hostilities to the bitter end: the conqueror is not unaware that he will mobilize against him his initially indifferent rivals, that his enemies will multiply as he reaps victories and accumulates forces. Before the crisis provoked by the French Revolution, war generally resembled armed observation; although the wars of the future must remain national and although the barriers of custom will be torn apart by the turmoil and not restored, Clausewitz none the less predicts the return to moderation more often than not. In the final analysis, meditating on history at the end of his life, he casts the responsibility for twenty years of war less on France itself than on the Revolution and the erroneous policy of other states.

When, in the last decade of the last century, there occurred that remarkable upheaval in the art of war in Europe which rendered useless a part of the art of war of the best armies, and which allowed military success on a previously inconceivable scale, it certainly appeared at first that the art of war should bear the responsibility for these false calculations. It was plain that this art, confined by custom to a narrow circle of conceptions, had been surprised by the possibilities which lay outside this circle though not outside the nature of things. But, is it true that the real and stunning surprise was in the conduct of the war and not in the political circumstance itself? That is to say: did the misfortune proceed from the influence of policy on the war or from a wrong policy itself? The remarkable effects of the Revolution abroad were clearly caused less by the means and new ideas of the conduct of war than by the radical transformation in state craft and administration, in the character of government, in the state of the people. That other governments failed to appreciate all these things, that they sought to hold their own with ordinary means against crushing forces: all of this arose from mistakes in policy. . . . Only a policy which would have had a just appreciation of the forces which had sprung up in France, and of the new relations which resulted in the politics of Europe, would have been able to predict the result, the great lines of war which were taking shape; only in this way could policy arrive at the mobilization of necessary means and the choice of the best paths.

Judgment of probability is based on experience and judgment is deduced from concept. Judgment over the nature of war lacks a basis as soon as new phenomena arise with a revolution. The understanding implied by the limitation of military effort involves respect for custom, homogeneity of the modes of government, the mutual confidence which is born of a certain familiarity – all conditions which vanish in a revolutionary period. Clausewitz thus concludes with two ideas, when he reaches the end of his meditation on personal experience, on the twenty-three years of war, 1792–1815. Wars, having become national, will so remain; wars approach the absolute form when revolutionary novelty prevents the implicit communication which favours moderation. History has confirmed both.

How, in real war, are the necessity of law (or the necessary laws) and the laws of probability brought together? What is the outcome? The necessity which leads logically to the rise to extremes results from reciprocal action, from the fact that each imposes his law and draws the benefit. The first example, the most quoted, returns us to the opposition between wars. 'If the enemy chooses the path of great decisions by arms, our own will be changed by this fact alone, against our will.' The logical necessity of the rise to extremes does not translate into a natural necessity, into a law of the real world; it nevertheless gives to each of the belligerents the capacity to impose on the other the constraint of great decisions. Whoever imposes his law on the other, whoever places the other under a constraint, is thus the stronger, the bolder, the more resolute. As Clausewitz never speculated over the implicit understanding which allows the limitation of violence, one can see why he has been considered a doctrinaire of war to the death – which perhaps he was for a part of his life.

Beyond this first meaning of the formula – imposing one's will on the other – a second takes form, suggested by the comparison with card-games. Who imposes his will on the other – in other words, who, by his action, creates constraints, obligations or prohibitions to which the other must be subjected? The one who starts play or the one who plays second? The one who attacks or the one who defends?

The book devoted to defence suggests that in spite of recognized opinions, the attacker, although he benefits from a moral advantage, does not impose his will on the other. Very often it is the party on the defensive who chooses the field of battle, who accepts or refuses to wage battle. Thus in Chapter 8 of Book III, a book which does not belong to the final stage and which exalts combat most, he nevertheless writes, having shown that broken terrain is no longer an obstacle and that it is no longer enough to choose a favourable position to dissuade the enemy from attacking:

> The defender, it is true, can today, if not refuse a battle, at least avoid it as long as he gives up his position and the role with which that position was connected: in such a case the success of the attacker represents a half-victory and an acknowledgment of his superiority for the time being.

A few paragraphs later, according to his usual method of converse arguments, he himself provides the opposite view.

> On the other hand, he who today wishes to retreat cannot be forced to fight. As the advantages which fall to the attacker by the opponent's retreat are often not sufficient and a real victory is a matter of urgent necessity to him, the few means which exist for compelling such an opponent to fight are often sought and applied with particular skill.

These means involve turning the opponent in order to cut off or make difficult his retreat, and (or) to surprise him. The latter means, due to the mobility of troops, does not unilaterally favour the attacker: quite the reverse, it allows, as is explained at length in Book VI, retreat into the interior of the country.

On one particular point – who possesses the advantage of laying down his hand the last (*der Vorteil des Hinterlandes*) – Clausewitz apparently contradicts himself from one passage to another. In Chapter 28 of Book VI, it is the defender who possesses this advantage. It is true that the defender takes measures before the attack, he has in hand stocks, fortifications, the organization of troops, and these measures so to speak guide the attack (which thus plays second in relation to the preparations completed in peace-time). But it is the attack which starts hostilities or which penetrates the theatre of operations: it is therefore the defender who keeps the advantage of the riposte.

On the other hand, in Chapter 16 of Book VII, entitled 'Attack of an Indecisive Theatre of Operations', he attributes to the attacker the advantage of playing second. The reason given leads us to the very centre of debate, to the essence of the duel: Who knows the other side better? Who foresees better the intentions and capacities of the other? In Chapter 28 of Book VI a defence with a decision is under consideration; in Book VII, an attack without a decision. In the latter case, it is the attacker who has the better chance of seeing through the enemy's plan: 'Dispositions with a view to a great counterattack are very different from those which aim at an ordinary defence, whereas the dispositions of an attack only differ according to whether the attacker's intentions are of a greater or lesser importance.' Clausewitz in Book VI is probably thinking of the independence of the decision which he attributes to the defender faced with the attacker seeking decisive victory and in Book VII, of the comparison between Frederick II foreseeing the conduct of his opponents whereas the latter showed themselves to be incapable against an army which conformed to the customs of the time but which was led by a bold and resolute leader. Whoever, in an indecisive war, limits himself to the defence of his theatre of operations, already betrays the absence of positive intentions and ambitious plans.

Whether or not we can reconcile these two texts in the reference to the dual type of war, these partial analyses touch on communication between the duellists, on the capacity of the one to foresee the intentions or capacities and movements of the other. By this approach, Clausewitz returns to the psychological relation between the opponents (which of them enjoys superiority) and to the principle of victory always mentioned in military literature: surprise. Now, Clausewitz, without denying the effects of surprise, tends to reduce their number and importance. 'It would be a mistake to think that it is by this means principally that great results in time of war can be achieved. The idea is very attractive, but in practice this means is paralysed by the friction of the whole machine.'

Why does surprise present so many difficulties at the higher level? The thesis appears to contradict the repeated assertions of the incomprehension of the opponents of Frederick or of Napoleon. In fact, Clausewitz is dealing at this point with strictly military surprise. In 1806, Prussia was not surprised by the war, she was badly prepared for it – which is a different matter. Even the course taken by Napoleon's troops in 1806 did not really constitute a surprise. It is thus at the tactical level, in matters which change from one moment to another, that surprises are most often produced, without necessarily involving decisive consequences.

Does this mean surprise due to activity, to rapid decisions, or to forced marches? Clausewitz uses the example of the two virtuosi in this field, Frederick and Napoleon, to show that unexpected, unforeseen and unusual movements do not always bring about the anticipated success e.g. Napoleon, withdrawing twice from Dresden in 1813, to strike Blücher, only to find nothing. If, by the same method, he reaped the equivalent of a victory over Blücher in 1814, this was due more to chance, and to circumstances of which Napoleon himself was unaware, than to his own initia-

188

tives. Clausewitz then comes to the somewhat mysterious remark which, he writes, bears on the essence of the question (*das Innern der Sache*).

Only he who dictates the law is capable of creating surprise; the law is dictated by whoever is in the right [*wer im Recht ist*]. If we surprise the opponent by a mistaken measure, we shall perhaps suffer, instead of favourable results, a severe setback; in any event, the opponent need not trouble himself much about our surprise for he finds in our mistake the means of avoiding the evil.

It is a strange formula. What is meant by being in the right or acting correctly? In relation to what is 'mistake' (*der Fehler*) defined? Clausewitz ends the chapter on surprise by returning to moral superiority. The proposition 'whoever is in the right dictates the law' none the less suggests that in the contest of skill, in combat between sabres, sufficient regularities are manifested for the art to be subjected not to laws but to rules.

These three uses of the concept of law – laws of inevitability in the universe of concepts, laws of probability in the real world, the reciprocal action of opponents, each attempting to impose his law on the other – do not contradict the conclusion of Chapter 4, Book II. None of them implies either the equivalent of a physical law in warlike phenomena or the utility of unconditional imperatives. There remains in his theory the fact that he has not explained the laws which are derived from the nature of things – a nature of things which are only represented in the real world in a more or less modified form.

3 Primordial law, general law and dynamic law

These three laws require the same kind of analysis.

In the first page of Chapter 12, Book II, we read:

War is the shock of opposed forces; from this it immediately follows that the stronger not only destroys the other but sweeps it along in its movement. This in principle excludes gradual action of forces; the simultaneous application of all forces destined for the shock appears as the primordial [*Urgesetz*] law of war.

Leaving aside the question of the nature of the law (inevitable, natural or prescriptive), let us see what use Clausewitz makes of it. Commanders do not always apply it since some of them often continue to believe in the notion of strategic reserve. Furthermore, it is only valid in so far as the contest resembles a mechanical shock. Where it resembles the reciprocal action of destructive forces (the exchange of actual fire), the successive engagement becomes conceivable and even, more often than not, expedient. All depends on the relation which is established between the engagement of fresh forces (for the side which has kept reserves) and the moral superiority that the first success, secured by numbers, has given the other side. At the critical moment, in the disorder and weaknesses induced by combat, even in the case of the victors, the shock of fresh troops can overturn the fortunes of war. Once this critical moment has passed there only remains the moral advantage of victory, and the fresh troops, incapable of making up the losses, risk being swept along in the disaster.

This analysis relates to the combats as they evolved in his age, as he observed and experienced them. Clausewitz draws the conclusion that

189

there exists, in this case, a major opposition between tactics and strategy. The first allows and even requires the successive use of forces; strategy demands the simultaneous use of forces. The reserves escape destruction by fire and by hand-to-hand fighting; they can intervene and reverse the outcome of the fight as long as it has not finished; sometimes, by reducing the number of troops engaged, they even limit losses. It is quite different in the field of strategy. The losses do not increase with the number of troops engaged, they sometimes diminish and at the same time they ensure success.

Clausewitz himself points out an objection to this proposition (*Satz*): he has so far only dealt with the combat (*Kampf*). Now, another principle of destruction is added to destruction by combat, exertions (*Anstrengungen*) and privations (*Entbehrungen*). Can one not have regard to how the army is at the end of a combat? Cannot the appearance of fresh troops be decisive in the case of one as in the case of another? Clausewitz replies that the victor and vanquished normally wait for reinforcements at the end of a campaign, but 'this is not an issue here because this increase in forces would not be necessary if they had been much greater in the first place'. On the other hand, these fresh troops, far from being of higher quality for not having fought, come up against soldiers to whom victory has given a moral superiority – to which is added the experience of fighting, the habituation to war 'which constitutes a clear gain'.

It remains to be shown tacitly that exertions and privations, as regards food or quarters, do not increase in strategy with numbers, though it is difficult to prove it to men. Even on this last point, Clausewitz attempts to prove his thesis by alleging that numbers allow an advance on a wider front. At the most, he concedes that in Russia Napoleon perhaps went too far in applying the principle.

Thus what finally remains of the primordial law? The analysis appears to invert its meaning: according to the primordial law all the forces must be engaged in the shock whereas their successive use is recommended in tactics, their simultaneous use in strategy. In fact, the contrast tends to disappear if we remember that the simultaneous use of forces in strategy is meant to prepare for the decisive shock initially to bring victory, and concentrate the contest into one single battle, according to the mechanical model of the clash of opposed forces.

In a way, the analysis and conclusion arises from a mental process, i.e. from reasoning. Clausewitz ends by asserting that time as such has no proper virtue in strategy – which does not exclude the possibility that it might acquire it in certain circumstances. The established truths – combat, by its duration, weakens the troops engaged, whereas it saves the troops in reserve; time by itself does not weaken troops strategically engaged – remain abstract and, all things being equal, valid enough.

Chapters 11, 12 and 13, lead to the summary in Chapter 14. In the final analysis what remains of the primordial law? The chapter begins by taking up the classical themes or ideas. The path of reflection never narrows into a single, simple line. There always subsists a certain margin of play as in all the practical arts of life. The decision finally falls to the act of judgment which, arising from natural perspicacity and based on reflection, almost unconsciously grasps the right. 'Sometimes it must simplify the law by reducing it to some striking characteristic points which form rules; sometimes the adopted method must become the staff upon which it leans.' The law gives way to three other concepts, judgment, rules and methods.

The original law can have no lesson to offer. As such, it applies to the most primitive, the least intellectualized forms of war, or again to the simplified model of the contest. (When a wrestler tries to floor the other, can the latter reserve his forces while risking being counted out?) It also retains a praxological significance for the more modern forms of war. War to the bitter end returns to the primitive forms of contest; the primordial law becomes a kind of abstract precept which commands less than it prohibits: it prohibits leaving troops out of use while others fight, it prohibits not engaging all one's forces and has its decisive moment. The law becomes an instrument of the mind, a kind of mnemonic – not original. Prescriptive law, natural law. We are dealing with a necessary relationship arising from the nature of things, a solution overlooked by all commentators except, if I may be allowed the statement, the formal one.

In the following book, Clausewitz introduces a general determination of the contest, close and complementary to the original law, namely the twofold effort of assuring the security of one's rear on the one hand, and of threatening that of the enemy on the other. This twofold effort becomes a kind of instinct. 'We cannot imagine a combat in which this effort does not manifest itself alongside the pure clash of violence.' He presents this instinct a few lines later as a general natural law of combat (*allgemeines Naturgesetz des Gefechts*). Why natural law rather than original law? Probably because combats evolve in greater conformity with this law than with the primordial law modified by many circumstances.

This law appears to concern tactics rather than strategy, since the latter touches the results of combat, successes or setbacks, as the means (material) of its art. Strategy, too, must take into account this general and natural law which is based on facts of a moral order rather more than a physical order. The danger of fighting on two fronts simultaneously, of losing the line of retreat: all this weakens resistance. The threat to the rear makes victory more probable and more decisive. In short, the effort to envelop characterizes the contest as such in the same way as the shock and the concentration of forces with a view to the shock.

At this point, Clausewitz, contrary to his usual practice, uses the term 'manoeuvre' in the wider sense and not, as elsewhere, in the limited meaning of 'manoeuvre-strategy' or the game of fencing. 'This natural law is effective everywhere, it presses everywhere with its natural weight and becomes the pivot around which nearly all tactical and strategic manoeuvres turn.'

This analysis of the most general natural law is enough to reject the caricatured presentation of the Clausewitzian doctrine. This extols the direct, brutal, concentrated shock, unhesitating and direct. Even in Book IV, which comes closest to the caricature, the mutual effort to envelop introduces an element of manoeuvre in all combats: even in small-scale warfare, the rivalry of skill is combined with the trial of strength. In this way, Clausewitz remains a theoretician of the same genre as those he criticizes or derides, even though he stresses other principles and reduces the significance of the non-human geographical and geometrical elements. The primordial law (of the concentration of forces in time) and the natural law of combat (the mutual effort to envelop) are both derived from the concept of the contest even though the second is confirmed by experience while the first becomes a kind of instrument of the mind. The dynamic law of war which appears in Book III (Chapter 18) explains the alternation of rest and tension (*Ruhe und Spannung*) which is characteristic of military operations.

This dynamic law applies to historic reality, to events themselves. It is connected with the problems posed by Clausewitz which we have already dealt with: how can the opponents both consider it to be in their interests at the same time to do nothing, to make neither peace nor war? Clausewitz gives two answers to this question, one valid in the abstract world of reasonable conduct on both sides, the other based upon human psychology, the tendency of each to overestimate the enemy and the natural inclination towards fear and irresolution. In Chapter 16, the order of these three factors is the opposite of that which we have just followed, the opposite of the order in Chapter 1, Book I. It is human nature which comes first, the dissymmetry of attack and defence last.

The dynamic law adds to these partial analyses at least two major ideas relating to the suspension of hostilities. First of all, even in the war of the first type, which was transformed by the Revolution and Napoleon, the long alternation subsists. Hostilities do not continue without interruption. The concept of *Ruhe*, tranquillity or calm, thus roughly corresponds to that of *Stillstand*. On the other hand, that of *Spannung* or tension offers both greater rewards and ambiguities because it touches on the frontier of political and military affairs. It is the degree of tension that determines the place of a war on the scale which ranges from armed observation to the will to disarm the enemy. One cannot always see a proportional relationship between tension (politics) and the violence of combat; tension sometimes gives a combat of secondary importance an extreme significance. 'The cannonade of Valmy had a more decisive result than the battle of Blenheim.'

The introduction into strategic thought of the concept of tension (important in Chapters 1, 11 and 18) is equivalent to considering the motives of war, the ends sought, the relations between states and within each of them.

At the same time, this chapter goes in the direction of the dual type of war. A doubt remains at the end of the chapter and the end of the book. After reflection that, in most of the wars of the past, the state of equilibrium lasted for a greater part of the time, and that events, whether successes or setbacks, rarely assumed a decisive character, Clausewitz briefly considers the Prussian campaign of 1806; here, measures which conformed to the spirit of former times proved ruinous in the new circumstances. He concludes with the following paragraph:

> This speculative distinction which we have made is equally necessary for the development of this theory because all that we have to say on the relation of defence and attack and on the performance of this dual act concerns the state of the crisis in which the forces are placed and during which tension and movement arise.

We can only treat all the activity which can take place in the state of equilibrium as a corollary, for that crisis is the real war and the state of equilibrium only its reflex.

Clausewitz was still inclined at the time he wrote these lines to recognize only the first type of war or the real war. The greater part of Book IV only in effect deals with real war or with war of the first type. Only the last chapter explicitly analyses the defence of a theatre of operations where there is no decision. It looks as though Clausewitz only managed to conceptualize the opposition of the two types of war by writing Book IV, as he brought to light the diversity of defensive practices according to the plans of the attacker.

The dynamic law remains no less valid for all wars because it explains as it were the pulsations of violence, the discontinuity of action which results from both the nature of men and the matter within the nature of the duel, that is the dissymmetry of attack and defence.

4 The propositions of the 'final note'

What conclusions may be drawn from this analysis? It seems to me possible to distinguish five different diverse contexts in which Clausewitz uses the notion of law.

First, he connects law and necessity and from this, given the nature of things, laws which govern the universe of the ideal will enlarge. On the other hand, as soon as one returns to reality, to modified war, one passes into laws of probability, or, more simply, into judgments of probability made by the actors in the light of the uncertainty of given facts. This explains how reason can lay down fewer laws in war as the latter departs from its absolute form.

The notion of policy as lawgiver (*Gesetzgeber*) implies no more than the idea, expressed several times in other ways, that the instrument must be subject to the intentions of the user. The latter cannot require from it more than is possible nor use it without an awareness of its proper nature.

The expression 'imposing one's will on the other' refers to the initial scheme of the duel. Neither opponent is free to determine alone the intensity of the combat. Neither can avoid the decision by arms if the other is firmly resolute. The very idea of 'dictating one's law' suggests, without rigorous formulation, that one of the duellists determines the conditions of the fight according to his own interest. If Clausewitz asserts that one must act correctly in order to acquire a dominant position, it is probably because he is thinking of juridical controversies (which, he writes, have much in common with war): right must be on one's side, justness in action if not justice.

In the same category belongs the supreme law of the decision by arms, the primordial law of the simultaneous application of all forces with a view to the decisive shock, the general natural law, the effort to turn the opponent's flank and to fight him on several sides at the same time. None of these laws lays down a command (order, positive or negative); none translates mechanically into precepts. All three are still of praxological significance. The supreme law of the decision by arms, subordinate to the legislation of policy, serves as the ultimate reference to the antagonism of wills. The original law changes its meaning according to the decomposition of the totality of war. The general natural law makes intelligible the diversity of manoeuvres in combat or in a theatre of operations without, for all that, being explicit in precise precepts which are valid for a given set of circumstances.

The dynamic law of tension and rest applies to the very reality of war or, according to Schering, to *Geschehen*. Hostilities do not evolve in a continuous manner, they are interrupted by moments of rest. As the belligerents find themselves in a state of equilibrium or in a state of tension, events – combats, movements, battles – take on a quite different meaning.

None of these laws characterize the theoretical revolution which Clausewitz dreamed of. None of these laws is in the list of propositions (*Sätze*) enumerated in the final note to show the sceptics that a theory of the conduct of war is, despite enormous difficulties, after all possible.

The first two propositions concern defence (the stronger form with negative end) and attack (the weaker form with positive end); propositions which are in one sense obvious, in another equivocal. If the defence were not the stronger form why would the weaker side nearly always remain on the defensive? But does the reasoning apply in the same way to strategy and to tactics? Do not arms and methods of fighting favour both forms of war?

The third proposition – that great successes shape lesser ones – forms the basis of a fourth proposition which is presented as a precept, albeit vague: that strategic action must involve a small number of centres of gravity. The first proposition is deduced from the total character of the battle or campaign, and so applies both to the concept and to historical experience.

There follows the assertion that the show of force (or diversion) is a weaker use of forces than true attack and must therefore be justified by particular circumstances. Great successes, centres of gravity, the futility (as a general rule) of a simple show of force – all these assertions came from the same idea, in unique, great and decisive events which must be dealt with individually.

The following propositions relating to victory are also first deduced from conceptual analysis. Victory consists less of conquest on the battlefield than of the physical and moral destruction of the enemy fighting force. The disarming of the enemy represents in the first two chapters of Book I the natural or ideal finality of war. The battle logically, as the decisive act of war, follows from this. However, the assertion that this destruction is more often achieved during retreat is based on experience and is valid by way of empirical generality, even if reasoning can find the cause of the fact: retreat, after a lost battle, weakens an army both physically and morally and threatens its disintegration.

The following propositions contain for the second time a precept drawn from the structure of the reality of war: since great successes at the same time determine the lesser ones, and since success is the greater where victory has been won, the sudden change from one direction or one line to another must be considered all the more a necessary evil.

The next proposition does not take on the form of a precept even though it demonstrates the possibility of a theory of the conduct (or entails one):

the justification for envelopment lies in superiority as such or in the superiority of one's own lines of communication and retreat; and likewise with flank positions. The account ends with the formula: every offensive becomes weaker as it progresses.

Clausewitz declares these propositions obvious. The majority of them are connected with the structure of the object of war or with the goal of the action in war: war constitutes a totality, and the dialectic of attack and of defence explains the reciprocity of action in a contest which evolves across space and time. None of these propositions, characteristic of theory, constitutes a law in either sense of the concept (law of nature or prescriptive law). None of them even constitutes a principle of action, but they contain instruction for the commander to the extent that he thinks of the field of battle and of the war commander with the help of major concepts: centres of gravity, destruction of enemy forces, strength of the defensive, attrition of the offensive, the total character of the battle or of the campaign, etc. Compared with the maxims of the military theoreticians of his time or of ours, these propositions are of such abstract character that they seem to belong to another world, and they earned Clausewitz his reputation as a philosopher or metaphysician. Now, he considers himself above all an analyst or observer: with good reason.

Two questions remain, suggested by the laws and propositions of the final note. Supposing that rational, theoretical reflection offers a way out of the antithesis of an unacceptable theory and of a radical scepticism, are the truths of this theory founded upon concept or upon experience, upon the experience of an age or of all ages? Since rational thought rejects the simplifications of dogmatic instruction yet seeks to be of use in action, which instruction does it suggest should be followed? The two following chapters attempt to give an answer to these.

Chapter 8

Theory and History

The distinction between the conduct of war, in the narrow sense of the term, and the subsidiary headings of the art of war (the armies' armaments, organization and supplies) leads naturally to the question of the relation between theory and history. Does strategy or the conduct of every war, in practice or in theory, change with the times, the organization of the armies and the type of weapons used? Is it a historical theory or an eternal theory, or a theory in itself for Clausewitz?

1 Law, rule and method

On the history of war in general, Clausewitz confines himself to a few remarks. He makes a distinction between barbarous or rough people (*rohe Völker*) and civilized people; he also sometimes opposes antiquity and modern times (from the sixteenth century onwards).

The first opposition inspires him with a pessimistic judgment often quoted from Book I, Chapter 1: the violence of the combats is not necessarily tempered by the culture of the people because it remains a function of the size of the interests involved. He even explains by pragmatical calculation, and not because of moral progress, the disappearance of some practices such as the killing of prisoners and the devastation of land. Intelligence has a greater influence on the conduct of war, it inspires more efficient methods in the use of violence than in former days the more brutal explosions of the instinct did.

In short, civilization increases the role played by intelligence in the conduct of war without eliminating or even reducing the role of primordial wrath. Not that civilized people always hate each other at the start of wars: it is the fight itself which generates, feeds and exasperates hostile passions. History has not refuted this gloomy diagnosis. The bombings of Dresden and Hiroshima by the British and American air forces outdo the atrocities of the Athenians and Spartans. The charnel-houses of Katyn, the gas-chambers, *Einsatzcommandos* whose task it was to exterminate the Jews, will always stupefy all who refuse to despair of humanity – no matter how much time has passed.

The opposition between antiquity and modern times provides the basis for a rule of historical method. Differing in this from most of his contemporaries, Clausewitz rarely uses examples derived from the distant past of the ancient world. Is it because he knew little Latin and no Greek? It would be peculiarly superficial to explain his reluctance by such ignorance. On this point he has never wavered. The man disliked pedants, drawing-room strategists and the lecturers who solve the political problems of our times by referring to Athens and Rome. But a rule or method also dictates his caution. The further events go back into the past, the less we know them both as a whole and in their details. Now, the only really instructive examples, as soon as one aims at confirming or disproving and not only illustrating a principle, demand that the case should be analysed in its slightest peculiarities. If that is not done, there will be no difficulty in finding examples to support false principles.

A few references to antiquity deserve mention. In particular, the case of Fabius Cunctator obviously interested him throughout his career. In the 'Strategy' of 1804, he refused to praise Fabius, attributing his behaviour, motivated by circumstances, to the temperament of the Cunctator. The proof he gives is the opposition made by Fabius to Scipio's campaign in Africa, and he concludes that Rome would have perished had Fabius been king, The example is used to illustrate the influence exercised by the psychological disposition of a war leader, to underline the difference between time and circumstances: the Romans could refuse to do battle; today this refusal must be paid for by sacrificing space. It must not be forgotten either that in 1804, and 1809, Clausewitz passionately reproaches the Prussian or European sovereigns for their hesitation. The contrast between the severity of 1804 and the judgments of the Treatise remains none the less significant.

The first time, in Chapter 8 of Book IV, he notes that the refusal of combat by Fabius in no way proves the physical or moral superiority of Hannibal, but only that Fabius' plan excluded combat. In the same chapter, he quotes him to illustrate a sort of resistance which relies above all on the enemy's self-destruction. He quotes him a third time during the indecisive campaigns in the course of which, superficially, the belligerents show some activity thus, Hannibal and Fabius, Frederick and Daun, all of them are warriors on the same level.

The comparison between the two allusions to Fabius in the 'Strategy' of 1804 and the three allusions in the Treatise makes it possible to conclude that there is development in the thought or mood of Clausewitz. Just as resolution tends to replace boldness, temporizing in a Fabius no longer tends to replace boldness, or reveal a weakness of character which happened to have served the circumstances and to have contributed to the salvation of Rome. A strategy *à la* Fabius, a refusal to combat, represents a defence strategy or, to speak in more precise Clausewitzian language, a kind of resistance. No doubt, this kind of resistance is not carried out in the same style as in the obscure days of the third century BC and in 1812. The camps in which the legions would settle made it easy for Fabius to refuse battle and Hannibal would offer it in vain (and this gives us an example of influence of tactics over strategy). In our time – and Clausewitz already recognized this fact in 1804 – loss of space for refusal to fight is the price paid. 'Nowadays battle usually can only be avoided by sacrificing a great deal of ground. Sometimes this advantage is not paid for too dearly by such a sacrifice, as for instance against the French at the Russian frontier.' On the other hand, in the Treatise, the strategy of Fabius, which in 1804 was compared with that of Daun and to which he gave no chance against a Hannibal, illustrates a sort of resistance which at all times deserves to be taken into consideration: a strategy which relies for victory on the wearing out of the enemy's armies in a hostile country, on the ordeals which the conqueror imposes on his own troops.

He mentions, once more, Scipio's expedition in Africa whilst Hannibal, unvanquished, was still very much on Italian soil. Whereas in 1804 Clausewitz used this bold decision to belittle Fabius who had criticized it, he now uses the example towards a completely different end, to rectify his judgment: thus the example of Scipio is instructive and we have a right to use it because we know well enough the general conditions of the states and armies on which depended the efficiency of this indirect resistance.

To paraphrase an expression of Leon Brunschvicg's, we could say that history is the laboratory of theory. From the early texts to the intellectual testament, the relationship between theory and history remains at the centre of Clausewitz's thinking. In 1804 he quotes Machiavelli's famous formula – measures must adapt to times and circumstances – which must not be considered as trivial, for it does not refer to details but to general measures:

> This rule is currently forgotten. Governments usually choose their war leaders without any consideration of time and circumstances, and the war leaders do no better as far as their system of war is concerned. This war system is a mere expression of their way of thinking and feeling, and is seldom something they have reasoned out.

In the same way, in Chapter 6 of Book II, he discusses the *condottieri* to illustrate how the conduct of the war depends upon the instrument which is used: he adds that at no other time did the armed forces have to such an extent the character of a tool, separate from the life of the state or its people. The conduct of war is confused with the art of war or the theory of this art; to state that the conduct of the war depends on the instrument is to state also that strategy – theory or practice – depends on the armed forces through tactics which uses them immediately (whereas strategy only uses them indirectly).

The commentator may be inclined to reverse the construct established by Clausewitz between tactical theory and strategic theory, the first being easier than the second. Indeed, if history – the difference between time and circumstances – is taken into account, it is tactics which change most, since the instrument, that is to say the armed forces, changes with the industry which supplies the arms and with the state which organizes the troops. Moreover, when he deals with tactical analyses, either he stresses the successive transformation of ways of attack or defence, or he explicitly specifies that he is dealing with the conditions of the next war or battle.

The most striking example of the historicity of tactical art can be found in Chapter 2 of Book VI. In Books IV and V, Clausewitz does not repeat in each chapter that he is dealing with the armies or the combat as they have developed in his own day, but the unprejudiced reader cannot doubt it. The distribution of troops between the three kinds of arms, or the deployment of troops on the battlefield, do not obey 'transhistoric' principles though sometimes, in accordance with specific weaponry or organization, tactics lend themselves better than strategy to the establishment of principles; in general they can be taught dogmatically with a positive doctrine.

Considering again the four concepts stated in the previous chapter – principles, rules, regulations and methods: principles, as we know, from a prescriptive law which is imposed in action, differ from law by its lesser rigour, by the certain amount of freedom it leaves to ordinary, to intuitive perception. Principles are easily found in tactics: 'Not needlessly to send the cavalry against an infantry which is still in good order; to use firearms only when you can begin to be sure of their efficiency; in combat, reserve as far as possible some force for the final phase.'

These three principles are all based on experience in the two meanings used by Clausewitz: the knowledge drawn from experimental sciences and 'which without any doubt form the foundation of the art of war', and historical experience. Experimental sciences teach us the effect of firearms at various distances, but the actual losses caused by the artillery also depend on many varying circumstances, not to mention the moral effect of a weapon which varies in accordance with the quality of the enemy's men and of their resilience in combat.

If detailed, historical, concrete experience – and not only knowledge established by experimental sciences – is necessary in tactical theory, the latter still requires more positive doctrine (*positive Lehre*) than strategical theory. I have restricted the significance of this statement by clarifying a consequence of other analyses, that is to say the evolution of the instrument (the armed forces) and the way it is used. Even with this reservation, a question remains, which the critics of Clausewitz have raised and which the most sympathetic commentator cannot put aside: How does the principle of reserving troops for the final phase of the battle differ from the principle of using all one's forces strategically in the decisive battle; in other words, how do the tactical principles differ from the strategic principles?

The examples of a rule given by Clausewitz are singularly like the examples of principles. If we establish a rule, to attack the enemy with increased energy as soon as he starts, in the course of a battle, to withdraw his batteries, the reason is that this sign reveals the whole situation and the intention of the enemy; and the enemy, when he gives up, can neither resist vigorously nor escape. The withdrawal of his batteries reveals most often his intention of abandoning the battlefield, just as the charge of the cavalry against a well-ordered infantry is most often doomed to failure. But the principles of action, based on the generality of cases and on probability, can also be found in strategy. For instance, usually it is better not to change the direction of attack and not to disperse during a retreat (concentric and eccentric retreat).

If need be, one can put forward a difference in degree between the principles of tactics and the principles of strategy; the relations between cavalry and infantry, at a certain time, in terms of a given efficiency of the weapons, are put to the test and confirmed by historical example which are both more numerous and more alike than the historical examples which are available to confirm tactical principles.

I believe that there is another argument which determines the need for tactical regulations and, consequently, for tactical methodism as opposed to the freedom of choice which pertains to war leaders. The nearer one is to the base and the further from the top where the leader is, the more necessary are the *Vorschriften* and the *Anweisungen*, the prescriptions and instructions which are expressed in regulations, both for exercises and for field service. Freedom of choice for the leader and a rigorous method inculcated upon the soldiers and the leaders at lower levels, is the Clausewitzian combination, characteristic both of the Prussian and German armies.

Why do the same unreliability of data and diversity of cases require the various levels to submit to regulations or trust the intuitive perception of judgment? Hundreds and thousands of commissioned and non-commissioned officers could hardly be expected to have the perspicacity, insight and intellectual mastery which are required (mostly in vain) from those who exercise the supreme command. Rather than trust individual initiatives which might at any moment be wrong, it is better to keep to the prescriptions and instructions which indicate the correct decision in the majority of cases, to adopt regularly the same deployment of the troops, the same order of battle and the same relationship between different arms, provided that these regulations for field service are modified according to changes of weapons and organization.

The second reason derives from the very nature of the military system, which consists of men but is intended for use as a tool, though a human one liable to break down. The soldiers, so to speak, are inoculated with the prescriptions and instructions, which become an integral part of their being, of what they do. In an exercise, regulations are universal, whereas in field service methods and complicated procedures including prescriptions and instructions come into play; this hardens into a schema when the method becomes schematic, automatic and foreseeable.

Clausewitz admits that, even at a higher level, 'methodism' though deplorable, remains inevitable as long as theory, as he himself calls it (i.e. rational study), has not trained the mind of the war leaders, enabling them to rise above contradictory theories and simple experience. For want of this theoretical revolution, the 'methodism' of the Prussian generals, who imitated the oblique order of Frederick the Great or the 'methodism' of French generals, repeating the brutal, massive and bloody attacks of Napoleon, will to a certain extent remain inevitable. Still, any 'methodism' that would determine the plans of war or campaign, and would deliver them ready-made, like a machine, is to be wholly condemned.

2 Limitation of experience and validity of theory

The preceding paragraph leads to two propositions, which are not contradictory but divergent: tactical theory requires more principles, rules or methods than strategic theory, because the phenomena are more regular, and because it is impossible to give to thousands of officers the same freedom of initiative as the war leader or chief of state. But if, in every age, prescriptions and guidance must guarantee the efficiency of the instrument, the instrument itself still changes from age to age, according to weapons and political circumstances themselves. The question already formulated thus remains: Does strategic theory in turn have a historical character? Does it change with times, societies and ways of thinking? Is it possible to apply the same criteria to the campaigns of Frederick the Great which can be applied to those of Napoleon? Or to criticize Frederick with reference to the Napoleonic model? In short, what solution has Clausewitz given to the problem of the relationship between history and theory, concepts and experiences? These expressions are, in the final analysis, almost equivalent, since historical examples, essentially, make up experience (beyond the technical knowledge to be derived from experimental science), and since concepts form the structure for theory.

Here again we must take Clausewitz's work as a whole, since any quotation wrenched from its context may be misleading.

One, probably quite late, passage may be taken as our starting point. In Book II, Chapter 2, there is a short paragraph entitled, 'Strategy derives from experience only the means and ends that it seeks'. Here, Clausewitz questions the validity of any theory based on historical experience, and only on limited experience at that. Pure philosophical inquiry, he says, would become highly confused if it set itself to discover a transhistorical theory, because logical necessity, at that level of inquiry, would have to be excluded. Therefore, philosophy must turn to experience, and consider the various cases that have already been noted in the wars of the past. Hence, there emerges only a limited theory, applicable only to the factors or circumstances that the past can supply as examples. Then comes his conclusion:

> Such limitation is in any event unavoidable for any theory, because any theory is constrained by virtue of its own construction, either because it will be an abstraction from the history of war, or, at least, because it has to be compared with actual historical experience. This limitation is in any case more formal than substantial.

Here, Clausewitz's expression is obscure: 'mehr dem Begriff als der Sache nach'. The opposition of 'concept' (*Begriff*) and 'object' (*Sache*), which Naville renders as 'more theoretical than practical', is not found in the usual vocabulary of the Treatise, let alone the earlier writings. This sentence can really have no other meaning than the above.

A theory drawn from a limited part of experience is *eo ipso* logically limited. However, the formal limitation does not extend to the content of the theory, which will explain the nature of phenomena and how they interrelate. We wonder, therefore, which principles or propositions of his theory Clausewitz himself wished to exclude from the heading 'historical experience'.

There is a first difficulty in comparing the text of Book II, Chapter 2, with another equally famous passage in Book VIII, Chapter 3. In the passage where Clausewitz distinguishes two types of structure in war, one in which only the final success will count, and the other where final success will be the outcome of a series of partial successes, he makes it plain that the first type derives its truth from a concept, whereas the truth of the second is based on experience. It would seem, therefore, that the theory has a twofold origin – in the analysis of both ideas and experience. With a little ingenuity and good will, he can reconcile the two passages: after all, it might have been supposed that the conception of absolute war was just an intellectual game if history, through Napoleon, had not offered a concrete case, close to the idea itself.

Whatever the origin of the theory, I cannot doubt that it results from a combination of conceptual analysis and historical experience. In this respect, Clausewitz did not change between the early writings and his intellectual testament, whatever progress had been accomplished between the fragments of 1804 and the conceptual cathedral of 1830. Even if the final texts sometimes seem equivocal to us, the reason is that Clausewitzian conceptualization, which is characteristic of eighteenth-century thinking, oscillates between two poles, the ideal type, the essence of the simplified model, on the one hand, and the concrete reality on the other.

In modern parlance Chapter 1 of Book I starts with a model and on the way encounters 'polarity', or the drawn game in which equality between loss and gain recurs. But in the notion of absolute war or the absolute form of war, Clausewitz puts more meaning than we do in a model or ideal type, as a simple instrument used by a mind eager to grasp a complex reality. There is no doubt that Clausewitz holds as true the conceptual series which unfolds in Book I, Chapter 1, just as Marx holds as true, as conforming to the logic of reality, the conceptual dialectics of Book I of *Capital*.

The example of Book I, Chapter 1, is, I think, simplest because it is the only case where theoretical analysis confronts history and makes it possible to understand its diversity rationally. The threefold definition of war substitutes for the opposition between absolute war and real war another formula, which is more satisfactory: any war will include the three elements in variable proportions. Real wars do not merely result from a modification of absolute war but from the uneven weight of each of those three elements. Clausewitz, like Marx later on, had the idea of social activity at the basis of his thought. Combat is a form of action between man and man. If we start off with two violent wills in conflict, two wrestlers in a ring, we find the same progression to extremes. The struggle will not stop until one of the two wills is broken or one of the two fighters is unable to resist – and the conditions of descent – the enemies do not need to understand each other or kill each other, but they need to communicate to overcome their passions and limit their losses.

Substituting states for individual wrestlers, and setting out the chain of concepts of war as Marx unfolds the concepts of the economic worlds, we find that since human beings are involved we cannot neglect moral factors. Since men fight with the tools which science puts at their disposal, and since armed forces require food, ammunition and reinforcements, there are three obvious targets: the armed forces, the natural and primary targets; the resources needed for their upkeep (the country); and the will which animates them or sustains their strength (morale and the resolution to fight to the end). By substituting states for single fighters, we have divided in two the will – the governing body and the people – and similarly with the forces, i.e. the present soldiers and potential troops, which are themselves divided between the mind which commands even savages (the political understanding) and the free activity of the spirit of the military leader. Armies fight in the spatial dimension. Hence the importance of distance, marching, details of terrain, climate, and all the material data that may appear as obstacles or as aids to be exploited; and hence, too, the importance of time, since armies, unlike single fighters, cannot be brought forward and used in a moment. The dialectic of attack and defence is a byproduct of the space–time pair, to take and to hold. The distinction between tactics and strategy, between combat and use of combat, derives from the original distinction between the fight and the human goals of the fight. Human fighting aims at a goal.

This conceptual system forms the foundation of theory in as much as the theory confines itself to rational consideration of the object of the war, without attempting to build a *Lehrgebäude* or doctrinal structure. In this sense, it confirms the formula of Book II, Chapter 2: the limitation of historical experience will limit the validity of theory only formally and not substantially.

Beyond this, there are many questions as to the relationship between concept and history:

(a) First, does the conceptual system suggest propositions as regards the general course of history? There is one in particular. Clausewitz as usual contrasts the two extremes: original violence and hatred, and understanding. Understanding plays an increasing part in the conduct of war, because war moves further and further from the blind, direct clash of warriors borne by instinct. The concept of the totality, and the insistence on the proposition that war is not composed of a series of separate battles but forms a whole, derives at least in part from the original concept of war, a test of strength between warriors.

At a certain time or, if my suggested chronology is not acceptable, at certain places, Clausewitz explains the pursuit of the decisive battle in Napoleonic times as a return to the original nature of war, in which war leaders' intelligence re-establishes a unity in the fighting that the complex nature of armies and societies had seemingly made impossible. 'If we imagine the state and its military force as a unit, then the most natural idea is to see the war as a single great combat; which is, after all, more or less the case in the simple condition of savages.'

In other words, the total character of war derives both from concept and from experience. The nearer war is to its absolute state, the nearer it is to its original nature. Intelligence can restore to wars their pristine unity, despite the complexity of circumstances and the multiplicity of battles. Finally, Clausewitz recognized that the wars that conformed to the original nature of fighting were neither the most frequent nor the most desirable among civilized peoples. But he maintained until the end that the intervention of intelligence did not guarantee any lessening of primitive cruelty – perhaps because war is *selbst nichts Menschenfreundliches*, i.e. is itself no friend of man.

(b) This first question naturally leads to a second. Any war forms a whole, but the totalities have various structures. We know that Clausewitz has distinguished two historical kinds which still, I think, have significance: one where only the last battle counts, the other where the result depends on the total successes and failures.

In sport today, championship and cup final describe the equivalents of the two structures. The championship is won by the side which, at the end of the year, has most points, with each victory giving a certain number of them. In the Cup Final, any failure represents elimination: here, victory or defeat has a decisive character. In other words, the structure of the totality of war will suggest a historical typology that Clausewitz indicated only fleetingly, but that really illustrates the combined use of concept and historical experience which is characteristic of his method.

How do the two totalities of war and the two types of war relate to each other? To my knowledge, Clausewitz did not explicitly link the two typologies, though there is an obvious enough link. If, on the one hand, the last battle determines everything, it has to be deoisive, and mean the overthrow of one side while securing the other a crushing ability to dictate the terms of peace. If, on the other hand, once hostilities have ceased, every piece on the board will be counted, then, neither side having won, peace must be negotiated. Neither side will have supremacy to dictate terms; so the whole action and not just the final bout will have its part to play.

However, one of the typologies results from a chiefly military, and the other from a chiefly political goal. A military victory, even if decisive, does not necessarily mean an ascent to extremes, and if the war is purely between states that recognize each other's rights to exist, then the decisive victory of one of the armies may resolve the conflict but without provoking the equivalent of a revolutionary crisis. Clausewitz's German commentators, in the last century, regarded this as normal: a militarily decisive victory would not spark off the ascent to extremes, and would take its place in the European system of balance. The circumstances that enabled Bismarck to conduct such policies have not recurred in our century.

Clausewitz's conceptual system did lead him to a typology reduced to two terms, and did not suffice for systematic classification of the various wars. In Book VIII, Chapter 3 (B), he surveys wars waged by quite different peoples or states – half-civilized Tartars, republics of the ancient world, feudal lords and cities of the Middle Ages, and kings of the eighteenth century – and he formulates the major proposition: all will wage war in their own way, each one differently, with different means and ends. We must remember that the theory of war can apply either a narrow or a broader meaning. The conclusion is obvious: that there is not a single theory of the conduct of war, valid at all times, but theories as different as the practices, the principles and customs of which they elaborate.

Book VIII, Chapter 6 (B), ends with a few already quoted lines: each age has its specific wars, subject to limiting conditions: and its own philosophical principles and theory. Clausewitz comes to a conclusion that underlies historical knowledge, and we must take account of its particular features. We can only understand or judge the war leaders by restoring them to their own time, and by taking account of the means at their disposal, the aims they pursued and the prejudices (or ways of thinking) that restricted their options.

This seems to finish off Clausewitz. To restore the unity of the concept of war, or rather, to give back its unity to the idea of war and put all real wars under the same concept, we have to look at these real wars in the light of their socio-political circumstances. Otherwise the 'cabinet' wars and the Tartar wars would cease to be 'things of a kind'. Whilst the political character of any wars explains the historical diversity of wars, this diversity seems to rule out any possible general statement. Does it not, by the same token, rule out any transhistorical strategic principles?

On the one hand, Clausewitz claims that the limitation encountered in historical experience does not limit the application of theory; on the other hand, he states that any age implicitly has its theory of war, and he even states that we must not classify the various practices as if they could be placed on an increasing scale of perfection.

How do we resolve this antinomy? Which solution does Clausewitz suggest? To answer this, we have to examine his methodology of historical examples and criticism, and his principles of strategy.

3 Examples and criticism

Let us suppose, at the outset, that theory does not teach commanders the rules of war as an art, but only attempts to analyse war as an object.

Whether with concrete cases or with criticism, Clausewitz writes as a historian or even, it could be said, as a historicist. He scrupulously takes into account the conditions of the time: the material as well as the moral conditions, the composition of armies and the prevailing ideas of their epoch. Whereas Bülow or Jomini or Rustow judge the commander with reference to eternal principles – Jomini for instance criticizing Frederick the Great by quoting Napoleonic principles – Clausewitz, in his campaign accounts as well as in the Treatise, recalls the political circumstances, the organization of supplies and the relationship of army and people in each case.

Clausewitz's historicism or historical sense explains his reluctance to use examples drawn from distant times that are not well-known. It also explains the limited period from which, on the whole, he draws most of the cases he analyses (from the seventeenth to the nineteenth centuries). In Chapters 2, 5 and 6, he attempts a methodology of strategic thinking applied to history, or based on history, in which historical study is the basis of strategic theory.

In Book II, Chapter 6, he distinguishes four different uses of examples: to clarify or illustrate an idea; to apply one; to show the possibility of something or some action; to draw a lesson or to prove a general proposition. Of these four uses, only the last two demonstrate something of interest to us, the last one in particular deserving attention.

To show that in some circumstances a fortified camp can fulfil the function assigned by strategy, needs only one instance, assuming that, as in logic, it is legitimate to move from the real to a possible situation. The example chosen is the case of the Bunzelwitz encampment which Frederick the Great made his troops hold from 25 August to 25 September 1761, at the most desperate moment of the Seven Years' War. In Book VIII, Chapter 8, Clausewitz cites this instance again, stating unhesitatingly that Napoleon would speedily have been able to rip up such a cobweb. He reminds us, however, that we cannot judge the conduct of a war without taking account of time and place, and he puts forward two of the arguments he uses to justify historical assessment of war leaders: the unequal strengths involved, and the character of the enemy. Frederick the Great was quite right in employing against a Daun and the Imperial Austrian army methods that would have been useless against his own troops.

He does not, in Book II, Chapter 6, mention a further use of historical examples that seems to fit between his third and fourth uses: to demonstrate a negative but general proposition, e.g. that a state can seldom take another by surprise by initiating a war or by instructing its troops to prepare. However, he does admit that surprise is less rare at a lower level: the enemy may be surprised by a quick march and be deprived of a position, or observation point, or road. History is also appealed to as a demonstration that small-scale surprises of this kind seldom lead to great results, and he takes this opportunity to clear up a historical legend concerning a manoeuvre of Frederick the Great in 1761, in illustration of the great difficulty of obtaining large-scale surprise effects. Similarly, he cites failures by the two 'virtuosi', Frederick and Napoleon, in July 1760 and 1813 respectively, and concludes that though successes of this kind may be conceivable, they have always required favourable conditions. Bonaparte's victories over Blücher's army ensured his success and, in the night of 14–15 August, Frederick similarly altered the disposition of his army from the chosen earlier one.

To demonstrate that a certain type of operation – it may be termed strategic surprise – rarely succeeds therefore needs a thorough survey of the cases, at least in the period to be considered, as well as a deep study of the exceptions. In Book VII, Chapter 19, he studies the attack of an enemy army from the headquarters viewpoint. In order to refute the opinion that such attacks are the acme of military art he surveys famous examples of operation, and analyses each one, discussing breadth of results, conditions, errors made by the vanquished, etc. Finally, he is able to list rules (though he avoids the word) to govern an operation of this kind, which will lie on the frontier between strategy and tactics.

In other words, even when Clausewitz draws up examples, he draw lessons not so much from the numbers of successes and failures as from the general conditions in both. In using history to demonstrate a general proposition, it is the detailed analysis and not the number of cases that has demonstrative value. This justifies his preference for studying wars of the modern era and his reluctance to study those of ancient times. It confirms yet again the dependence of tactics on armaments, or of strategy, at least in some aspects, on tactics. Thus, depending on whether armed camps can sustain attack, strategy will or will not use such devices.

The main idea that Clausewitz clearly expresses is now part of the common stock of the methodology of social science. It involves contrasting the illustration of a general proposition by arbitrarily chosen examples, and demonstration of the same proposition on an experimental basis. With strategic or tactical problems, for instance the placing of infantry and cavalry (e.g. whether behind or beside the other) or an eccentric attack, it is easy enough to find a few favourable examples for one or other side of the argument. A theorist, so long as he simply stays close to the bare facts, will hardly be able to decide between two opposing views. To illustrate the ambiguity of the facts alone, in the absence of analysis, Clausewitz returns to the two war leaders whom he happily refers to most often: was Daun a model of wise prudence or of irresolution, and was Bonaparte's crossing of the Dolomites in 1797 a great decision or merely rash? Similarly, was the disaster of 1812 owing to foolhardiness, or only to sluggish movement?

It still remains to determine what constitutes the detailed analysis of cases that makes proof of a general proposition possible. Criticism, which Clausewitz deals with in the chapter before the one that lists examples, certainly requires detailed analysis of cases. This leads us to additional aspects of the epistemological question, and helps clarify the Clausewitzian relationship of concepts (theory) and history.

To suggest plausible hypotheses as to what might have happened had a war leader taken a different decision, we have to go into questions of cause and effect. These questions are not dissimilar to matters affecting the relationship of means and ends, which will concern prospective rather than, as in the earlier case, retrospective study. Napoleon won the battle of Borodino because the Russians withdrew from the field, and because the victory must go to him who is master of the field. But did this victory, which did not destroy the Russian army, reflect Napoleon's real intention and the goal he must have had in mind? If he wanted to destroy the Russians, he failed. If we suppose that he did not want to destroy them, can we also say that he failed in his planning?

The difficulty of criticism that this instance represents comes from the divergence between the thinking of the actor before the event and the judgment of the critic who knows its outcome. The critic cannot fail to know what happened, whereas the actor will have wondered about the consequences of his various decisions. If history followed a rigorous necessity, we should know its lesson in advance. If it were merely a matter of chance, it would not teach us anything and strategic theory could not exist. As Clausewitz adopts an intermediate position between Bernhorst's scepticism and Bülow's pseudo-scientific pedantries, his critique has seemingly to follow contradictory guidelines: first identifying with the actor, but then placing his decision (the choice of a means with a clear end in view) in a larger, increasingly broad, context, and even, in some circumstances, endorsing the judgment that reality made on the actor.

Of the four examples analysed by Clausewitz, to the great indignation of his French readers he rated one very highly – the offer of armistice that eventually produced the Peace of Campo Formio. The next two, the raising of the siege of Mantua so that the two separated Austrian corps could be individually defeated, and the decision, after the victories of Champaubert and Montmirail, to turn against Schwarzenberg's Austrians, can certainly be contested, since a different strategy might have produced better results. The final example is dealt with in a complex and paradoxical verdict that recurs quite often in the Treatise.

Clausewitz approved of the Peace of Campo Formio after a set of political as well as military arguments, which are quite interesting in their internal logic. In fact, they emerge from the application of two notions that we have learned: on the one hand, the hierarchy of means and ends, from which arises the overall unity of the war, including proper conclusion, peace; and on the other hand, the relationship between morale and the combatants' willingness or otherwise to pursue the fighting to the very end of their resources.

Bonaparte had the means to threaten Vienna: the strength of his army and the armies of the Rhine under Hoche and Moreau outnumbered the Austrians by 130,000 to 80,000. But these forces could never have contemplated such a thing. However, the peace that Bonaparte did obtain, on favourable terms, was such as to suggest that the Austrians would have been reluctant to take on the effort and loss needed for a war fought to the bitter end, even had it produced a final victory. The same Austrian government was overwhelmed by defeat, and collapsed in discouragement without properly measuring its chances of obtaining final victory by fighting on. Clausewitz certainly meant to contrast the wisdom of the

207

young Bonaparte, who could use the fear he inspired to arrive at a favourable but still moderate peace, with the overconfidence of the older Bonaparte who, given the gradual exhaustion of the terror he inspired in Europe, strove for a last success in Russia, only to lose the gamble because he had misjudged his enemy.

It is strange that the first example, the only one where criticism leads to entirely positive appreciation, affected politics rather than strategy. But the two following instances deal with the purely military decisions in two of the most brilliant and most widely admired campaigns of Napoleon.

Bonaparte raised the siege of Mantua of 30 June 1796 and defeated the two separated relief corps under Wurmser. According to Clausewitz, Bonaparte could have used a different method, circumvallation, given that the 40,000 men of the best infantry in Europe had nothing to fear from Wurmser's 50,000. Mantua would have fallen in a few days whereas, once the siege was raised, it resisted for six months. This, according to Clausewitz, supplies educative criticism. Napoleon probably did not think at the time of circumvallation because it was quite out of date, and his critics did not do so either. But it is important to shed prejudice and acquire the freedom to examine all ways and means: such an examination, is needed wherever it leads.

Clausewitz was even harsher as regards current opinion when he refused unreservedly to admire the campaign of 1814. Why was not Blücher, the most enterprising and hence most dangerous of the enemies, pursued to the Rhine? 'I am sure that a complete change in the fortunes of the campaign would have occurred, and that the Grande Armée would have re-crossed the Rhine instead of falling back on Paris.' Criticism here is based on three arguments: in principle, it is better to carry on an attack consistently; Blücher's losses were tantamount to defeat and would have given Napoleon the decision; Blücher, because of his personality, was the enemy's centre of gravity, and not Schwarzenberg.

The fourth example provides a case for criticism's supreme question: To what extent does the end result judge the enterprise? Clausewitz found it impossible, as we know, to condemn Napoleon's Russian campaign outright, arguing that there was no choice and that the responsibility for calamity did not lie in mistakes made during the execution of the campaign. Napoleon staked his army in the game, and lost it, but his brutal blow was the only way to extract peace from the enemy. Perhaps the campaign ought not to have been undertaken, but, once it had started, it could hardly have been waged otherwise. In Book VIII, Chapter 9, Clausewitz returned to one of his favourite comparisons, that between war and a card-game: Napoleon lost his stake in Russia. Similarly, in Book II, Chapter 5 he insists that Napoleon took risks in all of his campaigns, even the victorious ones.

And yet we cannot accord to chance the same meaning in war as in card-games; we persist in seeing a subtle accord between events and the way they are consciously shaped. It was not chance that explained Napoleon's run of victories, nor was it chance that explained the disaster of the Grande Armée in Russia. In 1805, 1807 and 1809, Napoleon correctly judged his enemies, but in 1812 he miscalculated.

Considering all of the elements that depend on planning and on men's thinking, criticism must let events speak for themselves, especially those the secret and profound significance of which is not to be readily discerned by analysis, since they represent judgments delivered as it were *sotto voce* by the Supreme Legislator. The observer must protect this from the confusions of vulgar opinions, and try to prevent the gross misuse that such opinion can apply to this Higher process.

Given that the effect of a measure taken by one side against an opponent is bound to be a most individual matter, is foresight at all possible? Or, can we challenge the verdict of history? Even where Tsar Alexander held on, so that Napoleon lost?

Can we draw any general conclusions from these four examples for the methodology of analysing historical cases or of historical demonstration? The case of the siege of Mantua shows that strategic judgment does not rest on tactical data, and also cannot be deduced from transhistorical principles. The Peace of Campo Formio shows how much decision will depend upon the whole politico-military machine created by the war itself. It reminds us too, as does the fourth case, of the sometimes decisive effect of the war leader's psychology, on whichever side. The only example where Clausewitz applies strategic principles is the third one: not to change direction, and to strike preferably at the enemy's centre of gravity.

We thus come to the crux of the debate concerning the relationship between history and theory, concepts and experience. How do singularity of circumstances, diversity of epochs, and influence of morale, which cannot be quantified, and strategic principles combine both in theory and in its application?

It may be useful to distinguish between theory, in the sense of conceptualization of conceptual system, and principles. As regards so-called scientific theories, Clausewitz recognized that they constituted progress in their analytical application, but not in their synthetical part, i.e. prescription and rules. The entire conceptual system of the first chapter of Book I can be considered as an analytical part of the theory, to which may be added the military concepts, taken from the then theories, i.e. bases, lines of operations, surrounding, interior lines, concentric attack.

The difference between the analytical part of a Jomini and that of a Clausewitz stems from Clausewitz's addition of analytical plans of things, that Jomini regarded as irrelevant, to strategic science though he did not deny their existence. Whereas, according to Jomini, strategy presents scientific problems that have some aspects of drama, Clausewitz saw war as a drama that still needed intelligent thinking.

It would appear that the analytical part does contain more than the concepts necessary for prospective thinking and retrospective criticism, but Clausewitz does not explicitly distinguish between general propositions, valid for one era only, and generalizations that are universally valid. The proposition, 'tactical success decides all', is apparently universally true, and, similarly, propositions concerning defence and attack (the stronger form with the negative intention, the weaker form with the positive intention). These differ from the principles since they do not suggest any prescription that reflects the experience from which it arises: as a general rule the weaker side will be on the defensive, for instance.

209

The principle of annihilation, the original law, is deduced from the concept of war; the most general law, too, is founded, if not on the concept, at least on an assumption linked to probabilities and the nature of man, individual or group, that it is not solely valid for one era (e.g. the impossibility of fighting simultaneously to front and rear). On the other hand, the principles, though not necessary, like laws, but arising above particular cases and indicating probability or general truth, derive simultaneously and yet equivocally from experience and concept.

Thus, over the contrast between the need for tactical use of reserves (or staggered use of troops, tactically) and his condemnation of strategic reserves, the description given by Clausewitz of a modern battle does show the need for tactical reserves. The battle involves prolonged attrition, and so fresh forces must be kept for the moment of breakthrough or decision.

The principle of tactical reserves does not, however, depend exclusively on the singular characteristics of today's war. As each side wishes to turn or surround the other – the overall law of combat – it is vital to keep reserves to parry such enemy efforts, which can be foreseen though not perhaps precisely. The troops that are tactically committed will suffer loss through fire or shock, though for the moment we can forget the further matter of numbers, by which worn-out troops in close order will have to be replaced by fresh ones.

Although the intervention of fresh troops has often a decisive influence, given the disorder and the weakened or disorganized state created by combat, things are very different at times other than the moment of crisis, where strategy is concerned. Concentration of force, in strategy, does not disproportionately increase loss: on the contrary, it even tends to reduce the loss. When strategically arranged forces have created victory, those that have not been involved will not have suffered at all. The scale of the success will then make it possible to inflict serious loss on the enemy, defeat and pursuit being the cause rather than battle. However, this thesis needs proof, for it may give rise to an objection that the second principle of annihilation, beyond fire and combat, is effort, fatigue and deprivation, which may also cause losses. In strategy the effect of this principle increases over distance and time. Why should the appearance of fresh troops at the end of the campaign, when the army leading the attack is already worn down, not be decisive, as with Desaix at Marengo or Blücher at Waterloo?

Clausewitz replies to this with two arguments, moral and material. A failed campaign deprives troops of their courage and moral strength, whereas a successful one will increase these. In most cases, the effects balance out; all that is left is simply battle experience, a pure gain.

The material argument rests on the connection between the size of the army and the size of its losses. Whereas in battle losses increase proportionately with the effective strength, it is different in strategy where number makes it possible to reduce danger and effort. Deprivations are different in this material sense, and may be multiplied by the size of the effectives, as was shown by the French experience in Russia in 1812. Clausewitz concedes that in this case Napoleon perhaps pushed too far the application of the principle that you cannot be too strong at the decisive point, or else of the principle of simultaneous engagement of troops in trategy. But it was important for him to extend his front, and in this case he size of the effectives made it possible for him to do so. Superiority nabled him even to reach Moscow, and he probably could have gained >eace from the tsar if he had destroyed the Russian Army.

The examination of the notion of strategic reserve adds an extra dimenion to this analysis. Tactical reserves fulfil two functions: to prolong or enew the battle with a view to decision, and to take precautions against he unforeseen. Does this not involve a strategic necessity? Clausewitz loes not deny the need to guard against the unforeseen, and to take iccount of the unreliability of data. But he states – and this is a judgment of act, perhaps connected with historical circumstances – that as a campaign s seen as a whole, from an overall standpoint, the part of the unforeseen leclines. 'Time and space are so great, circumstances which cause action ire so well-known and change so little that they can be perceived at once or :ven in advance.'

Against the idea of strategic reserves, Clausewitz uses another argument :hat cannot be separated from his concepts and analytical propositions: :hat great successes entrain small ones. In a battle, the success gained by :resh troops will lead to an overall decision; in strategy, if a large part of :he army has been destroyed, successes gained later or elsewhere will be no :ompensation for the defeat. Finally, the law of simultaneous use of troops :ends to put the final decision (though it does not have to be final) towards :he beginning of the campaign, whereas at a tactical level it is delayed :owards the end. It should, however, be clear that if the principal decision :akes place at the start of the campaign, the notion of strategic reserve will become absurd for the simple reason that, by definition, after the main decision, the intact troops that have not seen action will have been of no use at all.

Is it possible to specify the share of historical experience and argument in this kind of strategic analysis? In a way it might be said that everything, including the proposition that concrete tactical successes decide everything, is demonstrated by experience. Even then, the right questions have to be asked; offered, simulated and model combat have to be made equivalent to real combat, otherwise the historical experience would appear to teach something quite different. Similarly, the lesson of the Russian campaign seems to be in contrast to the one drawn by Clausewitz if we do not accept, as he does, that Napoleon could only win by discouraging an Alexander who would have made peace after the loss of his army and the occupation of his capital. Clausewitz does not specify at each step whether he is arguing or observing; he observes history through his concepts. The demonstration of the staggered use of troops implies a distinction between the two moments in combat or battle of attrition and decision. The condemnation of the notion of strategic reserve implies the concept of principal decision; the near impossibility of strategic surprise depends on technical, political and changeable social conditions.

In his portrait of Scharnhorst, Clausewitz pictured the type of intelligence and kind of method that are adapted to the study of politics and war. 'In the art of war, imagination is without creative force and the indispensable truth is the one drawn from an approximation of concept and reality'; and later,

211

A penetrating intelligence without imagination can only approve of systems and speculative thought in the limits laid down by their agreement with the real world. If imagination leads to an exaggeration of system, then intelligence will come into play so as to link thought with reality and associate them; so that, according to the nature of the reality, speculation can pursue its quest for overall concepts.

The analytical part of the theory provides the concepts through which theorists examine history. Historical experience confirms or rejects principles that arise from a synthesis of abstract reasoning and concrete observation.

So far I have been concerned at a rational and theoretical level, where I believe the practice and theory of concepts will agree, provided that we remember that all principles involve exceptions and that all general propositions will express only what most frequently, though not always, is the case.

Any circumstances have singular characteristics so that decisions cannot be deduced from principles, though they may be inspired by them. Principles remain possible in spite of the infinite diversity of alterations because the nature of the means – armies, violence – introduces simplification. The factors of success and failure are few; in the same way, there cannot be many combinations of space and time, and movement. To concentrate superior forces at a decisive point, to threaten the enemy's lines of retreat while protecting one's own, are problems that do not need the thoughts of a superior intelligence. However, here again the simple turns out to be difficult.

There are still exclusively intellectual obstacles, and they are never quite mastered by Clausewitz himself, in the procedure from analysis to synthesis or from theory as observation to theory as prescription. In fact, according to the work as a whole, the conduct of war, in its narrow meaning of strategic art, is subject to three conditions. Tactical data form one. In Book IV, Chapter 2, Clausewitz writes that, with given definitions of tactics and strategy, it is obvious that a change in the first must influence the second. 'If the tactical phenomena are quite different one from another, the same must be true of strategic phenomena, if they are to be logical and rational.' Clausewitz always took this first condition into account in his historical narratives and strategic criticism, though did not do so always as regards principles. Which are valid for a particular era, and which for all time?

The second condition applies to the structure of the whole. In Book VI, Chapter 30, in Book VI generally and in Book VIII, Clausewitz exploits the distinction between campaign or battle whether decisive or not. At the higher level of war, dualism prevails: one aspect is unified in the final decision, whereas another is a whole set of partial decisions and failures that are independent of each other. Even though in the end this is all part of the same thing, the contrast between the two aspects makes it impossible to apply the same principles to both.

There is a further condition in the political goal of the war. This goal comes before the determination of the war plan which will dictate the course of the war according to means and ends involved. But the limited number of military objectives is contrasted with the variety of possible political goals, and Clausewitz wavers between various solutions. He lists the three objectives of any warlike activity – armed forces, resources, will (armed forces being the primary objective) – and then at a lower level of abstraction he distinguishes the various centres of gravity – the army, capital, allies, leader of popular revolt – against which decisive blows are to be struck. Proceeding from the annihilation of armed forces to overthrow of the enemy state may involve another method of fighting, since the armed forces of all nations do not always constitute the first objective. In Book VIII, Chapter 2, he finds general applicability and necessity only in the absolute form of war, since no real war is the same as the absolute concept.

These do not contradict each other: they are only so many rough paths through difficult matter. That was how Clausewitz himself saw it in Book VIII. Still, it is hardly surprising that, in searching for a military doctrine, men should have given up reconciling the historicity of strategic theory, subject to the inevitable change of tactics bound up with changes in arms and movement, with the duality of final decision and partial decisions, and finally with the dual character of wars, some of which aim at the enemy's overthrow so as to dictate terms of peace, while others are meant to gain limited advantages. We can see why generals bore in mind only the striking and simple formulae of the principles or deriving from them. In the same way, Marx had some responsibility for Marxism–Leninism: clever theories produce coarse doctrines that falsify them. One day, perhaps, scholars will be able to restore the theories in all of their subtlety – with a view (perhaps vain) to teach the theory rather than to rehabilitate the theorist.

Chapter 9

From Theory to Doctrine

At the end of Book II, Chapter 4, Clausewitz acknowledged that 'method-ism' at its highest level would remain unavoidable, and perhaps necessary, so long as theoretical reflection had no place in the training of leaders. However, this 'methodism', which could never be wholly eliminated, was not to derive from the passive or blind imitation of a Frederick or a Napoleon; rather, from the conclusions of rational study.

These conclusions cannot be reduced to the statement that any set of circumstances is *sui generis*. If we were limited in this way to partial truths, theory would leave judgment without directive or guidance. Clausewitz repeats that his theory must be useful, without being regarded as dogma. The logical problem is therefore reduced to the questions: How can argument or doctrine emerge from theory? What implicit or explicit teaching did Clausewitz mean to impart? The answer here is no less difficult than in Montesquieu's case, and for the same reason.

1 Principles and spirit in 1804

The answer to both questions derives, as it must, from examination of the *Principles of Instruction*. Although they do not have the rigour of laws, they are in fact formulated as imperatives. The text of 1812, which is a summary of the teaching given to the crown prince, is a form of doctrinal teaching, since it consists of a series of principles. The 'Strategy' of 1804 also contains numerous imperatives. We must again follow the chronology in order to answer our questions.

In this instance, paragraphs 12 and 13 of the 'Strategy' of 1804 seem to me the most instructive. Clausewitz formulates apparently unconditional imperatives, based on the spirit of war as an art. He says, for instance,

It seems to me that the art of war tells us this: choose the greatest aim [*Zweck*] and the most decisive one you feel you can attain, take the shortest road you can manage, and take the road you feel most equal to following.

Two ideas result from this: the war leader must decide according to his self-confidence, and if he remains rational he can never be bold enough. For boldness and the choice of a decisive aim derive from the very spirit of war. Subjectivity will intervene only to adapt the greatness of the end to the self-confidence of the leader. Clausewitz therefore reproached ever Charles XII for excessive caution, not boldness, in marching to join Mazeppa rather than on St Petersburg.

In the Treatise, Clausewitz did recognize the greatness of Frederick who unlike Charles XII, could limit his ambitions to his strength. The 24-year-old officer dreamt of nothing beyond attack, dash and great victories

214

When he compared Frederick with Napoleon (paragraph 29 of 1808) he tried to find excuses for the Prussian strategies of 1759–61 – themselves the result of a lack of courage as well as a lack of resources. Lion-like, he was only aroused in situations of extreme danger. It is true that in 1808 Napoleon had only known victories whereas Frederick had met the vicissitudes of fate. Nevertheless, at that time the hero, as seen by the young officer, possessed the virtues required for free play of the spirit, rather than wisdom or balance.

From this moment, he played down the importance of the principles to stress the importance of character and moral qualities. Even so, he did not defend Frederick against Jomini's criticism by citing the customs of the time, as he does later, both in the Treatise and elsewhere. He stressed the inevitable impact that numerous setbacks have, even on a hero. All the remarks and analysis of 1804–9 suggest a single way of conducting war, a single strategy conforming to the spirit of war.

The principle governing us, when we choose the most decisive operations according to our means, has to do with the spirit and significance of war, and a veritable art is involved in applying the idea – employing the armed forces available in the best possible way so that they will do their uttermost.

This definition does not involve reference to the political goal, and it implies confusion between results that are militarily decisive and those that are most advantageous overall. It states that 'the spirit and meaning of war', equivalent to the initial definition in Book I, Chapter 1, of the Treatise, dictates the imperatives for action.

Clausewitz contrasts these imperatives with the maxims inspired by economy, e.g. choice of an operation that promises maximum success with minimum expenditure of force. To him, such a formula would smack of pedantry, redolent, he says, of a spirit of mediocrity. He rejects maxims that include contradictory considerations, e.g. choosing the operation to combine them in such a way as to gain both success and security. These are 'empty shells from which the spirit of war has escaped'. Such contrasting considerations have a central place in the dialectic of the Treatise, although it does not explicitly, in the form of maxims, take up again any opposition between size of success and security of operations. It leaves open to the end, to the war leader, the responsibility of choosing between terms that are by nature opposed. But – and this is the decisive point – it no longer equates the spirit of war with the greatest dash.

The use of the concept of 'spirit' (*Geist*) inevitably recalls Montesquieu. 'Spirit' in action expresses the nature of an institution or art or people. It is even possible that the *Grundsätze* of Clausewitz, or some of them, derive from the notion of principle – in the meaning given by Montesquieu – complementing the meaning of nature. Just as virtue is the principle of democracy (i.e. makes it what it must be in accordance with its nature), energy and activity are the principles of war as such. The maxim, 'war must be waged with the highest degree of effort that is necessary or possible', tends to fulfil the nature of war. Paragraph 17, entitled 'Principle of Activity', could as easily be quoted. It seems to me that in the notes of 1804, the concept of spirit has two uses, of which the equivalents can be found in *De l'esprit des lois*: there is the spirit of an institution or regime, i.e. of an abstract entity built by a theorist, and there is the spirit of a people (e.g. the warlike one of the Swiss in paragraph 6).

Clausewitz, perhaps inspired by Montesquieu, used in his youth the two concepts of spirit and principle to formulate his thought in the form of imperatives. The remarks of 1812, which I did not enlarge upon in Chapter 1, i.e. 'The most important principles in the conduct of war, to complement what I have already taught His Royal Highness the Crown Prince', lie in the same line of thought.

There is an obvious difficulty in interpreting this last: Clausewitz was teaching, and therefore could not write that a theory was wholly different from a teaching. The teaching is summed up in the *Principles*, as rules for action: (a) principles valid for war as such; (b) general principles of defensive and offensive tactics and principles for use of troops in the field; (c) general principles of strategy, whether defensive or offensive. However, he notes in passing that theory is nothing other than a rational reflection of situations that have to be faced in wartime, and this is not different from the definition of it in the Treatise. Moreover, most of the principles in the 1812 text can be found in the Treatise itself, though of course the reverse is not true, for all the ideas of the Treatise are not found in the *Principles*.

Several of the principles listed in the notes of 1804 appear differently expressed in the later *Principles of Instruction*. Even in 1812, he recommends boldness rather than prudence, and he regarded this as an important maxim, though to him the war leader would still be responsible for decisions to be taken according to his courage and self-confidence. Strategy obviously must ensure physical and moral superiority at the decisive point, but must enable the leader to face situations of inferiority, i.e. operations that he must conduct though he can hardly count on success.

This insistence is partly explained by circumstances. Clausewitz was addressing the grand-nephew of the Prussian king, at a time when the monarchy was destined for disaster under the blows of the French emperor. He called on his royal pupil to be ready for a glorious death – an idea familiar to the great monarch who drew from it his strength for heroic decision.

The reference to the nature or spirit of war recalls the 'Strategy' of 1804. Clausewitz did not as yet distinguish laws from principles – in the Treatise it was purely theoretical – and also tended to underestimate the importance of strategy and the effect of political conditions ('In reality the few strategic principles that are based on states' constitutions or on armies' natures can be briefly summed up'), but it is interesting to speculate how these principles, had they been written fifteen years later, would have differed from the summary version in 1812.

The epistemology of the *Principles* is in no way elaborated, though the teacher expects history to shed light on them. He insists on the gap between war in the abstract and war as actually experienced. He therefore recommends the reading of history, particularly of books that offer plain, unvarnished reality – a model for him is Scharnhorst's famous account of the siege of Menin and the victorious sortie of the garrison. This returns in the Treatise, where he praises the *Memoirs* of Feuquières for their accuracy, though not for any method of proving by example. Moreover, from

1804 to 1814, Clausewitz fully developed his concept of 'friction' and argued that, though the intellectual problems of strategy are quite simple, application of the strategy is very difficult. Before dealing with practical principles, the fourth section of the *Principles* lists and analyses the causes of 'friction': unreliability of information about both the enemy and one's own armed forces; resistance of the human machine to the required efforts; imprecision of operations in space and time; difficulties of supply because of requisitioning or storing. It is through such friction that chance plays its inevitable part in war, because risks have to be taken, calculations of probabilities trusted and, finally, the carefully worked-out principles adhered to, even when men are troubled and confused by many contradictory impressions that can divert the leaders from their chosen course. There is no substantial difference between the fourth paragraph of the *Principles of Instruction* and Chapters 3–7 of Book I.

Nor is there much difference between Sections II and III of the *Principles* and Books III, IV and V of the Treatise. The text of 1812 deals separately with principles of tactics, but much the same is easily to be found in the manuscript of 1830. In tactics, the highest principle is that of the successive, or *échelonné*, use of troops, i.e. deployment in depth. A large part – a third, or even half – of the troops must be kept in reserve, away from the action. The three arms are placed according to constant rules and become the object of inevitable and useful 'methodism', which did in fact allow the French army to do extremely well. Similarly, the principles concerning terrain, especially defence in mountains and marshes, can be found in the manual of 1804 as in the detailed analysis in Book VI.

In the main, the principles do not change because they are based on good sense and historical experience; generally, for instance, it is better not to defend a mountain range from the summits, or to hold a river over its whole length. Clausewitz's arguments are not, in the end, metaphysical, and they lead him to two practical questions: What conditions can normally ensure superiority for a leader? What are the moral qualities required? If defenders wish to hold a mountain at the summit or in the valley, they will give attackers the chance to concentrate their forces at one or other of the re-entrants in the mountainous area; whereas, if defenders wait at the openings of these, in the plains, they will usually have a better chance of ensuring their superiority.

If we add the attempt to outflank or to strike at enemy centres of gravity, we thus arrive at the major principles of both defensive and offensive warfare. A very ambitious aim must be chosen, and striven for with the utmost energy and resolution; by keeping back part of the troops and by deploying in depth; enemy efforts to outflank can be thwarted, and the enemy in turn can be attacked in flank just as they attempt envelopment. If both sides have chosen an ambitious aim, each one will strike at a different centre of gravity; and the result will depend on the resolution displayed by the two sides, as well as on their capacity to limit the effects of each other's successes. Thus in the battle of Wagram, both Napoleon and Archduke Charles kept their left wings on the defensive, and both attacked with the right. Charles's brave efforts were made nugatory by the superior resolution and energy of his opponent.

According to the most general law in the Treatise, attackers must try to attack the enemy front concentrically, whilst defenders must strive to buttress their line by impregnable flanking positions. Terrain can be exploited in many ways – e.g. for protection of one or both flanks, or to create obstacles on the battle front, or to conceal reserves, or to obtain good observation of the enemy, or to provide good lines of retreat through broken country. The simplest and most instructive principle here is at the end of Chapter 11: 'Do not expect anything from terrain alone, and never be tempted towards passive defence.'

The essay of 1812 rectifies certain impressions of the Treatise that the French have criticized. The Clausewitz of 1812, at least, well understood that battles need planning and manoeuvre, that attacker and defender alike will choose a sector in which to concentrate superior forces. He certainly did not fail to see (as Camon accused him of doing) that planning the battle or selecting in advance the spot where an attack can break through will win the victory. The Clausewitz of the Treatise had also witnessed Borodino and Waterloo – the one fought on both sides as a slogging-match, and the other decided by the failure of a strategic manoeuvre on interior lines when the Prussian army, beaten the day before, returned to the field to decide the issue. In the text of 1812, he ascribes victory to the resolution and energy devoted by one side to the sector it had chosen to attack; in the Treatise, he stresses the gradual attrition, the successful army being the one that has the last reserves of material and moral strength. In both cases, the chief principle is applied – theory is knowing how to maintain superior strength and material advantage at the decisive point, and where this cannot be done, then moral strength must compensate for material inferiority.

Section II, covering strategy, shows better than the other three what progress Clausewitz made between 1812 and 1830, reflecting on war after 1815 and especially in his last years. The tutor of 1812 confined himself to the conditions and armed forces of his own day, hardly alluding to the past – that was the nature of his task – and he did not demonstrate a contempt for history or an unawareness of its relationship with tactical principles. Here he confined himself to stressing the contrast, valuable enough in the context of his remarks in Chapter 2, Book II, of the Treatise, between teaching a methodical system of tactics on the one side, and the need for initiative by commanders on the other. Indeed, he does not require much knowledge or intellectual training for war leaders: experience will teach them how to combine forces successfully; when you know how to fight and win, that is enough. If, however, we consult Chapter 1 of Book VIII and the first two chapters of Book I, we can see how far he progressed and his growing insight into the difficulties confronting theory once it moves into the higher level of the war plan.

The analytical section of the strategic theory is confined to a listing of three targets – armed forces, inert material and public opinion – and the methods of striking at them. The synthesizing part consists mainly of two kinds of imperative, the first giving rise to the second.

He starts with the principle that all available force should be used with all available energy against the objectives listed by him: if the first objective, then operations must be directed against the larger part of the enemy's chief army; if the second, then against chief towns, stores or fortresses; if the third, then towards victories or capture of the enemy capital. This logically leads to a principle of concentrating force for the main action, of not wasting time, and of exploiting success with maximum energy. All available forces must be committed if the army is to achieve the great objectives that the warlike spirit will certainly demand.

These principles lead Clausewitz towards judgments regarding geometrical pattern. In tactics he did not much believe in encirclements, and in strategy, similarly, he sees that any concentric operation will require considerable superiority. Here he is erudite, measured and open-minded, and close to Jomini, the advocate of manoeuvre on interior lines, when he shows that Napoleon never risked strategic encirclement. Using the instance of Frederick the Great's campaign of concentric advance towards Prague in 1757, he illustrates the danger of such a manoeuvre, and the way in which tactics decided its fate. Concentration on the main point will prevent any encirclement, he says.

The wording changed between 1812 and the Treatise, but the leading ideas were much the same. He deals with defence first, and attack second, for defence interested him the more, as it led only indirectly to ending the war, whereas attack did so directly. The principles of war were really the principles of the offensive, and comparison between the *Principles* of 1812 and those listed in Chapter 9 of Book VIII suggest that he did not even shift his approach, although the latter are more imperative in tone.

There was also hardly any evolution in his thoughts regarding the contrast of boldness and prudence. He three times emphasizes Napoleon's prudence – it had nothing in common with the false prudence of the half-measure – and shows how he never attempted strategic encirclement and how he guarded against panic, even in his boldest undertakings, by leaving troops to hold the rear, support the attack or cover the retreat.

There is, it seems, no clearer or more logically simple military philosophy: the spirit of war dictates objectives and lays down moral imperatives such as energy and boldness; the scale of the objectives dictates a concentration of strength on the decisive point in battle (though the troops may be thrown in successively, rather than simultaneously, whereas in the spatial concentration required in strategy, simultaneity will be needed). Manoeuvre with a view to battle will develop according to two patterns – concentric attack at a tactical level, and interior lines at a strategic one – since both favour concentration of greater strength.

Clausewitz could easily have laid out this kind of theory systematically: dividing it into material and moral parts, subject to laws of boldness and scale of objectives, based on the search for superiority at the decisive point or in the decisive battle; explaining how terrain could be used, though never forgetting that in the end it is men who fight. It is a theory that appreciates the gap between the speculations of cabinets and the actual fighting, accepts uncertainty, chance and friction, and therefore sees the responsibility of commanders and the difficulties of even simple operations once they leave the drawing-board. However, the Clausewitz who wrote the *Principles* and taught the crown prince had no fascination for posterity; his myth comes from what he wrote between 1812 and 1830. To decide whether he deserved this fascination, whether his myth comes from language rather than philosophical value, we have to confront what Clausewitz himself would have called the main decision.

219

2 From the Principles of 1812 to the Treatise

The Treatise is not a set of teachings in the manner of the *Principles* of 1812; it does not consist of principles, rules and methods. The calculus of a war plan could not be conceptually laid down even by a genius; theorists do not construct iron laws when they formulate a principle or reveal a truth intended to inform, not to dictate, thought. At the end of Chapter 8 of Book VI, Clausewitz again emphasizes that his aim is not to discover new principles or methods, but only to analyse a subject long familiar in its inmost structure, and to reduce it to its simplest elements, i.e. to reason his way towards an understanding of what war means, and which abstractions derive from study of the concrete cases of war.

However, the contrast between this and the imperatives or principles of 1812 is not as sharp as it might seem if we merely juxtaposed the practical guidance of 1812 and the theoretical remarks of 1826 or 1830; even in 1812, he took the view that principles were necessary guides that expressed, not a law to be scrupulously observed, but regular patterns revealed by observation and confirmed by reason, i.e. ways of doing that ought normally to be adopted unless certain circumstances rule them out. Matters of morale, friction, description of war as an experience, the wish to develop a theory as close as possible to practice all indicate that principles, even though presented as imperatives, will remain conditional, their basic validity subject to the reservations 'all things being equal' or 'in most cases'. Theory cannot dictate rules to genius, and although, of course, rules do apply to genius, it spontaneously acts in accordance with them, and it is up to theory to elucidate them. Here Clausewitz as a 24-year-old officer thought no differently than he was to think as a 50-year-old general.

The Treatise, even though it does not use the term 'principle', often suggests something equivalent to the *Principles* of 1812. In Chapter 2 of Book IV, for instance, where Clausewitz speaks contemptuously of generals who want victory without bloodshed, he writes: 'It is not just arrogant or foolhardy commanders who aim at boldness to crown their doings; so do all successful leaders' – suggesting, implicitly, a principle quite close to the earlier one of 1812, that you must have an ambitious aim. Moreover, in Books II and V of the Treatise he also deduces principles from the spirit or significance of war. The contrast of concept and experience – or rather, the combination of abstract thought and experience, i.e. Clausewitz's constant method – justifies his effort to deduce, from the concept or spirit of war, general aims that may be modified according to circumstances. The essence and the aim of war are in fact difficult to separate, the one revealing the other.

In rethinking, if not converting, his approach, Clausewitz had to consider more fully what, in his youth, he had called the spirit of war, and what later he called the concept or idea of it. His study of history made him see how strategy depended on goals and political circumstances, though he took account of this without its affecting his original concept of war: alterations owing to the instrumental character of violence would have to govern the aims the war leader could or should entertain. The significance of the rethinking or conversion can easily be seen from the section of Book VIII that alludes to the book's first chapter as it was to have been, in the final version.

This first chapter, according to the passage, was to have dealt with 'Your own strength; the enemy's strength; the combination of these; features of the peoples and governments, etc.' All of these are political matters, and since they govern war, they are parts of a greater whole that may be called the political intercourse of states and nations. Even if war were to develop quite naturally, according to the spirit or concept, and even if unlimited hostility occurred, it could still only be understood in a political context. In most cases, however, it does not occur purely according to its abstract logic. History shows wars that do not end in a 'decision', so there are two kinds of war, two entities or types that lead to the decisive idea that war has only a grammar, not a logic: political intercourse by fighting, rather than writing.

What remains of the idea of determining concrete aims from ultimate goals? It will now be meaningless to call for the utmost boldness and the greatest goal, in accordance with the spirit or concept of absolute war. The war plan requires so many variables to be considered, that the calculation would need Newtonian genius, for only genius could cut through the mass to the essentials, the particular character of the war at its particular time and place where the great decisions have to be made.

The breach in the evolution of Clausewitz's thought and his theory of war really occurred between 1826 and 1830, when he realized how his earlier theory was impossible – not because of moral theories or virtues, but because of accidents and the underlying variety of circumstances. His arguments did not prevent men from trying to find out what most often happened or from formulating rules and principles to sum up practices most widely applicable. The great change really comes from the fact that military operations do not always aim at destruction of the enemy state, and campaigns are not always meant to produce a decision: therefore the typology of wars will rule out any principle deriving from the final goals of battles, campaigns or wars; the goal that directly emanates from concepts of decision, destruction or overthrow is thus conditional. If we follow its logic, we will see in Clausewitz's intellectual testament not a repudiation, but rather a rethinking of his life's work. Principles, like those of 1812, that appear here and there in the Treatise – at least those which, in 1804 and 1812, came from the inner logic of the spirit or concept of war – are valid only on two conditions: that the enemy is to be destroyed, and that the particular circumstances allow the rules to operate.

If this is so, then Chapter 9 of Book VIII – which in style is closest to the work of 1812 – does not contradict the preceding arguments. The two principles of Chapter 9 – maximum concentration against enemy centres of gravity, and maximum speed, without halt or diversion – reproduce almost word for word the general strategic *Principles* of 1812, which then become the principles of attack; and that is because attack is directly aimed at the goal of the war. However, these principles, which in 1812 were applied to strategy overall and to any attack, are now valid only in one kind of campaign – when the enemy is about to collapse – and therefore for only one kind of war.

Clausewitz also practises some casuistry here. When, for instance, a subsidiary operation promises unusual advantages, then an exception has to be made, he says, to the rule. He lists the arguments that could be used against concentration of strength, and discusses concentric advance by separated armies which may bring great success, though at the cost of no little danger. He sets out the reasons for subordinating parts to the whole, hence for accepting inferiority and loss at secondary points and areas. Even so, whatever the exceptions to be recognized, the war plan must still be directed towards overthrow of the enemy, and this chapter, the last in the book, and probably written in 1826, had much the same source as the *Principles of Instruction* and proposed the same imperatives and practices as had been derived from the spirit or essential nature of war.

That is why the teachings incorporated in the Treatise have so often been called ambiguous. The main reason for a belligerent to stand on the defensive is because he is inferior in strength. Yet defence, too, is intended to destroy the enemy, at least in the indirect sense that retreat to the interior and choice of a favourable battlefield will compensate for the initial inferiority, or will allow the defenders to hope that the situation can be reversed. Now, real war tends to produce, if not an overthrow of one side, at least a decision. Yet Clausewitz applied all of this only to the case of superior, attacking force: the *Principles* of 1812 also apply in the Treatise when a war plan is made to overthrow the enemy – i.e. spatial concentration of strength, subordination of secondary to primary actions, no weakening of the main point in order to guard against risks elsewhere, choice of the direct path to the decisive battle.

This is the Clausewitz of Liddell Hart's pages: he is not even a theorist, for he is crude in interpretation and brutal in distorting realities, but merely a strategist despising or ignoring manoeuvre, seeking crude and bloody clashes of arms; he is a doctrinaire, obsessed with national armies and conscription, directing the Prussian Marseillaise towards the butcheries of Eylau and Borodino, and preparing the way for, if not wholly justifying, the slaughter to come in Flanders or on the Chemin des Dames.

The essence of the other extreme interpretation has been set out in earlier chapters. In this, Clausewitz's analysis of war is stressed, i.e. the conceptual system that I outlined in the first chapter, of the two contrasting movements of war, upward to the extreme, and downward to armed observation. Here, Clausewitz's real contribution to the theory of war lies not so much in the ideas that dominate the preceding interpretation discussed above as in the subordination, pushed to its logical extreme, of the military tool to political calculation; what is here stressed is Clausewitz's awareness, which is so obvious in the correspondence with Major Roeder, that all earlier theories (and military teachings) had neglected the essential feature of wars, that they were of various types because of the variety of political circumstances in states and nations that could occur.

The intellectual testament does not repudiate all the consequences deriving from 'spirit of war' or Clausewitz's original definition; it only makes them conditional. They become analytical propositions, true in a conceptual world but not applicable to a real war. In 1827, he considered 'intellectualizing' this by introducing everywhere the distinction between the two kinds of war. But it is not clear that such revision would, in 1830, have met the demands for final synthesis, even though it might, I think, have brought to light the fact that principles (in the imperative sense) are conditioned by political goals as well as by type of war. Similarly, he might have clarified the difference between theory and doctrine, conceptual analysis and rules for action, limited number of means and great diversity of political goals, and universally valid theory and principles valid only for particular periods of history. We should not have regarded as rules for action the analytical propositions that he drew from the nature of the means, the military objective or the geographical and climatic circumstances. These propositions can supply arguments on which to base a decision, especially one inconsistent with current practice, and they can shape a strategist's mind or limit his unreflecting spontaneity; but equally the strategist, knowing what he is about, will avoid the trap of excessive systematization of method. Thus, the theoretical revolution Clausewitz had in mind was meant not only to discriminate between analysis and doctrine, or permanent data and historical diversity, but also to demonstrate how to use principles based on the majority of cases: neither dogmatism nor heedless improvisation. Clausewitz could have written, like Suntzu, 'Whoever can win by modifying his tactics in accordance with the enemy's situation deserves to be regarded as divine.'

No one has yet stated this interpretation in full, since it remains, in part, implicit. Passages on the priority of destroying the enemy's main forces, and which deal with the military decision to overthrow the enemy state, occur very often; all stem from the analytical definition of war, the uniqueness of its means and the limited number of circumstances to be considered. Passages stressing the superiority of political considerations and not limiting their intervention in the fighting or conduct of operations, and which bear out the only proper (threefold) definition of real war, are few: they are concentrated in Books I and VIII, those that Colonel de Vatry even thought he could omit when he first delivered his translation of the Treatise at the end of the last century; in the same way, A. Rapoport believes we should miss out Book VI, dealing with the defensive, whereas this book explains both in political and military terms why the defensive is superior, and if we neglect Chapter 6 of it we can hardly imagine the balance-of-power world of the European system of states that Clausewitz knew and studied.

This interpretation is only possible through study of the formation and evolution of Clausewitz's thought; indeed, it only really started with my friend Rosinski's article in the 1930s. For a century, Clausewitz was read as he feared he might be, by men looking for recipes and ready-made formulae, not by men looking for authoritative reflection on war. If today we can understand him it is because the doctrinaire belongs to the past, whereas it is really the theorist of 1826–30 who interests us.

3 The dialectic of concepts: Kant and Hegel

At the end of this effort at overall interpretation, we can perhaps turn to the often asked question as to the kinship between Clausewitz and Kant or Hegel. As I have shown, I am convinced that Clausewitz's thought and method were to some degree dialectical, but we have to see how this is so.

In the three pairs of concepts analysed earlier, the relationship between the ideas changes from one pair to another. Means and ends are organized in a hierarchy so that the lesser or immediate ends are the means towards higher or less direct ends. Thus the military instrument is subject to the political end. However, the laws particular to the instrument are imposed on politics as constraints and limitations. Thus also, battles provide the matter for strategy, whilst the strategic plans create conditions for tactical victories.

Material and moral forces refer respectively to objects and to human beings, i.e. to different parts of reality. But the strength of an army comes from the junction of these two forces, with the weight and power of action on the one side and the soldiers' confidence in their leaders, their memory of past victories, their battle experience and their leader's genius on the other. Heterogeneous as all of this may be, it will still determine the strength of an armed force. Similarly, the strength of a state cannot just be measured in terms of numbers of uniformed men and weight of mobilized resources; it will also depend on the people's confidence in their rulers, and loyalty to the state and its institutions.

Attack and defence appear to be rather more contradictory. Either you are on the attack, or you defend; you try either to take or to hold, for there is a positive intention, to alter the *status quo*, or a negative one, to uphold it. But in reality the offensive will sometimes contain a defensive element because it will have, at some stage, to stop; and defence also has an offensive element, unless peace comes as soon as the enemy attack has been repelled. Besides, the offensive at a higher level – fighting on enemy soil – hardly rules out defensive fighting, any more than defensive action will rule out some attacking action on one sector.

These three conceptual pairs dominate his thoughts on strategy, and we may add two others at least – the contrast between boldness and caution, between ambition and risk. There is a kind of proportion between size of victory and size of risk, an incompatibility between prudence and gain. The inversion of principles, as regards strategy and tactics, is a further instance of dialectic, for reserves, fresh troops and the successive commitment of troops will determine the outcome of battles, whereas in strategy, where a decisive battle can affect the whole campaign, it would be absurd to withhold any of one's strength.

Since there were few non-military readers or commentators of Clausewitz, and since officers had at best only second-hand knowledge of Hegel or remembered only trite formulae based on his maxims, the Hegelian aspects of the thought of Clausewitz came to France and America only through mists of ignorance, both of Hegel and of Clausewitz, although in an official address on 17 March 1883, at Marburg, Hermann Cohen laid stress on the (less probable) influence of Kant on Clausewitz.

To discuss this, we must call on both history and philosophy. Did Clausewitz know Kant or Hegel, and did he know them directly, or indirectly? Is there essential agreement with the thought of either?

History can make short work of the first part of this. In Berlin, studying at the military acacemy, Clausewitz attended lectures given by J.G. Kiesewetter, who popularized Kant. Schering found in the family archives some notes taken on one such lecture, a mathematical one, and Clausewitz must also have attended the philosophical ones, for a contemporary in his memoirs wrote that Kiesewetter taught philosophy 'in homeopathic doses'.

Hegel does not come up even once in the Treatise or in the letters and papers in Clausewitz's archives. Neither does Kant, in fact, though we know that Kiesewetter formed a link in this, though not in Hegel's, case. True, Creuziger supposed he had found a link with Hegel in one Major Griesheim, a military teacher and Hegelian friend of Clausewitz's. However, Griesheim's personal records show that he taught at the military academy only for a few years after 1838, the year of Hegel's death from cholera – though this hardly matters, because there must have been several Hegelians among the group of lecturers at the academy.

Clausewitz's own Hegelianism was based on one unquestionable fact, that he was director of the military academy while Hegel reigned unrivalled in the university of Berlin. Clausewitz's method is also unquestionably dialectical, and we must ask how much it owed to Hegel's example.

Clausewitz, the educated and cultured soldier, with literary talent as well as an exceptional analytical mind, had undertaken to work out the conceptual system of a phenomenon, and to give rigour to the elements underlying decision and action. During the last ten years of his life he profited from the leisure left to him by his administrative tasks, and composed and corrected the Treatise while also writing accounts of various campaigns. He probably did not know Hegel before 1806, and from then until 1813 he would have had little time for leisure. Between 1816 and 1818 he did work, at Coblenz, on a first draft of the Treatise. He may have heard of Hegel at Berlin between 1820 and 1830, but he does not seem to have studied Hegel far enough to modify his own ideas, and in any case the final version of the Treatise would have to show clear traces of Hegelian influence for us to accept this not very plausible hypothesis.

Let us take the most obvious example of possible Hegelianism, the relationship between defence and attack. We could suggest, as has been written, that

> Clausewitz, looking for a Hegelian pattern of thesis, antithesis and synthesis, must have felt that he had hit upon something remarkable when he found this: thesis: defence; antithesis: offensive; synthesis: defensive–offensive. The terms are wonderfully opposed, and seem to promise a proper theory. But that was Clausewitz's mistake.

Schering attacked this interpretation with reference to the sources, showing that the defensive–offensive strategy really came from Scharnhorst's teaching, of which archives gave the proof. Unfortunately, Schering, as ever, could support his assertion only on documents that are now lost; he does not specify which documents they were, and historians disagree as to this, so that I cannot take over Schering's arguments here. But in any case, Clausewitz does not lead to a defensive–offensive synthesis. Sometimes, the stronger side must launch as unbroken, brutal and rapid an attack as is possible, whereas the weaker side may be reduced to pure resistance, almost passivity, in the hope of tiring the enemy, or waiting for the unexpected to alter the balance of forces. The doctrine of offensive–defensive is only one variant of the central thesis, which is that the defensive is the superior form.

However, even the defensive–offensive is quite different from a synthesis in the Hegelian meaning, for the third term does not come from a negation of the second that is itself a negation of the first; nor does the result form, at a higher level in the conceptual hierarchy, the starting point for a new triad.

Each of the two first elements contains its opposite: no offensive without an element of defence, and vice versa. The defence, by paralysing the attack, condemns it to failure, but attack crowns defence and ensures its ultimate success. The defensive retains what is best in the offensive, whereas the offensive takes from the defensive what is its worst side. Strategy oscillates between these opposites and has to seek out the best compromise between the opposite term's good and bad aspects. In no way is such oscillation or compromise the equivalent of a Hegelian synthesis.

The essence of Hegel's historical dialectic is the synthesis that rises above temporal contradictions and gives a rational significance to the progression; but it has no place in the Treatise, a wholly foreign work. If we are to guess at Clausewitz's historical philosophy, it would be set in the Machiavellian tradition, of political labours being valid only for a time, and leaving posterity indifferent, and art alone being capable of defeating time. It is not that action thereby loses its validity or dignity, but man cannot know the meaning that Providence gives to his sacrifices, struggles and victories at any given moment.

It might be suggested that Clausewitz's conceptual dialectic, as distinct from the historical one, is close to Hegel's, but this is clearly not the case. There is no contradiction between means and ends, numbers and morale, attack and defence. The contrast between these dissolves strategically at the point of battle, and tactically when the fighters clash, such that if, for instance, hussars parry the blows of lancers, who can say which is the attacker, and which the defender? It would be easier to find Hegelian elements in the positive and negative poles of electricity.

Again, Hegelianism could be found in the ideas of positive and negative aims, but I do not accept this. The positive goal is defined by intention to capture, conquer or destroy, i.e. to alter the *status quo*. It corresponds in a way to the Hegelian dialectic of master and slave, but without Hegelian recognition being involved.

Chapter 1 of Book I, which I called the spiritual testament of Clausewitz, is considered by Creuziger to reveal, better than any other chapter, the influence of Hegel. This suggestion is attractive, because triad, rather than, as elsewhere in the Treatise, pair, appears: absolute war leading directly to the extremes is made out to produce 'an interplay of chance and probability', which is subject to 'the free activity of the soul' that can canalize the nations' passions and produce a 'political understanding' that will dominate the boldest efforts of the war leader. We may wonder if this trinity belongs in a Hegelian world, but I do not think so, for it really stems from the same philosophy as shaped the rest of the Treatise.

The pure concept of war rules out moderation, and so cannot produce the second element; the first element cannot be shown, by conceptual analysis, to contain a second one that is its negation. This is the difference between the example of the duel between two men and the war between two states, in which there are significant alterations and an implied downward movement towards armed observation. The third element, the supremacy of the political, is implied in the second one, because war brings states rather than armies into conflict. There is therefore no contradiction between first and second, or second and third elements. In each case, they emerge from the substitution of real belligerents (peoples, armies or states) for the duellists of the initial scheme.

Creuziger, for obscure reasons, regards the cessation of hostilities, because of asymmetry between attack and defence, as an instance of the Hegelian method. If true, it is a very broad interpretation of the Hegelian method. In fact, Clausewitz would have accounted for such cessations as he did in his younger days, with reference to human frailties, fear of great decision or the tendency of each side to exaggerate the strength of the other and to underrate its own. Such cessation of hostilities, though quite possible in reality, contradicts the logic of absolute or ideal war; there is even a parallel in economics, as for instance when we theorize as to whether equilibrium can be gained without full employment. Clausewitz, stating that attack and defence are of unequal strength, makes it rationally possible for hostilities to be suspended even where each side has perfect knowledge of the other.

It might be possible to describe as dialectical the distinction between the polarity concerning the two sides' desire for victory and the non-polar relationship of attack and defence, but it hardly stems from any specific part of the Hegelian dialectic. In any case, the descent into mere armed observation is simply the outcome of proper planning, consideration of risk and the costs and likelihood of success. The reconciliation of opposed wills is not the outcome of mastery and slavery, the slave's revenge or the master's defeat, but of dictated or negotiated peace.

Creuziger's belief that Hegel can easily be found in Clausewitz comes from his accepting that they have a logico-conceptual method in common. This is, I think, incorrect: Clausewitz's method does not make him or other theorists a Hegelian. It all depends on the relationship between concept and reality. This relationship, which I have already discussed several times and to which I will return, can be interpreted in several different ways. None the less, it is clear enough that the duality of ideas and experiences does not lead to the Hegelian concept of concrete universals. *Vorstellungen*, ideas, notions – whatever the term we use – are always to do with the thinking mind, to understanding in the Kantian meaning, or intelligence in our own sense.

If we are to look for a philosophical origin for the strange trinity in the first chapter, I prefer to look to Kant's table of categories. War in the abstract always lends itself to universal judgment because it has a nature that it necessarily obeys. Men are mortal; all wars, by nature, tend to rise to the extreme because each side aims at overthrowing the other. But men are not identical, and no two wars are exactly the same. All men have mortality in common, but real wars do not always rise to the extreme even if, in all, violence is involved. If wars are different from each other, it is because the elements involved in them are in different proportions: each one is an entity in itself, and if we cannot meaningfully synthesize these entities, we can still approach them all with three common terms in mind – passion, free activity of the soul, and understanding – whether we mean to theorize as to differing manifestations of war, to understand a particular historical war or to arrive at a particular military decision.

227

To adopt the philosopher's vocabulary, if we are to place Clausewitz in a philosophical tradition, it must be the Kantian one of understanding rather than the Hegelian one of reason or *Vernunft*. True, Hegel did see war as an outstandingly political act, and also saw that war is armed politics, but Clausewitz did not need the lectures on the philosophy of history to reach the goal of his thought. There is in any case no evidence that these lectures of Hegel's contributed to Clausewitz's final evolution after 1827, even though Hegel's influence had been powerful elsewhere for some time. The Clausewitzian duel of single combatants has nothing in common with the duel of master and slave or the rivalry of historical states at the end of *The Philosophy of Right*. The combatants aim to impose their will, not to obtain recognition, but ransom; war pushed to the extreme does not have moral stature because each side is fighting to the death, but rather because it comes from furious passions, the size of the stakes and revolutionary change. Intelligence will adapt the effort and sacrifices to the gains it expects, and will deal as willingly in sham or threatened battles as in ones that are fought out. It sets limits to states' ambitions so as to avoid hostile coalitions which would sooner or later be formed out of the fear aroused by the conqueror or the disturber of the peace. That trend towards equilibrium in Europe which Clausewitz analyses suddenly in Chapter 6 of Book VI, and the political ideas he derives from it, condemn Napoleon, and also the Kaiser and Hitler before their time.

But if Clausewitz is not a Hegelian, he could still be a Kantian. Cohen cites some sentences and expressions that have a Kantian ring – 'the realm of the mind' (*geistreich*) or 'that same spirit of analytical research that creates theory must also be used in the business of the critical' (*Geschäft der Kritik*). Comparison between Kant's classification of temperaments in his *Anthropology* and Clausewitz's classification of temperaments in his chapter on military genius may not show any direct influence from Kant, but does prove that Clausewitz was familiar with Kantian tools, which were current themes of the time.

It seems possible that Clausewitz read Kant's remarks on the connection between theory and practice. The relationship of rules and judgment, and the role attributed to sense of judgment are quite similarly explained in the Treatise and Kant's pamphlet, although it has to be said that these ideas were familiar enough in the aesthetic literature of the age, while the concept of reciprocity, or *Wechselwirkung*, belonged in the Kantian list of categories. These (and other, similar) observations may only lead to a prudent, banal conclusion that Clausewitz probably knew Kantian thinking, at least indirectly. Is it possible to go further, to see him as a disciple of Kant, and to view his system as an application of Kantianism? Reasons for doubting this far outweigh the arguments in favour of it.

Clausewitz's ethics or, if we can use the term, morality, do not square with the categories in the *Critique of Pure Reason*. Some of the Reformers, especially Boyen, were regarded as Kantians since they were inspired by an ethic of duty and of respect for the law because it is law. Clausewitz, like all of the Reformers, fought Napoleon in the belief that he was obeying a categorical imperative. Gneisenau insisted on the ideological nature of the conflict; he, too, was defending a principle when he fought Napoleon and the French. But, though he made resistance a categorical imperative,

228

Clausewitz only advanced a political motivation. After Jena, Prussian patriots wondered about the purpose of their existence and their future, and the words 'honour' and 'citizen' constantly recurred in the writings of Clausewitz, who was then, as a young aide-de-camp to Prince August, a prisoner of the French both in France and in Prussia. The individual deprived of his country is thereby shorn of his dignity; if he is respected abroad, it is from generosity, not obligation. Clausewitz wishes to be an honoured citizen. But 'citoyen' had a Jacobin ring; whereas the German word, 'Bürger', implies what Clausewitz wished to be, a citizen loyal to Prussia and to her king, for the honour of the king merged with that of his state or nation. These are honourable, patriotic ethics rather than ethics of duty, and are not based on religion or metaphysics. Here, what applies to Clausewitz might also apply to Machiavelli. Both were believers in a vague way, but their thought developed beyond their faith, whatever it was. Clausewitz, at least, unlike Machiavelli, had no grievance against the teachings of the Church.

He never seems to have had the same hopes in the French Revolution that Kant had, or the same hopes in political Reason; nor did he place any faith as Hegel did in the greatness of the hero who could unify Europe, even if that meant temporary French supremacy. Since he never experienced the lyrical illusions of the revolutionary dawn, he was profoundly affected by the new German nationalism that the French provoked against themselves. Though he was a thinking man of action, he left moral law to the philosophers and historical destinies to Providence.

It might be argued that his language and vocabulary were close to Kant's, or derived from Kant's; but many qualifications must be made here. Generally, he confuses 'philosophic' with 'scientific'. At the end of paragraph A of Chapter 1 of Book VI, 'philosophical argument' is said to encounter difficulties when the downward movement towards armed observation is substituted for the rise to extremes. In paragraph 3 of Chapter 1 in Book I, the formula that 'a principle of moderation can never properly be introduced into the philosophy of war' implies that it is logically necessary for the ascent to extremes to occur from the very concept of war. Thus, in the works, philosophy simply merges with conceptual analysis of the nature of things.

There is a somewhat different problem in a text that I have already quoted, from Chapter 30 of Book VI, in which a 'war involving great decisions' is said to be 'much simpler, much more in conformity with nature, much freer of internal contradiction, more objective, more governed by laws of inner necessity', which is the reason that '*Vernunft* can prescribe forms and laws' for it. Here, for once, Clausewitz uses *Vernunft*, not, as usual, *Verstand*; perhaps this might be an echo of the Kantian distinction between these two. However, I hesitate to base any general interpretation on this exceptional use of *Vernunft* which, here, seems to mean 'source of laws and necessity', whereas the term *Verstand* means the intellectual activity of everyone in war, especially the commander, i.e. what *Intelligenz* usually meant in Clausewitz's day, rather than Kant's precise meaning. Some other words, for instance *Vorstellung*, are also used by Clausewitz in their current rather than philosophical sense – *Vorstellung* being for him 'idea' or 'notion' in the vague sense, or 'concept' without any connotations regarding image, representation or concreteness.

We thus arrive at the decisive question, whether Clausewitzian method, as I analysed it in the preceding chapters – i.e. his conjunction of concept and experience – owes anything to Kantian thought. If the answer is positive, then it must be added that Clausewitz wrote in a philosophical style, but without any understanding of philosophy – a remark that would also suit Montesquieu if we tried to interpret De l'esprit des lois using Kant's categories.

4 Clausewitz and Montesquieu

Commentators really made difficulties for themselves when they supposed that they had hit upon extraordinary contradictions in Clausewitz's thought by comparing him with the German Idealists who were his contemporaries – hence the questions as to whether he was Kantian, Fichtean or Hegelian. None of these German commentators gave much importance to the passage in the first note where he said that De l'esprit des lois had been something of a model for him. These commentators all wrote off this allusion, taking it to refer only to the style of writing – short chapters, ill-connected and unsystematically organized. I should not go to the other extreme and present him as a disciple of Montesquieu, but there is no doubt that he was much more familiar with the military and political writers than with Hegel or Kant. The questions he asks and the methods he uses derive from the philosophers of the eighteenth century and, to understand him, we have to put him where he belongs, among the men whom Meinecke examined in his Die Entstehung des Historismus, and not see him as a reader of Kant or Hegel.

The central problem that governs the Treatise, and on which Clausewitz was reflecting at the end of his life, was the diversity of wars and the contrast between absolute and real war. It was, and is, the problem of the relationship between ideas (concepts or notions) and historical, concrete reality. The relationship of concepts and realities governs the problem of the relationship between rational thinking (or knowledge free of theory) and positive teaching (or doctrines and instructions). It is no different in Montesquieu, and interpreters constantly wondered as to the praxological consequences to be derived from De l'esprit des lois.

In both authors, abstract or conceptual analysis began with the idea of nature. One meaning of this idea, today, would be what we call 'essence' – the spirit of a nation or institution necessarily implying certain expressions of itself, or objectives. The concept of 'nature' or 'spirit' is sometimes contrasted with the diversity of historical experience, and sometimes also defines specific historical circumstances. There must therefore, be two different relationships between concept and reality – either the nature of war, unchanging throughout time, or the historical kinds, i.e. the two types of war. Experience, in Clausewitz's sense, has nothing in common with that in Kant's meaning – not, as was suggested by one recent commentator, because Clausewitz used a pre-Kantian epistemology, but because his research is at a lower level. When economists contrast their models with reality, they do not mean a crude reality, unaffected by human subjectivity, but rather a perceived reality which has not been simplified by the creation of a few variables.

Experience in Clausewitz's sense has either to do with historical events – hence his question, for instance, as to whether strategic surprise has ever succeeded – or, at a level even further from abstraction, the actual experience of fighting. At the end of his *Principles* he tells his royal pupil to read the accounts of battles that the combatants themselves have written.

But the significance of these problems – of which many instances have been given in preceding chapters – is reduced if an effort is made to see in them a transposition or application of the *Critique of Pure Reason*. Clausewitz's aim, like Montesquieu's or all sociologists', was to make history intelligible and action rational, by adapting means to ends. This intelligibility is to emerge from a constant cross-reference from abstraction to history, or from concept to experience, which is typical of the Clausewitzian method.

This would never have been doubted had not obsessions with Kantianism introduced the erroneous, even absurd, idea of a relationship between absolute war and *Ding an sich*, in which real wars were to become a phenomenal manifestation of war *an sich*. Absolute war is a device, a mental construction, which has nothing in common with Kant's *Ding an sich*, something that may be thought about but cannot be known. The initial duel of two warriors is not to be projected through time and space in the way that the *Ding an sich* is projected through the forms of sense-perception as they affect consciousness. The process is simply a closer and closer approach to experienced or perceived reality, as the initially poor model becomes gradually more complex.

In short, Clausewitz belonged to the eighteenth, and not to the nineteenth, century. His thinking was shaped in his garrison years at Neu-Ruppin, and then at the military academy under Scharnhorst's influence. In his political opinions, his vision of the European family of states, he is faithful to the Enlightenment tradition even if he has also been impelled by the thunderclap of revolution into a spontaneous discovery of nationalist passion, and into becoming the doctrinaire of *levée en masse*, the *Landwehr* and reserve divisions based on popular conscription. His reaction after 1815 to the Prussians' behaviour, and his admiration for England, show that his loyalties were really with the pre-revolutionary philosophy of the European system of states.

His use of the concepts of nature and spirit in the 'Strategy' of 1804 and then in his *Principles* for the crown prince of Prussia is not, of course, a direct demonstration of Montesquieu's influence, but it does reveal a way of thinking that is characteristic of *De l'esprit des lois*. As he says himself, the brief chapters of Books I and II are written in Montesquieu's style. Where he differs is in his attempt to systematize and relate to all of the concepts needed to apprehend the object, war, whereas *De l'esprit des lois* can be seen as a kind of rhapsody, in which the parts are greater than the whole. It was shown long ago that that book had some internal structure, just like the Treatise.

Both books reveal the same problems of interpretation, and similar ambiguities, as soon as we try to work out their implications for practice. There are two kinds of implication, here, in Montesquieu. Each kind of regime, whether republic, monarchy or despotism, will require different laws. Each type will depend (according to a rather questionable determinism) on various factors such as numbers, climate, spirit of the people, etc. Conditional imperatives will arise from the nature and principle that govern a regime, as well as from historical circumstances. On what basis are we to choose a regime? Can politics or morality lay down unconditional imperatives? Do politics and morality, separately or together, even make it possible to choose the regime? If each regime is the necessary result of the circumstances, the environment or the spirit of a people, is there in fact any margin left for choice at all?

The types of war correspond to the types of regime. The strategy suitable to one type would be contrary to the nature of the other. Choice between types of war is not the outcome of the governing will of one of the belligerents, let alone of both. It is the political situation that dictates the main lines of the hostilities, and they are determined in advance by the nature of the relationship between and inside the states.

I do not think that the influence of Montesquieu matters very much. It might have been confirmed in the notebooks of Clausewitz that are now lost, but I should be quite prepared to give up any suggestion of Montesquieu's influence on Clausewitz, provided that we agree that there is some kinship as regards problems and methods. I am more concerned with the objection that Clausewitz's reference to nature, spirit and the determination of abstract aims becomes less obvious in the Treatise than in the earlier works. It may be that the interplay of conceptual opposites, which more and more prevails, betrays a different origin; can we be sure that the Kantian table of categories or the intellectual style of Fichte and Hegel did not contribute something to the development of Clausewitz's thinking?

However, at bottom I should find this difficult to believe. The Treatise is a study, by Clausewitz himself, of problems that arose from his own conception of things. All of the seeds of what we may call Clausewitzian dialectic, that of war and politics, emerge in the 'Strategy' of 1804, in the distinction of goals within the war and goals of the war, and here, again, are strongly outlined the dialectic of defence and attack, which again receives stress in the letters to Gneisenau in 1812. From the start, the dialectic of material and moral set Clausewitz, as a young officer, against the great builders of systems. Clausewitz was one of those minds who find their themes early on, and are still discovering new variations when they die: minds rich in intuitive perception, and also inclined to build their perceptions into a system. Such work can only be understood as a whole, the meaning being determined by the structure of the whole.

Unfortunately, the Treatise, which ought to have been read as a whole, has often been approached only in part. Today, in the universities, there are still readers who are willing and even eager to follow its cruder elements. We must ask whether now, in the nuclear age, the real Clausewitz has lessons to offer; and the hatred that the expression 'neo-Clausewitzian' has aroused at least will justify the investigation I propose to undertake in the remainder of the book.

Introduction to Parts IV and V

The greatest military writer of our age, Sir Basil Liddell Hart, shared with Keynes a belief that the legacy of Marx, despite official versions of Marxism, has been to justify the proposition that ideas influence the course of history. According to Keynes, the most influential economist of this century, governments and businessmen both apply theories that they learnt from their teachers twenty years earlier; and between the wars, Liddell Hart wrote, 'the influence of thought upon thought is the most important factor in history'. The inspiration provided by new ideas and the introduction of new approaches to military organization, strategy and tactics have played a role 'no less significant than the exploits of military genius'.

To illustrate this point, he took the example of Napoleon, who was regarded neither as an innovator in the field of armaments nor in that of troop organization. Napoleon rejected projects that his engineers suggested; and the division, as a large unit of men capable of independent action, had existed before he used it. Napoleon's contribution to the art of war was methodological, especially in the first campaigns of 1796, 1805 and 1806, and even that amounted to elaborating the ideas of Marshal Saxe and Guibert as regards troop concentration and mobility.

Liddell Hart thought that the true lesson of Napoleon had been lost, because he distorted his own past at St Helena, and because two men, Jomini and the Prussian, Clausewitz, failed to understand the spirit of Napoleon's actions. Jomini's approach was, however, scholarly, and less dangerous, Liddell Hart thought, than the philosophical outlook of Clausewitz.

Jomini wishes to reduce the art of war to a science, in which the governing principles of strategy would be immutable. In his opinion, manoeuvre on interior lines was a unique and constant feature of victory; behind the ostensible flexibility of Napoleonic manoeuvre there lay a strategic stereotype barely concealed by esoteric jargon. In Liddell Hart's opinion, it was obsession with security that threatened to paralyse initiative and lead to defeat.

But if Jomini's influence was pernicious enough, then that of Clausewitz, he said, was worse – not because he was the prophet of Napoleon, but because he was a prophet of Clausewitz. Liddell Hart called him 'the Mahdi of mass and mutual slaughter'. More specifically, he said that Clausewitz had caricatured and oversimplified Napoleon's method, emphasizing troop concentration, whereas its essence lay in mobility and the size of the network covering the theatre of operations, in which the different divisions or armies interrelated at both levels, so as to act as reserves for each other. Clausewitz was said to have exalted the clash of

233

armies, because he concentrated on mass strength and superiority of numbers rather than on operations or decisive sectors of the front.

The English writer blamed Clausewitz for two errors: his overrating of number and his underrating of manoeuvre. He did, however, also appreciate that Clausewitz was not responsible for all of the ideas attributed to him. Unlike most Germans, Liddell Hart appreciated that the formulae – war as the continuation of politics, and war as aimed at overthrow of the enemy state – contained an element of contradiction.

It is strange that he did not see the contradiction. For if war is a continuation of a political strategy, it must be waged with a view to postwar advantages. But a state that uses up its forces to the limit is condemning itself to political weakness.

Clausewitz, probably unwittingly, propagated the idea of war to the death, *à l'outrance*, and Liddell Hart thought that it was Clausewitz's bold generalization and trenchant formulae that affected the course of European history, rather than other parts of the Treatise, which abound in qualification, nuance and repetition.

I have quoted Liddell Hart at length because he seems to me to be the most intelligent, and also the most typical, opponent of Clausewitz writing in the English language. He is too intelligent to fail to see that Clausewitz was greater than his disciples, and too English to devote months to unravelling his skein of logical and empirical propositions, of theory and doctrine. Liddell Hart did like two features of the Treatise: the importance it gave to moral factors, and the supremacy of politics. But he condemned the rest of it – the implicit prescription of a fight to the death, the rejection of manoeuvre and the quest for brutal conflict between huge armies. At least he could, in part, attribute the bloody follies of the First World War to the fascination exerted by some of the theories in the Treatise.

I do not intend to offer a defence to this English attack. In Parts IV and V of my study, Clausewitz will appear sometimes as the accused, sometimes as the accuser, and most often as witness. To begin with, I would maintain that an attack on Clausewitz requires more attentive reading of the Treatise, and less summary historical analysis. Even in Germany, the case of Clausewitz cannot lend itself to simple categorical judgments. The first edition of the *Hinterlassene Werke* of 2,000 copies took twenty years to sell.

The first general study was written by a Frenchman, an officer of Polish origin, at the request of Louis Philippe's eldest son, the Duke of Orléans. After the elder Moltke's victories, the tribute paid to Clausewitz's genius took on a ritual flavour. Schlieffen wrote a preface for the fifth edition of the Treatise, and stressed, yet again, the work's permanent value, although he did add that its philosophical tone no longer corresponded with readers' tastes. The tone of the work had probably never pleased nineteenth-century readers, who were almost all officers, but if we eliminate the conceptual formulation that Schlieffen called philosophy (the French called it metaphysical fog) as well as the supremacy of the political, which general staffs did not accept, it is difficult to see what remains of the Treatise that readers could not have found elsewhere.

After the First World War, Hindenburg also paid tribute to the man whom Moltke's victories had turned into the founder of the German heory of war: 'There is a book, *On War*, that will never date. Clausewitz vrote it. He understood war and he understood men. We had to listen to him, and when we followed his advice, it was to our advantage. The contrary meant disaster.' However, on the decisive question of the link between war and politics, even Moltke, as we shall see, broke with Clausewitz's teachings, which had been too crudely expounded in Chapter 5 of Book VIII. Only Ludendorff, who was to Hindenburg what Gneisenau had been to Blücher, broke the taboo and stated explicitly that the Treatise belonged to a past age: war was no longer to be placed in the service of policy, but rather the other way about. At least he, unlike certain American teachers, did not regard the two formulae as interchangeable.

Clausewitz's works became familiar in France after the defeats of 1870 and thus coincided with the rediscovery of Napoleon. Perhaps the Treatise, whether understood correctly or not (in my opinion, not), played some part in the French generals' deliberations in 1914. However, once more it should be stressed that looking for a guilty party will not produce an indisputable conclusion, as I have demonstrated in the first volume. You can find what you want to find in the Treatise: all that you need is a selection of quotations, supported by personal prejudice.

Which of the chief ideas best guides us towards an understanding of Clausewitz's aims? An interpretation may take as its starting point either the supremacy of politics over the military machine, or the annihilation of the enemy, as being the inherent purpose of the act of war, and the overthrowing or disarming of the enemy as the ultimate goal of war. These two themes are more or less confused. In his youth, Clausewitz tended to follow those precepts on war that he found temperamentally satisfactory, but he also came to see that, historically, wars to the death have not been very common, and so are neither more nor less a natural expression of the concept 'war' than the 'cabinet wars' of the eighteenth century. The intrinsic goal of war may be contrasted with the real or historical goals, and such ideas can coexist in the same framework, so that when the particular circumstances are taken into account, the main goal will still remain the destruction or annihilation of the enemy. Of course, destruction and annihilation do not have to mean wholesale massacring. The two words really mean that the enemy should be made incapable of carrying on the fight. Is this, in the end, very different from two wrestlers trying to floor each other? Particular circumstances, of course, do make for a radical difference between an army obliged to withdraw from the field, and one crushed by the enemy. Thus the Prussians were only fractionally more exhausted than the victorious French after their defeat at Ligny, and they were victors themselves two days later, at Waterloo. Similarly, if an enemy is defeated, territory becomes open to conquest, but the converse is not true, for occupation of ground does not guarantee the destruction of enemy armies or the capitulation of the enemy state.

The translation of destruction and annihilation into concrete terms does not much alter with circumstances. But we can interpret in various ways the idea of overthrowing the state, on the model of the wrestling bout; the centre of gravity to be attacked will vary from generation to generation, in accordance with the structures of government. The various ways in which a state can be overthrown inevitably govern the various ways in which wars are planned. The theory, therefore, points to the supremacy of the political in the subjective and objective senses: conclusions derived superficially from the outcome of military struggles are corrected or rejected in the plan of war. It is not difficult to reconcile this intellectually once it is subjected to the logic of the final synthesis, though in practice military specialists have invoked their own speciality as the final arbiter, and even those who, like Bismarck, inclined towards a different approach, acknowledged indirectly that the destruction of the enemy forces was the goal of war. The strains between civil and military, between those who fight the war and those who fight the battles, result not from theory but practice, and the pre-existing state of affairs. As long as the Treatise as a whole is misunderstood, extremists in both camps will present exaggerated versions of both lines.

If the Treatise is read carefully, the conclusions that it reveals are contrary to those normally drawn from it. It is not dogmatic as regards armament, conditions relating to movement and supply, dependence of war plans and tactics on the political and social context, and the state's intentions, the adaptation of the plan of campaign to the type of war, or the account to be taken of the effects of chance, the event itself and the enemy. If Frederick the Great's defensive methods had been used against Bonaparte, they would not have been very effective. By which irony of history has this theorist, who rejected dogmatism, hard systems of method and the illusion of eternally valid maxims, been turned into a fanatical 'Mahdi' of mutual butchery?

Clausewitz has been the victim of an inevitable muddle in readers' minds that has confused his analysis and vision of reality with his utterances about the desirable state. De la Barre, Duparcq and Jomini condemned partisan warfare, as Moltke did when the French took it up in their turn in 1870–1. Liddell Hart disliked partisan warfare as much as million-strong armies: in conformity with the English tradition, he wanted wars fought by small armies, by experts dispositionally inclined towards the profession of arms and pursuing their tasks dispassionately and fearlessly. Clausewitz, who saw the wars of the years 1792–1815, felt that henceforth wars would be waged by hundreds of thousands, and that the oppressed would in the last resort arm to expel the invader. It is all *sine ira et studio*: he does not approve or disapprove, he merely takes note.

But Clausewitz was a victim of his method. The importance he attached to numbers was limited to cases where both sides were similarly organized and equipped. This is logical enough, but is dangerous in a work like the Treatise. He does not rule out manoeuvre in so far as conditions of superiority result at significant points which lead to battles being fought in such a way that decisive results follow (for instance, envelopment leading to a battle on reversed fronts). But in many places, especially in Chapter 9 of Book VIII, where he is trying to justify Napoleon's Russian campaign (a particularly clumsy operation), he gives arguments to those historians who had failed to distinguish between the manoeuvring strategy of the eighteenth century, which he despised, and the manoeuvre more or less centred on the battlefield, which he was well aware of, and in which mobility can ensure success.

As the book was unfinished, the final synthesis exists only as a draft. But the logic of the synthesis allows us to resolve all or almost all of its apparent deviations and incompatibilities, though on one condition: the commentators must base his remarks on the final note which attests the vital importance of the first chapter. Clausewitz's commentators have never come to terms with the logic of this final synthesis which, as presented, does not quite cohere as a whole.

Whether we wish it or not, as we go from Books III, IV and V to Book VI, we breathe a different air. Books III and IV abound in phrases that Liddell Hart could use to illustrate his 'Mahdi' thesis. Clausewitz seems to exalt battle, bloodbath, the grandeur of conflict and the cult of the supreme chief, mastering his emotions and still, at the height of the storm, clear-sighted and cool. By contrast, Book VI lists the advantages that a military and political defensive can give: defenders fight for independence, wish to keep what they have, and do not try to seize what belongs to others. They can choose the battlefield, and can draw the enemy, in some cases, into the depths of their own territory, where the native population can take up arms against him and, even if unarmed, can still in many ways harass, annoy or spy on the invader. Chapter 26 of Book VI has a no less subtly descriptive tone than Chapter 9 of Book VIII. Again, there is no logical contradiction: an offensive war strategy, aimed at overthrowing the enemy, does not mean attacking a neighbour: similarly, when Aristotle analysed the ways of maintaining tyranny he was not recommending it, though perhaps in Machiavelli's case it was different. The enigma of Clausewitz works at a lower level of abstraction or subtlety because as a strategist he stopped short of solutions that would produce a quick peace, and because he only vaguely indicates what these solutions are.

Is it possible to go further, and assemble from Clausewitz a body of doctrine that the work does not explicitly contain? I am not sure, for neither the man nor the work can be unequivocally summed up. All of it means something; but men who have been forced by the results of a first battle to hope against hope still find him more a master of morale than of technique. Clausewitz was sure that future wars would involve whole nations, but he did hope to preserve the European comity of states, to avoid the pitiless cruelty that occurs when all are armed and guerilla warfare is waged by peoples themselves. Though Clausewitz admired 'the god of war', and thought himself the kind of compulsive gambler who might, at the end of the day, flee like a beggar, without a thaler, he was a preacher of moderation, not excess, and preferred defensive, patriotic war to wars of conquest, even though he also expected German unity to emerge from the wars between German states. Strategically, he liked the defensive, provided it was a just one, or calculated because in some circumstances the defenders would be inferior to the attackers' strength, and thereby justified in waiting for their initiative.

Clausewitz was theorist of an art to be cultivated by study and reflection, one that cannot be learned. He inspired, rather than instructed. He sought to include everything that pertained to the business of fighting in a coherent whole, and to combine abstractions, the application of which would vary with circumstances, with a highly detailed analysis of the particular circumstances, denying the existence of hard-and-fast rules, but suggesting guidelines and maxims, qualified by exceptions. It is his resonance that accounts for his fame and for the frequent misunder standing of him, for his successes and for his failures.

Part IV
Defender or Prosecutor?

Three Themes

Nowadays, the wars of the French Revolution and Napoleon seem almost rehearsals for the two wars of our century. Violence disrupted tradition, and Clausewitz emerged. We will not, of course, blame our disasters on a book: it was not Clausewitz who set peoples so whole-heartedly against each other in August 1914, nor was it he who gave supreme power, in a Germany scourged by unemployment, to a demagogue who combined hatred, limitless will-power, and callousness with a trace of genius.

However, on both sides of the Rhine, generals referred to Clausewitz. Even Lenin gave the formula a new twist when he adopted the principle of just and unjust wars rather than that of the superiority of the political to the military; wars henceforth had an ideological dimension. In the next chapters, three of the themes of Clausewitz will appear, in the context of three different readings of the Treatise.

In the First World War, both sides wanted a fight to the finish, but it was the Western Powers who subdued an exhausted Germany, even if her military forces had not been decisively beaten in the field. Hitler and Stalin, both of them springing from revolution, did not fight their war in the generals' tradition, but as ideologues and conquerors. Stalin rallied the Russians to a patriotic cause, while Hitler caused the whole of Europe to revolt and resist him. Mao Tse-tung armed the people in a way that only the Prussian patriots had dreamt of (and that Clausewitz himself, and others, had sketched in theory); his methods became the essence of revolutionary war, one leading, through the creation of a regular army consisting of irregulars, to victory and annihilation. The generals of 1914–18 concentrated on one thing: decisive battle. Lenin, too, concentrated on one thing: the class struggle that would explain the historical and moral purpose of war. Mao went one further: arming the people is not only a feature of war between nations, but the decisive factor in a civil war.

Chapter 10

Annihilation and Attrition

In the nineteenth century Germany, united by Hohenzollern Prussia, became the greatest power in Europe. Up to 1945, hers was the best army in Europe and the world, and it won spectacular victories in the two wars of our century – though maybe 'lost victories', to use the title of Manstein's book, showing the *Ohnmacht des Sieges*, in Hegel's famous expression. Now, the Reich has gone. There are two Germanies, west and east, side by side. The greatness of Germany and that of Europe collapsed together.

For or against whom is the Treatise to be used? Or is its purpose only the exacting and bitter one of enabling us to understand the tragic development that runs from the Prussian patriots who confronted Napoleon to the resistance of the peoples of Europe to the tyranny of Hitler?

1 Bismarck and Moltke

After 1945 historians frequently went back to Bismarck and his work to understand the causes of the German catastrophe. This was an inevitable and often justified search, but it has always been in vain. No doubt Louis XIV prepared the way for the French Revolution, and Bismarck no doubt made Hitler possible, but a divided Germany, or a Germany unified by means other than blood and iron, suggests that diplomacy and war might have taken a different course, and I do not see how we can condemn the unification of Germany without falling into the trap of fatalism and making out that the consequences of that unification were unavoidable.

If we go back to history as it happened, to the policy of one of Europe's last real statesmen, we can see in Bismarck's work a masterpiece of the traditional processes of *Machtpolitik*. The wars that turned the King of Prussia into German emperor conformed to the principle of annihilation but equally did not infringe the restraints imposed by the balance of power. It seems doubtful that Bismarck, who was responsible for this achievement, had ever read Clausewitz, to whom he never refers in his memoirs, even though he might have found in the Treatise arguments that would have confounded his partner and rival, Moltke – arguments, moreover, that would have justified his actions with reference to the writings of a man whose authority the military could not reject.

Historians have often told the story of the battle of skills between the two heroes of German unification, the statesman and the general, and I shall add nothing to what they have said. The ideas of Bismarck, and the events of the time, enable us to see why the Germans used Clausewitz without realizing the contradictions inherent in the many interpretations of what he wrote. Distance in time now allows us to let Bismarck and Moltke speak for themselves, and allows me to forget what these names would mean to me as a French schoolboy during the First World War.

To judge from his *Gedanken und Erinnerungen*, Bismarck saw war as a tool, and did not condemn it as such, whether politically or morally. He acknowledged that his generals had a taste for it. Noting Moltke's pleasure in finally knowing that force would be the arbiter after the trick of the Ems telegram, Bismarck shared his aims, but the two men were not emotionally compatible. Bismarck never disguised the fact that he wanted war with France – which at the time he could have avoided – so that the conflict between northern and southern Germany could be subsumed in common bloodshed. However, when he abandoned his opposition to preventive war over Luxembourg in 1867 and over the too-rapid French revival in 1875, he did so with the reservation that only wars into which states are forced are justified. As regards the army's bellicose spirit, 'its absence would be deplorable; however, the task of containing it within the limitations of people's legitimate peaceability is one of the main tasks of the state, in the political rather than the military sense'.

At this stage he sketched an apparently Clausewitzian doctrine on the relationship of war and statecraft, though also contrasting his own with the often cited Moltkean one, which may be summed up with the sentences:

Statecraft uses war to achieve its ends and shapes the start and finish of war decisively, while reserving to itself the right to increase war aims or alternatively decrease them while hostilities proceed. Given this indecision, strategy may always concentrate upon the highest goal that can be attained with the means at its disposal. These means, therefore, can best serve statecraft, or at least its goals, while the activity is wholly independent.

It hardly needs to be said that Bismarck never accepted a doctrine like this which, though the military favoured it, manifestly contradicted common sense and Clausewitz. Bismarck talked ironically of these soldiers who wished to free themselves from the control of the foreign ministry, but only as long as they did not feel like 'closing the gates of the temple of Janus'. The symbol of the two-faced Janus really tells us that governments in wartime have to look beyond military aspects. Bismarck's conclusion had a Clausewitzian ring, despite its terminology:

the task of the army commander is to annihilate the enemy forces; the aim of war is to gain, through contest, a peace on terms that suit the state's policies. In setting and limiting the aims to be achieved through war, consultation with the sovereign, both before and during hostilities, is always a political matter, and the manner in which it is carried out must influence the way the war is fought.

The intervention of statecraft – in this case the foreign ministry – appears to be pragmatic. Bismarck, as a statesman of the old school, thought that he had done most to create the twentieth century in Europe. His policy in 1864, 1866 and 1870 had been to localize war and resolve it to Prussia's advantage, without taking out any mortgage on the future; and if his advice to the king was always governed by a desire to limit the conflict and prevent the intervention of other great powers, it was because he was not a conqueror or adventurer of genius. He wanted to preserve the European *status quo*. Bismarck was a civilized Machiavellian.

242

Bismarck's quarrels with the generals splendidly reveal his Machiavellian streak, since at times he would oppose an operation suggested by a general and at others would recommend a purely military venture that the soldiers regarded as useless or harmful. During the Danish war, before Moltke became chief, Bismarck had great difficulty in imposing his will on the commander in the field. In the first place, he was against a campaign in Jutland, so as to maintain his understanding with the Austrians; but General Wrangel exceeded his orders, alleging a threat of Anglo-French intervention. Then Bismarck pressed the wavering generals to attack the lines at Düppel, because he needed a military victory before the London conference, which in any case he regarded with equanimity, because he reckoned correctly that the obstinate Danes would provide him with a final opportunity to achieve what he wanted. The Danes did in fact resign themselves to submitting to the victors' will after negotiations broke down and after a few days' fighting. Bismarck had achieved what he wanted.

In 1866 there was a quarrel with Moltke. Bismarck gave direct orders to Falkenstein, commanding the army of the Rhine, to march on Frankfurt without even taking the precaution of crushing the Hanoverian army; and on this occasion it was the generals who bore a justified grudge against the civilians.

After the victory of Königgrätz (Sadowa), Bismarck suspended military operations and on 18 July agreed to a five-day truce to avoid the threat of French intervention, which Moltke thought unlikely. He was very careful to obtain the consent of Napoleon III, by negotiation, to the aims he had set himself, the exclusion of Austria from Germany, Prussian supremacy in north Germany, Prussian administration in Schleswig-Holstein, and annexation by Prussia of the Grand Duchy of Hesse, Frankfurt, Hanover and Nassau. In exchange, he left Austria intact, and did not give his sovereign or the generals the satisfaction of parading through Vienna. The king finally listened to the voice of reason, though he felt cheated of the fruits of victory.

In the war of 1870–1 Moltke had almost as much prestige and authority as Bismarck. But the state's structure did not allow him the kind of control that Frederick the Great or Napoleon had had. The king was the supreme leader, and although Moltke drew up plans and gave directives to the army, he did not have the same role as Schlieffen at the end of the century, or Hindenburg in the First World War.

The quarrel with Bismarck started over the addressing of military dispatches: Bismarck, properly, wanted to see them, and had the king's support. The most heated and best-known of these quarrels concerned the bombardment of Paris, and later the way in which the city was to be occupied after surrender. Bismarck wanted to finish off the campaign in a hurry as there were threats of foreign intervention, but Moltke was against, on military rather than humanitarian grounds. Paris, he said, would have to surrender from famine; why bother with a bombardment that might not work, and did not conform to current military orthodoxies, when hunger would inexorably produce the same result?

The dispute was fuelled by the support that the generals had from some of the court. The empress and crown prince were sensitive to an English

243

opinion that was turning against Prussia, and put pressure on Bismarck, who also did not scruple to use the German press to his own interest. In his memoirs, he denounced the humanitarian argument: was not hunger just as cruel as shelling?

The idea that Paris, a fortified place and the most solid enemy bastion, should not be attacked like any other fortress filtered through from Berlin. Expressions such as 'the Mecca of Civilization' and other distortions of the usual humanitarian sentiments suited the hypocritical public in England, a country that expects other powers to share such feelings, though it does not always allow its enemies to reap the benefits of them.

Once Paris had surrendered, Bismarck again became moderate. Whereas Moltke wished to have German troops occupy Paris, in conformity with the laws of warfare, Bismarck, once he had won victory and gained his political aims, did not want, gratuitously to humiliate the French for the sake merely of satisfying his soldiers' self-esteem with triumphal ceremonies in the Roman style. Once more, the 'emperor and king' decided in Bismarck's favour, and the Germans' parade through Paris was a small affair.

In his memoirs, Bismarck – it seems, rightly – defended himself against the allegation that he planned preventive war against France in 1875 to forestall her recovery. He said that such a scheme of prestige and power politics would have been no different from the kind of thing that had ruined the First and Second French Empires. After 1870 his task was to reconcile Europe to the new powerful Germany: his aim, in other words, was to gain decisive victories, but only by destroying enemy troops in limited conflict. In this way, the Prussian Germany could be created but without upsetting the European balance, and without Germany's power seeming to be irreconcilable with the traditional liberties of states such as England and Russia. To the very end, Bismarck succeeded in the way that such an expression will apply to a man like him: he gained what he set out to gain. The two great men of German history, Frederick and Bismarck, owed their success not only to force and guile, but to moderation, whereas the French persisted in regarding Louis XIV and Napoleon as heroes, even though they lacked wisdom and balance.

When I describe Bismarck's thoughts and practice on the vital subject of relations between statecraft and warfare as 'Clausewitzian', I may be considered in many ways provocative. Can we, after all, call the Treaty of Frankfurt 'moderate'? Did not the annexation of Alsace-Lorraine create a gulf between France and Germany that nothing could fill? Did it not sow seeds of hatred that, some day, would explode into life?

True, Bismarck's success did contain the seeds of retribution. In the tragic game of power politics, it is only on the last day that victory can be counted upon; and, for a country, there never can be a last day short of complete disappearance into the ocean's depths, as happened with the Celts or Carthage. Had it not been for German unification or the Bismarckian compromise between Prussia and the German states, the Kaiser would never have known the temptations of *Weltpolitik* and Europe would not have committed suicide as she did.

To judge Bismarck fairly, we have to use rules that Clausewitz suggested in his critique: we must identify intellectually with the man, without crediting him with knowledge he could not have, or applying a code of rights and duties to which neither he nor his contemporaries could adhere. The strictures of pacifists can be ignored. Bismarck was unquestionably convinced that war in his day continued to be a proper way of pursuing the aims of statecraft. He would not let humanitarian considerations clog his path while he was fighting a war, though, of course, he could not imagine massacring prisoners or civilians. He was simply cleverer than his enemies or colleagues, and more cynical – sometimes brutal in order to terminate a conflict that dragged out, sometimes showing moderation in order, for example, to preserve the chance of reconciliation with Austria or prevent the futile humiliation of the defeated side. As a statesman he was conservative, but in his memoirs he admits unambiguously that if need be he would at once have supported the Hungarian revolutionaries in 1866 or the Italian ones in 1870. The terms of the Treaty of Frankfurt, though thought harsh at the time, did not prevent the recovery of a France that no doubt did sink to the second rank, but only because of a fall in population and a decline of science such as precedes any military disaster. The country paid off her indemnity of 5,000,000,000 francs without difficulty, and the benefits that the Germans obtained with their 'most favoured nation' claim did no damage to French economic progress.

True, there remains the annexation of Alsace-Lorraine, against the clearly expressed wishes of the populace, and it is this, and probably always will be this, that is the most contentious point for the French and for any objective observers (if they still exist). Bismarck meant to unify Germany, without Austria, under Prussian leadership, in conditions that would safeguard the balance of power in Europe. Even after a century has elapsed, is it possible for us, knowing about the bunker and the suicide of the Führer, to condemn, morally and politically, the consequences of Bismarck? It is not really certain, even today, that what happened to the Second Reich was inevitable: ought Bismarck, the last German statesman, to have foreseen that he would have no heirs?

The annexation of Alsace-Lorraine had been demanded by German patriots even in 1815. When it happened, it was at the point of transition from one era to another, and two interpretations of it can be given. At the time of the French Revolution, conservatives like Friedrich von Gentz thought it would be appalling and destructive for the French to base their annexation of Alsace not on the Treaty of Westphalia but on the Alsatians' wishes; Bismarck, too, quite consistently opposed those of his compatriots who in 1815 had demanded the return to the Reich of provinces that were German in culture and language, for he too adhered to the Treaty of Westphalia and the ideals of the century.

But Bismarck also belonged to a different era, for German unity, even though won through blood and fire, was implicitly based on the idea of nationality. The intellectuals who pleaded the cause of annexation did so because the Alsatians were German, even if they had lost consciousness of this, whereas the French intellectuals replied, with Renan, that nations were made by a common past and could be strengthened by the common will to achieve future greatness. On the one side lay nationality; on the other, the self-determination of a populace. Bismarck, probably gladly, abandoned the task of appealing to, or flattering, public opinion to the writers, as Frederick the Great had done earlier with the jurists. To him, military considerations required annexation of Lorraine, including its French-speaking part, and political ones demanded that of Alsace, to cement the still-fragile unity of the empire, even if he was well aware that the price would be the impossibility of long-term reconciliation with France. He probably hardly supposed that he was breaking the unwritten rules of the European state system: Germany was replacing France as the dominant power, but was not destroying the age-old tendency towards balance.

There are two ways of condemning Bismarck. The Reich, by virtue of its power, was fated to engage upon what the next generation called 'world politics': indeed, a journalist of little importance, Prévost-Paradol, proclaimed in *La France Nouvelle* that there would be another war, that France would be defeated, and that there would be a new coalition, against the newcomer, of the British, the Americans and the Russians. The other way of condemning Bismarck is simply to condemn power politics generally: moderation is better than excess. However, to that a sceptic might answer that, in the power game, moderation cannot succeed in the longer term: the restoration after the Congress of Vienna, though it preserved European society for a century, was still only an interim arrangement. Clausewitz himself sometimes saw this, at the time, though he sometimes also entertained illusions. Even in his equivocal version of them, conscription, the *levée en masse*, the principle of nationality and the arming of the people were all emanations of a revolutionary dynamism that, one day or other, would sweep aside the rulers of a monarchical and aristocratic Europe. The miracle was that German and Italian unification came without general war.

2 The French disciples: Foch

There is a twofold task confronting us if we wish to attribute historical responsibility to Clausewitz in the First World War, for we must ask what influence he exerted on the military thinking of the French, for instance Marshal Foch, on the one side, and on that of the Germans, such as Schlieffen, on the other.

I am not aware of any overall introductory study of Clausewitz in French, although an American historian did provide the essential information in an article published in 1940. The first person to lecture on Clausewitz and *Vom Kriege* at the École de Guerre appears to have been Commandant Lucien Cardot, later general, in 1885. In 1886–7 a second translation of the Treatise, by Lieutenant-Colonel de Vatry, appeared. Foch entered the École de Guerre in 1885, the year in which Cardot outlined Clausewitz's ideas to the future leaders of the French army. The discovery of the 'god of war' and his prophet coincided, for comparison between the campaigns of 1806 and 1870, between the master's genius and the disciples' talents, became a stock theme of military and historical writing: thus also, in elaborate form, of the outstanding military authors of the period, such as Georges Gilbert whose *Étude sur Clausewitz* soon became a classic, Commandant (later General) Bonnal, whom Foch succeeded at the École de Guerre, and Commandant Maillard. Between 1885 and 1890 Clausewitz was part of the training of the officers who drew up the staff plans early in the twentieth century and led the French armies in 1914. The ideas of the Clausewitzian school did not, of course, spread without objection. For instance, H. Camon alleged that Clausewitz had failed to grasp the essentials of Napoleonic strategy, and he deployed arguments similar to those of Liddell Hart. It is important to find out what the French found, or thought they had found, in a Treatise that they could read only in faulty translation, complemented by the German original; and Foch's *Principes de la guerre*, published in 1903 but containing his lectures of 1900, demonstrates better than anything else to what extent officers of the time were arriving at Clausewitz's real meaning. By failing to obtain a total picture, they ended up, in fact, by caricaturing him.

Foch starts by positing the permanence and immutability of 'fundamental truths' and 'guiding principles', despite historical change. In 1911, even after the experience of the Boer War and the Russo-Japanese War, he could still say in his Preface, 'War is still, in its conduct, subject to the same laws as in the past. Forms evolve, but cardinal principles remain.' In the earlier Preface of 1905 he had said, 'the manoeuvring offensive will finally overcome all resistance, while supine defensiveness will unfailingly be defeated'. It is striking, though not surprising, that Foch could see no third way between manoeuvring offensive and supine defensiveness, whereas Clausewitz, though ruling out passive defensiveness as contrary to the spirit of war, thought there was more intrinsic strength in defence than in attack. The French followed their German contemporaries in neglecting the advantages of the defensive as set out in Book VI, whether political, strategic or tactical.

Foch did respect Clausewitzian ideas as to the value of history and the lessons to be learned from military history. Clausewitz himself concentrated on the last three centuries, and explained his reasons for this – incomplete knowledge of distant events, especially in ancient times, transformations in the military machine, and the need to know the details of battles if they are to supply lessons for the future. However, though Foch argued the cause of history, he exhibited a curious lack of historical sense. In support of his thesis, he gave an approximative rendition of Jomini's idea that 'war, far from being an exact science, is a terrifying and compulsive drama', but he did not seem to appreciate the differences between Clausewitz and Jomini, who drew contrasting conclusions from their studies of Napoleon. Foch stressed that in 1870 France's enemies had learned history from concrete examples, and 'with such a background, Scharnhorst, Willisen and Clausewitz trained the Prussian high command from the early nineteenth century'. But he himself stayed with the Napoleonic wars and with 1870. He viewed historical experience, in other words, only very narrowly.

Why? He started with a conviction that modern war, of the kind for which France must prepare, would be national and hence would involve 'Napoleon's true lesson, that of absolute war'. He confused the reality of absolute war with that of national wars, and explained these latter in terms that were not always coherent.

A new era had dawned, that of national wars that were to be limitless in their nature and to involve the complete resources of a nation in the struggle, because their initial aim would not be dynastic, or the conquest and occupation of a province, but rather the defence and propagation of philosophical ideas, and then the pursuit of principles of independence, unity and material interest of various kinds; the maximum potential of troops were to be drawn out from their sensibility and emotion; in short, aspects of strength hitherto untapped were to be exploited.

Foch had taken a Clausewitzian idea, that the character of a war was determined by political and social circumstances and especially their more significant elements. But where, in 1903, was the counterpart of the Revolution or the ideas that shook thrones a century before?

Foch curiously supplied an answer that comes as a surprise in the writings of a Catholic conservative, a man of faith and untainted patriotism. 'The war of interests', he writes, 'will be less and less interesting, but more and more interested'; and he goes on, 'new markets will be opened up by cannon-shot'. This national, ideological and commercial war would, he thought, go on until the nations had mobilized all of their resources, 'because the defeated will not negotiate until they have exhausted all of their bargaining counters, so we must aim to destroy these counters'. Did events confirm his view? They did indeed, though only because this was a self-fulfilling prophecy. Foch, like Colmar von der Goltz, did not distinguish between absolute war and actual war. The concept of absolute war drew him towards total war, i.e. the total mobilization of resources towards a radical solution.

It is worth emphasizing these last words, because Foch sees the mass confrontation not in the shape of a prolonged struggle but rather, with a view to 1806 and 1870, as a great battle, one in which the fate of nations is in the balance. He not only adopts the Clausewitzian formula that 'tactical results give the only real advantages in war, and armed victory is the only result of any worth because it alone leaves a victor and a vanquished'; he also thinks that 'the first offensive will be the most decisive', and he asserts that 'the improvement of firearms is an advantage to the offensive when it is properly used: history proves this, and common sense supports it', because

> a thousand defenders may fire ten thousand rounds in a minute with a rifle that can fire ten rounds per minute. But with the same rifle, two thousand attackers can fire twenty thousand rounds – ten thousand more. Thus the material superiority of fire swiftly comes more and more to the attackers' aid as weaponry improves. How much more, then, will the attackers' ascendancy and moral superiority engulf the defenders, and the strong oppress the crushed?

In his first chapters, Foch did not distinguish between tactics and strategy, and did not appreciate the Clausewitzian dialectic of strategic defence and tactical attack. He regarded the offensive as superior at all levels – divisions, corps, armies. In part, this lack of conceptual rigour came from circumstances. Foch had succeeded Henri Bonnal, who lectured on how an army was commanded under Napoleon; Bonnal had succeeded Maillard who, 'by studying the division and the corps, showed why they were necessary formations'. Foch did not much distinguish between strategy and tactics, between strategical and tactical security, and it did not occur to him that he might be wrong in attributing to Clausewitz principles alleged to apply both to tactics and strategy. How mistaken he was is shown in that, after listing the principles of economy of force, liberty of action, free placing of force, and security, he tailed off into an 'etc.'.

Foch, obsessed with the idea of a massive, crushing attack on a selected point, wondered how to gain superiority and (or by) surprise. He elaborated his predecessor Bonnal's studies on vanguards, and used rarely quoted parts of Book V for this purpose. When he discusses leadership in wartime, morale and decisive action, he frequently refers to Clausewitz. It was not the Roman legions, but Caesar, who conquered Gaul; and, Foch adds, 'the influence of command and the enthusiasm it generates may account for those unconscious movements among the mass, as in the solemn moments when an army in the field feels drawn forward imperceptibly, as though it were sliding gently down a slope'. He quotes the famous words of Joseph de Maistre, 'a battle lost is a battle thought to be lost', and he goes on to praise the great attack of Macdonald's confused troops at Wagram, or d'Erlon's at Waterloo, which are certainly 'the negation of the tactical' and which show 'in the very principle of it all', 'the ultimate brutality of this kind of slogging match'.

There would be little sense in condemning this impassioned, irrational book: it would be too easy, and history has already condemned it. We wonder what Foch took from Clausewitz. He did borrow some themes and expressions from the French translation of the Treatise, but if he was a pupil, he was not a good one. Of the two links between war and policy he mentions only one, the social and political circumstances that determine the character of a war, and even here he does not particularize which circumstances may impel European peoples into a war to the death. The second kind of war, that in which hostilities are waged with a view simply to achieving advantageous peace, he ignores: with even greater simplemindedness than Moltke and his successors, he suggests that fighting will only stop when one or other side has lost the practical and moral capacity to continue.

Of the two kinds of war, offensive and defensive, Foch would only acknowledge the former, and even then he failed to distinguish between its political, strategic and tactical aspects, on which manoeuvre has to be based. Clausewitz did give the offensive a moral advantage, but he came to understand the benefits of defensive strategies. Foch ignored these: for instance, he failed to derive a tactical lesson from German attacks on open ground, as at Gravelotte, and seemed to accept Goltz's explanation for the French defeat, that the French had lost their grasp of the attack, and had been led to disaster by pursuing defensive tactics. What in reality had happened was that the improvidence and cumbersomeness embodied in the charge of the cuirassiers had become a symbol for the blind and nonsensical deployment of the tactical offensive.

It is impossible to find any systematization of ideas in Foch's *Principes*. He did subscribe to the historical method, but did not apply it: he laid down first principles, without supplying arguments for them, and he exhorted his readers to feel free to have their own ideas. He upheld reason as sole criterion, but at the same time really required a process of thought that implied total intellectual conformity. The end-product jars, instead of providing a harmonious structure: some of the main ideas come from Clausewitz via Goltz, while the vocabulary (economy of force, freedom of action, guarantee of security) is Foch's own, or someone else's. Chapters 5, 6 and 7 – 'Guarantee of Security', 'Vanguards' and 'the Vanguard at Nachod' – deal with tactics rather than strategy. Not surprisingly, there are ideas in this book, such as 'the psychology of peoples', that have persisted through centuries of military literature. 'Here was a combatant, a soldier incontestably superior in racial qualities – agility, spirit, sensitivity, sense of service, patriotism. Such was the French cavalry officer as opposed to the mameluke.'

If I quote from Foch, it is not because he strikes me as the best or most orthodox of Clausewitz's French commentators, but because his very mediocrity shows, though crudely, the notions that French officers, following Lucien Cardot, borrowed from the Treatise. Expressions such as 'economy of force' and 'security', clumsy and ambiguous though they are, can help resolve problems arising from the doctrine of offensive war as seen from the perspective of the decisive battle: how can numbers in the field or at the front be concentrated when the enemy is in the same position of constantly increasing his numbers and fire-power?

Hence the odd definition of 'economy of force':

> It is the art of directing all resources at a given moment at a specific target; of utilizing all troops at this point. To make this possible, the troops must always link up to confront a fixed, unchanging point instead of remaining compartmentalized. Then, once the result has been achieved, they can again converge and move against a fresh, separate goal.

In one way or another, all French commentators on Clausewitz, the unrivalled exponent of the Napoleonic method, debated the part of manoeuvre in Napoleonic strategy. Isolating a few phrases, such as 'advancing straight for the goal on the direct route', 'concentration of force in the intention of fighting decisive battle', or 'concentration of men on the field with a view to overwhelming the enemy or breaking through', these commentators looked for the operational means of administering the decisive blow in the best conditions. Camon maintained that a manoeuvre against the enemy rear, which ended in a battle on reversed fronts, would give the greatest trouble to an enemy already half-beaten before the action began. Colin's explanation of the Napoleonic style is almost identical with Liddell Hart's: the objective remains the decisive battle, and all formations in the campaign will converge towards this. Once the objective has been chosen, the Napoleonic method is to spread the army out over vast areas, though divisions will still be mutually supportive and act as reserves for each other. The war of movement derives its strength from the constant expansion and concentration of divisions. Napoleonic strategy was characterized by its flexibility: any placing of troops must not be immutable or limit future freedom of action; the high command will not give up its plans at a single setback and 'what helps to delude or puzzle the enemy is . . . capacity to vary movement'.

It is therefore wrong for General Gambiez to say that before 1914 Clausewitz was Napoleon and Napoleon, Clausewitz. Some writers also attacked Clausewitz for ignoring the manoeuvre used by Napoleon to arrive at decisive battle. Even those who did not criticize him for this did not ignore the preliminaries to the great event, the attack that led to the decisive result. Foch, under the influence of his predecessor, Henri Bonnal, and in the light of the catastrophe of 1870, dedicated his lengthiest passages to questions of 'high tactics', and the role of the vanguard in reconnoitring enemy lines, pinning the enemy down and thus ensuring the safety of the greater part of the army. Unfortunately, by simplifying Clausewitz's own simplifications, Foch ended up by advocating them. 'Here, and elsewhere, even in politics as well, the entry of the masses, with their emotionality, into the equation will inevitably produce oversimplification.'

It is not surprising that the Clausewitzian school – Foch, Cardot and Gilbert – became associated with the veneration of out-and-out offensive warfare and with approaches to strategy that were partly responsible for the disasters of 1914. Compared with these men, who dominated the army's general staff around 1910 (though, as Camon has shown, Clausewitz actually fell out of fashion in that year, when Napoleon was 'rediscovered'), Grouard appears as a sage whose ideas clashed with those of the men in charge. His two chief works are remarkable for rigour and common sense.

Whereas the great leaders dreamt of an offensive, of decisive battle, Grouard concluded that such an offensive would be totally impractical. The strategic offensive presupposed that 'we should be the first off the mark, should have a conviction of greater strength, that our army should have the confidence based on a run of past victories and that we could choose the easy line for operations'. Grouard had no problem in showing that none of this fitted the case.

The book, published in 1913, concluded with prescriptions which, unlike so many others, have stood up to the test of history. A war, it says, must be both politically and militarily defensive: politically, because it is only thus that France can count on her allies to intervene, and militarily because the mobilized armies will obviously face each other as blocks and the nature of the frontier country will force France onto the defensive. It does not follow, however, from conducting a defensive war that resistance should be passive: on the contrary, it must be positively active. Grouard therefore recommended that no great advance should be undertaken beyond the frontiers, that penetration of the Ardennes and Vosges would be unwise, and that immediate concentration of the French forces should not be contemplated.

Clausewitz's admirers would answer that an intelligent reader of the Treatise would have arrived at the same conclusions, and that Jaurès, with reference to Book VI, came to similar propositions. None the less, Antoine Grouard, the most reasonable of the French strategists before 1914, portrayed Clausewitz in the same way as Jomini – in the end, the prudent Swiss, Jomini, was a better guide than the bold Prussian.

251

3 Schlieffen: the new dogmatism

In France after 1918, Clausewitz appeared to be in the dock along with the accused: had not the cult of the offensive been part of his influence? Was he not responsible for the triumph of the Young Turks which culminated in Michel's resignation in 1911, in Joffre's appointment and the blunders made by the high command in the first weeks of the war? In Germany, Clausewitz was more accuser than accused: he played prosecutor in a trial concerning the relationship of policy, statecraft, the power of the state and the general staff. There was a further trial concerning the Schlieffen Plan, and both Falkenhayn and Ludendorff called him as witness.

I will not here analyse in detail the considerable literature on these cases. I only wish to highlight the concepts and distinctive aspects of the Treatise that suddenly acquired historical significance in the twentieth century. In 1870, thanks to Moltke's military victories, Bismarck had attained the political objectives he had set himself through a war which was local when viewed from the perspective of the state system. In 1914, the war became universal and went from victory to victory until the final humiliation. Who had been to blame: politicians or soldiers, Clausewitz or Schlieffen, Falkenhayn or Ludendorff?

On one initial point the German writers had to call on Clausewitz against the leaders of the Second Reich because these leaders did not, before or during hostilities, respect the subordination of the military to the state as Clausewitz had understood this. He had claimed that it was absurd to create a war plan solely in military terms. Historians have now established that the Schlieffen Plan was in fact known to the chancellors though not apparently to Admiral Tirpitz, but it was never jointly discussed by the various authorities, civil and military, whereas the French plans were studied by the supreme war council, chaired by the prime minister.

The Germans insisted that Wilhelmine institutions had been defective; that the allies had been quite wrong in suggesting Germany had a resolute will to fight and win, because she did not have a strong leader at the helm. The fact is that the chancellor never discussed with Schlieffen and his successor, the younger Moltke, nephew of the victor of Sedan, the political consequences of the plan he adopted, even though it involved violation of Belgian neutrality and virtually guaranteed British intervention. The war minister had no real authority over the great general staff, and the man responsible for the naval construction programme could claim later that he had had no foreknowledge of the Schlieffen Plan. In any event, it seems that the leaders of both navy and army had never in advance considered an overall policy for conducting land and sea operations.

Gerhard Ritter has convincingly shown that Schlieffen, contrary to legend, never pushed for war during the Moroccan crisis of 1905, nor was he disloyal to successive chancellors between 1890 and 1905. He never concealed his plans, but the chancellor found any civilian interference with military affairs inconceivable. Bethmann Hollweg was unfamiliar in any detail with the plan adopted in 1914, in particular being unaware of important aspects such as the aim to capture Liège by *coup de main* on the third day of mobilization, according to a plan conceived by Moltke and Ludendorff and to be executed by Ludendorff. The German general staff had only prepared one scheme for a war with France and Russia. This forced the chancellor to precipitate hostilities when German troops invaded Luxembourg before any ultimatum had even been sent to Belgium. The ultimatum sent to France, with the added condition demanding the handing over of Toul and Verdun as a pledge of French neutrality, made Germany appear the aggressor. In 1870 Bismarck, who had wanted war, had made France the aggressor. Without considering questions of war guilt, it is clear that in 1914 diplomatic improvisation (resulting from lack of either co-ordination between foreign ministry and general staff) reinforced the conviction held by the French that they had become involved in a war of national defence, which turned a large part of neutral opinion against the Central Powers.

A condemnation in 'Clausewitzian' terms of the haphazard war plan that the German generals drew up without an overall framework is understandable and poses no historical problem. However, with the Schlieffen Plan it is different, as with its chance of succeeding in the conditions of modern war. Was it, too, an application of Clausewitz's theories on 'absolute war'? Did this theory inspire Schlieffen and Moltke, who executed the plan, or, later on, Falkenhayn and the Hindenburg–Ludendorff team?

One factor, known to specialists but not more widely, deserves emphasis. After 1871, the elder Moltke was sure that the next war would be fought on two fronts, but he did not foresee a swift or total victory. In his last speech in the Reichstag, in May 1890, he expressed doubt as to whether one side would be totally crushed if the great European powers, with their reserves of manpower and armaments, went to war. 'It could become another Seven Years' War, or even a Thirty Years' War', he remarked. This prophecy was correct. Moltke, despite his lightning victories over Napoleon III, remembered all too well the second phase of the war – the risks taken by the German forces and the incipient dangers involved in extending the combat into 'a people's war'. 'Germany must not suppose that a rapid and easy campaign in the west will rid her of one adversary so that she can turn against another.' Hitler, who saw in Schlieffen the evil genius of Germany, tried to widen the distance between the theories of the Bismarckian period and those of the later date, and he does seem to have proved a central part of his thesis, that neither Bismarck nor Moltke counted on total military victory (*Niederwerfung*) against a coalition of the French and the Russians. Moltke foresaw defensive operations in the west and offensives in the east that would not involve the conquest of vast Russian spaces. Finally, Moltke did not see any incompatibility between modern industrial society and a lengthy war. But to judge from his writings, especially a famous article, 'Der Krieg in der Gegenwart', Schlieffen himself did not believe that long wars were possible:

> such wars are impossible at a time when the existence of the nation
> is founded on uninterrupted pursuit of commerce and industry; a
> strategy of attrition [*Ermattungsstrategie*] is ruled out because the
> supply of millions will take thousands of millions.

However, this article was written after Schlieffen's retirement, and we may hesitate before deciding whether it provided rational answers or merely a rationalization of strategy. Schlieffen described the European situation in the darkest terms, revealing a Germany encircled by jealous and hostile powers. In his view the arms race became a continuation of the Franco-German war, and at the same time he rightly saw that 'England cannot eliminate German trade without irreparably damaging her own'. The understandable objective of the English was to keep their hated competitor going, because the Germans were their best clients, and although the future did confirm this, Schlieffen still did not doubt that the English wanted war and felt hostility to Germany, even though it did not make economic sense.

In concrete terms, this article of 1909 contained the seeds of the Belgian invasion: an exclusively military process of thought saw such an invasion as the only solution to the problems Germany had to face. Future wars would be waged by armies consisting of millions of men, even though Germany had neither the superiority of armaments she had had in 1866 nor that of numbers she had had in 1870. Germany took 250,000 men annually from a population of 62 millions whereas France took 220,000 from one of 40 millions. The increase in effectives and the growth of fire-power led Schlieffen, rightly, to foresee an inevitable extension of the front line. Tactical changes, the impossibility of close order and attack by column, and the advance of individual infantrymen using all possible protection all pointed to the need for an area of battle four times the size of the Königgrätz field for armies of the future. If we go on from where Schlieffen stopped, and demonstrate that the French fortifications had made the eastern frontier impregnable, then the violation of Belgian neutrality results from a double military need: to extend the front and outflank the fortifications.

It was an argument that could not be refuted, though only on condition that the military objective was total overthrow of the Franco-Anglo-Russian combination, i.e. that the objective was political and only to be achieved by overthrow of the enemy states. As I remarked earlier, Delbrück compared the strategy of Pericles with that of Frederick the Great in order to show the rules Germany must observe when fighting a war against a coalition of landpowers with an island power: to prevent the enemy coalition from winning, but not to seek decisive victory herself. Writing after the vain attempts of the Kaiser and Hitler to achieve total military victory, Gerhard Ritter has tried to show that the origin of all this, the Schlieffen Plan, was not the product of an ambition to win mastery, or a *Griff nach der Weltmacht*, but of a bifurcation of military and political thinking, previously denounced by Clausewitz. What did Schlieffen's military philosophy owe to the 'malign' influence of Clausewitz? The basic tenets of his thought did in fact come largely from the Treatise.

However, examination of the two volumes of the *Gesammelte Schriften* discourages comparison with Clausewitz. Apart from the article quoted above and the various maxims, these volumes contain historical studies collected in the main after his retirement from active service. Schlieffen, though an extraordinary military technician, had none of the philosophical leanings or the disposition towards meditation or political insight of the author of the Treatise. Was Schlieffen to Clausewitz as Lenin was to Marx? In both war and revolution, technician will supersede philosopher, but this is probably a hazardous comparison. The elder Moltke had used

254

modern transport – the railways – and modern weaponry in the artillery to ensure annihilation of the enemy in the field. The French army was encircled at Sedan and shut in at Letz. The geometric form of manoeuvre, which Clausewitz himself thought dangerous, led to victory thanks to the improvidence of the French high command and the Germans' numerical superiority. Schlieffen, unlike Clausewitz, was obsessed all of his life with operational geometry, probably because he hoped to avoid direct confrontation which would involve heavy losses and produce no decisive results given that mass armies and fire-power were increasing. He ended by seeing encirclement of the enemy as the supreme goal, the enemy army being drawn forward in the centre and its flanks falling into traps created by the joining up of two wings so that the enemy troops would either be killed off or captured.

Schlieffen admitted that a complete Cannae would be rare because it presupposed on the one side a Terrentius Varro as much as a Hannibal on the other. But he studied the campaigns of the previous century in the light of this single principle. Under his pen, none of them became a replica of Cannae: the great Napoleon for him died in 1807 for, although he created the modern army and attempted to lead 200,000 men in the same way as, earlier, 76,000, and to dominate extended fronts from a single position, 'this was no longer possible, and he was forced into setting mass against mass, double against single, two against one'.

Schlieffen thus arrived at a view that overwhelming or enveloping the enemy attack from flank and rear is part of the technical apparatus of the commander. There is no longer any question of applying the maxim 'on s'engage et puis on voit'. Mobilization, deployment and advance of troops must be planned beforehand. 'The future military commander will be required to foresee how his reserves will be needed hours or days in advance', he wrote.

Schlieffen, in the Clausewitzian tradition, provided the model for the military commander and his role. He will sit far from the front, in an office, surrounded by maps, and communicating with army commanders in distant places, controlling masses of men and equipment. He is able to do this, having thought out in advance and organized, not only the place and time for preparatory mustering of troops, but also the successive phases in the execution of the plan. According to the elder Moltke's formula, strategy is no longer 'a system of expedients' but, in the age of science, the execution of an idea and the victory of organization.

In his work published in 1956, Ritter for the first time revealed the complete, accurate text of the memorandum Schlieffen gave to Moltke, his successor. There were various corrected versions, leading to the final version prepared by the old marshal, on the eve of his death, in 1911 which recommended enlarging the area of operations and violating Dutch as well as Belgian neutrality. Ritter concludes that the chances of this succeeding without the necessary means were slim, while the political inconvenience would be considerable. Despite the favourable circumstances – the success of the *coup de main* against Liège and the blunders of the French high command – defeat on the Marne tends to confirm the conclusion that convinces most critics.

Immediately after the war, many of them put responsibility for the defeat on the younger Moltke alone. He recognized that he had erred in withdrawing two corps before the battle of the Marne to reinforce the eastern front. When they arrived there, the situation had already improved with the victory of Tannenberg. On the other hand, Moltke, in agreement with Ludendorff, had reinforced the front in Lorraine rather than, according to Schlieffen's prescriptions, reducing the strength there, and so the huge manoeuvre on the right flank was limited in size, at least relatively if not absolutely. Considerations of supply probably ruled out its being increased.

Can any conclusion be drawn from this brief exegesis to throw any light on our own problem, i.e. the influence of Clausewitz on the conduct of the war in 1914? Strangely enough, the Treatise seems to have influenced the French side, though it was incorrectly understood. The logical outcome of Book VI was to pursue a defensive strategy. On the German side, Schlieffen attempted to solve a twofold problem, that of million-strong armies and the fortifications of the French frontier. If we accept the premises generally used at the time – the impregnability of the French defences in the Vosges and Lorraine, and the need to obtain total victory within a few weeks – the Schlieffen manoeuvre becomes intelligible and even the only possible one. Had an enormous and concentrated army on the right wing crossed Belgian territory, the French would have been trapped against their own eastern fortifications, and the entire French army would have been destroyed in a single battle of encirclement. The manoeuvre did not faithfully copy the model of Cannae, because the encirclement resulted from the movement of only one flank, but the outcome would have been the same. The reality showed that total success was unlikely, because the offensive gradually lost its strength even though the French high command blundered; the apogee came on the Marne, long before the turning wing of the German army could reach Paris from the west. None the less, it has to be said that the Germans, though defeated on the Marne, still controlled French territory, where operations carried on up to the end of the war. The Marne was a failure in terms of the objectives involved but it was not a disaster.

Was Schlieffen's solution to a problem that Clausewitz could not have known in conformity with the spirit of the Treatise? We cannot answer this categorically, though the question is implicit in many historical studies. Schlieffen's thinking processes were simplistic, superficial and dogmatic, although the plan to which he gave his name did possess a certain kind of genius. The man who presided over the destiny of the German army between 1892 and 1905 thought, however, as a man of action and not as a strategist in the Clausewitzian sense. In the Treatise the destruction of the enemy armies constitutes the natural aim of a war, as a test of strength; however, the destruction of the enemy in a single decisive battle constitutes only an extreme example. Offensive strategy which leads directly to a solution requires superiority of force because the defensive forces themselves enjoy advantages and the offensive carried on in enemy territory exhausts itself. The elder Moltke, who not only considered himself to be Clausewitz's disciple but was probably a better disciple than Schlieffen, did not aim to topple France and Russia after 1870.

Clausewitz neither condemns nor condones Schlieffen, any more than he does Moltke as regards the chosen form of manoeuvre. The Treatise calls envelopment of the enemy – i.e. an attempt to strike on more than one side simultaneously – 'the natural law of combat'. This tactical law is transposed to a strategic level: for a battle to produce decisive results, it must be fought on reversed fronts; the enemy's lines of retreat must be cut, or the enemy front ruptured or outflanked to bring about his disintegration. Contrary to Schlieffen, Clausewitz rejected dogmatism of all kinds. However, in conformity with the teachings of his times, he preferred, as did Jomini, operations conducted on interior lines, and he regarded a plan such as Frederick the Great's in 1757 (the concentration on the battlefield of converging but separate armies) as dangerous. But he did not think there was a rule applicable in all circumstances: thus the elder Moltke also could have taken risks, given his superiority of force and against such an incompetent enemy high command, which Napoleon I would have made him pay dearly for; and the same was true for Frederick the Great when he had a Daun against him.

Schlieffen, the leader and technician of huge armies, inherited from the French Revolution and German unification armies augmented by compulsory military service (after 1870 France copied Germany in this) and equipped by great industry. Clausewitz had foreseen that from then on wars would involve the entire nation, although he never considered the further question – would national wars approximate to the ideal of absolute warfare?

Both Foch and Schlieffen attempted to answer this question at the same time and in the same way. The leaders on both sides could only imagine one contest: to the death. It would be a contest that could only be ended by a radical military solution. The statesmen held, albeit implicitly, the same view of the nature of war. From Day One, they adopted a very un-Clausewitzian formula, namely that there is one goal, which is victory. This relapse into extremism would have confirmed Clausewitz's fears and his predictions rather than his actual teachings.

There were two exceptions: A historian like Delbrück who remembered the lesson of Pericles, and Clausewitz's own distinction between the two types of war (according to the note of 1827) was faithful to the lessons taught by Bismarck and the elder Moltke. Delbrück longed for a defensive strategy with limited war aims, in other words the Reich's own policy before Schlieffen came to hold supreme power. And a soldier, Émile Mayer, a fellow student of Foch's at the École Polytechnique, declared that a war to the bitter end would damage irreparably the era of democracy and industry.

4 Delbrück, Falkenhayn and Ludendorff

As we know, Clausewitz refused to make any conceptual distinction between policy, conduct of war and strategy. This refusal came from a simple distinction: either the armed forces remain in the domain of tactics and battles, or the outcome of these is examined in such a way that the domain of strategy comes to have supreme importance. As strategy develops, so will a theory held by the chief of staff or the cabinet as to the nature of the war. From this will flow the plan of war, and the plan for campaigns will then be resolved in accordance with the course taken by the hostilities.

The European chiefs of state did not formulate any explicit proposition about the nature of war. The more perceptive of them anguished over entering an unknown world and the risk of a tragic dénouement. They handed over responsibility to their chiefs of staff. Did these men have any opportunity for thinking differently from the way they did? If we stay with Germany, from 1914 to 1945 she adopted the position held by France in Clausewitz's day. Whatever her leaders' intentions, she was a disruptive entity because victory would turn her into an imperial power. Nothing forced the main belligerents to set their sights on total victory and a dictated peace. For a start, the allies foresaw neither the dissolution of the Habsburg monarchy nor even the reconstitution of Poland within the frontiers of 1919. Neither France nor Great Britain needed any more colonies. Why, then, does Delbrück's thesis (first discreetly advanced and then, after 1918, repeated with greater vigour) not hold water?

Could the leaders of Wilhelmine Germany have adopted a strategy different from the one they did adopt? Could they have turned to the east, striking at Russia, and taken a defensive stance in the west? There was no need for them to become involved in a campaign comparable with those of Napoleon or Hitler, and be stuck in the depths of Russia. The Russian armies fought on the borders, in accordance with agreements reached between Russia and France; and the successes won by the Germans in the east, together with the lengthening of the conflict, led to the collapse of the tsarist regime. Had the German armies been larger, the successes would have been greater, without there being any serious threat in the west, even if pure defensive there had been adopted. It can hardly be wrong to pursue this reconstruction of events for, though they did not happen, they easily could have done. That the general staff in advance chose the western offensive, and that commentators approved of this, does not prevent us from seeing what would have happened if the decision had gone otherwise. This method does not differ substantially from Clausewitz's when he compared circumvallation and the siege of Mantua.

Those who, either before or after the event, spoke for a western defensive and an eastern offensive had a different view of war. In the light of Delbrück, they read the narrative, not of Cannae, but of the Peloponnesian War. They recommended Pericles' strategy – or perhaps the strategy attributed to Pericles by Thucydides – of shifting the blame to the demagogues of the popular party who were unable to limit the ambitions and enterprises of the democratic city-state.

The concept that Delbrück claimed to see in the note of 1827 suffered, as we have seen, under the equivocations that can also be found in other places in Clausewitz. The two types of war show essentially different ways of arriving at peace – dictated peace, after decisive victory, and negotiated peace, without any knockout blow. This transhistorical distinction reflects differing ways of fighting, whether manoeuvre in the style of professional armies, comparable to that of fleets, or search for decisive battle. The strategy of Frederick, according to both the anti-Delbrück commentators and Delbrück himself, differed from Napoleon's for material reasons – such as the professionalism of the army, the cost of soldiers, their weakness in numbers, and the nature of supply lines – as much as for political reasons, i.e. the 'cabinet' war, fought with no regard to popular opinion.

It would have been miraculous had the German general staff of 1914 – even if it had taken a professor's words seriously – recognized any of the circumstances underlying the strategy of Frederick the Great. Delbrück himself would have had to illustrate the contrast between dictated and negotiated peace treaties as being valid for all eras, whatever the military instruments. And yet, the example of the Peloponnesian War was a very good one.

Even if we imagine that the German generals had realized that the Central Powers were strong enough to avoid defeat but not to dictate peace *auf Gnade und Ungnade*, the historical circumstances would still have had to be such that a different strategy could have been adopted. Thucydides exalts Pericles' lucidity, but he still always contrasts the reasonableness of the advice with the dynamics of the passions involved. He shows why and how city-states involved in total war will not stop until one of them, exhausted and overwhelmed, begs for mercy, even if there are wise men who impotently remind the two sides that they are part of a common civilization.

The events of the fifth century BC recall, not the sovereignty of reason and compromise, but the blind determinism of catastrophe. The same political circumstances, dictating the nature of the war, governing the violence of the struggle and the volume of mobilized resources (in Clausewitz's terms), also led in 1914 to a war of the first type – a war to the death, forming a whole to be decided only in the last battle. Serbia was not worth an overall war, but once the war had started the prize at stake became immense and even measureless. If we cannot explain the extremism of the combat by the stake, there is still a further, also Clausewitzian, explanation, that popular passions can be unleashed, which political intelligence will find very difficult to control. In 1914, in a bourgeois Europe that was regarded as pacific and anxious only for prosperity, patriotic enthusiasm aroused the peoples, drove them towards the borders and to death in the field with unanimous *élan*, which was only gradually diminished by the absurd cruelties of trench warfare and *Materialschlachten*.

These Clausewitzian explanations of what did happen do not prevent us from guessing at what might have happened. The political reality created the situation, but intelligence in the government was still marginally free. The technical side of the war – fixed fronts, trenches, avalanches of fire, thousands of deaths for a few kilometres of ground – led to the notion of attrition or *Ermattungsstrategie*, but in a meaning far from Delbrück's. It was not a strategy to tire the enemy to the point of negotiating a peace, it was a strategy to dictate a peace of victory, through total exhaustion of the enemy resources. Of the three men who succeeded each other at the head of the great general staff, only one vaguely conceived a strategy that sought only to prevent the enemy from defeating Germany. Delbrück was not wrong in favouring Falkenhayn and being severe towards Ludendorff, though Liddell Hart, judging as a soldier, pronounced different verdicts.

Perhaps Falkenhayn was right in limiting his aim to the annihilation of the enemy's positive will. The means he chose – the offensive at Verdun –

became the symbol of an idea (or non-idea) of strategy, and one for ever condemned because of the way it was carried out and because it failed. We know that the high command, in the famous memorandum of December 1915, started off with a position contrary to that on which the initial plan of 1914 had been based. It renounced not only manoeuvre, but even breakthrough, which was thought to be impossible in the west. But what could be done against a well-armed, resolute enemy who was as numerically strong, if not stronger, than the attacker? The answer was to inflict losses such that he would lose hope of winning and come round to negotiation. In this sense, the intention resembles that of many other strategists. Clausewitz himself, though regarding the destruction of the enemy forces as the natural goal of battle, did not ignore other possibilities, for instance a straightforward weakening of the enemy. What strikes military writers, even today, as appalling and even an abuse of science, is that a commander should have launched an attack on this scale purely with a view to 'bleeding the French army to death' (*Ausblutung*), and that he admitted that the art of war was over, having been replaced by mere mass slaughter. Both the breakthrough and envelopment, the two classical methods of good tactics, now existed as a goal; the aim was simply to force as many French divisions as possible under the axe, and the land lost or gained hardly mattered, for the only definition of victory or defeat was the ratio of losses. Falkenhayn foresaw what the French would do. He himself did not care about Verdun, but he was sure that the fortress would have symbolic value for the French, who would throw all of their forces into a battle to save it. 'An engagement limited in manpower but considerable in *matériel*, and attack against a sector which France must defend with her last man – that will amount to a battle of *Ausblutung*.'

The plan – if that is the right word – failed simply because German losses were hardly lower than French ones. The defeat had many causes, not least that the high command left its subordinates in ignorance as to the true objectives. It wished or allowed people to believe that Verdun was the real aim, so the *Ausblutung* affected the Germans as much as the French. Such an operation would, however, hardly have had any sense in the context of a war aimed at negotiated peace. Falkenhayn also suffered from the solitude of the military leader, in the absence of any political direction in the war. But as regards 'moral' condemnation of the mutual massacre, can it really apply only to the general who appreciated that it was impossible to break through in the conditions of the western front in 1916 or 1917? French generals who talked of 'nibbling' at the enemy line, and who redoubled their attacks so as to gain a few hundred yards at the cost of losses twice those of the enemy, can hardly be excused for their blindness. Why should Falkenhayn's decision be thought 'satanic' because he planned to throw away thousands of soldiers to kill twice as many, whereas attacks launched by both sides during the war in the west had no other sense than that? There has been nothing so absurd in the history of military Europe than this clash of mass armies in a hail of steel. Since techniques and methods of breakthrough were lacking on both sides, Falkenhayn was merely making his logic plain whereas the others did as he did, but unconsciously.

He also failed in the enterprise because the German army emerged from 'the mincer' as worn out, and maybe even more so than the French. The strategy of Delbrück became confused with Verdun and mutual slaughter, and fell into total discredit. This was wrong. Delbrück had wanted to teach moderation in aims, both political and military, to his compatriots, so as to make negotiated peace possible. But was there ever a chance for such a peace in 1916 or 1917? Historians have not made out a convincing case for changing what contemporaries thought. There was, in 1916 and 1917, a vague peace party in the political classes in England and France, but could the French one ever have accepted a peace 'without annexation or contribution'? Or could any German government have ceded even the French-speaking part of Lorraine without being compelled by defeat to do so? It was in England, and there alone, that a peace party might have responded to a different German policy. However, in 1917 the new team of Hindenburg and Ludendorff would not consent to simple restitution of an independent Belgium.

Delbrück's criticisms, here, remain pertinent. Ludendorff did appreciate that American troops would gradually give the Allies an irresistible superiority. He undertook a race against the clock: to win decisively before the ratios were reversed. He lost the gamble, and at the same time deprived Germany of the means to negotiate peace terms: in signing the armistice, she laid down her arms. This – to use Ferrero's term – 'immeasurable and hyperbolic war' ended paradoxically, and in an unprecedented way, because the German army, which was the best in the world, ended the fight without having been defeated in the open field. The victor dictated peace to a state that had been effectively overthrown, even though its army returned in good order. From this paradox there emerged the 'stab-in-the-back' legend. The armistice sought by the Germans did save the army from defeat – a perhaps Clausewitzian decision by a Ludendorff who was the first great doctrinaire of the general staff to reject Clausewitz's teachings.

All of this brought to light two separate themes that in the past had been confused. Exhaustion might force one of the parties to accept a dictated peace, comparable to the peace that would have ended 'absolute' war. For, if we include under 'manoeuvre', as Delbrück sometimes did, blockade, or action against inert resources that nourish the living ones, then the strategy of attrition did in fact end the struggle, more slowly, but not less radically than 'the knockout blow' of annihilation. Strategy in the wider sense, as Clausewitz understood it – the employment of violence against the armed forces, resources or morale of the enemy – attained goals that allowed a peace to be dictated: total victory came as much from exhaustion as from annihilation. In 1763 Maria Theresa lost her will to win because she feared Frederick and reckoned that the cost of winning would be disproportionate. The Reich in 1918 was exhausted in a different sense, or at least in a different way, than the Austria of 1763.

In his polemic against all whom he blamed for the disaster, a German officer, Rudolf Leinveber, quoted a disciple of Delbrück's:

> With world war, we have returned to the age of the strategy of
> attrition: not, of course, for the same reasons as in the eighteenth
> century, i.e. because of lack of manpower or weakness of armies,
> but for opposite reasons, such as the creation of armies of millions,

with limitless supply requirements and needs for *matériel*, and with the great advantage that defenders will have intact railways at their rear.

Leinveber was of Schlieffen's school, and he looked to the Treatise for arguments against this theory. None of the conditions for eighteenth-century strategy really existed in the twentieth, he said, and was the situation not more like that of Napoleonic times, when there had also been an avalanche of hostility, popular passion, mobilization of all resources and extreme energy in the conduct of the wars? This was irrefutable, provided that a real link can be established between 'cabinet' war and strategy of attrition. To make Delbrück's thesis plausible, Thucydides rather than Frederick the Great should be the model, and the alternatives have to be posed as decisive victory or preventing the enemy from gaining decisive victory – in short, either win or do not lose.

These alternatives, in the event of a rough equality of force, or a superiority of the one side on land and of the other at sea, compel commanders to choose between war to the death, pushed to the exhaustion of all belligerents, or compromise. Delbrück's idea, that in the long run Germany would not win against the great coalition against her, turned out to be right. Today we can still argue on behalf of the profound thinking of Falkenhayn, for he appreciated that he must discourage the entente, not attempt decisive victory.

There exists, of course, the objection Leinveber made to Clausewitz, that 'if it is true that peace has often been brought about through exhaustion, the cause lies in the imprecise nature of war; we cannot therefore use philosophy to arrive at any general objective or to plot the outcome of any particular defence'. The latter part of that quotation reduces the scope of the objection: to reduce the enemy to a state of exhaustion is neither the philosophical goal nor the ideal objective of defence. It may be the objective in the real world. Clausewitz says it more clearly still in Book I, Chapter 11: a negotiated peace is often brought about because the side that could effectively win reckons that 'the game is not worth the candle', that the effort will cost more than the profit which can be achieved through negotiation. Did the war of 1914 have such an imprecise character? Would it have been possible to count on the lassitude of the stronger?

The generals on both sides wanted to win, forgetting that victory is a tactical, not a strategic, notion. In other words, they intended to present the statesmen with the means to dictate peace even if they wanted a moderate one. As for the statesmen, it may be believed that they were being forced to choose between revolution and total victory.

What remains of the responsibility of our 'Mahdi'? Nothing, or very little. The Young Turks in France, who preached the gospel of out-and-out offensive without distinguishing between tactics and strategy, referred to Clausewitz by quoting passages of the Treatise wrenched from their context; Gilbert rejected Book VI *in toto*, with its thesis of the intrinsic superiority of the defence. None of the French officers had wide enough understanding of ideas to put them on the alert. They flattered national self-esteem by becoming disciples of a Clausewitz whom they often – though not always – regarded as the leading exponent of Napoleonic method. The French were simply recovering property stolen by the enemy.

On the German side, the Preface written by Schlieffen indicates that he had hardly read the Treatise and retained only one lesson from it, or rather a quotation: how could the victories of annihilation of Leuthen, Jena and Sedan be repeated with thousands of men under arms?

Are we to blame Clausewitz for the swelling of armies and the increasing number of men under arms? That would be absurd. An insular power could, if necessary, make do with a small professional army. After the French disaster of 1870, a continental power had to oppose numbers with numbers for its own safety. There was no need to return to the *Professions of Faith* or the Treatise to see that twentieth-century societies were set for national, not 'cabinet' wars.

Is it true that the desire for a radical solution, a peace dictated when the enemy's means of resistance were destroyed, did originate in the Clausewitzian vision of a society of states? Book VI, Chapter 6, shows that statesmen and generals were wrong to suggest this. Moltke the elder, who certainly knew the Treatise much better than Schlieffen did, saw no contradiction between the master's words and a defensive strategy conducted with a view to negotiated peace.

In fact, when a historian returns to the fatal year, what strikes him most forcefully about every country is the unanimous feeling of passion, the patriotic fervour of peoples. In this search for glory, both ministers and generals shared the emotions, suddenly unleashed by war, which were born in the depths of old Europe. The French and German high commands – Germans with better reason than French – looked for the outcome in a great battle comparable to those of Napoleon which Moltke had waged and won. More or less rapidly, both sides found what at least two men, a French officer named Émile Mayer, and a banker from Warsaw, Jan Bloch, had said before.

Mayer constantly denounced the ideas of the future marshal: 'ideas that are even more dangerous than they are false'. As early as 1889 he wrote in the *Revue Scientifique*, 'We may say that any movement is dangerous, given the new strength. Immobility is power. Is this not tantamount to asserting that a defensive strategy should have the advantage?' Ten years later, he said, 'Each seeks to see and not be seen . . . that is the strength of the defensive.' Émile Mayer found his ideas borne out by the Boer War. By 1890 he no longer believed in the virtue of the offensive and could easily imagine 'two enemies facing each other like statues, remaining in that position until death, or more precisely ruin, comes'.

At the same time, Jan Bloch foresaw the radical novelty of the future war in its length and siege-like character. Compulsory military service, which was responsible for the huge size and complexity of armies, with the improvement of weaponry and fire-power, would lead almost to the impossible: 'The true chimera, the true utopia is now war.' He did not say that the impossible war would not take place, but that it would end in common ruin and revolution. The strength of fire-power that ruled out battles as they had been fought in the past would lead to mutual destruction by troops. Men would look for solution in a prolonged conflict that would end when one or even both sides were exhausted.

In an article in the *Revue militaire suisse* of 1902, Émile Mayer plotted the course of battle with even greater precision: the defensive battle would be a kind of siege with two walls of men poised face to face for months, or even years. Unable to break through the enemy line, each side would try to extend its own in an effort to outflank the enemy, but this would end somewhere – at the sea, a mountain or a neutral frontier. The outcome would be governed by events elsewhere – in finance, political conditions or the inability of public opinion to tolerate sacrifice.

Clausewitz taught that tactical results settled everything. This is not refuted by the lessons of the war of 1914. The French high command blundered from the start in wrongly interpreting the defeats of 1870. On the one hand, they misunderstood fire-power, and on the other they adopted a strategic offensive that common sense and the Treatise warned against. Is an author to blame for the folly of those who cannot reason, count or argue?

Chapter 11

The Meeting of Two Revolutions

Before the First World War, readers of the Treatise such as Foch and Goltz did not clearly distinguish between the two notions of absolute war and total war. They clung to a few aspects of war that corresponded with Clausewitz's absolute type, such as involvement of the populace, victory by annihilation of the enemy forces, and overthrow of the enemy state. They prophesied that the future wars between European peoples bent on accomplishing their 'civilizing mission' would be 'true war' or 'absolute war'.

Various passages in the Treatise suggest ways in which the expression 'absolute war' can become meaningful: 'a point of general reference', 'the original measure of all our hopes and fears', 'a fundamental notion that must always provide the foundation'. None of these phrases translates easily into the philosophical language of the times. None suggests Fichte, Kant or Hegel. Clausewitz was searching for an exact formulation for his thought. The final synthesis dissipated uncertainty: absolute war marked the limit of his journey to extremes, the kind of limit with which the hostile or violent will must come to grips. Similarly, the function of the concept is revealed. The theoretical function is to allow people to understand how far the logic of war in the narrow sense would develop when separated from the aim and origin of the war itself. It has a praxological function, too: reminding each of the adversaries the risk he runs if the other follows the law of extremes. Perhaps it might also remind both sides of the risk of mutual suicide.

No real war can be termed an absolute war, but Clausewitz none the less mentioned some of the circumstances that tend to provoke the emergence of a pure and ideal war, most notably the participation of the people. In Chapter 3 of Book VIII such participation is the decisive innovation that suppressed traditional limitations of efforts and means. Although at first sight there is no necessary or rational connection between the participation of the people and the overthrow of the enemy state, Clausewitz always indicated, even in Chapter 1 of Book I, that such participation was as natural as the final 'collapse'.

Even if Ludendorff did not create the idea, he at least popularized the concept of total war. In his first book, *Kriegführung und Politik*, he still followed Clausewitz although he was to part with him at a decisive point. Many years later, in another book, *Der totale Krieg*, he broke the taboo and openly declared that the author of the Treatise, *Vom Kriege*, belonged to a past age.

We can sum up Ludendorff's ideas in the following way. As an interpreter and observer of the Revolution and the Empire, Clausewitz correctly grasped the predominant changes that the art of war underwent in his time. The participation of the people disrupted the customs adhered to by professional armies as well as the diplomats' chess games and the generals' fencing bouts. Armies, however, still remain both the subject and the object of hostilities. The Franco-Prussian War had demonstrated another method of fighting during its second phase. Gambetta's national defence ought to have awoken memories of the Spanish guerillas and of Prussian patriots, but it only worried and irritated Moltke. In 1914 the decisive stage that led from Napoleon to total war was crossed.

Materially and morally the entire nation becomes the subject and object of the struggle. Aircraft take munitions factories as their targets, to paralyse the supply of *matériel*. Propaganda has an insidious goal, 'the spiritual cohesion' of the people, which is the basis of total war. Such faith, in the form of a nation involved in a spirit of sacrifice, gives the troops the morale of victors. The enemy will therefore try to break the national unity which is the prize in a game that is pitiless and secret. Ludendorff, conscious of the errors made by the leaders of the Second Reich in 1914, remarked quite rightly, 'People do not respond to the call of aggressive war, but they will allow a struggle for life, even if they easily see a will to aggression in any declaration of war.'

Ludendorff dismissed with indifference or contempt speculation about the respective weights of attack and defence. He continued to believe in the power of numbers, hoping to achieve a radical victory by attacking the enemy's weak points and repeating such an attack if the first effort failed to produce a decisive outcome. In the light of the experiences of the war of 1914–18 he wanted to see a high command entrusted with co-ordinating the various activities of the services (what function did the German High Seas Fleet have?), but also with using at the same time military, diplomatic, economic and psychological methods, both inside and outside the country, to achieve the final goal. He was probably wrong in thinking that a single man could carry the load of *global* (overall) policy: that was his way of reacting to the leaderless situation of Wilhelmine Germany, and the idea of *Globalpolitik* can be deduced from the nature of modern war, which includes popular participation.

By contrast, Ludendorff was wrong in reproaching Clausewitz for shrinking the ambit of politics by confining it to foreign policy and thereby subordinating the military to the diplomatic machine. Clausewitz exposes himself to this attack because he did not elaborate on the various meanings of 'political', and only once indicated the true extent of politics: 'to reconcile and unite all the interests of the internal administration with those of humanity, and all the arguments that intelligence can advance'.

Where does the breach with Clausewitz occur? It is important to remember that 'absolute war' is only a concept, not the same as real war, the design or ideal type of war in the narrow sense. The concept of total war describes the phenomena characteristic of the First World War. However, *Globalpolitik* is compatible with the thought of Clausewitz or its implications, though this changes when we read, in the sentence ending Chapter 1 of *Kriegführung und Politik*, that '*Globalpolitik* must exist in the service of war'.

This inversion of the Formula contradicts the general spirit of the

Treatise. There is nothing to permit the staff officer, Ludendorff, to adopt a metaphysic that turns war into the supreme test for society, a verdict passed by history. Conscious of the dangers that lurk on all sides for land-locked Germany, Ludendorff noted that Europe oscillated between two themes: moderate wars are 'anomalous' in terms of the concept; but they are also the most frequent. Which is right – the few wars fitting the concept, or the many not fitting it?

The error in Clausewitz's thought lies in the areas just quoted: here are the germs of the philosophies of Ludendorff and Hitler, and of Lenin and the Bolsheviks. 'Politics is nothing less than the directing of all interests against other states', he wrote, and added: 'That politics can take the wrong road, serving ambition, private interest and the vanity of rulers is not of concern here for the art of war can never be looked upon as the tutor of politics, since we regard the political as standing for society as a whole.'

In other words, the 'political' to which Clausewitz gives the supreme authority is the political as it should be, not what it necessarily is. It embraces all the interests of society as a whole, and governments (Frederick the Great is here the model) act as servants of the state itself. In any event, if rulers serve ambition and vanity rather than the state, the art of war will not put them back on the right path. By definition, an instrument cannot serve as mentor to those who employ it. The state cannot be put at the service of war. Ludendorff would have replied that in our day the state cannot help being put at the service of war, and Lenin would say that the political cannot stand for society as a whole.

1 Lenin as interpreter of Clausewitz

In 1915 Lenin read the Treatise with close attention, and copied extracts in a notebook after his own and Marx's habit. These extracts, with short notes, have been published.

Lenin used the first, three-volume, edition. In the first volume the extracts were taken from the first two chapters of Book I, Chapters 2, 3 and 6 of Book II, and Chapters 5 and 6 of Book III; in the second volume, from Chapters 2 and 4 of Book V and Chapters 2, 3, 5, 6 and 9 of Book VI; and in the third volume, apart from some extracts from Book VII and the *Principles of Instruction*, the essentials are from Book VIII (Chapters 2, 3, 6 and 9). For anyone familiar with the work, this choice of extracts is self-explanatory – Lenin was concerned with the relationship of war and policy (Books I and VIII), moral greatness and the dialectic of attack and defence, i.e. the ideas useful to his political strategy, or able to justify its military extension.

From the first chapter, Lenin copied out in full paragraph 24 and fragments of the two following paragraphs. Paragraph 24 is entitled 'War is the Simple Continuation of Policy by Other Means'. The following paragraphs take up the conclusions drawn from this thesis and sketch out what might be called the dialectic of ascension and descension in politics, the determining cause of the intensity of the struggle. Lenin stressed two words that were not emphasized by Clausewitz: violence and ideal. The more motives and tension weaken, the less the proper warlike element, violence (the essence of the specific means), harmonizes with the path fixed by policy. The more, then, that war is diverted from the objective of ideal war, the more it will become a political war.

This analysis (at this point Chapter 3 of the first book becomes relevant) marks the last stage of Clausewitz's thought. In the earlier texts, especially in his narratives of campaigns, he alludes to the fact that politics become more important in certain wars, as if these two terms were essentially different, as if war ceases to be politics to the degree that approaches the absolute form, i.e. its objective of annihilation. Paragraphs 24–7 not only have the consequence of putting all wars, moderate or unlimited, on the same level, they also illustrate what Lenin calls the dialectic in Clausewitzian thought. In fact, wars that approximate most to the ideal seem to be the least political; but they are in reality as political as the others, for it is politics that gives them a character approximating to the ideal. He therefore sees in them an example of the opposition between appearance and reality (the warlike appearance and the political reality); in the same way, the many expressions used by Clausewitz to designate the natural or logical tendency of war (ascension to the extreme, pure violence) are interpreted by Lenin as a distinction between subjective and objective.

Therefore, he found in the first chapter the main ideas that he was to use in the following years against the social democrats of the Second International: war is not something independent, it is only an instrument for the state or for the revolutionary and takes its particular features from its political source. Politics in Lenin's mind constitutes the essence, the deep meaning of war. Thus, when he copied the trinitarian definition (Section 28) in his notebook, an annotation in the margin shows how the interpretation is steered to the left. In effect he writes absolutely right as regards political heart, the essence and content of the war, the popular element and the foreign side. Clausewitz had nothing like this in mind, but Lenin managed in this way to simplify and trivialize the people's emotions, or the masses' adherence to war. Although he was far from denying that war could sometimes exacerbate people's hatreds, he corrected Clausewitz, who wrote in Chapter 2 of Book II that national hatred is rarely absent in our wars, with the marginal query: 'rarely?' And he added that there is national hatred in all wars.

In a way, the extracts from Chapter 3 of Book II (the comparison between trade and politics), and Book VIII take up, broaden, comment upon and correct the themes presented in Chapter 1 of Book I which contains the essence of the whole work.

I shall, however, mention a few passages that struck Lenin, the meaning of which, though implicit in Chapter 1 of Book I throws a light on the main themes. Thus Lenin repeats two objectives of war: to conquer territory and destroy the armed forces. And he adds: with a view to what? To which he answers: with a view to breaking the enemy's will so that he will proclaim his readiness to make peace. War as a trial of will: this formula attracted the revolutionary leader as much as the head of state or the army. The last lines of the paragraph noted down by Lenin in his notebook none the less reveal the historical distance between the Prussian patriot writing, gratefully, during the restoration, and the professional revolutionary kicking his heels in Berne while the First World War was raging. Clausewitz saw that a signed peace treaty does not necessarily mean the radical solution of problems, a finalization of the conflict. But he added, 'nevertheless, a number of the flames are doused, when peace comes, that otherwise would continue to burn; tensions do lessen'. At this stage there appears the phrase most characteristic of Clausewitz's way of thinking (he being, of course, still a member of the European tradition). 'Whatever is the case, it must always be borne in mind that with peace the end is reached and the business of war is over.' There can be no clearer way of refuting modern reversals of the meaning of the Formula.

In Book VIII, Chapter 3, Lenin found for the first time an illustration of Marxism, namely the historicity of all economic and social phenomena. Chapter 3(B) reviews the various aspects of war, the motivations, bloodshed and final outcome. Lenin either copied out or emphasized the many passages where Clausewitz attributed changes in the art of warfare, as well as the victories of the armies of the Republic and Empire, to the French Revolution. It was popular participation that had broken down the obstacles preventing the warlike ingredient, namely violence, from being unleashed. This historical fact was compelling to the Bolshevik mentality. Finally, there is the idea, implicit in paragraph 24 (Chapter 1 of Book I) and developed in Chapter 6(B) of Book VIII, that the reality or meaning of war is defined by the political situation. War is a totality which is defined by a dominant characteristic rather than by a motley collection of separate features. In the same way, a picture takes its overall coloration from one particular colour.

Clearly, Lenin did not bother to pick out what I have called objectivized politics (in other words, the body of socio-political conditions) which contains implicitly the particular features of the war and the policy adopted, the state's astuteness in directing the interests of that society *vis-à-vis* other states. Naturally, he does not object to any vacillation in respect of the use of the words 'policy' and 'politics'. On the contrary, anxious to unify theory and practice, he is careful to leave in a reciprocal relationship those things which the dialectic must not confuse. As long as the sociology of war highlights the part played by the socio-political conditions in the development of battles, victories and defeats, Lenin is there to take note, copy and approve. He approved no less when he adopted the extreme formula in which war and politics are the same. War has the grammar though not the logic of politics, it replaces the pen with the sabre, dispatches armies and shells rather than diplomatic notes, although notes are sent just the same. On one decisive point he is in agreement with Clausewitz and he writes without hesitation: 'Here is something akin to Marxism.' He noted that definition of policy which stood for the interests of society as a whole as against other states. The passage from Chapter 6(B) of Book VIII, noted above, implicitly dissociated active policy as it should be from active policy as it risks being when in the service of ambition, private interests and the vanity of rulers.

When writing about the Treatise Lenin never pointed out the utopian nature of a policy which represents all the interests of society. On the contrary, he felt that, by evoking the private concerns of a government, the Treatise suggested the possibility of an outcome that Marxism viewed as inevitable while societies contained hostile classes, namely that an overall policy for society cannot be carried through. Between 1915 and 1917

Lenin pitilessly condemned the 'social traitors' of the Second International by applying this thesis and Clausewitzian sociology. National hatreds did not matter to him; they were only the outward trappings of a reality of which politics alone revealed the meaning and essence.

The other two Clausewitzian themes that captured Lenin's attention, though less interesting, call for a short discussion. The relationship between defence and attack in the Treatise contains variations that could be called dialectical in the wide sense of the term. Clausewitz's remark that the defender begins a war because those opposing him would like to win without even fighting amused Lenin, although he attached no philosophical connotations to the observation. He was drawn basically to Chapter 6 (the means of defence) and Chapter 8 (varieties of resistance). He stressed the contribution people made to the war even in the absence of insurrection, and he found, particularly in Chapter 8, the influence of politics, the strength of the offensive and the resources possessed by the defence relative to the strength of the offensive. Briefly, he was interested in this passage for two reasons. First, political conditions help to explain the course taken by the hostilities. In other words, the strength or weakness of the political tensions determines the potential of the military. Wars become half-measures, yet their essence and their nature – in the form of violence – are not modified (this is an example of the dialectic).

Second, relative strength continues, generally speaking, to be the dominant cause of the means of resistance adopted even if it is sound judgment, that offers a solution rather than exact calculation of the forces involved. Lenin, the political leader, readily admitted that in wartime decisions are reached by simple intuition, and he also admitted that this was so not only in wartime. Thus, he again observed in Chapter 30 Clausewitz's appeal for judgment to be exercised in indecisive campaigns involving neither principles, rules nor strategy.

Clausewitz's antidogmatism (despite the clear-cut formulae from which a doctrine has been deduced) goes hand in hand with his awareness of the uniqueness of circumstances and a sense of the opportunities to be seized. The Clausewitzian combination of principles and awareness of the uniqueness of situations seems to me to be more philosophically satisfactory than the Leninist version where a determinist philosophy of history and action is jointed in a Machiavellian way. But both men, like all those who have thought about politics, knew that any solution is adventurous and that to win you must gamble.

Lenin certainly found in the defence–attack dialectic a scheme capable of adaptation to the requirements of revolutionary practice. He recognized that the class struggle did not always exhibit the violent character implicit in war. But he arrived at an inverted version of the Formula implicit in his rejection of national unity. Clausewitz said that all violence is physical. Moral violence does not exist beyond the realms of the state and law. In Lenin's version of Marxism, the state and the law are themselves the results of physical violence which has been more or less camouflaged. In a class society any peace disguises struggle.

In the same way, the dialectic of defence and attack reaches a decisive point in Leninist strategy. The distinction between defence and attack

270

disappears once the battle starts. The need to retreat to restore the balance of strength, the bold nature of the decision to strike: these Clausewitzian themes became Lenin's practice. Of course, they are themes dictated by common sense. But Clausewitz, like Lenin, would recommend common sense as the guiding strategic principle while adding that judgment should accompany the application of all these principles. Art rather than science rules – although historical study and reflection remain indispensable for the development of sound judgment.

Curiously, Lenin seems to have taken an apparent interest in Chapter 30 of Book VI where there is an analysis of the general staff: 'that part of any army that writes and prints the most'. In reality, narrative accounts of campaigns by members of the general staff contribute to a false impression of events. They also contribute to geological and geographical theories being accorded an exaggerated importance. Lenin emphasized those numerous passages in the Treatise where the makers of systems, the doctrine of key-points, accentuation of inessential material factors, the men and the army are dealt with. On the other hand, it is not at all surprising that Lenin latched on to a passage about Frederick the Great where Clausewitz stressed the need for a dominating and imperious will to control the armed forces, all the pieces on the board, from above. He who regularly searches for the best man would be unsuitable to command an army. Lenin summed it up thus: 'command of an army equals distrust as regards men'.

These extracts complete those taken from Chapters 5 and 6 of Book III. Lenin again took up the Clausewitzian commentaries on the subject of the professional army and *esprit de corps*. He also copied Clausewitz's praise of audacity and his account of the growing problems met by the audacious as they mount the hierarchical ladder. The part played by intelligence must increase with responsibility when it tends to supplant character or finer feelings. The leader's audacity becomes all the more admirable for its increasing rareness.

It seems that Lenin was not very impressed by Clausewitz's portraits of Frederick the Great and Napoleon as war leaders. Readers of both Lenin and Clausewitz often feel tempted to construct a portrait of the revolutionary leader who would possess, in effect, the qualities Clausewitz attributed to the wartime commander, such qualities being a sense of equilibrium in difficult situations, the courage to take responsibility, the astuteness to grab chances and unique opportunities as they arise, knowledge of different nations and their major preoccupations, ascendancy over a crowd, faith in oneself and one's destiny, and simultaneous mastery over the armed forces and the political field. But in my own view there is a difference between a Frederick the Great, a Lenin and a Mao Tse-tung which touches upon an essential issue. Lenin placed his realism and tactical clarity at the service of a utopian future. What makes the revolutionary leader unique is his combination of apparently contradictory qualities. He saw the present as it was, stripped of illusion, and he imagined a future uncluttered by the experience of centuries. The use that Lenin made of Clausewitz between 1914 and 1918 illustrates the dual nature of the revolutionary chief who was flexible in action and ruthless in his certainty.

271

2 Lenin and the typology of war

Lenin's short but faithful summary of the Treatise, made in 1915, might not permit us to pose the often futile question: What is the influence of one thinker on another? But in this case, there seems to me to be a possible answer.

In 1914 Lenin did not hesitate; from the first day he opposed the war and the national support given to it. Between the autumn of 1914 and the spring of 1915 he studied the Treatise at Berne although he probably knew it to some extent before that. The notebook on the Treatise belongs to the corpus of philosophical notebooks which also includes one on Hegel. The references to Clausewitz date from the spring of 1915, and after that time they increase until Lenin's takeover of power, even continuing during the civil war. The conclusion to be drawn is obvious: for Lenin and the Marxist–Leninists from that day to this Clausewitz's thought has provided a theoretical framework for legitimizing ideology. If the reader recalls the importance attached by Marxists to Clausewitz he will be able to understand the shifts by which Napoleon's adversary became the apologist for the greatest revolutionary of our time.

Let us take as our starting point the notion that policy constitutes the whole of which war is a part. During the latter the former is continued perhaps, but Lenin preferred to think (still conforming to Clausewitzian orthodoxy) that policy continues in wartime without its essential nature being modified. What emerges from this interpretation is that policies upheld by nations and by parties or groups within parties, before the outbreak of war are expressed by language and conduct during the war. The nature and essence of a war can only be determined by study of the political whole. With impeccable logic Lenin therefore concludes that the war of 1914 was an imperialist war for both sides. The motion passed at the Congress of the Socialist International at Basle had condemned the Great European Powers' diplomacy as imperialist. This imperialism continued after 4 August 1914. Therefore, any socialist who subscribed to the *union sacrée* (i.e. the notion of national unity in defence) was betraying the doctrine to which he had adhered in 1912 and was an accomplice of imperialism.

These 'social traitors' might say that the masses were responding to the call of the fatherland. True, replied Lenin, but all wars inflame national hatreds. This subjective, or apparent, aspect of a conflict should not be confused with the nature of meaning of the conflict. Let the philosophers justify their position by reference to popular sentiment; let the lovers of anecdote ponder over the crisis started when an Austrian archduke was murdered and try to discover who drew his sword first. A Marxist will not be taken in by this ruse of the class enemy and will eschew such a superficial version of events. After all, the social democrats had all admitted that the great powers rivalled one another as imperialists in their search for colonies, markets and zones of influence. By what miracle could such imperialist rivalry be turned overnight into a just war for liberty and the future of civilization?

The social democrats would object that Marx did not hesitate to support one side or another, Prussia or Germany against Napoleon III, at least until the empire fell. The only question that remained once war had broken out was who would win, and what were the consequences for socialism of the victory of one side or another? At this juncture Lenin introduced into the thought of Clausewitz a historical theory which can properly be called Marxist: the French Revolution, bourgeois in inspiration and colouring, instigated a phase of national struggles. This phase continued until 1871:

the truly national wars, especially those which took place between 1789 and 1871, were the expression of mass national movements, the struggle against absolutism and the feudal system or for the abolition of oppression and the creation of states on a national basis which was the essential feature of capitalist development.

Lenin recognized that the French revolutionary wars contained an element of pillaging and conquest of foreign countries. But this fact does not alter the historical significance attached to the wars that shook or destroyed the feudal regimes and absolutism of old Europe, the Europe of serfdom. During the Franco-German wars Germany despoiled France, but this does not alter the fundamental historical significance of these wars which freed tens of millions of Germans from the feudal partition and oppression practised by those two despots, the Russian tsar and Napoleon III.

In other words, during Marx's lifetime socialists had only one choice, between despotic (or feudal) regimes and bourgeois ones. Today the progress of socialism offers another perspective: socialist revolution. Those who yesterday preached in favour of that revolution and denounced imperialism deny themselves if they rally to national defence or retire to the Aventine. Clausewitz himself condemned them because the war is dictated by the political whole which contains it, which reveals and highlights the conduct of all. The same continuity should make it possible for men to grasp the nature of the conflict (the struggle of the greedy for a share of the booty) and let them understand the treachery of the leaders of the Second International.

The enthusiasm of the masses neither explains nor excuses such treason. To the Leninist way of thinking, historical truth is uncovered by Marxist analysis rather than by votes or mass sentiment. If, therefore, the Right Wing of the social democrats is converted to social chauvinism, if the Centre says 'no' to war but also 'no' to defeat, Lenin, by analysing the struggles within the factions of social democracy, manages to explain doctrines he regards as being incompatible with Marxism (or rather, his version of Marxism).

Social democracy had been exposed and shaken by the struggles between factions during the twenty years that preceded the war. 'Economism' and opportunism had exposed the essential problem: the inescapable class struggle and the road to socialism by violent revolution. All who had tolerated class collaboration, all who had subordinated the class struggle to economic development, all who had substituted reform for revolution – all of them were now social chauvinists or in a mess. What did they represent? The higher echelons of the working class to which the bourgeoisie distributed crumbs, cheaply bought, from their feast. Thus Lenin found that pre-war politics continued both in the factions of social democracy and in the states themselves.

There remains the last objection Lenin's opponents made to his thesis.

What would happen to the right of nations to determine their own fate? What of the principle of national liberation? If the Franco-German war of 1870–1 meant the liberation of Germany's masses rather than pillage by Bismarck, did not the European war of 1914 (though in essence imperialist) contain a component of national liberation? Lenin provided two answers, one easy, and the other uneasy.

He recognized without hesitation that Serbia was waging a war of national liberation. But what set Serbia apart from the other belligerents? All the great powers waged an imperialist war because they owned colonies and wanted those of their enemies, in order to exploit their populations and thus the globe. The secret treatise, denounced by Lenin, and which he published after the Revolution, left no doubt in his eyes of the similarity between the two camps. Both of them were involved in prolonging pre-war politics in wartime. Russian imperialism looked to Constantinople, French imperialism towards Morocco (or the left bank of the Rhine) and German imperialism looked towards Baghdad or Africa.

This argument helped Lenin in his attack on the provisional governments that emerged from the February Revolution, that of the Kadets as much as that of Kerensky. All of those who professed their loyalty to alliances and proclaimed their determination to fight the war repeated the blunder or crime of the Second International, i.e. they refused the only epithet worthy of a socialist, that of transforming the imperialist war into a revolutionary war. During the century of national and bourgeois revolutions, Marx, as well he might, wondered which side would benefit from victory – capitalism or the liberation of the people. The progress of socialism in the twentieth century allowed another attitude to prevail, which was hostile to all imperialism in the cause of the socialist revolution.

Just the same, an obstacle emerges at this point: what will happen to the right of peoples to self-determination proclaimed, though violated, by the European powers, in Africa and in Asia? Throughout his years of struggle Lenin did not hesitate for a moment in dealing with this: socialism, without discussion or reservation, would adopt the idea of self-determination. In an article devoted to analysing the pamphlet by Junius (Rosa Luxemburg), he rejected the thesis that 'in an era of unleashed imperialism there can no longer by any national wars'. On the contrary, imperialist war, namely war between imperialist states to partition the planet, would inevitably provoke national wars between colonies or semi-colonies (China, Turkey, and Persia).

> The wars of the Great Revolution began as national wars, which was what they really were. They were revolutionary in that they aimed to defend the Great Revolution against the coalition of counter-revolutionary monarchies. But when Napoleon founded a French Empire by enslaving a series of European national states that were large, viable and long-established, then the French national wars turned into imperialist wars which in their turn sparked off wars of national liberation against Napoleonic imperialism.

In the same way, but inversely, today's imperialist war could be turned into a nationalist war: a probable, even inevitable, transformation in the

:olonies and semi-colonies outside Europe. After declaring such a trans-
'ormation improbable in Europe, Lenin stressed its possibility, apparently
with regard to the liquidation of Austria-Hungary and even to the rebels in
non-Russian territories within the tsarist empire.

What would happen in Russia in the event of a socialist revolution?
Here again Lenin's answers ruled out ambiguity and compromise. He
quoted one of Engels's phrases with approval: 'Only one thing is certain:
that the victorious proletariat cannot impose happiness on any foreign
people without thereby compromising its own victory.' Anxious above all
else for the internationalist education of the proletariat, Lenin looked for a
way out of a 'very confused situation' with this formula:

> the Russian and German social democrats demand 'the
> unconditional right of Poland to be separate'; the Polish social
> democrats are anxious to bring about the cohesion of the
> proletarian struggle in small and great countries without for a
> moment launching the slogan of Polish independence.

Therefore, the founder of the Third International never failed to recognize national claims, nor did he confuse economic with political liberation
during his years of struggle. When he came to analyse imperialism he
discerned in the economic exploitation and forms of political domination
between colonies and semi-colonies only a difference in degree. The essential nature of the phenomenon of imperialism does not change though
Persia is an independent legal state or India a colony of the English crown.
By contrast, he radically opposed ideas that were widespread among
socialists by which the slogan of national self-determination, reactionary
in inspiration, would paralyse the necessary evolution towards large
economic units. He opposed annexations without reservation and unconditionally demanded the right of nations oppressed by the Great Russians
to separate. 'As long as the German proletariat tolerates Germany's
oppression of Poland it will remain in a situation worse than slavery, in the
role of a brute who helps to maintain others in slavery.'

Did Lenin present himself as a militant without taking this theme of
propaganda seriously? I do not believe it. In one document, where he
defends most passionately the right of self-determination, he rejects the
hypocrisy behind any protestation that would not involve a programme of
action. 'If a socialist party declares that it is against "keeping down by
violence those who are oppressed within their own frontiers by an occupying power" then the party itself implicitly promises to renounce that
violence when it takes power.' As to annexation, Lenin defines it simply as
violence (attachment by violence) and the notion of the foreign yoke, and
also by a violation of the *status quo*. A socialist would not oppose violence
as such, nor violation of the *status quo*, but would oppose annexation – in
other words, yoking a people to a foreign power by violent means. The will
of the people would decide whether or not to use violence.

In an article written in 1916 called 'A Caricature of Marxism' and 'On
Imperalist Economism' answering P. Kievski (Pyatakov), Lenin returned
to the question of self-determination and put foward his deepest thoughts
on the subject. These can be summed up in a dialectical formulation:

> There is not, nor could be, any contradiction between, on the one
> side, the propaganda that recognizes the right to independent

nationhood and the strict determination to bring such liberty about
when we are in government and, on the other side, propaganda in
favour of the linking up and fusion of nations;

or again, 'We are in favour of the fusion of nations but it is impossible at
the moment to go beyond such fusion imposed by violence toward
voluntary fusion, without the right to secede.' The separation of nations is
the inevitable intermediary stage before nations fuse and it will have the
same function as the dictatorship of the proletariat. The dictatorship of the
proletariat prepares the way for the extinction of the state just as the
separation of nations prepares for their fusion. 'The separation of Poland
and Finland after the victory of socialism can only be for a short time.'

Once again Lenin had compiled this study attacking imperialist
economism not in order to abuse readers but to instruct them. If we take
together Lenin's works written between 1914 and the taking over of
power – *Imperialism, the Highest Stage of Capitalism, The State and
Revolution* and the many lesser works on 'Self-determination of peoples',
the synthesis of Marx with Clausewitz becomes obvious. The nature of
the war results from the nature of states, parties or factions before hostilities break out. In this sense war is the continuation of policy by other
means. The imperialist war that the imperialist states are fighting
imposes a duty on socialists to bring about a revolution that will overthrow the state and, before the disappearance of the state, itself to substitute the dictatorship of the proletariat. Which proletariat? A national
proletariat, because a people that oppresses another would not be free. A
war becomes national, even in the era of imperialism, when a people
great or small, fights for its liberty.

Lenin's thinking, before 1914, had not yet shifted towards Stalinist
simplification: the nature of a war did not depend exclusively on the
particular regimes of the countries involved. Unjust wars were fought
during the French Revolution and the oppressed peoples fought wars of
national liberation. In the same way, the Leninist synthesis of Marx and
Clausewitz does not justify any and every war fought since by the Soviet
Union. Of course, Lenin had said that the liberty of peoples would not be
infringed by a socialist regime because, he thought, imperialism had its
roots in capitalism. However, he admitted that

the fact that the proletariat have accomplished the social revolution
will not necessarily make it saintly and will not prevent blunders
and lapses of weakness from occurring; national antipathies will
not disappear that quickly; hatred – albeit perfectly legitimate – of
the oppressed towards the oppressor will remain for some time.

The Leninist thesis suffers from an inherent weakness or contradiction.
In defining the nature of war, Lenin swept aside national passions indifferently and continued to follow the Marxist interpretation of the society of
states. But in defining annexation he referred to the will of the people. He
condemned the patriotic fervour of 1914 and approved in advance the
desire of Finland, Poland and even the Ukraine to be independent. Once
master of the state, and with the absolute power of the Bolsheviks overwhelmed by the dictatorship of the proletariat, would it be possible to
resist the temptation to qualify events and give them meaning by recourse
to an ostensibly Marxist analysis without referring to mass sentiment

supposedly corrupted by bourgeois propaganda? By Lenin's time the third element in the thesis – people's right to self-determination – had in effect disappeared. There remained only two extremes: on the one side imperialist states and on the other socialist states. The first would be condemned to warfare by internal contradictions; the second destined, beyond the dictatorship of the proletariat, to the union of peoples and its own disappearance. This double-think way was typical of the revolutionary leader who was lucid when unmasking enemies but a prisoner of a *Carbonaro* faith when he came to dream of the conclusion to his own efforts.

Must we follow Professor W. Hahlweg, the leading Clausewitzian expert in West Germany, and admire Lenin's interpretation of the Treatise? Do we judge it *sinngemäss*, i.e. in conformity with Clausewitz's own understanding of his writings? I doubt it. Lenin certainly understood one element in Clausewitz's thought: war is only an element in the political whole, a partial element, including what happens during the course of hostilities. On the other hand, a philosophy of history that simultaneously acknowledges the correct significance of a war and the justice possessed by a cause seems to me markedly foreign to the Prussian officer. The theory he sketched of the European balance of power still belonged to the intellectual world of the century of Enlightenment, even though it also encompassed the principle of nationalities.

Lenin certainly pointed out one possible meaning of the Formula. If we put forward the proposition that the class struggle is the ultimate cause of struggle between men, that a class prepares for the future and the end of all conflicts, it becomes possible to interpret particular wars using the criteria of class that determine the politics of the belligerent state. According to these propositions, politics does not reconcile the interests of the community or of humanity in general unless that class is the proletariat. But what are these propositions worth? The Leninist interpretation of the Treatise moves beyond theory into the quicksands of ideology. Sixty years later it was refuted, not by the lackeys of the bourgeoisie, but by a tribunal recognized with unease by Marxists, namely history. The Soviet Union and the People's Republic of China both point to one fact that has not been disguised by their struggles.

3 Hitler: The wager of the political leader

Had Hitler read Clausewitz? Did this provide him with inspiration? I do not believe it. Historians have not mentioned the Treatise as being among the works from which he sought material for his intellectual bric-à-brac. On the other hand, he knew Ludendorff personally and understood the revolutionary techniques of a Lenin. In a racial community as conceived by Ludendorff he used the methods of agitation and power-grabbing used both by proletarian parties and by fascism. Finally, he used the military machine inherited from Frederick the Great's Prussia, Bismarck's Germany and Seeckt's Reichswehr to initiate an enterprise more immoderate even than that of Napoleon.

Hitler also turned the Formula upside-down and extracted from it one possible meaning. International relations are as full of tension in peacetime as they are in war, though not in the same way or to the same degree.

The relationship between states is defined by hostility even when it is not expressed through the taking up of arms.

Hitler, like Ludendorff, substituted the racially pure community for the state as the subject-matter of historical destiny. To a greater extent than Ludendorff he demanded the elimination of all elements hostile to that racially pure community. But in the same way as Ludendorff he looked upon war as being the supreme test of peoples. Hitler remained superior to the machine – like a general as long as he was conducting a diplomacy appropriate to civil war and while he was paralysing his fascinated opponents by using ideas, not on a level with those of the professionals who were the products of the great general staff and the Schlieffen school. He was superior as long as he wanted to combine all the virtues of Frederick the Great with those of Napoleon and lead armies at the same time as waging war.

He gained victories at every turn between January 1933 and September 1938 by using procedures similar to those used by national political parties. He challenged his rivals and made sure that the eventual outcome would be a national *coup* based on mass sentiment. Rearmament, the introduction of conscription, the reoccupation of the Rhineland were decisions which immediately received the support of the majority of Germans and restored the Reich to a position of equality among states. While conforming to politico-moral judgments and public opinion – even when it remained neutral – the Germans created a series of *faits accomplis* which were passively accepted by French governments who would have had to resort to arms to put a stop to it all, and this they reckoned they could not do.

In March 1938 Hitler's gamble again came off even though his advisers feared the worst. His demagogic intuition triumphed over the experience of professionals, diplomats and the army. The professionals lost face but the Führer sailed on, fuelled by a mystical faith both in himself and in his destiny. In 1938 the Munich agreement again proved him to be right and probably saved him from the hazards of a military *coup*, although perhaps he regretted missing the opportunity of waging a local war. It was only in 1939 that he crossed the threshold between war and peace. On that September day, Hitler was set on a journey from which there was no return, which led from victory to victory and then to the bunker in Berlin. And he dragged his people with him towards apocalyptic catastrophe.

On this occasion Clausewitz does not figure as one of the defendants despite the ingenuity of Liddell Hart, though maybe as prosecutor or witness according to preference. The bombing of Germany (by zone in English parlance, by terror in the German) could not be put down to any principle of annihilation for the simple reason that neither the English nor the Americans had read the Treatise. Therefore the devastation of cities and the countryside alluded to in Chapters 1 and 2 of Book I are no examples of the principle of annihilation that Clausewitz particularly ascribed to the armed forces. After defeat the German generals also confided to Liddell Hart that they had not given enough thought to Clausewitz and the notion of subordinating the military to political strategy.

In fact, in 1940 Linnebach, one of the leading specialists on Clausewitz and an editor of the Treatise, had rediscovered the secret of victory by rereading Chapter 2 of Book I, Chapter 6 of Book III and Chapter 11 of Book IV. How could the dagger of the courtier resist the heavy sword of the *seigneur*? Once more the God of War (Hitler now taking the place of Napoleon) would strike at the party which refused to pay tribute and which looked for ways to circumvent difficulties while trying to avoid the bloodshed.

Indeed, the course taken by the war from 1939 to 1945 lends itself to two different Clausewitzian criticisms. One involves the conduct of the war by the Russians, the Germans and the Western Powers. The other relates to the conduct of operations by both sides. In the narrower and wider senses of the word it may be said that, after the defeat of the French in 1940, 'strategy' was planned by four actors, both individual and collective: by Hitler or the generals in the Third Reich; by Stalin above all in the Soviet Union; by Roosevelt and his military advisers in the USA, and by Churchill and the cabinet in Great Britain. The two traditional heads of state were Churchill and Roosevelt, the two revolutionary leaders were Stalin and Hitler. The generals, including those in Germany, were still traditional in outlook.

Until 1941 Hitler, waging the war as a statesman, gained unprecedented victories. In two weeks the Wehrmacht had destroyed the Polish army and, together with the USSR, wiped Poland from the map of the world. It took him four weeks to knock out the French army, neutralize the French navy and North Africa under the cover of armistice and remove all British bases on the Continent. Four weeks after the beginning of the Russian campaign Hitler ordered arms production to be reduced as the war on land seemed to be nearing its end. Four years later he committed suicide in the bunker.

After 1939 Hitler successively continued the wager but by military means rather than empty threats. The general staff reckoned that neither the economy of the Reich nor the army had been mobilized and got ready for a long and all-consuming war. In the west only some thirty divisions were left, eleven of them first-line.

After the Polish campaign the arms reserves were reduced by half and the weapon reserves were not sufficient to cover the next four months, according to the high command of the army. The Third Reich had the advantage over the Allies in terms of superior organization and operational methods but they were not so advanced in the field of mobilization. I do not believe that Hitler renounced policy, as his latest biographer, Joachim Fest, has suggested. He gambled eagerly, first on achieving a lightning victory in Poland before the French army were alerted, and he won. Then he gambled on a breakthrough in the Ardennes which he achieved with the superiority of the German army using both tanks and Stukas at the same time implementing the Manstein Plan which he imposed on the two army leaders, Brauchitsch and Halder (who were respectively chief of the army and chief of its general staff). He followed his intuition and, using the language of Clausewitz, judged his enemies correctly – the French people, who had not recovered from their terrible blood-letting, and the French government, paralysed by the divisions in the country. Unlike Liddell Hart, I do not believe that the course of the history of our time was changed with profound consequences for the future of all countries when Hitler's armies crossed the western defences on 10 May 1940, the narrow breakthrough at Sedan soon becoming a vast gulf, and the disaster bringing about the fall of France and the isolation of England. Although England managed to shelter behind her maritime defences, safety only came with a long war which became a world conflict. In the end Hitler was defeated by the combined weight of America and the Soviet Union, but Europe was exhausted and living under the shadow of communist domination. A prolonged battle in the west would have given the Soviet Union an even better chance of extending that shadow over the whole of Europe.

If we subscribe to this historian's judgment we must suppose that the distinct failure of Hitler's gamble would also have undermined gradually the confidence of his troops and the population. When the Germans were held up at the western front the strong internal opposition to Hitler would have been given a reasonable chance of gaining strong points and applying plans to overthrow him before negotiating any peace. This was possible, but then the French generals would for the second time have had to sustain the burden of the struggle, and nothing leads us to suppose that the German generals would have overthrown Hitler unless Germany had been defeated in the west, which was ruled out by the *Wehrmacht*'s superiority in 1940. Anyway, both kinds of conspirators, generals and nationalists, would have encountered the same kind of suspicion in London and Washington as they did in 1944.

During the period of lightning victories which, more than those of Napoleon, resembled *coups de main* on a vast scale, Hitler took two decisions that bore the seeds of reversal and the final disaster. 'In a large measure it was the personal intervention of Hitler that allowed the British Expeditionary Force to escape in 1940,' wrote Liddell Hart. 'Hitler made his tanks stop for three days.' We shall never know if this decision was made purely for military reasons or if he hoped to encourage the conclusion of peace by sparing the vanity of the British after the French defeat that had already become likely. This last hypothesis is not incompatible with Hitler's personality or his long-term political plans: perhaps he was not prepared to go to any lengths to destroy the British forces.

In much the same way the abandonment of Operation Seelöwe was caused by many reasons, among which probably figures Hitler's admiration for the British Empire. Marshal von Manstein thought that invasion of the British Isles was the quickest and perhaps the only decisive way of dealing with the British before the intervention of the USA and the USSR. 'From that time on, it was clear that Hitler had not put all his heart into the project,' wrote Manstein.

> There can be no doubt on this subject: Hitler always wanted to avoid a struggle with England and the British Empire. . . . He admired England as a politician. . . . Hitler knew that if this empire was destroyed the heirs would be neither himself nor Germany but the Americans, Japan or the Soviet Union. . . . His political outlook was opposed to the strategic necessities that imposed themselves after the defeat of France. The misfortune was that he encountered no sympathy on the British side.

Marshal von Manstein expresses the opinion of that part of the army

280

that believed in victory and pushed ahead with preparations most vigorously. As commander of an army corps himself he belonged in the first wave of the landings. It is not my task to speculate on the outcome of a bold operation that never took place. It is true that the German high command had not prepared a plan of attack against the British Isles before the fall of France. Hitler himself had launched the campaign in Poland without any plan, somewhat in the manner of a poker *coup*. As with the reoccupation of the Rhineland, he improvised the conduct of a war he wanted and had not thought things out, in advance, even in the most general terms. Hitler operated on the spur of the moment, hoping to gamble and win on each occasion and not repeat the errors of the First World War. In 1914 the high command had had only one plan, that of a victory of annihilation in the west before turning against Russia.

By the end of 1940, it was intended that Operation Barbarossa should take place in the spring of the following year. Hitler thus became embroiled in a war on two fronts despite the lessons he had learnt from the experience of 1914–18. Once Operation Seelöwe had been abandoned, might not the Third Reich have managed to force Great Britain to sign peace, or to defeat her completely before the Soviet Union was in turn attacked? Hitler was not deceived when he postulated the basic hostility of the Soviet Union. During celebrations in Moscow for the signing of the German–Russian pact Stalin evoked the love of the German people for their Führer, and Ribbentrop acknowledged the meeting of two revolutions, a meeting that did not survive the partition of Poland. A Germany that ruled from the Vistula to Brest and from Hamburg to Athens inspired in the USSR the fear of a new invasion, only this time the horde coming from the west would be mechanized. Hitler might still have hoped to discourage the English will to win in the war *à l'outrance* by operations in the Near East, by an intense submarine war and by bombing English towns.

It seems to me that he followed the logic of three arguments, two of them military and a third political. He believed he was safe from any English attempt to reconquer the Continent for several years. He also reckoned that it would only take a few months for the Wehrmacht to destroy the Red Army (a winter campaign had not been predicted) and he respected the British Empire while hating Marxism and communism.

Of course, he also adopted the old German idea of the drive to the east to conquer new lands in order to extend *Lebensraum* at the expense of the Slavs, the *Untermenschen*. The Reich would find fields of grain in the Ukraine that would provide guarantees against a famine like that of 1918. There were oil wells in the Caucasus without which a motorized army would turn out to be paralysed. He preferred to overthrow the Soviet Union rather than the British Empire and he did not impose the same regime on the occupied French as he did on the Poles, the Belgians and the Russians. During the war he achieved certain *faits accomplis* which he regarded as war aims, for instance the extermination of the Jews. Even on 27 January 1944 he gave a lecture to the commanders of the eastern front on the need to introduce national socialist education in the army.

Did Hitler therefore disprove the thesis of the supremacy of politics, given that the First World War had revealed the fatal consequences of a particular interpretation of the principle of destruction? He would have disproved it if Clausewitz had afforded priority to political logic rather than military grammar. What Clausewitz wrote was that military grammar must be subordinated to political logic, or rather that the errors of logic are not corrected by referring to grammatical rules.

Like Napoleon, Hitler had a run of victories (between 30 January 1933 and 15 August 1941), but only for as long as he played the revolutionary leader, intuitively grasping the moral and material weaknesses of his enemies. First of all, he misunderstood the resolution of the British, the traditional enemies of conquerors, and the unquenchable hostility the island power had towards him. Then he misunderstood the obstacle presented to invaders by the immensity of the Russian land. He misunderstood the lesson Clausewitz himself had learned from his own experience – that conquests in Europe are only made possible by dissensions within nations.

Let us reread the last few lines of the Russian campaign as narrated some fifteen years after the event by Clausewitz:

> Bonaparte wished to conduct and conclude the war in Russia in the same way as he had conducted and concluded his other campaigns. Using decisive blows to start with, and using the advantages thus gained to deliver new blows, he always gambled to win on a single card until he had broken the bank. This was his only method and the method to which he owed his colossal success. It was therefore imperative for him to end this war in a few campaigns. Until this time the plan of most wars had consisted of knocking out and destroying the enemy's armies, seizing the capital and throwing the government into the farthest corner of its territory, thus winning peace with the first wave of panic. In Russia he had to contend with the immense area of land and the fact that there were two capitals, far apart. He hoped to compensate for the moral outcome of his military success in two ways: by exposing the weakness of the Russian government and by sowing dissension between the government and the grandees of the empire. These hopes were misguided. Bonaparte realized that the war would not finish without two campaigns, but it was a great achievement to have occupied Moscow during the first campaign. By holding on to Moscow he could hope to stifle all preparations for later resistance by using those troops still loyal to him to impose his will, perturb public opinion and turn the population from the path of its duty.

This appraisal remains valid today on condition that the expressions 'weakness of government' and 'dissension between the government and the grandees of the empire' are transposed into relations between the Stalinist regime and the peoples of the Soviet Union. There lurked in the USSR dissensions between the government and the populace. Historians free to say so do not doubt that non-Russians and even Russians themselves welcomed the German troops in the initial stages of the campaign.

Even Erich von Manstein, a great soldier but an indifferent politician, and one of the German generals most indulgent towards Hitler, noted the contradiction between Hitler's overall aims and the means he employed. Hitler's first mistake (to say the least) was to underestimate the strength of the Soviet regime, the country's sources of power and the Red Army. Consequently, he began by thinking that he could defeat Russia in a single campaign. To do that he should have simultaneously attempted to provoke the internal collapse of the regime. But the policy Hitler exercised in the occupied eastern regions through his Reich commissioners and the SD, against the wishes of the military authorities, could only have the contrary effect. Whereas he desired to defeat the Soviets as quickly as possible he acted in the political arena in a way diametrically opposed to this strategy. In other words, contrary objectives frequently occurred between the political and military leaderships, which in this case were both in Hitler's hands, the outcome was that his eastern policy was contrary to his strategic needs. Thus the only chance of a rapid victory that may have existed disappeared.

Even after the defeat of the Wehrmacht before Moscow there was a Russian general who joined the invaders out of hatred for the regime, in spite of the fact that he had taken part in the decisive victory of December 1941. As a racially pure community the Third Reich fought those who were racially inferior in order to gain and populate living space. Manstein never fully understood the substitution of the 'racial' state for the traditional state, which logically brought about a 'racist' conduct of the war and which contributed to Stalin's victory and the twilight of the German gods.

It was an irony of history that the two regimes which, according to Erich Ludendorff, wished to build a spiritual community with an end view of total war had more traitors than the democratic regimes. Hitler's policy in the occupied territories restored the unity of nations in the face of the invader. And Stalin, unlike Hitler, rallied his people to a 'patriotic war' and not to a war fought for Marxism–Leninism. In 1944 the German patriots hoped to save Germany and her honour by overthrowing Hitler. At the same time there was no hope left for the anti-Stalinist Russian patriots – the Reich wished to use them, not to help them, and the English and Americans handed them over to Stalin. While the two revolutionary leaders waged a political war Roosevelt adhered to the principle of annihilation in a narrow military sense.

4 The impossible compromise

The Third Reich mobilized more during than before hostilities. In May 1940 the Germans were neither superior in divisions nor in tanks. Only their airforce had a thousand or so planes more than the enemy. Two factors explain the suddenness of the victory: the tactical and operational innovation of armoured divisions acting in close liaison with the bombers, and the Manstein Plan substituted for the plan of the great general staff when the latter (which would have been applied had the offensive been launched according to Hitler's wishes in November 1939) fell, by chance, into Belgian hands and thence into the hands of the allied staff.

The French high command let the Supreme Council, i.e. the political leaders, adopt a risky manoeuvre. As in 1914 it took the decisions desired by the enemy. There was time to repair the error in 1914 but there was not the slightest chance in 1940. By 15 May, Paul Reynaud could write that 'the battle is lost'. Almost all the Anglo-French divisions that were capable of mobility (the spearhead) had been sent to help Belgium and Holland with a view to a head-on battle. The breakthrough across the Ardennes and the hurtling of tanks towards the North Sea condemned the Belgian army to destruction as well as the French divisions sent ahead. To illustrate the radical difference between the annihilation of an army and mutual massacre, the Wehrmacht only lost 27,000 men, as against 135,000 on the other side, in the battle of France.

Specialists discussed and perhaps still discuss the relationship between Clausewitz, the Schlieffen school and the victories of destruction in the west and east in 1939, 1940 and 1941. To a layman these discussions appear to be equivocal. As Rosinski maintains, the German generals under the influence of Clausewitz (although others believe it was the memory of Moltke's Napoleonic victories and the teachings of the military academy) continued to be obsessed by the idea of annihilation and of a crushing victory. These ideas are as attributable to Clausewitz as they are to Moltke and Schlieffen; however, for Clausewitz this kind of victory was only one example, to be obtained by offensive, given enough superiority, whereas the others were gamblers. No geometric formula possessed a predominant value in all circumstances, according to the author of the Treatise. The antidogmatic Moltke succeeded in operations that Clausewitz reckoned to be dangerous, and gathered together armies that had come from different directions on the battlefields of Sedan and Königgrätz.

Whereas Liddell Hart sees in the author of the Treatise the prophet of mutual slaughter, Rosinski attributes to the persistent, maybe unconscious influence of Clausewitz the idea of mobility, of taking by surprise, the seeking out of the offensive and the envelopment or outflanking of the enemy army with a view to gaining a decisive success. Schlieffen obviously connects with Clausewitz as a master of mobility and annihilation.

On the other hand, the Schlieffen school, according to its ardent opponents, committed the error, denounced by Clausewitz, of choosing a geometric formula as if this was always superior to other explanations. Schlieffen and his school come within the tradition of 'oblique approach' according to this hypothesis. In order to outflank and then envelop, the strategy of attack is transposed on to one wing. In 1911, as Schlieffen foresaw violation of Dutch neutrality, he was still extending the scale of the manoeuvre.

If we see the essence of the Schlieffen school in envelopment and the refusal to break through, then the Manstein Plan which was based on a breakthrough in the Ardennes no longer belonged to the provenance of that school. But above all Schlieffen was an operator, even one of genius. With the state of the military as it was, he did not believe in the possibility of breakthrough. A disciple of Schlieffen who had refused in 1939 to see the possibilities afforded by tanks and the spread of motor transport would have committed the fault in strategy that Clausewitz called 'methodism'. Thus from 1919 to 1939 General von Seeckt's Reichswehr was an elite professional army based on mobility.

The idea of using armed divisions and tank raids over long distances came from the English Liddell Hart and Fuller, though the general staff in both London and on the Continent was conservative and gave the Germans the privilege and advantage of exploiting it to the full. Rupturing the front by tanks provided a new way of encircling and annihilating the enemy.

During the Russian campaign Hitler and his generals got into disputes several times, but it seems to me impossible to blame the Schlieffen school any more than the influence of Clausewitz for the errors commited by Hitler or the high command of the army. The Führer and his advisors were parties to the same illusion; and by 3 July Halder was writing in his diary, 'It is not too much to say that the Russian campaign has been won in a fortnight.' For his part, Hitler thought that operations would be over by mid-September. The armament effort was shifted towards submarines and aircraft. Those reponsible were already thinking in terms of the return of the troops.

A month later, in August, there was a debate of as great strategic importance as that which in the previous year had led to the abandonment of the Seelöwe project and the 'Barbarossa' decision: should the Germans put their best troops in the centre to head straight for Moscow? Brauchitsch and Halder begged Hitler in vain to launch a direct attack on the capital. They were repeating, probably without realizing it, Clausewitz's retrospective justification for Napoleon's plan. An area as vast as the tsarist empire could not be captured, only armies could be destroyed and the capital taken. Hitler chose to destroy some armies but he put off for two months the assault on the capital. The armies of the centre put their motorized units at the disposal of the northern and southern sectors of the front. When, two months later, Hitler decided to launch a last offensive on Moscow after spectacular, but not decisive, victories, Brauchitsch and Halder lodged several objections in vain.

According to Marshal von Manstein, the disagreement between Hitler and the high command was about radical differences concerning the objectives in war – to use Clausewitzian language: Hitler's strategic objectives above all resulted from political and economic calculations. On one side, they consisted of taking Leningrad, which Hitler considered to be the cradle of Bolshevism and which would gain him a link with the Finns and mastery of the Baltic. On the other side, he wanted the Ukraine, the land of raw materials, with the industrial region of the Donets, and finally the oil regions of the Caucasus. He thus counted on paralysing the Soviet war economy. By contrast, OKH argued with reason that the conquest of these regions, although of undoubted strategic importance, necessitated the precondition that the Red Army would already have been knocked out. The fall of Moscow would nearly have halved Soviet resistance and placed the Russian command in a situation where they could not organize an overall operation. The dispute broke out in August 1941 when a choice had to be made between a solution based on the wings or on the centre. It affected the whole course of the campaign. Hitler did not achieve his aims, which were anyway too remote, while at the same time he spoiled the ideas of OKH.

On two more occasions after 1941 Hitler's political obsessions probably influenced military decisions. In Hitler's mind the siege of Leningrad and, even more, the battle of Stalingrad, had symbolic importance as they possessed respectively the names of the founder and the ruler of the Soviet Union. He attacked the communism that he hated by striking hard against the cities that bore the hateful names of Lenin and Stalin. In the grip of this mania Hitler had already departed some way from the path of normal thought.

In the second phase of the campaign, when the respective strengths of the adversaries were reversed, the conflict between Hitler and the generals was essentially concerned with defensive methods. Early in the winter of 1941–2, when the German army was suddenly debilitated by the freezing conditions hundreds of miles from base, the army commanders Brauchitsch and Halder, who had recommended retreat, even before the final Moscow offensive, in order to shelter the army in the winter against Soviet counterattacks, insisted that the traditional method of an elastic defence was necessary. Hitler decreed an altogether different *modus operandi*: 'No retreat.' The outcome of this was the 'hedgehogs', the exact opposite of that mobility to which the German army owed its victories in 1939–41. 'This decision seemed to lead to disaster, but once more events proved him right,' says Liddell Hart who, in support of his view, quotes the German General von Tippelskirch:

> the main objective was to hold on to the large towns and the centres
> of road and railway communications. In accordance with Hitler's
> methods we formed a 'hedgehog' around these towns, thus
> surrounding them with a protective belt and we managed to keep
> them. The situation was therefore saved.

General von Tippelskirch continues, 'Men remembered Napoleon's retreat from Moscow with apprehension. If they, too, had been forced to retreat it would perhaps have become a rout.' To which Marshal von Rundstedt answered, it seems to me without contradicting his interlocutor, 'It was in fact Hitler's decision to stay put that provoked danger. If he had given his men the opportunity to retreat the danger would not have arisen.'

Politically, Hitler's greatest mistake was to submit people in the occupied territories to a pitiless regime and thereby encourage them to rally to Stalin and the patriotic war. From a military point of view, the major weakness was to delay the Moscow offensive, then to launch it when it was too late, and finally to put off the order to retreat until the moment when only resistance on the spot could be resorted to. Perhaps he saved the army by obeying his intuition against the advice of his military advisers. But the price, both in terms of men and material, was enormous. In the end Hitler, convinced more than ever of his own genius, no longer listened to anyone.

The Wehrmacht was still winning victories in 1942 but we look in vain for the main threads of its operations. The economic experts demanded the taking of the Caucasus oil which they regarded as indispensable for the conduct of the war. The generals at the front did not know the exact economic details and argued in favour of the destruction of the Soviet army. A dispersal of forces resulted. The Wehrmacht managed to put up resistance without oil from the Caucasus until 1945. Stalingrad could have been taken without a shot being fired in July 1942 but that town did not constitute one of the main objectives of the offensive. Hitler made it that later, thus symbolically marking Stalin's victory over him. The Russians defended their territory against the invaders and the heroism of each side was equal.

I have found only one reference to Clausewitz in the writings of the German generals. 'For the members of my generation,' wrote Liddell Hart, 'the teaching of Clausewitz had dropped out of fashion even when I was at Sandhurst and a member of the general staff.' He was still quoted but he was no longer studied with any attention. It was thought that his writings were part of military philosophy rather than having any practical worth. We were much more interested in Schlieffen's works which seemed to be more practical because they dealt with the following problem: How could an army with less capability than the enemy armies in coalition (which was the case in Germany) defeat the enemy on two fronts? However, Clausewitz's reflections were always valid, especially his doctrine that war was a continuation of politics by other means. The fault of Germany was in thinking that a military victory would resolve political problems. Under the Nazis the moment came when we virtually revered Clausewitz's maxim and came to the point of considering policy as a continuation of war. Clausewitz was also correct in predicting the difficulty of conquering Russia.

In spite of everything, Hitler had a better chance of conquering Russia than Napoleon as he was superior in arms and the populace was discontented with the rigours of Stalin's rule.

Contrary to legend, the German generals by 1914 had become disciples of Schlieffen more than followers of Clausewitz, or even Moltke. As Kleist has pointed out, they considered the means of decisively defeating a coalition of superior force thanks to their operational virtuosity. The famous Schlieffen Plan, simple yet brilliant, presented a solution to this problem. Soldiers, participants, and historians in large numbers put the blame first on the younger Moltke and then on Falkenhayn. Germany had to triumph or perish: *tertium non datur*. The only First World War leader probably influenced by a different approach discredited it by the slaughter of the Verdun 'mincer'. Liddell Hart, the most intelligent military historian, viewed Falkenhayn basically as an intractable realist, 'the most capable and scientific of the generals, penny-wise and pound-foolish, who ever led his country to ruin by a refusal to take calculated risks. The limiting of risks leads to bankruptcy'. Liddell Hart separated the military decisions taken at the highest level in war from political leadership of the war, i.e. the objectives *in* war. He seems to be saying *a priori* that the only aim the high command could and ought to have had in mind, at least on the German side, was a decisive military victory. On this point Ludendorff, as against Falkenhayn, was right. But Falkenhayn probably refused to accept this idea. If the war could not be won after the defeat on the Marne in 1914, as Liddell Hart wrote elsewhere, then the strengths of the Hindenburg–Ludendorff alliance would be as catastrophic as the prudence of the isolated chief. In any event, the shift in 1917 from a strategy aimed at a compromise peace to a strategy of total victory, in spite of American intervention, contained the maximum risk.

Conversely, Manstein, when drawing up the balance sheet of the winter of 1941–2, concluded with astonishing naïvety:

> From all the evidence it appears that the high command ought to have reached the conclusion that it should have tried to come to an understanding with at least one of its enemies at any price and see that only one goal should have been pursued on the eastern front, that of containment.

He explains elsewhere why he was against any attempt to overthrow Hitler by *coup d'état*. It never struck him that there was any contradiction between the desire for compromise with one of the enemies and the maintenance of Hitler in power. Moreover, the English and Americans wanted to destroy not only the National Socialist regime but Germany herself, as he says some pages later. So there was no way out apart from another encounter between the two revolutions, a second Hitler–Stalin Pact. Let us not reproach the German generals too much for this; on several occasions Roosevelt and Churchill feared such a compromise. The German generals shared with the American president the same lack of comprehension of revolutionary despots.

Why should Stalin have welcomed another encounter between the two revolutions even if he had public opinion under his control? How could Hitler have got him to forfeit his victories? Of course, by the spring of 1942 a Frederician strategy offered the best chance of avoiding defeat. It would offer resistance in the east and also mean opposing the invaders in the west with greater force than that used to contain the Western Powers' advance in North Africa, Normandy and the Ardennes. But how can we fail to repeat the reasons given by Clausewitz to explain Napoleon's refusal to adopt a methodical approach to conquering Russia?

Between August 1914 and November 1918 the will to eliminate the enemy replaced the ambition to achieve defined objectives. Peace would be dictated when the armies of the enemy were annihilated. Revolutions and the allied victory were the end-product of the paralysis of Russia and the great powers.

Waged by revolutionaries, the Second World War was in essence, rather than by accident, revolutionary. Neither the Soviet Union nor the Third Reich could survive defeat. The same was true for the liberal democracies of Europe. But the leaders of these countries never fully understood the war fought between these two men and the regimes they incarnated. The monstrous Hitler and Stalin betrayed their own ideologies, the one through criminal acts, the other by putting those ideas into practice. Armed combat favoured the one who was not pursuing the triumph of a monstrous doctrine, and that was just.

Between 1939 and 1941 Stalin's propaganda followed the example of Lenin between 1914 and 1917 and pointed a finger at all the belligerents, accusing them of imperialism. In the spring of 1942 the war, which had been imperialist until then, changed direction. Stalin cited Lenin in a speech made on 6 November 1941 and 'distinguished between two types of war: wars of conquest which were by definition unjust, and wars of liberation which were just. The Germans at present are fighting a war of conquest, an unjust war that aims to take other people's territory and subjugate the native population. . . . Unlike Hitler's Germany, the Soviet Union and its allies are fighting a war of liberation, a just war aimed at liberating the enslaved peoples of Europe and the USSR from Hitlerian tyranny.' He went even further in the defence of his allies because he recalled that in England and the USA there 'exist trade unions of workers and employees, parties of the working classes and a parliament, whereas in Germany all of these institutions have been abolished by Hitler's regime'.

Given the state he was in in 1942, Hitler could not have been converted to the wisdom of Frederick the Great. An adventurer or demagogue cannot act like a legitimate sovereign. Even after Stalingrad he was to become stubborn with his once-and-for-all method of resisting on the spot – a method which had probably led to avoidance of the worst in December 1941. A conversion to Frederician strategy could not have saved the Third Reich and by 1943 Hitler had, through his crimes, linked the destiny of Germany with his own. He was not interested in the future of his people if they were to be defeated.

None the less, Hitler's chiefs lived in hope up to the end. On the day of Roosevelt's death Goebbels invoked the Peace of Hubertusburg which had saved Prussia after the death of the Russian empress. The last recourse was to wait until there was no hope of winning or even holding on. For what? Nothing, except the unforeseeable. Hitler would never have surrendered. If the 20th July plotters had been successful it would have cut short the agony of the Third Reich without saving Germany from demands for unconditional surrender. Roosevelt did not wish to repeat the mistakes of Wilson.

Circumstances obliged Stalin to speak a language different from Lenin's in 1914. But in deed rather than by word he refuted Lenin's interpretation of the Formula. In November 1941 he proclaimed:

> We do not and cannot put forward war aims such as the
> annexation of other peoples' lands and the subjugation of foreign
> peoples. . . . We cannot and do not aim in the war to impose our
> will and our regime on the Slavs and the other peoples of Europe
> who count on us for help.

We know where this was to lead.

Chapter 12

Arming The People

The Convention proclaimed the *levée en masse*: mobilization of the whole population against the enemy and the counter-revolution. The patriots of Prussia even tried, in vain, to arm civilians without dressing them as soldiers, so making them partisans.

After 1815 Clausewitz meditated upon the events of his time, on those in which he had taken part, like the Russian campaign, and those he studied from afar. Succinct narrative accounts in French of the Spanish War and an account of the war in the Vendée were found among his papers. The fate of the militia or territorial reserve, the *Landwehr*, became the stake in the quarrel between patriots and reactionaries. The success of the latter compounded Clausewitz's bitterness as he kicked his heels in the administrative command of the military academy.

The Treatise retains the imprint of the experiences of an officer who fought against the victor until 1815. In the second chapter of Book V the reader will suddenly discover a striking remark in the context of the definition of an army:

> It would be pedantic to lay claim to the name of army for one partisan in some distant province; still, it must be said that no one is surprised when the 'army' of the Vendéens is referred to during the revolutionary wars even though it was not often much later.

The doctrine of national defence emerged most completely in Book VI – the book that the French officers refused to understand between 1880 and 1914; a book not included in the extracts published in the USA, and the implication of which only revolutionaries have grasped. For a century the Prussian and German general staffs, even the general staffs of all European armies, overlooked Chapter 26 of Book VI. This was an essential chapter because Clausewitz, who had for two years delivered the course on guerilla warfare to officers, is writing within here the framework of the dialectic of attack and defence as though the course on guerilla warfare was designed for a people in armies.

1 The arming of the people, 1813 and 1871

Let us for a moment ignore the political aspects associated with arming the people and concentrate on the military or tactical aspect of guerilla warfare. As we have seen, it is defined by the limitation of effective strength taking part at the same time in battle (at most 300 to 400 men). Guerilla warfare is thus reduced, in the eyes of theorists, to a small war fought by irregulars, by an improvised soldiery who have had no military training and who, unlike professionals, are not commanded. The theory formulates principles or rules valid for a guerilla war waged by irregulars.

In accordance with his usual method, Clausewitz first laid down conditions in which the arming of the people becomes a possibility. The war must be fought inside the country, the issue should not have been finalized by one lost battle, the theatre of operations must cover a sufficiently large area, the people must be dispositionally inclined to support the measures taken and, finally, the territory must present difficulties of access in the form of mountains, valleys, marshes or even the way the soil is cultivated.

According to this method the means of deploying the armed peoples can be deduced from both idea and reality. Once more Clausewitz shows his taste for paradox; in other words, he reasons dialectically. Guerila warfare, considered as part of a large war, is concerned wholly with tactics because it is defined by the use of troops. None the less, it remains possible and legitimate to distinguish in general between the deployment of those armed (the strategy of guerilla warfare) and the means of deploying irregulars in a fixed combat.

Contradictory principles express a contrast between regular troops and improvised irregulars. The more a war fought between regular armies is intensified, the more will it concentrate on decisive battles and, at the extreme, a campaign will be able to be decided in a day. On the other hand, popular warfare is characterized by the dispersion of the combatants and the progressive diffusion of hostilities. Partisans cannot and must not attack the main enemy forces. They concentrate on detachments, convoys, the rear and the lines of communication. By their very nature they are geared to tactical offensive and strategic defence. If they are to bring about a conclusion alone they need an immense area of land, as only Russia has in Europe, or a huge imbalance between the area to be held and the invading forces. Therefore, Clausewitz thought that popular warfare was not valid when conducted in isolation but only as a subsidiary means of defence bound up with the activities of the regular army. In the end, however, he confesses that his analysis is inadequate due to lack of experience. Those who observed popular war did not write about it with sufficient precision.

The few ideas and illustrations set out in Chapter 26 of Book IV none the less deserve more attention, since comparisons may be found, sometimes of a literally accurate kind, in twentieth-century writings as, for instance, in those of Mao Tse-tung. Clausewitz compared popular war with a fire that flares up in small spurts and is extinguished, then flares up again until the time comes when it spreads to other hearths and lights up an entire plain unless the blaze consumes itself and dies out. Or again,

> If it comes to the question of destroying roads or blocking narrow routes, the means that can be applied by patrols or flying columns of an army are in proportion to those means forged by an insurgent peasantry, as the movements of a robot can be compared with those of a human being.

It was still his way to accord priority to the psychological or moral aspects of the fight. The enemy army will only dispatch weak forces against the first rebels. At the same time local victories present an opportunity to inflame the situation. Courage and ardour grow and the combat gains in intensity until the culmination when the outcome will be decided.

The 'fire that spreads from small beginnings', popular war 'dispersed like fog or clouds suddenly condensing in a few places, not coherently, like a regular army' – beyond these images Clausewitz sketches a doctrine of structure and a doctrine of practicalities.

In respect of organization, the main rule acknowledges co-operation between the rebels and the regular army. Small contingents from the permanent army will reinforce the first groups of partisans who will attack the enemy rear, the isolated garrisons. Neither too many nor too few regular army soldiers must be detached. By dint of taking part in the popular war the army risks, on the one side, being weakened and, on the other, exposing the people to heavy enemy attack. The risk would arise of the people being separated from the fighting forces. Partisans would no longer appear as peasants in arms but as soldiers. The people would leave them to pursue the fighting.

One principle remains dominant in terms of practicalities: avoiding a tactical defence. The partisans are fierce in attack but, like all badly trained troops, lack balance and the power to concentrate. When they take the risk of establishing themselves in a position so as to defend it they should, at least, choose a favourable one, like the entrance to a pass or a river crossing. Even in these circumstances they must not resist on the spot up to the end. A people in arms defends itself by dispersion not by getting killed *in situ*. Clausewitz wrote, 'However courageous a people are, however warlike by habit, however great their hatred for the enemy, however favourable the terrain, it is incontestable that the popular war cannot be sustained in an atmosphere thick with danger.'

Let me repeat: this theory of popular war comes within the framework of a defensive theory, in that arming the people implies a kind of resistance which involves retreat into the interior and repeated use of force. It also offers the ultimate recourse in the case of a lost battle. There is a Gallic resonance about these lines:

> No state must believe that its fate and entire existence depends on a battle, even the most decisive one. . . . There is always time to die and in the same way a man who is drowning will by instinct clutch on to a piece of straw. It is part of the natural moral order of the world to seek ultimately for salvation even when tossed over the edge of a precipice. So, however frail and weak a state is in comparison with its enemy it must not spurn great effort without which it would appear to have lost its soul.

In 1870 the situation was reversed. Opinion in both Germany and the world denounced the French *francs tireurs* as outlaws who were violating the rules of war and they were treated accordingly. The view put forward on popular war afterwards by Helmut von Moltke was typical for a general in command of the invading army. From a humanitarian viewpoint, he wrote, it would be desirable for a popular army to show that it would be adequate to guarantee its country's independence.

> We have all had experience and have been forced to admit that the mobilization, even in large numbers, of energetic, patriotic and courageous men will not be capable of resisting a proper army. Those who preach the arming of the people should recognize this when observing how feeble were the results achieved in 1870–1. An

292

armed mob is a long way from an army in constitution, and it is cruel to hurl it into a battle.

Moltke's judgment was harsher still on the subject of the *francs tireurs*. They did not impede our operations on one single occasion but we had to respond to their provocation with bloody reprisals and this meant that our conduct of the war eventually assumed a brutal quality that could be regretted but not modified. The *francs tireurs* were dreaded by all the villages on which they brought down misfortune.

Strangely enough, a generation later another German general appreciated more accurately the work of Gambetta as well as the actions of the *francs tireurs*.

If ever, which heaven forbid, our German fatherland should have to suffer defeat like that suffered by France at Sedan, I hope that a man would appear who would be capable of sparking off resistance to the extent that Gambetta wished.

He still accepted the same thesis as Moltke on the inferiority of militia and improvised armies who had been deprived of the training and education that professional armies had received. 'If the army of the Loire was indeed the best militia that ever existed, its failure only confirms with greater force the superiority of professional troops and the vital importance of being prepared during peace-time.'

By contrast, he did not in any way share Moltke's contempt for the *francs tireurs*.

The forces led by Prince Friedrich Karl had behind them a magnificent campaign, achieved against an enemy who almost everyone before the war had thought would defeat Germany. That the will to win and the warlike ardour in their camp should have weakened once they faced a new enemy and a new war starting up immediately, can be explained with ease. We have shown how justified the French dictator was in his appreciation of this state of affairs and in his confidence in the calculations he had made on that basis. None the less, he made a very serious error in his method of waging war. The most dangerous thing for armies already exhausted by their efforts is national, guerilla war. In isolated, decisive combat, courage, discipline and trust still prevail. It is continual fighting that causes enervation, starting anew daily, producing a permanent state of tension in a brave and numerous populace, which rushes to arms to the last man. Its major elements will weaken, the more an invading army penetrates a country; the baggage becomes more cumbersome, young recruits show more independence and the lack of a sufficient number of subalterns to head operations is felt. All this helps the enterprise of the enemy free corps. But Gambetta wanted to fight a proper war. . . . It was only towards the end of the war that he wanted to pursue a wiser course. This is revealed in many of his declarations. In fact, from the start he tried to ignite a national war but this was only successful in a small part of the territory and to a limited extent. It is very difficult to create this kind of hostility where the inhabitants have not been driven to despair. For that to happen the people must possess special qualities and a particular civilization. I do not wish to revive a quarrel which some historians enjoyed because their passions overtook their desire simply to know. Could Gambetta have immediately begun a partisan war in the whole of France instead of assembling armies that were imposing in terms of their size but too inexperienced to win? Ought he to (as opposed to could he) have objected to peace as it was negotiated by the three Jules? Did both sides recoil from arming the people in the Clausewitzian sense?

I shall restrict myself to establishing that the traumatic experiences of the period of revolutionary crisis were forgotten by both sides, apart from the Prussians *vis-à-vis* number and conscription. The *francs tireurs* were often treated mercilessly by the German army, and in general they were put to death because they failed to respect the rules and customs of war. Despite their failure, they still left a memory of fear among victors, commanders and soldiers. The second part of the war, after the defeat of Napoleon's armies, often worried Moltke and Bismarck. Finally, the conflict remained within European traditions: a decisive campaign without overthrowing the European system of states degenerated into what seemed to be a fratricidal struggle to German eyes. When they returned home from captivity the imperial soldiers restored order and, with universal suffrage, the bourgeois republic emerged.

Terrible though it was, the First World War stopped short of arming the people – at least in Europe. Fixed front and trench warfare did not promote intervention by *francs tireurs* in the west. The regime of occupation behind the German lines was in conformity with international law. Propaganda, particularly that of the Allies, did have a role to play in 1917 and 1918 when deprivation, lack of foodstuffs and American intervention successively weakened the resolution and confidence of the German people. Still, the conflict was essentially national: each country fought for a cause thought to be its own, but none of them produced an ideology which they put into practice in the same way that Hitler imposed and applied his racialist politics throughout Europe.

Even the Russian civil war set armies against each other, although the Red partisans fought in territory occupied by the Red Army. It was in China from the 1920s onwards that Mao Tse-tung adopted the Leninist interpretation of Clausewitz and enriched and renewed the meaning of the Formula. In Europe after 1939, the encounter of two revolutions (Ribbentrop–Stalin), and then the alliance of one of them with the ideological enemy (capitalist imperialism), led not only to the extension of arming the people but also to the dissociation of two historical characaters, the *franc tireur* and the partisan. The same act also brought about civil war within the resistance.

2 Mao Tse-tung and the dialectic of defence and attack

I do not know if Mao Tse-tung read or studied Clausewitz. He quoted the Formula, referring to Lenin's pamphlets of 1915–17 where the revolutionary condemned social democracy and national defence. He employed a military vocabulary which often recalls the Treatise. But the expressions used – defence–attack, time–space, interior–exterior lines, destruction or attrition – belong to the vocabulary of his own time. Moreover, we would have to examine the Chinese characters to see if they correspond to those used by Clausewitz's translators who based their work on the Russian version.

Mao Tse-tung adopted Lenin's interpretation of an issue that strikes me as being fundamental to Marxist–Leninists although foreign to Clausewitz and his mental universe. Wars extend or represent the internal regimes of the states involved. When wars are waged by capitalist or imperialist states they express the injustices inherent in these countries. They either fight one another, in which case the proletariat's duty is to prepare the way for revolution, or they attack the weak, the poor and the colonized, in which case justice is all on one side, injustice on the other. As long as there is only one socialist state this process continues unhindered, on one condition: that war waged with a view to proletarian revolution, or revolution itself once linked with a war, will tend towards perpetual peace. 'As soon as humanity has destroyed capitalism it will enter a period of eternal peace and will not need war,' wrote Mao. 'It will not need armies, warships, military aircraft or poison gas. In centuries to come man will not know war. The revolutionary war that has begun is in part a war for eternal peace.'

A philosophy of history – the millenarian vision of perpetual peace which lies beyond the proletarian revolution and involves all mankind – completes Clausewitzian sociology. War reflects the policy from which it emanates. Moreover, Mao Tse-tung combined in the Leninist style two sociological theses. On the one hand, discrimination between just and unjust wars emerges from a simple analysis of class because the class struggle constitutes the basic root of all strife. The oppressed, the liberating class, will bring justice and the way forward in its trail. On the other side, the capitalist states became involved in a war to the death in 1914. In order to safeguard this entire system of interpretation it has to be admitted that war between capitalist states necessarily and directly follows from commercial policies within states. Mao wrote,

> When policy has reached a certain stage of development when it can no longer develop independently, it explodes into a war which raises obstacles on the political tracks. For instance, the semi-independence of China became an obstacle to the development of Japan's imperialist policy, and Japan entered into a war of aggression to destroy this 'obstacle'.

I can see no substantial difference between this 'explanation' of Japanese aggression and the Leninist 'explanation' of the 1914–18 war, although Lenin wanted to show antitheses of an economic nature between capitalist states and tried, in vain, to show that these antitheses would not permit compromise or regularization on friendly terms.

Mao Tse-tung's contribution to the synthesis of Clausewitz and Marx, or rather the transfiguration of Clausewitzian thought into a revolutionary doctrine, seems to me to be twofold, both political and military.

Clausewitz wrote that the political element, understood as the relationship between hostile states, does not come to an end when war breaks out. Despite the military, he taught that non-violent means must not be abandoned even though violence is being used. As soon as the war becomes a civil war continuing for years, even decades, the conjunction of war and politics reveals a clear character. War is waged with a view to the over-throw of capitalism and eliminating the exploiting class, thus converting the people to the socialist truth. How can a war, fought with such ends in view, not contain, even before victory is achieved and in order to reach such victory, psycho-political methods of persuasion and government?

The enemy troops belong to those same people who are the victims rather than the perpetrators of exploitation. The logic of civil war pre-scribes that they should be treated well, as Sun-tzu taught (and Mao probably knew his works better than those of Clausewitz). 'Treat the prisoners well and take care of them,' he wrote. And Chang Yu said, 'All those soldiers taken prisoner must be treated with profound magnanimity with a view to our making use of them.' Mao Tse-tung wrote: 'The fighters of the Red Army take good care of prisoners and give them a friendly send-off.'

A conceptual distinction arises from this example which I believe to be fundamental. The lone *franc tireur* makes a surprise attack on an isolated detachment, a marauder, a straggler or a badly defended outpost. He takes few prisoners because his method of fighting and living does not allow him to do so. The partisan serving a political cause (whether as a party militant or as an armed soldier) tries to win round his enemies and the majority of the population. To simplify matters, I am tempted to say that the *franc tireur* becomes the more partisan the more he embraces militancy.

Guerilla warfare, as understood in the eighteenth century and by Clausewitz, involved a high degree of mobility. This is a quality common to all weak detachments who take up a position to block a road or interrupt supplies and do not foresee the likelihood of pitched battle but, at most, quick manoeuvres aimed at striking a surprise blow. By its very nature the light cavalry must show 'a high degree of mobility during active combat'.

This type of fighting is imposed on irregulars as they have no arms, discipline or trained regular troops. From this results the principle, ordained by Clausewitz and adopted by Mao Tse-tung, of avoiding the tactical defensive as far as possible and of always reserving an escape route and retreat by splitting up. The combination of these two criteria – the theory of guerilla warfare with a theory of national defence – represents the partisan as conceived by Clausewitz.

The Spanish *guerrillero* and the Russian peasant emerged from the lands they were defending to fight the invader. Would it be correct in those cases to stress the extent of their political commitment? If we suppose that rebellion did not arise because of the arbitrary requisitioning and pillaging of land, then political commitment becomes confused with the defence of the country. I do not mean the nation but the country, the simple country of their fathers. The political commitment of the Vendéens was long thought to be essentially counter-revolutionary and therefore partisan (in the sense of being the expression of a political party). Modern historians, looking into the origins of the revolt, have given a more prosaic version that is less in keeping with the mythology of throne and altar (which the people had accepted themselves for more than two centuries and by which they continued to define themselves). None the less, the Vendéens remained linked to their own land. Clausewitz seems to have taken his interpretation of the war in the Vendée from Alphonse Beauchamp who described summarily the ways of this armed people who never left their homeland. Once the expedition was over, the Vendéen, whether victorious or defeated, would return to his farm and resume work in the fields. The behaviour of the Spanish *guerrillero* against the French army, and the Vendéens and Chouans against the soldiers of the Republic, confused political commitment (if that expression can be sustained) with the defence of their homeland and their customs. The partisan in the twentieth century, the ideal version that emerged in China, was recruited from among the peasantry, from among potential or active *francs tireurs*. By remaining mobile and avoiding prolonged confrontation with enemy troops he could gradually organize. A regular army emerged from the mass of peasantry provoking duality and rivalry between army and partisans in mid-war. It may also be said that in order to arm the people during the Chinese revolution the party encouraged the peasant revolt, and from these armed people there emerged at one and the same time a regular army and a partisan army both serving the same cause. The political commitment of the communist soldiers of the VIIIth Army was no less strong than that of partisans. Perhaps it was even stronger. At least the army performed as many and perhaps more political tasks than the partisans did themselves.

Mao's writings of the first period before the Japanese attack, like those of the later period, never distinguish between political and military action. Politico-military aims, i.e. taking power by total military victory, were summoned up and emphasized on each occasion. For war, as Mao like Clausewitz writes, constituted a totality governed by the ultimate goal that was to be attained.

Mao Tse-tung's arguments on the relationship between political and military tasks, between the operations of the partisans and those of the regular army, develop dialectically, but it is a dialectic that is probably traditionally Chinese and also approximating to Marxist–Leninist dialectic as vulgarized by Stalin. A middle way must be found between the two errors. Neither underestimate nor fear the enemy, do not sacrifice political work, the improvement of the lives of the peasants, agricultural progress, agitation and propaganda in order to rally the masses; but do not neglect the armed struggle, which in the last analysis is the decisive matter. Do not forget the usefulness of artisans or that the regular army will strike the final blow against the weakened enemy. This search for a balancing point between the errors of either side or between diverging tendencies reproduces, I think, the true nature of what might be called the Clausewitzian dialectic, though Mao Tse-tung probably never took the Treatise as his model. The magnitude of the success is not without the ingredient of greater risk. The wartime leader, isolated and ultimately responsible for everything, chooses a strategy suitable to his own confidence and the imperfectly judged facts of the situation. The three aspects of war – hatred, the free play of the spirit and understanding – each obey their own rules and none must be neglected. Theory must remain, as it were suspended between these things, these three gravitational centres. Mao Tse-tung, a war leader and not just a simple theoretician, says that there is a correct way without denying the risk of error. Whatever the circumstances there is a single way between Scylla and Charybdis, between sectarianism and dogmatism, between adventurism and defeatism, and between those who believe in a short war and those who see no hope of salvation.

In Mao's theory of the armed revolution the unity of policy and war goes considerably further than what Clausewitz wrote or even thought. During hostilities the army will pursue the essence of revolutionary policy. Political and military action are complementary although the pendulum is always swinging too far in one direction or the other. The duality between military objective and political aim which is equivocal in Clausewitz – because it varies with each war – gives way to unity. Destruction of enemy forces remains the objective (for once, in both senses) of war. But such annihilation is equivalent to the armed populace or the peasant working class united in the Communist Party taking power. Whereas in a classical war, victory, even when total, results from tactics (in the Clausewitzian sense), in civil war tactical victory cannot be distinguished from political ends defined by the taking of power. Both civil and imperial war achieve the same politico-military annihilation of the enemy.

The military part of Mao's theory of war seems to me to be more original than the political contribution. As I have presented it, the latter takes up the Leninist interpretation of Clausewitz. On the other hand, the military documents in particular sketch a theory strategic and tactical of both foreign and civil war.

I am leaving aside ideas which do not present a continuation of Clausewitzian themes (for example, the provision of bases for the partisan war). What strikes me is that Mao applies methodological rules which can be taken from the Treatise (although he expresses them in semi-Marxist vocabulary), and also that his dialectical expression of attack–defence, and strategic–tactical, seems to be an application to particular cases of the dialectic that Books VI and VII of the Treatise had tried to formulate.

Returning to the sequence of concepts: war constitutes a totality which is represented here by a war of the first type. The end and the end alone decides who will win and who will lose. Hostilities are prolonged but will cease with the annihilation of one or other of the belligerents. The revolutionary chief, said Mao Tse-tung, therefore resembled Clausewitz's description of a war leader, one who possesses the capacity of mastering the drift of events and turning them to his will, capacities which Tolstoy denied the hero. There is only one difference between the two although it is of considerable importance. The one believes in the inevitable unfolding of history whereas the other gives in and resigns himself to the outcome of chance. The one is a short-term realist who believes in permanent peace made possible by the intermediation of war. The other is a long-term realist and does not believe in any permanent victory over blind fate. Marx, Lenin and Mao wanted to reconcile Machiavelli, or Clausewitz, with Hegel. The reconciliation *post eventum* of the event with the destiny of reason justifies the same reconciliation postulated in advance by the revolutionaries. These dialectical acrobatics are haunted by the ghost of Stalin.

In order to understand this peculiar war – the Chinese revolutionary war – laws of war themselves, followed by laws of revolutionary war, and finally laws resulting from the peculiarities of China, have to be understood. Mao said that all wars constitute a whole, but detailed knowledge of each situation is the only way of reaching the right decision.

The laws governing revolutionary war themselves depend on political laws and the laws of warfare because, though war extends politics, it differs in the means and subject-matter at its disposal from laws bound up with the nature of the means.

The main strategic principle, which is also Clausewitzian in a sense, adds up to the dyad: conserve–destroy: destroy the enemy's forces and conserve one's own. The result is that in the last analysis the offensive which is aimed directly at destroying the enemy forces will finally succeed. But it is still suitable to distinguish between political, strategic and tactical offensives. In a political sense all revolutionary wars are essentially offensive because the revolution is itself offensive. The offensive looks for change; the defensive wishes to preserve the *status quo*, according to Clausewitz. Revolutionaries therefore promote and wage a just war. Reflecting on the European state system, Clausewitz was inclined to come to the opposite conclusion, namely that the assailant, i.e. the would-be conqueror, attracted the sympathy of others for his victim.

If the revolutionary war is offensive in political terms it normally contains a prolonged period of strategic defensive action, because the main reason a party remains on the defensive is inferiority of strength. In this case, the defence consists of sacrificing space to gain time. If we suppose that in the initial stage the revolutionary war does not involve anyone other than partisans, the mass of people will ally themselves with the defenders (theatre of operations, and the people, in Clausewitz's language). When the revolutionary party holds the two instruments, the party and the army, strategy first of all consists of co-ordinating the actions of each and later combining tactical offensive with strategic defensive. The Clausewitzian dialectic of defence and attack, which always struck military writers as bizarre, immediately interested the politicians, Marx and Engels. Every war spontaneously starts up the tactical method of multiple and sudden offensives within an overall policy of defence. This involves both refusing to be drawn into battle and the giving up of territory.

As a consequence of the transformation of the civil war into war against the Japanese invader, Mao Tse-tung, without renouncing the aims and conduct of civil war, presided over three turning points: from the partisan war against the Kuomintang to regular army operations, then from regular operations to partisan methods in the foreign war, and finally from these to regular operations against the invader. Up to the third and last phase of the general counter-offensive, partisan and regular operations were both characterized by mobility, but partisan activities kept what Mao called an irregular character for a war that was organized rigorously from a centralized leadership. This organizational distinction was accompanied by another distinction of military importance – that of dispersion and concentration. The operations of the regular army required a concentration of forces but not without a mobility equal to that possessed by the partisans.

Arguing in accordance with the concepts of classical strategy, Mao used two Clausewitzian antitheses: defence–attack and interior–exterior lines. According to the Clausewitzian formula, attack is directly aimed at destroying the enemy's armed forces. Defence serves directly to conserve force, but at the same time it provides an auxiliary means of offensive.

299

Mao Tse-tung concluded that the offensive was the principal method. The original is worth quoting:

The offensive, as the fundamental method of destroying the enemy forces, plays the main role, and the defensive, as a means of conserving one's own strength, plays a secondary part. Although more time is spent in practice during war on the defensive than on the offensive, the offensive still remains the chief means if we consider the overall course of war.

This quotation does not reproduce exactly those in Book VI of the Treatise but, despite fidelity to Chinese tradition, it preserves completely the principle of annihilation and thus the offensive as the ultimate and decisive form of war, without neglecting those periods when strategic inferiority necessitates defensive action.

According to documents relating to the civil war, the strategic offensive of the Kuomintang before the war with Japan developed on exterior or eccentric lines. In his study entitled *The Strategic Problems of the Revolutionary War in China*, Mao Tse-tung drew lessons from the five nationalist army campaigns waged against communist-held regions, emphasizing the fifth which forced the Red Army to seek safety in the Long March in order to transfer its bases towards the north. As a good Clausewitzian, Mao Tse-tung pleads the necessity of retreat and the abandonment of ground to a too-strong adversary, insisting on popular assistance and the need for positions from which the defender can gain advantage. In political language, to refuse to lose ground is 'ultra-Leftism'. 'In the event of a great enemy offensive the Red Army executes what can be called a "converging fall-back".' Clausewitz had also recommended the converging fall-back. In reply to the Kuomintang offensives, Mao Tse-tung preached action on interior lines and concentration of Red Army forces with a view to a unique and massive attack in one direction. He attributed the failure of the fifth counter-campaign to a misreading of this principle and to defensive action stretched out across the entire front which resulted in a dispersal of strength. Defence must not be passive; it leads by nature to the counter-offensive. It must not be adopted with a view to attack which will give the weaker party superiority on the battlefield as a consequence of manoeuvre on interior lines. Thus Mao rediscovered the secret of victory where Clausewitz, under quite different conditions, had placed it: 'Victory during the course of strategic defence depends essentially on the concentration of forces.'

The same dialectic of attack and defence, where the weaker party concentrates his forces during a strategic retreat, can be found in the relationship of exterior to interior lines. When the armies of the Kuomintang divided into several columns and attacked the Red Army's bases, the Reds fell back in order to gain strength and attack an enemy column or division so as to destroy it. But in a defensive campaign this partial attack could involve a manoeuvre on exterior lines against a fragmented part of the enemy army which itself operated, in an overall way, on exterior lines.

In later writings concerning the war against Japan, Mao Tse-tung combined, somewhat similarly, strategic defence and tactical offensive, exterior and interior lines. For example, in his study *Prolonged War* Mao sets out 'offensive operations for a quick outcome behind the lines', a lesson indispensable for the realization of a strategic plan 'of a long defensive war on exterior lines'. By using space, number and tactical means of destruction, the strategic defence gradually alters the balance of strength.

Then by taking advantage of all other favourable conditions over and above these victories, including modifications in Japan's internal affairs and the favourable international situation, we will be able to reach a balance of strength and superiority over the enemy. It is then that the hour of our counter-offensive will strike with the enemy being expelled from our country.

Clausewitz with greater effect talked of 'the shining sword of vengeance'.

Another example of the same thought processes is afforded by answering the question: Which side will encircle the other? Once more the answer lies in the relationship between the whole and the part, between the war and the extent of operations, between tactics and strategy. The enemy's concentric attack tended towards encircling the Red Army and its bases. But the Red Army responded on the offensive, tending to encircle, in a limited operation, one of the enemy's attacking columns. Each partisan base was encircled by the enemy, but overall the enemy armies were encircled by the Red Army and the partisan bases.

Does all this mean that Mao Tse-tung studied Clausewitz? I cannot say so. The thought processes seem to be the same for the simple reason that they reflect common sense and use the same concepts. In the middle of the object (war) is man as both subject and object because war is struggle and involves two enemies, each with a brain. Clausewitz and Mao Tse-tung both state that man decides all. Clausewitz did not ignore the role of *matériel* but he assumed hypothetically the same *matériel* to be present on both sides because that was the case in his day. Mao decreed 'man decides all' because the defender, i.e. the power in occupation, originally has material superiority during a revolutionary war. Civil war, even more than foreign war, obeys the annihilation principle. Enemy states coexist after and before a war, but between the revolutionary will to take over and the possessor's determination to hang on there is no compromise nor can there be one. Glory, or whatever, can be shared but power cannot be. Civil war thus brings about the identification of the military objective with the political end. Power belongs unequivocally to the revolutionaries when the enemy armies are annihilated. Of course, in its own way, power becomes, according to theoretical assumptions, the means to political ends. The construction of socialism, begun during the civil war, will continue after victory. To some extent this activity is presented in military language. The civil war is aimed at the enemy class, which must either be won over for a time or destroyed at once, but in any event eliminated in the end. Victory does not stop the destructive capacities of this class and the political war is carried on against them after power has been taken. However, Mao Tse-tung remained essentially Clausewitzian: the class struggle does not always have a warlike character even though it remains the root and foundation of all other struggles. The laws of war retain their specificity as against the law of the class struggle. All politics is struggle (at least this is so before the universal spread of socialism), but not all struggle is war even if the class struggle, inasmuch as it refuses the enemy his right to exist, is in every sense more pitiless than war in the usual sense of the word.

Some people are inclined to see Mao as anti-Clausewitzian, as being more in the tradition of classical Chinese writers or advocates of man-oeuvre. Certainly Mao sometimes quoted Sun-tzu, and inasmuch as a non-Chinese-speaking commentator, who is also ignorant of the military thought of classical China, can risk a judgment, he appears to have been inspired by certain aspects of the age-old wisdom forged by the oldest empire in the world. Besides, wars fought between conflicting states before imperial unification in some ways resemble the civil wars. It is only too easy to list the maxims of wisdom borrowed by Mao from the man called Sun-tzu: the importance of moral influence 'which sets people at harmony with their leaders'; 'treat prisoners well and look after them'; 'when you are superior by ten-to-one divide up and if you have equal numbers you can engage the enemy'; 'know the enemy and know yourself'; 'invincibility resides in the defence and the chance of victory in the attack, therefore defend when the means are sufficient'; 'those who are experts in military art make the enemy come to the battlefield and do not arrive there at the same time'; 'I concentrate my strength whereas he disperses his. I can use all my forces to attack a section of his'; 'just as water has no stable form, so there are no permanent conditions in war'; 'you must leave an escape route for an encircled enemy'; 'do not push on to the end against an enemy who is against the wall', etc.

None of these maxims seems to me to contradict the Clausewitzian spirit, except perhaps the last of them. Moreover, if Mao Tse-tung applied the maxim of 'not pushing on to the end' he did so, in all probability, only on a tactical level: in a strategic and political sense he did not abandon the annihilation principle which is first of all a means of modifying the ratio of strength and then concentrating on settling the matter. Those who oppose the two extreme schools, that of Sun-tzu (the school of ruse, deceit and indirect action) and that of Clausewitz (the school of brutal shock, attack at the strongest point and direct attack), reduce the teaching implicit in the Treatise to a simplified, parodistic version. The Maoist theory of prolonged warfare and strategic defence may be derived as much from Book VI of the Treatise as from the 'invincibility' of defence – the oscillation and complementary nature of opposed terms, the truth at the higher level that becomes falsehood at the lower, all of this Clausewitzian dialectic must be apparent to a reader of Mao Tse-tung who is acquainted with the German theorist.

I will go even further. The two Clausewitzian themes stressed by Lenin that of war and policy and that of defence and attack, were enriched by Mao, the latter more than the former. He enriched the former by requiring the same means (for instance, dispersion of partisans) to have both a political and a military function. Militarily, partisans cannot be seized yet they are ubiquitous, which increases their strength and gives the enemy the feeling of permanent threat. Politically, the partisan sets light to numerous hearths, and the fire, travelling from neighbour to neighbour, lights up the plain. He enriched the second by combining defence–attack and strategy–tactics with two others, namely exterior–interior lines and parti-sans and regulars. Moreover, he found a way out from the opposition between partisans and regulars when the Japanese army replaced the army of the Kuomintang in the part of chief enemy. The regular army fought in the style of the partisans.

Finally, and above all, the whole war is orientated towards the only possible conclusion: destruction of the enemy. The Clausewitzian concept, passed on through Lenin's Marxist translation, governed Mao's historico-political judgment at least until the victory of 1949. After that the victorious revolution can no longer be separated from the Chinese empire. The Chinese revolution remains an integral part of the world revolution but People's China continues and reinvigorates millenary China.

3 1813 – 1942: Tauroggen and Algiers – the resistance

The German army did not encounter a popular war in Europe that was as intense, revolutionary and lengthy as the one met by the Japanese army in China. Hitler's victories none the less provoked dissension and cries of conscience within the conquered lands comparable to those that occurred in the countries defeated by Napoleon's armies. Moral resistance, both passive and diffuse, was turned into guerilla or partisan war in some areas and at certain times. The partisans sometimes resembled the Spanish *guerrilleros* or the French *francs tireurs* of 1871. As regular soldiers sometimes fighting as irregulars, or as irregulars politically involved in the revolutionary cause, they were motivated beyond the liberation of territory.

Among western European countries only France had a government, legal in origin, which aspired to legitimacy yet refused legitimacy to those who continued the struggle. Legitimacy escapes all objective criteria the more it comes into contact with historical judgment. As regards legality, the Pétain government had all the signs of it in July 1940, whereas General de Gaulle was recognized by no foreign government and had no trappings of it. Clausewitz and the few Prussian officers who served with the tsar's army acted as patriots and obeyed their consciences. They did not imagine they were bearers of legitimacy, which at that time was incarnated in the state, or rather in the sovereign's own person. Thus the period 1792–1815 conserved some features of the *ancien régime* while prefiguring the age of nationality.

Officers passed from one army to another without any absence or betrayal of professional ethics. German troops fought at the side of the French up to and including the battle of Leipzig. Jomini, who was Ney's chief of staff for a long time, went over to tsarist service, and he instructed the heir to the Russian throne, yet he ended his days in France under Napoleon III. Nobles who emigrated fought the armies of the Republic, faithful to their sovereign if not to their country (but could they have regarded a regime that guillotined their sovereign as their fatherland?). The 'German patriotism' of the Prussian Reformers contained, in kernel, the nationalist passions of the nineteenth century. The psychology of particular peoples and national stereotypes held sway. However, there were two schools among Napoleon's enemies: that of the conservatives who refused to take Alsace from France in 1815 because after a century and a half the Treaty of Westphalia constituted a proper title, and on the other side, the patriots who invoked the new principle of nationality and longed for German unification. The one turned towards the past, thus impeding the flow of ideas and events, while the other prepared for a future without foreseeing the disasters that would result from the explosive mixture of conscription, industry and Napoleonic strategy.

At first Clausewitz refused to go to General von Yorck to negotiate the terms of a possible armistice; he knew what hostility desertion for patriotic reasons provoked among those who had continued to serve whatever their true feelings might be. He only took part in the last phase of negotiations when his interlocutor wanted him to be there. General de Gaulle immediately enlisted a few thousand followers and his few hundred officers against the troops who followed the legal Vichy government. He did not resign himself to the Syrian campaign but drew the British high command into it. In his own eyes he mingled France's destiny with his own exploits. So as not to abandon the spoils of victory after 18 June 1940, France would have to embody herself in him. In the same way he made civil war – which had not existed before November 1942 – inevitable. Instead of being grateful to the British who landed in North Africa without Free French participation (having learned a lesson from the experience of Dakar and Syria), he denounced a policy that prevented conflict among Frenchmen but would harm the 'legitimacy' of Free or fighting France.

If the regular French forces were divided into two camps by June 1940, one faithful to Vichy and the other to General de Gaulle, the first more numerous in 1940, but gradually absorbed by the second, then the American landing in North Africa in November 1942 turned the smouldering civil war in the Free French favour. Some generals and admirals were punished, unjustly in their own as well as the law's eyes, for hesitating at that moment when the fact became clear that they had to take sides. As long as the English and Americans found their interests served in a neutral Vichy and North African France there was a place for a 'third' who would not choose. In November 1942 this typically Clausewitzian common cause between the belligerents disappeared. The Anglo-American forces did not yet have sufficient strength for a landing in France, but they were sufficiently equipped to take North Africa which the French would not defend to the death.

The civil and military chiefs in Rabat, Algiers and Tunis had immediately to assume the responsibility that falls to a chief of state: to choose the enemy. General von Yorck had not even chosen the enemy by his own initiative: he had stopped fighting Russia who was deemed the enemy by his ruler. Admiral Esteva and Admiral Derrien had to abandon neutrality and choose the enemy. Was it to be the one suggested by their inmost feelings or the one the legal government had ordered them to fight, albeit passively? Neutrality was disintegrating. By defending neither the aerodromes nor the ports the military and civil leaders of Tunisia were putting themselves indirectly at the service of the forces of the Third Reich. This was decided by the tribunal that condemned those military chiefs to forced labour or imprisonment who had refused to choose the enemy and who 'betrayed' France by obedience.

I have put that word into inverted commas: the Tunisian leaders were in no way different from those in Algiers or Casablanca either by their virtues or limitations. Circumstances there permitted them to join the Allies in stages after a flourish for the sake of bravado. The decision in Tunis was forced on them by a German invasion. The cruel punishment these men endured was obviously a reflection of political justice, which is always more political than just. Was it necessary in both senses of the word? Only in the light of the tragic conception of history and the *raison d'état* implied by the legitimacy, retrospectively proclaimed and applied by General de Gaulle. In Tunis, in their own universe, the admirals believed they were innocent because they were obeying Marshal Pétain who had a mandate from the national assembly and to whom they had sworn an oath. In 1940 the dissidents had put patriotic duty above legality. By 1944 the Marshal's government no longer possessed any of the material or moral attributes of a legal government, but in November 1942 doubt persisted and a choice had to be made. But there was no doubt that the choice could only be justified by a political judgment. The governor of Tunisia, like General von Yorck, could neither follow his conscience nor his inmost wishes, but had to substitute himself for his enslaved sovereign and act as a politician according to the duties imposed on a military leader acting at the highest level. There is no reason to introduce Carl Schmitt's definition of politics to appreciate that at least in wartime designation of the enemy is the first task for that person who is responsible for the state. This choice, which was made in 1942 between two alternative camps, was the kind of thing that happens when war, in extreme circumstances, is pushed into its original state of being a duel.

But let us not go too far. In 1942 those who represented French authority in North Africa had, in effect, to join one or other camp, and refusal to do so – to oppose neither the Germans nor the Americans – was thought to be criminal. In fact, the Tunisians favoured the Germans, with whom they had concluded an armistice. But the Allies' side, joined by the French, contained a schism which events between 1939 and 1941 had made plain and which were manifested after the war. According to the Clausewitzian formula as understood by Lenin, with Stalin as a faithful disciple, on this point each state continued its policies in war but also by other means. From 1939 to 1941 France and Great Britain continued with their own imperialist policies. The USSR's policy was free from imperialism by definition because imperialism is the product of capitalism and classes born to exploit others. When Stalin and the communists said that the war had changed meaning in June 1941 they applied the logical consequences of their ideology: that the British and Americans could only get away from imperialism by an alliance with the socialist countries. Perhaps they were even prolonging their imperialist tendencies despite the alliance, but temporarily they fitted in with socialist interests.

In the language of Mao, the chief contradiction separated the invaders – Japan and the Reich – from the representatives of the working class – the USSR and the Communist Parties everywhere who had temporarily allied themselves with certain capitalist countries and bourgeois parties. In ordinary language, Japan and Germany were opposed by a heterogeneous coalition whose various members had a common objective, the military defeat in Europe and Asia of Hitlerian Germany and 'Co-Prosperity' Japan. Beyond their immediate objective the Allies did not pursue the same goals though they did not suspend political decisions during hostilities.

The French communists denounced the imperialist war in 1939 and only fully entered the arena in June 1941. The final government of the Third Republic had imprisoned some of their leaders while Thorez fled to the USSR. General de Gaulle freed the imprisoned deputies and took some of them up as ministers. But he had no illusions about his partners nor they about him. Gaullists and communists fought the war, but not the same war. The duality of the Maquis symbolized the duality of the policies pursued under the deceptive cloak of unity.

The communists had baptized the irregulars they controlled or led as *'francs tireurs* and partisans'. According to the vocabulary I have used above, these irregulars corresponded more to partisans than *francs tireurs*. I suggest that we should use the term partisan to apply to the irregulars whom a party organizes and to whom it accords proper revolutionary tasks. Clausewitz and the Prussian patriots wanted to put partisan warfare at the service of the established government and against the invader alone. The appointment or confirmation of officers by the king spared the people the temptation of taking up arms against their legitimate masters. The *francs tireurs* of 1871 resembled the *guerrilleros* of 1808 or 1809. They were from the people and obeyed a sort of instinct, defending themselves against the foreigner who sacked their country and ate into their meagre resources. The French maquisards of 1942 or 1943 who wished to escape forced labour also belonged to this traditional category. On the other hand, those maquisards who were led by Communist Party officials no longer corresponded to the historical notion of *francs tireurs*. Those revolutionaries delegated to fight with the Maquis went into the Maquis from a clandestine existence. They were urban dwellers, sometimes from the intelligentsia and often of working-class origin. They took over *francs tireurs* in order to recruit the first soldiers of a possible Red Army of the future.

In the west this takeover lasted for only a few months after the Liberation. Stalin did not intend to form a 'Red Army' in France or Italy while the German armies still resisted. Moreover, the intervention of British troops in the Greek civil war revealed that British and American leaders in the west had limits to their innocence and tolerance. None the less, the Maquis or resistance workers led by the Communist Party conducted for some months the policies that brought them to power in eastern Europe. This involved eliminating their enemies, especially the trade-unionists, who were rightly or wrongly accused of collaboration. Even the coalition government presided over by General de Gaulle had to take communist requirements into account in the execution of what was called the 'purge'. He forgot, and ordered people to forget, what had happened between September 1939 and June 1941. Could he have behaved differently once he had retroactively deprived the *de facto* Vichy government of all legality? From June 1940 General de Gaulle had pointed to the marshal's government as the chief enemy in the French civil war (the communists did not represent France and from the first he regarded them as virtual allies). Because of this he implicitly accused every member of the country's government, both civil and military, of treason and obedience to traitors. The judges refused to allow Pétain to be accused of signing the armistice, but the whole business of purging became a judicial monstrosity. Between

1939 and 1945 France had had three legal governments: that of the Third Republic, that of Vichy and that of General de Gaulle – the latter from a time that can be placed arbitrarily anywhere in 1943. The communists had refused to obey the first, the Gaullists the second, and the collaborators the third. Most Frenchmen had successively obeyed all three. Which orders given by the Vichy government ought they to have resisted? Who had taken initiatives or assumed responsibilities of their own beyond the limits set by discipline and restraint? Put in the pseudo-judicial form of *raison d'état*, there was a settling of accounts. The French purge will always have a hateful side because the Vichyites could not be confused with collaborators and because the judges, some of them Gaullists, others communists, did not pronounce their verdicts according to the same laws or in the name of the same ideals.

There was no such equivocation in eastern europe (in Yugoslavia and Poland) during or after the war. Tito's communists fought Mikhailovitch during the hostilities and wiped out Četriki wherever possible. Churchill also lent his support despite his own views on the kind of government the partisans would introduce. In Poland Stalin had wiped out some 10,000 officers of the old army at Katyn and allowed the heroic but senseless Warsaw rising to be put down. The war against the Third Reich, fought in alliance with some imperialist countries, afforded the chance of bringing the 'representatives of the working class', the Communist Party, to power. In a few years all those non-communists who had resisted had disappeared – to exile, prison or execution.

Comparison to the writings of Mao Tse-tung with Stalin's methods leaves no doubt as to what they had in common. Frenchmen, Englishmen and Americans had only themselves to blame if they felt they had been duped. It is true that according to the circumstances Stalin welcomed the encounter between two revolutions, or the relationship between Bolshevism and bourgeois liberalism and social democracy. But he himself had elaborated the theory of these tactical variations, as had Mao Tse-tung. It was a simple, even oversimplified theory which resulted wholly from Lenin's synthesis of Clausewitz and Marx. The historical root of all struggle is the class struggle. The ultimate goal of the fight waged by the proletariat is the elimination of class war. Meanwhile, the party that incarnates revolution and future peace must always decide which is the major enemy and then exploit conflicts between the different enemies to further its own cause. The Communist Party and the VIIIth Army fought the Japanese invader at the side of the Kuomintang, but they did not abdicate a jot of their autonomy and always kept in mind the future confrontation with their chance ally.

The Chinese communist army was indeed formed during the civil war. The party and the people were organized and armed and they took the power 'which is on the end of bayonets'. On the other hand, the parties of eastern Europe, except for Yugoslavia, were handed power by the Soviet army. The Communist Party had played a greater or lesser part in the resistance according to the particular country. The Polish resistance obeyed almost exclusively orders sent to them by their London government. In Romania there were only a few thousand communists in all. In applying the same ideological vocabulary to wholly different political situations Marxists–Leninists pursued a course of action that led to Stalinist paranoia. If a few hundred communists personify the proletariat, why should Stalin alone not become the Father of Peoples? Why should his sovereign will not be socialism, peace and liberty?

Let us return to the partisans in the Second World War: as resistance workers they were carrying on policies by other means, each group with its own policies and methods. After 1946, as after 1815, the two questions posed by Clausewitz at the beginning of Chapter VI arose: Is it militarily efficacious to arm the people? If so, can the political damage and the habits of violence and illegality which have spread be counterbalanced by the military benefits? In the eyes of a Liddell Hart (and he interpreted the Treatise in his own way) the desire for peace in the future ought to dissuade governments from inciting civil populations in occupied territories to take up arms in resistance. It was one thing to organize a collection of information, but quite another matter to organize a senseless guerilla war.

I shall not pronounce on this. In western Europe the resistance workers wanted to demonstrate something as well as to act. As part of their demonstration they aimed to be efficient militarily. And the demonstration itself served the political ends of reconstituting the community and legitimate power. The calculation of cost and return would defy the genius of a Newton or Einstein, and some of the variables cannot be calculated.

Perhaps the Russian experience should once again be exemplary. The partisans constituted an autonomous branch of the military organization of the Soviet Union with a central staff in Moscow subordinate to the Committee of National Defence chaired by Stalin himself. The committee co-ordinated the activity of the armies and of the partisans, the latter fighting behind the front. In the same way the notion of partisans turned out to be dissociated from that of irregulars. The guerilla or partisan war is a method of fighting that can be practised by soldiers or armed civilians or even, as Clausewitz thought, by civilians reinforced by army personnel. Simultaneously, the Russian partisans (though organized by the legitimate authorities) kept something of their revolutionary origin because, in most cases, command of the partisans fell to the secretary of the local party committee (or the chairman of the executive rural committee or the director or member of the bureau of a collective farm).

Of course, the contrary could be argued, that the leadership of the partisans guaranteed the loyalty of the people in arms to the government. It is a good enough argument, but in 1941, less than a quarter of a century after the revolution, the Communist Party remained a minority group which could still go underground, and which was under direct threat from Hitler.

On the one side, regular schools in Moscow, Leningrad and other towns trained soldiers or partisans. A *Manual for the (Partisan) Bands* included general instructions for the conduct of operations. Technical training was contained in radically different chapters. The partisan learned to destroy railways, bridges, aerodromes and to jump by parachute. He also learned how to procure false identity papers, how to behave in the event of arrest by the Germans and how to read a map and collect information.

The Wehrmacht in turn replied by elaborating a theory and practice of anti-guerilla warfare. Following the example of Manstein, who on 29

November 1941 published an 'Order for the Organization and Conduct of Anti-partisan Warfare', all armies took steps, which the Americans twenty years later tried to codify under the name 'counter-insurgency'. The Russian bands were answered by *Jagdkommandos* (flying columns) guided by native civilians who had been tried out when fighting against the partisans. The anti-partisan war, supplementary to total war, must have absorbed a large part of the Wehrmacht and the allied divisions.

Political effectiveness increased military effectiveness, which in this case was incontestable. In theory, according to the official instructions, the German army had to distinguish between suspects, sympathizers and partisans. Suspects were not to be shot because suspicion is only a state of mind in the accuser. Sympathizers fell into the same category as partisans if they had been of any effective help. If they conformed to four conditions, the partisans themselves became legal combatants: if they were led by a leader and his subordinates, if they bore a distinctive sign that was recognizable at a distance, if they openly bore arms and if they conducted operations in conformity with the laws and customs of war. Even if these conditions were met, partisans were not to be executed before being condemned legally and seen to be guilty of an established crime. In fact, the Russian partisans did not conform to these conditions and the Germans barely applied their own instructions.

Hitler waged war on communists and in any event wanted the political commissars to be eliminated. Units over which he and Himmler exerted direct authority were required to have racial contempt towards a population called inferior. Hitler's political conduct of Russian operations led to the spread of guerilla war which provoked anti-partisan warfare and reprisals. The logic of hatred provoked extremes. One historical entity, the racialist state, confronted another historical entity, although the latter held open the possibility of converting its enemy after victory. The racialist state intended that those they defeated should endure permanent serfdom.

4 The strange alliance: the formula turned upside-down

It has often been said that the Americans fought the last war only intending to overthrow the enemy's armed forces; this would be followed by unconditional surrender. Put in this extreme way the proposition is inaccurate. Roosevelt was also thinking about the postwar situation when he set himself the military objective of demolishing the Wehrmacht and the imperial Japanese army. His action was guided by two major considerations: not to repeat what seemed to him to be Wilson's mistakes, of taking on commitments towards the enemy state without destroying its army and of negotiating peace without securing the support of Congress and public opinion. The setting up of the United Nations represented to Roosevelt one of the goals governing the conduct of the war, and he discussed its methods of organization with Stalin during hostilities.

The American president implicitly interpreted the Formula in the way Moltke had done. Between the beginning and end of hostilities no political consideration should be allowed to compromise military decisions. Of course, the latter were not wholly self-contained. The diffusion of resources between the two theatres of war depended on the president who bore his military advisers' opinions in mind among a whole complex of factors. What I think still remains true among otherwise banal accusations made against the simple-mindedness of Roosevelt, Truman and Eisenhower is that they waged war as if the objective, the destruction of Germany and Japan's armed forces, would not create situations which diplomats would later hammer at in vain. It was the gathering of foreign ministers in London (between Teheran and Yalta) who traced the zones of occupation and thus the frontiers between the two Germanies. For political reasons (a pejorative expression), Eisenhower and Truman refused to accelerate the advance of American troops on Berlin and Prague.

The two atom bombs that were dropped on Hiroshima and Nagasaki in August 1945 seemed to extend the principle of destruction to whole populations and not just to the enemy's armed forces. In that sense they extended the aerial bombings of the British and Americans which had devastated German towns but which had failed to halt production substantially. In both Europe and Asia the USA stood against zones occupied by the Russian army obeying a Communist Party. The two Clausewitzian themes took historical shape. On the one side there stood a power possessed of a hitherto inconceivable destructive capacity, on the other there was an army bearing ideas, a regime and party which pitilessly eliminated its enemies one by one.

Does this mean that Clausewitz, the 'Mahdi' of Verdun and Flanders, espoused the doctrine that led to the Iron Curtain and the atomic bomb? Is he responsible for the bodies reduced to ashes or for the hero of the Bulgarian resistance who was hanged by his new masters? Let us leave these disputes, these accusations and defensive exchanges. Let us not rival in ingenuousness those Parisian intellectuals who even see in the *Phenomenology of Mind* seeds of the nuclear age. Clausewitz did not foresee the extermination of whole populations. For him the objective was to destroy the armed forces after which the victor would dictate the conditions of peace to the vanquished. The possibility of suicide which is implicit in a duel is perhaps present in filigree form in Hegel, but it cannot be easily traced in Clausewitz. As for the Americans, it took them years to surmount the antinomy between the capacity to destroy and the supremacy of policy – in the new sense.

The installation of Communist Parties in east European countries responded symbolically, as it were, to the nuclear explosions at Hiroshima and Nagasaki. MacArthur, who had had the honour of accepting the unconditional surrender of the conquered Japanese, was installed in Tokyo and the emperor himself came to pay homage to him. The navy and the air force had been destroyed, but a large army that could have resisted invasion was still in existence and some of its leaders wanted to continue fighting. But an island army cut off from its sources of supply becomes comparable with a continental power whose army has been decimated. None the less, the aerial weapon, the one favoured by the British and Americans, devastated, at least in appearance, the Japanese towns without at the same time destroying the Japanese armed forces.

Without excessive ingenuity we can discern common features and dissimilarities between the Soviet and American methods of fighting. But finally both sides proclaimed that the war was fought against the enemy regime and not against the people themselves. 'The Hitlers come and go, the German people remain.' Such a declaration inspired Roosevelt and Churchill when they were anxious about Stalin's real intentions. But the talks at Teheran about the division of Germany, and the Morgenthau Plan, clearly demonstrated the frivolous nature of those who conducted world affairs and the unreason governing those superior minds carried away by passion or asphyxiated by the smell of powder.

In both the east and the west the logic of total war put the peoples in the front line. Millions of Germans left their homes, fleeing in advance of the Red Army, and abandoning provinces that became either Russian (East Prussia) or Polish (east of the Oder–Neisse line). Millions more Germans sustained the violence unleashed by their fighting men to whom their supreme command accorded the age-old privileges of soldiery if only for a few hours or a few days. At the same time, bombs destroyed 70–80 per cent of each German city, and in one night Dresden, filled with refugees, suffered the deaths of tens of thousands. The distinction between civilians and military was blurred, and the laws of war, elaborated in Europe and codified from the eighteenth to the early twentieth centuries, were blown away in the tempest.

In applying his racialist philosophy in the occupied territories Hitler violated the laws that limited and guaranteed the rights of the occupying authorities. On their side, *francs tireurs* and partisans (the Maquis or underground in the towns) engaged in the war in ways that the German army regarded as being contrary to laws and custom. Clausewitz had not ignored this when he extolled the people's war. This kind of war unleashes hatred which is cruelly repressed. This exacerbates the cruelty of the partisans and the thing develops in a vicious spiral. Still, in the last analysis he thought that the desire for effectiveness would bring the authorities back to their senses. Organized in conjunction with the regular army or not, the partisans' war adds a further dimension to the battlefield and cuts down a barrier limiting the extension of hostilities. In this respect the Russians and the Western Powers differed only in degree. Churchill preferred a partisan chief who perhaps fought better and more often than a partisan chief who was anxious to spare civilian life; he preferred someone who would keep an eye on the communists and safeguard a certain kind of social and political regime for the postwar period.

In the same way the Soviets as well as the Western Powers added the political dimension to the war by refusing to treat with Hitler or any head of state who succeeded him. They wanted to annihilate the regime they considered to be responsible for the war. Therefore, they pursued a political aim beyond achieving the destruction of the enemies' forces and beyond the surrender of its government. The difference, and it was not small, lay in the methods to be used to install the regime that followed the one that was to be annihilated or condemned. Their own outlook obliged the Western Powers to tolerate in their zone of influence the activities of people supporting the other kind of regime. True to themselves, the Soviets did not tolerate the western democratic partisans. According to the classical exposition, in the west the communists demanded liberty in the name of liberal principles and refused it in the east in the interests of ideological coexistence. Mao Tse-tung's political objective (the gaining of total power by annihilation of political enemies) was achieved by the Communist

311

Parties of eastern Europe because the instruments of total power were handed to them by the Russians.

The failure of the Americans to grasp immediately the meaning of their opposition to the Soviets was demonstrated in two now-forgotten episodes which occurred immediately the war ended. The American secretary of state, General Marshall, was sent to China to forestall civil war and push for negotiation between Chiang Kai-shek and Mao Tse-tung. On the spot the American mediator rightly saw the impossibility of his task and the impossibility of a coalition government being formed or a compromise being worked out between communists and nationalists. States and peoples still survive after defeat or unconditional surrender at the end of war with a foreign power, but in the event of a civil war a party must win or disappear. In that sense civil war more than international war demonstrates the principle of annihilation: the police and the army have only to cease obeying the established government and join their new masters.

The second episode involved the attempt to merge the communists and socialists in the western zones of Germany. The Soviets imposed their own merger in their zone of occupation. In the west the communists took the same initiative: it was blocked by a social democrat, who had been in Hitler's concentration camps, under the initially indifferent eyes of the Americans.

Inasmuch as the global war, both during and after hostilities, was involved with civil war the American leadership was soon to discover that the end of military operations does not always settle the conflict. Nowadays, so-called 'revisionist' historians in America make Truman and his advisers responsible for the Cold War. The two notions of responsibility and cold war are so ambiguous that I shall take care not to participate in this uninteresting debate. What cannot be denied is that the Soviets brought with them a regime that accorded monopoly of power to one party and did not tolerate legal opposition to the existing government. The regime was gradually established in all the eastern European countries between 1945 and 1948 by a process of 'revolution from above', which was equivalent to the workings of civil war although the revolutionaries who had the instruments of violence from the start were able to dispose of their rivals without any fighting. The Americans could not use the atom bomb against the communist powers. During the war the Soviet army and the Communist Parties had laid the ground, and they immediately installed their own rulers. Having eliminated the fascists the Western Powers went on to hold elections out of which emerged legitimate governments based on democratic principles. Such was the scenario in western Europe. The Western Powers and the Soviets nowhere set up a common regime of occupation. In Italy and Japan the British and the Americans reigned alone. Korea was split into two zones that became two states.

It was in these circumstances that the Americans pondered about the relationship between war and policy. They debated the requirements involved in unconditional surrender and criticized the strictly military conduct of operations. In short, they criticized the practical implications of the Formula. The Korean War also taught them harsh lessons. Neither the North Koreans nor Stalin were led down the opposite path by means of nuclear weapons. The American expeditionary force provoked Chinese intervention by pursuing the North Korean army as far as the Yalu. The conduct of the war extended beyond the traditional framework: this was first to achieve a military victory and then to discuss political questions. As a world power, the USA ended up permanently enmeshed in a complicated network comparable with that which had involved the European states over the centuries. In the same way, the Formula ceased to have a militarist ring about it and became a banality, a truism or a simple instance of common sense. War constitutes quite simply a phase in the relations between states, a phase distinguished by the use of physical violence. What required analysis was not the Formula but rather its inversion. Do not the proletariat and its representatives wage a long war against the capitalist states or world imperialism? Do they not have the same aims both in war and peace-time? Do they not usually employ the same means, apart from the regular army they may occasionally send in? Are we to conclude that the society of states is becoming the universal theatre of civil war extending across frontiers and oceans? Once more, I do not believe that we should talk about *war* when classes or nations oppose and rival one another.

The two aspects of arming the people (the last recourse of an oppressed people as well as potential revolutionary insurrection) clearly faced Napoleon's contemporaries. The conservatives who feared that kind of war were perhaps more farsighted than the Jacobins or even the Prussians. Clausewitz does not pass any more judgment about this new phenomenon in the Treatise at least. He remarks without any enthusiasm that the war of people against people develops its own logic. Effective members of the regular army increase in number, territorial militias or reserves join the regular army and civilians join in the fighting. How could one or another of these things be abandoned without arriving at a position of inferiority?

Are we to regret that the 'warlike element' is growing stronger? Is this intensification of violence salutary or otherwise for mankind? The same question, when asked about war itself, would not produce a categorical response. Clausewitz himself concluded: let us leave that to the philosophers. Was he being ironic or serious? I am tempted to answer that he was speaking in earnest. Usually when employing the adjective 'philosophical' he meant analysis or conceptual definition. In this sense he regarded the Treatise as scientific or philosophical. Montesquieu, in sketching out the necessary relationships belonging to the nature of things, belongs to philosophy, and it is the same when Clausewitz confronts experience with the implications contained in concepts. This kind of philosophy left to Kant and Hegel the responsibility of making ethical judgments or ultimate historical explanations. But the principle of physical annihilation (the atomic bomb, armament of the people, the world class struggle) tends to demonstrate the permanence and ubiquity of violence. In this sense another question once more poses itself: Was it not historical reality itself which accomplished the inversion of the Treatise?

Part V
The Nuclear Age: The Gamble of Reason

The Neo-Clausewitzians

Professor A. Rapoport sketched out a comparison between Clausewitz and those he classed as being 'neo-Clausewitzians' at the end of the introduction he wrote to a selection of extracts from the Treatise. He put himself in their company, even adding a compliment or two to me, and reserving his sarcasm and indignation for Hermann Kahn. In what way is one 'neo-Clausewitzian'?

> None the less [my] 'world sociology' (for such is the ambition of the book) rests on the same Clausewitzian foundations: ideas are born in violence and relate only through violence which they will continue to do in the foreseeable future. The advice of those who do not accept this basic truth is useless or dangerous.

I do not subscribe to this last phrase: the hopes of peace-lovers or pacifists must not and cannot be abandoned. Moreover, the Clausewitzian fundamentals (to use Rapoport's expression) are confused with those of classical philosophy. It is only necessary to note that independent states contain a possibility of violence rather than that it must be permanently present.

If it is sufficient in order to be a neo-Clausewitzian to admit that the world is a collection of states, then I am in the company of many. Rapoport adds, it is true, that 'the objective of international politics is power and power is gained and maintained through violence'. These two propositions are unacceptable to me: violence or the use of force remain components of international relations, but they do not constitute their ends or their exclusive means.

I do not intend to discuss Rapoport's interpretation of Clausewitz and the 'neo-Clausewitzians' in the following three chapters. I should like to test the Clausewitzian thesis by applying it in order to understand the world today. An expression from the Treatise will be used at the head of every chapter and will symbolize each theme.

The 'deterrence cheque': what remains of strategy when the nuclear threat can do nothing other than deter, i.e. forestall its own use?

'War is a chameleon'. What of the diversity of wars and the complexity inherent in each one over the last thirty years, the initial period of the nuclear age?

'Policy or the expression of the spirit of the state': is it legitimate to imagine the state as an intelligent being and policy as being the product of that being? At the end of these analyses perhaps the reader will be able to judge which of us deserves the epithet 'odd', an authentic 'neo-Clausewitzian' or A. Rapoport.

Chapter 13

The 'Deterrence Cheque'

The destruction of Nagasaki and Hiroshima by atomic bombs marked the ultimate barbarous expression of the principle of annihilation. Retrospectively, the same events seem to lie behind a contrary impulse. Today it is sufficient to quote the Formula – war is a continuation of policy by other means – to receive the somewhat obvious answer, that nuclear war is no longer a continuation of policy by other means.

How could the destruction of towns and the blind extermination of human beings by means of thermo-nuclear war be regarded as a method comparable with any other of attaining the normal objectives of nation states? The effective use of these weapons would eliminate the significance of these relations, the human will-power, without which only brute strength remains.

The neo-Clausewitzian would reply sensibly to this simple idea that the threat of war, even nuclear war, has not disappeared since 1945. One aspect of Clausewitzian thought is succeeded by another: after orgies of violence politics again find some reasonable foresight. The spirit of moderation is born again from the excesses of the potential of destruction. Threat is substituted for action, deterrence for decision.

This answer leads in turn to another. The opposition to the two preceding propositions provides an outlet. If the threat is intended only to forestall its own execution, as theory pretends, is the result not a sort of contradiction or paradox? Can we always live on credit? The combat consists of honouring the 'drafts' or 'cheques' of diplomacy or strategy. How long can these 'bills' circulate and remain credit-worthy without being honoured? Must we suppose that an inter-state system that does not test the strength of the great powers corresponds accurately to this abstract notion of a monetary system with no sound base in some good merchandise? If we push the comparison could we not say that the absence of basic merchandise feeds permanent inflation and, in the other case, permanent warfare or anarchy?

1 Non-experimental analysis and synthesis

Clausewitz drew distinctions between the three constituents of strategic theory: knowledge taken from the natural sciences, conceptual analysis and the prescriptions or principles valid in the majority of cases.

According to the Treatise, theory is based first on knowledge borrowed from the experimental sciences. Although such knowledge derives from the nature of things it is better to confirm it by experiment. In fact, in their application so many varied circumstances exert their influence that only experimentation makes it possible to determine with any certainty the efficacy of the various branches.

This does not mean that the warlord must personally have detailed scientific knowledge of the manufacture and effect of arms. War is not made with saltpetre, copper or lead but with powder and guns. The warlord need not know how to make guns or maps. On the other hand, he must have a sense of space so as to use maps and the terrain. Similarly, he must study the various branches to order their proper use. Of course, the use of arms belongs to tactics rather than strategy. But when tactical phenomena change, strategic practices must also change to remain 'coherent and reasonable'.

Let us apply these common-sense observations to so-called nuclear strategy. The warlords, Brezhnev and Nixon, did not need to understand the workings of the atom and hydrogen bombs or of ballistic missiles in the scientific sense. They only had to comprehend the effect of each of these weapons and the speed or penetration of the different vectors (capacity of penetration, trustworthiness).

At this point the first difference appears between the weapons of the past and those of today: ours have never been tried in actual situations, only in tests. Theoretical physics, supported by tests, leaves hardly any doubt as to the destruction and loss of human life that would follow a nuclear strike at an unprotected town or population. Theory and experience combined show how many missiles may be needed to destroy other missiles hidden in silos and protected by a given thickness of cement. Knowledge of this kind is extremely complex. It is complicated in an extreme degree by the many variables that have to be taken into consideration: the mean distance that missiles of a given type have to travel to their chosen targets and the distance from which a nuclear warhead of a given explosive strength can destroy a silo of given resistance capacity, etc. Such knowledge possessed by experts who are not always in agreement is presentable in probabilist form: X missiles will destroy a fraction Y of silos with a probability Z. At the time of the rocket crisis the chiefs of staff are said not to have guaranteed the president more than the destruction of 90 per cent of the Soviet launching-ramps (in the event of non-nuclear bombing). The remaining 10 per cent served, at least, as a pretext for John F. Kennedy to oppose the chiefs of staff in their pleas for an immediate attack on the Soviet installations.

How far does today's situation differ from that of yesterday? Knowledge concerning weapons and vectors, taken from the natural sciences, is becoming increasingly complicated and impenetrable to amateurs. Whereas Clausewitz himself had authentic knowledge of the armament of his time (artillery, engineering, fortifications) the supreme leader of today, i.e. the chief of state, takes advice from military chiefs who, for the greater part, fall back on 'simplified knowledge', that which is indispensable at the highest level of the hierarchy of command.

Uncertainty is an added factor in this body of complex knowledge which has been simplified for the sake of the warlord. If it is a matter of the volume of destruction, uncertainty hardly matters as even 'weak' estimates are enough to inspire terror. It is not the same with the uncertainty that relates to the use of missiles against 'armed forces', primarily the enemy missiles. Uncertainty as to the number of missiles that would deviate from their trajectory and fall at a longer range than was estimated is important, because the imaginary attack would be aimed at destroying the enemy's power of retaliation. This uncertainty would weigh on the minds of leaders and would incite them to prudence, the more so as these arms, let us repeat, have never been tested in real fighting (if a nuclear attack against an enemy's nuclear forces could be called fighting).

This last example brings the conceptual analysis to an end as regards what the Treatise calls the analytical part of the strategy. In the same way that Clausewitz borrowed concepts from his predecessors and recognized analytical progress in them (base, lines of operations, eccentric or converging movements, superiority of numbers, mobility, requisitions, supply etc.). While rejecting theories based on an arbitrarily isolated element (that of supply in the writings of Bülow and interior lines in those of Jomini), the theoreticians over the past thirty years have worked out the conceptual system necessary for positing the various kinds of confrontation between the nuclear powers – first strike, second strike, action taken against forces or resources (or towns) etc. If we add two more – partial–total (or flexible/massive) and conventional weapons – nuclear weapons – the reader can easily imagine the number and diversity of models that authors, particularly the Americans, worked out in the first years of the nuclear age.

Of course, when the nuclear age began in 1945 two bombs were used. They forced a decision in the traditional sense of the term. The emperor, who had wanted to enter into negotiations for several months, was able to surmount the resistance offered by a military resolved to fight to the end, even to the point of the whole country being destroyed. The Americans for their part wanted to avoid landing a large army on the islands (which would ensure a radical but costly military victory) and appearing to negotiate, contrary to the doctrine of unconditional surrender. The atomic bombs allowed the two adversaries to achieve their respective goals: the emperor imposed his will on the fanatics who were committing national suicide and the president of the USA obtained formally an unconditional surrender, though also quietly allowing the imperial government to remain in existence.

What lesson could be drawn from this one example of effective use of the atomic bomb? At the time few newspapers or commentators bothered about the savagery of the episode. In any event, the attack on Tokyo with phosphorus bombs had caused no fewer victims than Hiroshima. The bombing of Dresden, which was filled with refugees, caused indignation in Great Britain (but only after peace had been declared). In brief, the events of the Second World War show that 'unthinkable' horrors take on the appearance of normality once passion is set on fire and massacre unleashed.

Reduced to essentials the events of 1945 remain conceivable because they belong to a banal area of military history. A town can be bombarded or threatened with bombardment until no stone is left standing, to force it to surrender without a direct assault. Apart from the intensity of the bombardment Truman used the same means against Japan as Bismarck had deployed against Paris in 1871. Let us remember Clausewitz's triple target: living forces, inanimate forces and morale. Bombardment attacked the two latter in order to reduce the cost of direct attack on the first.

However, it would probably be wrong to assume that the effective use of nuclear weapons would appear normal tomorrow even if it was limited to a few nuclear warheads of relatively weak strength. The 1945 episode occurred at the end of several years' pitiless combat. Government and people were accustomed to horror. Specialists had not yet grasped the gigantic step that man had taken in the art of massacre rather than war. A British Nobel prize-winner in physics could still write a book during the Cold War to demonstrate that the effective use of nuclear weapons in the event of war would not be decisive. Finally, the atomic bombing of 1945 did not constitute the execution of a threat or the failure of a deterrent. It constitutes the first and probably the last use of nuclear explosives as if they were no different from chemical explosives. If we are to suppose that nuclear weapons will be used through misfortune in the future, those responsible would not be acting with the same naïvety or inconsequentiality as they did in 1945. The deterrence theory cannot therefore draw any conclusion of practical importance from this one experience. It confirms the calculations of specialists. The memory of towns in ashes and the mushroom cloud creates only vague and diffuse dread.

Does this mean that crisis in the nuclear age is the equivalent of payment in specie in the classical theory? This formula, which I used in *The Great Debate* (*Le Grand Débat*, Paris, 1963), seems now to be more attractive than convincing. I shall not analyse again the nuclear crisis of the autumn of 1962. I believe there is no more to be said after T.H. Allison's book, at least not until the Kremlin archives are opened. The Cuban crisis lends itself to many interpretations: two states, both with nuclear weapons, were opposed to each another, neither threatening the other with the use of them head on.

President Kennedy had stressed that he would not tolerate the installation of offensive weapons in Cuba, which was just off the Florida coast. Let us leave aside the classical definition of offensive weapons. Strictly speaking, any weapon thrown or fired is offensive compared with weapons that clash or are used face to face. But at what distance do weapons now meet? No one doubted that ballistic missiles and warheads are, according to the American definition, offensive weapons even if, everywhere else, they have been used for a deterrent purpose (defensively). Let us also leave aside the politico-ethical controversy that emerges from the American refusal to accept Soviet bases in Cuba whereas the Soviets accepted those of the Americans in Turkey. By what right does the USA arrogate to itself the privilege of forbidding the government of an independent state to conclude a security agreement, and to decide what, in the western hemisphere, is contrary to or in conformity with the Monroe Doctrine? I shall simply restate what I believe to be a fact despite all the equivocations involved: by establishing launching-ramps for medium-range rocketry in Cuba, the Kremlin flouted a formal warning from President Kennedy: one that was meant to deter the Soviets from indulging in an enterprise that would be hazardous.

The warning given was nothing more than a vague threat. For motives unknown to us, Khrushchev did not take it seriously. Soviet engineers began work on the island without camouflage. According to American

320

writers, a series of accidents (and to begin with, the scepticism of the president and his advisers) delayed the moment when Kennedy was forced to take account of the evidence and to conclude that, despite what Gromyko said, the Soviet Union planned to construct a nuclear base in Cuba, meant for nuclear weaponry.

In this sense the stakes in the Cuban missile crisis were nuclear. This does not mean that the threat of nuclear weapons was used by either side. The chiefs of staff of the three services only studied plans for aerial bombing using 'conventional' bombs. The president decided to put the island in 'quarantine', i.e. he prohibited Soviet vessels carrying a 'suspect' cargo from crossing the American navy blockade. It was later that an ultimatum was received through an unofficial channel: the Soviet Union must withdraw its nuclear missiles and, *a fortiori*, any nuclear weapons it might have shifted there.

One of the two great powers certainly imposed its will on the other and did so by threatening the use of armed force. The confrontation passed wihout loss of face or at least with the appearance of good manners. The ultimatum never appeared in the press in the exact form in which it had been sent. As a counterpart to the withdrawal of the missiles, President Kennedy gave the promise never to attack Cuba, which allowed Khrushchev to say that he had achieved the goal he wanted: the guarantee of the island's security. At the same time he obtained a secret promise from Kennedy to withdraw American rockets from Turkey, which had been given several months earlier but had not been carried out.

The Cuban crisis occurred between nuclear powers in the nuclear age. Does this mean that it was the strategic equivalent of the 'payment in specie' of the classical strategy? In reality there *was* the threat of using nuclear weapons, made openly or in secret. One of the two Ks was bluffing and he lost his stake; the other was not bluffing and forced the enemy to respect the prohibition which he had refused by his *fait accompli* to respect in advance. In the absence of nuclear weapons the presence of a military base hostile to the USA in Cuba would have been tolerated even less by an American president. He would have made sure that it was dismantled by the same method – diplomatic action supported by veiled threats of the use of military force. The same method used in the pre-nuclear epoch would have forced the Kremlin to face up to the same choice: either open up the crisis (because of inferior strength in the locality) or give in.

In short, the most spectacular episode of the Cold War – the direct confrontation of two nuclear powers which unquestionably had serious consequences does not exclude in any way an interpretation along the lines of that afforded by classical diplomacy. The only blood that was shed was that of a U2 pilot shot down over the island. One of the two Ks, guilty of adventurism, reasonably accepted diplomatic defeat; the other took up the challenge thrown at him when his adversary refused to take his warning seriously, and by doing so achieved his goal, the return to the *status quo ante*. Deterrence had finally played a part but only through the mediating diplomatic crisis and the warning of armed reprisals.

If we look upon this prosaic version of events as being a likely or true explanation of the events in 1962, that have been viewed as the most dramatic in the last quarter of a century, why have there been so many controversies and commentaries, and so much passion? Today the answer strikes me as being both obvious and paradoxical. The main participants, Kennedy and his advisers, lived through these testing times if not in fear and trembling, at least in anguish and resolution, convinced that there was a risk, and a serious one at that, of nuclear war. Were they the victims of self-induced inebriation or of the analyists? Perhaps both. They were in any event the victims of that strange universe created by armaments which have no other function save to prevent themselves being used, and which can only fulfil that function because there is a chance that they will be used.

2 Fictional strategy: scenarios and models

In the autumn of 1962, when we learned of the installation of launching-ramps for medium or intermediate range missiles in Cuba, the American president had the members of the Presidium discreetly informed that there would be an aerial bombardment of these installations and/or the army would invade the island unless the base was immediately dismantled. Khrushchev and his colleagues, knowing that they were unable to offer resistance on the spot, gave way and got in return an undertaking from Kennedy to abstain from attacking the Castro regime – a promise that lapsed with Castro's refusal of inspection on his territory. These are the salient facts, briefly stated: the movement of ships and arms, and the public utterances.

Human events should not be confused with material facts and public words. The mental attitude of Kennedy and Khrushchev and their innumerable advisers, their intention and behaviour, are integral parts of the 'event' and determine meaning and importance more than the facts themselves. This gives rise to two questions: why was there an incontestable and uncontested fear of the apocalypse in the White House? And why did Moscow decide to give way?

I think that there is a simple answer to the first question: the American leaders thought of the international scene as part of a conceptual system that involved fear. By studying the American–Soviet conflict over the use of nuclear weapons American experts calculated that their use would be to deter the enemy (considered to be the Soviet Union) from military aggression. In the first phase the leaders of the three services – especially the air force – conformed to the simple doctrine that in the event of attack Strategic Air Command would reply immediately with a massive show of strength.

The Korean War had taught world leaders that there are more things in heaven and earth than in models, and this brought about, for the first time, a distinction between aggression against the state which had nuclear weapons and aggression against an ally of that state. This distinction immediately suggests two others: aggression perpetrated by the chief opponent, or one of its allies, against a major, or secondary, ally of the other side. A technical aspect can be added to the political calculation. The offensive and defensive uses of nuclear weapons are considered strategically. As in Clausewitz's day, the offensive consists of attacking the enemy on home territory and in this case the old rule relating to the priority of the enemy's armed forces continues to be applicable. It is therefore manifestly correct to guarantee the survival of strategic forces for purposes of reprisal in the event of an enemy attack. Analysis by itself prescribes prudence in keeping the forces for reprisal as invulnerable as possible by dispersing bombers, strengthening silos and increasing land transportation as well as that in the sea and air.

The analytical distinction between the first and second strikes, between action against armed forces and action against towns, emerged at the same time in the 1950s as oversimplification of the doctrine of massive reprisals, as a means of universal deterrence, gave way to a less coarse doctrine. It was clear that the threat of massive reprisals was sufficient to deter any state from attacking American territory. But once the Soviet Union possessed weapons which could reach American territory, it was unlikely that an American president would seek to punish them for, say, occupying the western sector of Berlin by unleashing strategic air power or ballistic missiles.

Leaving for the moment the subtle analysis by American writers of ways of adapting nuclear deterrence to non-nuclear situations, despite the destructive capacity of both, let us confine ourselves to the fundamental antinomy: if we agree to say that stability (the concept which replaces equilibrium in defence strategy) is a situation in which the combatants are definitely required not to use their weapons because each has the capacity to destroy the other, yet neither has the capacity to disarm the other, then stability at the higher reaches of nuclear warfare logically reduces stability at the lower level. From the abstract point of view, the combatants are less frightened of using classical weapons because they appreciate the consequences presented by using nuclear weapons.

At the time of the Cuban crisis in 1962 the president's advisers considered relations with the USSR in the light of such abstract arguments. They had drawn some conclusions from them as regards the defence of Europe, in particular the reinforcement of NATO's conventional forces. Such measures avoided the all-or-nothing alternative and made the deterrent of gradual response credible. Escalation which forestalls minor outbreaks of aggression would be risky if the atmosphere was really tense.

In 1962 analysts had not considered the situation confronting the president and his advisers. They had all hypothesized a military attack launched by the Soviet Union, i.e. a politically offensive enemy. Politically, the installation of a missile base in Cuba had offensive connotations, but the Soviet Union was not effectively employing any weapon and was answering a request made by an independent state as the USA itself had done on many occasions.

In the face of these unforeseen circumstances, either the president or his advisers applied the rather obvious idea of gradually stepping up their use of force as if this reflected the subtleties of nuclear strategy. But just as the Cuban operation demonstrated the distinction between the nuclear and classical type of relations between conflicting parties, the American leaders, imprisoned by their models, could not avoid being afraid. Why should the Soviets not use their superiority in conventional weaponry in a place where it would be as effective as that of the USA in the Caribbean? Thenceforth the analysts became actors, because the actors themselves behaved as though they were analysts, and both sides affected the outcome of the crisis by the interpretation they gave it.

Some drew the lesson from the crisis that no state can protect another these days by deterrence. It was a wholly unsuitable interpretation: Kennedy had not attacked Cuba and Khrushchev had not guaranteed the security of Castro's republic. Like a poker-player, he had tried a spectacular manoeuvre that could perhaps have altered the nuclear balance in his favour, or perhaps made the American president offer concessions over Berlin. The reader will find elsewhere hypotheses about the motivation of Khrushchev or the military leaders. Let us for the moment conclude that the Soviet retreat in 1962 in no way adds up to something which enables us to determine the value of the nuclear deterrent.

More serious is the question posed by two hypotheses – was it the Soviets' nuclear inferiority that determined the decision to pull back? In other words, would Nixon and Ford ten years later have dared to reply to the initiative of another Khrushchev in the same way and with the same degree of success? It has to be stated that no one can give a firm answer to this question, though personally I believe the answer to be yes.

The comparison between Cuba and Berlin is only useful for the purpose of model building. To the Soviet Union a nuclear base off the coast of Florida represented a symbolic victory on which the Kremlin could not normally have reckoned. The exchange of this base for a promise of non-aggression simply marked a return to the *status quo ante*, the failure of a bold enterprise. On the other hand the USA would have considered the loss of the western sectors of Berlin as a symbolical defeat of the first importance. Militarily it could be argued that the Soviet Union had the equivalent superiority in conventional weapons in central Europe that the USA had in the Caribbean. There was no equivalence between the withdrawal of American troops from a West Berlin occupied by right of conquest. The Soviets thought politically rather than technically. If they proposed change it was related to comparable entities: American missiles in Turkey as against Soviet missiles in Cuba. Did the Soviet leaders attribute their failure to their nuclear inferiority? I do not know, but some American analysts have said that they only encouraged their Soviet counterparts to catch up in arms. In any event, the fact is that since the Cuban crisis and probably because of the lesson learned from it, Khrushchev's successors have abandoned the blackmail and bluff that was evident during the years 1958–62 and at the same time they have deployed so many missiles that by 1975 they had more than the Americans and the Moscow Treaty of 1962 allowed them superiority in missiles and megatonnage. However, this did not rule out inferiority in the number of warheads.

The unfolding of the Cuban crisis contributed to the prestige of the analysts, but the Vietnam War had the reverse effect – perhaps as unfairly in the one case as in the other. Although journalists sometimes used the term 'escalation' to describe the behaviour of Kennedy over a period of days and that of Johnson over several long months, the similarity only existed in the minds of commentators. Kennedy prevented the military chiefs from acting in accordance with their own inclinations, namely of using force without trying first of all to achieve their aims in other ways. On the other hand, Johnson used force progressively, but without choosing between the two possible ways of looking at such escalation: the threat of going to extremes or the efficient use of escalation.

The idea of escalation, evoked by H. Kahn, is perhaps comparable to Clausewitz's *Steigerung bis zum Äussersten*, although Clausewitz never explored the exact meaning of this phrase (in his correspondence he did sometimes use it as synonymous with the French term 'jusqu'au bout' or 'to the bitter end'). More often he had in mind not so much the total mobilization of resources as extreme vigour in the conduct of operations, a vigour that led towards the natural goal of the struggle – a tactical victory eliminating the enemy and dictating the terms of peace. His frame of reference and model was Napoleon. Therefore, Clausewitz's *Steigerung* is not the exact equivalent of Kahn's escalation any more that his concept of 'absolute war' (the pure ideal type of war) is the equivalent of total war, an expression that describes certain wars that had occurred and were characterized by certain features such as the total mobilization of resources. Kahn, by his own admission, hoped in the book to which he gave the title *On Escalation* to engage the imagination of statesmen by speculating on imaginary circumstances, inventing incidents or crises and suggesting possible answers to each. In the end there can be no way, though, of knowing whether the strategists to whom Kahn addressed himself were meant to stay clear of the topmost rung of the ladder of violence or never to give the enemy the initiative or the last word whatever the degree of violence.

Kahn's book exhibited all the weaknesses of fiction strategy which in theory does not end up by making prescriptions but which in reality does more or less point to an attitude if not a doctrine. The book, of course, did begin by saying that it would not deal with the question I had posed: Who can deter whom, from what, with which threats, and in which circumstances? But a reader could still draw three lessons, one of them sensible enough (there are many ways for a state like the USA to defend its interests without recourse to weapons on a massively destructive scale) and two others that are quite dangerous. First was the idea of an enemy, i.e. the Soviet Union, that would be evil, and against whom there could never be sufficient means for force or ruse. Second was the idea of manipulating risk, the capacity of showing muscle in a lower level of crisis and if need be mounting the ladder further and using greater means if the lesser ones do not suffice.

Nothing goes to prove or even suggest that Kahn's strategic fictions affected Johnson's, or his advisers', thinking on the way in which the Vietnam War should be fought. What seems to me to be the case, apart from all the criticism levelled at this kind of pseudo-strategic literature, is that far from training the minds of leaders it tends to give them false ideas by presenting a world remote from reality.

In *On Escalation* statesmen are confused with military chiefs: they appear to be free at any moment to choose the means, and are always able to master violence and act reasonably in the midst of danger. In reality the Vietnamese experience has shown to men in positions of responsibility for American foreign policy the limitation on their autonomy both as regards public opinion and as regards the international system; the same is also true in respect of certain political goals, of weapons that cannot be used, and that the enemy does not fear for the simple reason that he knows they will never be used.

There is only an indirect and tenuous link between *On Escalation* and the Vietnam War. Besides, if the book is read carefully then it provides the lesson I have tried to elicit from it, namely that a particular war – of national liberation, for example – will be fought on the conditions and terrain chosen by the enemy and not by the United States government. In an interview with *US News and World Report* (7 June 1965), Kahn himself said,

> You can – and that is the case with North Vietnam – try to strike at the sanctuary which may or may not be a help. In most cases wars of national liberation will probably be fought in the interior of the country in conditions laid down by the rebels and, so to speak, their government.

Therefore, despite the legend, Kahn was fully conscious of the lack of continuity and the virtual impossibility of winning a military victory in Vietnam by the simple threat of arms that are not intended to be used.

But, on the second rung of the ladder, he takes as an example a press article from the *Washington Post* of 10 July 1964 which added up to a series of leaks and warnings to the enemy. The article set out in detail the fact that the Americans had drawn up a plan to answer each Vietcong attack on a South Vietnamese village with the bombardment or destruction of a village in the North. The article even foresaw that the murder of prominent local figures loyal to the Saigon government would be 'punished' in turn by the destruction of industrial installations in the North (the workers having been warned in advance so that they could evacuate the place). Kahn mentioned this theory without approval or criticism although, according to the 1965 interview, he was rather sceptical of its effectiveness, while making no political or moral judgment.

The bombing of North Vietnam marked the return to an old way of fighting – the devastation of enemy territory – something regarded by Clausewitz as being anachronistic or, at least, out of fashion. Both sides during the First and Second World Wars, and especially the Western Powers – resorted to this method of fighting with its twofold aim: either to reduce the enemy's means of fighting or to inflict such suffering on the population that the will to resist would collapse and the government would be forced to give in. Robert McNamara ended up convinced that the stepping up of the bombing reduced its effectiveness and that the bombing itself was not affecting the resolution of North Vietnam to help the 'rebels' in the South by sending in arms and soldiers.

Just as *On Escalation* did not dictate the conduct of the Vietnam War, the concept of 'compellence' did not supply anything other than a theoretical rationalization. In an analysis that was, as such, theoretically correct, T.C. Schelling applied to the strategy of the nuclear age the Clausewitzian distinction between attack and defence. His starting point was the thesis that diplomacy has become violent, i.e. that it contains, on a more or less permanent basis, the threat of violence, or uses that threat to impose its will on the enemy. Therefore, strategy is not reduced to the science of military victory but becomes the art of compulsion, intimidation or deterrence. In this art of 'the diplomacy of violence', or of violent diplomacy, he logically distinguishes between violence (which leaves to the other the responsibility and initiative for the act that will unleash punishment or reprisal) and what he calls 'compellence' which consists of forcing the other to do, or not do, something by way of threats. Deterrence maintains the *status quo*, while 'compellence' modifies it since it aims to make the other do something or cease to do something. Inevitably, the bombing of North Vietnam appeared to be the application of the concept of 'persuasion by violence', the degree of violence giving to the violence itself the character of a threat or a message. Besides, Schelling referred to the example of the reply to the attack on American torpedo-boats in the Gulf of Tonkin as well as to the bombing of North Vietnam. He approved of that reply without being sure of what he thought about the bombing.

The Gulf of Tonkin episode seems rather different today from what it did in 1965 when Schelling wrote his book. Today he would not write:

the next step was up to the North Vietnamese and the Chinese. The reputation of the United States for moderation as a civilized country and for resolution and initiative was at stake. However, the most important audience for whose benefit the action had been undertaken was the enemy.

Schelling continued with an almost aesthetic appreciation of the reply — the adaptation of words and acts by President Johnson to the attack on the American torpedo-boats. Schelling refused explicitly to analyse the political problems in Vietnam or South East Asia. But it was not difficult to read into this book approval of American action, as if approval or disapproval of the means could be separated in a diplomacy of violence from a verdict on the policy itself, i.e. the goals, if not the moral justification for the goals or means.

Some years later Schelling regretted even more his conditional approval of the bombing of North Vietnam. He noted that the American government itself had a poor understanding of what it was asking of the North Vietnamese. He implicitly defended Johnson against the reproach: how could the North Vietnamese satsify him when they did not know what it was he wanted? And he used various arguments, plausible in themselves and in some ways valid. It is less humiliating for a state (or an individual) not to cede too obviously to a precise threat by retreating or making the required concession. The use of violence or threats made with a view to gaining results from the enemy that the persuader has left vague means that such humiliation can be reduced or avoided. It is a fair enough proposition which a Sun-tzu could have made. But Sun-tzu had principles or moral views (however immoral others of them are). Schelling deals with events which are happening even while he is reflecting on the dialectic of the relations between states. He is anxious to rediscover in the nuclear age many of the practices of the past. After all, how can we read the following lines and feel at ease:

We may even suppose that the government of the USA did not know in any detail the degree of control or influence the Vietnamese government enjoyed over the Vietcong; we may even suppose that the North Vietnamese themselves did not know with any certainty the degree of influence they would have if they ordered retreat or sabotage of the movement that had their material and moral support.

We know now that the bombing campaign was preceded by a threat transmitted to Hanoi through Canadian mediation: unless Hanoi abandoned support for the Vietcong, North Vietnam would be attacked by American aircraft. Therefore, there was coercion by violence itself accompanied by a threat of stepping up the intensity of the violence. Abstract analysis of this 'violent diplomacy' without considering its historical, psychological and political context turns out, with hindsight, to be irrelevant. I am tempted to repeat Clausewitz's simple formula: 'the effect that a certain step will have on the enemy is the most relevant of all the factors in the action'. It might be argued that the destruction of a North Vietnamese village (possibly abandoned by its inhabitants) is equivalent to the murder of representatives of the Saigon government in the South. But this has to be argued so as to convince American and world public opinion.

Schelling's brilliant book occasionally touches on the traditional ideas that A. Rapoport would call 'neo-Clausewitzian', namely that the idea of victory inadequately expresses what a nation wants from its armed forces. Clausewitz had said with more clarity that victory only has tactical significance, and that at the strategic and political level both ends and means have to be considered. Schelling, like Clausewitz, distinguishes between brute force, which can be compared to the explosion of a bomb, and the intelligent, calculated use of force made with certain ends in mind. Again, like Clausewitz he specifically distinguishes between examples that prove and those that provide illustration. After all, in his Preface he confessed to having doubts about the bombing of North Vietnam. However, there is no radical difference between this kind of literature and that of the authentic neo-Clausewitzian.

This difference results first from the refusal to distinguish explicitly between war and peace or, in other words, the implicit assumption that the permanence of deterrent menace is the same as the permanence of war in its weakened form of armed observation. This will be discussed in Chapter 15. Then a neo-Clausewitzian would submit the use of scenarios and models to criticism comparable to that of Clausewitz at the expense of Heinrich von Bülow. Bülow foresaw that small states would be absorbed by larger ones as a result of the new way of fighting. Today others speculate about the levelling power of the atom bomb while yet others draw the opposite conclusion from the existence of nuclear weapons. Both are guilty of arriving at the same intellectual error: that of isolating the weapon and its use (or threatened use) from the spectrum of international relations, i.e. of getting the meaning of the Formula – which is more apt today than it was in 1827 – wrong.

3 Intimidation, deterrence and persuasion

Let us return to the origins of the atomic age. The USA possessed nuclear weapons, whereas the Soviet Union did not. But the two countries were not at war. Together they had just fought a war against the Third Reich, but they disagreed on the conditions of peace, and each imposed or promoted in the countries it occupied a government conforming to its own ideological persuasion. In Europe during the initial phase the nature of the regime dictated the diplomatic orientation. The peculiarities of the line of demarcation in the middle of Germany and in Berlin gave the impression of precariousness to the territorial status. Heads of state, journalists and professors saw American nuclear superiority as having a stabilizing function. As for Stalin's diplomacy, it exhibited extreme aggressiveness: the Berlin blockade and efforts to paralyse European countries through their Communist Parties or by propaganda campaigns, or the Stockholm appeal, etc.

When the USSR acquired nuclear weapons in turn analysts wondered what the conditions would be to restore American superiority in the maintenance of the deterrent. In the book that made his reputation, Henry Kissinger foresaw the tactical employment of nuclear weapons to restore to the USA the position it had lost, or risked losing because the Soviet Union now possessed nuclear weapons and vectors. No one followed his analysis, which he dropped anyway several years later, as all military operations showed the contradiction between concentrating troops using conventional weapons and the dispersion that was indispensable in the event of nuclear weapons being used.

On the other hand, the second problem – how to maintain the American deterrence against that of the USSR – brought about an immense literature without reaching a universally accepted conclusion. In asking the abstract question, under what conditions can one nuclear power deter another from aggression which does not directly affect it, there is a theoretical choice between several answers.

The first, which Kahn tended towards in his book on the thermo-nuclear age, emerges in the following formula: make the first strike credible. Starting with this imperative the 'deterror' must be able, if not entirely to eliminate the enemy's capacity for reprisals, at least to weaken it to the point where the chance of reprisal will disappear. A country would not risk complete annihilation by striking at enemy towns if it had already lost the greater part of its nuclear strength. The credibility of the deterrence would be even greater if the population could be given shelters in anticipation of passive defence and the building up in advance of the resources necessary for reconstruction after a possible nuclear war. The doctrine put forward by Hermann Kahn could be called 'deterrence by superiority' which is displayed in a unilateral capacity for the first strike.

Kennedy soon refused to embark upon this course (opinion was wholly opposed to shelters) and he chose another – deterrence by means of conventional weapons with an implicit threat of escalation. How could the USA convince the Soviets that it would sacrifice New York and Washington to save Hamburg? It is easy enough to answer: Why should the Soviets risk Moscow and Leningrad to take Hamburg? It was a theoretical dialogue and perhaps a meaningless one. Early in the 1960s the USA tried to convince its European allies that a stronger deterrent in terms of conventional weapons would add to the value of the American deterrent. The Europeans, and especially the French and Germans, would not accept this. The French, anxious to have nuclear weapons, imagined, and could only imagine, massive reprisals. The Germans in the front line feared that apparent acceptance of a limited war fought on their soil would only make it more probable, whereas the Americans thought that the ability to fight a war for several days or weeks without recourse to nuclear weapons would deter the Kremlin from any temptation to use its superiority in conventional weapons.

In the context of this line of thought westerners, including the farsighted like Liddell Hart, got into a panic over Berlin. Indeed, any military analysis of the situation of the former capital of the Reich ended with the unquestionable conclusion that the game was lost in advance. The Soviets could always rely on their local superiority and could always outbid their opponents' hand. Why did the Berlin crisis of 1962–3 end peacefully?

Of course, once again the events occurred in the heads of the protagonists in Moscow and elsewhere, so we are reduced to guessing. Let us assume, as everyone does, that the existence of these monstrous weapons weighs on the calculations of statesmen and inclines them to moderation. I wonder if, at the last analysis, the behaviour of states today cannot be interpreted in the traditional pattern. The USA and USSR, former allies, were not at war if we define war in terms of arms, the specific means. To take West Berlin (symbol of the common victory over Hitler) by force would have added up to a *casus belli* in any age. Why did some Americans fear that this would happen? Because they drew logical conclusions from abstract schemes, limited to the ratios of military strength. Berlin did not represent a stake that justified nuclear war but, as Berlin could not be defended in any other way, Berlin would be lost. The argument could proceed in another direction which is logically defensible. Berlin enjoyed maximum security because the USA could preserve it only by going to extremes.

There is a third and simpler argument which I prefer. By building the Berlin Wall the Soviets had achieved their first objective, that of preventing the emigration of East Germans to the West. They had a second objective in mind – that of consolidating East Germany and obtaining for it official diplomatic recognition. They certainly wanted to eliminate or reduce to the minimum western presence in the old Reich capital. But this goal, less important than their final ambition of stabilizing the territorial dispositions in Europe (something they could achieve without war), did not possess the value or urgency proportionate to the risks and consequences which would mean, at the very least, a return to the extreme tensions of the years 1948–53.

Khrushchev, perhaps inspired by the speculations of the Americans themselves, did attempt diplomacy by intimidation during the years 1957–63. I call 'intimidation' the attempt by vague threats to obtain from someone a change of conduct. He tried to intimidate countries that had allowed their aerodromes to be used by U2s and to intimidate the Europeans and Americans who refused to accept Berlin's change of status into a free city. The intimidation differs in degree from what Schelling calls 'compellence' and from what I have called 'persuasion' by explicit threat of violence or the 'progressive stepping up of violence'. The language of intimidation remained sufficiently indeterminate for Khrushchev not to lose face in this game of bluff.

The failure both of Khrushchev's intimidation by words and American persuasion through bombs perhaps evokes, in a new form, the Clausewitzian idea that it is easier to contain than to take and that the defensive is the stronger form. At the political level, or rather at the level of strategy by means of threats of violence, it is indeed easier to contain than to take. The offensive needs a comfortable superiority to win. On the other hand, on the level of the strategy of actual threats, the advantage lies with him who strikes first; who would, in other words, weaken the enemy's means of retaliation. However, the defender who has taken the precautions necessary to parry the enemy blows must not fear them. What stakes would make a nuclear exchange 'credible' or 'reasonable'?

The likelihood that nuclear weapons will provide a deterrent rather than a persuasive threat can be easily explained. First of all, it is defensive by definition, leaving responsibility for the initiative with the aggressor. Persuasion is offensive and forces him who uses it to honour his side of the bargain, to pay in specie at the victim's expense, and at his own expense if his countrymen rebel against these threats being put into effect. Persuasion by way of threats (what used to be called the ultimatum) worked over Cuba, but the precise threat did not involve the use of nuclear force. By contrast it involved payment in a specie that was perfectly feasible, namely the invasion of Cuba or the bombing of Soviet installations there.

The American theory of deterrence has remained, by and large, as it developed in the 1960s with two complementary factors, both of which are controversial. First, there is the place accorded to tactical atomic weapons in the panoply or deployment of deterrence and, secondly, there is the accentuation of the co-operation between enemies to avoid common disaster.

These two factors were present in the 1961–2 approach and they gained in importance as theoreticians developed the implications of the schemes they had constructed. Let us suppose that a theoretician argues about deterrence in abstract, strictly military terms. That is, if we return to the contrast mentioned above, let us suppose that the theoretician does not ask who can deter whom from what, with which threats and in which circumstances, but debates about how to secure the credibility of the threat of nuclear reprisals. There will be hesitation over using threats of increasing horror, however improbable they may seem by contrast with less apocalyptic but more plausible threats. The first alternative appears in the form of massive reprisals; the second in the form of stepping up reprisals. The first becomes the less credible as the nuclear powers become more equal.

Stability in Soviet–American relations involves, by definition, instability at the lower level where hostilities are conducted by means of conventional weapons. This sort of instability means that a state anxious for some gains will have little need to fear recourse to nuclear weapons which, *ex hypothesi*, it wants to avoid. Moreover, conventional weapons like tanks and aircraft mean that substantial results can be achieved by surprise within a few hours or days. They may even allow for a stake in the conflict to be seized because the aggressors would achieve a *fait accompli* at a blow and in turn become the *beati possidentes*. Those defending would need to resort to force to restore the *status quo*.

Some analysts therefore recommend the installation of tactical nuclear weapons, something in between nuclear and conventional weapons. It would be more sensible to refer rather to weapons used on the battlefield (weapons themselves being neither strategic nor tactical, but rather of greater or lesser strength). Here again, there is an antinomy – the emplacement of nuclear weapons in the very theatre of operations increases the risk of an escalation and therefore of deterrent action, but at the same time it blurs the distinction, in a situation where deterrence is not involved, between the various methods of combat. By definition, everything that increases the likelihood of escalation in advance also makes the limitation of the war, which would, after all, have started, more difficult. According to the geo-political position of their respective states, analysts worry over reinforcing the deterrent or underlining the line of separation between non-nuclear and nuclear combat.

This antinomy probably reflects a more fundamental antinomy involving the twofold aims that the analyst attributes, and cannot avoid attributing, to the participants. Clausewitz distinguished between victory as the natural goal of combat and the ultimate aim fixed by policy: the supreme rather than the despotic lawgiver in such matters. It is policy which, by virtue of the stakes and the passions involved, defines the necessary effort and energy needed and the resources which need to be committed. Even in classical strategy error would result from comparing war with a game. Thus Clausewitz did this when referring to military operations only in order to stress the reciprocity of action, when each side reacts to a living, intelligent force; and also to stress the part played by chance, the dialectic of one side anticipating the other and the advantage of coming second, i.e. of knowing the enemy's dispositions and intentions. He never presented war as a whole as in the doctrine of the Trinity or as assimilable to a game.

Napoleon threw the Grande Armée – or a grand army – into the Russian campaign with a view to imposing a certain peace on Tsar Alexander. There resulted two stakes: the Grande Armée and the possible victorious peace signed in Moscow. The heterogeneity of the tactical means and the strategic ends of the military commitment and the political objectives gave the war a structure radically different from that of a strategic game considered overall. The apparent or initial stake in a conflict continues in the same way as hostilities develop. This is not only because the military victor does not confine himself to his initial demands but because the stakes come to include the cost of the fighting. The defeated lose not only provinces but men, an army, prestige and their position in the international system.

The disparity between the stake and the winnings becomes striking once all distinctions between strategy (in the sense of the organization of armed combat) and policy (in the sense of the states' conduct) disappear by virtue of the supposed use of the nuclear menace. If we reason like Clausewitz, we must keep some proportion between political and military aims. But it would be difficult to find a partial aim that would justify the nuclear exchange. Doctrinaire Soviet thinking concludes that nuclear arms would only be used in the event of total and final war between the two sides. They add that this war is not inevitable, and doctrinaire American opinion concludes that a 'mastery of armaments' is necessary.

This notion is in many ways new, yet it is typical of the nuclear age in that it develops the simple idea of an interest common to the nuclear powers of not annihilating one another. The principles governing the Soviet Union and the USA may be quite different extraterritorially yet they agree on one essential point, that there should never be a nuclear war. From this vantage point American theorists have elaborated a calculus of co-operation between enemies to avoid escalation and to ensure the stability of deterrence which would be pursued at less expense.

The calculus of co-operation between enemies in a period of crisis is curiously combined with one of deterrence. In fact, deterrence, by threatening recourse to extremes, suggests imperatives which contradict those inspired by the need for enemies to communicate in order to avoid escalation. In Robert McNamara's day this contradiction sometimes took on a comic aspect if the observer could forget the realities behind these speculations. Sometimes the American defence secretary insisted on the Americans' capacity to destroy a large part of Soviet nuclear might to reassure Europeans, and by contrast he incited the Soviets to protect their ballistic missiles so that they would not be tempted to strike first in a period of crisis through fear of being caught unawares by a first American strike. The expression, 'you can't have it both ways' is the obvious rejoinder here.

Nowadays the anxious demand for a stable deterrent has won the day over deterrence by threatening escalation. In any event, the American leaders have accepted the thesis of equality, symmetry or equivalence. The first phase in the mastery of arms (arms control) after the defeat of Khrushchev's attempt at intimidation has involved the red telephone (direct and personal communication between enemies), the stopping of nuclear tests in the atmosphere and the non-proliferation treaty. The second phase ended with the Moscow agreement in 1972 when the installation of anti-ballistic missile defence systems (ABM) was abandoned and a provisional limitation arrived at of the number of authorized missiles.

The Moscow agreement marked the partial realization of projects drawn up some twenty years previously by American analysts. Since then these armaments have served only as agents of mutual paralysis – why not make do with a few hundred missiles instead of several thousand? Now that a thermo-nuclear bomb destroys an entire town, some hundred bombs of this kind will be enough to guarantee stability provided their vectors remain invulnerable. Arms control does not imply disarmament or even reduction to a minimum, but rather the implicit or explicit co-operation between enemies with a view to establishing a ratio of strength that will deter either from having recourse to war. With the exception of non-proliferation treaties which extend the principle of arms control globally, the control is only applicable to American–Soviet relations.

I probably expressed my views too sceptically in *Peace and War among the Nations*, not on the principle of arms control, but on the fixing of a ceiling for each side by treaty. This scepticism derived from two sources, one technical, the other political. Would the negotiators be able to agree in their calculations of equality? Would the pursuit of competition or rivalry be compatible with this kind of nuclear non-aggression pact? Or again, would it be possible to slow down or stop the arms race by a treaty that would not also provide a settlement of political conflicts between the great powers? The credit operations would, as it were, be suspended as unworkable because each side would rule out the possibility of payment in specie or real money.

4 Arms control and deterrence

What are the obstacles negotiators would have to overcome in order to conclude a treaty by which the antagonists would promise to limit their nuclear armaments and this alone? First of all, the antagonists would have to accept the same objective, stability through equality. Second, they would have to allow arms to each other so that neither would be threatened by the coalition of their *alter ego* and small nuclear powers. Third, since rivals continue to mistrust one another they must continue to put on a good show of force in the event of the agreement being violated or of any technical innovation. Fourth, either side must be sure that methods used to gain agreement would not put it into a position of political inferiority.

The first condition was met when Richard Nixon arrived in the White House. For several years in the USA the number of ballistic missiles in silos (Minutemen) had not risen beyond 1,054 whereas in the USSR it had risen rapidly – to some 1,700 in 1972. The Vietnam War dragged on, but public opinion in the USA was rebelling against this burden of imperialism. Congress would not have voted the credits necessary to accelerate the arms race which were only justified by arguments for the need for superiority. This superiority would be the equivalent of Soviet superiority in conventional weaponry. For technical reasons the thesis has now been abandoned: what can superiority mean, if it does not allow for elimination of a large part of the enemy strength? This is partly for political reasons, for neither public opinion nor Congress would have supported action aimed at gaining superiority.

At the same time, improved techniques overcame some of the obstacles the USSR put in the way of inspection. Satellites made it possible for the number of ballistic missiles to be counted without inspection on the spot. Other obstacles at least provisionally remain – how do we with certainty determine the number of multiple-head missiles and distinct trajectories (MIRV)?

The English and the French do not appear to have played a large part in the discussions. Whatever the judgment of their effectiveness may be, they do not substantially alter the quantitative ratio of the Soviet and American forces. As for the Chinese force, it does not affect calculations of number at this stage. Even in the least favoured of the hypothetical cases each great power still has a surplus or reserve of missiles.

In the final analysis, difficulties are concentrated on two points: first, how can equality be established as a fact? Second, would this involve changes in the nature of peaceful coexistence or the development of crises?

Negotiators and analysts renounced the word equality, which assumes that there is a similarity between the American and Soviet forces, whereas the technicians had occasionally chosen other solutions. To sum up the essentials crudely, the Americans had miniaturized their weapons and inserted into each missile several nuclear warheads (three in Minutemen II and ten to fourteen in the Poseidons), each with an explosive power of some dozen or hundred kilotons, whereas the Russians had missiles capable of hurling bombs of five to twenty-five megatons at their targets. The agreement presupposed accepting the equivalence of American superiority

334

in nuclear warheads with Soviet superiority in the number of missiles and overall explosive power, or 'megatonnage' in the current parlance.

This agreement about equivalence involved a decision to be made at first that was in some ways paradoxical, namely limitation of two of the sites that were protected by missile-launching ramps. The great powers had renounced protecting their cities, apart from their capitals and one missile site. The doctrine, conceived by the analysts, of *hostages* became reality. For the first time the Russians admitted that the means of defence could compromise stability as much as the means of attack. This concession was, so to speak, logically self-evident. When stability rests on the capacity of two countries to destroy each other's cities, the improvement of defence as much as the means of attack risks a destabilizing influence, or, in ordinary language, risks creating superior destructive capacity in favour of one or the other.

This view of arms control lent itself to criticism from those who had defended and illustrated the principle. Those opposed to this agreement posed the question: was it mad or common sense to use the common capacity for destruction as a foundation for peace? Mutual Assured Destruction: the initials spell 'mad'. Could not the same stability rest on a lesser capacity for destruction and a higher capacity for protection? Such stability achieved through the reduction in the number of hostages (or a developed ABM), though preferable in theory, was ruled out in 1972 if the negotiators at least wished to reduce it to print: the American ABM system which was in the process of installation was thought to be superior to the Russian system which was already out of date. On the American side, those in command had decided that abandoning or limiting the ABMs was the greatest concession that would force the Soviets to negotiate, and in particular not to increase their numbers of SS9s or heavy rockets capable of being used in a first strike to eliminate rockets that were hidden in silos.

Does the 1972 agreement prove the success of the doctrine of arms control? It is still too soon to be sure. Indeed, officially it has only a provisional character, which does not put an end to the qualitative arms race and requires another definitive and overall accord. The Russians and Americans subscribed to a parity which was by nature transitory, and involved, on the one side, more numerous nuclear warheads with, on the other, more powerful missiles. Brezhnev said that it was nuclear warheads that kill, not missiles, whereas any American president would answer that the day when the Soviets put multiple warheads on their heavy rockets they would have an overall superiority that would be contrary, by our definition, to stability.

The partisans of 'overkill' would then answer that such superiority would be fictional and without any reality. God is on the side of the big battalions at least when armies of the same kind meet. And what is the point of destroying for a second time a town or the same population? There is no need for 5,000 warheads, each with a potential for destruction greater than the Hiroshima bomb, to maintain parity between the American and Soviet forces. If this argument is pursued then the conclusion is self-evident that beyond a certain point equality or inferiority is meaningless.

Negotiators and analysts used the scenario method in turn to reply, adopting both technical and political calculation. According to the experts' calculations, development of nuclear warheads and missiles had reached a stage of extreme precision. The capacity to strike the enemy forces depends on precision, and therefore in 1975 theorists returned to the idea of a strategic anti-force, abandoned by McNamara and his successors. Not that the then defence secretary believes that the USA could be disarmed by a first strike aimed at bombers or land missiles. Technique does not permit a nuclear Pearl Harbor. But it would be simple-minded to foresee only the alternatives of apocalypse or passivity. As experts assert that anti-force action has been made possible by the precision of targets for missiles, theorists think up scenarios, and ministers and analysts take advice or lessons from these, which in turn create events, i.e. affect arms budgets and American–Soviet negotiations.

In January 1974 the American secretary of state put forward a doctrine by suggesting the possible development of a crisis. Let us suppose, he more or less argued, that the USSR takes the initiative in using nuclear weapons. Of course, this first strike would not 'disarm' the USA and would not remove all the means of reprisal. But would it leave us with 'selective' means of reprisal against the Soviet forces, which themselves would have launched selective anti-force reprisals, it would in this scenario be condemned to take the initiative by attacking cities, i.e. of provoking the total catastrophe that all wish to avoid.

This scenario presupposes the possibility of limited nuclear exchanges against precise targets in the manner of military exchanges in the past. The hypothesis includes the presence of statesmen who keep their heads and control events while nuclear warheads explode in the semi-desert regions of Arizona or Siberia. The participants on both sides – the president, the armed forces and their advisers, the Party's secretary-general, the presidium, the heads of the armed forces – increase the bidding and forget what the initial stake was. Instead of the dilemma of the prisoner there emerges the game of out-staring one another. Here, entente; there, bluff.

Do analysts or ministers sincerely believe in these scenarios? I prefer to be careful and not to pronounce on this. Many commentators answer without hesitation that analysts and defence ministers merely serve the military and industrial complex when they look for and find rationalizations of human folly in the accumulation of more and more costly weapons which are thrown away after a few years.

This is an obvious enough explanation, which perhaps contains an element of truth, although during the past thirty years several presidents of the USA have not hesitated to provoke unemployment in the aircraft industry by suddenly reducing orders. Moreover, each of the two great powers has not so much an arms industry as research teams. Neither of them can break such teams up without a guarantee that the other will also do so something that cannot be achieved. Researchers discover improvements in existing weapons if not new weapons themselves. These improvements may perhaps contain the balance of terror. All depends on the way in which the theorists understand such balance and how they are led to realize it. If the Russians and the Americans deliberated in the naïve manner of General Gallois then the world would be comprehended by small children. But the fact is that they think differently and that the analysts in the USA work out models of increasing subtlety while, at the same time, the technicians elaborate increasingly sophisticated weaponry. The models exist only in the minds of the analyst-strategists, whereas the weapons exist in silos or under water. Do these weapons result from models or from the irrepressible dynamism of technical progress? It seems to me that technical progress is the answer, but this also drives the analysts on to improve their theories by thinking up a use for the weapons which is as refined as the weapons themselves. Is it a material or effective use or is it merely a deterrent? No clear answer can be given. The deterrent uses risks, becoming an effective if not material use. In other words, we can imagine (as the scenario forces us to) that the capacity to manipulate risk affects the development of crises, and this capacity in turn depends on the means at the disposal of the two great powers including the means of selective attack in the event of a nuclear exchange.

It is a strange, Kafkaesque, surrealist literature which American strategists produce along with the qualitative arms race. Such literature achieves a total unity between policy (in the sense of external relations with other states) and strategy (conduct of the armed forces to attain the ends foreseen by policy). The latter does not involve the payment of real money, at least in terms of nuclear weapons, and thereby substitutes threats or offers to fight in the place of real fighting. But is this surrealist strategy in any way real? Has it really affected what happened as regards the outcome of crises or wars like those of Korea or Vietnam?

It is easy to say that the presence of nuclear weapons in the background of the diplomatic game haunted the minds of statesmen and forced them to act with prudence. Such a proposition is vague enough to be irrefutable. These weapons did not stop Stalin from challenging Truman with the blockade of Berlin and Korea (whether or not he wanted, or just tolerated, the North Korean move). Nor did they prevent Mao Tse-tung from sending volunteers to overthrow the VIIIth Army. Contrarily, despite the parity of nuclear forces, Nixon ordered the bombing of Hanoi at the risk of killing Soviet sailors. In short, are we forced to say that the ratio of nuclear strength has affected the outcome of crises? Or that it will affect the future course of events?

Some years ago I had private talks with Henry Kissinger about this, which were contradictory in content. Just when the newspapers announced the installation of a naval base for Soviet submarines in Cuba he confided to me that the parity in nuclear forces prevented him from resorting to the means tried in 1962. While he was trying to conclude a new agreement on strategic arms limitation in 1974 he said with the same sincerity and conviction that the ratio of nuclear strength had never affected the outcome of crises. In both cases he justified his action by alternating between incompatible justifications which in a man as self-aware as he probably betrays the uncertainties of the participants themselves. What could the Soviets do about Cuba and Hanoi without armed forces on the spot? Reply in the same way elsewhere? But where outside Europe (for, as I have pointed out, Europe has greater significance) is more important than a Caribbean base or a small South Asian people for those thinking in political rather than technical terms? The Soviets and the Americans supported their respective protégés during the autumn of 1973 in the Near East, but the Americans seem to have deterred the Soviets from sending troops even though the theatre of operations this time did not rule out local military action.

There certainly remains an equivocation in the circumstances created by the partial arms-control agreements. Do they not imply at the nuclear level a rupture or radical split between political rivalry and stability? Is this stability inconceivable in the long run without weakening political rivalry and without the rules of moderation laid down in the 1972 Moscow Declaration or the Washington Declaration of 1973? In short, obvious logic leads to the conclusion that the weapons to which only a defensive function is attributed (that is, to deter rather than persuade by threats) can be the object of limitation acceptable to both sides. Technique raises a first obstacle and compels search for parity rather than equality. Once this obstacle is surmounted, there is another. What remains of the deterrent value of weapons once stability, in the form of the guarantee of mutual destruction, is arrived at? Once more, analysts think up scenarios which are meant to give some credibility to the diplomatic (or political) use of the nuclear threat. But in their heart of hearts, politicians cannot fail to see that strategic arms limitation requires semi-connivance between rivals for the security of everybody.

Let us put this in dialectical form. The thesis is that nuclear weapons as tools which deter, rather than decide the outcome, lend themselves to forcing enemies to reach agreement rather than destroy one another and so impose common moderation. Disarmament would remove the premium on moderation, and an unlimited arms race would be useless, would cost too much and would suddenly perhaps create a *de facto* instability. The antithesis is that if recourse to the use of nuclear weapons brings about guaranteed mutual destruction, it ceases to be credible, and thenceforth the former method regains validity and only the ratio of conventional forces remains in any circumstance efficacious. The synthesis is that if one of the great powers used its local superiority in conventional weapons to harm its rival's vital interests, the rival would then feel, in an ill-defined but powerful way, that he had been duped or that the other was not respecting the unwritten rules of arms control. A pact based on millions of hostages requires that its signatories should in no circumstances have to make a fearsome choice in the end. Therefore, there is an unwritten promise of moderation accompanying this (a political promise) and analysts can accordingly imagine the deterrent use of weapons, despite the pact of mutual destruction, thanks to precison, i.e. to technical progress and a new version of the arms race or arms rivalry. Sisyphus then has to start pushing the rock uphill again.

5 The moral problem

Strategic literature, especially that of American origin, has been the object in the USA itself of many attacks among which the book by Philip Green seems to me to take first place. I do not intend to comment on the whole of his critique. I am interested in the relationship between Clausewitzian thought and so-called neo-Clausewitzian thought, in the changes occurring between the one and the other, in the lessons that the first can offer to the second and in the faults that the successors inherit from their ancestor.

Unquestionably, American analysts have adopted or rediscovered ways of arguing that are characteristic of the Treatise. They assume that war or, more generally, violence resembles not the explosion of a mine or the spread of an illness but a tool that the human will can use after reflection towards attaining its goals. In *Arms and Influence* T.C. Schelling even distinguishes between brute and intelligent force as Clausewitz did.

Does this premise of strategic reasoning falsify reality? Does it lead to errors in thinking? I am tempted to ask: which other premise do we use? Statesmen certainly resemble neither chess-players nor poker-players. The decision is not for one person alone conscious of his particular goals and their relative value. Historians rightly warn us against the perhaps inevitable tendency to confuse our schemes with the political process at the end of which a man or a group arrives at a certain decision of war or peace. But to reject the fiction of the 'rational participant' is to condemn oneself to despair. If we suppose that individuals, secretaries of Communist Parties or presidents of the USA remain, as Tolstoy wrote, the playthings of mysterious or profound forces, if war results from causes that are immanent in the structure of all societies, what do we do while we wait for salvation through revolution or death by the nuclear apocalypse? The doctrine of subordinating the military being to political understanding, which I discern in Clausewitz's testament, becomes necessary and even indispensable in the age of nuclear weapons. If we do not wager on reason, what do we wager on?

It may be argued that the reason on which I am depending goes no further than instrumental thinking and that this, by definition, formulates no categorical imperative or unconditional prohibition? All speculation on nuclear weapons sets itself *ex hypothesi* on the consent to use such nuclear weapons against civilian populations with, in certain circumstances, the monstrous resolution to use them in certain circumstances. The reasoning of nuclear strategists is essentially immoral because it accepts or conditionally resolves upon a perverse act, namely the killing of millions of human beings.

I recognize the force of this objection and to some extent it is irrefutable. Theologians have not managed to overcome the antinomy. Once these arms are in existence the threat to use them contributes to the prevention of war (at least great wars), but even the conditional threat of using them is no less monstrous than the realization of the threat would be. The doctrine of graduated reprisals in the form of using these arms against the enemy's forces and all the subtleties of nuclear strategy do not resolve the paradox although they weaken it. In multiplying the conditions for realization of the threat, and in shuffling responsibility for such realization on to the other, the doctrine of deterrence implicitly comes close to a rule often mentioned: 'No first use.' Each state possessing nuclear arms would promise not to be the first to use them.

So far no nuclear power has subscribed to such a rule, which would favour the great powers with their possession of both conventional and nuclear weapons. On the other hand, countries that only possess small forces which are bound to an anti-city strategy commit, conditionally, the worst crime. Whether or not we judge the probability of the crime taking place as being infinitesimal, nothing in the ethical debate is changed and the anticipated acceptance of such means violates the principles of armed conflict traditionally adhered to by the Catholic Church – the duty to save populations wherever possible, to keep some proportion between the fault (the aggression) and the punishment, to absolutely refuse to resort to certain practices like the indiscriminate killing of millions of men, women and children. Clausewitz left to philosophy the task of judging whether arming people, or war itself, is healthy or harmful for people. Strategists in our day do not act differently. They ignore the ethical debate that neither the pope nor Jean Guitton will resume. A strategy that even conditionally recommends a criminal act like bombing cities is itself criminal. Perhaps it preserves an immoral peace.

Once the ethical antinomy which none can resolve is admitted there remains the real problem: do analysts have any effect on statesmen? If so, is that influence favourable or otherwise to peace or the limitation of violence? That they have had an influence seems unquestionable to me, although no one can determine exactly how much. The various measures lumped under the heading of arms control have been thought out in advance by panels of professors and experts in universities and institutions christened 'think-tanks'. But the red telephone, limitation of nuclear experiments, and agreement on limitation of strategic arms are all rather in accordance with what the critics of nuclear strategic literature have sought.

These critics, Green as much as Rapoport, still formulate three objections that I shall sum up in this way: (a) The analysts present or suggest a terrifying universe with the USA facing a diabolical enemy. (b) They look for the means of avoiding nuclear war but they are still the victims of a military obsession. By multiplying intermediary steps between peace and apocalypse they end by describing a world where there is permanent war – in which, so to speak, violence never lets up. (c) They give a scientific aura, a fictional rigour, to implicit or explicit prescriptions that have no obvious authority. I believe that these three objections possess an element of truth, but that strategic analysis in the nuclear age inevitably has a semi-surrealist aspect because of the dialectic between technical and political calculus, the first based on objective probability, the second on subjective or psychological probability. By referring to Clausewitz we are helped in grasping the nature of the problem and the weaknesses inherent in any solution.

(a) The process of escalation results necessarily from the scheme of a duel between two wrestlers, each of whom wants to impose his will on the other. The de-escalation process may result from the victory of political understanding over passion, the maintenance of proportionality between stake and wager, on communication between the duellists, each hazarding guesses as to what the other wants, i.e. what he must fear and what he has the right to hope for. If the analysts posit a diabolical enemy in their calculations, or even if they suggest that reference should be made to the capacity rather than the intentions of the enemy, he will inflict panic upon himself.

Indeed, American analysts, if only as an intellectual exercise have at times presupposed that the Soviet Union or the People's Republic of China were looking for opportunities to do harm, inspired by the blackest of designs and ready to undertake the boldest gamble. Nuclear weapons do confer an almost unlimited capacity for destruction and the infliction of suffering. Analysts are not wrong in recommending the taking of precautions against a surprise attack and the protection of the tools for reprisal. But unless they are to condemn their own side to live in a climate of anguish the analysts must distinguish between the enemy they themselves have constructed, with a view to envisaging all possible hypotheses, and the real rival who is sometimes opposed but occasionally co-operated with. Of course, they insisted themselves on co-operation between enemies to avoid nuclear war. Have they insisted on co-operation between enemies in other fields strongly enough? I do not know. Everyone approaches the literature in his own way. Personally, I read into it the need for communication between adversaries with a mixture of promise and threats.

(b) Does the real world resemble that which presents such a terrifying image in *On Escalation* or *Arms and Influences*? To some extent there is a resemblance, but perhaps it differs on an essential point after all. When we read the analysts we sometimes have the feeling that there is no distinction but absolute continuity between peace and war – in other words, an inversion of the Formula. Clausewitz wanted policy to continue in wartime rather than violence to continue in peace-time.

Of course, it might be argued that the permanent presence of a deterrent implies that the threat of violence is permanent and that Clausewitz saw violence in threats themselves. In a sense the whole of this chapter can be reduced to a reflection on the consequences of substituting threats for combat or, again, the idea of credit without the payment of real money. The outcome does necessarily seem to me to be permanent warring. In fact, all this has happened as if the leaders of the nuclear powers had gradually got to know one another and, while taking precautions, no longer fear the sound of a thunder-clap in a clear sky. The Soviets also stress the other meanings of the Formula. War results from a political situation and the class struggle never stops, even though it does not always have the appearance of an armed struggle. Provisional or definitive peaceful coexistence is equivalent to the absence of armed struggle, i.e. to what we call peace. Arms create permanent risk, not permanent war. It is men not weapons that start wars.

(c) The third objection seems to me to be at once irrefutable and to a large measure unfair. In our age the Clausewitzian distinction between rational consideration and doctrinal teaching becomes both more necessary and more uneasy. We cannot derive a strategic doctrine from the angle formed by the operational lines. What doctrine can we derive from the explosive power of nuclear warheads? If we put forward the common interests of the combatants – not to go to extremes, to start with – we arrive at the advice given by McNamara to the Russians to guarantee the invulnerability of their force for reprisals. If we add to that end the idea of neither losing nor winning all the bouts we would have to try to keep superiority either at a nuclear or lower level in order to manipulate risk and burn the bridges behind us. These abstract precautions of a general character have been baptized 'theory' by many writers, whereas they vacillate between fictional strategy and doctrinal tendencies suggested by the model.

Here again I can invoke Clausewitz against the descendants of von Bülow and the system makers. As some dogmatists in the nineteenth century took the needs of supply as the basis for vast deductions including, in the end, permanent peace, so other dogmatists today base serene hopes on the equalizing power of the atom. Bülow saw the disappearance of small states over the horizon owing to the futility of resistance to the great powers. Contrarily, so some now see the equality of everyone thanks to the possession of an absolute weapon.

The argument begins with certain indisputable facts. A single atomic bomb of 20 kilotons destroyed the greater part of Hiroshima and caused the death of some hundred thousand people. A dozen strikes by bombs of some 100 kilotons would mean catastrophe even for a country the size of the Soviet Union or the USA. The threat of such punishment must have some deterrent effect on a country's leaders. The argument can be reinforced by rigorous presentation. Is it not in conformity with reason to admit a certain proportionality between the stake and the prize that a gambler will risk? The stake 'France' can be protected at a lesser cost in deterrent strength than the stake 'USA'. Three nuclear submarines carry a threat on the scale of the French stake. Thus that country becomes a sanctuary – meaning, in the language of the French analysts, that war may not cross her borders. Provided resolution is shown in advance the French government would be able to deter any aggressor.

How does one create the impression of inflexible resolution? The great power exposes a few towns, the smaller one its very existence. Which president of the French republic would press the trigger knowing that he would bring about the deaths of millions of Frenchmen in a few minutes or hours? If we cannot imagine a French president making the fatal gesture, why should a possible aggressor reckon that such a threat is possible? At this point theorists of the atom's equalizing power insert a supplementary hypothesis: to deter, the smaller power must always, so to speak, commit itself in advance and dispose of any escape route. Some generals seriously assert that by running down conventional forces France would make her nuclear deterrent seem more credible. Other analysts adopt the idea expounded by Schelling, without drawing from it any prescriptions – during negotiations he who acts like a lunatic sometimes wins points at the expense of a sane interlocutor. Between equals it is better to take the dilemma of prisoners as a model: the duellists will wager on implicit entente, on reciprocal confidence. A smaller power can only hope to bluff a great power, for he will meet death a second sooner than his opponent.

The French theorists of deterrence by nuclear threat do not convince all officers or overall opinion. They cannot convince any more than they can be refuted. France does not possess a common border with the USSR. But in present circumstances, which other state would strike at the French force? Does that force have the job of deterring the USSR from aggression when war is waged by conventional forces against the German Federal Republic? No theorist dares say this. As for nuclear attack against France and France alone, no one regards this as being plausible. So long as present circumstances pertain, so long as American troops are stationed in Europe no one can imagine a scenario in which the French forces would deter the

Soviets from launching an attack which had bypassed the American deterrent. At most it could be argued that the French force adds something to the effectiveness of the American force.

A dogmatic stand over the power of the atom to make equal, of 'sanctuarization', seems to me to be surrealistic, because it is based on simplified models abstracted from politico-historical circumstances. Let us begin by imagining a confrontation separated from the defined context of a country like France or one the size of the USSR. It is strangely simple-minded to imagine aggression answered by atomic attack or the peace of the sanctuary as the simple alternatives. Cuts with a scythe, salami tactics, moderate demands, the sudden occupation of frontier zones, banging on the table: neither aggression nor deterrence can be reduced to all or nothing. Of course, I do not really conclude that the possession here of a nuclear force by a smaller power would not influence relations with the great power. In all probability it would force the great power to exercise, at least, prudence. I claim that the pseudo-certainty based on the relationship between prize and risk (or wager) which in turn is based on rational calculation attributed to the possible aggressor, is worth no more than the dogmatism of the Maginot Line. How do we know if a great power could rationally attack a small one when the value of the small one cannot be properly calculated beyond a defined historical entity? This kind of rationality comes in the wake of Bülow, false science and false security.

The debate about tactical nuclear weapons involves uncertainties of the same kind. In the abstract, and even in the laboratory, theoreticians show or make it likely that simple and clear discrimination between conventional and atomic weapons assists communication between enemies which can forestall recourse to the extreme. If, once the fighting has actually begun, we can foresee the situation – i.e. after the failure of the initial deterrent – it will be correct to withhold the use of atomic weapons, an important stage in the riposte that will provoke a riposte from the other side. But, seen in advance, the risk of such a riposte itself constitutes a deterrent because our starting point is the hypothesis of a common will to avoid extremes in the person of aggressor and of defender. Thereby the immediate or rapid use of these tactical weapons brings us close to the thesis of massive reprisals, given that these arms raise the possibility of non-limitation. What can be concluded from this, if not that the same measures, though they are desirable inasmuch as they are deterrents, become deplorable on the hypothesis that they will have failed to prevent minor aggression? This contradiction, inseparable from the double goal of deterring all aggression and not creating automatic recourse to extremes, cannot be resolved. But general staffs have to choose some doctrine. Which one?

Let us abandon the terrain of pseudo-theory and consider the theatre of operations actually involved in all this, namely Europe. The two great powers maintain armies there on either side of the demarcation line. Each has a vital interest to defend for each has invested more than his capital in his prestige and moral authority. Neither side can here accept defeat, neither the USSR by allowing Hungary to be free or Czechoslovakia to be liberalized, nor the USA by making West Berlin into a free city. If the Presidium accepted or envisaged the hypothesis of a great war it would eliminate the western presence in the middle of the Soviet *imperium*. So long as such a hypothesis is impossible there will be no recourse to arms, not even conventional ones.

However, this does not make NATO doctrine indifferent. The ratio of military strength exerts a vague, not measurable, influence on international relations. The refusal to increase the volume of conventional weapons on the Europeans' part does not seem to prove inflexible resolution as harbinger of the use of nuclear weapons, except to dogmatists. This refusal shows rather the tendency of Europeans to leave to others (the Americans) the responsibility for defending themselves.

Of course, I cannot in a few words take sides in a debate that has continued intermittently for years. I suggest only a doctrine of common sense based on a distinction between theory and teaching. Theory suggests divergent prescriptions as the goals are incompatible, namely to deter minor aggression by means of nuclear threats, and yet to avoid escalation if fighting has started after all. There can be no solution that combines the advantages of contrary doctrines. Choice must be made in the light of concrete circumstances, with all the political and psychological data before one, rather than from a scheme of abstract reasoning. Whether they want to or not, analysts become inspirers of strategy if not strategists themselves. They should not be ignorant of this and should take it into account. Whether he is in heaven or hell, Clausewitz knows that he erred in repeating again and again that theory trains the minds of strategists without giving them a concrete doctrine. Most analysts leave this distinction vague, while some seem to be searching for a theory that will resemble quantum physics or economic equilibrium or, at least, Lenin's idea of imperialism. But all so-called theories of nuclear strategy are only in reality heuristic models constructed in imitation of games theory. However, these models rule out the rational solution in the stronger sense of the term, because neither the theoretician nor the players know the values attached to the various results as the game does not obey the rules accepted by the players. The beginning and the end are not fixed and the players would probably prefer to abandon the game if they could do so.

Differences between stake and prize, between the resources committed by each combatant and the consequences for them of losing or winning the game without violence, radically alter the strategic calculation. Indeed, the wager seems disproportionate to the initial stake. If Kennedy was right in thinking that his own measures were creating a one-in-three chance of war, was the consequence not an unjustifiable disparity between the initial stake (the presence of Soviet missiles in Cuba which did not greatly affect the ratio of strength) and the millions of lives that were being endangered? I think that Kennedy's calculations about the chances of danger were wrong. But suppose that he did measure it exactly. Ought he to have accommodated a Soviet nuclear base off the Florida coast? Perhaps the pressure of Congress and public opinion stopped him accommodating such a move. In any event Khrushchev substituted for the limited material stake (a few dozen missiles on Cuba) one that was immaterial and unlimited in the form of the credit of the American president. In the absence of payment in cash the gambler must guard his own credit with care. Without this, arms which only become redundant, become ineffective. When is this credit staked? The art of strategy in any case requires that the hazarding of it should be avoided and that the circumstance should be recognized when, whether desired or not, it is actually at stake.

Do nuclear analysts merit the title of neo-Clausewitzians? If we apply this honourable or shameful title to those who imagine that the European or global family of states is free from higher call, legal authority or physical force and therefore composed of autonomous centres of decision, then they are unquestionably neo-Clausewitzian. But so in this respect are all the classical interpreters of international relations from Thucydides to Morgenthau via Machiavelli, Hobbes and Rousseau. The more important and specifically Clausewitzian factor seems to me to be not only the idea that violence is a means but the thesis of heterogeneity of materials and product, of colours and the picture, of violence and its political end. Napoleon made a grandiose wager in Russia in the form of his army. If he had destroyed the Russian army, or if Alexander had signed the peace after the occupation of his capital on terms that conformed to the conqueror's ambitions, then Napoleon would have achieved his goal and a different political *status quo* would have resulted in Europe. Kennedy threw millions of human lives into the equation to maintain his credit.

In the same way analysts have rediscovered the intrinsic unity between warlike and political acts at which the Prussian general arrived only by reflection at the end of his life. The laws proper to the military instrument exist even in the intellectual testament of the theoretician. Rigorously speaking, there are also laws for the effective use of weapons, even nuclear ones. These scientific laws teach us how missiles can be aimed with precision, and the destructive range of nuclear warheads according to their power in kilotons or megatons. But if the American analysts had learned their way of thinking from Clausewitz himself they would, for reference, have taken as their starting point the two movements of ascent and descent, schemas of the logic of the duel in Chapter 1 of Book I which now seem to be expressed in the climb towards the inconceivable 'thermonuclear spasm' and the re-descent towards armed observation. Perhaps in a way Clausewitz missed posthumous destiny just as, in his own eyes, he did not live up to his own promise because he did not clarify two ideas derivable from his conceptual system – to make the stake and the wager proportionate and to maintain communication with the adversary so as to avoid errors of excess and default. If these maxims had dominated the minds of European war leaders after 1835, then the course of history would have been as different as the imagination could freely roam.

It is self-evident that the sceptic has a ready-made answer. It is not statesmen but war leaders who lead nations or armies. This is true enough, but if Tolstoy was right, if the use of nuclear weapons obeys the same blind forces as the ebb and flow of peoples, what hope for us remains? The anti-Clausewitzians who do not believe in revolutions, who wish to make combat into a game or a debate, remain, albeit unwittingly, neo-Clausewitzian although they are more optimistic than the others. They do not escape from the paradox of our age, which is that the possibility of unlimited violence restrains the use of violence without any threats even being proffered.

Chapter 14

'War is a Chameleon'

Let us take as our starting point the historicity of all wars and their internal complexities. Clausewitz emphasizes the relationship between the army and the people as one factor of this historicity, but he is not unaware of the others – the weapons, the scientific inventions, the organization of public authority, the nature of political organizations and the limitations and rules imposed on the family of nations.

The present family of nations has an original feature in relation to earlier state systems from which all others result. It extends over the entire planet and thereby includes basically heterogeneous states. This heterogeneity is apparent from all perspectives, so to speak: the dimension (small and large states, those with 600–700 million people down to those of hundreds of thousands), the culture, the degree of economic development (in terms of extremes of poverty and prosperity), ideological or constitutional principles of the state and structure of the military. Out of all these, three have a visible and immediate influence on possible or real wars: the plurality of weapons, the incompatibility of ideologies and the immense power gap between the two giant states and all the others.

The plurality of arms, especially of nuclear weapons, tends to localize, limit and moderate wars – at least in relation to the maximum violence that is abstractly conceivable. The incompatibility of ideologies tends to add the dimension of civil war to all armed conflict. The crushing superiority of the great powers forces states, which, while opposed to one another geographically, constitute a half-separated system or a sub-system, to create for themselves the means of pursuing an autonomous foreign policy by their alliances or their neutrality.

The combination of these various aspects within the same, single family of states produces consequences that are perhaps unprecedented. Some states have military machines out of proportion to their technical and economic potential, which does not permit them to indulge in prolonged fighting. One state can envisage several kinds of war. Another country will prepare for a war that it cannot foresee. In his historical survey Clausewitz enumerated 'half-civilized Tartars, classical city-states, feudal lords and commercial cities, eighteenth-century kings and the princes and peoples of the nineteenth century'. What would today's list consist of? Let us limit ourselves provisionally to contrasting the 'unthinkable war' (that which has not taken place and which would, so to speak, abolish time and space) with 'popular wars' which depend on terrain and duration even more than classical wars. Between the equilibrium formed by terror and individual terrorism fall those wars that are closest to those classical ones – the Indo-Pakistan War of 1971, the Six Day War of 1967 and those rapid wars that may or may not lead to the attainment of the political goal.

346

1 War of national liberation and revolutionary war

In thinking of today's wars in Clausewitz's terms we do not have mechanically to apply the concepts peculiar to the Prussian officer but rather to apply his method faithfully. Since war is a chameleon the first task of the statesman is to determine the proper nature of such and such a war that he has to understand or wage.

Journalistic language nowadays tends to confuse popular war, war of national liberation and revolutionary war. Rational means of classification require us to look at three levels, the political, the tactical and the strategic. The war waged by the Vietminh against the French in Indo-China was a war of national liberation in so far as all Vietnam, Tonkin, Annam and Cochin-China, etc. were 'colonized'. Perhaps parts of the population worked with and for the colonizers whether from interest, conviction or fear. Those who waged the war justly saw themselves pursuing the goal of national liberation – a legitimate end in the view of both sides who were involved. After 1945 the Europeans no longer believed in the legitimacy of their authority or in a civilizing mission.

The party fighting a war of national liberation uses psycho-political and military means at the same time, the military effectiveness of the former being no less evident than the psycho-political effectiveness of the latter. The notion of strategy has therefore to be extended, which, of course, conforms with Clausewitz's thought. The belligerent party attacks existing strength (or the armed forces), inert strength (or resources that can be mobilized) and will or opinion (of the army and the population). Strategy determines how violent or non-violent means should be rationally used in order to strike at one or other of the three goals – the theatre of operations, the colonizing power's territory or the United Nations. I consider this extension of the concept of strategy to be logical because Clausewitz, unlike most other military writers, does not distinguish between strategy and tactics by the size of the field of vision but through the nature of the means. Tactics involves armed strength and strategy is the result of combat. In effect it is strategy that fixes where, how and when combat or battle should take place, always in terms of the final objective of the campaign which is directly linked to the political ends of the war itself. We can speak of tactics of psychological, political and military operations. Strategy conceives of and combines the various kinds of operations in the light of the military objective and/or the political goal.

Is the military objective related to the political end by the conjunction of ends and means or through the objective of the war? In fact, in wars of national liberation, as the liberators themselves conceive them, the relationship between the objective and the end varies with circumstances. All depends on the colonizers' will to resist and on international circumstances. In Indo-China it took a Dien Bien Phu for the French government to resign itself to negotiation. That the Vietminh was communist-led caused the USA to give financial support to the war fought by the French Expeditionary Force before sending such a force itself nine year later. The French government decided to negotiate in Algeria though the guerillas had won no serious military victory. The 1954 Geneva agreement caused a second war. The Franco-Algerian agreement of 1962 was not respected but normal relations were established between France and the former departments which had gained independence as states.

The strategy of wars of liberation therefore differs essentially from the strategy of revolutionary war as worked out by Mao Tse-tung. Revolutionary war remains a war of annihilation. The enemy, the team or the government cannot surrender because they would then cease to exist. Surrender is by flight rather than by negotiation. The war of national liberation sometimes achieves its ends from one tactical military failure to another. It is these wars of national liberation that support the now obvious proposition that the partisans need only refrain from losing in order to win.

In fact, a whole set of circumstances promoted decolonization at the end of the Second World War. The European homelands emerged weakened from the storm. The two major powers, sometimes acting independently, sometimes as a team, supported the liberation of colonized peoples. The colonists had lost the prestige authority demanded and the colonized had lost the respect that brings obedience. Economic development enriched the homelands and made defence of the colonies costly. Economic reasoning reinforced the arguments of the idealists. Orators by the dozen argued the cause of the colonized in the United Nations. All European countries gave way. Great Britain started the ball rolling when Indian independence brought down the entire edifice and because the political class, either by foresight or resignation, enjoyed considerable freedom of manoeuvre as regards public opinion. In Rhodesia the white minority refused to give way to majority rule and proclaimed independence. Even with South African help this situation cannot in the long run survive.

France had difficulties when she entered the last stage of decolonization in Algeria where more than a million French citizens lived. The FLN or GPRA achieved their political ends without a military victory by aiming at the divisions within France, by putting pressure on international opinion and by the exhaustion of the enemy's will-power. Even then, it was relevant that the million French citizens had somewhere to go and that the Algerian insurgents had bases for their regular forces in Tunisia or Morocco. The global unity of the state system was symbolically expressed through the United Nations, a platform for orators and demagogues and a sounding board. All those who waged wars of liberation could find advocates in New York. The states that furnished asylum and gave help to the Maquis fighters escaped the censure of the lawgivers.

Guerilla warfare acquired a usurped reputation for invincibility though Clausewitz himself had warned against this. In reality he had only had direct experience of guerilla warfare with the Russian peasants in 1813. What struck him and what apparently inspired him towards writing Chapter 26 of Book VI was the scale of the forces kept by Napoleon in Spain. Historians still debate the effectiveness of the Spanish guerrilleros. Perhaps the Prussian people's refusal to obey the edicts of 1813 and take part in the revolt is to be explained by the passing remark that a nation of poor men used to work and deprivation will usually be stronger and more warlike.

Arming the people (which the patriots' Prussian adversaries called a 'legally proclaimed state of anarchy') is initially thought of as being an auxiliary means of national defence to resist the invader before it turns to

the political offensive and strategic defensive in a war of national liberation. It is politically offensive, in that the aim is to deprive the colonizer of
what he has. It is strategically defensive because superiority of arms and
numbers belongs to the possessor, the *beati possidentes*. But superiority in
numbers if not in materials risks being turned about in the long run by
tactics. The armed populace proclaim 'legal anarchy' in the service of
national liberation, i.e. they reject once and for all the existing legality and
treat those who obey it as enemies. They bring and proclaim their own
legality, i.e. the state they intend to set up, in which the liberators proclaim
themselves to be the incarnation of the first active element.

Tactically, there is no difference between the first phase of a revolutionary war (as with the activity of the Communist Party in China) and the
first phase of a war of national liberation. The difference between the two
comes with political circumstances. The first phase sets two claimants to
power against one another, recruiting within the same national boundaries from the same population. The second sets apart one party against
the colonial authority (in the ideal type of case) and another party
recruited from that part of the population which inevitably supports the
colonizer. Confusion between these two concepts can be explained for two
reasons — the tactical similarity between the two kinds of war and the
multitude of intermediate cases.

The Chinese Communist Party was fighting a proper revolutionary war
before the Japanese attack; although Mao Tse-tung recognized the semi-
colonial and semi-feudal character of the Chinese, he wished to liberate
them by taking power. But it does seem that the campaigns and counter-
marches that took place before the Long March involved two armed
parties in a civil war, both aspiring to government and both claiming to
represent the people. In Maoist terminology this civil war belonged to the
class struggle with the final victory of the world proletariat bringing
eternal peace. Unlike the French officers after the wars of Vietnam and
Algeria, Mao Tse-tung never separated China from the world context. He
took into account the help he and Chiang Kai-shek could get from abroad.
Looking at the overall situation he concluded that the partisans would
inflame the situation and gradually crush the Nationalist forces. Once it
was admitted that Chiang Kai-shek's plans were imperialistic then the
revolutionary war would become in part, at least, a war of national
liberation.

At the other extreme, the revolt launched by the Algerian FLN in 1954
was aimed at national liberation while using tactics similar to those used in
the revolutionary war. The Fellagha — partisan, or *guerrillero* (the name
hardly matters) — fulfilled the function of missionary as well as fighter: he
was a bringer of the Word as well as a soldier. It is true that he also used
revolutionary language with words that suggested a common front of the
oppressed against a common front of the well-to-do. None the less, the
FLN eliminated the Communist Party as an autonomous entity during the
eight-year war of liberation.

From the beginning the Chinese Communist Party waged a revolutionary war with a view to taking power and establishing a regime whose
initial ways of doing constituted, at the same time, tools for the struggle.
The FLN waged a war of national liberation from the beginning, without

determining in advance the kind of regime that would govern an independent Algeria, and without managing to create any military-political base within the national territory before hostilities ended.

Following Clausewitz's method, I have intentionally chosen two extreme cases: the revolutionary war which assumed the character of a war of liberation thanks to Japanese aggression and American support for Chiang Kai-shek, and then the Algerian war of liberation which assumed a revolutionary aspect because of the international nature of the ideas involved. The Algerian bourgeoisie did not take the initiative but joined the insurrection gradually. They did not supply the next class of politicians. Liberation in this sense brought social revolution. As a by-product of revolution, the war had involved substituting an independent Algeria for the French-Algerian departments. On the other hand, the revolutionary war in China was openly waged when Chiang Kai-shek broke with the communists. This did not involve the independence of China as the China of Chiang Kai-shek would have been no less nationalist than that of Mao but choice between two men, two parties, two regimes and two ideologies.

In abstract terms let it be said that Clausewitz, Marx, Lenin and Mao agree in their view that war only becomes meaningful in the light of politics and policy, in the circumstances that cause war and the intentions of the combatants. The Chinese reformers were divided into two parties, each one intent on a war to the death. Early on, a group of Algerian activists attached to the Nationalist Party instigated, with derisory strength, an armed struggle, despite the overall scepticism of nationalists.

The case of Vietnam suggests a third variant between these extremes. If national insurrection is led by the Communist Party then the war involves the two extremes from the beginning. It is revolutionary because national liberation would bring communists to power and install a regime approximating to the Russian and Chinese models. The aim it sets itself and the effective target is to achieve national liberation. As long as it attacks foreign troops it continues to justify national ideology and the partisans' aims that inspire some with enthusiasm and others with fear. The theory of revolutionary war developed by French officers was based on the similar tactical methods of modern partisan wars. These methods necessarily involve common features that are determined by the specific nature of the instrument. Militarily, partisans cannot oppose regularly led troops for long, since they have neither the weapons nor the organizations required. They fight a defensive strategy, whether they are on the political offensive (like the Chinese partisans) or politically on the defensive (like the Tyrolese against Napoleon or the French resistance fighters against Hitler). According to the consecrated formula, they give up space in order to save time, avoiding battles and fighting only by surprise when they are sure they have the advantage in numbers and the nature of the terrain. These elementary rules do not have to be learned from books by the partisans any more than by the *francs tireurs*; they are culled from experience and common sense, which teach what it costs to ignore them. In order to make these ideas clearer let us now abandon the equivocal expression 'partisan war' and instead use the concept of 'partisan tactics'.

These tactics obey the principles laid down in Chapter 26 of Book VI of the Treatise, but Clausewitz's two functions take on a different aspect with each case. As long as they are few in number the partisans are less anxious to strike at the enemy than to gain new recruits and win sympathy – especially help from as much of the populace as possible. Clausewitz's metaphor, which was adopted by Mao, illustrates what is involved in the partisans' fight against their enemy: are the fires in the hearth to be extinguished one by one before China is ablaze? Or, by contrast, will the incendiarists oblige the 'forces of order' or 'the enemy side' to run vainly from one hearth to another to extinguish the flames?

The fight for the population (of which the struggle of some to extinguish, and others to set limits to, the blaze constitutes the first phase) can be found on all occasions when the people are armed, whether in popular resistance to an invader or in revolutionary war or in a war of national liberation. The ways and means of this struggle obviously vary according to circumstances. In 1870–1 the Germans took hostages and inflicted collective punishment on the villages. In short, they did not try to convert the mass of ordinary men to their cause but rather to mobilize ordinary men in favour of their side, men who were not traitors or heroes but prepared to leave the job of fighting within acceptable limits to the professionals.

In revolutionary wars or wars of national liberation this simple type of fight for the population continues to play an important part. The forces of order or repression must give villagers a minimum sense of security without which they will submit alternatively to one side and the other, liberated by the partisans at night and then by the army during the day. Nevertheless, there exist extreme diversities. The struggle for the population between the Vietminh (or FLN) and the French showed that the Vietminh (and the FLN) could convert the masses and even minorities hostile to the cause of liberation, if not those hostile to the method used the regime installed by the liberators. In terms of a wider perspective, the French could not convert the Vietnamese or Algerians to their cause.

In Asia the French remained obvious foreigners and conquerors. In most cases the expeditionary forces' officers were not fighting against communism but for the retention of empire. Of course, the French promised in their turn to give independence to the associated states between 1946 and 1954. None the less, the troops of these associated states were still fighting on the side of the ex-colonists. Ideologically, the advantage lay with the partisans.

In Vietnam the partisans always possessed politico-military bases and rapidly organized three kinds of unit – the regular unit, territorial militias and auxiliaries. After 1950 the army was strong enough to bring off offensive operations on the borders, and by 1953 or 1954 they could beat the best expeditionary force battalions in pitched battle. The Vietnamese war of liberation of 1946–54 developed on the same lines as the Chinese revolutionary war, involving joint action by regular troops trained in the hostilities and partisans. Among the latter some were stationed in barely accessible regions and others hid clandestinely as peasants living in villages.

In Algeria neither the guerillas of the *djebels* nor those clandestinely in the towns became invincible in the sense that even if the fire is put out a single spark can rekindle it. France could not win decisively nor take the army back home. If the FLN attained its political aims it failed to achieve the goals that its military campaigns were meant to gain. The French became tired of an unending war and General de Gaulle became convinced that retreat to the metropolis was in the national interest.

Until 1974 those who were inconsolable pointed, in the contrary sense, to the example of Portugal and her empire. In fact, as an underdeveloped country Portugal resisted ten years longer, under an authoritarian government. The myth of the multi-racial Lusitanian empire collapsed at the same time as the Salazar government.

2 Classic war: military decision and political aims

The war between India and Pakistan in 1971 illustrates the transformation from national insurrection to classic war in a global situation. Pakistan consisted of two provinces, 2,000 kilometres apart, with the seats of central government being in the western province at Karachi and that Islamabad. The eastern province represented part of Bengal where a language (Bengali) was spoken quite unlike the language of the capital (Urdu). The authoritarian regime led by Marshal Yahya Khan organized free elections that gave 167 of the 169 seats in the eastern province to the autonomist party led by the first head of the state of Bangla Desh, Sheik Mujibur Rahman. After the failure of negotiations between him and the head of the state of Pakistan, troops from the western province hit hard at the autonomists, especially those who inspired resistance. It seems that the Muslims of the west, who were powerful warriors, were determined to decapitate the Bengali movement which was also Muslim but of a quite different character. The response to repression was the beginning of the revolt. On the borders a few Awami League militants proclaimed the new state of Bangla Desh with the agreement of the Indian government.

From then on two things could happen: either India would intervene, as so many other states have done in the past 25 years, by supplying and arming the partisans or she could send a regular army across the border to settle things in a few weeks. Pakistan could not reinforce the 70,000 odd soldiers she had sent to the eastern province to restore order. Guaranteed complete superiority, India could choose whether to liberate Bangla Desh in a war 'of aggression' (by crossing frontiers with regular armies) or to support the partisans, perhaps for years. Mrs Gandhi took the expeditious method, which was less legal but more humane. Within three weeks the Pakistani troops had been forced to surrender. The Awami League became the party of government with Mujibur Rahman leader of the new state, and the Biharis who had fought for Pakistan now replacing the freed Bengalis in the camps.

Nothing could be more classic than this war which, in its way, was a total surprise. India had complete liberty in the east, provided that China was paralysed. The alliance with the Soviet Union (a security alliance conforming to the old European tradition) guaranteed Chinese neutrality. Committed to Vietnam, the USA, whether hostile or not, had no one to fight the local battle. To quote Clausewitz, blows levelled at the economy or lines of supply act slowly, whereas blows levelled at the enemy's armed forces produce immediate results. The 1971 war – the third since 1948 when the two states were born – followed that of 1965 over Kashmir,

352

which was both local and limited and had a classic form. Two armies collided and then the government of the victor gained its objectives which, here, was not territorial conquest but the dismemberment of Pakistan, or rather the independence of the eastern province under the name of Bangla Desh. The diplomatic game that preceded, accompanied and followed the short war again underlines its classic character. The alignments show no trace of ideological considerations. The representative of People's China argued not for repression but against the dismemberment of Pakistan, i.e. for Marshal Yahya Khan, China's ally and the intermediary between her and the USA. The USA made a symbolic protestation against the military operation by sending an aircraft carrier. The USSR defended the cause of the freedom of peoples. China defended the territorial *status quo*.

War of this kind within a sub-system might be compared with a local war within the European system. The great powers tolerated a war between two European states provided that the victory of one or the other would not endanger the overall balance of power and that the victor would refrain from widening his claims beyond the limits custom had fixed. Despite the United Nations, things today are hardly different. Two other considerations weigh on the deliberations of those who decide to take up arms: the need for a rapid decision, and the frequent inability of the belligerents themselves to produce the arms they use to provide the field of battle with reserves and produce from their factories.

The Indo-Pakistan War of 1971 seems to be an almost unique global war: it was substituted for a war of national liberation according to partisan tactics and it definitely provided a solution to the problem. In this sense it differed from the Israeli war which involved victories of annihilation in 1956 and 1967 but without attaining the political solution that was sought by the victorious army.

In 1948, 1956 and 1967 Israel set herself the ultimate task of achieving peace, which meant recognition by her Arab neighbours. In 1956 Israel evacuated territories occupied during the war. In 1967 she refused to do so and set up her line of defence on the Jordan and the Suez Canal. In 1967, no more than in 1956, did she obtain peace and recognition. Clausewitz tells us that Napoleon would have signed a victorious peace at Moscow if he had destroyed the Russian army. If this was right, the verdict was based on the customs of the age. Napoleon, with an army reduced to 100,000 men, could neither force the tsar nor hold the country some hundreds of miles away from base. Today the destruction of an Egyptian army means nothing. The Israelis send back prisoners some days or weeks after the cease-fire. The Soviets replace the lost equipment. After two or three years at most, the Egyptian army will turn out to be better than before. In 1973 the Israelis discovered a truth as old as the world: defeat is a good mentor, victory an enervating drug.

Compromise was made more difficult by the disharmony between the situations of the belligerents. Within her 1967 borders Israel could not lose a battle without losing the war and even her existence. If the Syrian tanks had broken through the line of resistance in 1973 and emerged from the Golan Heights anything, including the destruction of the country and the state, could happen. On the other hand, the Arab states can lose battles without losing the war. Even after losing the war, i.e. accepting Israel, they are not in danger of extinction. Defeat for Israel would mean the death of the state, perhaps the death of part of the population.

The Israelis are therefore inclined, according to military logic, to extend their territory. Within the 1948–67 frontiers they could only defend by attacking. Therefore they took the initiative twice, the first time at the instigation of the British and the French, the second as a response to Nasser's provocation. In 1973, with the southern frontier far from their vital centres, they did not believe they were endangered and therefore they were taken by surprise. In any case, they experienced the contradiction between their political objective and the military requirements necessary for their security. The Arab states will never accept that Israel should hold territory larger than that of 1967. If the Israelis reinforce their military security they reduce the chance of political recognition. Either it is a new battle or a retreat – producing, in both cases, permanent insecurity.

If forced together, face to face, without a third interested party being present, will the Israelis and the Arabs arrive at peace? I do not believe so. One side will continue to enjoy numerical and territorial superiority, the other a better army. The army can succeed in one battle, perhaps in several. But it alone cannot bring about the achievement of any and every objective. Again, in this case the conduct of war is a matter for governments and it requires at this stage the use of non-violent means. But from 1948 to this day, Israel has acted according to the doctrine of security, the military effectiveness of which is partial but incontestable and goes in direct opposition to its political objectives.

About a million Palestinians fled from towns and villages that are nowadays inhabited by Israelis. Dispersed between Lebanon, the West Bank, Jordan, Syria and the Gaza Strip, some are in camps and others are more or less integrated into the host countries. They are mostly uprooted and irreconcilable. They have lost their homes and they want them back. They cannot get them back without expelling those now in occupation. Millions of Germans expelled from lands annexed by the Russians or Poles have taken root in the Federal Republic; thousands, indeed hundreds of thousands, of Palestinian Arabs have not been able, or did not want to find a new fatherland. By 1948 the Israelis had organized themselves to fight guerillas and resist incursions or *coups de main* from the other side of their border. They applied systematically the tactic of deterrence by reprisal to force the governments of the Lebanon, Syria, Jordan and Egypt to put a brake on the activities of the Palestinians and to do so made then responsible for the commando raids the Palestinians launched. It was a tactic that proved militarily effective except as regards the Lebanon, as the leaders of that little country did not have the physical means to control the organizations or the fighters of the Palestinian resistance. But it was also politically counterproductive as Israel was involving herself in a war that the Arabs had every interest in prolonging.

The combination, characteristic in our day, of regulars and irregulars takes on an original shape in the Near East. Neither the Arabs who have remained in Israel since 1948 nor those of the West Bank tried to or succeeded in setting the fire alight. Trained in neighbouring countries, Palestinian commandos crossed the frontiers to attack a farm, a school, a military detachment, to lay mines or to take hostages. During the pitched battles of 1956, 1967 and 1973 their contribution was insignificant. On the other hand, they recruited from all corners of the world and refused to adhere to the limitations custom lays down concerning the theatre of operations. If they had cut air communication between Israel and the rest of the world, terrorism – the hijacking of aircraft and the taking of hostages – would have had some rational explanation. In fact, any rationality it did possess was through psychological or moral objectives, namely the 'bearing witness' of the Palestinians to their resolution and sacrifice, thereby discharging their resentment and preventing the world, through violence, from forgetting them; the world was forced to witness their misfortune. Israel, supported by the USA, had declined in the opinion of Left-wing intellectuals to the position of vanguard of imperialism. Among the Jews of France and the USA many inclined to the Left but many also felt solidarity with Israel. Some inclined to an ideological vision of world government while others made their minds up according to the particular, i.e. Israel's, case. The Japanese terrorists at Lods knew nothing about Israel; they only knew about world imperialism. Claude Lanzmann puts the survival of Israel above anti-imperialism.

The Israeli secret service responded to the spread of Palestinian terrorism throughout the world with counter-terrorism. Israeli agents and Palestinian resistance fighters wage a merciless war in the shadows, of which a few incidents or failed *coups* occasionally make the press. It is ubiquitous guerilla war, an integral part of the prolonged war between Israel and the Arab states.

What has happened in the Near East since 1948 is a single war interrupted by truces and the suspension of hostilities resulting from the superiority of defence over attack. Between 1948 and 1956, and between 1956 and 1967, the Arabs had not the necessary superiority to attack and the Israelis twice won battles that did not win them their political objective and risked pushing these further into the distance. The Arab–Israeli conflict, preceded by a phase of guerilla activity accompanied by partisan warfare, ended up with the 'globalization' of guerilla warfare, which reached heights of cruelty. The battlefield stretched over the entire universe and anyone could be a target. Terror becomes ever greater if the terrorists refuse to distinguish between the enemy and neutrals.

The contrasts and similarities between the Indo-Pakistan and the Arab–Israeli wars are striking. The military victories of Israel were no less spectacular than those of India in 1971 and they were more decisive on the ground than the outcome of the fighting in 1948 and 1956. In the Indian sub-continent as well as in the Near East the states attained a military instrument they could not themselves produce or maintain without foreign help. Today India as well as Israel (with the exception of her aircraft) makes the greater part of her armaments, but the Jewish state now possesses armed forces, the cost of which is out of proportion to the resources of a population of 3–4 millions. In 1956 and again in 1967, Israel still managed to win the battle without receiving supplies from abroad in the course of the war. In 1973 she had to ask (and obtained) arms and munitions, the USA improvising an air bridge in answer to that of the USSR organized a few days previously.

Between countries at odds with one another and their respective armed

355

forces there is discord: either society cannot keep up with armaments technology or it supports armed forces requiring larger GNPs than exist. The money spent by the west on oil allows the Arab states to finance in their turn the purchase of Soviet arms. Israel cannot keep up with the arms race without American help.

The similarity between the tank battles on the Indian subcontinent and those in the Near East did not disguise the radical differences in the two political situations. Even if, in the last analysis, India one day refuses Pakistan's right to exist, or even if the partition of West Pakistan one day follows the separation of the two provinces, this refusal, whether possible or likely, would have nothing in common with the refusal of the Arab states to recognize Israel. India and Pakistan both belong to the Third World as do the Arab states. Israel does not. Therefore the Israeli war lends itself to two interpretations: is it fought to achieve the liberation of the Jewish people or as a bulwark of imperialism?

3 The wars of Vietnam and Latin America

Marxism–Leninism, according to the articles of 1915–17 and the famous book *Imperialism, the Highest Stage of Capitalism*, describes imperialism not only as a regime or a model regime, defined by such and such features, but the historical entity where countries have a regime of this type. Thereby the countries of the Atlantic Alliance constitute the imperialist system, or imperialism in action. Torn by contradictions comparable to those that provoked the 1914 war, the interests of national capitalism are contradictory and the most powerful of these, American capitalism, exploits the subordinate ones. To this system are attached, as objects or victims of exploitation, states which are developing and sell raw materials in conditions of 'unequal exchange', or which import foreign capital and exploit the national resources for the greater profit of companies that are called multinational. The gaining of sovereignty, symbolic of European palaeo-imperialism, now gives way to juridical independence and neo-colonialism, economic as regards investment and political as regards manipulation of parties or social groups.

The Vietnamese wars fought by the French from 1946 to 1954 and lost by the Americans between 1954 and 1972 illustrate, in the one case, European decolonization, and in the other the ambiguities of American hegemony. Both in their similarities and in their differences they require analysis at three levels: political, strategic and tactical.

The events of 1940–5 had ruined French prestige and, so to speak, the mandate of heaven without which the Europeans could not rule in Asia. Government is never conducted solely by force, a truth still more self-evident when it is carried on by a minority from the other side of the world in a foreign land and civilization. To have defeated the Vietminh revolt it would have been necessary to separate the mass of the rebels from the population as the British did in Malaya, thus providing a political perspective. The military blunders that led to Dien Bien Phu were not inevitable but the Vietminh victory was. If any further proof was needed then it was supplied by the Algerian war. A liberal democracy cannot wage a war indefinitely in order to maintain a costly and questionable sovereignty over an unassimilable populace against its own principles. What seems mysterious today is not decolonization but colonization. If the French rulers, including General de Gaulle, had obeyed reason in 1945 rather than following their desire to wipe out the humiliation of 1940, the simple whim of reconquering Indo-China would have seemed to them to be senseless.

The American leaders had only one aim and that was to preserve South Vietnam, a non-communist state. To this end they sent an expeditionary force of over half a million in strength in 1966, and from 1965 to 1968 they bombed North Vietnam and intermittently did so until December 1972. They did not win but neither did they lose the war militarily. The annihilating victory by the North Vietnamese over the South in 1975 crowned the political defeat of the USA.

The Americans had set themselves the task of saving a non-communist government in the South to prevent the southern rebels, supported by the government in the North, from taking power in Saigon. The Vietcong waged a 'revolutionary war' of the Chinese type which combined the three approaches – psychological, political and military. It also combined regular troop operations with procedures close to terrorism of individuals, i.e. the murder of local notables and representatives of the government they wanted to eliminate. The number of civil servants murdered during the first phase of the war, and the cruelty of the Vietcong at Hué during the few days when the rebels occupied the imperial city in the course of the Tet offensive, once more make plain (if that is needed) that the struggle for popular following does not just involve debate, a kind of tournament in which the most convincing propagandist wins. This struggle for the masses involves deterrence as much as persuasion. It means making any service provided by the reigning authorities seem dangerous. Military success seemed to Clausewitz to be the best way of influencing opinion in guerilla warfare as well as in large-scale wars. If a particular part of the fire goes out, another must be rekindled while the embers still burn. In Vietnam those who disobeyed the clandestine government were surrounded by danger, both passive and active, which revealed the cruelty of the struggle for the people.

The now well-known characteristics of a revolutionary war that aimed at being a national revolt were combined. There was no front, only the joining of regular armies: one of which fought in the style of the partisans (strategically defensive and tactically offensive operations which covered assassination of persons linked to the Saigon government or the execution of a Vietcong agent) to operations involving several thousand on each side. The rebels controlled their own zones and supplies coming from the North across territories that were legally neutral or of difficult accessibility. They created a parallel administration according to the technique perfected against the French. Neither the Saigon government nor the Americans knew who controlled a particular village at night time, to whom the peasants paid their taxes or who took the rice harvest.

The overall Vietcong offensives of 1967 and 1972 did not succeed. A moral success was won in the USA by the Tet offensive which contributed to the change in American policy. It caused the rebels enormous losses on the spot and gave the South Vietnamese army the idea of independence, a sort of self-confidence. The 1972 offensive, which took place between

357

Nixon's journeys to Peking and Moscow, also failed after initial success. The North Vietnamese had not mastered the use of tanks as well as the weapons of guerilla warfare. By contrast, after the American defeat, in 1975 they provoked the collapse of the government and the army in the South.

Materially this war did not differ from that of the Vietminh against the French except in scale and in the existence, in the refuge zone of North Vietnam, of a legally recognized state with a regular army whose units could enter the theatre of operations in the South. Aerial bombardments by the Americans turned out to be ineffective in two ways: if they were meant to break the morale of the people they succeeded no more than area bombing had done in Germany. If this was intended to paralyse the economic, administrative and military machine in North Vietnam it was no more successful. Neither Kennedy nor Johnson fought the war in the South according to a politico-military and rationally thought out plan. They came, without the help of a rational solution, to the assistance of the threatened government. The idea of counter-insurgency, a struggle against the revolt, was a slogan rather than a doctrine and played much the same part in the USA as the idea of 'revolutionary war' had done in France. The guerilla operations mounted by the Americans in North Vietnam constituted the equivalent of the psychological conditioning of FLN prisoners by the French army's re-education programme in Algeria. Civilians and soldiers were making the same mistake in both cases by isolating one aspect of overall activity and giving it an effectiveness it could not as such have and which it really owed to the overall context. Certain southern commandos could not create the insecurity in the North that was created by Vietcong militants. The FLN could inflame the Algerians with the vision of an independent Algeria and no technique of crowd-rape could convert them to French patriotism.

I shall not discuss the tactical problems faced by the Communist Party in their struggle against insurrection. The best book on the subject seems to me that by Sir Robert Thompson. Like Mao Tse-tung, he distinguishes the successive phases of the struggle: subversion, insurrection, guerilla war, the establishment of a regular force, and the measures appropriate to each of these phases, namely the distribution of judicial, law-enforcing and military functions and the likely response to tactics deployed in the revolutionary war. But although, according to the vocabulary I have adopted, the book deals essentially with tactics it initially sets down the fundamental principles of strategy. The leaders of the revolt will know what they want and will use a set of psychological, political and military factors, one reinforcing another, to achieve a single objective. A government that is coping with a revolutionary war, whether or not it is led by a Communist Party, must in turn 'know what it wants', organize strategically to the political end in view and adopt the tactical means appropriate to this end.

The French gradually discovered that they had to fight in order to leave Vietnam. Yet, they never fully made their minds up about this. In Algeria they fought for French Algeria. The objective that they gave to their struggle guaranteed that it would fail. No 'trick' of psychological warfare, no 'gadget' of clandestine technique could restore lost legitimacy to the

French in Vietnam. Even, to the west and east of Algeria, the existence of independent states, which had been restored to their sovereignty at an earlier date, ruled out true pacification, although part of the population consented to French rule. Militarily, the army could not lose the war; electrified lines on the frontiers prevented the reinforcement of partisan units and the temptation which they probably would not have resisted of forming larger units. What made the so-called revolutionary war in Vietnam invincible (although it was in reality a war of national liberation) was not the Communist Party, nor the methods of subversion and insurrection, nor the guerilla war; it was the weakness of the resistance that a France, herself hardly liberated, was trying to put up to restore her authority against the dictates of common sense.

From the start the war fought by the American expeditionary force in Vietnam did not suffer from the same contradiction. The Americans did not have the slightest desire to replace the European palaeo-empires by a neo-empire of the same kind. Whatever their intentions were – and they changed according to the passing years – they never conceived of founding a colony of Cochin-China or a protectorate of Annam. They were not fighting in order to remain there (at least, in the military sense). Therefore, they had to give the population the feeling that the American expeditionary force was not purely and simply replacing its French predecessor and that the South Vietnamese army was fighting for itself, for an independent state and against an aggressor, or even an invader. The contradiction that had to be surmounted was inherent in the situation itself: the Soviet Union and China supplied the North Vietnamese with arms but the latter relied on their own troops; the Americans, however, actually took part in the combat. The strategy, in keeping with the political solution of the war, would have been one giving priority to reinforcing both the government and the army in Saigon. The American army, accustomed to material profusion and without colonial experience, in no way came close to what was required. The French officer who was a social and educational reformer in Algeria entertained illusions about the extent of his experience and duly extrapolated from a large-scale to a small-scale war. But his behaviour did, at least, conform to the requirements of the situation. An Algerian government to which the French could have given the authority to defeat the FLN or GPRA would have approved. By contrast, the more or less indiscriminate bombing of villages in the Vietcong areas cemented the population to the rebels and compromised the Saigon government. On a more general level, the American army tried to organize a South Vietnamese army in its own image, an effort that was also absurd because an army must mirror the country from which it comes in the way that the war itself does.

Could the USA have achieved its objectives by adopting immediately rational priorities (by reinforcing the government in Saigon and the army) and by combining suitable externals with the tools of revolutionary insurrection, i.e. by withdrawing their troops and leaving a regime capable of resisting the insurrection alone from within, with outside support? Or, by contrast, was the undertaking to create South Vietnamese nationalism with American help to combat nationalism in the North doomed from the start because, although necessary, it compromised the independence of the

Saigon government? I incline towards the first hypothesis, taking note that after the Paris agreement (which 'legalized' the presence of Vietcong and North Vietnamese troops in enclaves in the South) General Thieu seemed to be able provisionally to maintain his authority over a large part of the Vietnamese population and sustain a war that the Vietcong intended to wage until they achieved a final victory. The events of 1975 do not prove that this undertaking was condemned from the start.

Let us take up the Clausewitzian analysis again: to rely on bombing to break the will of the Vietnamese was to forget the lessons learned in previous wars and the rule propounded in the Treatise, namely that the same step can produce contrary results according to the nature of the enemy. The communists do not allow themselves to be intimidated by threats of escalating to extremes, which in any case were not very effective. Because of its relatively primitive nature their economy survived destruction. The war fought according to the principles of political annihilation was forced to fail by the war that obeyed political intelligence.

The war of liberation in the South was only partially successful because it faced a partially national government. The population in the South did not help the Vietcong towards national insurrection in 1967, or in 1972 or 1975. No two wars are the same – tactics can be subject to rules because these derive from the tool itself. Strategy depends on the major features characterizing a particular war. From 1945 to 1954 this major feature in Vietnam was the end of European domination. Could a form of nationalism different from that offered by the North Vietnamese and the Vietcong come into being?

It was Fidel Castro rather than the American failure in Vietnam that nourished the myth of invincible partisans. If some few dozen men disembarking on an island and taking refuge in the Sierra could take Havana and the whole island two years later, does this method of fighting not possess a magical power and a recipe for victory? Once more the theoreticians returned to their persistant aberration of turning geometric form, strategic manoeuvre or tactics into an overall truth. A year after disembarkation Castro and his colleagues had neither raised the peasants nor rallied thousands of fighters. President Batista's regime was collapsing on its own under the rebellious blows in the towns. This was a bourgeois and liberal revolt rather than a peasant and communist one, to which the guerilla fighter added the death blow without, as it were, himself striking. Fidel Castro became the leader of the victorious revolution, the harbinger and the hero, thanks to the miracle of radio. The Communist Party, having been hostile to the adventurer at first, joined the 22 July movement some months before the flight of Batista and the victory of the 'bearded men'. Legend was born with the Cuban revolution.

Revolutionary wars against legal governments within independent nations (or half-nations) had not been won in Korea, the Philippines or Indonesia. It is also true that the British had put down the revolt in Malaya by exploiting the divisions in the population (between Chinese rebels and the Malay population in the countryside). The methods of fighting a revolutionary war had been used in the service of national liberation. In the eyes of the Left any state that is integrated into the world market is semi-colonial and therefore revolution automatically brings about national liberation. It is not the same with the bourgeoisie who acknowledge other forms of nationalism apart from the communist version. Neither is it the same for the peasantry who are more or less capable, according to circumstances, of being mobilized by a few professional revolutionary troops.

The Che Guevara epoch in Bolivia crowned the defeat of Clausewitz's teachings and also those of Lenin and Mao by which the creation of centres of insurrection by *guerrilleros* themselves would make it unnecessary for the rebels to wait for the socio-political conditions of revolution to ripen. Che had drawn three lessons from the Cuban experience: that a people can defeat a regular army (true in some circumstances); that in Latin America the countryside is the theatre of operations for armed struggle (which is not always the case); and finally that it is not necessary to wait for a revolutionary situation to mature, for the centre of the revolution itself will cause the situation to ripen, which is not always wrong. Fidel's colleagues perished trying to apply this principle derived from the Cuban experience, but falsely interpreted by them. The peasants were probably not ready for revolution in Cuba, but revolution was growing in the towns. The Fidelistas refined the revolution they had proclaimed to their own advantage.

Guerillas did not have any success either in Venezuela, Brazil, the Argentine or Uruguay. Guerillas did not manage to defeat a regular army in either the town or the country in Latin America, nor did they provoke disintegration of the civil authorities, or mobilize the population. The 1960s marked the end both of the spectacular victories attributed to revolutionary war, the doctrinal and historic split between the two great powers of the socialist world and the birth of the myth of the partisan which at the same time brought about the spread of Left-wing violence. This latter form of violence was based on Mao's teachings, until his meeting with Kissinger – a meeting that marked the conversion of People's China to the 'nationalization' of revolutionary ideology. Neither the Soviet Union nor People's China stopped sustaining a revolutionary war in conformity with their ideology or their great power interests. Usually a revolutionary movement can find an interested third party which will supply it and argue its cause, but the duel between the socialist camp and the imperialist camp is disintegrating into a system of growing complexity. The Nigerian government received arms from Great Britain and the Soviet Union. In Sri Lanka, Mrs Bandaranaike had them from everywhere – from the Soviet Union and People's China, from the USA and Great Britain (I have probably forgotten others). The rebels of Sri Lanka (the only country to have two Trotskyite parties), peasants and their sons who had gone through university, failed to arouse the sympathies of anyone, not even the intellectuals who specialize in indignation.

Returning to the modern origins of arming the people: the Prussian patriots dreamt of this but conservatives objected that it would be equivalent to a generalized state of anarchy, and the German peasants and bourgeoisie refused to take up arms. The edicts of 1813, though soon annulled or left to lapse, none the less demonstrated a warlike rather than a revolutionary form of romanticism that the excesses of Napoleon had inspired in officers. Lenin and Mao Tse-tung, with the help of circums-

361

tances, transformed a way of fighting into an instrument of revolution. Of course, Scharnhorst, Gneisenau and Clausewitz understood that people could take up arms against an invader only with a view to changing society. Once a partisan, the civilian would no longer resemble the Frederician soldier who had to 'fear his officer more than the enemy'. The armed civilian or partisan had to know why he was fighting, to show a spirit of initiative, to know the ground, move quickly and adapt to circumstances – all of them qualities foreign to the infantryman of the line trained by 'drill'. As Delbrück suggested and as W. Hahlweg bears out in the light of the present day, we can descry an elective affinity between the citizen who emerges from the revolution and the partisan emerging from small bands of troops. But this kind of interpretation can easily turn into legend.

The Spanish *guerrillero* fought on and for his ground from 1808 to 1811. The French armies of 1793 employed *tirailleur* (sharpshooter) tactics and also mass attacks in columns-in-depth. Nothing is less like partisan tactics than the 'magic square' of Napoleon. The only things the partisans and Napoleon had in common were speed and mobility. In this sense alone the Prussian officer's formula – that the 1806 campaign was like a partisan *coup de main* – counts not as a pithy explanation but only as partially true. If we agree that Scharnhorst, Clausewitz and Gneisenau wanted social change as a condition and objective of national insurrection, they did so at most in the manner of General de Gaulle in 1940–5, never in the manner of Lenin or Mao. To evoke revolutionary war to explain the activities of the Prussian patriots is a falsification of what they were, a false idea of what they represented in their day. They still belonged to the century of Enlightenment and of handicrafts. They dreamt of arming the people, not of revolutionary war.

The material relationship between the processes of guerilla warfare and banditry reappears in full view once violence against individuals – murders, indiscriminate terrorism, bombs in cinemas and trains, hostage-taking and the hijacking of aircraft – ceases to be organized by any party with a view to liberation or revolution. In the illegal war conceived by the patriots, legality was guaranteed by the officers. Later, communist commissars fulfilled the same role. When each of these goes, guerilla warfare becomes more and more like crime and the partisans resume their medieval aspect: no longer peasant on his land, no longer professional revolutionary, no longer Communist Party militant or even a Che Guevara, an Argentinian bourgeois carrying the revolutionary torch into the Latin American countryside, but simply an outlaw, protesting against a world he cannot change, even through violence. The revolutionary International, led for almost half a century by the Kremlin, has divided into at least two Internationals, neither keeping complete authority over parties that proclaim their allegiance, retrospectively, to one or the other. On the other hand, we can see the beginnings of another International, that of pure, naked violence, salvationist as such, which Fanon exalted in his book and of which Sartre sketched out the theoretical framework in his Preface. Seen in this light, the Japanese atrocity at the Israeli airport of Lods takes on a symbolic importance.

The events of the 1960s, including those of May 1968 in France, the failure of the revolutions in Latin America (including the non-violent

362

revolution of Allende in Chile), the urban guerilla in the USA or the Argentine, the activities of undergrounds in many countries including industrial countries like Italy, the multiplication of atrocities for no obvious reason, all of these things are the phenomena that shake regimes, whether liberal or authoritarian, but they do not necessarily prefigure the onset of a revolution or a revolutionary war. Italian anarchy may bring the Italian Communist Party to power whether it shared or monopolized (shared to begin with, perhaps monopolized later on). The urban guerilla in Uruguay, or the armed struggle of the Left and of the extreme Right-wing commandos in the Argentine, reveal the tensions present in societies too poor to satisfy the aspirations of the majority, with political classes unable to improve living conditions or to obtain popular support. Neither the murder of notables nor the taking of hostages are sufficient to release revolutionary war. The partisan bears witness through his actions and sometimes by his martyrdom. The sons and daughters of the Parisian bourgeoisie who stick portraits of Che on to their walls are honouring a hero, but a defeated hero who was mistaken on the essential point, even according to his own viewpoint, i.e. analysis of the political situation.

The Vietminh or Vietcong assassinated the civil servants of Saigon or the village notables so as to spread terror and turn the poor peasants against the rich. This kind of terrorism, organized and conceived according to a precise objective, does not contradict the Bolshevik doctrine of opposing the terrorism of the socialist revolutionaries. It was the fashion of the 1970s to accord anarchy the form of 'rationalized' terrorism. It also marks a return to the earliest forms of terrorism: individual spontaneity where small groups play a part first of all. In their latest incarnation partisans are the Jesuits of the Revolution: worshippers of a faith but devoted to crime; exalted by the theologians of violence, but condemned by communists and liberals. They express their rejection of the world by killing some of their fellow human beings whether picked out in advance or chosen haphazardly. Though the actual outcome of their activities may be derisory they believe in the political solution to their rebellion, and the moral value of their witness. They forget that terrorists without a cause simply resemble highwaymen.

4 Carl Schmitt and the partisan figure

Readers familiar with the works of Carl Schmitt, *Der Begriff des Politischen* and the *Theorie des Partisanen*, will have recognized in the above pages ideas similar to his, or perhaps a different interpretation of the same themes. As my intentions coincide with his ('The theorist must take care with his concepts and call things by their names. The theory of partisans involves the notion of politics, the search for the real enemy and a new view of the world') I have felt it necessary to point out areas of divergence affecting the very notion of partisans, and as I have done, Carl Schmitt moves from the Prussian edicts of April 1813, from Clausewitz and Gneisenau, to the French *francs tireurs*, the European resistance to Hitler, and Che Guevara, travelling via Lenin and Mao. But he arrives at an analogy between General von Yorck and General Salan that is unacceptable in my eyes. In the historical process a short article by Lenin has an essential place, whereas his articles of 1915–17 are hardly mentioned. By contrast, Hitler, or the substitution of race, as distinct from state or people, as historical subject, does not figure. Finally, the link established between the partisan and the particular hostilities is intellectually unsatisfactory. Curiously enough, Schmitt, though a jurist, ended by forgetting the inevitable relationship of the partisan to the state, which does exist at least for as long as the partisan is more than a bandit or a rebel and aspires to play a political role.

The conceptual difficulty of the theory is illustrated by the listing of features stressed by Carl Schmitt to define the partisan: irregularity, a high degree of mobility, intensity of political commitment and telluric character. But it is obvious that the first two features are linked most frequently and seem inseparable while having nothing much to do with the others. Moreover, political commitment, far from explaining the telluric character tends rather to rule it out. Again, to be more precise, political commitment has a different meaning according to whether the irregular is still rooted in his terrain.

At the start, in the eighteenth century, partisans belonged to a party or detachment that covered the countryside. Of one such detachment, Marshal Saxe wrote that it could cross an entire kingdom without being observed. Let us turn to one of the classic works of the period, *La Petite Guerre ou traité du service des troupes légères de campagne (Guerilla Warfare, or a Treatise on the Function of Light Campaign Troops)*:

> Without returning to the ancient past where the Numidian cavalry gave great service to Hannibal, particularly at the famous battle of Cannae, and where the Parthians by their speed and by their agility in combat maintained some freedom as against the Romans' power, the French have formed battalions at different times and in different names to go forward and prepare for the campaign, to find out information about the enemy, intercept his convoys, remove posts and fall on supply lines in a campaign.

Light troops or parties thus filled the functions both of the vanguard and Maquisards to today. The latter acted tactically in the manner of light troops. They differed from eighteenth-century partisans in that they did not belong to the regular army. Mobility does not imply irregularity, but irregularity does imply mobility. Fighters without uniforms, training or officers act by surprise and cannot sustain prolonged combat against regular troops. Regular army contingents often constituted the nuclei or framework for the *guerrillero* bands in Spain.

Was there an intensifying of political commitment in these latter? We must at least draw a distinction between policy and politics. The more politics is confused with home and hearth, with the fatherland in the eternal sense of the word, the more the Maquisard or *guerrillero*, the *franc tireur* or partisans will seem politically committed. Yet no one could be less· like the Maquisard than Che Guevara or Régis Debray. On the one side there is the peasant on his land; on the other, the intellectual from the town, the professional revolutionary. Of course, Carl Schmitt could not completely ignore the contrast presented by this obvious and striking point. He alludes to it first of all when he is discussing the influence of 'technicallization' on the partisan of the past, and he does so on a second occasion in the paragraph entitled 'From Clausewitz to Lenin'. He does not grasp the essential, for lack of rigorous discrimination between the levels of policy, tactics and law.

Tactically, the irregular does not fight anyone other than the regular light troops. The participants and the light troops must be mobile (in the eighteenth-century sense) as must the detachments of irregulars. Thus the light troops behind the German lines in the Second World War were composed both of regulars and irregulars. International law tried to give status to irregulars, Maquisards and resistance fighters. But for the latter to have the benefit of protection awarded by the laws of war, required circumstances basically incompatible with the requirements which made this kind of war effective. How could a Maquisard 'openly bear arms'? How could he have a sign fixed and 'recognizable at a distance'?

The principles of mobility essential to guerilla warfare which go back to the most distant past have not been altered in nature by technique, though the resources available have been multiplied by it. Maquisards communicate with each other and their leaders almost like fighters in uniform. Technique enriches the means of the guerilla war, of both regulars and irregulars, but it has not changed the concept. On the other hand, the dual nature of arming the people – for national defence or revolution – became a reality in China and during the Second World War when men of a political party took charge and organized the Maquisards for revolution (or, if the term is preferred, *francs tireurs* or Maquisards). In the end there is something *teluric* about Mao but not about Che. The political commitment of the Spanish *guerrillero* in 1807 differed radically from that of the communist partisan in 1944. If we use the same expression 'political commitment' then, following Clausewitz's lesson, we must add that the combat can only have meaning in terms of the political end: the one *pro aris et focis* and the other for revolution. The strategy and even the tactics are influenced by the political aim.

Therefore, I put Mao Tse-tung in a different place from Carl Schmitt – between Clausewitz and Che Guevara. He attaches great importance to an article of Lenin's entitled 'The Partisan War' that appeared on 30 September 1906 in the review *Proletarian*. He sees in it 'a clear, and logical development of the notion of enemy and hostilities, of which the discovery began in *What is to be Done?* in 1902, chiefly in opposition to the objectivization of Struve'. Unquestionably the little work of 1902 appears, retrospectively, to be the theoretical origin of the professional revolutionary, though at the time Lenin still based his ideas on those of Kautsky who derived consequences from the role of intellectuals in the transfer to socialism that were quite different from those arrived at by Lenin. As for the article 'The Partisan War', I see in it a contemporary document without further relevance.

Lenin obviously never ruled out the possibility of armed revolution, the taking of power by violence. The memory of the barricades, the *guerrilleros* and the *francs tireurs* had never disappeared even though Engels, a specialist in military affairs in the Marx–Engels team, rightly saw the changes that arms would bring to the tactics of street fighting and, more generally, to the violent phase of the proletariat's struggle.

What does Lenin say about partisans in 1906, or about those individuals organized in small groups that executed spies who had collaborated with the police, and that also raided banks or public establishments to take money with which to finance the proletarian party? That he was not opposed to violence was, so to speak, self-evident. That he refused to condemn methods used more or less spontaneously by militants equally needs no subtle explanation. It was important to him not to be counted among 'Anarchists, blanquists or Terrorists', all of whom represented types of social action condemned by international social democracy at the time.

He therefore presents such partisan activity as the consequence of the insurrection of 1905 and as preparation for the revolt to come. In reality, according to the doctrine that was and remained that of social democracy and the Bolsheviks, the class struggle, but not the armed struggle, is permanent. The explosion of partisan activity after the revolt of 1905 is not to be condemned by him (because he does not condemn the militant's fighting) but he none the less recognizes the risks involved in this for the organization of the workers' movement. He ends up with a historical interpretation: 'The partisan struggle is an inevitable form of struggle at a time when the mass movement is heading for revolt and when there are more or less considerable gaps between the great battles in the course of the civil war.' In other words, it seems to him in 1906 that, because Russia is a theatre not only of the class struggle but of civil war, he must permit partisan action in the intervals between insurrections.

He also adds immediately: 'What disorganizes the movement is not partisan activity but the weakness of a party unable to lead it.' In 1906 Lenin did not doubt that the revolution would result, in Russia at least, from a civil war and that in such circumstances the militant party must become the fighting party. Provided the Communist Party retained overall control, he was not opposed to the murder of 'spies' or the expropriation of money in banks, but only because a situation of class struggle and civil war had been hypothesized. The synthesis of Clausewitzian strategy and partisan theory (or, perhaps, the reading of the Treatise in the light of Chapter 26 of Book VI) was the work of Mao Tse-tung.

As regards the contribution made by Lenin to the theory of absolute war and absolute hostility, which, following Lenin's article, Carl Schmitt analysed, this suffers from ambiguity because the German jurist substituted his own notions for those of Clausewitz and Lenin.

He says that in Lenin's eyes only revolutionary war is true war because it emanates from absolute hostility. All the rest is conventional games-playing. Lenin would never have been so silly. When, in the margin of a passage from Chapter 30 of Book VI, he contrasts war (*voyna*) and game (*igra*) he is content, following Clausewitz, to stress the contrast between buttoned fencing, or subtle manoeuvre suitable to the armies of the eighteenth century, and the pitiless fighting between armies and people after the French Revolution. A moment of reflection is sufficient to remind us that the wars between capitalist states are anything but games according to Marxism–Leninism. Hostility will escalate between European states trying to partition the world and unable to do so peacefully, just as it rose between monarchical states and revolutionary France. Is it 'absolute hostility'? The notion is not Clausewitz's for he was content to say that the opposed interests are very great, but to the question, is it Lenin's notion, I can only say 'no' rather than 'yes'. Up to a point, it can be found in Lenin, but only in a particular sense: 'absolute hostility' results from the class struggle, the ultimate root of all conflict. When commenting on Clausewitz and Lenin it is better to avoid concepts that belong to another way of thinking. In Clausewitz's eyes absolute war is only a limited case – the concept of war waged to the end with all the available means and all possible energy. In no way does it imply the 'criminalization' of war. Napoleon did not put his defeated adversaries on trial. Sometimes he took all or part of their land from princes and kings. It was Prussian officers who wanted to execute Napoleon there and then, while the kings and the English wished to send him to Elba and then to St Helena, so that 'the usurper' could not live beyond the fame of his arms which, in any case, he did not believe he could do because he refused all hints of compromise peace that his father-in-law, Emperor Franz of Austria, could have promoted in 1813. The Prussian officers Clausewitz and Gneisenau 'theorized' the arming of the people of which the Spaniards and Russians supplied the model. They dreamt of it and managed to draw up the edict of April 1813 and convince the Prussian king that it should be signed, but it remained a dead letter. Major Schill, Andreas Hofer, a few free corps in the service of Austria: such were all the episodes of the 'national resistance' to Napoleon. On the other side were Hegel, Goethe and a large proportion of the cultivated classes. Sentiments of hatred towards the French were really present only among intellectuals like Fichte, who had at first acclaimed the Revolution, and some officers like Gneisenau and Clausewitz whose pride and patriotism had been wounded.

All the elements of later history, all the implications of a war of one people against another, already appeared in nucleus or blueprint from 1792 to 1815. The tradition of European individual rights and the limitation of means required by this tradition resisted the storm. Arming of the people only occurred in two theatres of war – Spain and Russia – in spite of the French party at the head of things in the first case, and with the approval of the authorities in the second.

The makers of the Versailles Treaty who, in Carl Schmitt's formula, 'criminalized' war on the one side, and Lenin with the Bolsheviks doing so on the other, had nothing in common and belonged in thought and action to different compartments. Bismarck was prepared to help the Hungarian revolutionaries to defeat the Austrian empire. Ludendorff did not hesitate to facilitate the return of Lenin to Russia and to finance the Russian partisans of peace at any price. The Allies did much the same. Statesmen in London and Paris did not have to face the question of whether to make peace with the Hohenzollerns. The revolution that broke out in Berlin decided the question for them. In the war of people against people, each side organizes enthusiasm and blames anything, whether autocracy or militarism, for the catastrophe, all the while promising reconciliation once that element is done away with, so as to strike at the morale of the other side.

The article in the Treaty of Versailles making the Central Powers responsible for the war came from two sources. After beginning a 'war like all the others' of which a rapid outcome was expected within a few months, the leaders of Europe were forced to find a real goal and guilty parties on the same scale as the sacrifices they were asking from their peoples. As for the president of the USA, he did not and could not consider the war to be in a tradition that looked upon war as an intermediate stage between pacific relations. In saying, or suggesting, that war of aggression was criminal and that Germany was guilty, the Treaty of Versailles introduced (or tried to) into positive law a distinction reserved by the classics for morality.

Lenin ignored the 'criminalization' of war in this form just as, whatever Carl Schmitt says, he ignored 'absolute hostility'. He substituted one historical subject for another without denying the reality or even the ferocity of war between capitalist states. In the framework of a philosophy of history inspired by Hegelian Marxism he used the Treatise to demonstrate that all belligerents were equally belligerent and to preach the gospel of the single war that would now be just: that of the working class against all the capitalist states.

In 1919 the Allied and associated powers decreed at Versailles that their war had been just because it had been forced on them by the Central Powers. From 1914 onwards Lenin had said that the war was altogether unjust because it was only a phase in a political whole that was itself unjust. Neither absolute war nor absolute hostility resulted from either statement. The nationalists took the notion of 'total war' from the experience of 1914–18, which was translated into one of the possible meanings of absolute war. The Marxist–Leninists took a tactical lesson from it – joint action of partisans and armies – and a political lesson – the exploitation of imperialist wars with a view to revolution.

Ludendorff, or 'Ludendorff–Hitler', is an indispensable link in the conceptual series which ends at the present day. They alone gave a precise meaning to what Carl Schmitt calls 'absolute hostility' which the makers of the Versailles Treaty or the Marxist–Leninists or the victors of the Second World War in the west did not do. Ludendorff and Hitler posited the racial community as a historical entity and the enemies of such a racial community as transhistoric enemies of the German people, even of all peoples. I would call this 'absolute hostility' as it alone deserves the term 'absolute', since it ends logically in massacre and genocide. As interpeted by Goltz and Foch, absolute war was a contradictory concept. Both the German and the Frenchman believed that great conquests were impossible in Europe because of the very strength of national feeling, this same national feeling that, for obscure reasons, set people against one another. They both imagined a sort of fight of the Horatii and Curatii in which not all the citizens of Rome and Alba, but their delegates, would fight. It would represent the judgment of God as between peoples, each united as a single man. The consequence of the postulate of absolute hostility (and to be paid for very highly) was the common will to dictate peace.

Compared with that of Mark Antony and Octavian, the hostility that Lenin and then Mao Tse-tung bore to the enemies of revolution was absolute. Of the two claimants to the throne of the empire, one must perish. Again, the hostility expressed by Marxist–Leninists to the defenders of a regime condemned by history may be broken down, in theory, into indulgence or pity. Good men, the prisoners of a world upside-down, may fight for a lost cause. In China, the Maoists often acted as if they thought that they could redeem their adversaries. Everyone can judge for himself whether death through fidelity to oneself or conversion after brainwashing is more humane.

By contrast, hostility becomes physically 'absolute' when based on a biological or racist philosophy. If Jews and gipsies infiltrate a people like microbes they must be eliminated as pitilessly as microbes. The means in the gas chambers resembled pesticides.

Of course, I do not ignore the fact that Stalin probably massacred more people as enemies of the revolution than Hitler did in the name of the purity of the race. In practice the Stalinists showered insults ('poisonous vipers', etc.) on the enemies of socialism just as Hitler's followers did with the Jews. Hostility based on the class struggle has taken on no less extreme or monstrous forms than that based on the incompatibility of races. But if we wish to 'save the concepts' there is a difference between a philosophy whose logic is monstrous and one which can be given a monstrous interpretation.

Because he failed to locate properly the two Marxist–Leninist interpretations of Clausewitz's thought (in Lenin's articles of 1915–17 and Mao Tse-tung's documents on lengthy conflict), Carl Schmitt recognizes without giving it a central position the duality of the 'telluric partisan' and the 'professional revolutionary', the war of national liberation and war fought with a view to revolution. To distinguish the nature of the fighting we must start from politicization, from the political aim which is in view.

There is no historic character in the partisan, as there is in the knight, builder, prophet or hero. It would be futile to define the resister of 1939–45: there was not one type, but several. Some of the 20 July conspirators in Germany wanted to bear witness, save their country's honour; but they could hardly act as *francs tireurs* or professional revolutionaries. The resistance incarnated conscientious objection in its partiotism and hope of a better tomorrow. These men were one, fighting a war of the shadows, each man and woman submitting to a discipline without uniform and without direct mutual help. However, they were not fighting the same war because they did not have the same ends, even if the immediate objective of all was the liberation of their country.

Carl Schmitt, failing rigorously to apply the Clausewitzian theory, called his little book *Theory of the Partisan* although implicitly he realized that there are several partisans, not just one. He even managed to set up an analogy between General von Yorck and General Salan, which was a remarkable achievement.

Comparison can obviously be made between the few Prussian officers who served with the tsar in 1812, the Prussian corps that served in the Grande Armée, and General de Gaulle with his companions. Even so, in 1940 Marshal Pétain did not ask the officers on land and sea to fight the ex-ally on the ex-enemy's side. He incited them to neutrality. For reasons not entirely military, Churchill would not accept the neutrality of the French fleet and the tragedy of Mers El-Kebir resulted. In agreement with the British government, General de Gaulle tried to rally West Africa to his cause and he forced the Free French to fight other Frenchmen, which he had promised not to do. General de Gaulle refused to command a French corps that would fight for the greater glory of His Britannic Majesty. He immediately set up a *de facto* legal authority while waiting to be recognized as president of the National Liberation Committee and then as head of the Provisional Government of the Republic. Thereby he introduced an element of civil war that was perhaps made inevitable by the armistice, but which he could have delayed or weakened.

The case of the French generals and admirals in North Africa compares with General von Yorck in 1812, after the defeat of the Grande Armée. Were they to take it upon themselves to choose the enemy despite orders, however fictional, from the government whose legality they recognized? How in 1942 (as in 1812) could they fail to see that the real enemy was the one who had imposed a humiliating peace, an alliance under duress and who occupied the national territory? This real enemy could be defined outside any ideology by traditional criteria. At the most, whether out of fidelity to an oath or to ideas, a few of the officers in North Africa hesitated to recognize the national enemy.

As for Salan, he exhibited the cardinal error against which Clausewitz warned and which Carl Schmitt does not always avoid: that of defining a combat or a combatant in terms of some methodology. The French colonels were obsessed by procedure – terrorism and counter-terrorism, parallel organizations, coexistence of a clandestine government and the legal administration – and they imagined that they could turn these procedures, as adopted by the partisans, against the partisans themselves.

This formula was applicable, but in a rigorous and narrow military sense Napoleon is credited with the formula 'when fighting partisans, you must fight like partisans'. Behind the front the Germans maintained *Jagdkommandos* (flying commandos) who behaved liked partisans. But they hardly differed from the soldiers operating like the *Parteigänger* whom Clausewitz knew, i.e. light troops (there was a further aspect of this in civilians among the partisans who often prowled secretly around the villages).

The French colonels did not realize that the psycho-political action of the Algerian rebels could not be turned against them. Of course, some Algerians, whether through fear or conviction, did oppose the FLN, which was divided into rival factions who continued their quarrels in the Maquis. But 'brainwashing', even of the most scientific kind, could not transform the mass of Muslims or Algerians into French patriots. The Vietminh managed to persuade French prisoners that France was fighting 'an imperialist war'. This proposition, true enough for the political system of the Vietminh, was at least plausible in the political system of the soldiers and officers of the expeditionary force. The conversion of the officers did not long stand up to the irresistible influence of familiar circles on their return home.

The French army always easily recruited the *harkis*, creating many secure zones where the population could continue with its daily life. What it could not do in Algeria was reply to Algerian patriotism by creating a French patriotism; nor could it inspire the metropolitan French with the will to maintain French sovereignty over Algeria at any price so as to make a million fellow countrymen permanently safe. The cardinal error committed from the start was to mistake a war of national liberation for a revolutionary war, conducted according to revolutionary techniques; and this resulted in a heavy price, for the OAS emerged from it.

Unlike Yorck, Salan defended an empire in Indo-China as well as in Algeria. What was it that led him into believing he could assume the mantle of the General de Gaulle of 1940, or the Vietminh revolutionaries or the FLN? As a defender of empire he was without allies in a world dominated by anti-colonialism. As a defender of the west he had suffered impatiently under American tutelage in Vietnam, and had no hope of obtaining the help of the leading power in the anti-communist coalition. If it were not to seem quite mad Salan's effort had to be based on an idea that the mass of Algerians would feel solidarity with the OAS. But even those Algerians best disposed towards France hardly liked the *pieds noirs* who dominated the mixed Algerian society.

In 1940 when de Gaulle would not obey a government more legal than his own he could, with some reason, justify this with reference to Pétain's position as 'captive prince' (as with the King of Prussia in 1812). Some miles away from the demarcation line the National Assembly had given full power under semi-duress to an 84-year-old general who chaired a semi-captive government. Many Frenchmen believed, almost to the end, that there was a secret agreement between the marshal and the general. At root, the operations of the OAS both in Algeria and in France suffered from a nonsensical element. In 1942 the unfortunate Admiral Derrien had been forced to choose the enemy. In 1961 General Salan had only to obey a government legalized and legitimized at the same stroke by the referendum and elections of 1958. Salan, transformed into a leader of the partisans against the legal government of France and against the French authorities and the FLN in Algeria, slipped into tragic buffoonery.

Like Lenin, the Marxist–Leninists have never confused war with the class war as such. War designates the violent phase of the class struggle. Peace does not therefore exclude the possibility of adopting various relatively non-violent procedures which strategists can, in turn, use in wartime propaganda: espionage, murder and the weapons of the guerilla have been a constant recourse of partisans from the fedayeen to Che Guevara. Are the partisans not guaranteed a hearing in the United Nations and a 'third interested party' to support their cause? All the wars of this century, and explicitly those since 1945, have a dimension of civil war. Because of the ideological rivalries peace will also have a dimension of transnational civil war. Is there still room for the 'intelligence personified' – the political element continuing in war – and to make distinctions in terms of the specific means of violence between war and peace?

Chapter 15

Policy or the Expression of the Spirit of the State

At the end of his life Clausewitz managed to reconcile history and ideas, not as Hegel had done but on the lines of Montesquieu or Max Weber. He neither wrote nor probably believed that meaning was accomplished through the vicissitudes of men's strife. That Clausewitz was a 'resister' and Hegel, at least in spirit, was a 'collaborator' (at Jena 'the soul of the world passed on horseback under his windows') meant that there were essential differences between the two men, not merely differences of personality. Both recognized that armed struggle between states was a fact. But the soldier could not conceive of peace except in and through the liberty of people organized into states. He was the precursor of the age of nationalism. Hegel, the philosopher, accepted the French empire as the accomplishment of an idea.

As the last quarter of a century dawned, the dialogue between the defender of the national state and the Marxist–Leninist ideology from Hegel via Marxism resumed. They read and used Clausewitz: the one to place violence at the service of policy as the expression of the state's intelligence, the other to put it at the service of the proletariat as expressing the spirit of the people personified. In this way the European society of states ceased to resemble states of the *ancien régime* and the restoration but rather those of the revolutionary period. The states were not all of the same type; they were not based on the same principle and did not adhere to the same vision of the just and the unjust. The same war could be just in some eyes, but unjust in others. Is all historical truth relative? The opinions of the democrat are seen as fictional in the eyes of the Marxist–Leninists, who do not recognize a state composed of people but only the class of the oppressors. Equally, the democrat does not recognize a 'proletariat' in the party that installs a totalitarian state everywhere it takes power.

This makes for many difficulties. Can a state, of whatever kind, have a spirit to be expressed? The Marxist–Leninist will answer 'no', if it is a question of the state in capitalist societies, but the positivist, the empiricist and the pacifist will also answer 'no', whatever the state in question is. The internal complexity of the body that takes decisions is said to be such that any comparison between a state and a spirit or intelligence becomes impossible. In this light, criticism by Americans of the 'fiction' of the rational actors comes close, if we generalize it, to the Marxist–Leninist critique.

But if the concept of the spirit of the state *is* legitimate, there is still another difficulty. Does the state retain the characteristics of the Clausewitzian spirit? In the Treatise, we do find a theoretical description of the combat 'on credit' or 'with deferred payment'. The uncertainties of nuclear strategy come largely from want of a 'payment in specie'; and, the further the sun of Los Alamos and the burning of Hiroshima and Nagasaki recede and are expunged from men's memories, the very term of reference will disappear. Threats that are never carried out are less and less like the proffered or simulated battle in which the side with the weaker credit will anticipate the outcome by treating it as though already fought and lost. Does strategy in the nuclear age resemble classical strategy? Can Clausewitzian strategy dispense with the concept of absolute war? Does that concept mean anything despite nuclear weapons?

This problem leads to a third. Clausewitz defined war as the use of physical violence, particularly by armed forces. However, nowadays, even in peace-time, submarines armed with missiles are on permanent patrol within range of a potential enemy's cities. If threats become confused with their own execution, then such a permanent threat blurs the distinction between war and peace. The very idea of prolonged conflict removes, or risks removing, the clear definition of a total entity that the Treatise presupposes.

There is another perspective in which today's world is seemingly beyond the range of Clausewitz's conceptualization. The word 'strategy' is no longer applied only to military action and leadership: now, anything may involve strategy, although in the last quarter-century states, at least the most powerful ones, have never employed their total resources to resolve even a major conflict. Wars have been fought within the confines of the American *imperium*, and Soviet troops have intervened to maintain discipline in the socialist camp; but military means have remained an instrument, and not the only or even the favourite one, for states to maintain themselves against an opponent. It may even be that an inversion of Clausewitz's Formula would better reflect present-day realities than the Formula itself.

Finally, we should consider the philosophical truth of the doctrines professed by the two groups of Clausewitz's descendants. Are we to look to people's war, fought for liberation or revolution, and ending, after prolonged conflict, in a victory of annihilation? Or should we look to a predominance of the political, in which the relative weight of the wager and the stake can be assessed, in which the deterrent threat becomes the solution in a situation of such disparity between the destructive power of nuclear weapons and the conflicting interests of states, and in which men are to be taught the art of avoiding mutual destruction while none the less not having to submit to the predominance of one state?

On the one side there is a Hegel, impoverished by the intellectual sterility of his disciples *à la* Bobigny; on the other, Kant, or maybe Montesquieu adjusted by Kant. Peace, like absolute war, is a concept, part of an ideal world – the one representing what we have to fear, the other what may be hoped for. Can the deterrent ever be a means for bringing about, for humanity as a whole, the ideal peace, which is not merely absence of war, but the fruit of human will?

1 Theoretical fiction and reality

Clausewitz did see that a government of a state would be subject to many influences – moods of sovereigns, class interests, cowardice or weaknesses of character so that it could hardly count as a single 'spirit' or intelligence. If in his view there was no contradiction between the political element and the armed force, it was because he could identify the – as it were – ideal–political with the spirit of the state. The incarnation of the state in the sovereign reduced, or seemed to do so, the gap between the real state and the central actors in it. In 1807, loyalty to the king was combined with German nationalism and echoes of the French Revolution to bring about a fervour among the Prussian patriots that was directed towards both people and state. The individual, if he were not a citizen of a respected state, would have only charity or pity from foreigners: it would be alms for the poverty-stricken, rather than respect for a man belonging to an independent political system. Prince August's aide-de-camp knew the distress of exiles and refugees in advance of the events of the next century – the Jews of a new Exodus, tossed from port to port as they looked for a land where they would have the Rights of Man, and would once again be fully-fledged citizens.

Americans and Europeans no longer regard their nation states with the wild passion shown in the letters written by Clausewitz as a prisoner when he was traumatized by the defeat. To believe that this is bad and anachronistic shows a lack of historical consciousness that is characteristic of American civilization. The democratic era begun by the French Revolution substituted the abstraction of the nation-state for the individual and concrete reality personified in the sovereign. Nor did this era end with the First or Second World Wars. Multinational states (and all are such, though not in the same degree) seem to be torn, more uncertain of themselves and their futures, than states which approximate to the national type. States born out of a movement for liberation from a negative nationalism against the occupant, colonizers or foreigners, aspire to positive nationalism. They wish to give individuals the feeling of belonging to a community and of being subject to the laws of the state.

What I think has aged, without disappearing, is the desire, often expressed by Clausewitz in the years of struggle, that the fatherland should impose not only respect but fear. His patriotism, whether Prussian or German, was expressed at times if not in bellicose then at least in martial language. Again, we must remember that Germany was just emerging from the period of division and impotence to which she had been condemned by the Peace of Westphalia and which was brought to an end by the victories of Frederick the Great. The collapse of 1806 seemed to bring about annihilation. Perhaps it is necessary to live through such a collapse to understand the delirium of rage often expressed by Gneisenau and Clausewitz who, though highly cultivated officers, gave way to savage hatred. Moreover, have we won or lost on the exchange when we substitute the fiction of class for that of state and nation?

When Clausewitz used the phrase 'the expression of the spirit of the state' to define policy he meant mainly to refute the narrow notion of policy that reduced it to the ruses or extrapolations of 'cabinet' diplomacy. He suggested the use of an expression equivalent to what writers of today would call the 'national interest'. The same idea occurs in Chapter 8 of Book VI in an even more explicit way: policy administers the multitude of interests in society as a whole. Of course, today's reader, acquainted with his Lenin and Mao, will object to the idea of 'all the interests of society as a whole' as being both logically and practically impossible. I do not believe that traditional writers would have disallowed this. The number of variables that must be taken into account in the equation of war would defy the genius of a Newton. What the mathematician cannot calculate cannot be grasped at once by the intuition of a war leader. In each war one aspect characterizes and colours everything. Society's interest requires the mobilization of all resources against the conqueror to safeguard the nation's independence. If the state is fighting for its existence, even during a period of crisis of this kind some individuals or groups do not wish to acknowledge or obey society's interests through blindness, cowardice or selfishness, and Clausewitz would certainly have understood this situation, because he fought those who collaborated with Napoleon with as much passion as he fought the enemy himself.

Criticism of the notion 'the expression of the spirit of the state' involves different meanings, according to philosophical viewpoint, for other actors than states are involved in the field where the 'old monsters' meet. It would be insane to ignore this patently obvious truth. The head of state who takes the final decisions alone (if we suppose that such an isolated creature exists) gets his information from many bureaucracies. A study by sociologists of the Cuban crisis in 1962, taken to the smallest detail, reveals the effective leadership of several people, each more or less rational according to the interests of society as a whole, rather than one organization facing another organization.

For all its precision and subtlety Allison's study plays an old tune. The chief, in all ages, depends on the 'apparatus'. Sociological analysis of the American apparatus cannot be applied as such to other states. In the present circumstances one of the unknowns concerns the precise means in which the Soviet apparatus functions. Historians now studying the German and Japanese apparatus in the last war have discovered conflicts between generals and admirals and between the various secret services and also between the Führer and some of his generals. It is a truism that any study of a state that neglected the gap between the spirit of the state and the real state would be committing grave errors. As long as the Kremlin archives remain closed the reasons for the installation of ballistic missiles in Cuba and the working in daylight on the launching-pads will remain a mystery. The landing in the Bay of Pigs and the catastrophe of Pearl Harbor remain mysterious as long as we fail to substitute the real people for a fictitious person and people who received information and interpreted it in the context of a mental outlook, who took decisions while loyally obeying an organization, their immediate leader or the political group to which they belonged.

Why not just abandon the fiction of the personified spirit of the state? I can give two reasons for not doing so, one secondary, the other fundamental. During the few thousand years of high policy men have never belonged to anything other than particular entities, limited in space and contiguous with other entities. The more these entities solidified, the more they imposed on individuals submission, discipline and sometimes sacrifice. According to the epoch, these entities either included or excluded those simple mortals who were outside noble affairs. Clausewitz lived during a period of transition from the monarchy of the *ancien régime*, where soldiers were recruited from the lower echelons of society, to modern societies where all healthy men were mobilized with a view to a conflict between nations.

But whether or not people participated in wars, armies took their orders from a chief, and the strategist himself took his orders from somewhere: the assembly of people in the agora, or the emperor who 'personified' the supreme authority of one entity as against another. Whether or not Khrushchev decided to install rockets in Cuba, or whether it was decided by the Presidium, or as a consequence of obscure quarrels between civilians and the military, Soviet soldiers would have been killed if American aircraft had bombed the launching-pads according to the deliberations of the chiefs of staff. For over half a century historians have discussed who was responsible for the war of 1914. Who took what decision? Who provoked the disaster? These uncertainties, often insoluble, cannot acquire the status of facts: armies and people responded to the appeal of August 1914 as 'one man' (or almost).

The behaviour of these armed masses becomes senseless if we refuse to see a spirit leading them. If it is philosophically necessary, I will agree that there are only individuals and that state, nation and army do not exist in the same way as individuals do. But if these concepts are suppressed then political history becomes incomprehensible and blind rage and chaotic tumult ensue. A conceptualization that dissolves the human object to which it is meant to give flesh is self-refuting.

Marxists might object that the interest of society as a whole is an ideology, for there is not and cannot be a common interest of enemy classes. No one denies that the external action of a state is partly determined by how such and such a class makes use of its interest or by the pressure exerted by groups on those who wield the power of the state. But two experiences in our century invite reflection. When he has been converted to Marxism the worker does not lose his national consciousness. If the majority of 'responsible leaders' or 'permanent heads' of the French Communist Party followed the directives coming from Moscow in 1939, the militants and electors of the party still fought as Frenchmen. To postulate that the only true struggle takes place between classes does not add up to an ideology, because it gives a meaning to history that would be rejected by the people who lived through it. The ideology could only become a philosophy when those parties to it had arrived at the state of affairs they decried, i.e. abolition of the class struggle.

The revolutions of the twentieth century have given more substance to the state. A Communist Party, after the revolutionary victory, hurries to 'regularize the irregulars' and legalize its own national claim. The Chinese empire lasted for thousands of years; the ideology of universal revolution lasted for barely ten years within the framework of coexistence between the two great states basing themselves upon it.

Let us be clear on this point. To call the Soviet Union 'Russia' is just as much ideological as calling it the 'Workers' Socialist State'. The Russian of the tsarist heritage has been taken out of the Communist Party. After taking power in the capital, the Communist Party reconstituted multinational empire without even stopping at the reconquest of a province that had set up a government with a different ideology. But the Soviet Union did not purely and simply begin where the tsars left off. The openings offered to the various races did not remain the same and the Bolsheviks had different geographical and traditional bases from the Romanovs from which to work. What makes General de Gaulle's ideology closer to conceptual truth than the ideology of Marxism–Leninism is that he seized upon an aspect of historical reality whereas the Marxists aimed for utopia – at a world that has never existed and, so far as we can judge, never will. Humanity does not constitute a politico-military unity: any party that takes power hastens to set up a particular state even in the name of the world proletariat; in our day this even applies to states that try to be national though they contain a plethora of people and races. The new masters introduce multiple interest in international relations and in inter-party relations. Since even a party-state is a state – that is, the members of the ruling party defend the interests of the country as a whole against other countries – why should these interests always be in accordance with those of any other party-state? The Sino-Soviet dispute was expressed and rationalized in the language of Marxism–Leninism which was common to both sides. You would have to be very simple-minded to think that the conflict only involves the interpretation of ideology or that ideology constitutes the only cause of the schism. The Soviet Union would not have any doubt about the terms of unequal treatise which the leaders of People's China on principle reject. If Mao's China ran risks in 1958 to throw the nationalists out of Quemoy and Matsu, does the USSR also have to do so? Even when they were trusting allies, Khrushchev and Mao were to discover the fatal implications of nuclear weapons. In the end Khrushchev behaved towards Mao as all American presidents have done towards France. The policies of the socialist and Atlantic camps call to mind the spirit of the state personified all the more as one man can press the button. Nuclear war restores its authentic meaning to the definition of policy as the spirit of the state personified.

There remains a final objection, the one most often raised. Just as the state machine, divided between competing parties, does not constitute a whole, so society torn by classes or its economy and dominated by the multi-national monsters cannot resemble the nation exalted by the French Convention and exalted in their turn by the German patriot against Napoleon. Are states alone to count as historical subjects? Must the study of social relations which cross frontiers be based on conflicts and exchanges between states?

Here again the objection seems to me to be both obvious and irrelevant. I either ignored or neglected international phenomena and what I have called the transnational. The Roman Catholic Church and the Communist International never confine themselves to territorial boundaries even if their leaders reside within the capital cities of single states. In the same way the gigantic conglomerate of IBM, though born within a national economy and directed by an American board, takes an international approach. Businesses wrongly termed multinational make no claims, in the manner of the Catholic Church or the salvationist religions, to transcend differences of nationality, race or linguistics groups. They accept frontiers and teach the leaders of their branches to adapt to the customs and requirements of the national state. They calculate investment and division of means as if the national economics belonged to a single economy. Even where they are part of a universal church the churches have a national stamp. It is no different with the branches of IBM. The meaning of this 'national stamp' varies from one case to another. Catholic priests spread the same words of salvation in Italy and France, in Europe and Africa, as to the children of Quimper and Douala. The transcendental truth the good word brought to each and every one crosses frontiers which vanish in the eyes of God. The strategy of multinational concerns crosses frontiers, using them for profit without denying their existence.

I therefore believe that transnational phenomena differ in their significance from international phenomena. Both of them involve what is known academically as 'international relations'. What is problematic is the principle stated at the beginning of my *Peace and War among the Nations*: the central character of international relations. Do they remain central to the socialist or capitalist worlds? Are armed conflicts like the Indo-Pakistan and Israeli–Arab wars merely peripheral in importance compared to the price of oil? Once possible solutions become the exception rather than the rule, and of only marginal importance to international relations, what remains of the Clausewitzian universe?

2 Nationality – Clausewitz to the American 'analysts'

There have been four stages in the framework of Clausewitz's thought leading from the European system of states to the world system of today: (a) Lenin, in which the national interest is supplanted by class interests; (b) Mao Tse-tung, where in the last analysis the political matters more than the technical and the people's defence of itself will succeed in the face of weapons of massive destructive power; (c) nuclear strategists, particularly American, who say that arms with huge potential for destruction rule out 'payment in specie' since, if such payment is resorted to, it would mean a risk of common suicide. From common sense they argue that the most devastating weapons are useless and a victory of annihilation is therefore impossible; whatever their fascination for generations of generals there can be no more Jenas or Sedans (whether of 1870 or 1940). (d) Brinkmanship and escalation: without the criterion of absolute war how are relations between enemies to be governed, enemies who traditionally proceed according to tests of strength of successful or potential combat?

André Glucksmann, one of the few French commentators on Clausewitz, has argued that there is a deep gulf between the Clausewitzian viewpoint and that of the American analysts. If I understand him correctly, his thesis at bottom offers marginal propositions. Clausewitzian strategy presupposes autonomous strategic calculations in the military sense even if their original point was political. Now, since the strategic and the political are the same, there will be total concurrence between military objective and political goal, so that surely argumentation will be irrelevant and only the language of deterrence will remain.

Glucksmann's sketchy interpretation of Clausewitz stems from a position I believe to be unacceptable. He bases a theoretical entity on a few phrases wrenched from their context which are incompatible with many ideas in the Treatise. He creates an abstraction out of the various occasions when the chapters were written.

In order to demonstrate the incompatibility between Clausewitzian reasoning and the reasoning of nuclear strategists, Glucksmann starts by suggesting that in the Treatise strategic calculation is autonomous, a calculation needing a solution comparable to that of a strategic game. He relies on a few lines in Chapter 1 of Book I to prove his point: according to this, disarmament constitutes the proper objective of warlike action and there is some gap between the political objective and actual war. This phrase, as we have seen, is in the first part of the chapter, but it is also legitimate to extrapolate from the model, as Clausewitz himself does, i.e. from the savage, original concept of war in which the two sides simply try to knock each other out, without motive or even political aim.

There is a second phrase in Chapter 1 of Book I that confirms this one: if the objective of a war is equivalent to the political aim, then as a general rule it will diminish in accordance with the political aim. Here again Clausewitz notes a proportionality that is not constant or necessary, but is still frequent and natural, between the size of the political prize and the intensity of violence. Neither phrase permits an exact correspondence to be made between the 'political' logic and its expression, and the strategic 'grammar' − a correspondence that might support the interpretation arrived at by Moltke and the great German general staff. Glucksmann, through sophistry and questionable analogies, paradoxically arrives at the crude and inaccurate conclusions of the military.

In effect, his aim is to show that Clausewitz's strategic calculation could lend itself to mathematical treatment comparable with a strategic game.

The aim of the great battle and the superiority of defence are not simply two transitory historical events. They form the background to any purely strategic calculation. *Vom Kriege* poses the fundamental problem for any purely strategic calculation and lays down the form of any solution. If we do not situate the problem, the warlike act, between the two limiting positions of decisive battle and strict defence, we should have to find other limiting positions with the same conceptual functions. Otherwise the existence of the problem as a theoretical entity would be impossible, whatever the publications and attention it provokes; the entire politico-strategic relationship has to be considered; recourse to the *ultima ratio* has no strategic, but only a political significance, and at the conceptual level, Hegelian dialectics will outweigh Clausewitzian strategy.

But the Treatise never uses such expressions as 'strict defence' which for Clausewitz would be meaningless: defence has to be active, and will always contain an element of the offensive.

Using both space and time, the defence will bring additional force to the weaker side and possibly allow it to make up for its inferiority. The symmetry of defence and attack is perhaps a necessary condition, but not, of course, a sufficient one, in the mathematical calculation of strength that Clausewitz declared to be impossible once and for all because of 'moral questions'.

Glucksmann suggests an analogy between one of the conditions of a 'mathematizable' game of strategy and the disparity of defence and attack: 'the players have contrasting interests, but the means used by them are not related in the form of mutual opposition'. In the same way, polarity or mutual opposition requires a solution (or battle) but the means, whether defence or attack, do not.

The decisive battle could even be ingeniously compared with the end-game while truce or armistice, the encounter of two strategies of prudence, could be equated with stalemate. None of these comparisons really survives examination.

The analogy implies that any war should belong to the first type, aimed at arming or disarming the enemy state and victory by annihilation of enemy forces. Strategic calculation is made out to exist in only one type of war because the decisive battle is not the goal of the other. Rational calculation in the sense of games theory is not possible even in a war of the first kind because, according to Clausewitz, in any real war, moral qualities, 'friction', the effect of accident on military operations will intervene and they are not quantifiable. The strategist knows his weaknesses better than those of the enemy. He must therefore take risks and wager on a particular set of circumstances which, in detail, will resemble no other. The war plan to which Glucksmann attributes a possible or theoretical rationality would involve the whole game and would contain several possible answers to the various possible enemy responses as well as the possible result of the encounter between the two strategies. Clausewitz would never have thought that plan of war could meet such demands.

Nothing is more foreign to Clausewitz than the idea of a system of thought based on calculations of strength, 'abstracting the players, their motives, whether overt or not, and their psychology'. He would have fought the pseudo-rationality of the calculations of strength as he fought the geometric forms of H. von Bülow and Jomini. A plan of war that exhausts all options and provides for everything cannot, and does not, even theoretically, exist. Clausewitz says it will lose all relevance and significance if it departs so far from reality.

Despite its subtleties the interpretation that I have attacked is an old tune. Clausewitz wrote that there is a grammar of war but not a logic of war. He never wrote that the grammar translates the logic point by point, nor that once the objectives have been set by logic grammar becomes self-contained and obeys its own laws. By distorting Clausewitz's thought in this way it is possible once more to justify the military leader in his desire to handle the military instrument as he thinks fit, once it is handed to him by the state. Moreover, international relations – the polarity that characterizes the hostility – are also raised to the level of politics and it can be suggested that political relations between states are a zero-sum game as a whole, which obviously contradicts Chapter 6 of Book VI. Between states that recognize one another interests are sometimes opposed, but in some circumstances they can be in harmony, and the tendency to equilibrium in the system results from the superior nature of the interests joined together against any disturbance. International relations do not resemble the strategic zero-sum duel. We have no right to attribute to Clausewitz the idea that peace is strategically prolonged and prolongable truce. Truce is the suspension of hostilities during war. Peace is non-war and non-recourse to violence. War does not suspend relations between states; rather it gives them a supplementary dimension – that of violence. By definition each wrestler will try to beat the other. But the simple polarity involved in the zero-sum game only concerns the outcome – victory – which is a tactical notion and not the real war. It is guided by political objectives and waged by states belonging to a complex unity. At every stage the conduct of war is a political act. The laws proper to strategic (or military) grammar are always subordinate to the requirement of political logic.

If, as according to Glucksmann, the warlike act and the political act were identical, any theoretical basis for nuclear strategy would be removed. This is plain and expressed clearly in the final synthesis of the Treatise. Such an identity does not mean that there is a break between the classical and modern theories. Both of them pose two major propositions: the political determines the war and its character; policy shapes it with a view to the objectives suggested or set out by the political. Like any tool, the military tool must be used in conformity with its nature and laws but that tool is in the control of the person who uses it. The act of force remains intrinsically a political act, an element in the dialectic of wills at odds.

The question raised by Glucksmann – does the strategic-political link have to be reconsidered in the nuclear age? – none the less remains legitimate and necessary; though not because the strategic calculation which was autonomous yesterday has ceased to be so today, nor because the *ultima ratio* or recourse to violence has changed its significance. By their very destructive power, nuclear weapons cannot be handled in the same way as weapons from the past. Neither decisive battles nor the intrinsic superiority of defence can exist as such in our epoch.

Space and time will be to some degree eliminated the more nuclear weapons are effectively used. A nuclear weapon of some megatons is sufficient to destroy a city. In half an hour a ballistic missile will cross the thousands of miles between its launching-ramp and a city. If one of the great powers was to strike the other with the greater part of its nuclear arsenal the other would barely survive as a historical subject fit to surrender. The risk of contamination would prevent the aggressor, assuming that the victim could or would not respond.

If the superiority of defensive forces constitutes the only way of preventing a recourse to extremes it would disappear if nuclear weapons were to be used against cities. If it is only the decisive battle that brings war to an end, then war will last without end and without a solution. The conditions laid down for 'a rational solution of the strategic problem' do not exist. But it is Glucksmann, not Clausewitz, who tries to lay them down. Logical dreaming or the recourse to extremes is stopped as soon as historical subjects replace wrestlers in the simplified model. States know one another and, approximately speaking, they also know what they have to fear. Communication between enemies based on historical experience contributes moderation to warlike excesses in a non-revolutionary period. The question continually posed by Glucksmann – who will limit the limited wars? – has the same answer in the nuclear age that it had in Napoleon's time, namely political understanding. The answer has not changed;

neither have the risks. Each party acts according to the desires he imputes to others and his *alter ego* behaves no differently. The dialectic of mutual suspicion – the response of A to the supposed intention of B, B's intention justified by the supposed intention of A with regard to the supposed intention of B, and so on *ad infinitum* – leads to extremes in all directions. Nuclear weapons have reactivated this without aggravating the process. American writers have gradually admitted that the two opponents have the supreme interest in common of not annihilating one another. Suspicion maintains arms rivalry; the common interest prevents an escalation to extremes and leads back to armed observation. The two solutions relating to arms and to deterrence are both political and strategic, inseparably linked. They both involve mutual understanding. Neither of the two great powers wants a victory of annihilation, which is ruled out by the opponent's capacity for a second strike. War between the two great powers if we suppose (wrongly) that rivalry is similar to war, belongs to the second type, involving limited victory with no radical solution. In the second type of war no necessity exists even in the abstract: reason lays down no laws. Politico-strategic understanding reigns and the rapier or button-rapier is substituted for the heavy sword.

None the less, there is a considerable enough difference between the dialectic of today and that of the past. In the past the size of interests and passions brought people near to mutual slaughter. Rightly or wrongly we suppose that from now on consciousness of a possible catastrophe is a buffer. We suppose that common suicide, the constant possibility of a fight to the death, will be rejected by the participants even if they become involved in a struggle that once would have been called a fight to the death. There is nothing to guarantee that this hypothesis will be confirmed in the future. At least we can conceive of a possible conflict in which the effective use of nuclear weapons seems plausible and in circumstances perhaps not too distant. The threat of common suicide acting as a buffer ought, after all, to be more effective than the greater effectiveness of defence, which the aggressive state can often make explicit by innovations in technique and method.

That the unity of politics and strategy does not permit other limitations on war except by agreement between the contestants is a proposition at least implicit in Clausewitz, and it has become both fundamental and explicit in American literature. It does not change our understanding of Clausewitz but rather stresses the political aspect.

The disappearance of decisive battle might deprive strategic thinking of an indispensable concept. But so-called deterrent strategy is not all strategy. In Clausewitzian vocabulary the use of a weapon involves tactics not strategy. If nuclear arms were to be used on the battlefield it would be tactics that would show how they should be used. Deterrence by threat only has a negative (defensive) objective which is to prevent the other from taking advantage or from attacking. As this threat is, or seems to be, permanent (all the year round the submarines patrol underwater), and as it has to forestall its own use, it belongs to the area of politics and does not lead to any solution. The USA and the Soviet Union are not waging a war in the Clausewitzian sense. The absence of any confrontation through deterrence results logically from the very concept of deterrence. Rivalry between nuclear powers can and must be pursued without a confrontation, although any conflicts that do arise will involve a result in favour of one side or the other.

The Clausewitzian way of looking at things always remains political. It wants to appear to be 'reasonable' even though no one can calculate how much reason can explain in the absence of a standard by which to measure the value of the stake and the size of the risk. At no point can it obey the necessities of reason. It canalizes passions, controls the freedom of the military leader and designates the centres of gravity or the weaknesses of the enemy. To the American writers, responsible for a diplomacy that involves if not violence, at least the threat of it, and that requires conceptualization of problems, strategic calculation means using scientific data as regards weaponry, so as to obtain the best military results with a limited budgetary outlay, to adapt the means to the end. It also means using military force to preserve the USA's interests and to acquire military force corresponding to the needs of alliances unless these alliances are subordinated to the military apparatus. This strategic thinking is not outside the pale for Clausewitz even if it uses some notions or expressions borrowed from games theory. It places force at the service of political ends and looks for rationality in the adaptation of means to ends and for what is reasonable in the choice of ends. It speculates on abstract situations so as to train the mind for controlling real ones.

What distinguishes this from the Treatise is that there the military elements were based on historical experience as well as on concepts and reason. However, in all areas concerning the link between political intention and the military, the Treatise clings to historical description and recalls theoretical truths and the maxims derived therefrom. The paradox of American strategic literature as observed in places by Glucksmann is that the writers implicitly recognize 'the unification of the strategic and the political' but do not accept the consequences of this. In other words, they limit themselves to analyses that are essentially strategic (in the sense of the use of force), whereas nowadays strategy contains a greater political element (in all senses of that word) than in past centuries. The result is the risk of misunderstood formalism, abstract controversies and doubtful prescription. Deterrence by nuclear threat uses the notion of rationality regularly without defining it. There is nothing to show that 'American rationality' coincides with Chinese rationality.

3 Clausewitzian principles in the nuclear age

American strategic literature concentrates on nuclear weapons and speculates on models that are more or less schematic. it invents scenarios and suggests ways of doing things appropriate to particular situations without making any prescriptions. It is equivocal and impure and lacks epistemological rigour. It moves in the world of what-is-likely, reflecting that world that it has partly contributed to forming, and provisionally resolving the contradiction between the capacity of states for mutual destruction and their refusal to fuse into a superior unity or to combine. We could also say that it resolves the contradiction between radical oppositions, which in earlier times would have led to a fight to the death, and the effective limitation of warlike violence on the global scale.

My intention is not to pass judgment on this literature but to sketch out a comparison between the politico-strategic calculation of today and that of the past in respect of two classical themes: dialectic of defence and attack: and the relationship between strength, ways and means of negotiation, i.e. trade on credit, in the absence of any payment in real money.

Referring to the three levels – political, strategic and tactical – for both nuclear and classical forces, we find that at a tactical level, i.e. in the event of the effective use of nuclear weapons, advantage belongs to the attacker (the first strike) as this would destroy the enemy's nuclear weapons, or part of them, and in any event creates the likelihood of chaos. Indeed, we could say that the lapse of time between attack and reprisals would be reduced to the point where the distinction between attack and defence would be almost wiped out, as happens in hand-to-hand fighting. Abandonment by the two powers of anti-missile defence as well as of passive defence signifies acceptance of common vulnerability, an acceptance based on a confidence in the other's use of reason (or rather, a common understanding of what is meant by reason).

The strategic level (or military threat) and the political level are indistinguishable as far as nuclear weapons are concerned. These weapons have only been used as a threat, both implicit and conditional, since Hiroshima and Nagasaki, always controlled by the head of state himself and never put at the disposal of military leaders. The very term deterrence or *Abschrecken* (*dissuasion* in French) suggests a negative or defensive approach in the Clausewitzian sense. Nuclear weapons abolish the enemy's offensive intent. Some doctrinaire approaches to nuclear weapons push the idea of the superiority of defence over attack to the extreme. Provided that it has destructive capacity due to a small number of nuclear weapons, any state could transform its territory into a sanctuary definitively sheltered from attack by the threat of reprisals.

This transposition of the superiority intrinsic to defence is said to illustrate, yet again, the truth of the Latin tag: *beati sunt possidentes* or the advantage lies with him who has control. It is easier to hang on to something than to take it. Since a duel conducted by threats is equivalent in the last analysis to the dialogue between the two states or two 'people' it can, as it were, be grasped intuitively that a deterrent menace meant to stop the other side from taking what it covets will operate more easily than a persuasive threat meant to force the other side to retire from an occupied area or to suspend operations which have already begun.

This thesis seems to me to be both plausible and psychologically probable, yet it has not been proven. The dialectic between two political wills is never wholly foreseeable. The thesis that nuclear threats are infallibly effective, even where the hypothesis demands that the forces engaged are unequal and that the enormity of the risk taken will compensate for weakness of credibility, remains a matter of opinion. The ability to quantify the amount of destruction needed for a small power to deter a great one remains for the moment an intellectual game without any demonstrable value. A proposition, even if general and vague, may none the less have some verisimilitude. Nuclear blackmail, or the use of the nuclear threat with a positive goal in mind, does not belong to the mental universe of statesmen. There has been no such example in the past twenty-five years. The Soviet Union did not resort to nuclear weapons to prevent People's

384

China acquiring them in turn. These arms help to abolish the (real or supposed) intention of the aggressor and they contribute to maintaining the territorial *status quo*, in so far as it is not changed by events inside countries or by armed conflicts taking place below the nuclear threshold.

At the level of tactics, classical weapons favour attack rather than defence in our day. In the tank battles and particularly in the desert the Arab–Israeli wars revealed the advantage of striking first. The battle was won in a few hours in 1967. The Egyptian army, with no air cover, was doomed from the first few minutes. In 1973 the advantage attached to surprise did not give the Syrians and Egyptians a decisive victory but it very nearly did. The Syrians were on the point of breaking through on the Golan Heights and pushing their tanks on to the plain. The Egyptians, perhaps, could have taken the key positions of the heights on the eastern banks of the Suez Canal.

The weapons that gave Hitler lightning victories in 1939 and 1940 still exist. Anti-tank and aircraft arms are available, but unequal technique and organization can allow the aggressor to exploit his own superiority on the battlefield and arrive at a *fait accompli* within a few days. If there were more wars fought with conventional weapons and ending quickly the cause would be the worldwide nature of the system. Classical arms that force a decision – armoured weapons and aircraft – can be produced in great quantities but only by the industrialized states who alone possess the economic means to fuel combat. Apart from 1973, the battles fought with modern weapons by partially industrialized countries have lost momentum, either because stocks ran out or the solution was reached. During the Yom Kippur war the belligerents were supplied by the Soviets and the Americans. The Soviets wanted to give the Arabs the chance of victory and the Americans wanted to avoid the defeat of Israel.

As for the industrialized nations, they have not fought a conventional war against each other for the last twenty-five years. The American expeditionary forces fought in Korea and Vietnam. These were troops from industrialized countries equipped with modern weaponry as well as aircraft. The only decisive victory was the landing at Imchon which allowed the Americans to cut the supply lines of the North Korean army which was fighting in the South, and to destroy the greater part of it. Otherwise such fighting resembles the second part of the last war where defence once more showed its intrinsic superiority. In Vietnam the regular army of the North fought in the style of the partisans, concentrating tightly to fight at one moment and then dispersing to survive without a continuous or marked front. The military draw in Korea resulted from the American refusal to increase the stake. In Vietnam it resulted from the regular army's inability decisively to defeat an army that refused to give battle and whose objective was to avoid being defeated. These wars, by their length, contrast with wars fought between small states.

Do nuclear weapons explain the length of one and the brevity of the others? I do not think so. It is circumstances in the outside world that explain the rapid stopping or the prolonging of armed conflict. The two dominant states, and particularly the USA, exert an influence on most conflicts, either by the mediation of the USA or directly in ways comparable to those used by the great powers or the 'concept of Europe' in local conflicts in the nineteenth century. Even though the belligerents join one of the two camps into which the world has divided, the Soviet Union and the USA try not to be involved in their conflict, though one of the great powers also tried to limit the defeat of its protégé. This struggle of one of the two great powers against an ally or protégé of the other may be prolonged, whether for want of a decisive victory or for want of a common interest. The Soviet Union thus profited from the American forces being stuck in Korea and then in Vietnam.

The diversity and forms of these conflicts have brought about the American concept of 'escalation', in which there exists something akin to the old idea of an ascent to extremes. This notion, which is never defined, contains two ideas, a moral and a political one. War in the past could be waged with extreme energy, leading to mobilization and then resolute and brutal use of a maximum of resources. The urge to defeat the enemy so as to impose one's will and dictate peace terms led, therefore, to the most direct (though not the only) method – destruction of the enemy forces. But since the end of the Second World War the greatest world power has not won a single armed conflict in which it took part. By contrast Mao's Chinese and the Vietnamese of Ho Chi Minh were victorious after prolonged fighting. In our age, annihilation at the end of a process of attrition takes on specific forms, but conceptually it belongs to the Clausewitzian universe. The national insurrection against the French of which he dreamt and the destruction of the Grande Armée in Russia prefigured the extreme solution in a revolutionary war or a war of national liberation, owing to retreat into the interior, the arming of the people and the defensive use of time, space and morale.

The contrast between nuclear indecision and the decisive nature of conventional weapons and popular war brings up the classical notion of the relationship of strength and involves escalation. The events of the 1950s were not a mystery. To quote Clausewitz, war is not fought with coal, sulphur and saltpetre or with iron and lead but with powder and guns. It is the courage of men and the effectiveness of their weapons that wins victories on the battlefield, not the statistics of the GNP. If the USA had thrown in further military divisions it could have achieved a decisive military victory in Korea. Truman and Acheson reckoned that they could or should be content with a draw because the political prize of success – the unification of Korea – did not justify the necessary gamble.

The case of Vietnam posed more difficult problems. In certain circumstances a regular army cannot win a decisive victory against irregulars if these people can last out until they finally tire the will of the regular army, the politicians at the helm, and the likely recruits. Irregulars can achieve all or part of what they want without carrying attrition to the end in the theatre of operations. Here again, history repeats rather than invents. Innovation on both regular and irregular sides concerns rationalization of the techniques employed in the form of arms, communications and psychological warfare and organization. With its methods of leadership the political party is the counterpart of the military.

In other words, experience suggests that there is a diversity between the levels of military action, every level being autonomous. The nuclear arms of the USA did not influence the Korean War. Late in 1950 China intervened to prevent an American victory even though she had neither nuclear weapons, nor any means of retaliation if those weapons were used. If the bombing of North Vietnam was meant to communicate a threat of the extreme in the form of nuclear weapons, it failed: either the North Vietnamese disbelieved the threat (and events proved them right) or they decided in advance to pay any price rather than give in.

Is the old idea of strength – ratios made obsolete by the relative, if not absolute, autonomy of the levels and the means of asserting force? The USA's influence across the globe, and its secretary of state's ability to act either as mediator or arbiter, reflect its overall potential, a potential that is military, economic, technical and financial. What proportion of this potential can be imputed to the military? And of that, what share is taken by nuclear weapons? This cannot really be precisely answered. Certainly, Sterling in the nineteenth century did not dominate because of the Royal Navy's control of the seas. The one lent nothing of significance to the other. In the same way the military power of the USA has contributed to the reign of the dollar but that would not have been enough to impose.

What remains relatively singular and novel is not that the overall strength of a state is expressed in its external actions, but rather that overall strength turns out to be so inapplicable that a negotiated settlement like Vietnam is ineffective. In spite of the diplomatic efforts of Nixon and Kissinger in Moscow and Peking, and the million tons of bombs dropped on North Vietnam and the Ho Chi Minh Trail, the clauses in the Paris agreement that failed to give Hanoi an immediate victory (a government under communist domination in the South) also officially allowed the Vietcong enclaves in which they could survive in the South; officially this opened the way to a third war, following the military defeat of the French and the Americans.

Virtually everywhere negotiated agreements, at least territorial settlements, in the last thirty years have become *faits accomplis*. Partition survives in Korea as it did for twenty years in Vietnam. These wars which end in a cease-fire but not in peace, these *de facto* partitions that one state will not accept, or *faits accomplis* that cannot be changed but which cannot be accepted openly, stem from many features in the modern world: from the worldwide extension of a system that both provokes a clash between radically different civilizations and rules out the coherent power of a universally recognized system of international law, and from the ideological rivalry that gives some conflicts a dual aspect of being at the same time foreign and civil. Logically, a civil war demands a radical victory for one of the sides whereas a foreign war can take a compromise solution. The great powers have created two claimants for power and only partition can offer an alternative to civil war, though in Vietnam partition itself did not bring the civil war to an end. Clausewitzian themes, altered in some ways by the existence of nuclear weapons, survive today provided that the unity of warlike and political acts is recognized, or, to put it differently, provided that the military always remains within the confines of political understanding. At the end of the chapter devoted to demonstrating the absurdity of the ideas he himself imputes to Hermann Kahn, Glucksmann concludes:

If the essence of nuclear strategy presupposes the interaction of these two gambits, where blackmail regarding escalation is harmonized with the conventional use of force, then the essentials of nuclear strategy and the credibility of threats depend on policy (Who threatens whom? Why?) and not on strategic calculation (How?).

Glucksmann has attributed to Clausewitz an autonomous strategic military calculation and then attributed the idea to American strategists only to discover when it is all worked out that the idea fails. In fact, the whole question does not involve speculation in the abstract about deterrence, but the knowledge of who can deter whom, from what, with which threats and in which circumstances. In other words, the credibility of deterrence presupposes a reference to all the circumstances and it can never be reduced to a simple military calculation (although such a calculation is an element in the whole).

The autonomy of the different levels leads him to the same conclusion:
If the thresholds are 'standards of behaviour' then the 'how' of the strategic game will depend on the 'against whom, for whom, why' of the political game at the level of the thresholds and not vice versa. Therefore it is the very beginning that invites rejection because it does not provide anything other than a purely descriptive and retrospective frame of reference which cannot be the basis for any calculation or foresight. The idea of an overall nuclear strategy as distinct from the game of the great thermo-nuclear powers must be abandoned.

The last phrase should be stressed because it expresses the thesis I have always upheld and that most American writers would except, though not without reluctance – Hermann Kahn with less reluctance, probably, than the others (W.W. Kaufmann, T.C. Schelling or even A.J. Wohlstetter). In substituting the concept of a scenario for that of a model he implicitly renounces the ambition of giving a theoretical status to his speculations or war games.

4 The definition of war and the ubiquity of violence
In the interpretation that I have given it, the identity of the political act with the warlike act does not compromise the Clausewitzian system. It would be quite impossible for conflicts between states to be reduced to a zero-sum game when such conflicts sometimes reach extremes and sometimes descend to simple armed observation. The heart of the problem, especially today, is the maintenance of the initial definition of war by violence within the framework of the final synthesis.

Three arguments are advanced here and there against this definition. Does not the Cold War represent a kind of international relationship that lies somewhere between peace and war and does not correspond to a radical distinction between the one and the other? Even when *détente* succeeds, cold war does not. Russian and American as well as British and French submarines are on permanent patrol; they can launch their deadly missiles at targets fixed in advance. Finally, is it right to reduce violence to physical violence embodied in armed force? Is there not in the present world a crystallized violence, without which the double hierarchy, within and between states, would cease to exist?

I shall pass over the first argument which is, I think, irrelevant even if correct. In both peace-time and war, changing customs fix the limits of harm that men and states will do to one another. Montesquieu's maxim – in peace-time do as much good as possible, in wartime as little damage as possible – has never been respected. However, human beings controlled centrally do not take up arms against one another unless they cross the barrier between peace and war. On the other hand, pressures exerted on allied states by non-violent means have always counted as normal. The activities of secret agents, spies or agitators especially are not unknown either to contemporaries or historians in the golden age of the European republic of states or of the 'concept of Europe'.

In 1866 Bismarck held in reserve the men and weapons of national revolt against the Austrian empire to impose his will. Elsewhere I have analysed the historical oscillation between the Holy Alliance of the sovereigns against all revolutionaries and their alliance with the internal enemies of their brother-sovereigns. The unity of the people, or the unity between governments and governed, constitutes one of the factors in the state's external power. In this respect there has been nothing new since the beginning of the nineteenth century and the Treatise.

I do not believe that the distinction between absolute peace and cold war, which can be found, for instance, in the books of General Beaufre, lacks conceptual significance. These two kinds of non-war present difficulties of degree, not of kind. When states coexist despite conflicting ideologies and at least one of them has a universal vocation, relations within societies in the margin of international relations have to some extent the aspect of a civil conflict or a partisan struggle. If the universal ideology of one of the two great states finds a party within the other states to incarnate and spread it, then psycho-political activity of each state to safeguard its unity and disrupt that of its enemy will become inevitable. The wars of religion presented an example of this intermingling of the internal and external, of military and ideological struggles comparable with those that occurred in the years after the Second World War. We could even say that the states of the twentieth century were more effective and rigorous in limiting the escalation of ideological struggles into violence.

The contrary impression results from the worldwide scale of the system. If we only take the relations between the two great powers, the USSR and the USA, the use of rebels, of racial or national minorities, by each against the other remains discreet. Of course, each of the great powers questions the very nature of the other, but essentially the activities of each hardly go further than secret agents, espionage propaganda. It was in a third set of countries, whether committed or not, that Russo-American rivalry became intense and adopted violent means that came close to war.

Must we regard the Korean War as an episode in the Russo-American war? I believe that we sow confusion if we do. The postwar period has been dominated by the leaders in the Kremlin and the White House trying to avoid war in the true but no longer conventional sense of the term. Korea became the theatre of operations for a war, the origin of which lay in the partition of the country into two zones of occupation. Stalin was probably responsible for tolerating if not ordering the North Korean attack; Truman was responsible for the intervention of Chinese 'volunteers', because he did not take seriously the warnings transmitted to Washington by the Indian ambassador, and because he trusted General MacArthur. The actions of the American ambassador to the Kremlin just after hostilities broke out made the Kremlin innocent of any responsibility. In other words, it tended towards the 'localization of the war'. In conformity with the principle of proportionality between the wager and the prize, the USA only committed forces that were limited as a proportion of their total resources and they did not look to a military solution. This conduct of the campaign, right or wrong, took account of the overall world situation. A limited war was waged having regard to the overall rivalry with a semi-spectator enemy but there was no total war in a limited theatre of operations.

Of course, these circumstances involved some original features, and to simplify I shall name only two. The Soviet Union did not stop supplying North Korea and China with weapons while the North Korean army and the Chinese 'volunteers' fought the American expeditionary force, which in theory was under the control of the United Nations. Between 1948 (or 1949) and 1953 Stalin reduced to a minimum not only diplomatic exchanges between states but also human ones, between countries. Soviet representatives did not appear at sporting competitions or at scientific congresses. During the past twenty years these extreme forms of fall-back or close-down have disappeared. The Soviet Union has a place in all assemblies where delegates of states or societies appear, although it continues to restrict individual exchange over the border, and although trade remains slight and subject to the requirements and highly detailed decisions of the competent ministry.

The second argument poses a more difficult problem. It is sufficient to quote the famous section of *Leviathan* on the state of nature to discover the equivalent there of present-day circumstances. The silos replace the eighteenth-century fort and ballistic missiles the gun. What is new is the instantaneous and total character of the threat from which results precautions against an 'atomic Pearl Harbor'. The Soviets have followed the American example without, it seems, sharing their rival's anxieties. Convinced of the primacy of policy, they never believed that weapons would go off by themselves or that a plausible scenario would arise through a massive attack in a period of calm.

The question that remains can be formulated in these term: does technique alone — the enormous space covered by the destructive power of a nuclear bomb, the thousands of miles crossed by a ballistic missile in a few dozen minutes — condemn mankind to live in anguish? To unite or to perish? To overcome the division into sovereign states? On many occasions I have been inclined to think so. Now I tend in the other direction. It is policy rather than weapons that creates the danger. Despite the ramblings of would-be experts, France does not consider herself to be threatened by the Soviet capacity. Is this because of the three nuclear submarines and the sixteen underground missiles in Haute-Provence? Of course not. In the absence of this strategic deterrent force, the anxiety (or serenity) of the French would remain the same. It is not machines that make history; they alter the conditions in which men make it.

Men thus become accustomed to the sword of Damocles and no longer fear that it will suddenly strike them. Does this provide a false sense of security or a dangerous illusion? No one can give a categorical answer. Of the two visions of the future that were seen twenty-five years ago there seems to be one that history is gradually bringing about: either one of the two claimants for mastery would decisively achieve it, or other centres of power would be constituted or reconstituted. It was the second alternative that always seemed more plausible than the first, and now, I believe, it has lost all credibility. The instrument of nuclear power provides neither a solution nor imperial power. It permits extermination rather than hegemony. Would a new Hitler some day manage to make a threat credible to the point of obtaining the surrender of his intended victims? No one can rule such a scenario out, but equally no one should give way to an obsession with the possible horror.

In the last twenty-five years the division of the diplomatic field, both horizontally and vertically, has become accentuated. Domination at the higher level of violence does not determine the outcome of a conflict waged at a lower level. The superiority of the defensive, in the form of popular warfare, is the counterpart of the tactical superiority of the attack thanks to improved weapons in the last war. Aggression and decisive success in a limited area, where neither great power can or will commit regular forces, may be allowed by conventional weapons. Once decolonization is over, popular war continues to make use of the tactical procedures common to wars of liberation and revolutionary war. Within a national framework it is no longer sufficient for partisans simply not to lose or survive in order to win against governments stemming from the same people and talking the same language. Despite their political inspiration the partisans fall back into the situation of the *francs tireurs*, or even banditry, as soon as murder, hostage-taking, bomb-planting and other practices of urban guerilla warfare, confined to inaccessible areas, fail to ignite the great bonfire.

In other words, despite popular war, the worldwide society of nations embraces new customs and defines the always floating limitations between peace and war. The USA and the Soviet Union live at peace, not at war, although each one of them supplies one of the belligerents with weapons in some of the limited wars (e.g. Israeli–Arab). The Soviet Union and China do not make war although they have not settled some of their differences, and they tolerate frontier incidents as if they were the normal activities of peace-time.

On the other hand, between 1950 and 1953 the USA and People's China fought a limited, though undeclared, war. This was a juridical and social phenomenon that invites reflection, but it does not dissolve the conceptual distinction between peace and war. The USA was defending a border of its imperial territory while China wished to prevent that zone from extending to the frontier separating Korea and Manchuria. The stake was more limited for the USA than for China, but all the same it was limited for both belligerents. The common interest of avoiding recourse to extremes, of preventing the consequences of the juridical state of war, explains the mutual consent to fictions – of 'volunteers' on the one side and of the United Nations on the other. Each side gave a different interpretation to events and used a different vocabulary. According to the North Koreans and the Chinese, the Americans were participating illegitimately in a civil war which became a war of national liberation for them. To the Americans the North Koreans had been the aggressors against South Korea and the Chinese in turn had committed aggression by sending regular troops disguised as volunteers. Despite the incompatible interpretations, the belligerents agreed on concrete measures for limitation.

The more the new states ossified, the more the great powers gave up worrying about the allegiances of the non-committed ones. The more the regional groupings of states acquired autonomy as against the overall system, so the incompatibility of ideologies weighed less in the real business of policies. As long as there are only two predominant states, the world of today will not see the equivalent of the 'concert of Europe' in the last century. The relative weakening of ideological and/or armed conflicts is greater, the more states become 'personified' and acquire recognition of their sovereignty over their territory from the international community. The less People's China can be penetrated by Soviet propaganda, and inversely, the more the dialogue between them will resemble that between individuals despite the multiple influences which, within each one, can be brought to bear on those few responsible for decisions on which will depend the fate of all.

It may be objected that a relationship between two intelligent individuals does not rule out extreme conflict. Certainly, if one wants to reduce the other to total impotence then extreme conflict will result. There is nothing to guarantee that things will not happen in this way one day, but the calculation of risks by one intelligence in the atomic age offers a better chance of controlling hyperbolic violence than the passions of crowds or the intransigence of ideologies. We must regret that states do not even more resemble intelligent people rather than deplore the personification of the state.

There remains an objection: is violence reduced to physical and armed violence? Is not the entire social order, that within states as much as between them, founded on violence? Is it not to be identified with violence? In this hypothesis it is impossible to regard violence as being the specific means of war because it is made out to contaminate the whole state and international structure.

This conceptualization, typical of a certain kind of sociology, ends up by dissolving concepts. Any society contains the threat of sanctions in the event of non-obedience or violation of prohibitions. There is no society where some people are not ready to disobey the social imperatives once the risk of punishment is removed. If we call coercion the act by which an individual or a group elicits behaviour from others by threats of punishment, then it is obvious that any social unit will contain some element of coercion. Moreover, if like some theologians, we suppose that violence can be measured not by the resistance of the governed but by the injustice of the privileged, with the observer being the judge of just and unjust alike, then the share of violence will increase yet more. Thereby the threat of violence or coercion, of violence crystallized or social injustice, covers everything or almost everything in the social field. The distinction between physical and moral violence dissolves because moral violence, that of the law and the state, has become established and maintains itself by physical

392

violence. There is only one more step necessary to end up with the concept of 'symbolic violence' as used by Pierre Bourdieu and his disciples, though without a definition being given, and to arrive at a theory of imperialism which is confused with a theory of international relations.

Symbolic violence may mean 'violence by symbols' or 'symbols of violence'. The gesture a mother makes when imitating a slap is a symbol of physical punishment, a pretence or a substitute. A gesture not accompanied by the physical action has the same effect as the action itself, making the child conscious of his fault and preventing its repetition. The symbolic gesture can even be the equivalent of deterrence.

The violence of the father, the schoolmaster and teachers of every kind and degree is the violence of symbols as seen by Pierre Bourdieu and, if I understand him right, it consists of imposing conceptual frameworks and moral norms, arbitrary because they vary from society to society, on members of society and particularly on the very young. To impose ideas, beliefs, and ways of living and acting that are called *habitus* ('ethos' in Weber's terminology) is said to be violence. Of course, everyone can choose his own vocabulary but this one strikes me, to say the least, as odd.

No one denies the evidence. If a French baby is taken from his cradle and handed over to German foster-parents he will become a German. Culture is not in the blood, it is transmitted by family, school and the many instances of socialization. For this employment of the term 'violence' to be justified, then socialization would have to be regarded as contrary to the aspirations of nature, or at least contrary to the aspirations of a particular category of men.

Freud said that socialization could not proceed without constraint on the individual, without the repression of desire and its expression. He would probably not have confused the constraints imposed on a child's development with violence if it is meant to mould him to the requirements of reality and the group. In any event, at the level of sociological analysis, confusion of the two terms leads to conclusions that are deprived of meaning, or rather conclusions that seem to have some kind of political or polemical motivation.

Generalization of the concept of symbolic violence to cover any kind of educative or pedagogical activity reproduces, with a different vocabulary, what Sartre argued in his *Critique de la raison dialectique*: any socialization will become alienation because the empty consciousness, pure and translucid liberty, is insidiously filled by these 'collective beings' or 'class beings' that enslave it and distort it. In calling the power of the father or master, of the family or school, 'symbolic violence' and in relating that power to the dominant class, sociologists, desperate to be scientific, try hard to present the end process whereby the child, unparticularized at birth, will have a role thrust upon him, as a form of violence. He will acquire the *habitus* – a whole way of seeing, believing and desiring that corresponds to his place in an all-encompassing society.

This is a bizarre vocabulary as it no longer allows a distinction to be made between the ways and means of socialization, the inevitable and diffuse influence of the social group on individuals, which tends to reproduce itself, and the constraint which presupposes conscious or other kinds of resistance by those in power. Violence can only maintain a specific meaning if it designates a relationship between men which involves the use of threats or physical force. Of course, in the context of current speech it is legitimate to talk of moral violence, but the expression does not extend to an unequal relationship between people. A does some moral violence to B when he makes B do something he considers to be morally repugnant, under the threat of force. The sanction involving constraint may be to ruin B and discredit him in the eyes of public opinion. A father is morally violent to his son when he forbids him to follow his own way when he has reached full consciousness. The Sergeant King was morally violent to Frederick the Great, and not without physical violence on occasion. Only he who resists, opposes and attempts to escape the restrictive will suffer violence. If all education is in essence violence, discrimination between violence and non-violence becomes impossible. A word that covers so many relationships can only have an affective or suggestive value. It inspires moral reprobation as regards the phenomena it designates, but it hardly helps in an understanding or appreciation of their complex nature.

The second generalization that is made, based on the concept of violence, seems to me to be less unjustifiable: that the whole of the international system is based on violence. The unequal order present in all societies certainly contains an element of underhand violence. Some who are thus dominated will respect the law and accept the regime only for lack of power. The controversy over the respective share of consent and force needed to maintain social order at this level of generalization remains indefinite and sterile. We can distinguish between regimes that permit criticism and those that do not. Similarly, we can distinguish between the methods adopted by the various socializing agencies, the authorities that tolerate or forbid religious heresies, demands and demonstrations. From the moment that sociologists become obsessed by the contrast between dominating elements (the privileged minority with power, prestige or money) and those who are dominated, they will see violence everywhere because it is indeed found everywhere in one form or another. But at the same time what ought to receive attention and arouse interest is the form this polarization takes and the way in which domination is exerted.

On the other hand, if we adhere to the contrast between the dominating elements and the dominated ones, or between and the centre and the periphery, nothing is easier than to construct a pattern that takes in the dual domination, both internal and external. The dominating elements of a dominant political entity find their natural allies in the centre of peripheral states (privileged people in an exploited society) without those dominated within the dominating society feeling any solidarity with the victims of an unequal relationship from which they themselves derive some advantages.

This theory, or rather, overall picture of the world, is based on certain incontestable facts. The territorial status of Europe in 1975 results from the overt violence of the years 1939–45 and contains 'crystallized violence'. In 1871 the Alsatians proclaimed their desire, through the voices of their representatives, to remain French. A century later they would have accepted their attachment to the Reich had there been no war in the meantime. Once the Alsatians had stopped protesting at their fate, would that have been tantamount to 'crystallized violence'?

394

Economic inequality between peoples constitutes a major factor in our day. The industrialized countries import large quantities of raw materials which they then manufacture. The USA invests capital abroad that usually produces a higher return than it would do at home. By the mediation of so-called multinational companies it contributes towards shaping conditions in which market prices are established. If we agree to call the unequal situation between states imperialism, comparable to the domination by the majority over the minority within states, then nothing can prevent us from calling 'imperialism' – not the taking of sovereignty, which the European states did in the previous century – but the system (excluding the socialist states) as a whole in which the USA has a dominant position.

I do not intend to discuss this theory of imperialism here or to assess its advantages and disadvantages for underdeveloped countries, of commitment to a world market in which the USA occupies the centre. I am interested in vocabulary and concepts. If we regard as 'violent' any social order which we call inequitable or against which part of the dominated element revolts, violence cannot then be conceptually grasped by virtue of its ubiquity. Inversion of the Formula is thus made out to be self-evident. It is not an error made by the Marxist–Leninists.

5 Nations, classes and empire

Why did Clausewitz, like the Marxist–Leninists, not subscribe to the formula that peace is a continuation of war by other means? For a single reason which is the same in both cases: because they define war according to its specific means. Clausewitz did not believe that the international relationship was comparable to a zero-sum game as such. He thought it possible that states could peacefully coexist for centuries to come; there might be occasional conflicts, but without any of the belligerents being eliminated. The Prussian officer's Marxist disciples put his strategic thinking into a philosophy of history, of which the total victory of a class and the elimination of wars would mark the end.

The possible identity between ends must not lead us to false ideas. It is not true that the international relationship as such, or the essential relationship between states, should imply a struggle to the death. The current expressions of psychological or economic warfare cannot be taken *strictu sensu*. In other words, war does not continue when armies have ceased firing?

What classical philosophers taught and what remains true is that, in the absence of laws, states do not escape the risk of violence and cannot rely for their security on the goodwill of their rivals. Even now the USA and the Soviet Union act according to such teaching. The nuclear arms race bears this out. As states the two dominant powers do not wage war to the end. Both of them are saturated by huge land masses so why should they become involved in conflicts, the prize of which is much less than the stake? Even after eliminating its rival the victory would not rule the universe. It is therefore sufficient for the two great powers to act as states did in the past, which in general they have done. Their rivalries, kept within certain limits, remain compatible with non-war and even the weakened warlike tensions of peace-time.

The confusion that needs to be dispelled involves the use of the word 'strategy' outside the context of war. This usage does not seem to me to be contrary either to the original sense of the word or to the Clausewitzian definition. In the framework of war or armed struggle, tactics and strategy are differentiated not by the extent of the horizon but by what is employed, troops in one case and battles in the other. Hitler's wider strategy between 1933 and 1940 lay in the prolongation of the traditional sense of strategy by using before military operations the psychological means that the Allies had used against the Central Powers during the First World War. Total strategy, to use the term of General Beaufre, becomes confused with the policy of the state itself, exploiting all means and methods to assert itself *vis-à-vis* other states.

Current conceptualization more or less clearly distinguishes as many strategies as types of means, economic, psychological and military. Total strategy combines the use of these various strategies. It becomes the means whereby plans conceived by policy or objectives that are laid down are executed. Here again I see no great difficulty in this way of talking, although it does contain ambiguity.

In another Clausewitzian sense, the nature of the means used, whether it be troops or battles, differentiates tactics from strategy. However, at the upper limit, the use of battles is subordinate to the political goal (the state's aims) and the political elements of making decisions, i.e. the attitude of neutrals, the morale of the civilian population and of each side on the front line etc. The conduct of war in the traditional sense takes account of policy in these two senses – policy in the way that goals are fixed and in the way that military strength is conditioned. In so far as the notion of 'total strategy' tends to reduce the autonomy of purely military strategy in order to subordinate it to an overall strategic conception which is itself governed by the political concept and worked out and executed by politicians, it is a continuation of Clausewitz's thought and, whatever General Beaufre's view, it can hardly be distinguished from the conduct of war or 'total policy'.

General Beaufre prefers strategy to policy for two reasons. I accept one and reject the other. He wishes to 'lay down a maximum of rigour in the conduct of war' (or peace). Of course, I agree, but I am not persuaded that the notion of strategy leads to great rigour or to methods of thought that are more reliable than policy. The other reason is his fear that rejection of the term 'total strategy' is a disguised return to an artificial separation of the two fields, the political and the military. What I fear is that the notion of the conduct of peace will confuse war and peace. General Beaufre's suggested definition of strategy oscillates between the two poles. Either it covers all methods of execution by which the self-ordained goals can be attained; in this case 'total strategy' designates the totality of means at a country's disposal for it to attain its ends with or without force or constraint. Or it is 'the art of using force and constraint to attain the ends fixed by policy' or 'the art of the dialectic of wills using force to resolve their conflict'. In this sense, we could never talk of business strategy or party strategy in a democracy since neither firms nor parties use strategy.

Provided we admit that strategy does not necessarily include the means of force or constraint there can be no objection to talking about 'total strategy' in times of peace. However, if strategy implies force or constraint, the permanence of strategy is equivalent to the permanence of war and the international world in all its phases thus involves conflict. In this case we move from the Clausewitzian or Marxist–Leninist conceptualization to the American one that ends in a sterile dialogue between pacifists and neo-Clausewitzians, both of them inclined, under the influence of the Cold War, no longer to distinguish between conflict and war. One side will recall that states have peacefully coexisted for centuries – sometimes fighting but never to the death – whereas Clausewitz's Marxist disciples use his strategic approach in a philosophy of history in which there are endless cases where force can be used and in which the enemy is envisaged as a diabolical figure, whereas to one's own side the use of force is a failure of the political, and an anachronistic way of settling things.

In making the Cold War into a 'level of war' General Beaufre suppresses the main distinction between peace and war, because only perfect peace would not be 'peace-war'. Again, choice of vocabulary is free but Clausewitz and the Marxist–Leninists can warn us of the serious consequences of confusing concepts. A rivalry or conflict of interests, for instance, between the Soviet Union and the USA, is not a war in which historians could attribute responsibility, beginning or end.

It would be possible to talk about 'the conduct of peace' or 'the conduct of a state's external affairs in peace-time' and call this 'total strategy' provided we also recognize that in the absence of armed combat the dialectic of wills is aimed at persuasion as much as at constraint, and at a negotiated settlement or a compromise, rather than the use of force, even if the possibility that force can be used is always present in the background of relations between states.

Does a sudden increase in the price of oil affect the European communities more substantially than an act of physical violence? It does, but it has been said that the dividing line between economic conflict and war remains intact in the sense of recourse to arms. Would the industrialized nations have submitted without armed reprisals if they had been refused oil (which would have paralysed them) or not? The answer depends on one's point of view. It is still the case that participants with differing interests, but who cannot do without one another, have so far decided to play the game without physical violence.

The point on which Clausewitzians and Marxist–Leninists differ is the nature of rivalry between classes and between countries governed by hostile classes. The Soviets and the Chinese do not ideologically renounce the Leninist interpretation of Clausewitz's thought. There are just and unjust wars which in the long run will lead to a peaceful outcome of the class struggle. Clausewitzians recognize the ideological dimension of wars, but wars remain above all confrontations between groups, each having a centralized command, the armed forces of which therefore constitute a means of action abroad.

Nowadays, as in 1807, the controversy between Hegelians and Clausewitzians, between patriots and collaborators, is over a view of history. The Maoists were considered to be the doctrinaire exponents of the class struggle waged to the annihilation of the enemy (the enemy being the capitalist bourgeoisie and the imperialism that was its expression) and they attributed the same end to periods of struggle without arms as to periods of armed struggle. According to this doctrine all struggle is essentially struggle to the death. Hegel and Clausewitz have joined forces.

However, the more the Communist Party strengthens its hold over the Celestial Empire and builds socialism, the same changes can be seen as have taken place in the USSR. A people's China accepted by the international community has behaved in the same way as capitalist and socialist states. The conflict between the two great communist powers forces them to exchange accusations of heresy and adapt themselves to strange connivances.

Moreover, the most official forms of Marxism–Leninism proclaim the sovereignty of every socialist state. Why should states never oppose one another? Even, which are the contrasting interests that could tolerate compromise or, if arms were used, would count against a radical conclusion? Is it not the same with all states in the nuclear age provided that they obey an 'intelligence' and manage to control the fanatics?

Between states of the 'free' world the struggle to the death now also seems to be inconceivable. The more 'national' the Communist Party becomes the more will it act as the manager of the state rather than as a missionary of the class struggle. The 'nationalization' of the two parties that have taken charge of the historic empires has broken the coherence of the socialist camp, while it also contributes to the forming of international relations in the overall system that exists today. This is more like relations of the classical type, playing down the ideological element in the form of civil war. The World War, fought between the victors of the Second World War, has not taken place.

No one can say with any accuracy who is responsible for the weaponry or the policy of this non-war. Let us merely say that the rejection of armed conflict corresponded to the normal workings of the state's 'intelligence'. Twenty-five years is too short a period on which to base any historical forecasts, but it would appear that countries will, we hope, resemble intelligent persons in their actions.

Empirical sociology easily demonstrates that rivalry between organizations, parties and classes forms the circumstances in which human beings take decisions. Still, it was on orders given by Kennedy and then by Johnson that the number of American soldiers in Vietnam was successively raised from 15,000 in 1961 to over 500,000 in 1965. The political system of the USA still functions, even if mysteriously. The spoken or written words of the president cause troop movements, bombings, ruin and death. At the time of the 'Great Purge' the word of Stalin terrorized a whole people and sent communists and non-communists, innocent and guilty men and women, to camps and prisons in their millions.

These examples underline the danger of confounding the state with the intelligence of one person, and show that policy could cease to be intelligent in becoming identified with one person. It is obviously too simple to impute passion to the people and intelligence to the state in the form of its rulers. It may even be that the rulers run the greater risk of becoming deranged the less they distinguish themselves from the state they personify. In the case of institutions, power-sharing and the balancing game are all the more in evidence as they are needed to prevent the despotism of one man alone.

398

If I argue that the equation of policy with the intelligence of the personified state is theoretically valid all over the world it is because the only substitute for this notion of the historical subject is the notion of class or some other group which embodied an ideology. But ideology or a world vision crosses frontiers and, as Hitler remarked, rules out compromises. Lenin and Mao Tse-tung transposed to the political debate the concept of annihilation by which Clausewitz characterized the immanent end of the collision of armies. As long as Marxist–Leninists direct their activities towards this radical end then the outcome of the Cold War or of peaceful coexistence remains that of war. On the western side, strategists tend to base models on the enemy and fail to see the implications of the specific means; they end by viewing the various phases of the Cold War in too exclusively military terms. Even General Beaufre sometimes forgets that peace-time strategy does not presuppose and should not presuppose only those relations that involve or require constraint or force between allies or between enemies. Marxist–Leninists want to see the demise of capitalism. Anti-communists want to convert communists rather than bring about the death of communism. But if nothing guarantees the moderation of states, the policy of an ideology personified or of a salvationist class rules out moderation and implies war to the death.

> The eternal little machine of common sense has it that it is contradictory to pursue a conflict to the very end, when it can end only with the common death of the enemies. Common sense will not hesitate to preach this great truth again and again. But when the single question is asked – *when* does this contradiction arise – it is silent. (Glucksmann)

But common sense is not silent: there is a contradiction between propositions but not between men, parties and states. Incompatibility of goals is not the equivalent of a contradiction – a logical concept – but rather of a conflict, or a concept of practice. If a man confuses conflict with contradictions, and if he thinks and acts as if he cannot survive unless the other dies, then nothing can stop him from carrying on with this logic until the struggle to the death, even if this logic ends with the simultaneous disappearance of both enemies. The only human sense in a struggle to the death is the recognition of the victor by the defeated. Extermination of people by nuclear arms would only leave contaminated ruins behind.

Mao Tse-tung was right, rather than the Americans, when he remarked that technical superiority in weaponry would never solve the class struggle. The Americans and Khrushchev were right compared with the rodomontades of Mao when Mao imagined a society incomparably finer than that of today built on millions of corpses: nuclear weapons do not distinguish between classes. Marxist–Leninists and westerners look at the world in terms of different catagories, but not to the point of losing a common language.

Both sides admit that nuclear weapons lead to deterrence and not to a decisive outcome. Nothing prevents the west from appreciating that its political goals require neither the use of nuclear weapons nor the physical destruction of the enemy.

Epilogue

A Farewell to Arms, or the Great Illusion

Patriotism, liberty and identification with the power of a state constituted the many elements united in the harmonious personality of Clausewitz. He did not need to have recourse to sophistry, to deceive himself or to raise a barrier between his intelligence and his humanity. Clausewitz was a whole man. Perhaps his religion was based on a God of evil, but he revered that God with his entire being. In short, retrospectively, we can see him as a sinister but noble figure in the unfolding of a tragedy. It is difficult to find a comparable role for the contemporary disciples of Clausewitz. (Rappoport)

Who in Europe who is sane would dream of reviving the romanticism of fresh and joyous war? Who can forget the mincer of Verdun, the mud of Flanders and the flower of European youth mowed down by machine gun, let alone the unspeakable horrors of the Second World War, the death camps, genocide and the area bombings?

Nowadays, anyone reflecting on war and strategy raises a barrier between his intelligence and his humanity. I am sure it is no different with the neo-Clausewitzians of Moscow and Peking.

I experience none of Clausewitz's passions – the cult of the fatherland incarnated in the sovereign, the exaltation of the martial virtues or the intoxication brought on by victory. I refer to the theoretician who in the evening of his life tried to transmute his experience into theory and to reflect on the object-war for generations to come. Through the musings of Lenin and Maeo Tse-tung he remains one of the masters of Marxism–Leninism. Provided that they understand him, democrats and liberals can at least learn conceptual rigour from him.

In Moscow in 1972 a book of military doctrine appeared in English translation; it had run to five Russian editions between 1957 and 1968 and won the Frunze Prize in 1966. Under the title *Army and War according to Marxism–Leninism* it deals with the nature and essence of the phenomenon of war, the types of war that exist today and the various armies in accordance with the economic and social systems. A western reader is struck by the mixture of theory, doctrine and propaganda, and more exactly by the refusal to separate arguments that he would class otherwise himself, partly as analytical or scientific thought, partly as the rhetoric of action.

Clausewitz as interpreted by Lenin remains the founding father of the

Marxist-Leninist theory of war. The authors take as their starting point, as I did myself in Book II, Chapter 11, a passage from Volume 21 of Lenin's complete works, taken from the pamphlet 'The Bankruptcy of the Second International':

The fundamental thesis of the dialectic deformed by Plekhanov with so much impudence to please the bourgeoisie is that war is a simple continuation of policy by other means (more precisely, by violence). Such is the Formula of Clausewitz, one of the greatest writers on the history of war, and whose thought was inspired by Hegel. This was also the viewpoint of Marx and Engels who regarded any war as the continuation of the policies of enemy powers – and of different classes within these countries in a defined period.

The trite criticism immediately follows this quotation: 'Clausewitz said that policy represented the interests of society considered as a whole. He denied its class character. Consequently, he developed a false, idealist view of policy, talking of the expression of the spirit of the state.'

Soviet authors reproach Clausewitzians of the bourgeoisie with allegedly reducing policy to foreign policy and misrepresenting the intimate link between internal and external policies. As a general rule, the latter reflects the former. A typology of war can be deduced from this essential truth, distinguishing just from unjust wars and pointing out the predictable victory of states waging just wars, etc. However, 'the dependence of foreign policy on internal policy (or again, the class structure) does not rule out the particular importance of foreign policy during world wars and when the fate of nations is in the balance'. Moreover, if the Soviets, as faithful disciples of Clausewitz, argue that the armed struggle, as such, is part of policy, they do not ignore the counterpart; 'the armed struggle represents the principal means, the specific element of war. Even if the chronological limits of war are not determined by the dates that mark the beginning and ending of military action this remains true'. Therefore, they do not commit the error of certain western Clausewitzians; they do not reverse the Formula.

'In peace-time the central role is generally played by non-violent means of policy, whereas violent means do not exhaust the nature of full-scale armed conflict'. The contrast between violent and non-violent means obviously does not rule out the use of non-violent ones during hostilities, whether economic, psychological or ideological ones. But these means, which involve policy in the wider sense, then become subordinate to the armed struggle, which is the specific feature of a state of war.

It is no different within states. Civil wars have specific features which distinguish them from all other types of war.

It would be inaccurate to give the concept of civil war too wide a meaning and to include the armed activity of a people against aggressors. The concept of civil war must not be used in such a way as to include all armed clashes between workers and the government or police force. Armed resistance by demonstrators or strikers against attacking troops is still not a civil war.

Civil war therefore constitutes a particular phase of the class struggle, characterized by its specific means. In the same way rivalry between

401

countries with different social systems, even in a period of cold war, is not equivalent to a war. In short, the Soviets who for many years have appreciated the continuation of policy, and the likely identity of the goals aimed at by policy and by war, do not then arrive at the conclusion that there is no distinction between them. As an activity, policy remains the same as regards its ends but varies as to means.

In general the Soviets, unlike Clausewitz, distinguish between politics and policy, politics being the object (the whole set of socio-economic circumstances) and policy the subject. Another Soviet theoretician, Vasily Yefisovich, in a work in the same series devoted to military thought, contrasts the objective laws of war, which are independent of men and their consciences, and the principles of the military art. 'The principles of military art are the fundamental ideas and the most important introduction to organizing a battle, an operation or an entire war.' As regards the laws of war and armed conflicts (the book under review carefully distinguishes between these), they determine the course of history through the unfolding of military phenomena just as the laws of physics or chemistry determine natural phenomena.

Soviet authors who agree on essentials none the less dispute the typology of laws and the confusion, legitimate or not, between armed conflict and war. On the other hand, they all subscribe to a formula like this: 'This revolutionary struggle, fought with a view to achieving the dictatorship of the proletariat, includes the use of open political coercion by the exploiters but does not necessarily include armed struggle'. Most of them would also accept that armed conflict is not the same as war. 'In the absence of a political goal, even the most ferocious battle will not be a war but simply a struggle, according to Lenin.' If we only see the clash of arms in war then we should neglect the other forms of struggle, the military and political conduct of the war by the government, the contribution made by the rear, and even the class nature of any war. In other words, the concept of war at once presupposes political aims and recourse to arms. In this respect the Soviets remain Clausewitzians. Without political aims men can fight, but they do not make war. Men or groups can aim for incompatible ends without recourse to arms and they are still not making war. An affray or a riot does not constitute revolution. The guerilla warfare of partisans is not the same as banditry even if it resembles it at the beginning and the end.

What changes in the theory of war are brought about by nuclear weapons? First, the 'ideologues of the bourgeoisie' are said to falsify the relations between policy and war. Some exaggerate the importance of policy and identify it with war and others 'reduce war to an armed conflict', without appreciating its political aspect. Neither group understands the dialectic, the constant and the variable elements in the fundamental relationship between war and policy. Without this dialectic some thinkers in the west reject Clausewitz's teaching while others retain only the permanent truth and do not perceive the historical changes (e.g. the October Revolution) which on the basis of Marxism–Leninism permit its application to present-day circumstances.

Second, the Soviets say that according to some writers in the west the Clausewitzian thesis as to the relationship between policy and war is now anachronistic and void of meaning. In this group the Soviets haphazardly include James William Fulbright, Claude Delmas, Edgar J. Kingston-McCloughry, Ferdinand O. Mischke, Stephen King-Hall and Fritz Sternberg. Their major argument is said to be the abolition of any distinction between front and rear and the threat of catastrophic consequences for all belligerents. The Soviets say that this argument has an element of truth but does not stand up to criticism.

If the arguments of the Formula are no longer valid, what is the nature of war? This thesis is made out to be aiming at discrediting Marxism–Leninism in so far as it retains and gives the true meaning to war: anti-communism is made out to have taken on the disguise of love of peace. Third, the sociologists or military writers of the west confuse two closely linked but distinct questions, the theoretical question of the essence, the content and character of nuclear war, and the practical question of knowing whether it can be used as an effective tool of political activity. Fourth, their unilateral arguments disguise the role that aggressive imperialist policy plays in the development of these weapons. Finally, the cardinal error of these arguments camouflages the predatory nature of American imperialism. They minimize the danger present in aggressive policies waged by this imperialism and its capacity to start a new world war.

I have happily set down the five objections expressed by Soviet writers so as to make clear the obstacles that arise in any honest discussion with Soviet ideologues, at least in public. The distinction between theory, ideology and propaganda does not exist for them because their theories include an ideology (the pacific character, by definition, of Soviet foreign policy) and are the basis for propaganda.

Only two of these five arguments are what the west would call theoretical. If the Formula belongs to a bygone age how can we define war? The Soviets say, moreover, that war, including nuclear war, is now, as it always has been, the continuation of policy by other means, i.e. it results from policies towards class and imperialism and aims at political ends as wars have done in the past. The qualitative changes of modern policy, on the other hand, and the revolution in the means and methods of armed struggle on the other, are said to affect the essence of a possible war fought with ballistic missiles and with nuclear warheads and so to distinguish it from the essence of past and present wars fought with conventional weapons.

This possible war 'would resolve the crucial historical problem that involves the fate of mankind as a whole rather than specific political interests'. 'Never before has such an immeasurable problem constituted the political content of a war.' A nuclear war would also differ in means (the destruction of the economic, scientific and politico-moral means of the enemy at the same time as his armed forces) and by consequences from the wars of the past. There is an inevitable outcome to this possible war, which is the victory of the socialist camp in conformity with the logic of history and its objective laws which prescribe the invincibility of what is new in social development.

The third argument uses the distinction between theory and teaching, or again, between knowledge and practice. Every war, including nuclear war, would remain linked to the policy from which it springs and the ends towards which the politician responsible for it tends. But unlike other wars, thermo-nuclear war, in certain circumstances, is not admissible as a means: it would be irrational to use weapons of massive destructive power and it is possible to preserve peace. In other words the Formula retains its scientific truth: the phenomenal features of thermo-nuclear war point to specific principles of action, i.e. the will not to fight such a war. Thereby the theoreticians answer the Left or the Leftist revolutionaries. These latter use the Formula, the link between politics and war, with a view to demonstrating that even nuclear war is inevitable or desirable as a means of policy or as a way to hasten world revolution. This is an erroneous thesis which merely helps the imperialist aggressors.

Between the neo-Clausewitzians of the west and the Marxist–Leninists of Moscow, nothing stands in the way of dialogue. Both admit the same facts – that there are sovereign states with armed forces at their command, the devastation that would be caused by nuclear arms, the rivalry between socio-politically incompatible regimes and the possibility of pursuing that rivalry without recourse to nuclear arms. Seen from Moscow the neo-Clausewitzians of the west appear merely bizarre. They are accused of idealism and are thought to misunderstand the class aspect of the policy that causes wars and the aggressiveness which the diplomacy of the capitalist states, by definition, causes. But they share a 'peculiarity' with me that a pacifist would notice, namely a way of seeing society and its conflicts, the use and limitations in use of force as a means of preventing the recourse to weapons of massive destructive potential.

Such an analysis of our universe requires the separation of intelligence and humanity, though more obviously in the east than the west. In the east – at least to the extent that such writers fully believe in their own ideology – right is accorded without hesitation or reservation to one side rather than the other or, in limited contests, to one of the belligerents rather than the other. Because we do not know the outcome of the historical drama, and because we are not fighting for a system as such, we in the west grope for the best or the least bad. It is not any non-communist or anti-communist regime that seems to us to be preferable to a communist one. Clausewitz said, and repeated, that in war everything is simple, but what is simple is difficult. Today we would say that in politics nothing is simple and the great simplifiers, Hitler and Stalin, were they to rise again tomorrow, would have the responsibility not of tens of millions but hundreds of millions of corpses.

As the almost legendary ancestor of Moltke and Schlieffen, Clausewitz belongs (provisionally) to a bygone age, at least if we are talking about relations between the great powers. The principle of annihilation has been given material reality with the bombing of Hiroshima and Nagasaki as well as in the British and American area bombings. It gave nuclear weapons a monstrous connotation to the extent that no one argues over this now. These arms inaugurated a deterrent strategy rather than an era of decision. As regards Clausewitz, 'the most remarkable military writer of the bourgeoisie' in whom Marx and Engels, followed by Lenin and Mao Tse-tung, found partial truths and corrected the idealist mistakes, he has remained the master common to the three interlocutors – Russian, Chinese and American – of the historic dialogue of our day, who in some ways reproduce his 'strange trinity'.

Conceptual confusions committed on occasion by western writers have to be cleared up. In his Introduction to *Strategy*, General Beaufre distinguishes five models. He baptizes the fifth one the Clausewitzian model: 'If the military means at one's disposal are sufficiently powerful, the outcome can be looked for in a military victory, in a violent and if possible short conflict.' Such is the teaching, indeed, that the German general staff (and the French one, too, before 1914) drew from the Treatise. The model is inapplicable as the objective of nuclear powers with a second strike capacity; disarmament of the enemy ceases to be accessible. In a sub-system, Israel unsuccessfully and India successfully acted according to traditional teaching.

The fourth model taken by General Beaufre from Chinese experience also belongs to the Clausewitzian universe though it takes on original features today. 'If the margin for freedom of action is wide, but if the disposable forces are too weak to obtain military victory, one may have recourse to prolonged conflict aiming at moral attrition and tiring out the enemy': this model reflects Mao Tse-tung's practice, but it can be found in Clausewitz, provided that we presuppose a state of war, either civil or foreign. The Russian armies' retreat to the interior in 1812 and the actions of the Spanish *guerrilleros* after 1808 offer examples of this. The formation of a regular army from an irregular base, the gradual alteration of the ratio of strength between insurgents and established powers, the victory of the regular army of the insurgents over the regular army of the former power, lie in the continuation of the Clausewitzian conception of the defensive and the arming of the people with the revolutionary will being added to the will to national defence, or replacing it.

The three other models listed by General Beaufre leave the reader uncertain, for want of fundamental precision: are the actors, as regards one another, in a state of war? 'If one has very powerful means . . . and if the objective is small-scale, a simple threat to use the means may bring the enemy to accept conditions that one wishes to impose on him and cause him more easily to renounce claims of changing the *status quo*.' The earlier expressions refer to the two possibilities – of defence (the maintenance of the *status quo*) and the offensive (imposing conditions) – without the alternative being confronted, of either recourse or non-recourse to violence. Similarly, the model that follows (a narrow margin of liberty, limited means, small-scale objectives) does not include recourse to violence. An authentic Clausewitzian would therefore reproach General Beaufre for committing the cardinal error committed by many westerners: the inversion, even if unconsciously of the Formula. Once we begin to list the types of strategy without contrasting war and peace we can easily slip into the thesis wrongly imputed to Clausewitz by pacifists, that peace is a continuation of war by other means.

Perhaps this is simply a matter of words. It may be, but it is also a matter of concept and theory. I admit without difficulty that we may talk of a peace strategy not in the sense of strategy conducted with a view to peace but as strategy in peace-time, provided that we define strategy as the art of using all possible means to arrive at ends determined by policy – each means (economic, psychological, – ideological, etc.) being tactical. There is still a difficulty. In order to keep part of the classical meaning of the concept we should include on occasions constraint or coercion, and in our definition of strategy, force, without even acknowledging the importance of this shift. But all individual and international relationships contain an element of conflict and, in one form or another, constraint. Therefore, if General Beaufre characterizes strategy simply by constraint he accepts the first definition – the choice of means adapted to the end in view – which is open to two objections, which are apparently different but are both valid. He neglects the element of partial accord between interests and wills which is also present in less extreme varieties of human relationships. He fails to appreciate the specificity of war, linked to the specificity of means, from which results the proper nature of the phenomenon of war and its development. To quote the Soviets: 'The essence of the laws of armed struggle is that they express the complex and contradictory nature of a specific socio-political phenomenon, the violent interaction of parties at odds, each trying to achieve definite politico-military ends.'

The internal equivocation in General Beaufre's thought is illustrated by his use of the expression 'strategy of indirect approach' borrowed from Liddell Hart. As meant by the English writer, indirect strategy certainly represents a model or figure for operational art which is above higher tactics and below the political conduct of war (although the choice of this figure of speech may be determined by political consequences). Wellington's landing in Portugal and the landing of allied troops in the Balkans during the Second World War illustrate this method which is opposed to the interpretation given by Schlieffen to Clausewitz.

On the other hand, when Beaufre presents the indirect approach of Hitler between 1933 and 1938 as an example he broadens the meaning of the idea to include non-violent as well as violent means. In 1935 and 1936 Hitler extracted approval from his adversaries less by threat than by defiance, invoking principles which he himself despised but on which the democracies were based. In 1936 he gambled on the reluctance of the French to use force again. In 1938 he ostentatiously brandished the threat of using force. Retrospectively, Hitler's diplomacy from 1935 to 1939 has the appearance of what I have elsewhere called 'extended strategy'. It was a preliminary to war and created a context in which the armed forces would deal the death blow. Here again, the Treatise gives inevitable yet dangerous advice: once war is inevitable, pragmatic calculation must say when it will break out.

Marxist–Leninist propaganda against atomic weapons at the end of the 1950s and the psycho-political activity between the two sides – particularly from 1948 to 1953 – did not act as a preparation for war but rather acted as a substitute. It led to an acceptance of the new territorial status; there were limited wars in Korea and Vietnam but there was no overall war or total war between the USSR and the followers of the USA.

Once again I agree: the frontier between peace and war, both within and between the states, is blurred. In times of peace methods of imposing force and threats are now tolerated through habit in a way that would have been condemned in the past. The class struggle is expressed here and there, through dispersed violence which does not quite add up to civil war, and which opinion has accepted in a resigned way as being normal. As Clausewitz would have said, to distinguish between opposing concepts we must consider extreme cases.

It might be argued – why should concepts be saved? If we regard all conflicts as so many wars, we attribute a bellicose character to all social existence. Some will find symbolic violence in the father's or schoolmaster's authority, others confuse the students' barricades in June 1968 with those of the workers in June 1848. On the pretext that rivalry between states continues in peace-time, this example could be called continuation of war by other means. On the pretext that the social order is threatened by brigands, gangsters or a political challenge, no distinction will be drawn between criminality, class struggle and civil war. All means of violent death can be put via statistical calculation in the same category.

But in my eyes a second category is more important. Perhaps the Marxist–Leninists in Moscow wish sincerely for American imperialism or capitalism itself to come to an end. But once the bearers of a transnational ideology take governmental responsibility over people, even without the aid of nuclear deterrence, they learn that frontiers survive and that victory through civil war leads to the end of prolonged conflict. If the west confuses cold war with war itself then it joins forces not with Mao but the Parisian Maoists who did not and would not distinguish a prolonged conflict, at the end of which the Communist Party seized absolute power, from the rivalry between states with different social systems that will take radical decisions only in the distant historical future.

In the strange Clausewitzian trinity of people, war leader and head of state, Maoist thought corresponds to the first category, westerners to the second and the Soviets to the third. The ideologues of Peking used to say that the truth lay with the people; diplomacy is violent, said the American strategists; the supreme law, according to the theorists of Moscow, lies in the political aims. Each interlocutor has something to learn from the other.

From Khrushchev the Maoists learn that nuclear weapons do not distinguish between classes. The west learns from the Chinese and the Russians that class war is not war because war is defined by the predominant use of armed force. From different axes Marxist–Leninists and westerners can agree to recognize that the nuclear weapon is not decisive for the class struggle or for the rivalry between states. It would only be decisive in a total war between nuclear powers, and again only on condition that the states survived to accept defeat or enjoy triumph. As a weapon of supreme recourse it throws the shadow of nothingness over the dialectic of violent wills because some will rule it out in civil war, and others in limited wars while all profess their determination to avoid the 'final struggle' that would wipe out both camps.

A paradox remains: I have put the Americans into the second category, headed 'war leader', through their belief in the free play of the spirit and their sense of gambling. In fact, it is westerners who believe they can use the Marxist–Leninists as an example when they reverse the Formula, whereas the latter are faithful to the Leninist interpretation of Clausewitz, adhering to the Prussian officer's authentic lesson, which involves the continuity of relations between states and the distinction between different phases according to the specific means employed. It sometimes even seems that the American strategists incline to regard diplomacy in terms of violence whereas the Marxist–Leninists, despite their vocabulary, adhere

407

to the traditional contours of the theory.

This reversal of roles gives Rapoport a valid object of criticism against those he wrongly calls neo-Clausewitzians. In passing, he himself admits that, according to Clausewitz, there is a threshold between peace and war. What he does not say is that Clausewitz foresaw zero-sum games, i.e. he inserted co-operation and communication between enemies into his system and coexistence between states.

What westerners, disciples of Montesquieu and Kant, and perhaps even neo–Clausewitzians, must teach the Marxist–Leninists both of Peking and Moscow is that history has decided in favour of Clausewitz and against Hegel. Even if all states were based on the same ideology they would not be united under a single ruler, nor under the legislation of a world parliament. For some time, how long no one can tell, humanity is condemned to more or less peaceful coexistence between peoples who misunderstand one another, states which want sovereignty and those with incompatible ideologies.

Because they are not waging a crusade to impose a dogmatic ideology, men in the west try to spread a modest ideology: the disappearance of absolute war also sees the disappearance of the absolute enemy, the enemy whose survival would endanger one's own existence. In the nuclear age no state tends unconditionally towards destroying another.

Some years before the holocaust of 1914, Norman Angell produced a book that denounced in advance the irrationality (in the economic sense) of the war that was feared between Great Britain and Germany. Linked to each other as client and supplier, each would suffer from the other's ruin. The foresight was accurate but the advice was futile. Why should men now win their wager with Reason? Is it not an illusion to hope that sovereign states will become wise? Or that they can for ever live on credit without acknowledging the nuclear threat even if it is implicit? Is it not again an illusion to imagine that governors take their decisions in a rarefied atmosphere where passions are cooled and intelligence reigns? After all, Rapoport concedes that, logically speaking, means must be adapted to military ends, but that psychologically the implications are interpreted in a contrary sense: 'Political ends are determined by military capacity.' This last proposition applies neither to Bismarck nor to Hitler, who both set themselves political ends – in the one case moderate and in the other unlimited. My own interpretation of Clausewitz is given plausibility only by the ending of Franco-German conflict and of European greatness. The owl of Minerva appears at dusk.

Even today a Frenchman cannot read without dread the letters and memoranda of a Gneisenau or a Clausewitz. These men of good education, inspired by idealism, unreservedly abandon themselves to a hatred of France and the French. German historians have not passed over the fanaticism of the patriots; the admiration they rightly feel for the makers of liberation conceals from them the danger that was being hatched in the heat of war. Even the victory of Napoleonic France did not mean the ruin of European civilization, as Gneisenau wrote, any more than the victory of the Second Reich would have brought barbarism. War propaganda remained for the first time in Hitler's case behind the truth, or rather it respected certain secrets, perhaps because the cruelties of Stalin were no less than those of Hitler.

Napoleon's immoderation – crossing Europe on horseback, mobilizing troops of allied or satellite states to fulfil his ambition and putting his brothers on various thrones – provoked a revolt that was equally immoderate. The victors always strike the vanquished as arrogant, and they probably are arrogant. In their hour of success they forget their own experience of defeat. After 1871 Moltke forgot the *Bekenntnisse* and condemned the French *francs tireurs* arrogantly and with an easy conscience.

According to the current historical version, it was at the time of the French Revolution that the conversion of German thought occurred from cosmopolitanism to nationalism, from rationalism to nationalism. Clausewitz fits into this phase of transition. The relationship between absolute war and the real wars, between the concept and the phenomenal diversity, had more, I believe, to do with the method of Montesquieu than with the transposition of the misunderstood duality between the thing-in-itself (*Ding an sich*) and phenomena. Besides, this simultaneous search for the concept and the concrete does not belong to the Germans alone. The equivocations of the concept in nature, sometimes close to the essence, sometimes to the original, sometimes against the mind and sometimes the object of intelligence, can be found in some form or another among eighteenth-century writers on both sides of the Rhine.

The radical originality of German culture compared with French rationalism or English utilitarianism constitutes, I believe, an ideological theme rather than a historical truth. If, during the last century, Prussia then Germany followed a path that took them away from France and England it was because of events rather than ideas. Within the Second Reich the army obeyed the king-emperor as though he were a feudal suzerain. A modern industry flourished in a state that exalted above all else the traditional and military values; the bourgeois abdicated and accepted a second-rate role. Before 1914 and after 1918, Veblen stressed the similarity between the German empire and the Japanese empire, between the explosive mixture of warrior-ideal and industrial technique.

Friedrich Meinecke's books mark the successive stages of the German liberals' meditation on their own fate as well as their country's fate. I should regard it as arrogant to give a categoric answer to their questions in one sense or another. After 1815 the reactionaries beat the Reformers. But, except perhaps for Gneisenau, the Reformers did not progress beyond the national-liberal framework: the national army in a *Rechtsstaat* but not a democratic one. The revolutionary notions of the patriots between 1807 and 1813 did not survive victory and the restoration.

No solution can be found in a continuation between the Reformers and the German generals of the two world wars. The same social class retained most of the higher posts although the increase in the number of soldiers did make it necessary to employ more and more middle-class officers. The same names crop up in 1815 and 1914, the same families furnishing incomparable servants of the king-emperor from generation to generation. Some of them, trained in the schools of the general staff or the military academy, acquired both high culture and an unrivalled competence. The French hated the Junkers just as the Germans hated the improvised gener-

409

als of the Revolution. Neither group was detestable, as such – at least no more or less than war itself. As long as there is success to be had, generals will justify their lives and their trade in terms of success. The tandem of Hindenburg–Ludendorff reproduced that which, a century earlier, sealed Napoleon's fate, the tandem of Blücher and Gneisenau at Ligny and Waterloo.

Ludendorff failed to match Gneisenau just as Schlieffen lacked the philosophical and historical sense of a Clausewitz. Strategic thought became impoverished as a mere technique of operations. However, I find it difficult to accept Rosinski's view of unreservedly admiring Clausewitz and Schlieffen while bitterly criticizing Ludendorff; or again Wallach, who attributes a cult to Clausewitz and puts Schlieffen on the wrong side of the barrier. The debate has persisted for more than a century and will continue until the – perhaps approaching – day when men will lose an interest in their fathers' experiences.

If I have to choose a thesis, I adhere to the political version even though it may be the coarsest one. Bismarck succeeded by limiting his ambitions and preserving the European system of states. The leaders of the Second Reich, whatever the origins of their ambitions, would have had grandiose objectives had there been a radical outcome in their favour. Still, looked at retrospectively today, it was, I think, H. Delbrück who talked the language of wisdom and vainly repeated the advice that Pericles gave the Athenians as war broke out. Germany, the empire in the centre, had to stand up to a coalition of enemies rather than to eliminate it. But Thucydides and Clausewitz both explain why such words remained unheard. Both of them leave the mind in suspense and do not decide between the passionate logic of what happened and the reasonable logic of what might have happened. Nor do I reach a decision; doubt remains and nourishes hope. The great illusion was dissipated long ago. As long as the principle of annihilation applied, war, even when absolute, and fought with the objective of disarming the enemy, could be used as a tool of policy (like the French campaign in 1940). In the nuclear age the only chance of saving humanity from itself is the intelligence of the state and arms control.

Must we fear that this gamble with Reason will also be baptized the 'great illusion' tomorrow. Who knows? Rapoport reminds us of the 'illusory nature of security through power, the obscene absurdities of total war, the poisoned fruits of militarism'. Yes, of course they belong to the past – commanders on horseback, regimental traditions, campaigns executed with impeccable rigour culminating in a decisive battle. But if the foundations of patriotism have perhaps been eaten away in Europe and the USA by contemporary commercialism and industrialization, is it the same in the USSA, China, India, Algeria and the Arab countries? In reality, the great illusion of today is not that which threw the people of Europe into suicidal opposition; it is the contrary illusion, that of the Europeans and sometimes even of the Americans, which ascribes a single rationality to all peoples and to those who govern them, namely that of the economists who compare cost and effect. The Europeans would like to leave behind history with a capital H, which writes its letters in blood. Others in their hundreds of millions are entering or re-entering such History. The weapons of mass destruction have provoked a mutation in the form of war, not a mutation

410

of international relations, i.e. a transfer to the rule of law.

The professors of political 'science' have discovered that international relations constitute only a fragment of a greater whole that includes exchanges between individuals, members of distinct societies, social movements, and businesses indifferent to frontiers – even supernational institutions. From that, some conclude that states hardly count any more, that legal sovereignties represent fictions. They end by forgetting even what obsessed them a few years ago: the fact that the central commands in Moscow, Peking and Washington still have the instruments of violence at their disposal – armies, fleets, aircraft and weapons of massive destruction. India, despite her povery-stricken masses, explodes a nuclear bomb. Despite *détente* the Soviet Union has never spent so much on arms as a percentage of a GNP that rises regularly. Tanks are built and the west provides motor-car, lorry and aluminium factories on credit. The USA failed to subject North Korea or North Vietnam to its will. Judging by its acts rather than its words, the Kremlin has not deduced from this that force is useless.

Moreover, the thesis that sovereignty is withering away spread in American universities even while the emirates of the Persian Gulf organized with other oil producers into a cartel to multiply the price of oil fourfold and produce a world economic crisis overnight. The economic sovereignty of the European states is limited by the constraints of a world market voluntarily accepted and through decisions, accepted willingly or otherwise, by the Americans. The political sovereignty of the states in Eastern Europe is exercised only within the limits fixed by Moscow. The economic sovereignty of Saudi Arabia permitted the rise in oil prices and in India it allowed the war against Pakistan.

The quarter-century that followed the Second World War risks appearing to us retrospectively as a time of peace, despite the Cold War, Korea, Vietnam, Pakistan and Israel. The predominance of the USA guaranteed the appearance of order, just or unjust, and of course unequal. The superiority of the American over the Soviet republic belongs to the past. The Atlantic Alliance remains, but only as an organization without soul, a half-spent force. In all the international assemblies, motions or resolutions attack the rich countries through the numerical superiority of the poorer ones. There is no need to have special insight to appreciate that the pseudo-parliament of the United Nations, composed of multifarious states, is a caricature of national parliaments and that world society remains anarchic. It becomes increasingly so the more the American republic for want of means or the will, reduces the stake and allows the others to play.

Perhaps the great illusion of the Europeans is not so much to gamble on reason but to misunderstand the counterpart of that gamble. To save men from destroying each other, they have to be saved from wars. The Europeans would like to go one step further and bid a 'farewell to arms'. Decolonization is ending as all or almost all peoples have acquired sovereignty. Just as the Europeans had to go to the end of the night and live through the horrors of absolute war in order to gain wisdom, would not the men of other continents, who until yesterday were humiliated and downtrodden, prefer co-operation to violence? They could work together

411

for a world society that would be more than a collection of states where each obeys no law other than his own will.

I am not unconscious of the responsibility of the theoretician. Each of us, even to an infinitesimal degree, makes a world conforming to the image we have of it. Whoever denies the authority of international law further weakens it. But the pacifist who tries to 'put the blame' on his adversary is too ready to present himself as a saint. War does seem horrible and absurd to us, the intellectuals of good will lacking ideological fanaticism, patriots without nationalistic or imperialist passion. But the Marxist–Leninists of Moscow acclaim civil wars. Jean-Paul Sartre shares the intoxication of the crowd that takes the Bastille by assault and carries its governor's head around stuck on a pike. The Jews of Europe learned at their own cost that it was not enough to refuse to resort to violence to escape death. The Palestinians, deprived of land they consider to be their own, and a fatherland of which they dream, mobilize the hatred of rebels from all corners of the world against the Israelis who still live in their ancestors' land or die fighting.

What is lacking in run-of-the-mill professors is the sense of history and tragedy. This sense is also lacking in those who are called neo-Clausewitzian and have never read Clausewitz. At least the American Neo-Clausewitzians have the merit of rejecting both the idea of total war (as symbolized by insistence on unconditional surrender) and international legalism (peace guaranteed by the rule of law), those twin illusions that peace can finally be secured when whoever threatens it is eliminated or when states at last cease regarding themselves as the sole fountainheads of justice. One of the main features of Wilsonian idealism, the illusion of the 'crusade for peace', has now been eliminated by the advent of nuclear weapons; another of its features, the illusion that acceptance by the society of nations of the majority principle would produce universal equity, has been dispelled by the voting record of the UN General Assembly. As for the final illusion, suffice it to say that even after the horrors of World War I, neither men nor states were ready to bid a 'farewell to arms'.

The general who wrote the Treatise, and even the young officer who dreamed of glory on the battlefield, knew all too well how precarious is our hold on those values to which we have dedicated our political efforts. Even now our own grandchildren can hardly grasp how my friend Golo Mann and I must have felt when we watched Goebbels, in an act revived from a more primitive age, hurled the works of Freud and Musil into a bonfire on the *Kurfürstendamm*. To remind myself of the passions of those earlier Prussian patriots who resisted Napoleon, I had to reread the memoirs and letters of Clausewitz and Gneisenau.

Future men will feel other passions. But today, how can I, as a Frenchman of Jewish origin, forget that France owes her liberation to the power of her allies, or that Israel owes her very existence to her arms and probably owes her future survival to her willingness — and, if need be, American willingness — to fight again?

Nor shall I feel guilty about this until the day when some great tribunal can at last decide who — Israeli or Palestinian — really has sole claim to a land held holy by all the three religions of the Book.

Index

413